THE RIGHTEOUS

THE UNSUNG HEROES
OF THE HOLOCAUST

Martin Gilbert

BLACK SWAN

THE RIGHTEOUS
A BLACK SWAN BOOK : 0 552 99850 8

Originally published in Great Britain by Doubleday,
a division of Transworld Publishers

PRINTING HISTORY
Doubleday edition published 2002
Black Swan edition published 2003

1 3 5 7 9 10 8 6 4 2

Set in 11/12pt Melior by
Phoenix Typesetting, Burley-in-Wharfedale, West Yorkshire.

Bantam Books are published by Transworld Publishers,
61–63 Uxbridge Road, London W5 5SA,
a division of the Random House Group Ltd,
in Australia by Random House Australia (Pty) Ltd,
20 Alfred Street, Milsons Point, Sydney, NSW 2061, Australia,
in New Zealand by Random House New Zealand Ltd,
18 Poland Road, Glenfield, Auckland 10, New Zealand
and in South Africa by Random House (Pty) Ltd,
Endulini, 5a Jubilee Road, Parktown 2193, South Africa.

Printed and bound in Great Britain by
CPI Antony Rowe, Chippenham and Eastbourne

Papers used by Transworld Publishers are natural, recyclable products
made from wood grown in sustainable forests. The manufacturing processes
conform to the environmental regulations of the country of origin.

Dedicated to Mordecai Paldiel
who has done so much to uncover
and to preserve
the stories of the Righteous

Contents

Preface

On 28 October 1974, while walking on Mount Zion in Jerusalem, I saw in front of me the end of a procession on its way to one of the city's Christian cemeteries. Surprised that most of the walkers seemed to be Jews, I asked one of them whose funeral it was, and was told it was that of a German Christian, Oskar Schindler, who had helped save the lives of more than fifteen hundred Jews during the Second World War.

Like most of the four hundred people in the procession, the man to whom I spoke was a Jew saved by Schindler. So too was the Polish-born Judge Moshe Bejski, a survivor of the Holocaust, who delivered the funeral oration. Bejski was then active in the search for non-Jews who had saved Jewish lives during the Holocaust, to enable them to receive formal recognition as Righteous Among the Nations. This recognition was being given, and continues to be given, by Yad Vashem, the Holocaust museum and archive in Jerusalem, as laid down in the law of the State of Israel.

The concept of Righteous Among the Nations – in Hebrew, *hasidei umot haolam* – is an ancient one in Jewish tradition. Originally those 'nations' were the non-Israelite tribes of Biblical times. During the Passover evening family recitation, according to a post-war tradition, Jews recall Shifra and Puah, the two Egyptian midwives 'who defied Pharaoh's edict to drown the male

9

children of Israel in the Nile', and the daughter of Pharaoh, 'who violated her father's decree to drown infants, and who reached out to save Moses'.[1] Seeing the new-born Israelite boy for whom death was the sole decree – her own father's decree – she took him in his basket from the river and brought him up as her own son. In the Bible she is given no name. The Jewish sages chose a name for her: Batya, daughter of God.

From that moment on Mount Zion in 1974, I began collecting newspaper items about the awards and award ceremonies at Yad Vashem, and spending time in that part of the archive there dedicated to the Righteous. Some of the material in this book derives from my researches at that time.

Many of those Jews who survived Nazi rule and occupation in Europe between 1939 and 1945 owed their survival to non-Jews. The penalty for helping a Jew hide was often death, especially in Poland and eastern Europe. Many hundreds of non-Jews were executed for trying to help Jews. Hostile neighbours could be as dangerous as the Gestapo, often betraying both those in hiding and those who were hiding them. At the beginning of the year 2002, fifty-six years after the end of the war in Europe, more than nineteen thousand non-Jews had been honoured as Righteous at Yad Vashem. As one century gave way to another, more than eight hundred non-Jews were being identified and honoured every year. Were a single printed page to be devoted to each person already recognized as Righteous, it would take fifty books the size of this one to tell all their stories.

In 1993 I was invited to speak in Jerusalem to a gathering of several hundred Jews who had been hidden as children during the war by non-Jews. These 'Hidden Children', as they called themselves, had first come

---

[1] *Haggadah Supplement*, The Jewish Foundation for the Righteous, New York, 2001.

10

together two years earlier in New York, and felt strongly that the time had come to seek public recognition of those who had saved their lives. Those who had hidden Jewish children, saving them from deportation and death, included Roman Catholics – among them Franciscans, Benedictines and Jesuits – Greek and Russian Orthodox Christians, Protestants, Baptists and Lutherans, as well as Muslims in Bosnia and Albania. They were priests and nuns, nurses and nannies, teachers and fellow pupils, neighbours and friends, as well as employees and colleagues of their parents. A single act, even a single remark, could save a life – as when a Polish peasant woman, hearing her fellow villagers say, of four- or five-year-old Renée Lindenberg, 'throw her into the well,' replied: 'She's not a dog after all,' and Renée was saved.[2]

Abraham Foxman, who had been saved by his nanny in Vilna, told the Hidden Child conference in Jerusalem: 'For the first fifty years after the Holocaust survivors bore witness to evil, brutality and bestiality. Now is the time for us, for our generation, to bear witness to goodness. For each one of us is living proof that even in hell, even in that hell called the Holocaust, there was goodness, there was kindness, and there was love and compassion.'[3]

The story of non-Jews who saved Jewish lives – the 'Righteous' of this study – was not one that had a high priority in the first few decades after the war. Understandably, Jewish writers wanted to tell the story of the suffering, the destruction, and the murder of loved ones, as well as of Jewish resistance and revolt. In his substantial study of the Vilna ghetto, published in 1980,

---

[2] Recollections of Renée Lindenberg (later Kuker), Hidden Child conference, Jerusalem, notes of the proceedings, 14 July 1993.
[3] Remarks by Abe Foxman, Hidden Child conference, Jerusalem, notes of the proceedings, 14 July 1993.

the historian Yitzhak Arad, himself a survivor of that ghetto and a wartime partisan, wrote only a few sentences about the Righteous, while stating emphatically: 'The Lithuanian populace in Vilna did not provide refuge for the Jews.'[4]

In commenting on the paucity of rescuers in Lithuania, Dr Arad noted: 'A possibility of haven in a non-Jewish surrounding was dictated by two basic conditions – the attitude of local inhabitants, and the punishment awaiting those who extended help. Both were disadvantageous to the Jews. A big segment of the local public was animated by anti-Semitism, profited by illicit gains from abandoned Jewish property, and favoured or was apathetic toward the extermination of the Jewish community. Those who might have been ready to assist the Jews were intimidated by the likelihood of punishment. Very few overcame their fears and extended help.'[5]

Yet Yad Vashem, of which Dr Arad was chairman for many years, has – since the fall of Communism made it possible – paid homage to more than four hundred Lithuanian rescuers, many from Vilna. As research continues in independent Lithuania, the cases of as many as two thousand more Lithuanians are being prepared for possible recognition in the first decade of the twenty-first century.

Focus on the Righteous is not universally welcomed. In response to my published requests for stories of rescue, a Polish-born Jew wrote in some perturbation that 'in my opinion, enough is being written on Christian help to rescue Jews. I feel that the focus is shifting away from the crimes.'[6] Another correspondent, a Polish-born survivor of the Holocaust, Ella Adler, who was living in

[4] Yitzhak Arad, *Ghetto in Flames*, page 444.
[5] Yitzhak Arad, *Ghetto in Flames*, page 196.
[6] Letter to the author, 14 October 2001.

Cracow when war broke out, wrote: 'Thank you kindly for your recent letter inquiring as to whether I had experienced a kindness from a non-Jew during my four years of incarceration during the Holocaust years. Sorry to say that I personally do not recall any such kindness during that period.' Such responses were not unusual. Yet at the same time, Ella Adler added that she does know 'of a person in our group of Holocaust Survivors who had such an experience', and that she was passing on my request to him.[7]

Baruch Sharoni, a member of the committee at Yad Vashem that recognizes the Righteous, has commented: 'The number of such cases was peripheral because so many more who could have contributed to the rescue did not.'[8] Yet Sharoni also reflected: 'I see the savers as true noble souls of the human race, and when I meet with them I feel somewhat inferior to them. For I know that if I had been in their place I wouldn't have been capable of such deeds.'[9]

Many survivors react with unease, and even anger, when they reflect on how few people were willing to help. Gerta Vrbova, a young Slovak girl during the war, asked: 'What were the reasons for the appalling behaviour of the local population when their neighbours were deported to unknown destinations?'[10] A Dutch survivor, Dr Maurits de Vries, wrote: 'I would like to stress again the fact that only the relatively few, who were saved, could bear witness, and that the voice of those who fell in the hands of the Nazis, by treason, cannot be heard.'[11] Professor Edgar Gold, who survived the war in Germany

---

[7] Ella Adler, letter to the author, 20 September 2001.
[8] Benek (Baruch) Sharoni, 'Man's Humanity to Man', *Mizkor*, October 2000.
[9] Benek Sharoni, letter to the author, 20 June 2001.
[10] Professor Gerta Vrbova, letter to the author, 18 January 2002.
[11] Dr Maurits de Vries, letter to the author, 12 January 2002.

as a hidden child, and whose father survived four concentration camps, including Auschwitz, writes that his father often told him 'that the Germans could not have done what they did without the assistance of their Ukrainian, Polish, Estonian, Latvian, Lithuanian, Hungarian and Croatian "helpers". Furthermore, the roundup of Jews in France, the Netherlands, Belgium, Italy, Greece, Hungary, Yugoslavia, and even Norway, would not have been so "successful" without significant local "help". My father also often mentioned that the cruelty and bestiality of Ukrainian and Baltic States' concentration camp guards often far surpassed the cold, calculated cruelty of the Germans.'[12]

Collaboration and betrayal cast a shadow on the story of rescue, raising the question of how many more Jews might have been saved had more people been prepared to take the risk of helping them; they also intensify the light that shines on those who did help, almost always at great risk to themselves. Henry Huttenbach, the historian of the Jews of Worms, writes of an elderly Jewish couple in Worms who were made welcome in a Catholic convent and thus escaped deportation: 'They had the good fortune of encountering brave and decent people who sheltered them in an otherwise overwhelmingly unfriendly and disinterested Europe. It must be remembered that those who did escape camps, ran away into societies poisoned by anti-Semitic sentiments. The vast majority perished at the hands of collaborators with Germany's scheme to exterminate the Jews, whether Swiss border guards refusing entrance to anyone over sixteen, or the French police arresting foreign Jews, or Poles refusing to hide escapees from ghettos, or Russian partisans who killed Jews seeking to join them in their fight against the Germans.' But, he added: 'In this

---

[12] Professor Edgar Gold, letter to the author, 5 November 2000.

morally depraved Europe, there were islands of exceptions, an occasional decent person who risked his life by opening his home, and a rare convent or monastery which had the moral backbone to extend sanctuary to persecuted Jews other than to those who had converted to Christianity.'[13]

Those 'islands of exceptions' and the 'moral backbone' of the rescuers are central to the story of a Nazi-dominated Europe within which righteous acts testified to the survival of humane values, and to the courage of those who save human life rather than allow it to be destroyed. In every country under Nazi rule or occupation, the instinct to help remained strong, despite widespread hostility or indifference. Six million Jews were murdered, but tens of thousands were saved.

In almost every instance where a Jew was saved, more than one non-Jew was involved in the act of rescue, which in many cases took place over several years. 'In order to save one Jew,' writes Elisabeth Maxwell, referring to the French experience, 'it required ten or more people in every case,' and she cites the story of Alexander Rotenberg, who crossed from France into Switzerland. On reading his story, she noted, 'I find that more than fifty people were directly involved and needed in his rescue from Antwerp, via France to Switzerland, and that takes no account of all those who were in the know or closed their eyes and did not talk.'[14]

The story of the Righteous is the story of men and women who risked their lives and those of their families to help save Jewish lives: people who, in the words of Si

---

[13] Henry R. Huttenbach, *The Destruction of the Jewish Community of Worms*, page 69.
[14] Elisabeth Maxwell, 'The Rescue of Jews in France and Belgium During the Holocaust', *The Journal of Holocaust Education*, Summer/Autumn 1998.

Frumkin, a survivor of the Kovno ghetto, 'ignored the law, opposed popular opinion, and dared to do what was right'.[15] According to Jewish tradition: 'Whoever saves one life, it is as if he saved the entire world.'[16]

Martin Gilbert
Merton College
Oxford

28 June 2002

---

[15] Si Frumkin, editorial, *Graffiti for Intellectuals* magazine (Los Angeles), 3 July 2000.
[16] Babylonian Talmud, Tractate *Sanhedrin*, folio 37a.

Acknowledgements

I am grateful to all those who wrote to me about their personal experiences, or gave me access to information. At Yad Vashem, the Holocaust museum, archive and research centre in Jerusalem, Mordecai Paldiel, head of the Department of the Righteous for more than twenty years, helped me from the breadth of his knowledge. I was also helped at Yad Vashem in the 1970s by Yitzhak Arad, the late Dr Joseph Kermisz and the late Chaim Pazner; and more recently by Shmuel Krakowsky, Dan Michman, Elliot Nidam and Sari Reuveni. Judge Moshe Bejski gave me the benefit of his experience both as one who was saved (by Oskar Schindler) and as the judge who, at Yad Vashem, had the primary responsibility over many years in honouring the Righteous Among the Nations.

At the United States Holocaust Memorial Museum, Washington DC, I was helped in the Photo Archive both with photographic and archival material, and would like to thank Genya Markon, Sharon Muller, Judith Cohen and Leslie Swift; at the Hidden Child Foundation, New York, I was assisted by its President, Ann Shore, as well as by Lore Baer, Rachelle Goldstein, Carla Lessing and Marion Wolff. Harvey Sarner gave me access to his personal archive regarding Righteous whose visits to Israel he made possible. The Holocaust Memoir Digest has been a valuable source, and its Project Director,

Esther Poznansky, a font of good guidance. I am also grateful to the archivists and staff of the International Committee of the Red Cross, Geneva; of the Polish Institute and Sikorski Museum, London; and of the Polish Library, London.

The rescuers remain to this day almost universally modest about their actions. Those who sent me details of their work included Jeannette Brousse, Pierre Golliet, Dr Michel Reynders and Dr Tina Strobos. Among those who were rescued, who wrote to me with their recollections and answered my queries, I am most grateful to the following, listed under the countries in which they were saved:

Belarus: Richard Vanger.

Belgium: Walter Absil, Nicole David, Rachelle Goldstein, Flora M. Singer, Bronia Veitch.

Czechoslovakia: Frank Bright, Hana Greenfield, David Korn, Jana Tanner, Henry Wilde.

France: Professor Amos Dreyfus, Betty Eppel, Gisele Feldman, Carl Hausman, Greta Herensztat, Lady Lipworth, Walter W. Reed, Helen Resnick, Anne Schwab, Felice Zimmern Stokes, Ines Vromen.

Germany: Professor Edgar Gold, Charles C. Milford, Evy Woods.

Greece: Jeff M. Levis.

Holland: Lore Baer, Ilana Drukker-Tikotin, Cecile Kahn-Kanner, Levie Kanes, Dr Robert Krell, Edna Heruthy, Donya Meijer, Steffi Robertson, L. I. Troostwijk, Dr Maurits Eduard de Vries.

Hungary: Pal Foti, Tibor Hegedus, David Peleg, Professor Gabor Vermes.

Italy: Marek Herman, Ursula Korn, Mario Lattes, Dora Herczog Levi, Elia Levi, Pia Levi, Adriana Bassani Luzzati, Dr Marcello Morpurgo, Luisa Naor, Ada Vitale, Marina Lowi Zinn.

Latvia: Maja Abramowitch.

Lithuania: Margaret Kagan (Lady Kagan).

Poland (pre-1939 borders): Ella Adler, Lydia Aran, Zwi Barnea, Benjamin Bender, Dora Bernstein, Alexandre Blumstein, Dr Leon Chameides, Ilana Feldblum, Lisa Garbus, Rachel Garfunkel, Halina Gartenberg, Myra Genn, Pearl Good, Helen Garfinkel Greenspun, Henry Herzog, Helena Horowitz, Marcel Jarvin, Lorraine Justman-Wisnicki, Jack Kagan, Michael Katz, Bianka Kraszewski, Jerzy Lando, Ben Meed, Vladka Meed, Betty Piechotka, Selma Rossen, Mania Salinger, Eugenia Schenker, Dana Schwartz, Ilana Turner, Dr Norris N. Wallach, Jane Weber, Bracha Weisbarth, Shewach Weiss, Joseph Wisnicki, Eli Zborowski, Harry Zeimer.

Slovakia: Professor Gerta Vrbova.

Concentration camps, slave labour camps, death marches and the last months of the war: Judge Moshe Bejski, Jack Brauns, Zvi Gill, Lea Goodman, Roman Halter, Lorraine Justman-Wisnicki, Jakub Lichterman, Anna Ostrowiak, Ilana Turner, Henry Wiener, Henry Wilde, Abraham Zuckerman.

Many other people have responded to my requests for material. I thank them all:

Roy Abrams, Jeffrey Adler, Ian W. Alexander (The Church of Scotland World Mission), Krik Ariens, Valerie Arnon, Aryeh Assan.

Professor Yehuda Bauer, Lorraine Beitler (Beitler Family Foundation), the late Arieh Ben-Tov, Leslie Blau.

Susan Caine, Daniel Chameides, M. Donald Coleman, Dr Kenneth Collins, Grazyna Cooper, Mel Cooper.

Dan Danieli, Yohanan ben David, Margit A. Diamond, William A. Donohue (President, Catholic League for Religious and Civil Rights).

His Excellency Giulio Einaudi, Apostolic Nuncio, Croatia.

Pearl Fichman, Alice Fink, Eitan Finkelstein, Sandy Flitterman-Lewis, Eddy Florentin, Frank Fox, Si Frumkin.

Ben Gale, Professor John Garrard, Nicky Gavron, Ben Giladi (*The Voice of Piotrkow Survivors*), Professor Edgar Gold, Helen Goldberg, Alain Goldschläger, Michael Good, Professor Richard Griffiths, Dr Andras Gröbler, Ruth Gruber.

Suzan E. Hagstrom, David and Dorothy Harman, Marilyn J. Harran, Marek Herman, Herbert Herz (representative in Switzerland and Savoie of the Yad Vashem Righteous Among the Nations Department), Agnes Hirschi, Jan Hoser, Michael D. Hull, Professor Otto Hutter.

Leonid Kelbert, Brother James M. Kelly (President, Mount Saint Joseph Xaverian Brothers Sponsored Schools), Roman Kent, Peter Kessler, Serge Klarsfeld, Rachel Kostanian (the Vilna Gaon Jewish State Museum of Lithuania, Vilnius).

Laya Labi, Sinai Leichter, Alexander Levy.

Mira Marody, Dr Elisabeth Maxwell, Leif Arne Mendelsohn, Professor Eric Mendoza, Ruben and Sandra Montefiore (Italian Immigrants Association, Israel), Keith Morgan, Francis J. Murphy.

Ambassador Dr Istvan Nathon (Budapest), Robin O'Neil.

Gottfried Paasche, Dr David A. Patterson, Aldo Perosino, Iris Posner (President, One Thousand Children, Inc.).

Uriel Reingold, Glenn Richter, Clive Rosen (Israel–Judaica Stamp Club), Lawrence M. Rothbaum.

Leonid Saharovici, Sister Brenda St Lawrence (Sisters of Sion), Professor Marc Saperstein, Bat-Sheva Savaldi-Kohlberg, Ruth Schijveschuurder, Henry Schwab, Per Kristian Sebak, Baruch Sharoni, Jay Shir, Stanley J. Stahl (The Jewish Foundation for the Righteous), Dr Ernest Stock, Judy Stoffman.

Aba Taratuta, Ida Taratuta.

Ricardo Vargas, Professor Irena Vesaite, Hugo Vickers. Janek Weber, Roman Weingarten (*Cracow*

Friendship), Leon W. Wells, Dr Simon Wessely, Dr Wendy Whitworth (Remembering for the Future 2000), Barbara Wind (United Federation of Metro West Holocaust Remembrance and Education Council), Dr Bob Wolf, Myriam Wolf, Dr David F. Wright.

George P. Young.

Harry Zeimer, Mark Zingeris, Dr Anna Zsigmond, Ronald Zweig.

Ben Helfgott gave me as always the benefit of his wise advice. My publishers, Marianne Velmans at Doubleday and Liz Stein at Holt, have been supportive throughout. Gillian Bromley provided essential editorial support; proofreading was undertaken by Judy Collins and Ruth Carim, and Deborah Adams; Mari Roberts and Katrina Whone co-ordinated the editorial process. Alice Corrie assisted me with the index. The maps were expertly crafted by Tim Aspden on the basis of my rough drafts. Arthur Wadsworth helped with filing and sorting. Translations have been provided by Deborah S. Jacobs, Carine Kennedy, Sara Rosen, Taffy Sassoon, Ilana Turner and Aliza Wurtman, as well as by Enid Wurtman, who also helped me throughout my researches at Yad Vashem. Kay Thomson made important suggestions of presentation and content, and helped organize the considerable mass of correspondence.

I am grateful to the Photo Archives, United States Holocaust Memorial Museum (USHMM), Washington DC, for access to, and permission to reproduce, the sixty-four photographs in this book. Additional acknowledgement for the use of these pictures is due to Gay Block and Malka Drucker, *Rescuers: Portraits of Moral Courage in the Holocaust* (photographs 1, 25, 26, 31, 57), Abraham Foxman (2 and 3), Museum of Jewish Heritage/Centre for Holocaust Studies, and Stanley Berger (4), Helen Wisgardisky Lewin (5), Rose Levin Weinberg (6), Anita Helfgott Ekstein (7, 8), Shalom

Foundation: Golda Tencer-Szurmiej Collection (9), Alicija Fajnstejn Weinsberg (10), Zydowski Instytut Historyczny Naukowo-Badawczy (11, 12, 13, 14), Jacky Barkan (15, 16), Annette Lederman Linzer (17), Jacques Leibman (18), Yettanda Stewart (19), Sara Lamhaut Boucart (20), Michel Reynders (21), Thea Rothenstein (22), Rachelle Silberman Goldstein (23), Marguerite Birnbaum (24), Bep Meyer Zion (27, 28), Thomas Stein (29), Nederlands Institut Voor Oorlogsdocumentatie (30), Memoir Juive de Paris (32), Hanne Leibman and Jack Lewin (33), Nelly Trocmé Hewett (34), Roger Waksman (35), Nadine Fain Thiberville (36), Gavra Mandil (37), Marion I. Cassirer (38), Babi Yar Society (39), Bernard Geron (40), Alice Slade (41), Lea Kalin (42), Sophie Zajd Berkowitz (43), Ursula Korn Selig (44), Frihedsmuseet, Denmark (45, 46), Hagstromer & Qviberg Fondkommission (47), Eric Saul, of 'Visas for Life' (48, 49, 51, 52, 53, 55, 61), Nina Gladitz Film Produktion (50), Schweizerisches Bundesarchiv (54), Agnes Herzer (56), Yad Vashem Photo Archives (58), Swedish National Archives (59), Thomas Veres (60), Comité International de la Croix Rouge (62), PFG International (63) and Leopold Page Photographic Collection (64).

List of Maps

CHAPTER ONE

Rescue in the East

Starting in 1933, as Nazi rule imposed harsher and harsher conditions on the Jews of Germany, many governments opened their gates to Jewish refugees. The United States accepted the largest number, more than a hundred and fifty thousand, followed by Britain with more than eighty thousand, including almost ten thousand children brought to Britain on the British government's initiative in what became known as the Kindertransport after the destruction of synagogues and Jewish property during Kristallnacht in November 1938. Many of these children were given new homes by Christian families. Even when governments, including Britain and the United States, imposed quotas on the number of Jewish refugees allowed in, individual diplomats made special efforts to issue as many visas as possible. Prominent among these diplomats were the British Passport Control Officer in Berlin, Captain Frank Foley, and the Chinese Consul-General in Vienna, Dr Feng Shan Ho. The visas they issued enabled several thousand Jews to leave Germany and Austria during the period when German policy was to allow Jewish emigration. On the Swiss border, a Swiss police officer, Captain Paul Grüninger, ignored the orders of his superiors and let more than two thousand Jews cross into Switzerland.

When war came, with the German invasion of Poland

in September 1939, other diplomats outside the Nazi sphere issued visas which enabled Jews to leave Europe altogether. In the Lithuanian capital Kaunas – Lithuania then being neutral – a Dutch diplomat, Jan Zwartendijk, and the Japanese Consul, Chiune Sugihara, enabled more than two thousand Jewish refugees from Poland to cross the Soviet Union en route for Japan, Shanghai and the Americas. Following the German invasion of France, Holland and Belgium in May 1940, a Portuguese diplomat stationed in southern France, Aristides de Sousa Mendes, issued transit visas that enabled many thousand Jewish refugees to cross into Spain before German troops reached the border and closed it. In Marseilles, an American citizen, Varian Fry, was head of an American Emergency Rescue Committee that, over a thirteen-month period, issued documents enabling more than twelve hundred mainly German refugees, including many Jewish intellectuals, writers, artists and scientists, to leave Vichy France for the United States. Fry and his team were supported in their efforts by the American Vice-Consul in Marseilles, Hiram Bingham.[1]

In German-occupied Poland, where all Jews were forced to live in ghettos, starvation took a terrible toll. More than two million Polish Jews were trapped in the ghettos; the Germans would not allow any emigration. Then, in June 1941, Hitler's forces invaded the Soviet Union, overrunning an area in which more than two million more Jews were living. Within a few days of the German invasion of this vast eastern region, the mass murder of Jews began on a scale hitherto unknown:

---

[1] The story of these diplomats, who together enabled as many as twenty thousand Jews to leave Europe before the Holocaust began, is the subject of the exhibition 'Visas for Life', prepared by Eric Saul, which has been widely shown in the United States, Canada, Britain and Europe since 2000, and is part of my forthcoming book *'Knights of the Spirit': The World's Response to Hitler's Persecution of the Jews, 1933–1941.*

hundreds, sometimes thousands, sometimes tens of thousands, being killed every day. This was the start of the Holocaust, the systematic destruction of the Jews of Europe. This mass murder was carried out by the Einsatzgruppen, SS killing squads, assisted by local volunteers, among them Ukrainians, Lithuanians and Latvians. By the end of 1941 as many as a million Jews had been murdered in the conquered regions of the Soviet Union.

In the face of such a systematic and sustained frenzy of killing, every act of rescue was remarkable. In Bialystok, the first eastern Polish city to be overrun, one of the first acts of the killers was to lock hundreds of Jews into the main synagogue and then set it on fire. At one moment, while the SS were concentrating on shooting Jews who were trying to escape from the front of the building, a Polish Christian – his name is not known – who had been employed as an odd-job man by the synagogue opened a small window at the back, and several dozen Jews managed to escape. By the end of that day of burning and shooting, two thousand Jews had been murdered.[2]

At Jedwabne, forty miles from Bialystok, more than a thousand Jews were murdered on 10 July 1941. Their killers were not the German occupiers but local Polish villagers, their neighbours for generations. During the massacre, a Polish woman, Antonina Wyrzykowska, sheltered seven Jews from Jedwabne in her home in the nearby hamlet of Yanczewka. Her courage was later recalled by two of those to whom she gave shelter, Lea and Jack Kubran, at that time eighteen-year-olds who had just married: 'For twenty-eight months', they wrote, 'this selfless and generous woman protected us, giving us bread, water and potatoes as we hid in two bunkers. Antonina kept her sheep on a floor over the bunkers for

---

[2] Szymon Datner, *Walka i Zaglada Bialystockiego Ghetta*, pages 10–14.

further camouflage. Constantly the Gestapo poked its guns around the farm looking for the seven Jews. We were ready to commit suicide if they discovered us. Ingeniously Antonina had spilled gasoline around the area covering the bunkers so that the Gestapo's bloodhounds could not smell their prey.'[3]

Another of the seven in hiding, Moishe Olszewicz, later wrote: 'Best friends, the goodness and virtue of these people cannot be described. No amount of money can adequately compensate them and no words can adequately thank them. It was not one day and not one minute, but two and a half years of fear and suffering, of anguish and fear.' When liberation came, 'We left the stable, just like the animals, into the lighted world, full of air and sunshine, which for us had been forbidden, and we embraced our saviours. Their joy cannot be described. They looked at our thin and pale faces, at our thin arms and legs, at our extinguished eyes which looked and saw nothing, the hearts which let out a cry full of pain knowing we had lost the best and most beautiful – our families.'[4]

After the Russians liberated the area, Moishe Olszewicz recalled, 'Antonina's Polish neighbours taunted her over having hidden the seven Jews. She was even beaten up once and she and her husband were forced to leave the farm. (He himself had only known about four Jews being hidden – not all seven.)'[5] Antonina Wyrzykowska's family eventually emigrated to the United States and settled in Chicago.[6]

---

[3] Szymon Datner, *Walka i Zaglada Bialystockiego Ghetta*, pages 10–14.
[4] Letter of 30 June 1964, Yad Vashem Righteous Among the Nations Archive, file 1011.
[5] Letter of 3 October 1975, Yad Vashem Righteous Among the Nations Archive, file 1011.
[6] Jan Tomasz Gross, *Neighbours: The Destruction of the Jewish Community in Jedwabne.*

In supporting her for a Righteous award, another of those whom she saved wrote to Yad Vashem: 'My Jewish brethren, these were terrible times, and the struggle for survival was unbearably hard. You can't truly appreciate and value what the Wyrzykowski family did for those seven Jews who survived and now have children of their own. I now live in Yedwabno – Jedwabne – and I am still the same Jew called Grondowsky. My Jewish brethren, I would like all of you who happen to read this statement to know that thanks to the Wyrzykowski family, seven Jews survived, and it is impossible to evaluate the reward this family deserves for rescuing us.'[7]

Menachem Finkelsztajn was also saved by Antonina Wyrzykowska. He had fled to Jedwabne from the neighbouring village of Radzilow, where local Poles had murdered a large number of Jews two days earlier, on June 23 – only twenty-four hours after the German invasion of the Soviet Union and two weeks before the Jedwabne massacre. Both the local priest and the local doctor had refused all Jewish appeals for help. Only the arrival of a group of German soldiers, who were shocked by the slaughter, saved the lives of eighteen Jews, including an eight-year-old boy who had dug himself out of the mass grave.[8]

Bronka Klibanski, masquerading as an 'Aryan' Pole in Bialystok while serving as a liaison for the Jewish partisans in the nearby forests, recently paid tribute to a Polish officer in the underground Polish Home Army, the Armia Krajowa. Dr Filipowski worked in a German pharmaceutical warehouse and 'provided me with medicines and equipment for the partisans'; he also guarded Mordechai Tenenbaum's underground archives, which

---

[7] 'A letter from Grondowsky . . . ', Yad Vashem Righteous Among the Nations Archive, file 1011.
[8] Frank Fox, 'A Skeleton in Poland's Closet: The Jedwabne Massacre', *East European Jewish Affairs*, volume 31, number 1, 2001.

had been smuggled out of the Bialystok ghetto. Bronka Klibanski also recalled that another Pole, 'an elderly man named Burdzynski, would come and visit one of us whenever it was necessary to allay a landlady's suspicions; these visits were interpreted as proof that we were Christians.'[9]

The Polish province of Volhynia, which the Soviet Union had annexed in October 1939 – today it is part of Ukraine – was overrun by the German army in the first weeks of the German–Soviet war. More than a quarter of a million Jews were living there. Starting in November 1941, ghettos were established for Jews in all the towns and villages where they lived. In one of these towns, Ostrog, the Germans regularly sent 'work brigades' of Jews out of the ghetto. These groups did not return. Realizing that there could be no safety in remaining in the ghetto, Lisa Dawidowicz and her family escaped into the countryside. 'We searched for a hiding place,' she later recalled. 'A poor farm woman agreed to hide our family of five in an underground potato cellar – there was no room to stand and we could breathe only through a hole covered by pumpkins. We remained there for sixteen months.'[10]

From the beginning of the German occupation, the position of Jews in hiding was precarious in the extreme. On 25 September 1941, the first day of the slaughter of the Jews of Ejszyszki (in Yiddish, Eishyshok), in which the mass murder of almost five thousand people was carried out by Germans and local Lithuanians, several Jews who escaped from the village made their way to the home of a Christian friend in the village of Dociszki. In

[9] Bronka Klibanski, 'In the Ghetto and in the Resistance: A Personal Narrative', in Dalia Ofer and Lenore J. Weitzman (editors), *Women in the Holocaust*, New Haven, Connecticut: Yale University Press, 1998, page 184.
[10] 'Name: Lisa Dawidowicz', United States Holocaust Memorial Museum, Photo Archive, Worksheet ID4381.

the words of Yaffa Eliach, the historian of Ejszyszki, herself a survivor and eyewitness, this man 'welcomed them with open arms and fed them bread, honey and warm milk'. Another non-Jew who took Jews in for the night at the time of the slaughter was Yashuk Kapitan: when the Jews arrived at his home his wife was already in bed, 'her head barely visible amid piles of pillows and goose-down quilts looted from Jewish homes'. After a night in the barn and a day in the hayloft, the Jews were asked to leave: Kapitan felt their presence had become too dangerous. Walking to the village of Korkuciany, they came to the home of a farmer who knew them. The farmer let them in, and agreed to take a message from them to the Radun ghetto, eight miles away, which had as yet escaped destruction.

Another local farmer, Zoludzewicz, took in a pre-war Jewish friend and his family who had escaped the massacre. But, Yaffa Eliach has written, the farmer's son 'feared that the farmers in the vicinity would betray them, burn the house down, and kill everyone in it'. The son even refused to eat or drink unless the Jews were sent away, and after two weeks Zoludzewicz asked the family to leave. Yaffa Eliach herself (then Yaffa Sonenson), her parents and sister, and several other members of her family, found refuge in the village of Korkuciany with a Polish farmer, Kazimierz Korkuc, and his mother. Korkuc was 'a completely honourable and generous man, who helped dozens, even hundreds, of Jews in the vicinity'. Near his bed was a trapdoor, covered with straw and manure: it 'led to a narrow shaft, which in turn led to a tunnel that was connected to a pit, a cave-like space beneath and beyond the house, with an air shaft consisting of a hole beneath a cherry tree'. In this pit, Yaffa and her parents hid with three other members of their family. So secret did the hiding places have to be that the Sonensons did not know at first that their first cousins had also taken refuge on the Korkuc property: nine Jews in all. Other Jews were also in hiding elsewhere on the property, and on nearby farms where Korkuc had found them a place. A Lithuanian shepherd on the Korkuc estate, Antoni Gawrylkewicz, would warn Jews in hiding when a Polish Home Army unit came into the area; some of these units did not hesitate to kill Jews when they discovered them. Many Jews on the run found food at the farm: Korkuc was willing, in Yaffa Eliach's words, 'to risk his life on a daily basis'. After the war, Kazimierz Korkuc and his mother were 'unable to return to their home in safety because of the help they had given to Jews'.[11]

Elsewhere in the Ejszyszki region, in one of her many hiding places, a Jewish woman, Miriam Kabacznik, nearly lost her life on account of her dumplings. A neighbour of the family who was hiding her, a man who belonged to the Polish underground Home Army, ate some soup with dumplings in it which Miriam had cooked. 'These dumplings could only have been cooked by a Jewess,' the neighbour remarked. That very night she was on the run again, in search of a new shelter.

In July 1942 the liquidation of the Volhynian ghettos began. In the city of Wlodzimierz Wolynski (in Russian, Vladimir-Volynsk; in Yiddish, Ludmir), it began on 1 September 1942 and continued for two weeks. Almost all the twenty thousand Jews in the ghetto, half of them refugees from dozens of smaller towns and villages, were murdered. While the killing was at its height, a Jewish woman, Ruszka Singer, escaped with her fourteen-year-old daughter Nechama into the woods. There they hid until the coming of winter forced them to seek shelter at the home of a farmer, Nikolai Vavrusevich. After the war, Vavrusevich fell on hard times. Fifty years later the Jewish Foundation for the Righteous, which at that time was providing him with financial help, described his

---

[11] Yaffa Eliach, *There Once Was a World*, pages 59, 617, 619, 683, 685.

response to Ruszka Singer's plea: 'Risking death, Nikolai took in this miserable mother and child and brought them to his shed. When Ruszka came to the shed, she found thirteen other Jews in hiding. Nikolai gave Ruszka and Nechama warm, dry clothes and food. The fifteen Jews lived in the shed, not venturing forth for fear of being noticed by a neighbour. The winter was very severe. The Jews moved from the shed to the house and to the forest depending on the circumstances. Nikolai and his brother Mikhail dug a bunker under the shed and this is where the Jews remained for the duration of the war until they were liberated in 1944.'[12]

When, fifty-five years later, Nechama was reunited with Mikhail and Nikolai Vavrusevich in New York, she recalled that in April 1943 the Vavruseviches had dug up extra potatoes and beets from their fields so that she and her mother could observe Passover and refrain from eating leavened bread. The Vavruseviches also helped those in hiding observe the Sabbath each Friday by lighting a makeshift candle: an oil-dipped piece of thread in a hollowed-out potato.[13]

When the Einsatzgruppen entered the small Volhynian town of Zofiowka (Sofiyevka), all two thousand Jewish inhabitants were forced into an open, unfenced ghetto, and strictly guarded. During a three-day 'Action' – the word used both by the SS and by the Jews to describe the moment of the destruction of a whole Jewish community – starting on 25 August 1942, all the Jews in Zofiowka were taken in small groups to a nearby forest to be murdered: shot down mercilessly in cold blood. Only thirty-six managed to elude their captors. Making their way with difficulty to the village

---

[12] 'Nikolai Vavrusevich: An Expression of Gratitude and a Story of Moral Courage', single-sheet information page, Jewish Foundation for the Righteous, New York.
[13] Somini Sengupta, 'Tearful Reunion for Friends who Defied the Nazis', *New York Times*, 28 November 1997.

of Cholopiny, the survivors sought out Alojzy Ludwikowski, a Polish farmer whom they had known before the war. He agreed to try to shelter all of them. Digging a number of pits in the dense forest, in which they could hide, and covering the pits with undergrowth, he provided them with clothing, food and even weapons. In February 1943 the Germans discovered one of the pits. The sixteen Jews hiding there opened fire in self-defence; all of them were killed in the ensuing battle. The other twenty remained in hiding until liberation.[14]

When the SS turned their attention to Lutsk, two thousand of the twenty thousand Jews in the ghetto managed to escape the round-ups. The historian of the fate of Volhynian Jewry, Shmuel Spector – who himself escaped from Volhynia to the Urals before the German occupation – has recorded that, with the help of Witold Fomenko, a Ukrainian, many of them hid first in the houses of Poles inside the city or in its outskirts, and then, under cover of darkness, made their way to the woods.[15] In the Volhynian village of Strumowka, near Lutsk, Fomenko had a hairdressing shop opposite the synagogue. David Prital, who had been a youngster in the ghetto, later recalled that it was said he 'would come to the ghetto with bags full of bread in order to distribute the bread to the women whose husbands were deported or shot during the first "Actions". This man tried to encourage Jews who were depressed by regaling them with cheerful stories and jokes about the Germans.'[16] David Prital himself was saved by a Ukrainian couple in the same village, Sawko and Okseniya Mironiuk. In 1992 he wrote to the Claims Conference in New York to obtain financial support for Mrs Mironiuk, then a widow, eighty-five years old and

---

[14] Yad Vashem Righteous Among the Nations Archive, file 2145.
[15] Shmuel Spector, *The Holocaust of Volhynian Jews, 1941–1944*, page 197; Yad Vashem Righteous Among the Nations Archive, file 392.
[16] Yad Vashem Righteous Among the Nations Archive, file 2655.

blind: 'To my knowledge she and her family saved a second Jew, Ignnetz Shetz, who after the liberation joined the Russian army and died subsequently fighting the Germans. I remember when Ignnetz was hiding in Mironiuk's house. The Germans were conducting house-to-house searches and Ignnetz wished to leave but the family refused to let him go. For no reason the Germans passed their house and all were saved.'[17]

However, the local Ukrainian population could also be terrifyingly hostile to those who sought refuge; it had, after all, carried out murderous pogroms of its own against the Jews in the first weeks of the war. A Jew who had fled from the ghetto of Dabrowica later recalled that, when he asked a Ukrainian peasant friend for help, the 'friend' told him: 'You've left all your property with the others in the town and you come to me asking me to help and save you. I thought you were smart but now I see that you're very dumb. Hitler has conquered almost the whole world and he is going to slaughter all the Jews because they crucified our Jesus. You think you can get away from this fate? You shouldn't have run away from the ghetto; at least you would have rested in the same grave with your family. Now who knows where you're going to die. My advice for you is to return to the ghetto. Take a loaf of bread and get out of my sight, for the devil remains the devil and the Yid remains a Yid.'[18] Such an attitude, widespread as it was, throws into even starker contrast the goodwill of those who were willing to risk their lives to try to help Jews.

In his testimony to Yad Vashem, David Prital recalled

[17] Letter of 6 November 1992, Yad Vashem Righteous Among the Nations Archive, file 2655. Many years later David Prital edited the annual publication *The Jews of the Soviet Union*, which played a prominent part in the campaign to allow Jews to emigrate from the Soviet Union.
[18] Dubrovitsa Memorial Book, page 541, quoted in Shmuel Spector, *The Holocaust of Volhynian Jews, 1941–1944*, page 241.

how the first Pole to whom he turned for sanctuary in Lutsk had demanded more money than Prital could even contemplate. He then decided to seek out the Bron family, whom he knew, and who lived in the village of Ozhenitsa. 'I had developed a friendly relationship with this family all year long, but they never promised to help me in a time of crisis. I arrived at their home in the evening and asked them to let me sleep for only one night. When Mr Bron saw the state I was in, he agreed to let me in. I felt the tension in the house caused by such a dangerous guest who could bring death upon the entire family. During that night I was thinking about my friends who remained in the ghetto. Early in the morning I got up with the same big frightening question. Where shall I go now? I decided that I must do something and went to the kitchen. I lit the fire in the oven and started to peel potatoes for breakfast. My hosts were surprised when they saw me doing the household chores when they woke up, but at the same time they were pleased to see that some housework had been done. "Not so bad," said Mr Bron, "you see, the night has passed and not a single German has come. Let's hope that no one will come, after all, how can they keep an eye on each house?" I felt that the tension eased a little.'

Bron and his daughters went to work, 'and his old, ailing wife stayed at home. I understood that I had to be of real help in this house, and I performed all kinds of household chores that day. When the family returned home after work, they were pleased to see that the floor was clean, and that I had helped the old lady. But I saw doubt reflected in their eyes. There was a Jew in the house! Yesterday the Germans had murdered the remainder of the Lutsk Jewry by shooting them at the outskirts of the town. Despite any doubts or hesitations which were reflected in his eyes, Mr Bron was a noble man and he didn't remind me that I had asked him to let me sleep in his house for only one night. Through the window I could see the first signs of the approaching Russian winter, cold and bitter, and my hosts' kindness didn't allow them to throw me out of the house. Therefore, I stayed in the house for another night, and on the next day I continued doing all the housework. Then I decided to talk seriously to Mr Bron about my plans, which were linked to the coming spring. I said: "Mr Bron, let me stay in your house only through the harsh winter months and in March or April I will try my luck in the Ukrainian woods." Radiating optimism, my host and my rescuer agreed to let me stay in the house through the winter.'

There were times when danger came very close. On one occasion a Jewish road-building contractor was caught in the house of a Polish woman, who was executed for the help she had extended to him. But other Christian families in Lutsk were hiding Jews; and this, David Prital recalled, 'undoubtedly encouraged the Bron family and raised their spirits considerably'. One problem for the young man was that one of the daughters 'was usually full of prejudice against the Jews, and she never tried to hide it'. Mrs Bron was also anxious at the continual presence of a Jew in her devout Roman Catholic home. But one day, after she had asked a priest to visit her, she told David Prital, with tears in her eyes: 'Now I am totally relaxed, as the priest, Bukovinsky, said I was doing a great act of kindness hiding a Jew in my house. Now I have regained my peace of mind.'

Spring came, the season when David Prital had promised to leave the house and try his luck elsewhere. 'Jews were caught in the town more often than before,' he recalled, 'and this heightened the atmosphere of apprehension in my host family.' His account continued: 'I realised that I must find people who are humanitarian by nature and by convictions. Where were such people? Who were they? During long winter nights I recalled walking with my grandfather on his business trips and visiting some villages. I remembered visiting a peasant whom my grandfather called a righteous person. He belonged to one of the many religious sects in the Volyn region. I also remembered prayers and strange rituals performed by the members of the sect on the banks of the Styr river. When I was a kid, I liked to watch the ritual of baptism and listen to their peaceful songs. Those were small groups of Baptists. I also recalled the figure of a housemaid in our yard who also belonged to one of those sects. I recalled her peace of mind and her love for the Jews, and I firmly decided to find these people . . .

'I left the Brons' house on a bright spring morning. Due to a curfew, I couldn't leave in the evening, and I had to take a risk of walking through the streets of the town in daylight in order to reach the village.' David Prital was fortunate to meet a German coachman who had been friendly with at least one Jewish family in Lutsk. 'I knew that the coachman was a friend of the Jews and when I saw him, my eyes filled with tears. I told him that I was looking for a hiding place after I had had to leave the house of a Polish family. He explained that he could not take me because he was already hiding a Jewish couple in his stable – even his wife was unaware that he was providing shelter to Jews. Nevertheless, he agreed that I should come to him if I could find no other place.'

Finding two Jews who were hiding in the granary of a Polish peasant who had taken them in, David Prital told them he hoped to get in touch with those peasants who belonged to the Baptist sect. One of the Jews, taking him to a small gap in the wall of the granary, pointed out a typical Ukrainian house and said to him, '"In this house lives one of the Baptists, but you should be careful because in the adjacent house lives his brother who will kill you without any hesitation. Good luck!" In the evening, I left the granary and walked in the direction of the house that was covered with straw. I walked in the path between two fields, and my heart was full of anxiety and apprehension. Suddenly I saw a figure of a Ukrainian peasant walking peacefully in the fields. My instincts, which served me well in many dangerous situations, told me that I didn't have to be afraid of this meeting. He approached me and immediately understood who I was. With tears in his eyes, he comforted me and he invited me to his house. Together we entered his house and I understood instantly that I had met a wonderful person. "God brought an important guest to our house," he said to his wife. "We should thank God for this blessing." They kneeled down and I heard a wonderful prayer coming out of their pure and simple hearts, not written in a single prayer book. I heard a song addressed to God, thanking God for the opportunity to meet a son of Israel in these crazy days. They asked God to help those who managed to stay alive hiding in the fields and in the woods. Was it a dream? Was it possible that such people still existed in this world? Why then didn't I think about them while I was still in the ghetto? With their help and proper planning we could save many people!

'They stopped praying and we sat down at the table for a meal, which was enjoyable. The peasant's wife gave us milk and potatoes. Before the meal, the master of the house read a chapter from the Bible. Here it is, I thought, this is the big secret. It is this eternal book that raised their morality to such unbelievable heights. It is this very book that filled their hearts with love for the Jews.

'After the meal, I started to talk to them. "Look, I, too, am a Jew," he said. I was shocked. In what world were we? "I am a Jew in spirit," he continued. "This encounter with you gives me more food for more thought and confirms the words of the prophets that the remnants of the Jews will be saved."'

Late at night the Baptist brought David Prital to the granary so that he could sleep there. 'As I have related, unfortunately for me, my hosts had a neighbour who was known for his hatred of the Jews. For the sake of caution, my host had to take me to sleep at another peasant's home who was of the same faith and who also received me cordially, and who was ready to help me in every way. However, there were serious problems caused by the special status of the Baptist community. They represented a small minority in the village surrounded by Russian Orthodox neighbours who hated them. Therefore, I couldn't stay for a long time at this other peasant's home and I had to wander from one place to another . . . I remember the following episode. One of the peasants said to me: "Normally, we trust our people but a person's real nature can only be tested in times of trouble. Tonight we ask you to go to a certain peasant and ask for refuge. He is not aware of your staying in the village and his attitude to you will be a real test for him. There is no personal danger for you. If he refuses to let you in, it will be a source of information about the depths of his devotion and his loyalty." Having received instructions on how to get to this peasant's house, I finally went there late at night, and after midnight I reached the house that corresponded to the description I was given – tin roof, a granary, a kennel, etc. I knocked on the door, and I heard the frightened voices of the family members. "Who is there?" I said: "A homeless person is asking for a shelter for a few days." Inside, they started to argue. The wife implored her husband not to open the door. I realised that these good people were indeed subjected to a strenuous trial. In 1943, every night could turn into a night of killings and conflagrations. I heard a voice saying, "We don't open the door at night." I said, "What a time has come when a Jew asking for shelter does not receive it." The master of the house turned to his wife: "This is a Jew, and how can we refuse him?" The door opened and the hearts of those good people opened, too, and I spent several days in this house.'

40

One night, when David Prital was sitting in the granary, his host came in and sat beside him. 'I see that you are sad and frustrated,' he said. 'I will sing you a song that may help raise your spirits.' The peasant then started to sing from the Psalms: 'When God returned the Jews to Zion' – and sang, Prital noted, 'in Hebrew!'[19]

From Kostopol, another small Volhynian town, two brothers, Szmuel and Josef Liderman, managed to escape the massacre there in which six thousand Jews were murdered in a three-day orgy of killing that started on 26 August 1942. Fleeing to the village of Antonowka, the brothers found the thousand Jews there still alive – only to be rounded up with them and taken to a clearing, where they were made to dig a mass grave, and forced to undress. The shooting then began, but the two brothers somehow managed to run away a second time, although Szmuel was shot and injured in the hand. Naked and exhausted, they reached the isolated farm, deep in the forest, of Stanislaw Jasinski, a pre-war acquaintance of their father. Although the relationship between Jasinski, who was elderly and blind, and their father had not been good, he agreed to take them in, telling them, 'The past is forgotten.'

Jasinski's wife Emilia bandaged Szmuel's injured hand, and gave the brothers clothes, and a mattress to sleep on in the barn. The couple asked for no payment. Instead, Jasinski let them dig a hiding place under the cowshed. A few days later, two more Jews who had escaped the massacre in the forest knocked at Jasinski's door. They were Szaje Odler and Akiba Kremer, who were also given shelter and assistance.

After the hideout had been in use for two months, a rumour spread in the vicinity that Jews were hiding on Jasinski's farm. The four fugitives were forced to leave

---

[19] Yad Vashem Righteous Among the Nations Archive, file 2656.

and penetrate even deeper into the forest, where they remained until their liberation by the Red Army in July 1944. A month later, Akiba Kremer, Szaje Odler and Josef Liderman were murdered by Ukrainian nationalists.[20]

In the small town of Hoszcza a Ukrainian farmer, Fiodor Kalenczuk, hid a Jewish grain merchant, Pessah Kranzberg, his wife, their ten-year-old daughter and their daughter's young friend for seventeen months, refusing to deny them refuge even when his wife protested that their presence, in the stable, was endangering a Christian household.[21] In the last week of September 1942, five hundred Jews were murdered in Hoszcza. The Kranzbergs survived. Their rescue, in the circumstances of the East, had been a rare act of courage.

After some of the mass shootings a few – a very lucky few – of those who had been forced into the execution pits managed to survive the hail of bullets, and to crawl away once night had fallen. One of these survivors was Rivka Yosselevska. As she made her way, wounded and bleeding, across the field around the slaughter pits of Mizocz, in Volhynia, a farmer took pity on her, hid her, and fed her. Later he helped her join a group of Jews hiding in the forest. There, she survived until the Red Army came in the summer of 1944. Nineteen years after her escape from the pit, she told her story, including that of her rescue, to a court in Jerusalem.[22]

Following the destruction of the Jewish community in the eastern Polish city of Nowogrodek and the surrounding villages, most of the survivors were sent to a labour camp in Nowogrodek itself. In November 1942 fourteen of these slave labourers, including Idel (now

---

[20] Yad Vashem Righteous Among the Nations Archive, file 3122.
[21] In 1967 Kalenczuk planted a tree in the Avenue of the Righteous, Yad Vashem, Jerusalem, Yad Vashem Archive; Arieh L. Bauminger, *Roll of Honour*, pages 82–3.
[22] Testimony of Rivka Yosselevska, Eichmann trial, Jerusalem, 8 May 1961, session 30.

Jack) Kagan, escaped, determined to join the Jewish partisan group headed by the Bielski brothers in the nearby forests. Their first refuge, in the Nowogrodek suburb of Peresika, was with the Bobrovskis, a well-known family of dog-catchers whose job it was to catch stray, unlicensed dogs wandering in the surrounding woods and countryside. 'They lived in an isolated house, far from the town, which no one ever visited,' Jack Kagan recalled. 'But it was the Bobrovskis who felt compassion for the Jews' bitter fate and helped as much as they could, smuggling food into the ghetto. The ghetto Jews knew about this humane behaviour.' Every Jew who managed to escape from the Nowogrodek ghetto and reach the dog-catchers' home was hidden for a day or two and supplied with food for the journey ahead. The Bobrovskis also kept in touch with the Bielski partisans, 'and they would tell runaway Jews where they might be found'.

After resting for about an hour in the Bobrovskis' house, the fourteen men went across the fields to where Boinski, a prosperous Polish farmer before the war, raised and sold pigs. He had many friends among the Jews of Nowogrodek. 'At midnight we knocked on Boinski's door,' Jack Kagan recalled. 'He came out, frightened, and told us that he lived in constant fear of the Germans, who paid him frequent visits. He agreed to hide us for one day. He led us into the barn and covered us with hay. At noon, the good man brought us some bread, potatoes and water, and when night fell we left the farm and made our way to the nearby road.' Seven or eight miles down the road they reached the home of a White Russian, Kostik Kozlovsky, who was known to take messages and letters from the Bielski partisans to the Jews in the ghetto. 'We arrived at dawn, exhausted. Kozlovsky said that no partisans had been there for several days, but that they might very well come that night. He suggested that we should wait for them in a nearby grove. We spent the whole day in that grove, lying in a trench from which we could watch the road, bustling with German military vehicles.' At nightfall, several young Jews from the Bielski partisans arrived at Kozlovsky's farm, and the fourteen escapees went back with them to the forest.[23] There they joined the Bielski partisans – as at least twenty more Jews were to do with Kozlovsky's help.

Jack Kagan later recalled how 'the name Kozlovsky and that of the dog-catchers (Bobrovski) became known. The story was that if you were planning an escape, you should go six miles from Nowogrodek to Lida to Kozlovsky's farmstead. He would then direct you to the partisans and of course everybody knew where the dog-catchers lived. And they also had contacts with the partisans.' The Bobrovskis, the family of dog-catchers, paid a high price for their helpfulness. During a German raid on their home a Jewish family was found in hiding. Rescuers and rescued were all killed, and the Bobrovskis' property burned down.[24]

We will never know how many Jews were hidden by Polish farmers in the Nowogrodek region, and how many were betrayed. As Jack Kagan noted: 'Very few farmers wanted to risk their lives and the lives of their families to save a Jew. The penalty for just having contacted a Jew was death. But there were some good farmers who risked their lives and hid children or entire families.' One of those saved was a baby, Bella Dzienciolska. 'Her parents had entrusted her to a farmer to hide. She was blonde and she did not look like a Jewish child, but at two years old, she already spoke Yiddish. So the farmer made a hole under the floor and kept her there during the day for a year until she forgot

[23] Jack Kagan and Dov Cohen, *Surviving the Holocaust with the Russian Jewish Partisans*, pages 57–9.
[24] Jack Kagan, in conversation with the author, 18 March 2002.

to speak Yiddish. He then took her out and told the neighbours that a relative's child was staying with them.' Bella Dzienciolska survived the war, thanks to that unknown farmer. Fifty years later she was to return to the farm, and found under the floorboards the hole in which she had been hidden.[25]

In Byelorussia, in the early days of the German occupation, a group of women in the capital, Minsk, worked with Jewish resistance groups in the ghetto, smuggling Jewish children out of the ghetto and placing them in Christian orphanages. In the course of several weeks, seventy children were saved in this way.[26] Twice, in Minsk, when Jews were being led out of the ghetto to their execution, Maria Babich managed to take a Jewish boy away from the march, hide him in the family home in the city, and then acquire papers for him as if he were a Byelorussian child. Maria Babich's daughter Emma noted that 'our neighbours could have been the reason of our death. If one of them or somebody else had informed the police of such an action we would have been immediately shot dead on the spot.'[27] Emma also remembered that as a seven-year-old girl, she herself would go to the local German headquarters and beg for bread, in order to help feed the children.[28]

During the search for help in Minsk, a Jewess, known only by her first name, Musya, met Anna Dvach, a Byelorussian woman with whom she had worked in the

---

[25] Jack Kagan and Dov Cohen, *Surviving the Holocaust with the Russian Jewish Partisans*, page 166.
[26] Wila Orbach, 'The Destruction of the Jews in the Nazi-Occupied Territories of the USSR', *Soviet Jewish Affairs*, volume 6, no. 2, 1976, London: Institute of Jewish Affairs.
[27] Letter of Emma Sandrigaylo (*née* Babich) to the Israeli Ambassador to Belarus (formerly White Russia), 20 January 1994, Yad Vashem Righteous Among the Nations Archive, file 7252.
[28] Letter of Emma Sandrigaylo to Yad Vashem, 7 October 1994, Yad Vashem Righteous Among the Nations Archive, file 7252.

same factory before the German invasion. Anna took her home, gave her food and shelter, and then sent her back to the ghetto with food for the other survivors. From that day until the arrival of the Red Army six months later, Anna Dvach ensured the survival of thirteen Jews.[29]

In the town of Radun, deep in the forests and swamps of Byelorussia, Meir Stoler was one of only a few survivors of the mass executions on 10 May 1942, when the two thousand Jews in the ghetto were killed. After being chased and repeatedly shot at by a German officer on horseback, the thirty-year-old blacksmith managed to reach the tiny Polish hamlet of Mizhantz, where the villagers took him in and gave him food. He survived the war and returned to Radun; fifty years later he was the only Jew living there.[30]

As many as twenty-six thousand Jews were living in the former Polish city of Brest-Litovsk when the Germans captured it from the Russians in June 1941. Almost all of them were murdered, many being taken by train to Bronna Gora, seventy-five miles to the east, on the Brest–Minsk railway line, and shot in huge pits specially dug to receive them. 'A tiny percentage – about one person in a given thousand – survived the Holocaust in Brest,' write John and Carol Garrard, historians of the destruction of the Jews of that city, and they add: 'Given the terror inspired by the German occupying forces and the hostility expressed towards Jews by most of the Polish and Ukrainian population, it is a wonder that anyone agreed to help the Jews.' Yet despite the fact that helping Jews 'was a crime punishable by the death of the entire family involved', the names of ten Righteous have been recorded. Among them were Pyotr Grigoriev, known to the Jews as

---

[29] Reuben Ainsztein, *Jewish Resistance in Nazi-Occupied Eastern Europe*, page 483.
[30] Dovid Katz, '"Radin's Last Jew" Recalls Nazi and Soviet Horrors', *Jewish Chronicle*, 7 November 1997. Radin is the Yiddish rendering for Radun.

a 'precious human being'; Floriya Budishevskaya, who saved the life of a ten-year-old Jewish boy (she was later shot by the Germans for her connection with the Soviet partisans); and Polina Golovchenko, who saved two young sisters and a young boy, and also hid a brother and sister, Khemie and Lily Manker.

On one occasion Polina Golovchenko learned that neighbours had denounced her to the Germans for hiding Jews, and that the Gestapo were on their way. She immediately took the Mankers to another hiding place. The Garrards describe how, when the Gestapo arrived at her home, she 'calmly handed them all her keys, and told them they were welcome to search her house and grounds. After combing her property for hours, they left, uttering more threats and imprecations.' She then 'went serenely to the hiding place, and brought the Mankers back into her home, even though she knew that she was under constant surveillance by neighbours seeking the bounty for handing over a hidden Jew'.[31]

After the destruction of the ghetto of Brest-Litovsk, several hundred Jews survived in hiding places known as 'malines', mostly in cellars and outhouses. Outside help was also essential for survival; a local couple, Ignacy Kurjanowicz and his wife Maria, helped the young Moshe Smolar to survive by giving him food to eat and to take back to his hiding place. 'The Kurjanowicz family took me in for a week,' he later wrote, 'and I was invited to visit them once a week on a regular basis. For greater safety, and in order not to make me look too obvious in the streets of the town, he accompanied me to the ghetto fence and from there I sneaked into the den (malina). From that day, I came there regularly for a full day once a week, until 4 January 1943, when peasants

---

[31] John and Carol Garrard, 'Barbarossa's First Victims: The Jews of Brest', *East European Jewish Affairs*, volume 28, no. 2, 1998/9, pages 38–40.

discovered my hideout, and I had to leave it for good. Then the Kurjanowicz family, after discussing the matter, decided to keep me in their house until there was a chance to escape.'

Moshe Smolar's account continued: 'I remained in their house till March 20 . . . about three months. Needless to say, all this time they were risking their lives every day. They did all this without any remuneration, financial or otherwise. On the contrary, keeping me in their home cost them a lot of money, and they had to cut down on their own rations to share their daily bread with me. When I ask myself what were their motives, I can only attribute their good deeds to their humanitarian feelings originating both from their compassionate feelings toward the Jews, deep emotional empathy with the persecuted, and truly deep and pure religious feelings. All these factors nourished their deeds, and helped them withstand the risk of paying a high price for what they did – if caught.'[32]

When Ignacy and Maria Kurjanowicz were being considered at Yad Vashem for a Righteous Among the Nations Award, someone noted on their file: 'This is a story that touches the heart – a real and dear Righteous Gentile.'[33] Moshe Smolar's family did not survive the war: his father, mother, sister and two brothers (one of them with his wife and three children) were murdered during the liquidation of the Korzec ghetto.[34]

Richard Vanger was ten years old when he managed to find help in the eastern Polish town of Stolowicze,

[32] Letter to Yad Vashem, 1973, Yad Vashem Righteous Among the Nations Archive, file 819. Smolar published his memoirs in Hebrew as *My Struggle for Survival* (Tel Aviv: Moreshet, 1978). I am grateful to Professor Yehuda Bauer for drawing my attention to his story.
[33] 'Protocol', 7 January 1981, Yad Vashem Righteous Among the Nations Archive, file 819.
[34] Testimony by Moshe Smolar, Yad Vashem Righteous Among the Nations Archive, file 819.

despite the hostility of many local Byelorussians to the Jews. It was a Polish family in the town who agreed to help him. His father, a book-keeper, had a Polish Catholic assistant, Mrs Teressa. Shortly before the liquidation of the ghetto, 'my father approached Mrs Teressa, and she agreed to hide us, and also the Rabbi's daughter, Gietl. We were hidden in Mrs Teressa's barn. Her house was the last one in that particular road, the last house before the cemetery on the east branch of the crossroads. I think we were there about two days and nights and on the third the Germans came and started liquidating the ghetto. I remember hearing lots and lots of shooting. I think I was too young to realise what was going on but Gietl was a bit older than myself and she knew. She said to me that the Germans were practising, just shooting into the marshes, which were all around the village. After a couple of days there was no more shooting. It was all finished.'

As the Germans, helped by Byelorussian police, intensified their search for hidden Jews in Stolowicze, Mrs Teressa kept Gietl in hiding with her, and managed to find a Polish Catholic woman in a neighbouring village willing to hide the young boy. This new rescuer had three children of her own, including a daughter, Yasha, who used to bring him food in the barn. 'I was always hidden, as they got frightened when I arrived. People began to ask questions. I was never really allowed to come out into the daylight. In fact I was in a locked room in the loft of the barn most of the time and sometimes things got worse because they had a relative who lived in Stolowicze by the name of Bruno who used to go and visit the family. When this happened I had to hide. Apparently in Stolowicze in the very early days of the German occupation he was in the police force and he was not one of the nicer people. Of course he would have recognised and remembered me very quickly.'

While he was at this Catholic family's farm, Richard Vanger recalled, 'I spent most of the days in the barn, sometimes the nights as well, but on cold nights I was allowed to sleep in the house. I remember that Yasha was the one who always used to bring the food to me in the barn. She would be coming over as if bringing food for the pigs or the chickens and in amongst it would be a plate for me.' As time went on, 'there was more and more trouble from the Byelorussians and it was getting dangerous for me to be there. There were one or two visits to the farm by the police searching for arms and luckily they did not take any notice of me. It was during the day time and they thought I was just a kid looking after the livestock, but the family decided I could not stay there any more.'

Richard Vanger returned to Stolowicze where, despite the great danger, Mrs Teressa agreed to take him in again. 'I was able to go into the house where I spent part of the time under the bed and part of the time in the loft in the barn. When I was hiding under the bed or in the loft I kept occupied as Mrs Teressa taught me how to knit. She showed me how to make a sock with wool and four needles. I used to knit something like a metre of sock, perhaps more, then undo it and start all over again. I also did a lot of reading . . . Mrs Teressa played the piano very nicely and every evening she used to play. Somehow or other I used to read these books and there was for me an association with the music. Even today when I hear certain Chopin pieces – and Chopin is what she mostly played – I immediately remember those particular stories.'

Richard Vanger remained with Mrs Teressa until liberation. In 1946 he was taken to Britain, where he had an aunt and uncle. In 1970 he went to live in Israel. Returning to Poland in 1991, he learned from Mrs Teressa's daughter Litka that, shortly after he had left Stolowicze for another village, two Polish policemen and an SS officer had, after a tip-off, gone to the barn in Stolowicze where he and Gietl had been hiding, and where Gietl remained. Pointing to Gietl, they asked Mrs Teressa: 'What is this Jew doing in your place?' As Mrs Teressa hesitated, Gietl said to her: 'Thank you very much for all you have done for me,' whereupon the SS officer took out a revolver and shot Gietl on the spot, in front of Mrs Teressa, her sister and Litka. 'He then pointed his revolver at Mrs Teressa and said: "Now I will kill you," whereupon Litka and her aunt started crying and they threw themselves on to Mrs Teressa. They said: "If you kill her, you will have to kill us as well," and somehow he did not shoot them. The SS officer said: "You are not to bury this Jew – leave her rotting there on your doorstep so that you will know what a Jew smells like." The men then left.'

At their meeting in 1991, Litka told Richard Vanger that four months before the end of the war Mrs Teressa had been arrested and taken to the concentration camp in Koldiczewo, four miles from Stolowicze. There she was questioned and tortured. 'Litka would not tell me the real reason why her mother had been arrested, but said: "Partly they were questioning my mother about you but there were other things too." That is all she would tell me. Mrs Teressa was beaten very badly at this place. She was made to stand in barrels of cold water and the month was March, which in Russia is very cold. Also, together with Mrs Teressa, a neighbour was arrested and this woman was shot about a month before the war ended. Obviously had the war gone on for any longer period Mrs Teressa would also have been killed.'

The war ended and Mrs Teressa was saved, although she was by then very sick. She died in 1952, 'perhaps as a result of her injuries from the beatings and the treatment she was subjected to in the concentration camp'. She was forty-two years old when she died, and was buried in the White Russian town of Slonim. Richard

Vanger added: 'No words of mine can adequately express what a wonderful, courageous and special person Mrs Teressa proved to be during those years of the Second World War. If it had not been for her and her family I would not be here to write my story.'[35]

Yad Vashem has recognized 1,755 Ukrainians – inhabitants of present-day post-Communist Ukraine – as Righteous Among the Nations.[36] A far larger number turned their weapons and their venom against the Jews. This made the acts of rescue all the more remarkable, and all the more dangerous for the rescuers, who were often betrayed, and killed together with those whom they were sheltering. Among those who risked their lives to rescue Jews in Ukraine were an Armenian, Arakel Mkrtchyan, who lived in Kharkov with her son, Vartan. They took into hiding in their house, where three of their cousins also lived, a Polish Jew, Iosef Trashinski, who had managed to escape eastward at the time of the German invasion of Poland in 1939. After the German occupation of the Ukraine in 1941 he was once more on the run. Vartan Mkrtchyan obtained forged papers for him, and he stayed with them for more than a year, until the city was liberated by the Red Army in August 1943. At that point, the two men, Iosef and Vartan, joined the army. Vartan was killed in action. Iosef completed his military service, returned to the Armenian family that had rescued him, and married one of the cousins who had helped save him, Knarik Shakhbazyan.[37]

---

[35] Richard Vanger, manuscript, 'I want to put on record . . .', sent to the author, November 2001.
[36] 'Righteous Among the Nations – per Country & Ethnic Origin,' 1 January 2002, Yad Vashem Department for the Righteous Among the Nations (list sent to the author on 29 January 2002).
[37] Yad Vashem Righteous Among the Nations Archive, file 8698.

Also in Kharkov lived Pan-Jun-Shun, an elderly Chinese labourer who, as a devoted Communist, had chosen, many years before the war, to live in the Soviet Union. At the start of the two years of German occupation he took in ten-year-old Ludmila Dvorkina and her mother, hiding them until liberation.[38]

In Kiev, a Russian Orthodox priest named Aleksey Glagolyev, the dean of the Pokrovsky Church, saved five Jews by hiding them in his home.[39] In the remote village of Yaruga, on the River Dniester, Fedor Kryzhevsky, whom the Germans had appointed the village elder, but who secretly organized local resistance, ensured, in an impressive act of compassion, that all four hundred Jewish families, as well as Jews from Bukovina and Bessarabia who had found refuge in the village, were found hiding places by their Ukrainian neighbours. Kryzhevsky also persuaded the local German administration to allow a number of Jews to live openly, as specialist winemakers, in a region where winemaking was an important part of the economy. To feed the large numbers of Jews in hiding, Kryzhevsky organized a secret food store. For eighteen months, the hidden Jews remained undiscovered: when the Romanian authorities took over the administration of the region from the Germans in late 1942 they ignored the Jews, whose survival was thereby assured.[40]

Seventy-nine Russians (defined as those living in the post-Communist Russian Republic) have been recognized by

---

[38] Testimony of Ludmila (Dvorkina) Lurie, 25 April 1993, Yad Vashem Righteous Among the Nations Archive, file 6437.

[39] 'Priest Aleksey Aleksandrovich Glagolyev . . .', United States Holocaust Memorial Museum, Photo Archive, Worksheet 67018, citing the Babi Yar Society.

[40] Wila Orbach, 'The Destruction of the Jews in the Nazi-Occupied Territories of the USSR', *Soviet Jewish Affairs*, volume 6, no. 2, 1976, London: Institute of Jewish Affairs.

Yad Vashem as Righteous Among the Nations.[41] In the Russian town of Novozybkov, as the Germans rounded up the Jews for execution in 1942, the Safonov family determined to save as many as they could. Digging a hole under their cattle shed, they hid nine Jews there, in almost total darkness. Three of them were their neighbours, the Mogilevskyis; three were members of the Gutin family, and three from the Uritskyi family. At night, under the security of darkness, the nine Jews would emerge from the hole for fresh air. The Safonovs fed them and cared for them for several months, after which Vasilyi Safonov and his sister Nadezhda led them to the forest, where Russian partisans protected them. Mrs Mogilevskyi, however, was too sick to make the journey to the forest; she stayed behind on the farm, and when she died was buried in the Safonovs' garden.

Mogilevskyi and his son fought with the Russian partisans: the son was killed in action against the Germans. Nadezhda and Vasilyi Safonov also fought with the partisans. Their parents were betrayed to the Germans, and shot – because they had hidden Jews. Mogilevskyi adopted Vasilyi as his son, and they fought side by side until the end of the war.[42]

By the end of 1942, German forces had overrun much of the Caucasus. In the north Caucasian town of Piatigorsk, the Germans announced that all 6,300 Jews in the town were to be deported. When a Russian sister and brother, Kira and Dmitry Belkov, went to say goodbye to their Jewish friends the Litovskys, the daughter of the house, Masha Litovsky, a classmate and close friend of Kira's, feared the worst and asked her friends to hide her. They took Masha home and asked

---

[41] 'Righteous Among the Nations – per Country & Ethnic Origin', 1 January 2002, Yad Vashem Department for the Righteous Among the Nations (list sent to the author on 29 January 2002).
[42] Jewish Foundation for the Righteous, website: www.jfr.org.

for their parents' permission to save their friend.

That night, the entire Jewish population of Piatigorsk, men, women and children, were loaded on trucks, taken to the outskirts of town and murdered. Masha's parents were both killed during that mass execution, but her older sister, Fira, managed to escape from one of the trucks and came to the Belkovs seeking shelter. The two sisters were hidden in the cellar. Kira and Dmitry took care of Masha and Fira, sharing food and clothing with them. It was, however, too dangerous to keep two Jews hidden for long in such a small town, so Dmitry Belkov helped the two girls escape to the town of Armavir, 150 miles away, where they made their way to the home of two Russian sisters, Adel and Zoya Zagurska, and their mother Mihalina, whom they had known before the war.

Without hesitation, Adel, Zoya and Mihalina took them in and provided them with food and shelter. The Zagurskas were able to obtain forged identity documents for Fira and Masha, and found jobs for them working in the local hospital. The five women shared a one-room apartment for over five months. There was little to eat and they lived in constant danger of being denounced. They knew from the notices all over town that the penalty for hiding Jews was death. In 1943, the Red Army liberated Armavir. Fira and Masha returned to Piatigorsk to find that they were the only members of their family to have survived. But at least they had survived.[43]

Ironically, German records sometimes reveal acts of would-be rescue. On 16 January 1942 the Einsatz-kommando unit at Kremenchug reported that it had shot a Red Army officer, Major Senitsa Vershovsky, because he had 'tried to protect the Jews'.[44]

In the late summer and early autumn of 1941, on their

---

[43] Jewish Foundation for the Righteous, website: www.jfr.org.
[44] Operational Situation Report, USSR, no. 156, 16 January 1942, International Military Tribunal, Nuremberg, Document NO-3405.

drive to Leningrad, which they besieged but never captured, the German army overran both Latvia and Estonia, then independent Baltic States. Yad Vashem has recognized ninety-three Latvians as Righteous Among the Nations.[45] In the Latvian capital, Riga, the forty-year-old Janis Lipke, who worked as a loader in the German air force stores in the city, was charged by the Germans to take a group of Jews from the ghetto each morning to the storehouse, and to supervise their work. Outraged by the massacres he had witnessed in the first weeks of the German occupation, Lipke was determined to find ways of helping as many Jews as he could. During his daily journey into the ghetto he would smuggle in food and medicine. He also befriended two Latvian drivers working for the German air force, Karl Yankovsky and Janis Briedys, with whom he planned to rescue as many Jews as possible from the ghetto.

On 15 December 1941, with the help of Briedys, Janis Lipke smuggled ten Jews out of the ghetto, finding hiding places for six of them in the cellars of houses belonging to his friends, and taking the other four to his own house.

When a further six Jews were smuggled out of the Riga ghetto, Lipke again took three of them to his home. It was then that he decided to build a special hiding place underneath a shed near his house. Using logs and cement, and building a hen-house above the entrance to the hideout, Lipke provided a secure haven, helped in his task by his wife Johanna and their eldest son, Alfred.[46]

As the German occupation continued, and the treatment of the Jews worsened, Janis Lipke continued to

[45] 'Righteous Among the Nations – per Country & Ethnic Origin,' 1 January 2002, Yad Vashem Department for the Righteous Among the Nations (list sent to the author on 29 January 2002).
[46] Information obtained in Riga by Aba and Ida Taratuta, Leningrad, and sent to the author, 1985.

devise methods of rescuing those imprisoned in the ghetto. One Riga Jew, Isaak Dryzin, later recalled that Lipke approached him and his brother, an engineer, while they were working in one of the work 'commandos' outside the ghetto. Lipke told the two brothers to go to the ghetto gate on the Day of Atonement, October 10. That morning, Lipke approached the guards at the gate. 'Give me some Yids to work in my kitchen garden,' he said, in what Isaak Dryzin later recalled as a tone of 'drunken familiarity', adding: 'Here, take two packets of cigarettes.'

For these two packets of cigarettes, Lipke received the Dryzin brothers, as well as a third Jew, Sheyenson, all three of whom had been waiting at the gates. Lipke took them to the nearest doorway out of sight of the guards, removed their yellow stars, gave them peasants' hats to put on and drove them out of Riga, to a farm of another friend. There, like the Jews whom Lipke had earlier taken from the ghetto, they were hidden in barns and haystacks.

His mission accomplished, Lipke told the Dryzin brothers: 'Tomorrow I will go to the ghetto again and will keep bringing people here every day.' That same night he began to plan a similar rescue, which he was able to carry out on the following day.[47]

After the war, it seemed puzzling to many of Lipke's neighbours that he and his family had saved Jews. 'Many of their countrymen saw them as traitors,' the writer Jeffrey Goldberg recalled. 'When I met the Lipkes in their hut in the winter of 1986, there were even rumours afoot in Riga that they were part-Jewish. How else to explain their inexplicable behaviour during World War II, when they rescued Jews from the Riga ghetto, a ghetto

[47] Material in the Vad Vashem Righteous Among the Nations Archive, file 207. Lipke and his wife received the designation Righteous in 1966.

maintained – and then liquidated – with the enthusiastic help of the Latvian people?' Of Latvia's pre-war Jewish population of more than eighty thousand, only around three thousand survived the war. Since then, ninety-three Latvians have been awarded the title of Righteous Among the Nations, Lipke among them. 'Lipke is known as the Latvian Wallenberg,' writes Goldberg, adding that of the fifty or sixty Jews whom he smuggled out of the ghetto, 'only a dozen or so survived, many of the others having been betrayed by Latvians in the countryside.' Asked why he had done what he did, Lipke told Goldberg that he was a 'man of action' who 'could not sit idly by'.[48]

Another Latvian, Yanis Vabulis, was a former officer in the Latvian army, who worked during the war in a construction company. On the eve of a night in which ten thousand Jews of Riga were slaughtered in a single massacre, Vabulis sheltered a Jewish woman, 21-year-old Zelda Shelshelovich, in an apartment in the city left empty by Jews who had been forced into the ghetto. Later he gave her refuge in his own apartment, where she masqueraded as his non-Jewish girlfriend. In that apartment Vabulis would often entertain his fellow Latvian officers, who would describe with glee the mass execution of Riga's Jews in which they had participated – and in which Zelda's entire family had been murdered. Vabulis made sure she was hiding in another room when the boasters came to call. After the war they were married.[49]

In the Latvian city of Dvinsk, only five hundred of whose thirty thousand Jewish inhabitants survived the war, Maja Zarch (later Maja Abramowitch) was offered

---

[48] Jeffrey Goldberg, 'Latvia's Empty Gesture', *Forward*, 27 February 1998.
[49] Sam Kiley, 'Secret Witness Tells of Nazis' Boasts', *The Times*, 3 January 2000.

refuge by her Gentile nanny, who had been surreptitiously getting food to her and her mother when they
returned to the ghetto after the day's forced labour. 'One
day,' Maja Abramowitch recalled, 'on our return to the
ghetto, we found my Nanny was waiting for us, upset
and agitated. She told us she had heard that graves were
again being dug. Her fervent plea was that we should
convert to Christianity, for she felt that because we were
Jews and she a devout Christian, it would be impossible
for us to meet in heaven. This deeply religious Catholic
woman risked her life every time she met us but, despite
this, she never failed to arrive. We agreed to be sprinkled
with her holy water. The following evening she was
there in the field waiting for us with a little bottle of
liquid to anoint us. She baptised my mother and me, said
a prayer and gave us both a medallion of the holy Mother
and Child. There in the field at night, under the lonely
stars, she was convinced that we had become Christians.
She was relieved and happy. The next time she met us,
shortly after our "conversion", she announced that she
had arranged with her uncle, with whom she shared a
cottage, for me to come and live with them.'

Maja Abramowitch went on: 'My mother agreed and
after our next meeting, all having been prepared, I was
smuggled from my mother's place of work, without my
yellow star, and safely reached my Nanny's house. She
lived in a very primitive, ramshackle wooden bungalow
on the outskirts of Dvinsk. The tiny property belonged
to my Nanny's aged uncle and was just large enough to
have a yard that coped with our needs. The house itself
consisted of the kitchen, a large, high, tiled stove on
which I slept at night and hid most of the day. Two small
bedrooms housed Nanny and her uncle who seldom
appeared. I remember this sojourn as a very hazardous,
lonely time.'

This was not the end of the saga. 'After two months the
neighbours became suspicious, and the uncle heard

people gossiping about a child being hidden by his niece. After a lot of soul-searching, Nanny decided to return me to the ghetto.' The sight that met them when they reached the ghetto was one of carnage: pools of blood, murdered children and dead bodies, 'mute testimony to a last useless resistance'. Surviving in the ghetto, and then surviving deportation, concentration camps, slave labour camps and death marches, Maja Abramowitch lived to tell the story of the woman who gave her at least a chance to live.[50]

In neighbouring Estonia, out of a small Jewish community of four thousand, three thousand escaped to the Soviet Union before the German army arrived. Of the thousand who remained, almost all were murdered by the SS killing squads. One of those who survived, Isidor Levin, owed his life to the help of his Bible teacher, Dr Uku Masing, and his wife Eha, who hid him and kept him from the danger of arrest and deportation. They are the two Righteous Among the Nations whom Yad Vashem has honoured for Estonia.[51]

In July 1941, Valentina Varnavina was fleeing by train from the Russian city of Zhitomir, seeking to escape the eastward thrust of the German army. Next to her on the train was a Jewish woman, Bluma Shtraim, and her two young sons, Ilya and Fima. During the journey the train was bombed, and Bluma Shtraim was killed. 'While other passengers tried desperately to escape the burning train,' writes Katia Gusarov – the person responsible for the Former Soviet Union section of the Righteous Among the Nations Department at Yad Vashem – 'Ilya and Fima remained rooted next to their mother's body.

---

[50] Maja Abramowitch, *To Forgive But Not Forget: Maja's Story*, pages 48–9.
[51] Isidor Levin, 'Uku Masing (11.8.1909–25.4.1985)'; Yad Vashem Righteous Among the Nations Archive, file 507.

Seeing the two helpless boys, Valentina grabbed them and tried to remove them from the horrifying scene. Three-year-old Fima could not run, so Valentina lifted him up and carried him. In the turmoil of the escape, ten-year-old Ilya got lost. Having failed to find the older boy, Valentina began her long journey home. As she wondered what to do with the three-year-old, little Fima clung to her even more tightly, caressing her with his tiny hands. Valentina, who did not have any children, knew at that moment she could not desert him.'

A few days passed, Katia Gusarov related, 'until the two somehow managed to return to Zhitomir. On approaching her apartment building, Valentina wondered how to explain the boy's presence to her neighbours. She decided she would initially conceal Fima, until he was able to respond to a new, less Jewish-sounding name.' The name she chose for him was Valik. Before introducing the boy, she told her neighbours that her 'nephew' was due to arrive shortly from the village. A few days later she emerged with Valik in public, and thus began Valentina and Valik's new life together. 'Over time, the two became very attached to one another, all memories of Valik's life prior to the war seemingly forgotten. But Valentina remembered: as well as his black, curly hair, the child was circumcised, and Valentina lived in great fear that her secret would be revealed.'

In November 1943 the Red Army liberated Zhitomir. 'One day, several months later, an unexpected visitor appeared on Valentina's doorstep. To her great surprise, it was Ilya, Fima's elder brother. Ilya had miraculously survived the war by wandering alone . . .'

There was a remarkable sequel to this story of rescue. One evening in the summer of 2001, Fima Shtraim (then known as Yefim Sklarsky, having lived in Israel since the early 1990s) was watching a Russian television programme dedicated to the search for missing persons. As he watched, he was astonished to see a familiar face on the screen. 'There before his very eyes was Svetlana Shubaliuk, the adopted daughter of his beloved rescuer, Valentina Varnavina. Her voice cracking with emotion, Svetlana was holding up a picture of a young child, imploring anyone who knew of the child's whereabouts to notify her immediately. Through heavy tears, Yefim identified the child in the picture; it was a photo of himself as a young boy, taken while he was under the care of Valentina Varnavina.'[52]

Despite the passage of time, the bond between rescuer and rescued, and between their families, is one of the strongest ties from that time of torment.

---

[52] Katia Gusarov, 'Valentina and Valik, Rescued from the Wreckage', *Yad Vashem Quarterly Magazine* (Jerusalem), volume 25, Winter 2002.

CHAPTER TWO

Eastern Galicia

In accordance with the terms of the Nazi–Soviet Pact of
August 1939, Eastern Galicia became part of the Soviet
Union after the German conquest of Poland. It was not
until June 1941, following the German invasion of the
Soviet Union, that the region, with its more than a quarter
of a million Jews, came under German rule. With occupation came the mass murder of Jews by the SS killing
squads and the establishment of ghettos where all
surviving Jews were confined, and from which they were
later deported to their deaths. Most East Galician Jews
who were not murdered in their towns and homes were
deported to the death camp at Belzec, and murdered there.

In Lvov, the Eastern Galician capital, those who
offered to help Jews included Wladyslawa Choms, a
Polish woman known as the 'Angel of Lvov'.[1] Following
the establishment in Warsaw of Zegota – the Council for
Assistance to the Jews – she became the head of its local
branch. Later she was to describe how both the Roman
Catholic Church and the underground Armia Krajowa or
Home Army assisted her and Zegota in making it
possible for Jews to be saved. 'The Catholic clergy were
of invaluable assistance', she wrote, 'in enabling us to
obtain certificates of baptism, for which they provided

---

[1] Yad Vashem Righteous Among the Nations Archive, file 6.

blank forms, instructions on what to do, and ready-made certificates. How much effort and nerves went into the making of one document! With time we became more experienced. Zegota from Warsaw began to supply us with blanks of documents and the Home Army legalizing cell with beautifully made official stamps. The fury of the Gestapo at our graphic skills was correspondingly great for they realized what was going on.'[2]

One of those who owed his survival to Wladyslawa Choms and to at least one other member of Zegota in Eastern Galicia was Zygmunt Chotiner. In a letter describing his survival he wrote of how, in the town of Brody, one of her representatives came to his aid: 'During the war I, like all of us fellow Jews, had been refused human rights and was doomed to await a tragic end. At the very critical moment, however, appeared at Brody, where a small group of us was hard working but still existing, a Mr Jukalo. The before-mentioned gentleman was representing Mrs Choms, a social lady, well known for her pro-Jewish sympathies. He was offering us help in the form of false papers, money, etc. At the beginning it seemed too unbelievable to be true and we were rather suspicious but finally he succeeded in convincing us.' Soon they were given the promised false papers and money, 'which we received every month from now on as a rule. Some of us found accommodation at Mrs Choms' friends over on the "Aryan" side and some disappeared, trying to take a chance on their own.'

Zygmunt Chotiner's account continued: 'It is to my knowledge that the honourable Mrs Choms had to be careful not only of the Gestapo but even of her neighbours of whom she could never be certain. She also had to change her name and place of living quite often. They say she despatched a letter to the late President

---

[2] Wladyslawa Choms, quoted in Kazimierz Iranek-Osmecki, *He Who Saves One Life*, page 50.

Roosevelt, asking him for help for the Jews. I personally know of many cases whereby she gave away her last food (which was so scarce in those days) to help the people. I am also glad to know that before the war Mrs Choms went for a trip to Palestine, which impressed her very much. Afterwards, she, together with the famous Professor Bartel, was editor of the democratic paper *Czarne na Bialem* ('Black on White') in which she inspired the Poles to be loyal to their friends the Jews, whose productive work she happened to admire in the Promised Land. I also know that Mrs Choms helped to hide the doomed Jews from the ghetto and the escapees from the underground water canals. Two of her Polish lady friends were tortured to death after the search and discovery of false papers for the Jewish people. My Jewish lady friend had to undergo a dangerous operation: Mrs Choms produced both the surgeon and the money to perform it. She placed a lot of Jewish children in the orphan houses too.'

It was Zygmunt Chotiner's 'deep feeling and conviction' that there were 'no words to describe what she was trying to do (and, in consequence, suffering) to help us'. His worry, many years after the war, was that he could not help her. 'Unfortunately, I am a hard-working, ordinary worker now, have quite a number of dependants and can hardly make ends meet. While living in Germany, I used to help Mrs Choms by despatching food parcels to her but that was not enough to cover our debt which no money in the world could ever pay off. She is a generous and noble, clean human being and we all who knew her feel very much obliged and thankful to her for all she has done for us, risking her own life to save ours.'[3]

From the first hours of the German occupation of Lvov,

---

[3] Letter of 21 May 1952, seeking funds to enable Mrs Choms to emigrate to the United States. In the event, the government of Israel invited her to Jerusalem. Yad Vashem Righteous Among the Nations Archive, file 6.

mobs of local Ukrainian hoodlums, incited by German proclamations and pamphlets, rampaged through the streets and houses, murdering Jews wherever they found them, or taking them to the city's prisons, where thousands were tortured and shot. In an attempt to halt the slaughter, Yechezkel Lewin, editor-in-chief of the Jewish weekly newspaper *Opinja* ('Opinion'), and rabbi of the Reform Synagogue in Lvov, went, in his rabbinical robes, to see the head of the Ukrainian Catholic Church, Metropolitan Sheptitsky. 'You told me once, "I am a friend of Israel",' Lewin declared. 'You have always emphasized your friendship to us, and we ask you now, at this time of terrible danger, to give proof of your friendship and to use your influence over the wild crowds rioting against us.' According to one account, Sheptitsky declined the rabbi's request to go out and ask the mobs to disperse.

Meanwhile, in the words of Philip Friedman – then a young Jewish historian in Lvov – 'the mobs were on the rampage, the howls of the killers mingled with the screams of the victims, and the slaughter in the streets continued.' Sheptitsky urged Lewin to remain in the security of the Metropolitan's episcopal palace until the violence had subsided, but Lewin told him: 'My mission is completed. I have come to make a request for the community, and shall return to the congregation, where my place is.' He then left and walked back towards his home. On the way, several of his Christian friends urged him to return to Sheptitsky's palace for his own safety, but he refused to do so. On reaching his own house he was seized by Ukrainian militiamen and taken to prison. There, still in his rabbinical robes, he was beaten with the rifle butts of Ukrainian soldiers before being shot down in the prison yard. Also among the thousands of Jews murdered in these prison killings was Lewin's brother, Rabbi Aaron Lewin, a former deputy in the Polish parliament, who was the head of the rabbinical court in the Western Galician city of Rzeszow.[4]

Metropolitan Sheptitsky arranged to find a hiding place for Rabbi Yechezkel Lewin's son Kurt and his brother, as well as for several other Jewish youngsters, including Leon Chameides – whom he placed in the Studite monastery in the town of Uhniv – Leon's brother Zwi, and a young woman, Lili Stern, who, with her mother and a Jewish couple, Jozef and Anna Podoszyn, were taken into Sheptitsky's palace in Lvov in March 1944, and kept there in safety for several months, until liberation.

Zwi Chameides (now Zwi Barnea) has recalled the many people who played their part in his rescue: first Metropolitan Sheptitsky himself, who took him to see his brother, Father Ihumen Sheptitsky; then Father Ihumen, who transferred him to a young seminarian called Ben; then Ben, who showed him how to make the sign of the cross correctly, and then went with him on foot to a suburb of Lvov, to a boarding school run by the Studite monastic order. The boys were hostile to him, however, and he had to move on. He was taken to yet another person willing to help, Brother Boyarskyi, a monk who gave him shelter, taught him the basics of Christianity and improved his knowledge of the Ukrainian language, which he would need to speak well if he were to pass himself off as a Ukrainian Christian. Brother Boyarskyi then took him by train to the town of Przemyslany, from where they walked for several hours to an orphanage attached to the monastery at Uhniv. 'Late that night I fell ill. A Brother who had some medical knowledge was called and gave me a hot infusion of berries to drink. I was probably feverish and half asleep when I heard Brother Boyarskyi discuss with a priest whether I could stay in the Uhniv orphanage.

---

[4] Philip Friedman, *Roads to Extinction*, pages 246–8.

The priest was explaining to Brother Boyarskyi that they could not accommodate me. First, they already had one other boy like me, and, besides, the situation was particularly dangerous because Przemyslany had just been cleared of Jews and the Germans were searching the surrounding villages for any who might have managed to escape.'

Zwi Barnea's account continued: 'At first I hoped that the priest might have changed his mind about letting me stay. The Uhniv orphanage was a very pleasant place after the ghetto and boarding-school experiences. The children were very friendly, and I now found that my Ukrainian no longer drew any attention to me. I also discovered that the orphanage had a number of books. One of these was a primer of Church Slavonic which explained to me the meaning of the many strange words in the basic prayers I had memorized. I taught myself the Church Slavonic alphabet, which is very similar to modern Cyrillic. I soon guessed which little boy was Jewish. After being allowed to rest for a few days, I was nevertheless obliged to return with Brother Boyarskyi to Lvov.'

In Lvov, Zwi was taken 'to an elderly Ukrainian woman who lived in a flat with a maid, Sofia. The woman was a widow whose husband had been a well-to-do engineer. The couple had close connections with the church. Both the woman, whose name I have unfortunately not retained, and the maid were extremely frightened to keep me and made elaborate plans of how I was to escape through the back door if the Germans should come. I stayed with them for about a week and then Ben the seminarian came to take me to an orphanage in Brzuchowice, a small town near Lvov.'

The orphanage in Brzuchowice accepted the young boy. On the first day, another boy asked him his name. 'When I told him, he said: "Oh, your brother is also here." I protested that I had no brother, only to be confronted with my brother Leon. Apparently, for the sake of good order we had both been assigned the surname Khaminskyi, and by resemblance we certainly looked like brothers. I knew it was bad for us to be associated with one another and therefore continued to maintain that my name was Khominskyi and not Khaminskyi and besides I had no brother. My brother Leon, following my lead, confirmed that he too had no brother. Fortunately, the children soon lost interest in whether we were brothers or not and the grown-ups did not even become involved in the matter.' Although all the children spoke Ukrainian, Zwi Barnea noticed that their command of the language varied considerably. 'I soon guessed that there were among the children at least two Jewish girls and another little Jewish boy, Dorko (Oded Amarant), about my brother's age.'

One of the Jewish girls was called Romka. One morning, as Zwi Barnea later recalled, a Ukrainian woman who worked in the orphanage office started questioning her about whether she was Jewish, what her Jewish name was, and whether the lady from the office was her mother. 'Romka denied the accusations and the woman became increasingly angry and started shrieking at her. Since the boys in my room crowded into the other room to see what was happening, I also went in just as the woman asked Romka to make the sign of the cross, which Romka, whom I had coached, demonstrated faultlessly. The woman became increasingly hysterical as little Romka, about eight years old, continued to deny everything with cool dignity.'

Still Zwi Barnea was not out of danger. One day a doctor arrived, accompanied by a young nurse. 'There was no advance notice and my bed being nearest the door, I was the first to be examined. The doctor looked at my chest briefly and then pulled down my pyjama trousers and then quickly pulled them up again. I could see dismay on his face and then saw him turn and scrutinise carefully the face of the accompanying nurse. The nurse's dull expression had not changed during the examination. She had apparently not seen or recognised what the doctor saw. I saw the doctor's face relax somewhat as he moved on to the next examination. I considered what had happened and concluded immediately that the doctor had no intention of reporting that I was circumcised. Nevertheless, I was, of course, extremely worried. At about nine that evening one of the nuns appeared and asked me whether the doctor had examined me. I nodded vigorously. The nun told me to dress and went off. She returned soon and when I came out she was waiting with my brother and Dorko.'

The boys walked that night to a small convent in Brzuchowice, whose nuns belonged to the Order of St Basil. They slept there that night, and the next day a nun took them back to Lvov, to the Studite monastery near the archbishop's residence. 'Here I met for the first time Father Marko (now recognised by Yad Vashem as a Righteous Gentile). Father Marko was a young, handsome priest with a smiling face and energetic manner. He laughed a great deal and when he conversed with us one felt his obvious affection. He listened attentively when I told him that there were two Jewish girls who still remained in the orphanage and then smiled and looked at me thoughtfully without replying. ('Romka' and her mother survived and sent me a message after our liberation but I did not meet them again and never got to know their names or story.) Father Marko told us that he would take my brother and Dorko to Uhniv. I was to wait for his return and in the meantime I was again placed with the engineer's widow and her maid Sofia who were now even more fearful than during my previous stay.'

Father Marko took the boy by train to Stanislawow, 'which we reached after much trouble. We stayed there overnight with Father Marko's friends who were very frightened to accommodate me. A group of Jews who were hiding nearby in a bunker they had built under a bombed-out house had just been apprehended. Father Marko tried to reassure his friends by telling them that I had family in England. I do not know how he knew this.'

From Stanislawow Father Marko took the boy on, by train, via Czortkow, to the end of the railway line. From there they continued by horse and cart to the village of Paniowce Zielone, where the River Zbrucz flows into the Dniester, which at that point marked the border between pre-war Poland and Romania. 'Father Marko brought me here to the house of his older brother, Father Stek, who was a parish priest and lived with their elderly mother who managed the household. Before leaving, Father Marko suggested that I tell his mother the day after his departure that I was Jewish. However, I was too frightened to do so and persuaded myself that this extraordinarily shrewd woman had already figured it out all by herself.'

In due course the boy was taken back once more to Lvov, to a church boarding school. The director, Father Kyprian, found out that the lad was circumcised but did nothing. When liberation came, the young man learned that his father and his grandparents had been murdered. Two months after liberation, on his way home from school, the young man encountered a funeral procession. 'I recognized immediately that it was the funeral of a very important person because of the large number of Greek Catholic bishops in full funeral vestments who followed the coffin. They were followed by a group of high-ranking officers of the Red Army. Next to me an elderly woman made the sign of the cross in the Greek Catholic manner and so I asked her in Ukrainian whose funeral it was. The Metropolitan Sheptitsky had died, she told me, wiping away her tears.'[5]

It was not only his Christian flock that mourned the

---

[5] 'Report to Sir Martin', sent to the author by Zwi Barnea on 14 May 2001.

Metropolitan. Those whom he helped to save were, and remain, determined to obtain recognition for the churchman whom one of them, Leon Chameides, calls 'this saintly man'.[6]

Bracha Weisbarth was only three years old when the Germans overran the Ukrainian village in which she lived. She escaped with her mother and brother, and recalls how, 'while we were in the forest, various individuals helped us. On occasion we were given shelter in their homes.' All three survived – as the twenty-first century began, her mother was ninety-five years old.[7]

Throughout Eastern Galicia, individual churchmen protected Jews. In the small town of Liczkowce, Father Michael Kujata hid eight-year-old Anita Helfgott, a fugitive from the ghetto at Skole, in his parsonage. Later a Catholic couple, Josef and Paulina Matusiewicz, gave her sanctuary. She survived the war.[8] Priests played a crucial role in many cases. Felicia Braun was just five years old when, after the death of her mother, she was taken away from the terrible scenes and cries and hiding places – including a coal-box – of the Warsaw Ghetto, to a village in Eastern Galicia. One summer day, she later recalled, her aunt dressed her up 'in a fancy dress. I had never worn such a dress before. She told me that she was taking me to my grandmother's house. We walked out of the apartment block toward the walls of the ghetto. All the while, my aunt was repeating out loud the address of my "grandmother". When we reached the gates, she bent down and whispered to me, "Felicia, you are as smart as Shirley Temple. From now on, you will have to be a little actress in order to stay alive. From now on,

---

[6] Dr Leon Chameides, letter to the author, 30 January 2001.
[7] Bracha Weisbarth, letter to the author, 20 March 2001.
[8] 'Anita plays in the parsonage yard of Father Michael Kujata', United States Holocaust Memorial Museum, Photo Archive, Worksheet 09316.

your last name will be Garbarczyk." She pointed out a bench outside the walls where she said I would find a man who would take me to my "grandmother". She told me that the guard at the wall would turn away when I walked by.'

Felicia Braun's account continued: 'I was five years old. I repeated my instructions dutifully. I kissed my aunt goodbye. I wanted to live. I skipped through the gates and saw the man. He rose to get on a bus. I followed him. He did not speak to me. I followed him when he got off the bus. He motioned me toward a building. We went inside and climbed the stairs to an apartment. Inside, he told me, "Lie down on that bed and don't move." I did as I was told, lying motionless in the severe heat, barely breathing so no one could hear me. That night, my father appeared. I had no idea where he had been or how long he would stay. I wanted him to stay with me forever. He bathed me and fed me and led me out to another apartment building. He settled me onto a sofa where I fell into a deep sleep, drained from fear and exhaustion. This was the first of the many places I was moved to. In each of them, I was taught Catholic prayers. It seemed to me that everywhere I was sent, German soldiers followed.'

Several months later, Felicia Braun recalled, 'I was taken by the same stranger onto a train. I had been told that I was going to live in the country. I was told I would be safe. I was told not to ask questions. The train was crowded. Soldiers boarded. Their dogs were straining at their leashes, snarling, snapping, biting at whomever the soldiers pointed them toward. They were sniffing out Jews, and when they found them, the soldiers unleashed the dogs to tear the Jews apart. I was so desperate to live that I laughed at the hideous scene, laughed at the Jews being mauled, pretending as if I were Shirley Temple. I was brought to a farmhouse far out in the country and introduced to a middle-aged couple whose names were Leokadia (called Losia) and Kazimierz Stroka. They were to be my new parents. Concerned for my safety, they, too, moved from one part of the country to another.'

One day, when the Strokas and their new 'daughter' were staying in a Ukrainian village near Rawa Russka, Felicia Braun's own father came for a brief visit. 'He appeared on Christmas Eve carrying gifts for all of us and stayed for three days. The night before he left, he took me into his arms and covered my face with kisses.' The next day he left. 'Watching from the window as he walked through the snow, I knew I would have to be brave like him. I knew I could never let anyone know that I was Felicia Braun, that I was a Jew. I was able to deceive everyone, even the German soldiers who visited the Strokas regularly. They would sit me on their knees and tell me how I looked just like their own daughters, like a good German girl.'

Felicia Braun recalled the day of her First Communion: 'I was tortured with apprehension. What if today someone doubts me? I thought. What if someone asks: "Are you sure that child is Catholic? Are you sure she is one of us?" I could not get my face to wear the right expression. No matter how hard I tried to put on my very best Shirley Temple smile, my eyes showed only terror. I was as frightened as I had been in any of the last few years of my life, frightened as I was in the coal-box, frightened that I would be found hiding – this time, in my Catholic disguise. I was terrified that I would be wrenched from the prison of my carefully crafted lies and thrown into a new prison where I would be tortured to death with the truth.'

The photographer who was taking pictures of the children who were about to receive their First Communion tried to cheer her up. 'He told me how beautiful I looked in my Communion dress. He took a photograph, but the expression on my face was so miserable that he had to take another one. "Come, you want to be bright for your Communion picture. You will keep it all your life to remember this happy day," he said. I was nearly sobbing. His second picture looked even worse. In disgust, he told aunt Losia that he would waste no more pictures on me, and that she would have to bring me back another time when I had some control of myself. I already knew how angry "Uncle" Stroka would be.'

The ceremony went ahead. 'I was shoved into the procession of children and felt my feet moving toward the altar. As I knelt, I heard the voice of Father Kaczmarek as he leaned toward me with the wafer. I looked up into the kindest face that had ever gazed at me, at a face whose eyes I could look into forever. They were eyes that accepted my lies and loved me despite them. What I saw was the face of my real father. I thanked God that it was him and that none of the people in this church had discovered Felicia's lie.'[9]

In the Eastern Galician city of Tarnopol, a Polish nursing student, Irene Gut Opdyke, worked as a supervisor in a German laundry. Located in a camp near the ghetto, the laundry also used Jewish women as forced labourers. The young Polish woman treated these women 'with special sensitivity'. At the camp, she worked for a German major who suffered from digestive ailments. Irene prepared special meals for him. His gratitude took the form of a willingness to overlook her bending the rules with regard to the Jewish workers. With his connivance, Irene acquired special passes making it possible for the Jewish workers and their families to leave the ghetto and remain in the laundry while deportation 'actions' were taking place in the ghetto. In July 1943, when the camp where the laundry facility was located was slated for liquidation, Irene urged the three hundred Jewish forced labourers to flee. She hid nine of the workers in the major's private

---

[9] Recollections of Felicia Braun, in Wiktoria Sliwowska, *The Last Eyewitnesses: Children of the Holocaust Speak*, pages 263–6.

apartment. When the major discovered what she had done, he berated her for placing him in jeopardy; but somehow, Irene managed to persuade him to allow the Jews to remain, and he even agreed to furnish his cellar with some conveniences to make their lives more comfortable. When the Gestapo became suspicious and came to investigate, Irene refused to allow them to search the premises, on the grounds that they were the private residence of a major in the German army; she suggested they call him at his office instead. The ruse succeeded, and the police left without conducting a search.

As the war turned against the Germans, Irene and other personnel in the German civil administration were ordered to evacuate Tarnopol and move towards the German border. Instead, Irene went into hiding with the Jews in the cellar, and then fled with them to the forests; there, before parting from them, she arranged for a Polish woman to look after them. They were subsequently liberated by Soviet forces on 23 March 1944. In the meantime, Irene had been taken with the retreating Germans to Kielce. She managed to escape and joined a Polish partisan unit. She survived the war, to be recognized as one of the Righteous Among the Nations.[10]

Walenty Laxander, a Pole living in Tarnopol, was working as an engineer in the nearby Czystylow labour camp when he was handed a bundle and asked to keep it safe until the end of the war. That bundle was a two-month-old girl, Gizela Ginsberg, the only child of a Jewish couple working in the camp. The child was born in April 1943, at the very moment when the Jews of Tarnopol and the surrounding towns – among them the

[10] 'Irene Gut Opdyke poses with Jewish forced labourers . . .', United States Holocaust Memorial Museum, Photo Archive, file 89819, citing Gay Block and Malka Drucker, *Rescuers: Portraits of Moral Courage in the Holocaust*; Paldiel, *The Path of the Righteous*, pages 210–11. See also Irene Gut Opdyke, *In My Hands: Memories of a Holocaust Rescuer*.

baby's grandparents – were being deported to Belzec and murdered. A Polish doctor helped Laxander smuggle the baby out of the labour camp, leaving the bundle on a street in Tarnopol for him to collect. He then registered the baby as an 'abandoned' Christian child, and raised her as his own. Gizela's parents were murdered when the labour camp was liquidated. Gizela survived. Shortly before being killed, her father had sent her a letter, asking that Laxander's memory be one day honoured for his act of rescue. The letter was dated 4 June 1943; fifty-three years later Laxander was recognized as a Righteous Among the Nations.[11]

During one of the round-ups of Jews in Warsaw in August 1942, Maria (Maryla) Charaszkiewicz, who had already saved a number of Jews in both Warsaw and Lvov, received an urgent message from her dentist in Lvov, Dr Kamila Landau, who asked for help. 'Maryla came to see me immediately,' Dr Landau recalled. 'She did not even let me say a word and she acted very quickly. She told me to put a hat on my head, placed a handbag in my hands, and she took me out of the clinic. We entered a streetcar that went to the Aryan side.' From Lvov, Maryla Charaszkiewicz took Dr Landau into the countryside, to Grodek Jagiellonski, where her sister Yula lived. Yula took in the fugitive, refusing to accept payment.

Dr Landau's account continued: 'Maryla sent food for me because Yula's material wellbeing was far from good. She was married to a worker at a railway station. My benefactors looked after me and they hid me without any compensation. I was sick and tired of sitting inside all the time, and in October 1942 I went for a walk. When I got back, I heard screams. It was Yula who intentionally

---

[11] Paldiel, 'A Last Letter and a Precious "Bundle"', *Yad Vashem Quarterly Magazine* (Jerusalem), volume 26, Spring 2002.

raised her voice saying: "What? My cousin is a Jew? How dare you say such a thing! When she returns from Lvov, I'll prove what kind of a Jewess she is!" I realized that she raised her voice to let me know what was happening. I fled from there, and I hid in the bushes. Some time later they left. I heard her husband's footsteps, who came home at that moment, and Yula's voice: "They came here to look for our Marylka (this is how she called me) and I do not know where she went. I am worried about her." Then I called her from the bushes and she was happy to hear my voice. It turned out that there had been an informant against me. Our neighbours' daughter who returned home after being sent to work in Germany understood who I was and informed the Gestapo. "I will go to Lvov tomorrow," I said. Yula accompanied me. She walked first, and I followed her, and thus we came to Lvov.'

Maryla Charaszkiewicz described what followed: 'The door opened, Yula entered and she said: "I brought you your dear friend, and she is waiting for you in St Anna's Church." A problem arose, where to hide our Marylka. I called my Ukrainian neighbour who had a room with an entrance from the corridor between our two rooms, and she agreed to lease me a room (for financial compensation). I made a kind of a garbage room, a real dump; and I told my neighbour I planned to store potatoes there. At that moment even my husband didn't know that Marylka was in the house. I put a bed in the room for Marylka. We decided that when we were not home, she could use our apartment. We had to reveal this secret to our domestic servant. I told her that my cousin was hiding in the garbage room because she had fled from forced labour in Germany and that my husband didn't know about her presence.'

Dr Landau later recalled how, when the Charaszkiewiczs were busy in their shop, she helped their maid with the housework. Then at seven in the evening, she would return to her room, 'where Mr Charaszkiewicz never entered. After the war he told me that he knew all about this but he pretended not to know. This proved the nobility of his character. He overcame his fear and he didn't prevent his wife from helping me.'

Maryla Charaszkiewicz remembered: 'We were terribly afraid all the time. We were often standing at the window looking into the street and thinking: maybe they are coming . . . Once we entered our apartment and saw Marylka standing in the kitchen. She obviously forgot it was already seven o'clock in the evening. I shielded the door with my body because I didn't want my husband to notice Marylka, but I couldn't hold myself up and I fainted.'[12]

Fanny Tennenbaum and her eleven-year-old son Dawid escaped from the ghetto in Lvov in August 1942. A Ukrainian professor who was a friend of the family assisted her escape and found her a temporary hiding place at the home of an Ethnic German in Lvov. Ironically, the son of the professor was serving as a member of the Ukrainian SS on the Eastern Front. After a month, the professor secured false papers for Fanny and Dawid, and found them a long-term hiding place in the village of Zimna Wola. They moved there in December 1942, to live in the home of an elderly retired schoolteacher, Mrs Sokolinska. Shortly afterwards their first hiding place was raided and everyone there was arrested.

In Zimna Wola, Fanny Tennenbaum hid under the name Franciszka Maria Wieczorkowska. Her son, who had grown his hair long, passed as her daughter, and was given the name Teresa Marja Wieczorkowska. He also pretended to be retarded, so as to avoid having to take the required physical examination to attend school. He

[12] 'Double Testimony' of Dr Kamila Landau and Maria (Maryla) Charaszkiewicz, Yad Vashem Righteous Among the Nations Archive, file 1028.

passed his time playing by himself and reading among the many books in the house. Occasionally during their first year in Zimna Wola, Fanny succeeded in returning to Lvov and visiting her husband, but he disappeared in the spring of 1943. He was almost certainly sent to the concentration camp at Janowska and later perished. The Soviet army liberated Dawid and his mother in September 1944: he was then thirteen years old.[13]

In Lvov, Katarzyna Rudawksa hid thirteen-year-old Halina Gartenberg for fourteen months, until liberation: her parents and her brother were also killed in Janowska. 'Katarzyna was a very simple woman, who could hardly read or write,' Halina later recalled. 'She was a very courageous woman of very high moral standards. She told me, at one point, that one day she will stand before her God and would have to explain why she let me die.'[14]

Donia Rosen, who later became head of the Department of the Righteous at Yad Vashem, responsible for seven years for submitting names for the Righteous award, was herself saved by two peasant women – one Polish and one Ukrainian – in the Eastern Galician town of Kosow. As a twelve-year-old girl, Donia had witnessed the execution of her parents; she then wandered, alone, in the forest until, as she recalled, she came to a village where she remembered a friend of the family lived, and she asked her for help. This woman, with all her good will, was afraid to take the risk – and even more afraid of her husband who, she feared, might not agree to hide the girl, and might even report her to the police. Nevertheless, she took Donia in for a while, and then introduced her to an elderly woman, Olena Hryhorysztyn, who was prepared to take the risk of

[13] 'Dawid Tennenbaum . . . dressed as a Christian girl . . .', United States Holocaust Memorial Museum, Photo Archive, Worksheet 60282.
[14] Halina Gartenberg, letter to the author, 12 March 2002.

helping her. 'Olena was an old, uncomplicated woman who was in strained financial circumstances,' Donia Rosen recalled, 'but she was extremely rich in spirit, kindness, and the nobility of her soul. She was lonely and poor,' but from the start felt attached to Donia, and set herself the goal of saving her.

Olena Hryhorysztyn – for whom Donia Rosen later acquired a Righteous award – found hiding places for Donia, and took various jobs in order to be able to bring her food. When her fellow villagers discovered that she was hiding a Jew in her house they beat her severely, and then reported her to the Germans, who arrested both of them. Miraculously, the two escaped from the place where they were imprisoned. Undaunted by what had happened, Olena swore to do everything in her power to ensure Donia's continued survival.

Helped by Olena Hryhorysztyn, the young girl continued to wander from one hiding place to another, hiding even in wells in the woods. Olena camouflaged these hiding places for her, and brought her food. Several times she was caught and questioned about where she had hidden the Jewish girl. Severely beaten yet again, she never broke down, never spared herself, and sacrificed everything so that Donia would live.[15]

Well aware that efforts to rescue Jews in Eastern Galicia were multiplying, the head of the SS and police in the General-Government in Cracow wrote on 7 October 1943 to the Reich Security Main Office in Berlin: 'According to reports reaching us from the Galicia District, the number of cases immediately pending before the special court in Lvov, regarding people providing refuge for Jews, has in the last period increased greatly in number and in scope. The death

---

[15] Donia Rosen, *The Forest My Friend*. New York: Bergen-Belsen Memorial Press, 1971; Yad Vashem Righteous Among the Nations Archive, file 144.

penalty is the sole punishment under the law for this crime. In the present situation, the special courts have had on occasion to carry out successive death penalties. Judicial circles more or less oppose this. The nature of their criticism is that the death penalty should be implemented by the secret police. Nevertheless, everyone agrees that the death penalty is entirely necessary since under present conditions, the Jews in hiding have the legal status of pirates.'

Philip Friedman, in quoting this report, comments: 'It appears from this that many death sentences were carried out against Gentiles who concealed Jews. In fact, at the time of the report, SS and Gestapo personnel did not always wait for a trial, but sometimes murdered both the "guilty" Gentiles and the Jews they were hiding. Court-ordered executions, however, which took place amid great publicity, served the Germans to impose upon the Gentiles a dread of offering Jews any assistance. Particularly infamous was the death sentence carried out against Kazimierz Jozefek, who had concealed a few Jews in his house in the Kleparow suburb. This execution instilled fear in the Gentiles, and greatly disheartened the Jews who still remained in hiding.' Friedman adds that dozens of Jews in hiding, or posing as Aryans, were caught every day, and either killed immediately or sent to Janowska camp and murdered there.[16]

The threat of betrayal was ever present. Near the village of Tluste in Eastern Galicia, a Polish farmer took in Baruch Milch and his wife, as well as his brother-in-law and his wife, offering all four safety from the destruction all around. The farmer and his family had known the two brothers-in-law, both physicians, before the war. But this farmer – to whom Milch, in his testi-

---

[16] Philip Friedman, *Roads to Extinction*, page 300.

mony in the Jewish Historical Institute in Warsaw, refers to only as 'B' – was not all that he seemed to be. While Milch and his brother-in-law went out in search for another shelter, they were betrayed. The two young wives were murdered, their bodies desecrated and then buried near a rubbish dump. 'The saviour turned into traitor,' comments Sara Rosen, herself a survivor, who translated Milch's testimony.[17]

A second family, by the name of Zielinski, who had not known Milch or his brother-in-law before the war, took them in, and kept them in hiding for nine months. In spite of the danger to their own lives, the Zielinskis gave the two grieving men both 'moral support and love', in addition to taking care of all their daily needs. Later, they found a hiding place for the two men in a convent near Tluste, run by three Sisters of Mercy and their Mother Superior. Baruch Milch later recalled: 'These heroic women ran the religious services of the parish, conducted the choir, played the organ and managed the kindergarten. Later in the summer they opened a secret shelter for foundlings. Among these tiny outcasts were about six or eight Jewish children left by desperate parents roaming the fields and forests, or just found abandoned at the monastery's threshold.' On one occasion the three nuns found in their backyard a four-year-old boy, speaking only Yiddish. 'They gathered him into their midst. As long as the murderers were unaware of what was going on behind the walls the self-sacrificing women shared their scanty provisions, fed their charges, cared for them and took them to the church.'[18]

In Lvov, a professional thief, Leopold Socha, and one of his pre-war companions in crime, Stefan Wroblewski – both of whom were sewer workers in wartime Lvov

---

[17] Sara Rosen, letter to the author, 16 January 2002.
[18] Testament by Baruch Milch, Archives of the Jewish Historical Institute, Warsaw.

– made it possible for ten Jews to survive the final round-up and executions in the ghetto on 1 June 1943. One of those who was saved, seventeen-year-old Halina Wind, later recalled how, as the Gestapo surrounded the ghetto that day, 'We did not know what to do. We went down with a group into the basement through a pipe, steps, water, a tunnel, other pipes. Finally we were crawling in the sewers of Lvov. We heard a rush of water. Suddenly we were standing on a narrow ledge against a wall. In front of us flowed the Peltew River. Along this ledge very slowly and carefully people were moving. Sometimes there was a splash, when someone slipped and fell in or couldn't stand the stress any more and deliberately jumped in.'[19]

With the group was Leopold Socha, who, in his pre-war life as a thief, had long been familiar with the sewers as a hiding place for his stolen goods. Now, as a sewer worker, his interest was professional. Socha and his friend Wroblewski took twenty-one of the Jews whom he found in the sewer, including Halina, to one of his subterranean hiding places, telling them to 'stay put' and promising to bring them food on the following day. Halina Wind later recalled that the group included one whole family: Jerzy Chigier, his wife Peppa, their seven-year-old daughter Christine and their four-year-old son Pawel. 'We were brought food every day,' she added, 'always by different manholes so as not to arouse suspicion.' Another of those whom Socha sheltered was a pregnant woman, Weinbergowa. She survived child-birth in these grim conditions, but her child died shortly afterwards.

Halina Wind also recalled how several of the group decided to leave that particular hiding place for some other refuge elsewhere in the sewers. 'None ever

---

[19] Testimony of Halina Zipora Preston (*née* Wind), Yad Vashem Righteous Among the Nations Archive, file 1379.

returned. Three of them left one morning and we found their bodies the same evening.'

Each week Leopold Socha would take the dirty clothes of those in hiding and return them washed. He also brought them a Jewish prayer book that he had found in the now deserted ghetto. At Passover, knowing that Jews could not eat leavened bread, he brought a large load of potatoes which he pushed down through several man-holes. 'We were careful of the potatoes,' Halina Wind later recalled, 'always eating the rotten ones first, until we realized that the rats were having a feast on the fresh ones.' On the day that the Red Army forced the German surrender at Stalingrad, Socha and Wroblewski brought the fugitives vodka to celebrate.

On 27 July 1944 the German army retreated from Lvov. Only a few hundred of the city's once flourishing community of a hundred thousand Jews had survived. Among those survivors were ten of the Jews hidden by Socha. While still underground they heard the firing of the guns in the streets above. Then they heard Socha shouting down to them, 'Get ready, you are free.' Halina Wind later recalled: 'The manhole cover was opened, and one by one we climbed out, some reluctantly, since they were still afraid.' The manhole cover was in the courtyard of the house, inside which Socha's wife Magdalena had prepared a table with cake and vodka.

Some months later, Leopold Socha was accidentally killed, run over by a truck in the streets of Lvov. 'As he lay on the pavement,' Halina Wind recalled, 'with the blood dripping into the sewers, the Poles crossed them-selves and said that it was God's punishment for hiding Jews.'[20]

Halina Wind later emigrated to the United States, where her son, David Lee Preston, was born in 1955. As

---

[20] Testimony of Halina Zipora Preston (*née* Wind), Yad Vashem Righteous Among the Nations Archive, file 1379.

a reporter for the *Kansas City Star*, he was to press for recognition of the man who had helped to save his mother.[21]

Throughout Eastern Galicia, there were non-Jews willing to risk their lives to save Jews. In Kolomyja, Vasilien Petrowski, a Ukrainian, saved eighteen Jews, men, women and children, in a secret bunker in his home.[22] Not far away, near the village of Rosochacz, a Jewish couple, Karol and Roza Bergman, and Roza's mother, escaped from the liquidation of the Kolomyja ghetto in September 1942 and found refuge on a farm where a Polish couple, Jozef and Katarzyna Lazanowski, and their daughters Bronislawa and Anna, took them in without hesitation. As quickly as they could, they dug an underground shelter in the barnyard, protected from the rain and camouflaged with branches and soil. The three refugees spent their days in this shelter. At night they came out to wash and breathe the fresh air. They remained in their hideout, with the Lazanowskis' sympathetic and devoted care, until the Soviet army liberated them in July 1944.[23]

On the eve of the destruction of the ghetto in Zloczow, Helena Skrzeszewski, from the nearby village of Jelechowice, 'came to us when we were outside the ghetto and took us to her home,' recalled Selma Rossen: 'us' was seven-year-old Selma, her eight-year-old sister Edith, her parents Lipa and Samuel, and her grandmother. Helena Skrzeszewski took them to her farmhouse in the village and hid them in one of the rooms. 'When we came, four other Jews were already

---

[21] David Preston, 'Horrors of Nazis recalled', *Columbia Missourian*, 23 April 1978.
[22] 'The Fund for a Memorial Film about Kolomea' (Kolomyja), note of the ceremony at Yad Vashem at which Vasilien Petrowski's sister Aniah received the posthumous honour on his behalf, 12 November 1997.
[23] Yad Vashem Righteous Among the Nations Archive, file 3851.

there, all in the same room,' Selma recalled.[24] The door was kept locked whenever the Skrzeszewskis had visitors; the windows of the apartment were covered with heavy curtains to prevent anybody seeing in.

Those in hiding were helped by Grzegorz Tyz and Marie Koreniuk – a teacher in the village.[25] One of those hidden there, Efraim Sten, later recalled: 'All of us – nine in all – lived in one room. In the event of danger we fled to a hiding place that was built near our room by Mr Tyz, and we entered the hiding place through a closet in our room. Mr Tyz wandered about the villages in the area and, bartering our clothing, bedding and other belongings, managed to bring us flour, barley and oil.'

In November 1943 the nine who were in hiding discovered, by chance, that five other Jews were in hiding in the stables. Then, at the beginning of 1944, German soldiers were billeted in one of the rooms in the house. For the fourteen Jews in hiding the risk of exposure was ever present. 'If our presence was revealed,' wrote Efraim Sten, 'we would all have been killed on the spot together with our rescuers.' Such a fate had happened in nearby villages.[26] It did not happen to them; all fourteen survived the war.

One of the very few survivors of the destruction of the Trembowla ghetto was a thirteen-year-old boy, Arieh Czeret. Escaping from the ghetto on the day of liquidation, he sought a hiding place in the remote countryside. 'On my way,' he later recalled, 'I stopped at the house of a Polish woman who used to work for my uncle. I stayed with her for about a week, but had to leave, as she was afraid to hide me. Towards evening I left to go towards my hometown. On my way three

[24] Selma Rossen, in conversation with the author, 13 May 2002.
[25] Samuel Tennenbaum, *Zloczow Memoir*, page 231.
[26] Efraim Sten, letter to Mordecai Paldiel, 2 January 1988, Yad Vashem Righteous Among the Nations Archive, file 3860.

Ukrainian guards got hold of me and started interrogating me. They decided to hand me over to the German police. I managed to break free, and started running in a zigzag as they fired their rifles, but they missed, because it was already dark. That night I reached another farmer who used to work for us before the war, transporting goods to our store. I told him that I was the only survivor of my family. He gave me a hiding place in the barn.'

Arieh Czeret stayed in that barn until the end of June 1943, hidden and fed by the farmer: 'I asked him for a prayer book and learned all the prayers of the Ukrainian Church by heart. At the farm there was a worker about my age who came from the Carpathian Mountains. I made a deal with him. I gave him my boots and in return he gave me his identity document without a photo.' After that, Arieh Czeret was able to masquerade as a Ukrainian until liberation nine months after he had been given refuge.[27]

Not far from Trembowla, in the small town of Budzanow, a Roman Catholic priest, Father Ufryjewicz, saved a whole Jewish family by baptizing them and giving them baptismal certificates, and forging his parish register in such a way that he created for them a complete set of Christian forebears. With the false identities that he had created they were able to move from place to place, away from those who might know their real identities, and thus to survive.[28]

In Turka, on the eve of the deportation of the Jews in August 1942, Sister Jadwiga, a nun who was also the head nurse at the local hospital, hid twelve-year-old Lidia Kleiman in one of the cubicles of the men's bathroom, which was used as a broom closet. Lidia stayed

---

[27] Arieh Czeret, letter to the author, 22 March 1995, quoted in Martin Gilbert, *The Boys: Triumph over Adversity*, page 131.
[28] Information provided in conversation with the author on 22 March 2002 by Grazyna Cooper, the daughter of one of those who was saved.

hidden in the hospital for several weeks. Sister Jadwiga then took her to her own home and taught her Christian prayers in preparation for placing her in a Catholic orphanage in Lvov under the assumed name of Marysia Borowska. There she was put in the care of Sister Blanka Piglowska, who knew that she was Jewish. When a suspicion arose in the orphanage that Lidia might be Jewish, it was Sister Blanka who obtained new false papers for her, with a new name, Maria Woloszynska. She then transferred the girl to another orphanage, at the convent in the village of Lomna, where the Mother Superior, Sister Tekla Budnowska, was hiding many Jewish girls.

In the early autumn of 1943, after an attack by Ukrainian nationalists on the orphanage, Sister Budnowska received permission to transfer her girls to Warsaw, and to establish an orphanage in an abandoned building in the former ghetto there. In Warsaw, she accepted yet more Jewish children. After the suppression of the Warsaw Uprising in August 1944, the orphanage relocated to Kostowiec, fifteen miles southwest of Warsaw.

Lidia's mother had been denounced to the Gestapo while travelling on false papers, arrested and killed; but her father had been hidden by a Russian Orthodox priest, and survived. Father and daughter were reunited after liberation.[29]

Each story of rescue reveals a remarkable person, usually acting quite differently from his neighbours, not so afraid to risk death as to be prevented by fear from helping, and willing to work out a whole series of different stratagems to protect those whom he or she had taken in. In the spring of 1942, six Jews escaped from the ghetto of Stryj,

---

[29] 'Group portrait of small children in a convent school . . .', United States Holocaust Memorial Museum, Photo Archive, Worksheet 44914.

making their way to the apartment of Boleslaw and Zofia Bialkowski, who lived in the town. The Bialkowskis took in the fugitives and hid them in their attic, in a narrow, dark cubicle no more than six square metres in size. The Jews were forbidden to speak among themselves in case the neighbours heard them, and betrayed them and their rescuers. To provide the fugitives with some light, Boleslaw Bialkowski made a small skylight for them in the tiled roof. In order to muffle their footsteps, the floor of the hideout was covered with straw, which also served as bedding. Each morning, Boleslaw Bialkowski removed the refuse from the cubicle. From time to time he brought them the local newspapers. His wife Zofia prepared meals for them and washed their clothes, hanging them up to dry in the apartment so as not to arouse the neighbours' suspicions. As so often, financial reward or recompense were not a consideration; for a short time the fugitives paid for their keep, but when their money ran out, Bialkowski provided for their keep out of his modest earnings as a tinsmith.

One day Bialkowski was visited by a Jewish acquaintance, Jakov Lewit, whose skills as an artisan were valued by the Germans. Lewit brought with him his four-year-old daughter, Erna, whom he asked the Bialkowskis to shelter; they agreed, and the child remained with them. Because she could not be expected to remain silent, the child was not placed in the attic with the six other Jews, but stayed inside the apartment. Erna became attached to the Bialkowskis' four children and played with them. Whenever visitors came, she hid in the cupboard. With liberation, the little girl, and the other six Jews, were finally safe.[30]

---

[30] Yad Vashem Righteous Among the Nations Archive, file 3589. As well as Erna Lewit, the Jews who were saved were Mosze and Rozalia Brenner, Aron Brenner, Janusz and Jadwiga Rozenberg, and a lawyer named Lehrer.

In his study of Ukrainian–Jewish relations during the German occupation, the historian Philip Friedman, himself a survivor of the Lvov ghetto, wrote of testimonies gathered by the Yiddish writer Joseph Schwarz concerning a Ukrainian engineer, Alexander Kryvoiaza, from the East Galician town of Sambor, who employed fifty-eight Jews in his factory and helped conceal them during an anti-Jewish 'Action'. Friedman also noted that in the nearby town of Zawalow, a forester, Lew Kobilnitsky, and his brother-in-law rescued twenty-three Jews.[31]

Before the First World War, Brody had been the border town in Austria-Hungary through which hundreds of thousands of Russian Jews had passed on their way out of Russia. Between the wars it was in the Polish province of Eastern Galicia. The Germans occupied it in June 1941. Many Jewish refugees from Lvov, fifty miles to the west, having tried to flee from the German advance, were in the town when it was taken. One of them was Ian Lustig, who later recalled that his mother, who had brought him to Brody, had spent her childhood there, where she had a number of non-Jewish friends, among them Marja Michalewska. 'We lived there in fear and one day when nearly all our relations and Jewish friends had been taken away by the Germans, Mrs Michalewska found out that another "Aktion" was about to begin and she told us about it and found a place of refuge at a peasant's house. I remember she took all our family at night to that peasant's residence in a village. We found refuge in the loft of the peasant's house. Mrs Michalewska told us she would do everything possible for us to keep alive and we knew she meant what she said. During the "Aktion" nearly all of my remaining relations at Brody were taken away by the Germans.

---

[31] Philip Friedman, *Roads to Extinction*, page 190.

After the "Aktion" we came back to Brody and Mrs Michalewska assisted us in our escape to Lvov. I was dressed as a girl and we went by train. I sat between Mrs Michalewska and her girlfriend and my mother was at the end of the carriage. In case anything happened to my mother, Mrs Michalewska would have taken care of me. Afterwards while we stayed in Lvov Mrs Michalewska sent us food parcels and brought my little cousin to us. She also took care of my aunts. Such exemplary help and assistance is not easy to forget.'[32]

In June 1943 the Podhajce ghetto was destroyed and almost all its inhabitants were murdered. A Polish shoemaker in the town, Wincenty Rajski, and his wife Stefania hid two members of the Herbst family, from whose leather store he had used to buy his materials before the war. The Rajskis took the risk involved even though they had two small girls of their own. Ziunia Herbst was three years old when she saw her father for the last time. She and her mother Sabina owed their survival, she wrote, most of all to 'the courageous humanity of a Polish, Catholic family who hid us in the attic of their barn for almost a year. They risked their lives in order to save ours.'[33]

At the time of the round-ups, a few of the Jews in the Podhajce ghetto managed to escape to the nearby woods. From there, a group of twenty-three survivors approached two Polish brothers, Lewko and Genko Bilecki, and their teenage sons Roman and Julian, whom they had known before the war. The Bileckis agreed to help. Roman and Julian's respective sisters, Jaroslawa and Anna, participated in the collective act of rescue.

[32] Letter of 2 August 1963, seeking funds for Marja Michalewska, Yad Vashem Righteous Among the Nations Archive, file 6.
[33] Myra Genn (Ziunia Herbst), letters to the author, 19 December 2001 and 1 February 2002.

Lewko and Genko showed the Jews where to build a bunker in the woods and for almost a year provided them with food. That winter the snows were very deep, and in order to prevent the Germans finding the bunker, Roman and Julian would bring food to the Jews by jumping from tree to tree so as not to leave footprints in the snow. Despite all the precautions, the bunker was discovered not once but twice, forcing the Jews to flee; each time the Bilecki family showed the fugitives where to build their new bunker, until, in the spring of 1944, they were liberated by Soviet troops. The courage and commitment of the Bilecki family had saved the lives of twenty-three Jewish men, women and children.[34]

A Polish couple, Jozef and Antoine Sawko, and their daughter Malwina, went every Sunday into the countryside near Podhajce, taking with them food for two Jews, Israel Friedman and his daughter Berta, who were in hiding in the fields. Israel Friedman's other two daughters, as well as his wife and father, had been murdered during the liquidation of the Podhajce ghetto in June 1943. That September, when the weather turned cold and the fields no longer provided adequate protection, father and daughter moved to the Sawkos' farm (they had not wanted to hide there earlier, for fear of endangering their helpers). When winter came they dug a small hole under the pigsty. The hole, which the Sawkos covered with straw and wood, was not deep enough for them to stand up in: the water table was too high to dig any deeper, so father and daughter had to live in the hole in a sitting position. When it rained, they were waist-deep in water. In February 1944, when Soviet forces liberated the region, Israel and Berta Friedman stole away from their hiding place in the middle of the night, so that none of the farmers nearby would know that Jozef, Antoine

---

[34] Harvey Schulweis, printed letter of December 1998, Jewish Foundation for the Righteous.

and Malwina Sawko had given them food and shelter – and life itself.[35]

In discussing the story of the rescuers in Podhajce – which he described as 'this terrible place full of anti-Semitism' – Glenn Richter, a leader of the Student Struggle for Soviet Jewry in the 1970s who had befriended Berta Friedman (then Mrs Weitz) in New York, reflected: 'It gives a sense of hope that there is something better among humans, that you can go far beyond yourself.'[36]

In the Zborow region of Eastern Galicia, two brothers, Kazimierz and Franciszek Barys, sheltered five Jews on their farm: Golda Schechter and her two children, Fryda, aged five, and Martin, aged one; Maria Nisenbaum; and another Jew by the name of Rozenberg. At first the brothers prepared a hideout in the attic of their home, but when they learned that the Germans frequently raided attics in their searches for Jews, they dug a bunker beneath the barn, and covered it with a box full of heavy tools. Taking care of the five Jews meant huge and sustained effort to bring food and drink each day, to ensure that they were clean and properly clothed, and to remove refuse from the hideout. The brothers had not known any of the five before they had sought shelter at the farm. Nor did they ask for any payment for the help they gave.

From time to time, German police and Ukrainian collaborators raided the house and farm buildings in search of Jews, but the hiding place was never un-covered. Then, in the summer of 1944, only a few hours before the village was liberated by Soviet troops, Rozenberg left the bunker; he was seen by a Ukrainian and shot on the spot. The Barys brothers were spared

---

[35] Material provided on the Jewish Foundation for the Righteous website: www.jfr.org/stories.
[36] Glenn Richter, in conversation with the author, 1 January 2002.

punishment for hiding Jews only because the Germans were already fleeing from the approaching Russians.[37]

When the ghetto of Brzezany was destroyed, Mark and Klara Zipper managed to flee to a nearby Polish village, where a Polish acquaintance directed them to the home of a basketmaker, Julian Baran, who lived with his wife and three children in one of the village houses. The Barans, devout Catholics, were extremely poor, but did not hesitate to take in the penniless couple who sought their help. Mark Zipper, who knew how to weave, helped the Barans with their work, repaying them to some extent for their kindness. In their testimony, the Zippers subsequently stated: 'We consider Mr and Mrs Baran to be angels from heaven, and shall remain eternally grateful to them.' After the war, the Zippers emigrated to the United States. They kept in contact with their benefactors, from time to time sending them money and parcels.[38]

The town of Drohobycz had one of the largest Jewish populations in Eastern Galicia – some twenty thousand. With the arrival of the German army on 1 July 1941, a ghetto was established; forced labour and near-starvation rations were imposed, and executions were frequent. Harry Zeimer, a survivor of that time of torment in Drohobycz, described how rare it was for any Jew to escape. The Catholic population in the surrounding area, 'though hating the German invader, believed that God chose those "brutal Huns" as a tool to eliminate the descendants of the crucifiers of Jesus. Not more than a few per cent of Poles were thinking otherwise. But to think and to act were not the same thing: A Pole hiding a Jew, or helping him to escape, was simply shot by the Germans! Therefore, I consider my late friend Tadeusz Wojtowicz (a true Catholic Pole) as a hero, who has risked

---

[37] Yad Vashem Righteous Among the Nations Archive, file 3610.
[38] Yad Vashem Righteous Among the Nations Archive, file 3167.

his own life to save mine. In addition, he refused my intention to get for him the Yad Vashem (Jerusalem) medal for "The Righteous People": in his opinion, there was no glory but human duty in what he did!'

Before the war, Harry Zeimer wrote, he and his rescuer 'were no more than schoolmates at the Polish State High School in Drohobycz. During the German occupation, his conscience didn't let him be a passive witness of the Final Solution. As a true Christian, Tadeusz Wojtowicz could not decide to join the Polish underground forces, because to kill – even a German – was a sin. In 1942 he found his solution: he will risk his life to flee with me to Switzerland! The papers necessary to enter the Reich for an Aryan Pole, volunteer to work there, the dangerous twists and turns to get them were incumbent exclusively on my late friend, because I was too much known as a Jew in our small town. At the same time, I bought an Aryan identity card, and as soon as my friend got his papers – we succeeded to add there my (false) name . . . and we were gone. With a lot of luck, the two "volunteers" reached Singen-am-Hohentwiel, a German town near the Swiss border, where we worked for eight days. There were numerous Polish workers, ex-prisoners of war, a very solidarity-minded group, who helped us to organize our leap into Switzerland. Except my friend, nobody knew that I was a disguised Jew. Among these courageous, hearty young people, I could statistically confirm the deep effects of the anti-Semitic education by the Polish Catholic Church, during the centuries. On 1 November 1942 we were in Switzerland . . .'[39]

Other than his father, who survived incarceration in three camps, all of Harry Zeimer's family perished. After training as an engineer in Paris, Zeimer left for Israel in 1960. His rescuer, Tadeusz Wojtowicz, his wife and children, went to Australia, where Wojtowicz became

---

[39] Harry Zeimer, letter to the author, 13 May 2001.

1. Gertruda Babilinska and the young Jewish boy whom she saved.

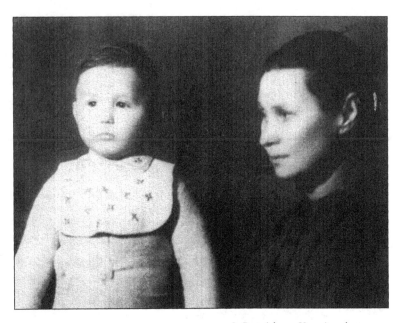

2. Bronislawa Kurpi and Abraham Foxman, the Jewish boy whom she saved in Vilna.

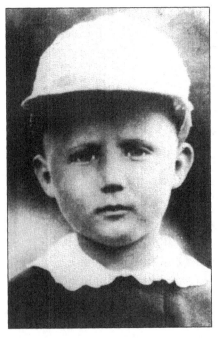

3. 'Henryk Stanislaw Kurpi', aged four.

4. Mr and Mrs Jachowicz, with Shachne Hiller, the Jewish boy they saved in southern Poland.

5. Henia Wisgardisky, a Jewish child in Kaunas, with Nijole Stankevic, the daughter of her rescuers.

6. Rose Levin Weinberg, cared for by a Lithuanian family, with her favourite doll.

7. Father Kujata and his parishioners, with Anita Helfgott (*centre*).

8. Anita Helfgott in the yard of Father Kujata's parsonage.

9. Three Jewish sisters hiding in a forest in Poland.

10. Helena and Jozef Biczyk with the two Jewish sisters whom they hid in Warsaw.

11. Henryk Wolinski, a member of the Polish Council for Assistance to the Jews (Zegota).

12. Tadeusz Stepniewski, a member of Zegota.

13. Zofia Kossak-Szczuka, a co-founder of Zegota.

14. Wladyslaw Bartoszewski, a member of Zegota who was later Foreign Minister of Poland.

Professor of Slavic Literature at the University of Hobart, Tasmania.

Boryslaw was another East Galician town with a substantial Jewish population. Among those saved there was a future Speaker of the Israeli parliament, Shewach Weiss. On 1 July 1941, when the Germans entered Boryslaw, local Ukrainians, supported by the Germans, started a day-long anti-Jewish pogrom in which three hundred Jews were killed. To escape the slaughter, the Weiss family sought refuge with a Ukrainian couple, Roman and Julia Schepaniuk, who took them all in: the two parents, their sons – Aaron, aged thirteen, and Shewach, aged six – and their nine-year-old daughter Miła. When the pogrom was over, the Weiss family returned to their home. However, in late November 1941 the Germans started periodic anti-Jewish 'actions' in Boryslaw, and at the beginning of 1942, following two mass killings of Jews in the town, the five members of the Weiss family decided to leave the Schepaniuk home and seek shelter with the Goral family. Michael Goral had been a friend of Shewach's mother, Genya, before the war. Fifty-five years later, Shewach Weiss recalled: 'On the first night we hid under Michael's and Maria's beds in the bedroom. In the following nights, we hid alternatively in the barn and in the stable, between and in the stalls. One day we were hiding in the granary, deep inside the straw, when the Gestapo suddenly entered, with their Ukrainian collaborators. They searched through the straw, picking it with their bayonets, while the Goral family watched. They did not utter a word and did not give us away, despite the certain death they were facing. Later we hid in a small prayer house that was built near the family's farm, as is the custom among devoted Catholics. There, on a concrete floor, I hid with my mother and sister. My sister and I were hiding under the crucifix's outspread arms, wrapped around my mother. To this day I remember the

97

lizards running over the chapel walls, and the envy I felt to these free creatures. I prayed silently. Let God turn me into a lizard.'[40]

As German and Ukrainian searches for Jews in hiding intensified – as they were throughout Eastern Galicia – Aaron Weiss and his father went out to look for an alternative hiding place. 'Mrs Gorlova, a Ukrainian peasant woman,' as Shewach Weiss recalled, let them hide inside her haystack. 'We were under the hay,' he recalled, 'and over our heads a German soldier checked the contents of the haystack with his bayonet.'[41]

The heightened searches and killings culminated in the 'big action' on 4 August 1942, when all the remaining Jews of Boryslaw were ordered to leave their homes and live inside the newly designated ghetto. The Weiss family gave their house into the care of the Schepaniuk family and moved into the ghetto. Some time later they decided to leave the ghetto and find a permanent hiding place outside it. Julia Schepaniuk immediately agreed to take them in again. This time, they built a hiding place in the double wall of the store-room. Two more relatives of the Weiss family joined them there, and later an eighth fugitive, Israel Bakhman. All eight lived in the one hideout, under the Schepaniuks' devoted care.[42]

Schewach Weiss's father had managed to take two books with him to their hideout: Alexandre Dumas' *The Count of Monte Cristo*, and an encyclopaedia. 'Thanks to the Count of Monte Cristo,' Weiss later recalled, 'I, little Shewach, could become a famous Count right there in the burrow. Thanks to the small atlas attached to the

---

[40] Shewach Weiss, interview with Zvi Zinger of *Yediot Aharanot*, Yad Vashem Righteous Among the Nations Archive, file 8939.
[41] Shewach Weiss, 'A 700-day nightmare', *Jerusalem Post*, 8 April 1983.
[42] Yad Vashem Righteous Among the Nations Archive, file 2820.

encyclopaedia I could add to my knowledge and roam all over the world. These two books gave me the loveliest moments of light in the darkness that reigned around me. Puntrzela, our good-hearted neighbour, sometimes brought us old newspapers that she had obtained. Through her we tried to guess what was happening in the world out there. I used the clay at the bottom of the burrow to mould my toys – tanks, motorcycles, animals and anything else that I saw through the window in the ceiling.'[43]

For her selfless act in housing the fugitive Weisses, Julia Schepaniuk, like all those who had helped the family to survive, was later awarded the title of Righteous Among the Nations.[44]

Also in Boryslaw, a Jewish couple, Zygmunt Kranz and his wife Franciszka, together with their three-year-old son Henryk, were warned by a Polish friend, Jozef Baran, that a deportation was imminent. Baran and his wife Eleonora offered to shelter the family until the danger had subsided; so that night the Kranz family made their way to the Barans' house. Thereafter, what had begun as a humanitarian gesture became a protracted personal obligation. Zygmunt, who believed that as a worker in the German arms industry he would be able to go on living in the Horodyszcze Hill labour camp even after the ghetto had been liquidated, paid occasional visits to his wife and son in their hiding place. When the danger of discovery increased, Zygmunt and Baran dug a pit under the floor of the house to serve as a refuge. Later, a second hideout was dug in the courtyard of the house, and in January 1943 Zygmunt escaped

---

[43] *Maariv* newspaper, Youth Supplement, Holocaust Remembrance Day, 1996.
[44] Protocol of the Meeting of the Commission for Commemorating Righteous Among Nations, Jerusalem, 28 May 2000, Yad Vashem Righteous Among the Nations Archive, file 8938.

from the labour camp and joined his wife and son. The fugitives were penniless, but Baran bought them a little food in exchange for their possessions. Eleanora assisted her husband in all that he did; she grew vegetables in the garden, in order to be able to feed the Jews in her care, and kept their existence secret from her children.

After liberation, for many years, the Kranz family sent the Barans a monthly stipend in gratitude for their 'heroic selflessness'.[45]

Among the Jews who had reached Boryslaw when it was under Soviet rule after the German defeat of Poland in September 1939 was Izabela Hass, known as Zula. She and her brother Eidikus had been sent to Boryslaw by their parents from Bialystok, for safety, to live with their two aunts. But on 1 July 1941, the Germans entered Boryslaw and, as Zula and her brother hid with their aunts, searched for Jews and led them to their deaths. When the Einsatzgruppen returned in the spring of 1942 – having killed thousands of Jews four months earlier – Zula's aunts, one of whom was a doctor, realized they must find a hiding place outside their home. Zula recalled: 'Aunt Rachela scanned the list of patients in search of those who would be most likely to hide us in their homes. She had ruled out Mr Lemecki who had been overheard saying that the Poles ought to thank Hitler for getting rid of the Jews. But it was that Mr Lemecki who volunteered to hide all of us in trunks kept in his cellar! This time the Jews had anticipated the *Aktion* and many had hidden. The Germans then resorted to a trick: they discontinued the round-up for twenty-four hours, thereby luring the fugitives, in-cluding us, into a trap. My aunts, Eidikus and I immediately returned to the Lemecki residence. But when we knocked on the door, we overheard Lemecki's anti-Semitic mother say, "Hide these dirty Yids again?

[45] Yad Vashem Righteous Among the Nations Archive, file 6136.

Never!" Yet Lemecki saved our lives once more. When we returned to Boryslaw after two days in Lemecki's cellar, many of our friends were missing. All of them had been sent to the extermination camp of Belzec. My hopes for survival were completely dashed and I wondered if my parents would ever see me again.'

Zula survived in the Boryslaw ghetto. But with each 'action' the number of Jews who remained alive dwindled, from thousands to only hundreds. A hiding place was constructed in the cellar of her aunts' home. But it was clear that sooner or later – possibly very soon indeed, as Ukrainian policemen initiated search after search – it would be discovered. Zula recalled: 'Some time in February 1943, Mrs Kowicki walked into Aunt Rachela's office. She was clad in black and she told my aunt about the tragic death of her fifteen-year-old daughter. My aunt then asked Mrs Kowicki if she would be willing to save the life of a Jewish mother's daughter in memory of her own daughter. When the bereaved mother said yes, I became the Kowickis' "niece", and they took me into their home. To legitimise the enterprise, all kinds of original and forged Aryan documents were purchased for me. These documents included the birth certificate of a dead Polish girl and I became Irena Borek.'

Zula's account continued: 'I loved my "Uncle Emil" and my "Aunt Sophie" but my stay there became precarious. Uncle Emil built a hideout for me over the veranda whose boards would be moved in the evening so that I could come in for the night. But one day neighbours inquired if it was true that the Kowickis were hiding a Jew in their house. In view of this new danger, a decision was made to have me live with Uncle Emil's relatives in the town of Sanok. On 3 June 1943, I was secretly baptized, given the rosary beads and prayer books of Janka, the Kowickis' daughter, and taught the essentials of the catechism. I was told that St Mary would now save

101

me. I was only fourteen years old and I had to pretend so many things. Would I be able to do it? I was now the daughter of Wladyslaw and Olga Borek née Partyka, Polish patriots whom the Soviets had exiled to Siberia.'

Danger lurked at every stage. 'When Uncle Emil and I entered the train to Sanok, I found a patient of my aunt staring at me. Will she give me away? Please, St Mary, don't let her do it! Then a German gendarme boarded the train, took one look at me and declared, "Du bist doch eine Jüdin!" (You surely are a Jewess!) Over and over, Uncle Emil insisted that I was a Polish Catholic girl, his niece. My papers were carefully checked while Aunt Rachela's patient remained quiet. The documents passed the test, yet when I saw the quizzical expressions on the other passengers' faces I thought, "They all know that I'm Jewish." But I said, "This is not the first time that I've been mistaken for a Jew." Then I stood by the window and felt nothing, nothing at all until we arrived in Sanok.'

Each moment of rescue could have its terrors, of the soul as well as of the body. 'Walking uphill towards my new home, I saw that the pavement beneath our feet bore Hebrew inscriptions. When I realized that these were Jewish gravestones, my soul began to cry. Shocked by the bleak reality, I felt like a trapped animal. There stood an outhouse by the side of the road and I dashed to it, locking myself in. I saw no sense in going on and looked for ways to end my life. But Uncle Emil kept reassuring me that I would be safe. There were trees and flowers around the house, and within this serenity I began to believe that maybe I will survive. The following Sunday I went to church with my new family. I was a careful observer, mimicking the melodious prayers and the cadence of standing and kneeling. That afternoon I returned to the empty church and, standing in front of the statue of St Mary, I pleaded with her for my life, making vows of gratitude: "Save me . . . please save me

. . . If you do, I will believe in you until the day I die."
Gradually, my fears disappeared. People treated me with
kindness but, of course, they were not aware of my true
identity. Time and time again, I saw Jews being led to
their death. There were no longer any enclaves of Jews
in Sanok, so I imagined with dread that they had been
discovered in their hideouts in Polish homes.'

Liberation came in the summer of 1944 with the
arrival of the Soviet troops. Zula remained with
the family that had saved her life. Then, more than a year
later, in October 1945, she learned that her sister Rena
had survived the concentration camps in Germany.
She had returned to Poland and was living with the two
aunts, who had also survived, and then lived in that part
of Germany annexed by Poland after the war. They
wanted Zula to join them, but, she later wrote: 'How was
I, an ardent Catholic, going to live within a family of
Jews? Since my parents and the rest of my Jewish family
had all been killed, I decided to remain a Polish Catholic
for the rest of my life. I went to Walbrzych and told my
sister that I would not go with her to Germany and wherever else she would go from there. Rena and I parted our
ways forever.'[46]

Zula Hass lived the whole of her post-war life as
Catholic. She married a Polish Catholic, a future member
of the Polish government and Minister of Public Works.
Both their son and their daughter became leading Polish
physicians. Only some fifty-five years after the war had
ended did Zula reach out to her Jewish past. As her sister
Rena – a retired high-school biology teacher in the
United States – has written: 'She has joined the organization of Children of the Holocaust in Warsaw and she
has allowed us to tell her son and daughter the truth. The
son alone chose to acknowledge his Jewish heritage. In

---

[46] Zula Hass, 'This Is How It Was', *Hidden Child* newsletter, Summer
2001.

August 1999, he joined his Jewish-American cousins in saying "Kaddish" at Majdanek's mass grave, which contained the ashes of his Jewish grandfather.'[47]

For many Jews like Zula, rescue involved eventual conversion to Christianity, absorption in the new faith, and a sense of belonging to the religion of the rescuers. It was the price – the penalty, from a strictly Orthodox Jewish perspective – that was paid hundreds, even thousands, of times for the gift of life.

The city of Brzezany lay in the centre of Eastern Galicia. The history of the relationship between Poles, Jews and Ukrainians in the town from 1919 to 1945 has recently been written by Shimon Redlich. He ends the acknowledgements to his book by thanking Karol Codogni and Tanka Kontsevych, 'without whom I would not have survived to tell the story. It is to them, for their humaneness in the midst of barbarism, that this book is dedicated.'[48]

Shimon Redlich was five years old when the Jews of Brzezany were forced into a ghetto. At the time of one of the 'Actions' in which hundreds of Jews were rounded up and killed, he was hiding in an attic with his mother and his grandparents. After a while, the heat in the attic with its tin roof became unbearable, and the occupants began to leave, looking for better hiding places. 'One night my mother took me by the hand and we walked into a neighbouring village,' he later wrote. 'The stalks in the wheat field were high, smelling with the ripeness of summer. We knocked on a few doors, but nobody wanted to let us in. We returned to the attic and stayed there.' Many years later he read of what had

---

[47] Rena Hass, 'This Is How It Is', *Hidden Child* newsletter, Summer 2001.
[48] Shimon Redlich, 'Together and Apart in Brzezany: Poles, Jews and Ukrainians, 1919–1945', manuscript.

happened to a young girl, Hermina, who was with them in that attic. 'This girl went downstairs one day and was intercepted by people who came to loot the deserted house. She bribed them and they let her go. It's a miracle that we weren't denounced by all those who left the attic and were, probably, caught by the Germans. Remaining in the attic now was our foursome, another boy my age with his grandmother and a single old lady. Our immediate problem was finding food.'

Redlich's grandfather decided that the only way to survive was to contact an old acquaintance, the Polish locksmith Stanislaw Codogni. Fifty years later, Codogni's son Karol recounted how, late at night, the grandfather and a woman 'knocked on our door. My mother gave them hot milk and they told me to go fetch some potatoes. We also gave them freshly baked bread and some onions.' From then on, whenever the old man came to their door, the Codognis would give him a sack of food which they had prepared in advance; but they lived in constant fear that he might be caught by the Germans, or that their other efforts to help Jews might be discovered. Forty years later, Karol Codogni wrote to Shimon Redlich: 'Our house wasn't far from the ghetto and we were watched at all times. Still, we were able to help a few people who escaped from the ghetto. During the day they would hide in our place and at night continue on their way. I don't know how many survived.'

For several months the hiding place was unmolested, but then new tenants began preparing the apartment one floor below. 'When grandpa and mother went down the stairs on their way to the Codognis,' Shimon Redlich recalled, 'a woman appeared in a door and warned them that if we didn't leave within a day or two, she would report us to the police. We had to get out, and fast. At that time my mother's younger sister Malcia, and Vovo, her young and good-looking husband, were hiding in

Raj, a village near Brzezany. Tanka Kontsevych, a young Ukrainian woman and a mother of two, whose husband was sent for compulsory labour in Germany, had been keeping them in her house since the "Judenrein" round-up. Tanka used to visit the Codognis, and carry messages between us and Malcia. A few hours after the new tenant demanded that we leave, grandpa Fishl, disguised as an old woman, went to the Codognis and asked them to convey an urgent note to Malcia, in Raj. My aunt persuaded Tanka to take us all in. The following evening my mother and I descended from the attic. The street was covered in snow, on the corner a lone figure, Codogni's young son, Karol. When we approached him, he whispered, "Follow me and pray to God."'

A woman was waiting for them further up the street. It was Tanka Kontsevych. 'Karol left and we started walking behind the Ukrainian woman. By now my limping mother could hardly walk. My own muscles must have atrophied in the attic and I could hardly move my legs. Tanka ended up carrying me on her back while holding on to my mother's hand. Slowly we trudged through thick, crisp snow, towards Raj. From time to time mother swallowed a handful of snow. When I asked Tanka half a century later what she remembered about that night, she told me that I was small and my legs hurt. She also recalled that the walking took several hours, since she preferred a roundabout track through the fields. We must have reached her house at dawn. I can still taste the freshly baked white bread and hot milk. I couldn't believe my luck when promised that from now on I could have all the bread and milk I'd want. After we had eaten we had the first warm bath in months.'

The Kontsevyches were devoted to those to whom they were giving shelter. But, as Shimon Redlich recalled, there were 'some frightening moments'. On one occasion, as German soldiers 'horsed around with Tanka downstairs, we sat just above them with bated breath. The tiniest creak could be fatal. I made in my pants, right there, in utter silence, like an animal. One afternoon, while Tanka was out two German soldiers walked in and started yelling for straw. The straw was with us, in the attic.' Ania, Tanka's ten-year-old daughter, remembered the event fifty years later: 'The Germans started to climb to the attic. I knew that up there was this little boy and if they found them they would take them away and kill them. So I grabbed one German by his trouser leg and started pulling him off the ladder. Then I pulled the ladder itself. We had a sort of tug-of-war. Then my mother returned, quickly went up to the attic and started throwing down the straw. At the same time she covered up with straw the people who were hiding up there. And then the Germans finally left.'[49]

Leon Wells was in hiding in a basement underneath a stable in Lvov after the revolt of the slave labourers in the Janowska camp on 19 November 1943. On 6 December 1943, he later wrote in his memoirs, 'As usual the owner came down, but this time he seemed very nervous. We realized immediately that something was amiss. He told us that in a neighbour's house, the Juzeks, only a few hundred yards from there, thirty-two Jews had been discovered. The hideout had been reported to the Germans by Juzek's own brother-in-law. From the thirty-two, twenty-six were from the Death Brigade, and among them was our leader, Herches. While they were being led to the truck, they had made a sudden attack on the Germans, and twenty-eight of the thirty-two escaped. Juzek and his wife had been arrested and next day publicly hanged in the market. Our host was very much afraid that the discovery of Jews in this neighbourhood would lead to a search of all the houses.

---

[49] Shimon Redlich, 'Together and Apart in Brzezany: Poles, Jews and Ukrainians, 1919–1945', manuscript.

A small search did go on during the following days, but nothing happened in our house.'

Leon Wells added: 'One story circulating at the time was that when the Russian Army came into Tarnopol a group of Jews came out of their hiding place in a Polish house. A few days later, when the Germans returned, this Polish family was hanged for hiding Jews. This story made our host ponder just how long he should keep us in the cellar after the Russian Army had liberated Lvov. Other stories about Poles hiding Jews resulted in new searches for Jews by the Germans. All the houses in the neighbourhood were very thoroughly searched except our house, and this was due only to the fact that our host was the chief representative of the local farmers to the German officials. We were just plain lucky.'

The month of May 1944 again brought bad news. 'A group of twelve Jews were discovered on Balanowe Street, only one block away from where I used to live. A daughter informed on her own mother, telling the Germans that she was hiding Jews. The mother was hanged, and the Jews were killed.'

As the Soviet troops advanced, pushing the Germans further and further back, Lvov became the front line. 'One day we heard many German soldiers come into the stable. They were going to use it for some purpose or other. To make it fit for this unknown purpose, they planned to pull out the whole floor above us. We heard the entire discussion. We sat paralysed, staring into the darkness of the basement. The work began; then suddenly an order came for the soldiers to move out. Again we were saved at the last second. At last the Russians arrived! Our host rushed in with this news in the middle of the day. The light went on, and everyone sat up and quietly listened to details of the news. We still could not talk loudly or make any noise because we were still afraid that the neighbours would find out that we were hiding here.'

Liberation brought its own restraints. Leon Wells remembered how it was planned 'that we would leave in the early hours of the next day, so that no one would see us. Even now our host asked us not to come back to visit him, or for any other reason; it would go hard for him if it were known that he had hidden Jews.' In a footnote at this point in his book, Wells wrote: 'How sad was the situation in Poland that when a man proved he possessed high, idealistic qualities, he would be ashamed and unpopular for doing such a great deed!'[50]

Of the quarter of a million Jews from Eastern Galicia, no more than a few hundred were saved as a result of the help of non-Jews. The examples of those who were willing to risk their lives to try to save Jewish lives are noble; but the dominant thought on reading the stories of the rescuers in Eastern Galicia is how few there were of those rescuers. Their heroism is all the more remarkable, given the extent of the indifference and complicity of the local population.

---

[50] Leon Weliczker Wells, *The Death Brigade (The Janowska Road)*, pages 236–9.

CHAPTER THREE

Vilna

Throughout the interwar years, Vilna was the largest city
in eastern Poland, having been seized by the Poles from
Lithuania after the First World War. The city had been a
centre of Jewish cultural and spiritual life for several
hundred years; the Jews knew it as 'the Jerusalem of
Lithuania'. Following the German conquest in 1941, most
of the city's fifty-five thousand Jews were murdered by the
Germans, with the active support of many Lithuanians;
the rescue efforts of a few non-Jewish Vilnaites – individual Poles and Lithuanians – enabled a few hundred
Jews to survive.

Gertruda Babilinska worked in Vilna as a nursemaid
for a Jewish family, the Stolowickis. After the German
occupation, when their son Michael was four years old,
his mother was taken gravely ill. Gertruda Babilinska
promised her that she would look after her child and,
after the war, make sure he was taken to Palestine. After
Michael's mother died, Gertruda went on looking after
the boy, pretending he was her own child, and persuading a priest to let him join a church choir. After the
war she set out with the boy, then nine years old, for
Palestine; but their boat was intercepted by the British
as it tried to land its passengers. All those on board,
including Gertruda Babilinska and her charge, were sent
back to Europe and interned in a displaced persons
camp in Germany. They made the journey again when

the State of Israel was established, and both nanny and child became citizens. Gertruda Babilinska remained a Catholic, but, as she had promised Michael's mother, she raised the boy as a Jew.[1]

Another Roman Catholic nanny in Vilna who saved her young Jewish charge was Bronislawa Kurpi. Abraham Foxman was four years old when she took him for safety to her own home and brought him up as if he were her own child, naming him Henryk Stanislaw Kurpi. It was Foxman, later head of the Anti-Defamation League in the United States, who exhorted the Jerusalem gathering of 'Hidden Children' in 1993 to bear witness to the goodness of those who had saved and cared for them.[2]

Rose Levin Weinberg was born in Vilna in March 1941. Four months later, shortly after the German occupation, her father was shot. Her mother then placed her with a Lithuanian couple, the Budrikenes. After the couple died, Rose was taken care of by their daughter, sixteen-year-old Lusia Budrikene, with whom she stayed until 1957, when an aunt from Canada found her, and arranged for her to emigrate to Toronto.[3]

Another rescuer from Vilna was Krystyna Adolph, a high-school history teacher in the city. Among those she saved was a former pupil, Lydia Aran, who had graduated on the eve of the German invasion, having been in her class for eight years. Lydia Aran later recalled how Krystyna Adolph 'was recently widowed and taking care of her three-year-old daughter and the old father of her late husband. She managed – God knows how – to send us a message, days before we were rounded up to be

---

[1] United States Holocaust Memorial Museum, Photo Archive, Worksheet 00901.

[2] Hidden Child conference, Jerusalem, notes of the proceedings, 14 July 1993.

[3] United States Holocaust Memorial Museum, Photo Archive, Worksheet 12471.

locked up in the ghetto, saying: "Girls, if the worst comes to the worst, just come to Ignalino." But sheltering Jews meant instant summary execution. Would she indeed endanger her own, her little girl's and her old father-in-law's lives to help us? Was it sensible to expect her to do so? Would it be fair to put her offer to a test? And what would we do if she refuses to take us in?'

Lydia described her journey to Krystyna Adolph's village, together with her twin sister Monica: 'We left Vilna at dawn after a nightmare of searching for a hiding place; the humiliation of rejection, the unbearable embarrassment of trying to impose ourselves on others and seeing them in their moments of truth and failure. The day before, we left the ghetto as usual with the labour squad and were cleaning the army barracks when the young officer who had introduced himself as chaplain approached me once again offering help. This time, I decided to accept the offer. That morning, on our way out of the ghetto we saw yet another young man hanging from a street lamp in the courtyard of the house we slept in. The cries from a nearby house were bloodcurdling. What was there to lose?

'That evening the officer told our guard that Monica and I would stay in the barracks to clean his rooms. At dusk, he took us to a small house in the military compound. A noisy drinking party was going on inside, and guards seemed used to seeing soldiers with girls milling around. We spent the rest of the night in a small storeroom at the back of the house. At dawn the officer came and we left the compound arm-in-arm, like friends. We decided to go to the house of our father's secretary, Mr Zielonkowski, who lived at the outskirts of the town with his old mother. He was very devoted to our father and we counted on his help in leaving the town. When we were nearly there, we took leave of the officer, who wished us good luck and said that he was sure he would not return home from the front. He gave us a small snapshot of himself to remember: a very young blond man on skis, laughing, a long scarf around his neck fluttering in the wind. I lost it when we had to abandon all personal things while crossing into the British-occupied zone at night, a few years later.

'Mr Zielonkowski panicked when he saw us and refused to let us in. He told us that Miss Sabina, our veteran seamstress, his neighbour, had been executed on the spot the day before, when somebody said she had been talking to a Jew. But he agreed to accompany us up to the city limits and also to tell our father . . . Indeed, we did meet father, as agreed through Mr Zielonkowski, in a clearing in the woods, near Waka. Very soon after that, father was handed over to the Lithuanian police who shot him. About two hours later we crossed a wide river in a boat with a young Gypsy woman, who gave us a knowing look and offered to tell us our fortunes. We had no money to pay her so the fortune-telling project was dropped but she agreed to take us to the other shore. While crossing, she kept looking at us with pity, humming a little song which sounded like a ballad, repeating the words: "You so young and pretty, your fate so ugly." We were not sure about her intentions, so we left her and the boat as fast as we could and continued on our way.'

Lydia and Monica reached Krystyna Adolph's village unexpected and unannounced. 'Krystyna was not home when we arrived. We were sitting there waiting for her to return, too tired to talk, too worried to care, oblivious to the possibility that we might be seen, too exhausted to think or plan. And then we saw her with Hania, walking up the road toward the house. Suddenly, she saw us. Without a moment's hesitation, she dropped the little girl's hand, and started running toward us, her arms outstretched in a gesture of welcome, and in a moment she was hugging both of us.'

That 'climactic moment', Lydia Aran wrote, 'extended

into a three-year-old saga of a heroic struggle by this extraordinary woman for the survival of three young people with a death sentence over their heads (at a certain stage we were joined for a year by a wounded Russian prisoner of war, who escaped from a transport), while each of us – if caught – would cause her own immediate summary execution. While all around us whole villages were burned to the ground and families executed on as much as a suspicion of having fed an escapee, Krystyna simply ignored the danger from gossip, denunciation or random discovery of ours and Nicolai's presence on the farm, and put herself serenely in God's hands in the simple and unshakable certainty that she was doing what a decent person ought to do.'

The moment of rescue, and the three years that followed, 'were crucial for us mainly because they saved us from a certain and cruel death. But beyond that they afforded us the rare privilege of surviving the years of the Nazi horrors in an atmosphere of goodness and true sharing, and of witnessing a rare instance of a triumph of courage and generosity over fear and instinctive egoism, under extreme conditions.'

Lydia Aran later wrote: 'I think that our case is not typical even among those in which non-Jews did help Jews, because of the exceptionally noble motivation and the extraordinary courage of Krystyna, who did not hesitate to put at risk not only her own but also her little daughter's life to do what she believed was right, who offered to shelter us in her home at her own initiative, and who, from the moment we came, accepted us as an equal and inseparable part of a four-member unit which would survive or die together.'[4]

Samuel Bak was only eight years old when the German

---

[4] Lydia Aran, letter to the author, 29 August 2001. In 1984 Lydia Aran had planted a tree in her rescuer's name at Yad Vashem. At the time she was teaching Buddhism at the Hebrew University, Jerusalem.

army entered Vilna. A child prodigy, he had the first exhibition of his drawings a year later, inside the ghetto. After his father was sent to a labour camp, he and his mother were taken in by Sister Maria, the Mother Superior of the Benedictine convent just outside the ghetto. 'In time we became very good friends, Sister Maria and I,' he later wrote. 'I always waited impatiently for her daily visit. She supplied me with paper, coloured pencils, and old and worn children's books, gave me lessons from the Old and the New Testament, and taught me the essential Catholic prayers. After several days Mother's sister, Aunt Yetta, joined us; later her husband, Uncle Yasha, and Father, after they managed to escape the camp in which they had been long interned, were granted the same asylum.'

Only the Mother Superior and one other nun knew that there were men hiding in the convent. Eventually, as so often, the threat of discovery or denunciation loomed, and a new hiding place had to be found. This was a former convent in which the Germans had housed the looted archives of a dozen museums and institutions in Vilna and the surrounding towns: 'Trucks loaded with confiscated riches arrived daily to be unloaded in the ancient building's courtyard,' Samuel Bak recalled. 'There the nuns, dressed now in civilian poverty, met a number of Jews who were sent every day from the ghetto to carry and pile the thousands of volumes, documents, and rare books that filled its rooms and corridors. One small group of them created a hiding place for the days that they foresaw would follow the final liquidation of the ghetto. The evening Mother and I arrived was a few months after that liquidation. Three Jewish families were now living buried under the books.'

Sister Maria and Father Stakauskas, a Catholic priest and former professor of history who was employed to supervise and sort the looted material, provided the hidden Jews with food and other necessities. 'Had the authorities discovered their selfless acts, they would have been tortured and executed,' Bak wrote. 'Their courage and devotion went beyond anything I have ever encountered. It was Maria who convinced the group in hiding to take in a woman and a child. She explained to them our state of total despair. Sending us back would have meant our death. The nine people had a hard choice to make, and they vacillated, as clearly we would take up a part of their space as well as some of the very limited portions of available food. Moreover, a few of them were afraid that our presence could increase their chance of being detected. But Maria made it clear how much she cared about us. The group could not afford to alienate her. All this came to our knowledge only later, but it provides one more link in our chain of miracles.'

Sister Maria visited every night. 'She would knock lightly on a wooden beam, three knocks that were the sign for us to dismantle the bundles of books inserted into our tunnel. She always came with some food, some necessary medications, and, most important, with good news that the German armies were losing on all fronts and that the days of our ordeal were numbered. Her optimism and her courage nourished the energies that were vital for our survival.'

Father Stakauskas visited once or twice a week. 'In his old black leather case that was stuffed with papers, he brought some hidden carrots, a few dried fruits, or a piece of cheese. But his main contribution to the boosting of our morale was his summary of the BBC news. A village friend allowed him to listen to a clandestine radio in the basement of his barn. The Germans were retreating on all fronts. A map of Europe of my own making and movable little red flags indicated to us all that the Third Reich was shrinking. It was a question of a few weeks or maybe a month or two. We had to hold out. The intensification of Soviet air raids confirmed our hope that the end was nearing.'[5]

Jan and Zofia Bartoszewicz, a Polish Christian couple, were hiding in their cellar one of Vilna Jewry's greatest poets and authors, Avraham Sutzkever. He had reached their door exhausted and starving. Having given the poet sanctuary, Zofia Bartoszewicz went into the city to find Sutzkever's son-in-law, who was in a German labour gang, and managed to hand him a loaf of bread. She then walked every day to the ghetto gate, a distance of more than three miles, to arrange for bread, potatoes and even meat to be smuggled in to Sutzkever's wife and mother.

While in hiding, Sutzkever fell ill. Zofia Bartoszewicz and her husband took him from the cellar and, despite the risk of discovery, brought him into their own rooms. Calling a doctor, they said that the poet was their own son. When he recovered, they refused to let him go back into the cellar, but insisted he continue to stay with them. All went well until a neighbour caught sight of him. To protect his rescuers from denunciation, Sutzkever returned to the ghetto. Later he escaped, joining the partisans in the woods around the city.[6]

Betrayal and denunciation were a constant danger: among those murdered at Ponar, outside Vilna, in September 1943, was a young Polish woman who had given refuge to a Jewish child.[7]

Wiktoria Balul, a devout Polish Christian in her sixties, found sanctuary for a Jewish couple, Moshe and Chawiwa Flechtman, in the home of her son Antoni. With the help of her husband Wincenty, Wiktoria provided those in hiding with food from Polish farmers outside the city. Chawiwa Flechtman was pregnant when she was taken to Antoni Balul's home. After the

[5] Samuel Bak, *Painted in Words: A Memoir*, pages 338, 357, 358–9.
[6] Yad Vashem Righteous Among the Nations Archive, file 2241.
[7] Archives of the Vilna Gaon Jewish State Museum, Vilnius.

baby was born, the Baluls made sure that it was safely hidden. They also took in a thirteen-year-old Jewish boy, Jakow Jakubowicz, who had escaped from the ghetto. All four of those in hiding with them survived the war.[8]

When David and Leah Gitelman decided to hand over their twenty-month-old baby girl, Getele – so named because she was born inside the ghetto – to a Polish woman, Wiktoria Burlingis, and her Lithuanian husband Pawel, the child was smuggled out of the ghetto in a sack while she was sleeping. The only language the child knew was Yiddish, which would quickly alert those for whom betrayal was a way of life (and a source of food, alcohol and money). Getele was quickly taught Polish, and then, as the risk of betrayal grew, a Polish nun, Aleksandra Drzwiecka, agreed to take the baby. She was already looking after a Jewish boy.[9] The boy and Getele survived the war; their parents did not.

Maryla Abramowicz-Wolska and her husband Feliks, both devout Catholics, took many Jews into their apartment, fed them and provided them with forged 'Aryan' documents. One of those whom they helped was the historian Dr Mark Dworzecki; another was the poet Shmerl Kaczerginski. For her work in saving Jewish lives, and in helping to cheat the Nazis of their aim of wiping out Vilna Jewry in its entirety, Maryla Abramowicz-Wolska was known as 'The White Angel of the Vilna Ghetto'.[10]

With the liberation of Vilna by the Red Army in July 1944, Pearl Good has written, 'several hundred Jews hidden by Gentiles on the outskirts of the town returned to the city'. Among them was her future husband, Vova

---

[8] Yad Vashem Righteous Among the Nations Archive, file 6311.
[9] Yad Vashem Righteous Among the Nations Archive, files 5520, 5510A.
[10] Yad Vashem Righteous Among the Nations Archive, file 2072.

Gdud, who had found refuge with a non-Jewish family after escaping from the death pits at Ponar, where as many as a hundred thousand Jews were murdered by the Nazis between 1941 and 1944.[11]

The courage of a few non-Jews, each one outstanding in his or her different way, had enabled a few individual Jews to survive. But Vilna Jewry had been destroyed.

[11] 'Life Story of Perela Esterowicz – Pearl Good', typescript (sent to the author by Pearl Good).

CHAPTER FOUR

Lithuania

Lithuania's independence was destroyed when it was annexed by the Soviet Union in 1940. Within a year it was overrun by the German armies that attacked the Soviet Union on 22 June 1941. Of the hundred and thirty-five thousand Lithuanian Jews who came under German rule, only six thousand survived the war. More than fifty Lithuanian towns had established Jewish populations; none escaped the killing squads and their Lithuanian helpers. Nevertheless, by 1 January 2002 more than five hundred Lithuanians had been recognized as Righteous Among the Nations by Yad Vashem in Jerusalem.[1] They are also being commemorated by a series of volumes issued by the Vilna Gaon State Jewish Museum in today's Lithuanian capital, Vilnius. The story of these Righteous, writes Emanuelis Zingeris in his introduction to the first volume, is 'about the spiritual people of Lithuania who opposed the infernal laws of the time in the name of thousand-year-long justice'.[2]

Among the Lithuanian Christians who tried to help

---

[1] 'Righteous Among the Nations – per Country & Ethnic Origin,' 1 January 2002, Yad Vashem Department for the Righteous Among the Nations (list sent to the author on 29 January 2002). The exact Lithuanian figure was 504.
[2] Emanuelis Zingeris, 'Introduction', in Mikhail Erenburg and Viktorija Sakaite (editors), *Hands Bringing Life and Bread*, volume 1, pages v–vi.

Jews was Bronius Gotautas, a monk in the city of Kaunas who changed the photograph on his own passport in order to save a Jewish doctor. In the village of Babrungas, a Lithuanian peasant woman, Julija Gadeikyte, and her brother Pranas hid six Jews in a hideout that they prepared for them underneath the hay in their barn. When it was safe for the Jews to come out for a while, Julija would enter the barn and quietly sing. Although it is possible that somebody in the village suspected that she and her brother were hiding Jews, nobody betrayed them.[3]

The first two Lithuanians to be recognized as Righteous by Yad Vashem were Julija Vitkauskiene and her son Arejas Vitkauskas. Asked to hide Jewish children from the Kovno ghetto, Julija, who was having difficulty in providing for her own son, agreed to take in a Jewish infant, and feed and house her, commenting: 'What is life for, if it is not to help other people?'[4]

One of the Lithuanians chosen by Mordecai Paldiel for inclusion in the 1990 *Encyclopedia of the Holocaust* was Ona Simaite. At the time of the German occupation she was a librarian at Vilna University. Using the pretext that she had to recover library books that had been loaned to Jewish students, she obtained permission to enter the ghetto, and went there every day, bringing in food and taking out valuable Jewish books, which she then hid in the university library. She also managed to smuggle a Jewish girl past the guards on the ghetto gate, and then to find her several hiding places, until she was accidentally discovered.

In the summer of 1944, Ona Simaite adopted a ten-year-old Jewish girl, registering her as a relative from

[3] Mikhail Erenburg and Viktorija Sakaite (editors), *Hands Bringing Life and Bread*, volume 1, pages 34–5.
[4] Mikhail Erenburg and Viktorija Sakaite (editors), *Hands Bringing Life and Bread*, volume 1, pages 106–7.

another town which, she said, had been severely bombed. Enquiries were made by the authorities, who discovered that the story was false. Cruelly tortured, Ona Simaite revealed nothing about her many Jewish contacts, or about any of the hiding places of which she had first-hand knowledge. Sent to Dachau, she survived the war, though much weakened by her incarceration.[5]

In Lazdijai, a Lithuanian priest was asked for help by a seventeen-year-old Jewish girl, Guta Kaufman, whose family had been murdered during the slaughter of the town's Jews. The girl had already been turned away by a former schoolfriend to whom she had turned for refuge. The priest took her in, and tried to persuade the school-friend to change her mind, but she would not. The priest then did what he could to help Guta, obtaining forged 'Aryan' documents for her, and in due course placing her in the home of Wanda Baldowska, an elderly Polish woman who, as a devout Catholic, regarded saving the Jewish girl as a religious imperative. Guta remained with Wanda until the area was liberated by the Red Army. With the aid of the priest's housekeeper, Wanda supplied Guta's needs out of her own funds. In the words of Yad Vashem: 'She linked her fate with that of her Jewish charge, and cared for her with love and devotion.'[6]

On 5 November 1943 the SS searched the Shavli ghetto for children to send to their deaths. Seven-year-old Ruth Kron and her younger sister Tamara were among 575 children – as well as 249 sick and elderly Jews – who were rounded up that day for deportation. Ruth was able to escape deportation as a result of the intervention of the ghetto doctor, who had earlier successfully treated the SS Commandant – who, in

[5] Mordecai Paldiel, 'Simaite, Ona (1899–1970)', *Encyclopedia of the Holocaust*, volume 4, page 1358.
[6] Yad Vashem Righteous Among the Nations Archive, file 3311.

return, allowed one of the 824 deportees to be spared.

A Lithuanian woman, Ona Ragauskis, who had recently lost her baby son to diphtheria, took Ruth Kron with her to her village ten miles from Shavli, where her husband Antanas was the schoolteacher. First, as the Canadian writer Keith Morgan has recorded, she had to ask her husband to agree to this. 'I want to save her,' Ona told her husband. 'It is the right thing for Christians to do. I saw the hollowness in the eyes of the mothers who lost their children when the Germans came for them. I have lost a child and I know their pain.' Having lost their baby son, she had only one remaining child, a two-year-old daughter, Grazinute. She continued: 'But Antanas, you must know that if we take her now she could be with us for the rest of her life . . . we would have to feed her and educate her.' Her husband replied: 'I will love her as my own.'

Ona Ragauskis returned to Shavli, where Ruth Kron's mother Gita begged her, 'Please take my little girl. We don't have much time.' Ruth was then smuggled out of the ghetto. Fifty-seven years later, Ona Ragauskis recalled how, during the journey to Kuziai, she was so frightened the driver would betray them that she made him drop them off a mile from the village.

At the Ragauskis' home, Ruth sat in a cupboard during the day so that none of the Lithuanian children would see her. By night, she could walk about and breathe the outside air. She slept in an outhouse at the back of the schoolhouse. Ona and Antanas Ragauskis fed her and did their utmost to keep up her spirits. Later, when it became too dangerous for the child to stay there, a priest, Father Kleiba, hid her in his home, where he was already sheltering a number of Jews.[7]

---

[7] Ruth Kron's story was told in Keith Morgan, 'Hidden from the Holocaust', a serial in four successive issues of the Vancouver *Province*, 24–7 October 2000.

Lithuanian priests who helped save Jews, or protested against the killings, are remembered by survivors to this day. One of those survivors, Joseph A. Melamed, has written with deepest appreciation of the elderly Father Dambrauskas from Alsedziai, 'who did everything in his power to save Jews and was even punished for this by his Bishop'. He also wrote of Father Bronius Paukstis from the Jesuit church in Kaunas who saved many Jews in that city; of Father Lapis from Siauliai (Shavli) who attempted unsuccessfully to help Jews there; and of Father Jonas Gylys, a parish priest in Varena, 'who delivered sermons against killing Jews, and tried to comfort the Jews whom the Lithuanian murderers concentrated in a synagogue before their murder'.[8]

The largest number of Jews in Lithuania lived in Kaunas, known to the Jews by its pre-1914 Russian name, Kovno. Once the city's thirty thousand Jews were confined in the ghetto, the only ones who left were those taken for execution at the nineteenth-century forts around the city, or those sent out each day to work in the nearby factories.

A Lithuanian medical doctor in Kaunas, Elena Kutorgene, helped not only those Jews who had been her patients before the war, but also many other Jews who turned to her. When, before the arrival of the Germans in the city, Lithuanian mobs rampaged through the streets, murdering Jews, she hid seven or eight Jews in her surgery for the night. During the short period after the creation of the Kovno ghetto, when it was still open, she went there daily with food and medicines. When the ghetto was closed, and non-Jews barred from entering, she went to the fence to hand over her packages. 'The situation in the ghetto is horrible,' she wrote in her diary. 'I simply cannot bear to live while knowing that right

---

[8] Joseph A. Melamed (editor), *Lithuania: The Land of Blood.*

next to me people are enduring such suffering and being subjected to such terrible humiliation.'[9]

Also in Kaunas, a Lithuanian couple, Jonas and Joana Stankiewicz, gave sanctuary to a young Jewish child, Henia Wisgardisky, who had been hidden in the ghetto during the 'Children's Action' of 1943, when the Germans embarked on the wholesale slaughter of the Jewish children in Kaunas, and then smuggled out. Before the war, Jonas Stankiewicz had been the foreman of the chemical factory owned by the young girl's father. Henia survived the war, as did her parents, who were hidden by a Lithuanian potato farmer in his cellar.[10]

In the village of Padrabé, the Tomkievicz family gave shelter to ten-year-old Mulik Krol, while the Wiszumirsky family found a place in their home for his mother – who hoped that, by putting her son somewhere different from herself, he might have a better chance of surviving. 'These people could not even risk mentioning to their neighbours that they were hiding a Jew: at that time even a next-door neighbour could be an informer. Therefore, the Tomkievicz and the Wiszumirsky families, whose farms were four kilometres apart, did not know anything about the other's night-time visitors and parcels of food left at designated places.'[11]

It was not until 1992 that Mulik, then living in South Africa, began looking for his saviours in Padrabé. By that time, the parents of both families that had rescued Mulik and his mother were no longer alive. Jolanta

[9] Quoted in Ilya Ehrenburg and Vasily Grossman, *The Complete Black Book of Russian Jewry*, pages 333–4.
[10] 'Portrait of a Jewish child in hiding with her Lithuanian "sister"', United States Holocaust Memorial Museum, Photo Archive, Worksheet 14637.
[11] Jolanta Paskeviciene, 'Childhood is not a dream', *Lithuania in the World* magazine, 2001. In South Africa, Mulik Krol took the name Sam Keren. Of the nine members of his family, he was the only survivor.

Paskeviciene, a Lithuanian journalist, told Mulik's story in an article in 2001: 'Mulik felt that their children are like brothers and sisters to him. He and the Wiszumirskys' elder son, Karol, used to tend cattle, they learned to ride a horse together, and tried to learn to swim. The Tomkieviczes hired him as a shepherd for several summers. Nobody suspected that the blond teenager was Jewish.'

The Tomkieviczes' daughter Olga Gulbinovicz recalled, at the age of eighty: 'Although almost half a century has passed since then, I still recall the awful, paralyzing fear that went on for several years. I cannot say even now which of the two feelings was stronger; the fear you would be turned in, and all your family would be shot dead; or the pity we felt for the innocent tortured children, the elderly, the sick and the women. I can remember very well how my parents got on with Mulik's parents, who ran a shop in town. We always shopped there. We could also buy on credit or borrow money from them. How could we possibly refuse them help in such a situation? My mother loved Mulik as if he was her own child. She would come to wake him up in the morning, but didn't have the heart to disturb the little shepherd's sweet sleep. So she would take the herd out to pasture herself. When Sara, Mulik's mother, was shot in the forest, we all mourned her for several days, and could not bring ourselves to break the news to the child who was now an orphan.'[12]

Those who hid Jews had to take extraordinary precautions. In the village of Parankova, fifteen miles from the town of Butrimonys, a farmer, Mikhail Shestakovsky, and his wife, Mikhilina, were among those noble souls who risked their lives and those of their family to hide Jews. 'It was harvest time for potatoes,' one of those in

---

[12] Jolanta Paskeviciene, 'Childhood is not a dream', *Lithuania in the World* magazine, 2001.

hiding there, Rivka Lozansky Bogomolnaya, later re-called. 'They locked me in the house to help out. All the neighbours were busy with the potato gathering so it was quiet and nobody visited anyone. Since I wanted to make myself useful I tidied up and polished the house. I cleaned the windows, taking the opportunity to check if anyone was coming. I made the beds and did whatever I could. However, when Mikhilina came home and saw what I had done and the order I had made, she let out a scream. She feared it would be immediately noticeable that there were Jews hiding because in the village nobody cleaned the windows like that or made the beds like that. She crumpled the beds; it was harder to do anything about the windows.'

When Mikhail Shestakovsky heard 'that runaway Jews were being sought in the barns he became very fright-ened. He didn't tell us to leave, but consulted his family, including his brother Ignatzia, who had brought us, and his sister Genya. His youngest brother was very much afraid, and warned that if they were tired of living, they should at least think of saving their children. In response Mikhail and Ignatzia dug a pit under the house (beneath the workshop – he was a carpenter). He said that if any of the neighbours saw and asked, they should say it was for the potatoes. But if this happened we wouldn't be able to hide there any longer.'

On one occasion, as Rivka Lozansky Bogomolnaya recalled, 'our protectors wanted to prove to the neigh-bours that nobody was in hiding with them, so they took off for three days to visit Mikhilina's brother. They brought a neighbour to stay in their house overnight. They left us a supply of bread and water, a jug of milk and a bucket with a cover for the necessary human func-tions. They covered the little pit with the lid, painted it with lime, and left. We were closed up for three days. It is very difficult to describe our suffering. It was dark and there was no air. In addition we couldn't even go out once a day. In the house it was forever cold, so the neighbour and her children sat all day on the oven, which was right opposite the pit. It was a miracle though that though the Shestakovsky children, who were three and four years old, saw us crawl out of the pit, they never even cast their eyes towards the pit when strangers came into the house.'

The Shestakovsky family, like so many of the Righteous, was poor. 'They would eat only twice a day – tea in the morning and in the evening a few boiled potatoes and onions (which were cooked together). They had two small children, so from their meagre food supply they had to manage to give us something too so that we wouldn't die of hunger. Though we were full of worries we nevertheless wanted to eat.

'Late at night when all the neighbours had long been asleep we would be let out for a bit of fresh air and for necessary bodily functions. All day long we suffered in the pit awaiting nightfall. Then we would be allowed to climb up on the stone oven to dry out from the dampness. One would stand guard at the window to make sure nobody was passing by looking for us, in which case we would have to sneak into the pit so as not to bring misfortune upon ourselves and, more importantly, on the householders.'[13]

Rivka Lozansky Bogomolnaya survived the war in hiding. Others whom she knew were less fortunate.

Five Lithuanians from a single family, Jaroslavas Rakevicius and his four sons, Ceslovas, Juozas, Zenonas and Algimatas, typified the bravery that could be shown when the will to save was strong. This one family saved thirty-five Jews, systematically smuggling them out of the Kovno ghetto and taking them into their own home

---

[13] Rivka Lozansky Bogomolnaya, *Wartime Experiences in Lithuania*, pages 69–71.

in the village of Keidziai, more than fifty miles away. Among those whom this family saved was a young boy, Aaron Brik – later, as Aharon Barak, the President of Israel's Supreme Court – who was taken out of the ghetto by Jaroslavas Rakevicius in a sack.[14]

In one of the factories in Kaunas, Johannes Bruess, the German director of the iron foundry, allowed one of his Jewish workers, Joseph Kagan, to build a hideout in the factory's attic. The factory's Lithuanian bookkeeper, Vytautas Garkauskas – who was himself hiding a Jewish child in his home – knew about the scheme and approved of it. But 'the heart and soul of the scheme', wrote Kagan's wife Margaret, who was also hidden there, was the factory foreman Vytautas Rinkevicius.[15] Joseph Kagan later noted that Bruess was a devout Jehovah's Witness, Garkauskas a Roman Catholic, and Rinkevicius a Protestant.[16]

Rinkevicius made plans to hide not only the newly wed Joseph and Margaret, but also Joseph's mother Mira, in a specially constructed refuge – little more than a wooden crate – in the attic. Rinkevicius's wife Elia knew nothing of her husband's plans to save three Jews. 'I took Joseph's unbounded enthusiasm for this wonderful man with a pinch of salt,' Margaret Kagan later wrote; 'thus when Joseph wangled for me to get assigned to his work brigade on a day pass, I went with some trepidation.' It was not until the lunchtime break 'that I was to get my first glimpse of Vytautas. Joseph pointed to a distant figure in a far corner of the foundry-yard. We were to go over and Joseph was to hand him the bundle of personal belongings we had smuggled out of the ghetto, while I stood on guard. The man we were approaching was tall

---

[14] Yad Vashem Righteous Among the Nations Archive, file 1072.
[15] Margaret Kagan, manuscript (sent to the author, 10 August 2000).
[16] Joseph Kagan, *Knight of the Ghetto: The Story of Lord Kagan*, page 77.

and lean, wore blue coveralls and a beret, looked alert, yet reassuringly relaxed. He wore heavy rimmed spectacles and their thick lenses seemed to set him apart from our ugly world. From behind these lenses his eyes exuded calm, hope and confidence. When I got back to my mother in the ghetto that evening, I found it difficult to explain just why this man had made such a monumental impression on me; but I did manage to convey my deep-felt confidence in Vytautas's integrity and goodwill. I sensed my mother breathe a sigh of relief. Once more I was to join Joseph in his workplace for a day and this time Joseph managed to take me up to the box in the loft, which was to be our home.'

Margaret Kagan later recalled how, on a prearranged signal from Rinkevicius 'that the coast was clear, we tiptoed upstairs. A wood plank wall sectioned off the loft from its gable end to which there was access through a small, secretly hinged door. Within that gable end there stood a nearly completed crate-like wooden structure, approximately 6 × 5ft, topped by a wooden roof slanting at the same angle as the loft. Inside it – two wood plank shelf-beds – the one along the 6ft wall to be Joseph's and mine, the other, a few feet above and across – Joseph's mother's. It all looked both comforting and frightening. How long would the three of us have to be cooped up here, afraid to breathe or move? What were our chances of survival? Was the ghetto a safer place to stay in, after all?'

The day came when Margaret Kagan left the ghetto for the last time. 'Vytautas and Joseph had done a wonderful job of completing and equipping our hideout. Its comforts exceeded all my expectations; hair mattressing plus sheets, blankets and pillows graced our plank beds; we had electricity; two bulbs – one inside plus another one outside our box, above an electric cooking ring, and a small electric heater. Soap and towels, next to a washstand with a bowl and bucket, a few knives, forks and spoons plus a couple of pots and pans, and even a radio – all bade us welcome.'

The three people whose lives Vytautas Rinkevicius was risking his own life to save spent their first night 'very conscious of the fact that come day and the morning shift workers, we would have to lie low, stop moving around or making noise for fear of being discovered. Towards dawn we slept fitfully and when, eventually, we started hearing voices and clanking, we hardly dared breathe. It felt like an eternity until we heard the agreed knock on the trapdoor outside our hut. This was built into the ceiling of the canteen food store of which Vytautas was in charge. Ever so gingerly we tiptoed to that trapdoor, opened it gently and were much relieved to read in the eyes of Vytautas's serious face that our illicit move had not been noticed. After a whispered exchange confirming that on no account were we to stir unless we heard the two plus one knock, Vytautas assured us that he would take every opportunity of visiting us, probably every few days. Then, to our surprise, a basket was hoisted up to us on a devil's fork, containing a traditional welcome of bread and salt, plus a chunk of bacon meat – a great luxury at the time.'

That hideout was to protect Joseph and Margaret Kagan, and Joseph's mother, for three hundred days, from the end of 1943 until late 1944.

Recalling the efforts that Vytautas Rinkevicius made on their behalf, Margaret Kagan noted that he was 'far more successful in keeping his worries and problems from us than we were with ours. Slowly, very slowly, we did, however, manage to piece some of his together. For instance, we did, eventually, realize how difficult it had been to keep us as his secret in order not to inflict his worries on his wife. Apparently she had noticed that Vytautas now seemed preoccupied and absent-minded more often than before; besides, valuable food items started going missing out of her icebox and pantry. This led her to start suspecting Vytautas of being involved with another woman. It was only when faced with this suspicion that Vytautas confessed to hiding us. Elia – a generous, kind-hearted person, as we were to find out – proved sympathetic to our plight, but questioned whether they, as parents, had the right to put the life of their own child at risk. Thus Vytautas had to continue carrying the additional burden of not being able to share many a dangerous moment either with us, or with his wife.

'We had come to depend on Vytautas's face lighting up our difficult existence. At the same time we worried ourselves sick about his safety and found it difficult to get reconciled to the fact that at any moment we could prove the involuntary cause of his undoing. So any day Vytautas did not materialize through our trapdoor would cause us double concern – one, we missed him, and two, was it a routine obstacle which had kept him away, or had some disaster befallen him?'

One particular February morning in 1944, Rinkevicius appeared at the trapdoor 'looking tense, pale and crestfallen. Our whispered solicitous enquiries elicited only that he had had a bad night due to a stomach upset, but we remained unconvinced. Later the same day – another knock, a most unusual occurrence. Vytautas had decided on second thoughts that he had to warn us that Mr Garkauskas – and he knew about our hideout – had been arrested the previous night. It had been impossible to ascertain whether or not his arrest was in connection with us; yet, as there seemed to be no indication it was, we were not to worry. But we all knew what this meant and none of us could have got much rest that night.'

On the following morning, earlier than his usual time, 'an exceptionally agitated Vytautas came to tell us that Mr Garkauskas had managed to smuggle a letter out of jail to tell us that his arrest was unconnected with us.

Sadly, he had been denounced by a neighbour for harbouring a Jewish child and the inevitability of tragic consequences marred our own relief at not having come to the end of our road. As it happened Garkauskas managed to escape death; the child did not. Reconciling our double-edged emotions of horror and relief was hard. Our inner turmoil was inexpressible. Gloom and silence reigned in our hut.'

Margaret Kagan recalls wondering whether, had they been denounced, they could have escaped 'through our unfinished emergency exit; and if so, how could we have destroyed the evidence of our hideout and Vytautas's culpability. Yet – life, such as it was, continued. We were learning to read Vytautas's deep set eyes, he – slowly, to share some of his worries. Half jokingly he would tell us about his recurring nightmares. One such was that as we were about to be discovered and with the sound of German jack-boots approaching he would shove all three of us under our plank bed and would then try, in vain, to squeeze himself in on top of us. Also, we would get special food treats more often than before. Now that Vytautas's wife Elia was "in" on us, the family would happily deprive itself in order to share rare goodies with us.

'Whenever a new threat of being discovered loomed up, such as an outsider discovering the fresh saw marks we had created in order to make a disused little gate into an emergency exit, or our parcel of refuse (excreta) landing on the roof, rather than on its designated resting ground, or a zealous meter reading reporting a suspicious increase in electric consumption, or indeed, the tragic Garkauskas episode, we would revert to discussing ways of leaving and somehow finding new hiding places. This not only to save our own necks, but also to get Vytautas out of the direct firing line of questioning and torture. But he would have none of it. Come what may, he would say, we were safer in our loft than at large, and he was ready and prepared to face any consequences.

'I still cannot imagine how we could have coped without Vytautas's extraordinary moral fortitude. For instance, one day my mother-in-law decided that she could not survive "buried alive", as it were. In her claustrophobic delusion the ghetto became her "fata morgana". It was Vytautas who, with the help of a letter from my mother living in the ghetto, dissuaded her from returning to the ghetto. We did all agree, though, that Mira, my mother-in-law, did need to get away in order not to crack up. Again, it fell to Vytautas to arrange for her to be given refuge for a short break, away from our hideout with another devoted family of Lithuanian friends – the Serapinases.'

Another Lithuanian couple, Antanas and Maria Macenavicius, had already taken in Margaret Kagan's eleven-year-old brother Alik, and were also looking after a little Jewish girl.[17]

In the small town of Naumiestis, a Lithuanian woman, Apolonia Shaparis, took in a Jewish girl called Rachala, brought her up as her own daughter, and enabled her to survive the war. When the war ended, Apolonia Shaparis and her family, including Rachala (then named Halina), fled from Lithuania, eventually settling in the White Russian town of Slupsk. There, at the end of 1946, by a miracle of perseverance, Rachala's father located her and took her home.[18]

Fifty-five years after the end of the war, a member of the Shaparis family began her quest for the Jewish girl who had been sheltered by her grandparents. In a letter to the *Hidden Child* newsletter in New York, asking for information, she set down everything that she had

---

[17] Margaret Kagan, manuscript (sent to the author, 10 August 2000).
[18] 'Looking For . . .', *The Hidden Child* newsletter, volume 9, number 1, Spring 2000.

learned from her family about the little fugitive child. 'We believe the girl's name is Rachala (Rachel) Goldberg. She was born around 1940 in the Suwalki region. Her father worked in the manufacture of textiles and her mother was a schoolteacher. They were taken to the Kaunas ghetto. In about 1943, the Nazis ordered the elimination of all Jewish children from the ghetto, and her father sought to hide her. My birth grandmother lived in Kaunas and apparently put bread on the fence for people walking to forced labour. The family asked her to hide Rachala. She agreed. The young girl was then taken in a sack by bus to Naumiestis. She spoke only Yiddish and a little Hebrew. Once in Naumiestis, she was renamed Halina and was raised by Apolonia Shaparis and her husband. The other children were told that she was their sister.'[19]

The 'children's action' in the Kovno ghetto, which Rachala Goldberg had escaped thanks to the willingness of a Lithuanian woman to take great risks, took two days to complete. Several thousand children were rounded up, driven away in trucks and shot. Only a tiny fragment survived, among them the five-year-old Zahar Kaplanas. This young boy was saved by a non-Jew, a Lithuanian, who smuggled him out of the ghetto in a sack. Later Kaplanas's parents were both killed in the ghetto. Zahar survived the war.[20]

At the very moment of the slaughter of the Jewish children in Kaunas, a Lithuanian doctor, Petras Baublis, the head of the 'Infants' House' in the city, risked his own life and the safety of his family by offering to smuggle

---

[19] At the time of writing (May 2002), Rachala Goldberg had not been traced.
[20] Information provided by Eitan Finkelstein. In 1984, Zahar Kaplanas was among more than ten thousand Soviet Jews who had been refused permission to emigrate to Israel.

Jewish children out of the ghetto and hide them in his institution. To ensure their safety, Dr Baublis, who had a number of close friends among the Lithuanian Roman Catholic priesthood, obtained blank birth certificate forms, which the priests then agreed to authenticate with church seals and signatures, stating that each was a Christian child.

Among the Jewish children saved by Dr Baublis was the two-year-old Ariela Abramovich, whose father later testified that he knew of at least seven other children similarly saved. Baublis also took in another Jewish child, Gitele Mylner, who had been born only a few months before the massacre. She had been handed to the doctor by her parents. Baublis gave her the name Berute Iovayshayte and a certificate stamped by the church authorities, stating that she was a Christian child.[21]

In January 1944, in the village of Lavorishkes, just outside Kaunas, Teresa Danilowicz found two exhausted strangers on her doorstep. Without her husband's knowledge, she took Slioma and Tamara Goldstein in, fed them, and offered them shelter for the night in the family's barn. On the following morning, the Goldsteins explained that they had nowhere else to go, knew no one with whom they could seek refuge. Teresa Danilowicz agreed to shelter them, still keeping this fact from her husband, who was not well, and who had already agreed to hide a Polish refugee. She did, however, share the secret with her daughters; and there the Goldsteins remained hidden for seven months, living in the attic above the stables. At night, they were allowed into the house to wash, and to warm themselves. They remained in hiding until liberation seven months later.[22]

---

[21] Yad Vashem Righteous Among the Nations Archive, file 1183.
[22] Yad Vashem Righteous Among the Nations Archive, file 5414.

*   *   *

On 12 July 1944 the surviving eight thousand Jews in the Kovno ghetto were ordered to assemble, and were then taken by train to the concentration camp at Stutthof, near Danzig. Hundreds tried to evade being taken and hid, only to be dragged out of their hiding places by German soldiers and hostile Lithuanians. Many were murdered in the streets. In the midst of this carnage, Jan Pauvlavicius, a Lithuanian carpenter, who had already taken several Jews into hiding, including a four-year-old boy, dug an underground hiding place next to his cellar for yet more Jews. He equipped the cellar with two bunks, on which eight people could lie, and made a small opening to the vegetable garden above, to provide the hideout with air.

Dr Tania Ipp, one of those whom Pauvlavicius saved, later recalled: 'He was like a father to us – a man only to be admired.' As well as hiding nine Jews in the hole that he had dug next to his cellar, Pauvlavicius also found refuge elsewhere for two Soviet prisoners of war who had escaped from a German camp, and for another young Jewish boy.[23]

One of those whom Pauvlavicius saved was a Jewish woman, Miriam Krakinowski, who had managed to break away from the line of deportees in the confusion of the moment. On reaching Pauvlavicius's house she had been taken into the cellar, whereupon Pauvlavicius took a broom, swept aside the wood shavings covering a small trapdoor, and knocked on the floor. 'I saw a small door being pushed up,' Miriam Krakinowski later recalled. 'He told me to go down the steps. I couldn't see where I was going, but I didn't say anything. Gradually the room became lighter, and I found myself in a very

---

[23] Testimony of Dr Tania Ipp, Yad Vashem Righteous Among the Nations Archive, file 2472.

small, hot room filled with half-naked Jews. I began to cry as they asked questions about the fate of the ghetto.'

The Jews hidden in Pauvlavicius's cellar remained there for the next three weeks, until the day of liberation. 'After liberation,' Miriam Krakinowski recalled, 'Pauvlavicius was killed by Lithuanians who hated him for saving Jews.'[24] He was actually murdered by one man.

That someone should be murdered by his fellow villagers, his fellow nationals – his fellow human beings – for an act of kindness (some would say, nobility) is hard to contemplate. Yet such incidents were repeated again and again. The story of Mykolas Simelis – as narrated by an American of Lithuanian origin, Benjamin Lesin – is another blot on the landscape of modern civilization. 'During the war, fourteen Jews, mostly strangers, found their way to Simelis's farm. He hid them and fed them, while he could barely feed his own family. He took care of their needs at great peril to himself and his young family. Indeed, his five small children, the oldest only eight years old, were robbed of their childhood because they could no longer play with the neighbourhood children. They had always to stay near their own farm in order to warn of any approaching neighbours or strangers.'

Benjamin Lesin, after recounting the family's story, writes: 'Had this been all their sacrifices, it would have been significant and noteworthy. However, this was only the beginning. In 1944 Mykolas's wife, Jadvyga, became pregnant with their sixth child. Not to further complicate life on the farm with their fourteen guests, Jadvyga chose an abortion. She died of complications in April 1944. After the War with the re-occupation of

---

[24] Testimony of Miriam Krakinowski, Yad Vashem Righteous Among the Nations Archive, file 2472.

Lithuania by the USSR, bands of Lithuanian Nationalists roamed the countryside. They were convinced that anyone who rescued Jews had to be Communist, an enemy. In July 1945, Mykolas Simelis was murdered by them. The children grew up in an orphanage.'[25]

---

[25] Benjamin E. Lesin, 'Lithuania, the Evil and the Righteous', *Los Angeles Jewish Times*, 2 August 1996.

CHAPTER FIVE

Poland: The General-Government

As the killings in the East continued, in those parts of
Poland conquered by Germany in 1939 the Jews
remained confined to ghettos, segregated from the local
population and forced to wear a distinctive Star of David
badge; their food was reduced to such meagre rations
that thousands died every month. Not only was any Jew
leaving the ghettos there 'liable to the death penalty' –
in the words of a decree of 15 October 1941 – but, the
decree added: 'The same penalty applies to persons who
knowingly shelter such Jews.'[1]

That penalty was ruthlessly applied throughout the
territory of the General-Government, the German-ruled
administration established after the conquest of Poland,
with its capital in Cracow. 'My parents suffered death for
having kept Jews,' recalled Henryk Woloszynowicz of
Waniewo. 'My father was murdered on the spot, my
mother was taken and murdered at Tykocin.'[2] The
memorial book for the town of Skierniewice recorded:
'Sometimes a mere gesture of sympathy shown to those
persecuted could easily cost a life. Thus, the Germans
organized a public execution of fifty Jews in Mlawa in

[1] General-Government Decree, issued by Governor-General Hans
Frank, 15 October 1941.
[2] Wladyslaw Bartoszewski and Zofia Lewin (editors), *Righteous
Among Nations*, page 600.

April 1942. All the inhabitants of the town were herded together to watch this grim spectacle for the purpose of "racial education". One of the Poles who could not control his feelings began to shout: "Down with Hitler! Innocent blood is being shed!" The Germans seized him and shot him dead on the spot.'[3] A month later, in the town of Czarny Dunajec, in the Nowy Targ district, a local notice recorded: 'Three persons (a Pole from Wroblowka and two Jews from Czarny Dunajec), names identified; shot by the Gestapo; the Pole for supplying food to Jews. Bodies buried in the Jewish cemetery.'[4]

In Sosnowiec, Frieda Mazia witnessed the public execution of two women, one a Christian and the other a Jew. A Jewish mother had bought an egg from a Polish peasant, determined that her child would not die of hunger. This normally innocuous act was seen and reported to the German authorities, and both the mother and the peasant woman were hanged. The two bodies were left hanging in public for a few days, 'so one couldn't avoid seeing them – if we wanted to go out we had to pass them.'[5]

Such terrifying punishment did not deter those whose instinct was to save. Also in Sosnowiec, Maria Dyrda protected a five-year-old girl, Mira Rembiszewska, whose parents had been deported. She kept the young girl safe until liberation, when her parents returned to claim her.[6]

Many Polish-born survivors of the Holocaust express

[3] Yitzhak Parlan (editor), *Sefer Skierniewic* (Memorial Book). Skierniewic is the Yiddish form of Skierniewice.
[4] Bulletin of the Central Commission for the Investigation of Nazi Crimes in Poland, volume 9, quoted in Kazimierz Iranek-Osmiecki, *He Who Saves One Life*, page 269.
[5] Testimony of Frieda Mazia, Eichmann trial, 4 May 1961, session 27.
[6] United States Holocaust Memorial Museum, Photo Archive, Worksheet 25904. As Mira Reym Binford, Mira Rembiszewska later went to the United States, where she became a film-maker, and made a film of her experiences, *Diamonds in the Snow*.

141

scepticism about the extent of Polish help to the Jews, and unease at too great a focus on the Righteous. During a discussion about the Righteous in Poland, Benjamin Meed, an eyewitness and a survivor of the German attempt to destroy Polish Jewry, commented: 'More Jews were saved by Jews than by non-Jews.' In Warsaw, he added, 'most of the bunkers on the "Aryan" side were built by Jews. They could not trust the Poles to bring in materials.' Ben Meed's wife Vladka, also a survivor, reflected: 'The percentage of the Righteous was so small compared with the numbers of Jews who were killed.'[7]

Poles who risked their own lives to save Jews were indeed the exception. Yet they could be found throughout Poland, in every town and village. The memorial at Belzec death camp commemorates not only six hundred thousand Jews but also fifteen hundred Poles 'who tried to save Jews'.[8] In as many as a thousand locations, often small, insignificant places on the map through which today's tourist drives quickly, almost without noticing them, someone, some family, was willing to risk their life.

Wladislaw Misiuna lived in Radom during the war. He was eighteen when it began. 'This man surely did something that is against human nature,' writes Baruch Sharoni, who served on the Yad Vashem committee that designates the Righteous, 'as he decided to infect himself with a terrible skin disease, in order to go to a Polish doctor and get medicines, to share them with a Jewish girl, and save them both.' Misiuna also stole food for the ten Jewish girls who were working under his supervision in a rabbit-breeding farm belonging to the commander of

---

[7] Ben and Vladka Meed, in conversation with the author, New York, 14 November 2001.
[8] Martin Gilbert, *Holocaust Journey*, page 210, 'Day Eight, Cracow-Zamosc'.

an ammunition factory in the city. Misiuna also did the girls' laundry in order to avoid the spread of infectious diseases.[9]

In the village of Bobolice, near the town of Zarki, Andrzej Kolacz, his daughter Stanislawa, his son Joseph, his daughter-in-law Helena and his one-year-old grand-daughter opened their small dwelling to Jews desperate to avoid deportation and death. One of those Jews, Joseph Dauman, later wrote: 'The entire house consisted of one large room, an adjacent chicken coop, a barn where a horse and one cow were placed. We, my sister Rachel and myself, stayed in the adjacent cubicle that had only an opening for light and air instead of a window. In the month of June, a third person joined us, this was our older sister Cywia Jonisz. About 7 August 1943 came three more family members.'

In September 1943 two more members of Joseph Dauman's family, having escaped from the nearby con-centration camp at Pionki, asked Andrzej Kolacz to take them in. As there was no room for the two newcomers, he took them to his sister's house in the same village. Still more Jews in flight sought refuge at the Kolacz home. In August 1944 Joseph Dauman's sister Zissel arrived, with her two sons, Eli and Mendl, and her daughter Tsila. The burden on the Kolacz family was considerable, and increasing. Their one cow gave only a small amount of milk a day. Joseph Dauman recalled: 'There was no water well in that village, Bobolice. The nearest well was two kilometres away in the village of Mirow and in summer and in winter, rain or snow, the fourteen – later fifteen and sixteen – year-old girl, Stanislawa Kolacz, was carrying water pails to provide the family and us with water. One had to be careful that neighbours should not wonder at the Kolacz family using too much water, a sign of perhaps hiding some

---

[9] Baruch Sharoni, letter to the author, 5 September 2001.

people. The same fear was in acquiring food. Apart from the difficulties to buy food, we knew how careful the Kolacz family had to act when buying food, as well as bringing water to the house.'[10]

The family continued to feed and protect those in hiding until the day of liberation. Yet, as one of the youngsters saved, Eli Zborowski, later recalled, the family that had saved twelve Jews had to leave the village after the war 'because of the attitude of the population, who were furious with them for hiding Jews. That is why they are no longer living in Bobolice.'[11]

Many rescuers lived in poverty. Before being taken in by the Kolacz family, Zissel Zborowski, her two sons Eli and Mendl, and her daughter Tsila had been hidden for twenty months in another village by the Placzek family. 'They were very poor people,' Eli Zborowski later recalled. 'We paid for the basic foodstuffs. Since they only had coupons for the three of them, it was very difficult to feed seven mouths.' Yet this peasant family did just that. Josef Placzek, a builder, built them two hiding places, a wooden one in the attic with a double wall, and one in the cellar with a double brick wall. There was no window, Eli Zborowski recalled, 'only an opening the size of two bricks for light and air. As difficult as it was to feed a family of three, the Placzek couple and an eight- or nine-year-old daughter found ways to get food for us. The food was very, very limited but thanks to their dedication we did not starve, even though we often felt hungry. While it was fraught with danger, the little girl was entrusted with the fact that Jews were hidden in the house. Once a day, in the evening, at curfew time, Mr

---

[10] Joseph Dauman, letter to Yad Vashem of 26 February 1998, Yad Vashem Righteous Among the Nations Archive, file 1322.
[11] Eli Zborowski, letter to Yad Vashem, 2 February 1978, Yad Vashem Righteous Among the Nations Archive, file 1322. Eli Zborowksi was later chairman of the International Society for Yad Vashem.

Placzek would come up to the attic to tell us some news and empty the chamber pot.'

In August 1944 a German policeman warned the Placzeks 'that neighbours were carrying rumours about Jews hiding in the Placzek home. One week after we left the place, German and Polish police came to the Placzek home looking for the Zborowski family. How lucky we were!! We know, all too well, what would have happened to us and to the Placzek family had the police come a week earlier and found us there.'[12]

Another peasant couple, Jan and Maria Wikiel, took into their farm near Wegrow a young Jewish couple, Lonia and Sevek Fishman, who had married in the Warsaw Ghetto, and then managed to escape. 'With bloody fingernails,' Lonia Fishman later recalled, 'we dug a dank cellar "grave" – lined it with straw, and lay motionless in the hole, concealed from danger for eighteen months. Jan and Maria risked their lives by bringing us food and emptying our chamber pot every day. Once a week they sponged us down.' After liberation, the young couple had to re-learn how to walk after their long confinement.[13]

Polish peasants could take the gravest risks to save a total stranger. Kazimierz and Janina Bialy were impoverished farmers in a remote village in the Lomza district of eastern Poland. When a Jewish woman, Estera Klejnot, escaped from a deportation train to Treblinka and arrived, utterly exhausted, at their small farm, they took her in without hestitation, and hid her in their barn. Soon afterwards a Jewish family whom the farmers had known before the war, Arje Chazan, his wife and three

---

[12] Eli Zborowski, letter to Yad Vashem, 2 February 1978, Yad Vashem Righteous Among the Nations Archive, file 1322; letter to the author, 30 April 2002.
[13] United States Holocaust Memorial Museum, Photo Archive, Worksheet ID3753.

children, also came to their door. When Mrs Chazan and her eldest son went into a nearby village to look for food, they were spotted as Jews, denounced by local Poles and killed. After this, the Bialys insisted that the husband and younger children stay with them. Arje Chazan later recalled: 'They scarcely had food for themselves, but nevertheless they gave us bread and a little soup in the evenings. I remember them as angels, devout people who loved their fellow men. They always said that history would not forgive our murderers.' From time to time, when the danger became acute, Kazimierz and Janina hid the children with the Stokowski family, farmers who lived in the same village. The Stokowskis paid for their generosity with their lives: neighbours set their house on fire and murdered them. The Bialys also gave food and clothing to other Jews who came to their door.[14]

In another village in the Lomza district, Jozef and Jadwiga Zalewski hid Felicja Nowak in a niche in the attic of their barn. Every day they brought her food, and news of the course of the war; and on Christmas Eve 1942 they took the risk of inviting her into the farm for a festive dinner. They refused to accept in payment the few pieces of jewellery that Felicja offered, which she had been given by her mother. 'I was experiencing the grace of compassion,' she later wrote, 'which flowed from the faith of those people who had taken me under their roof. They were deeply religious folk, and what they did for me, they did in the understanding that it was the commandment of God and their religion.'[15]

In the village of Czerniejew, in the Siedlce district east of Warsaw, it was another poor peasant woman, Stanislawa Cabaj, a widow, who gave shelter to two

---

[14] Yad Vashem Righteous Among the Nations Archive, file 4534. The village was Boguty Milczi.
[15] Felicja Nowak, *My Star: Memoirs of a Holocaust Survivor*, page 138.

Jewish girls, Batja and Ester, sisters who had escaped from the Warsaw Ghetto and wandered for several months through the Polish countryside. Their elder brother Janek, aged fifteen, had already been murdered by a Polish farmer to whom he had gone for bread; and their thirteen-year-old sister Halinka had been killed by the Germans while in hiding in a forest.

Fearing betrayals, Stanislawa Cabaj took Ester, aged eleven, and Batja, a mere five-year-old, for sanctuary to Sister Stanislawa Jozwikowska, in the Heart of Jesus convent near the village of Skorzec. 'I was dirty, ill, weak, full of lice,' Batja later recalled. 'The nuns washed me thoroughly, put me into soft pyjamas, and put me in a clean bed.' The Mother Superior, Beata Bronislawa Hryniewicz, nursed her back to health. 'She fed me, she strengthened me.' After she recovered, the young girl attended the local school, as did her sister. 'Once the headmaster checked my file and did not find my baptism confirmation. He asked my sister about it. My sister claimed that the church we had been baptized in, Bielany, a northern suburb of Warsaw, had been bombed, and hoped her answer would be acceptable. But the headmaster was a Polish nationalist, he did not give up.' He informed the local Polish police chief, and also the Mother Superior, 'who summoned my sister to the monastery and questioned her. Finally my sister confessed that we are Jewish. Ester knew that Mother Superior Beata Bronislawa Hryniewicz loved me a lot and she also would do everything not to harm us.'

At that time, half the convent was occupied by German soldiers. The Mother Superior, determined to strengthen the young girl's self-confidence, sent Ester on 'various tasks in the afternoons – precisely when the Germans were active around – as to deliver something to other nuns, to feed chickens, to watch bees, etc.'

Nobody knew the two girls were Jewish except the

Mother Superior and Sister Stanislawa Jozwikowska, who had brought them in. After the war, the Jewish organization which found the girls wanted to pay the convent for having looked after them, but Beata refused to take the money, saying: 'I did my duty as a Christian, and not for money.' Sixty years after having been given shelter, Batja reflected: 'Mother Superior Beata Bronislawa Hryniewicz healed me; she recovered my soul by great love; she pampered me as her own child; she dressed me nice and neat; she combed my hair and tied ribbons in my plaits; she taught me manners (she was from an aristocratic noble family). She was strict, but fair with my duties; to pray, to study, to work on my character, to obey, etc., but every step was with love, love, love!' On liberation, Batja had refused to leave the Mother Superior Beata, 'but I was forced to. In autumn when I was nine – in 1945 – I left the monastery.' At that moment, separated from her rescuer, 'I lost my child-hood forever and pure human love.' From 1946 until the Mother Superior died in 1969, they were in correspon-dence. 'I always longed for Mother Superior and even wanted to go back to her . . . Years after her death I told my story, and she got the medal of Righteous Among the Nations, in Warsaw. Sister Stanislawa Jozwikowska died on 7 December 1984, she also got the medal. Mother Superior Beata Bronislawa Hryniewicz is always in my heart, and I still miss her very much.'[16]

Others in a similar plight found sanctuary only briefly. When the Jews of Parysow were being transferred to the Warsaw Ghetto, three Jewish sisters managed to escape to the village of Puznow. There they were given sanctu-ary by a Polish villager. They would sleep in his home at night, and hide in the nearby woods during the day. Betrayed by another villager, they fled eastward,

---

[16] Betty (Batja) Piechotka, letter to the author, 17 February 2002.

towards the River Bug, which was then the border of the Soviet Union. They were never heard of again.[17]

In the convent at Wawer, six miles east of Warsaw, the Mother Superior, Johanna Reiter, took in four-year-old Felicja Sandezer, keeping her safe until the end of the war, when she was reunited with her mother.[18] At another convent in Wawer, that of Sister Felicja Nek, the young Alicja Pinczewska was given sanctuary, under the name Alicja Woloszczuk, masquerading as a Catholic. While at the convent she celebrated her First Communion. After she had been there for a year, an anonymous Polish informer wrote to the convent that he knew it was hiding a Jewish child. Forced to leave, Alicja was taken to Warsaw, where she was found a place of refuge by several Christian families in the 'Aryan' sector of the city.[19]

In the small town of Ksiaz Wielki, north of Cracow, Joseph Konieczny, and his two sons Stach and Sender, sheltered seventeen members of the Matuszynski family, hiding them in a bunker under his barn. A surviving member of the family, Aron Matuszynski, later recalled: 'This was our final hiding place. We came from various other hiding places, which no longer provided us with safety, and we had all reassembled in desperation at the Koniecznys. This righteous couple, risking their own lives, provided us with shelter and food.' Because conditions in the hiding place were so crowded, Aron and his wife left for another hiding place: they were given shelter by Wladyslaw Kukuryk and his wife in the nearby village of Swiecice.

The Matuszynski family was kept safe by its respective rescuers from 7 November 1942, the day of the final

---

[17] United States Holocaust Memorial Museum, Photo Archive, Worksheet 38506.
[18] Yad Vashem Righteous Among the Nations Archive, file 3359.
[19] United States Holocaust Memorial Museum, Photo Archive, Worksheet 05705.

149

destruction of Jews in Ksiaz Wielki – when all five hundred Jews still in the ghetto were killed – until 5 May 1944, a period of eighteen months. What followed was cruel, but not untypical of the risks and dangers of hiding Jews in Poland. It began with the arrival of a platoon of men from the underground Home Army. Armed with machine guns, they interrogated the Konieczny family. 'They beat Mr Konieczny and his sons Stach and Sender so mercilessly that they finally gave in and showed the secret bunker to the soldiers. These soldiers claimed they were partisans and that the hidden group would be taken as partisan members. But that was a lie. They took the entire before-mentioned group to the local forest in the village Adama. The soldiers told them to remove their shoes, boots, clothing. They placed the machine guns in a crossfire manner. This action alerted some members of the group to try to escape. My brother Jankiel Matuszynski, my brother-in-law Martin Hershkowitz, and Heynoch Leysorek, escaped. The rest of the members who had been sheltered by the Koniecznys were slaughtered.'

The soldiers counted the dead. 'Three of their intended victims had escaped. But twelve bodies lay in the forest. They had been told of seventeen members, and there were two more missing. Word went out to scour the countryside for the two missing members. Mr Wladyslaw Kukuryk came to my wife and me, and begged us to leave his bunker for two weeks. The soldiers would surely find us and then he and his family would be killed. We slipped out of the bunker during the night.'

News of the massacre spread rapidly throughout the area. On the following day, 6 May 1944, it was the Gestapo that came to Joseph Konieczny's property. 'Mr Konieczny and his two sons were already in hiding for they had feared that the Armia Krajowa was out to search and kill them too. At home on the Koniecznys' property the Gestapo found the men gone and only Mrs

Konieczny together with her eighteen-year-old daughter and youngest baby girl of about two years. They took out Mrs Konieczny from the house and then shot her. The eldest, eighteen-year-old daughter saw this and ran towards her mother and the Gestapo shot her as well. The youngest baby daughter was miraculously spared.'

Aron Matuszynski survived the war. His brother Jankiel also survived – but was killed six months after liberation by Polish anti-Semites.[20]

Despite the dangers, those Poles who were able and willing to help Jews could go to extraordinary lengths to do so. In Czestochowa, a shoemaker named Borowczyk obtained the necessary papers for a Jew, Joseph Wisnicki, to pass as a Polish worker, enabling him to get work outside Poland. As Wisnicki had no money, Borowczyk paid for the documents, and then accompanied him across Germany to the Austrian town of Bludenz, where Wisnicki found work in a garden nursery owned by an influential member of the Nazi Party.[21]

Also in Czestochowa, Genowefa Starczewska-Korczak gave sanctuary to a young Jewish girl, Celina Berkowitz, shortly before her parents were killed. When the Germans executed Genowefa's husband, she was forced to place her Jewish charge and her own two daughters in a Catholic orphanage. But each weekend she brought all three girls home.[22]

Helena and Waclaw Milowski hid a Jewish couple, Isaac and Bala Horowitz, and their son Gabriel, in their apartment in the centre of Czestochowa. Waclaw Milowski had collected them from the farm where they had been in hiding, but where the farmer had been

---

[20] Testimony of Aron Martin (Matuszynski), 29 December 1989. I am grateful to Bob and Myriam Wolf for sending me this testimony.
[21] Joseph Wisnicki, manuscript, 'My Fight for Survival', 1997, sent to the author 25 September 2000.
[22] 'Portrait of Celina Berkowitz while hiding . . .', United States Holocaust Memorial Museum, Photo Archive, Worksheet 29905.

attacked and robbed. There was one corner in the apartment, the couple who were saved later recalled, where
they could walk upright, but in other parts they had to
stoop so as not to be seen by somebody outside. If something unusual were to happen, they would have to go
down to the cellar, most of which was full of coal: if
forced to stay there, they could do so only in a sitting
position, with hardly any air. In this hiding place they
spent twenty-two months, without seeing even a patch
of sky. Every day Milowski brought two buckets of water
for washing and drinking; every day he emptied a bucket
of their excrement, which was burnt in an oven. When
Milowski was absent (because of work, visits to his
family, etc.) his brother Lucek would bring them water;
but since he was able to come only once a week, they had
to make do with two buckets for a whole week. Milowski
also used to bring them food which he bought with their
money – bread and potatoes. It later emerged that Helena
Milowski's father had also hidden two Jewish women.[23]

Uriel Reingold, who sent me the account of the
Milowskis, and who is related to the Horowitz family,
wrote about the Righteous: 'My thoughts on the subject
are, I presume, shared by many who feel, as I do, great
admiration for all those who endangered the lives of
their children, as well as their own lives, to save Jews. I
have no doubt that they are the true heroes of this dark
period. It is easy for me to reach this conclusion when I
ask myself: "Would I act as they did?" '[24]

In Tykocin, east of Warsaw, Marysia Rozensztajn was
not yet three years old when the two Polish women who
were hiding her and her mother were killed and her
mother arrested and sent to Auschwitz, as a Polish political prisoner. The little child was found wandering in

[23] Uriel Reingold, *Ha-reingoldim* ('The Reingolds'; in Hebrew; Tel
Aviv, privately printed, 2000), pages 55–9.
[24] Uriel Reingold, letter to the author, 20 January 2001.

the street by a Polish couple, Lucyna and Waclaw Bialowarczuk, who, realizing she was an orphaned Jewish child, took her into their home and looked after her until the end of the war. Her mother, Bela, who survived Auschwitz and Belsen, found her daughter in Tykocin in 1946. Two years later Bela was killed in a traffic accident. Marysia was adopted by a Jewish woman, and later left Poland for the United States. Her two rescuers were later recognized as Righteous Among the Nations.[25]

In Wolomin, north-east of Warsaw, Anna Grabowska and her husband hid a Jewish woman in their home for more than a year. But in 1943 Polish hooligans attacked the house, smashing the windows, and warned the couple that they knew they were hiding Jews. Because of the threats, Anna Grabowska took the woman she was hiding to Warsaw, where her sister, who was involved with the Polish underground, could look after her.[26]

Among those saved by non-Jews in Kielce was a young girl called Nechama Tec, who was later to write one of her first books about Christian rescuers in Poland.[27] She herself was hidden with a Polish family, the Homars, who also gave shelter to her parents. 'In day to day contact,' she recalled, 'they never took advantage of us, they never behaved cruelly or even inconsiderately, but treated us instead with respect and kindness,' and she adds: 'Considering our close quarters and the dangerous times, this was a real blessing. I often heard my parents say we were fortunate to come across such considerate people.'[28]

---

[25] United States Holocaust Memorial Museum, Photo Archive, Worksheet 25573; Yad Vashem Righteous Among the Nations Archive, file 4742.
[26] Testimony of Anna Grabowska, as presented to Yad Vashem, Yad Vashem Righteous Among the Nations Archive, file 2004.
[27] Nechama Tec, When Light Pierced the Darkness.
[28] Nechama Tec, Dry Tears: The Story of a Lost Childhood, page 178.

Doba-Necha Cukierman was also fortunate. She and her family were hidden in Lublin by the Prokop family. 'On the second evening,' she recalled, 'after Mr Prokop returned home from work, we sat around the kitchen table discussing the latest news of happenings in Lublin and reading the *Glos Lubelski* ('Voice of Lublin') newspaper. As we talked about the Nazi cruelty to the Jews, Mr Prokop revealed something that left me speechless and terrified. He said, "In principle, I am an anti-Semitic, but you and Jan are an exception. I like you both." I felt as though a knife had been struck into my heart, but as it was nighttime and having nowhere to turn, I stayed – silence enveloping me again. I felt that the Prokops, although they proclaimed to be our friends, and had in fact risked their lives to help us on many occasions, wanted to see me elsewhere, not with them.'[29] Anti-Semitic opinions were held by other rescuers as well; but being anti-Semitic did not mean that one could not save a human being from otherwise certain death.

In their comprehensive study of the fate of non-Jewish Poles who tried to help Jews in the face of what rapidly escalated into rampant barbarism, the writer Wladyslaw Bartoszewski, who himself was active in helping Jews, and his co-author Zofia Lewin, who survived through being hidden by Poles, give many examples of heroism, on the part of both individuals and husbands and wives. One such couple was the Malickis, who worked in the municipal population records office in Warsaw. Bartoszewski and Lewin record how, "Together with the local parish priest they forged entries in the register of births and deaths and gave us the Christian certificates of two deceased women. In order to prepare such documents three persons had to collaborate. The Malickis had issued documents for numerous Jews. Unfortu-

---

[29] Doba-Necha Cukierman, *A Guardian Angel: Memories of Lublin*, page 153.

nately, one of the latter fell into the hands of the Gestapo who thus learned the names of these persons. The parish priest was shot, the Malickis were taken to Treblinka where the Germans broke Malicki's arms and legs in order to force him to divulge the names of other rescued Jews. He did not betray anyone. Both Malickis perished in Treblinka.'[30]

Every non-Jew who decided to hide and feed a Jew risked death. Bartoszewski and Lewin record an incident in the town of Wierzbica, where, on 29 January 1943, after learning through Polish informers that three families in the town were hiding three Jews, the Germans shot fifteen people, among them a two-year-old girl. For trying to save three people, fifteen people were murdered.[31] In January 1943 at Pilica, in southern Poland, a Polish woman and her one-year-old child were shot for hiding Jews.[32]

Local records suggest that active sympathy for Jews was widespread in certain villages. In Bialka, on the edge of the Parczew Forest, Jews took refuge with the villagers to avoid a German manhunt. On the second day of the hunt, 7 December 1942, the Germans entered the village and shot ninety-six villagers, all men, for helping Jews.[33] Three days later, a few miles west of the Parczew forest, at Wola Przybyslawska, seven Poles were shot for concealing Jews.[34]

Some – rescuers and rescued – were luckier. Jan Nakonieszny hid five Jews in a hen-house which was

[30] Wladyslaw Bartoszewski and Zofia Lewinowna, *Ten jest z Ojczyzny mojej* ('He is my fellow countryman'), page 464.
[31] Wladyslaw Bartoszewski and Zofia Lewinowna, *Ten jest z Ojczyzny mojej* ('He is my fellow countryman'), page 110.
[32] Wladyslaw Bartoszewski and Zofia Lewin, *Righteous Among Nations*, page 608.
[33] 'Parczew District, Bialka', *Scenes of Fighting and Martyrdom Guide*, page 244.
[34] Wladyslaw Bartoszewski and Zofia Lewinowna, *Ten jest z Ojczyzny mojej* ('He is my fellow countryman'), page 362.

only two feet high, four feet wide and thirteen feet long.
The fugitives were Henryk Sperber, his mother, his
sister, his fiancée and his cousin. All five survived the
war. So, too, did their saviour.[35]

Jaffa Wallach and her husband Norris found refuge in
the house of a Polish mechanical engineer, Jozef
Zwonarz, who lived in Lesko. 'He was the only link we
had with the external world,' Norris Wallach later wrote.
'His wife and five children knew nothing about our
hiding in that house.' Jozef Zwonarz also hid Jaffa
Wallach's brother Pinkas and her sister Anna. He had
already taken their four-year-old daughter Rena out of
Lesko, on the eve of the deportation to Zaslaw, and
found the child a home with a Polish 'uncle', Jan Kakol,
who lived in the forest. 'It is important to emphasise',
Norris Wallach wrote, 'that Zwonarz, and the Kakols as
well, endangered their lives for pure human motives
without any financial gain nor expectations.'

Those whom Zwonarz saved were to honour his
memory for the rest of their lives; and to remember, too,
how he would use his knowledge as a mechanical engineer, while 'repairing' German vehicles, to sabotage
them – especially, Norris Wallach recalled, those that
were about to set out 'for hunting Jews'.[36] In the course
of seeking the award of Righteous Among the Nations for
this rescuer, one of those whom he saved, Dr Nathan
Wolk, was interviewed by Yad Vashem. His interviewer
noted: 'Jozef Zwonarz never received any compensation
and he, too, lived in very trying circumstances. He could
barely provide for his own family, but, nevertheless, he
provided for the needs of those he rescued, as well. His
wife wasn't aware of his rescue mission at all. Only a

[35] Wladyslaw Bartoszewski and Zofia Lewinowna, *Ten jest z Ojczyzny mojej* ('He is my fellow countryman'), page 470.
[36] Dr Norris N. Wallach, letters to the author of 29 May 1983 and 17 September 1984.

month before liberation, when a bomb fell on the shop and it was impossible to stay in the pit under the shop, Jozef Zwonarz transferred all five of those he rescued to the cellar of his house. Thus, his wife learned that for two years he had been hiding Jews in the house.' After liberation, Jozef Zwonarz returned to Dr Wolk 'the ten dollars and a watch he had given him when he went into hiding'.[37]

When two thousand Jews were murdered in the Rembertow ghetto in August 1942, Yehudis (Judith) Pshenitse was twelve years old. After the war she recalled how she was helped to survive. 'I went to see the priest,' she wrote, 'who had known me as a small child, when I used to go into the church with our Christian maid. I wept and begged the priest to save me. I told him what had happened to my parents. He calmed me and promised me that he would give me as much help as he could. He hid me in his cellar. Every day I went to church with him, and I became one of the best singers in the church choir. After a time he gave me false papers, with my name listed as Kristina Pavlovnia. I began to feel like a genuine, born Christian.'

That did not last long, however. 'One day, when I was walking to church, a Christian stopped me on the street and said, "What are you doing here?" I ran away in terror. When I told the priest, he calmed me, telling me to go back into the cellar and be as quiet as possible. That same day two Germans went to see the priest, demanding that he surrender the Jewish girl whom he had hidden. He denied that there was anyone in his house. They threatened to shoot him, but he continued to insist that he was hiding no one. The Germans tortured him in various ways, but he continued to refuse to give me up until he fell to the ground covered with

---

[37] Interview by Dr Bronowski with Dr Nathan Wolk in Haifa, Yad Vashem Righteous Among the Nations Archive, file 331.

blood. His body was pierced in several places, and his face was unrecognizable. Then the Germans left him as he was and went away. Before he died, the priest asked his housekeeper to take me out of my hiding place and bring me to him because he wanted to bless me.'

Her memory of this moment was terrifying: 'All I saw was a pool of blood and the priest's body, torn into pieces. I fainted. When I came to, he raised his crushed and broken hand and caressed me. Finally he told his housekeeper to give me over to trustworthy people, to behave toward me like a mother so that no one would suspect I was Jewish. Thus, leaning against him, I felt his body grow cold. Once again he asked that I be hidden in a safe place, and then he died. I can't remember the priest's name. He was a parish priest in Nowy Dwor. The housekeeper led me away from the priest and cleansed me of his blood. She changed my clothes, and at five in the morning she led me to Modlin. She left me there and disappeared.' After that, living by her own wits, posing as a Christian child, Yehudis Pshenitse survived the war.[38]

In the course of investigations that led to more than five thousand Polish non-Jews being honoured for saving Jewish lives, Yad Vashem in Jerusalem received more than ten thousand notarized testimonies from those who were saved. In one case, however, there was at first no witness, only a story that was eventually authenticated forty-eight years after the war, when witnesses were found. At some time during 1941, an unknown Jewish woman arrived at the house of the Krasucki family in Minsk Mazowiecki, and asked if she could leave a

---

[38] Yehudis Pshenitse, 'Wanderings of a Child', Pinkas Novy-Dvor (Nowy Dwor memorial book), quoted in Jack Kugelmass and Jonathan Boyarin (translators and editors), *From a Ruined Garden: The Memorial Books of Polish Jewry*, pages 177–8.

newborn infant there for a few days. Irena Krasucki and her husband, who had two small children of their own, took the baby in, despite the danger of the undertaking. No one came to claim the baby, which had arrived with no financial support nor hope of such. After a time the Krasucki couple gave the child the name Bolek Strzycki, telling neighbours that he was a relative from a far-off city.

In 1943, amid fears that little Bolek's Jewish identity would be discovered, Irena passed the child on to her mother, Jozefa Baranowska, who agreed to care for him until the end of the war. After liberation, the boy was handed over to Jewish institutions, and resided in various orphanages until his official adoption in 1948 by a couple named Kurtz, who emigrated with him to the United States.[39]

Nadja Goldberg and Heinich Laznik were married in July 1939, less than two months before the German invasion of Poland. Their daughter, Esther Rachel, was born in August 1940. The family were on friendly terms with a non-Jewish couple, Kazimierz and Janina Tworek. When the Jews of Piotrkow were confined to a ghetto, and compelled to labour in the city's factories, the way to work for Nadja and Heinich went past the Tworeks' house. Sometimes, as they passed by in the morning, the Lazniks would leave a note saying, 'We need bread'; and on their way back that evening there would be some bread left out for them.

When the deportation of Piotrkow's Jews began in October 1942, Nadja Laznik managed to break away from the round-up, carrying her two-year-old daughter with her. Her husband also managed to escape the deportation. Their granddaughter, Lisa Garbus, later wrote: 'After that escape, my grandmother asked a non-Jewish

---

[39] Yad Vashem Righteous Among the Nations Archive, file 5146.

family they knew (I don't know who that family is) if they would hide her and my mother. They were afraid to hide an adult, but agreed to take my mother. That family didn't keep her for long, though. They left her in a train station with a note pinned to her. She was found and brought to a Catholic orphanage where she spent the rest of the war as a Catholic child.'

Lisa Garbus's account continued: 'A few months after hiding my mother, my grandparents went to the Pietrusiewiczes' house in the middle of the night and knocked on the door. My grandparents told me that the father (I've forgotten his first name) opened the door, looked around to see if anyone was watching, and silently led them inside. "It was an unspoken agreement," my grandparents told me. I think they were hidden first in the attic of the small house, and then, when that seemed too dangerous, Mr Pietrusiewicz fabricated a hiding place for them outside, underneath the outdoor dog kennel that was behind the shed in their large backyard. He even created a ventilation system with pipes that came up into some bushes. I saw the shed and the yard when I was there (another house now takes up half the yard). The hiding place and dog kennel are no longer there. They crouched in that hole for around two years, and I can't imagine what it was like. My grandmother used to say, "Anne Frank, she lived in a castle compared to where we were." Then she would add, "But we are alive, and she is not."

'The family would bring them food every day, making it look like they were feeding the dog. I think there was some signal for the dog to move to free the access to the hiding place. The Pietrusiewiczes had four or five children (all of whom knew my grandparents were there), and there wasn't much food, but my grandparents told me that they always left a little food on their plate, so that the family would never think that they didn't have enough. Mr Pietrusiewicz would sit with them sometimes, and I think my grandmother did some knitting. At night they would use the bathroom and walk around the yard, but that became too dangerous in the winter when their tracks in the snow might arouse suspicion. They washed once a week, and my grandparents always insisted that they were clean. When the Russians liberated Poland, Mr Pietrusiewicz wisely advised them to remain in hiding for another month or two, because it was still not safe. "Just because the Germans are gone doesn't mean the Poles won't kill you," he told them.'[40]

Lisa Garbus's rescuer made money illegally distilling alcohol and selling it on the black market. 'One day,' she wrote, 'the Germans did a search of all the houses on their street. If they had found the black market operation, the family could have all been killed. But they skipped the Pietrusiewicz house. After the war, when my grandparents emerged from hiding thin and pale and unaccustomed to the light of day, they tried to thank their saviour. "You saved us," they said. "No," he said, "I didn't save you. You saved me. It was because you were hiding in my yard that the Germans passed over my house during their search."'

Reflecting on this remark, Lisa Garbus wrote: 'Who knows what he actually meant. Maybe he was superstitious and really believed they were his good luck charm. Or maybe by saying that they saved him, he meant that they saved his humanity, that they allowed him to be a decent human being in the midst of all that chaos. Whatever he meant, it is clear that his message to them was: "You don't owe me anything. You did the favour for me." This, for me, reveals the core of this man's virtue, and that of his family. It's one thing in these happier times, to tell house guests that it was a pleasure to have them over, and to turn the guests'

---

[40] Lisa Garbus, letter to the author, 21 November 2000.

appreciation around and thank them for coming. It's quite another to thank the people you saved by risking the lives of your whole family and to tell them that they owe you nothing, that you, in fact, feel you owe something to them. This is the ultimate gift, even more profound than the gift of life he gave them.'[41]

When the war was over the Lazniks found their daughter in the infirmary of an orphanage in Zakopane. 'The orphanage workers recognized that they were her parents,' Lisa Garbus wrote. 'My grandparents had a picture, and apparently, she hadn't changed much over the three or so years. And my grandparents recognized her. At first they just visited her, so as not to shock her; then they took her with them. She would cry to go to Church on Sunday, and she would hide bread in her clothes.' As to Esther Rachel's time in the orphanage, Lisa Garbus comments: 'When my mother was there, her name was Wanda. I don't know if she had false papers, but I think my grandmother did instruct her, before leaving her with the family, to speak Polish, not Yiddish. Not much is known of her time there. My mother remembers very little. She doesn't remember any Polish. She only remembers not wanting to eat. The children were at long tables, and they were supposed to clean their plates, but she threw her food under the table.'[42]

As a result of Polish Christians' courage, a family of three had survived. 'Both my grandparents saw their Polish saviour as a father figure. My grandfather carried a picture of that man in his wallet every day of his life.'[43]

Sabina Schwarz (later Sabina Zimering) was sixteen years old when the Germans invaded Poland in September 1939. In October 1942, shortly before all but two thousand of the twenty-two thousand Jews in the

[41] Lisa Garbus, letter to the author, 21 November 2000.
[42] Lisa Garbus, letter to the author, 10 January 2001.
[43] Lisa Garbus, letter to the author, 22 September 2001.

Piotrkow ghetto were deported more than a hundred miles to Treblinka and their deaths, her mother told her that if her Catholic friend, Danka Justyna, would give up her identification papers, she might pretend to be a Pole and perhaps survive. Danka and her sister Mala had been lifelong friends of Sabina and her sister Helka; both worked for the Polish underground. Incredibly, Danka's family provided three sets of false identification papers: one for Sabina, one for Helka and the third for their mother. The two girls, whose brother was in a labour camp, escaped the ghetto only two or three hours before it was surrounded.

Thus began an odyssey of 'Hiding in the Open', the title of Sabina Zimering's as yet unpublished memoirs. On their father's advice, the two sisters went to Germany as Polish volunteers, to work in a labour camp. At one point, on the verge of being discovered, they decided to flee. They were arrested at a railway depot. When the director of the camp was summoned to the police station to identify the girls, instead of angrily condemning them, he asked the police commander to return them to the camp, where, he said, they were good workers and well-liked. However, others had already accused them of being Jews, and they were forced immediately to run again. Trying to get to Switzerland, they managed to reach Regensburg, where they found jobs in the luxurious Maximilian Hotel. 'It was some time before she [Sabina] realized that the guests were all high-ranking German military officials. She was still working there when American soldiers displaced them all.'[44]

The two Jewish sisters, as well as their brother,

---

[44] Terry Hokenson, 'Sabina Zimering gets students' undivided attention', *The Voice of Piotrkow Survivors* magazine, number 24, October–November 2001. Sabina Zimering was telling her story to Jewish 8th grade students in Minneapolis on 13 May 2001.

survived the war: their parents, and fifty members of their wider family, were murdered.

Each story of rescue has its own remarkable features. From the town of Chmielnik, Kalman and Sara Garfinkel sent two of their seven children, their daughter Helen and their son Fishel, to a farmer in nearby Celiny. There, the two youngsters worked as shepherds by day, and at night slept on haystacks inside the barn. The farmer taught them how to pray, and how to cross themselves. Their story has been told by an American writer, Suzan Hagstrom: 'One day, fear, rather than loneliness, prompted Helen to take Fishel home. "I saw a sign," Helen said. "It offered a bottle of vodka and 100 zlotys for farmers to tell the Germans where the Jewish children are. My brother couldn't read. He was only seven. I got scared. The next day we walked home."'

Their father persuaded them to return to the farm. 'One day, as the children herded cows towards the barn, the farmer greeted them frantically, saying two Germans on motorcycles were approaching. He hid Fishel, and gave Helen a scarf and apron to wear, instructing her to milk a cow and not to talk, even if she were asked questions.' The German asked her, 'Where are the Jewish children?' She shook her head. 'I kept milking the cow,' she recalled. 'All I could think of was the Germans are going to find my brother, and my brother will tell.'

The Germans left, but after they had gone the farmer explained he could no longer keep them. 'He had a family, and he was afraid.' For a second time the two children returned to their parents.[45] There followed years in ghettos, slave labour camps and deportations: the fate of almost all of the two million Jews under the General-Government. Helen survived the war, as did her elder brother Nathan and three of her sisters; but her

---

[45] Suzan E. Hagstrom, *Sara's Children*, pages 79–80.

parents, her brother Fishel, and a younger sister, Rachel, were deported to Treblinka and murdered.[46]

The need for places of refuge in Poland spanned more than two years, from the start of the deportations in mid-1942 to liberation at the end of 1944 or early 1945.

By 1943, tens of thousands of Jews were in hiding throughout occupied Poland, Byelorussia and the Ukraine; and German searches for them were continuous and brutal. On 22 March that year a Polish eyewitness in the town of Szczebrzeszyn, Dr Zygmunt Klukowski, recorded in his diary one of the harrowing scenes he had witnessed: 'Yesterday they brought me a dangerously wounded peasant from Gruszka Zaporska. He had concealed six Jews from Radecznica in his cow barn. When the police appeared, he began to run and was shot at. He died last night. The gendarmes did not permit the family to carry away his body and ordered the Municipal Administration to bury him as a bandit. The Jews were shot by the Polish police of Radecznica and, shortly after the event, the gendarmes appeared in Gruszka and shot the peasant's wife and two children: a six-year-old girl and a three-year-old boy.'[47]

On 3 June 1943, during a deportation from Michalowice, three Jews had hidden in a barn, opening fire as the Germans approached. Tadeusz Seweryn, a Pole, later recalled how one of the Jews was killed and one escaped. The third fought to the end, and was burnt to death when the barn was set on fire. Enraged at the resistance, the Germans then killed two Polish farmers, Stefan Kaczmarski and Stanislaw Stojka, for hiding the three Jews.[48]

[46] Suzan E. Hagstrom, letter to the author, 22 March 2002.
[47] Quoted in Wladyslaw Bartoszewski and Zofia Lewin, *Righteous Among Nations*, pages 599–600.
[48] Testimony of Tadeusz Seweryn, in Wladyslaw Bartoszewski and Zofia Lewin, *Righteous Among Nations*, page 607.

On the night of 23 February 1944, in the remote Polish village of Zawadka, the Germans arrested a former primary-school headmaster, Aleksander Sosnowski, and his seventeen-year-old daughter, together with two Jewish women whom he had hidden and sheltered in an attic for a year and a half. All four were killed.[49]

Among the few Jews who survived in hiding in Lubartow was twenty-year-old Raya Weberman. Together with her father and her uncle, she had stayed in hiding since the final 'Action' against the Jews in the Lubartow ghetto in November 1942: at first in a hole under the kitchen floor of a Polish farmer, Adam Butrin; then, as the German searches began, in a pit that Butrin dug under the floor of his stables. After a further search, they had to live for three weeks lying down in a field, and then in the nearby forest, drinking stagnant water. 'The water was green, bitter and full of insects,' she later recalled. Then they returned to the hole under the stable. 'For two years we wore the same clothes,' Raya recalled. 'I read bits of newspaper, dozens of times each.' When liberation came in late July 1944, 'Butrin joyously told us the good news. Afterwards he returned and announced sadly: "The Russians hate Jews too." '[50]

Raya Weberman, her father and uncle owed their lives to the bravery of Adam Butrin. Another non-Jewish Pole who showed such bravery was Teresa Strutynska-Christow. She was fifteen years old when the Germans hanged her mother in the town square, and left her body hanging there for seven days in a deliberate attempt to frighten all the Polish inhabitants of the town. Teresa's

---

[49] Wladyslaw Bartoszewski and Zofia Lewin, *Righteous Among Nations*, pages 598–9.
[50] Testimony of Raya Barnea (Weberman), written at Hadera, Israel, on 10 January 1982. Copy sent to the author by Raya Barnea's son, 1985.

home overlooked the square. For seven days she saw her mother hanging there. As a result she decided to hide Jews – and did so.[51]

On 3 November 1942 the Jews of Zaklikow were deported to the death camp at Belzec. Dana Szapira, then seven years old, later recalled how, at the time of the deportation, 'there was a Jewish woman dentist. Her leg was broken.' A German official came; the woman told him that she was the only dentist in the town, and suggested that she might be of some use at headquarters. Having taken her out of the deportation line – she was on a stretcher – the German then went off to see if she could be employed, which would have saved her; 'while he was gone a German soldier known as "Moustache" came up. "What are you doing here?" he said, and shot at her, not to kill her, but to see her writhe. Slowly, here and there, here and there, she was killed.'

Dana Szapira and her mother, Lusia, were hidden by a Polish farmer who had no idea they were Jewish. They survived inside a cubbyhole in his cowshed. One day the farmer heard a knock on the door: it was a Jew, carrying in his arms his teenage son. 'I have been hiding in the woods for months,' the Jew told the farmer. 'My son has gangrene of his foot. I cannot cut it off myself. Please get a doctor.'

The farmer went to the Gestapo and told them about the two Jews. 'He got two kilogrammes of sugar for reporting them,' Dana Szapira recalled. 'They were taken away and shot.'[52]

Dana and her mother were exceptionally lucky: 'We went to great lengths to make sure that the farmer did not

---

[51] Information provided by Harvey Sarner (custodian of the Sarner Archive on the Righteous), in conversation with the author, 10 April 2001.
[52] Recollections of Dana Schwartz (Dana Szapira) in conversation with the author, Simi Valley, 2 November 1985.

know – or suspect – that we were Jews. That would have been the end of us.' To ensure that the deception worked, mother and daughter went to church every Sunday.

Sixty years later, Dana Szapira (Dana Schwartz) reflected: 'I am so sorry I cannot give you any Righteous in my life. In my life there have not been any Righteous Gentiles.'[53]

In his study of Polish–Jewish relations in the Second World War, Emanuel Ringelblum wrote of how in Lukow the Jews hid in the surrounding woods for some time after the 'resettlement action'. It was 'a frequent occurrence', Ringelblum wrote, 'for Polish children playing there to discover groups of these Jews hiding: they had been taught to hate Jews, so they told the municipal authorities, who in turn handed the Jews over to the Germans to be killed.'[54]

Confirmation of the flight of numerous Lukow Jews to the surrounding forests, as well as the part played by the local population in tracking them down and denouncing them, is to be found in the diary of a Polish teacher from Lukow, whose righteous instincts are revealed in the horrified tone of his diary entry. He wrote, three days after the event: 'On 5 November, I passed through the village of Siedliska. I went into the cooperative store. The peasants were buying scythes. The woman shop-keeper said, "They'll be useful for you in the round-up today." I asked, "What round-up?" "Of the Jews." I asked, "How much are they paying for every Jew caught?" An embarrassed silence fell. So I went on, "They paid thirty pieces of silver for Christ, so you should also ask for the same amount."'

---

[53] Dana Schwartz, in conversation with the author, 28 June 2002.
[54] Joseph Kermish and Shmuel Krakowski (editors), *Emanuel Ringelblum: Polish–Jewish Relations during the Second World War*, page 138.

POLAND: THE GENERAL-GOVERNMENT

The teacher's account continued: 'Nobody answered. What the answer was I heard a little later. Going through the forest, I heard volleys of machine-gun fire. It was the round-up of the Jews hiding there. Perhaps it is blasphemous to say that I clearly ought to be glad that I got out of the forest alive. In Burzec, one go-ahead watchman proposed: "If the village gives me a thousand zloty, I'll hand over these Jews." Three days later I heard that six Jews in the Burzec forest had dug themselves an underground hideout. They were denounced by a forester of the estate.'[55]

Rescue and denunciation: the range of conflicting responses demonstrated in human behaviour is astonishing. Eugenia Schenker, a graduate of the Cracow Conservatory of Music, recalled what happened after her escape from a labour camp. 'I was hidden by a Polish family until their neighbours denounced them to the Germans and I had to escape to another Polish family and the same thing happened after a short period of time and I had to run again. It happened the same way, but four families tried to help me without any compensation, really only out of the goodness of the heart.'[56]

The numbers of those who betrayed Jews and their rescuers must certainly have run, in Poland, into many thousands, perhaps tens of thousands. It is, however, due to other Polish men and women of courage and goodwill that Eugenia Schenker – and all those who have written to me about their rescuers – are alive today.

A survivor from the southern Polish town of Rzeszow, Henry Herzog, wrote from his home in the United States: 'I am alive today due to the courage of three Gentile

[55] S. Zeminski, diary entry for 8 November 1942, *Biuletyn* (Warsaw), no. 27, 1958, pages 105–12; quoted in Joseph Kermish and Shmuel Krakowski (editors), *Emanuel Ringelblum: Polish–Jewish Relations during the Second World War*, page 138, n. 25.
[56] Eugenia Schenker, letter to the author, 1 June 2001.

Poles.' Returning to Rzeszow long after the end of the war, he was able to pay his respects to two of his rescuers, Titus and Luiza Zwolinski, 'prostrating myself on their tomb'. Yet he knew that another Jewish friend of his had been betrayed by the Poles and executed. Henry Herzog added: 'I fully agree with you that the memory of those who at the risk of their own lives, as well as of their families, helped Jewish people escape the genocide should be held in sanctity, counted and recounted.' And he adds: 'The memory of Righteous Gentiles has to find its place of honour and gratitude in the annals of the Holocaust. The controversy due to acts of bestiality by other Poles is not negligible, but should not be allowed to cast a doubt over the acts of humanitarian courage of the Righteous Gentile Poles.'[57]

---

[57] Letter to the author, 20 April 2001. Henry Herzog's memoirs . . . *And Heaven Shed No Tear*, were published in 1996

CHAPTER SIX

Warsaw

Warsaw, with almost half a million Jewish inhabitants
on the eve of the Second World War, was to see by far
the largest destruction of Jewish life of any city in Nazi-
dominated Europe. In November 1939 the Jews of
Warsaw were ordered to live in a ghetto: more than
eighty-nine thousand were forced to leave their homes
throughout the city and to move into the predominantly
Jewish section of the city, where two hundred and eighty
thousand Jews already lived, many in crowded ten-
ements. A further twenty-six thousand Jews were forced
into the Warsaw Ghetto from across the River Vistula,
mostly from the suburb of Praga.

Many Poles looked with satisfaction at the Jews being
moved into the ghetto, even gloating; but there were
others who behaved decently. Writing in his diary on
19 November 1940, the Warsaw Jewish historian
Emanuel Ringelblum recorded that on the day after the
ghetto wall was completed, 'many Christians brought
bread for their Jewish acquaintances and friends', while
others helped Jews 'bring produce into the ghetto'. That
very day a Christian Pole was killed by the Germans
while 'throwing a sack of bread over the wall'.[1]

---

[1] Emanuel Ringelblum, diary, 19 November 1940, in Jacob Sloan
(editor), *Notes from the Warsaw Ghetto: The Journal of Emanuel
Ringelblum*, New York: Schocken Books, 1958.

For the first year of their existence behind the wall, some of the ghetto dwellers experienced individual acts of kindness by their non-Jewish neighbours of pre-ghetto times. Despite the risks incurred in doing so, some of these Poles even took Jews for a night or two into the calm and quiet of their homes in 'Aryan' Warsaw – the common term used for the non-Jewish sections of the city – where food, though scarce, was at least available in life-sustaining quantities. But on 10 November 1941 the German Governor of Warsaw, Dr Ludwig Fischer, who was determined to bring all such help to an end, issued an official decree, imposing the death penalty on 'those who knowingly give shelter to such Jews or help them in any way (e.g., by taking them in for a night, giving them a lift in a vehicle of any sort, etc.)'. The decree noted that sentences would be imposed by special courts. The Governor added: 'I forcefully call the attention of the entire population of the Warsaw district to this new decree, as henceforth it will be applied with the utmost severity.'[2]

Hundreds of non-Jews ignored this order. Maria Charaszkiewicz – who was to plant the second tree of the Righteous Among the Nations in Jerusalem in 1962 – was one of them. From the moment Fischer's draconian order came into force, she stole into the ghetto almost every day to help her Jewish friends. During one of her visits, which took place during an outbreak of yellow fever, she succeeded in smuggling out of the ghetto the members of the Pollak family and a girl named Henia, whom she hid in her apartment for the night, and for whom she afterwards found a hiding place among her relatives. In 1941 she made a journey to Lvov, where she had lived before the war, found shelter there for two Jewish girls whom she had managed to get released from a deport-

---

[2] Decree issued by the Governor of the Warsaw District, Dr Fischer, 10 November 1941.

ation, and then brought the girls' parents, Cesia and
Janek Lewin – friends of hers from before the war – back
with her to Warsaw, where she found them shelter.[3]

The deportations from the Warsaw Ghetto to the death
camp at Treblinka began in July 1942. All those deported
were murdered within a few hours of reaching the camp.
David Wdowinski writes of the journey on the deportation trains: 'Sometimes a humanitarian Ukrainian for a
piece of gold or a watch or a thousand zloty would bring
half a litre of water.'[4]

Jews who managed to escape from the ghetto into
'Aryan' Warsaw had to find families who were willing
to risk their own lives in taking them in. Each story is
different, and each one reveals the humane, decent
character of the individuals who took such grave risks.
The story of Bernard and Felicja Feilgut and their five-
year-old granddaughter Ewa is one example. At first,
posing as non-Jews, they rented a room in the home of
Stefania Laurysiewicz and her two daughters. When
their money ran out they had to tell their landlady that
they were Jewish – and they asked her for help. Yad
Vashem's archive records the sequel: 'Although aware of
the danger, Laurysiewicz and her daughters responded
in the affirmative. For humanitarian motives and for no
material reward, they protected fugitives and met their
every need.' Since Felicja Feilgut and her granddaughter
looked 'Aryan', spoke Polish fluently and frequently
attended the church near their place of hiding, 'the two
did not arouse the neighbours' suspicions'. But Bernard
Feilgut, 'whose facial features bespoke his Jewishness',
had to remain in the apartment at all times, and retreated

[3] Yad Vashem Righteous Among the Nations Archive, file 1028.
[4] David Wdowinski, *And We Are Not Saved*, page 68. Wdowinski
adds: 'But more often the Ukrainians were not so humanitarian.
Indeed they took the watch, but they did not bring the water. They
simply shot.'

to a hideout whenever visitors came. When in early 1944 Wanda Laurysiewicz married Jan Spychalski, who moved into his mother-in-law's apartment, the young man also took on the task of helping the three Jews.[5]

Four people had taken an enormous risk – and they continued to do so for almost two years. Both families, rescuers and rescued, survived the war. In another collective effort, seven members of the Brejna family worked together to save and protect Jews. Tadeusz Brejna was married to Stefania-Barbara, a doctor who worked in a fever hospital near the ghetto. Fearing infection, the Germans kept out of the building, which consequently served as a temporary hideout for Jewish refugees. Tadeusz obtained 'Aryan' papers for a number of Jews, while Stefania-Barbara performed operations to disguise the traces of circumcision and Tadeusz's sister, Stanislawa-Lucyna, a nurse, assisted Jews in need of medical care. In December 1942 a five-year-old Jewish girl, Teofila Raszbaum, was brought out of the ghetto, suffering from burns to her hands. She was taken to the Brejnas' home, where she was looked after by Tadeusz's father, Boleslaw Brejna, his wife, Wladyslawa, their son, Kazimierz, and daughter, Zofia. The Brejnas did not abandon Teofila; they kept her hidden in Aryan Warsaw throughout the Warsaw Ghetto revolt of April 1943, and kept her with them even after their own expulsion from Warsaw in the wake of the Polish Uprising in August 1944. (The Brejnas were supporters of the Armia Krajowa, the underground Polish Home Army, and Boleslaw and Kazimierz were executed by the Germans during the uprising.) In 1941–2, the Brejnas also gave refuge to Juliusz and Stefania Kepski, after Stefania had been denounced to the Gestapo as Jewish.

As devout Catholics, the Brejnas regarded it as their

---

[5] Yad Vashem Righteous Among the Nations Archive, files 2485, 2485a.

duty to save Jews, and asked nothing in return for their actions. After the war, the Kepskis and Teofila Raszbaum emigrated from Poland, but they continued to maintain contact with the Brejnas for many years to come.[6]

The need to disguise circumcision was also a concern of a Polish surgeon named Feliks Kanabus, who used the techniques of plastic surgery to reverse the operation. He also used false certificates to circumcised Jews stating that their circumcision was 'necessitated by an infection'.[7] In December 1945 two American Jews, Dr S. Margoshes and Louis Segal, who were on a World Jewish Congress mission to Poland in search of survivors, were told by several Jews whom they met of 'a legendary figure, a Polish doctor by the name of Kanabus who, at the risk of his own life, the lives of his children and his aged mother, had saved many Jews by hiding them and also by some remarkable operation which he performed'.

It was then, noted Dr Margoshes, 'that I resolved that I would seek out Dr Kanabus.' Eventually he found him: 'A youngish man with a pleasant Slavic face, blond hair and a ready smile, he immediately inspired confidence. He told me of his years at the Warsaw University, where he joined a Socialist group and befriended many Jews at a time when Jewish students of medicine were barred from the courses in anatomy. He also told me of his sense of shame and humiliation at the sight of many Poles aiding the Nazis in their perpetration of horrible crimes against Jews, and of his resolve to do what he could to save as many as possible.'

The rest of the story of Dr Kanabus the astounded Margoshes learned from Dr Michael Tursz, a physician who was one of many Jews saved by Kanabus. 'Both he and his wife had been dragged from their home to the

---

[6] Yad Vashem Righteous Among the Nations Archive, file 2314.
[7] Letter of 8 May 2001 from Peter Dembowski, Yad Vashem Righteous Among the Nations Archive, file 87.

Warsaw Ghetto. In sheer despair, Dr Tursz sent a message to his original friend of university days, Dr Kanabus, asking for aid. He was most surprised to receive a quick answer, for in those days of terror friendship counted for but very little. Before long Dr Kanabus managed to get into the Warsaw Ghetto, and by a ruse, to lead both Dr Tursz and his wife past the ghetto watch. For the next three years Mrs Tursz, on forged papers prepared by Dr Kanabus, served as a kitchen maid in Dr Kanabus' household, while Dr Tursz spent his days and nights in a cellar which Dr Kanabus secured for him with the connivance of his family and some of his friends.'[8]

Kanabus's wife Irena had helped with the operations, and had supervised the recovery of the patients. She too was honoured by Yad Vashem as a Righteous person.

Jan Zabinski and his wife Antonina were among the very first Poles to be recognized at Yad Vashem in Jerusalem as Righteous Among the Nations. When the Germans occupied Warsaw, Jan Zabinski was the director of the Warsaw Zoo. The Germans also appointed him superintendent of the city's public parks. As a result of the German air raids on Warsaw in September 1939, most of the cages in the zoo had been emptied of their animals. With the beginning of the deportations from Warsaw in 1942, Zabinski decided to use the empty cages as hiding places for Jews who were fleeing from the ghetto. Over the following three years, he provided several hundred Jews with temporary shelter in the animal houses, as well as providing refuge for some twenty Jews in his own two-storey home in the zoo grounds. During the uprising in August 1944, Zabinski, himself a member of the Polish underground, was

---

[8] Dr S. Margoshes, 'Dr Felix Kanabus, Rescuer of Polish Jews, His Deeds of Heroism, Welcome!', *News and Views* (New York), 7 September 1965. Kanabus was visiting the United States to attend the International Congress of Surgeons in Philadelphia.

captured by the Germans and sent as a prisoner to Germany; but his wife continued to help Jews who were hiding in the ruins of the city.[9]

Sister Matylda Getter was the Mother Superior of the Warsaw branch of the Order of the Franciscan Sisters of the Family of Mary. In peacetime she and her Order had worked mainly among orphans and the sick in hospitals. In 1942, when she was already ill with cancer, Sister Matylda took the incredible risk of taking in any Jewish children from the Warsaw Ghetto who had managed to escape and who were brought to her. She placed these children in various homes owned by the Order, many of them in the one at Pludy, seven and a half miles outside Warsaw. It has been estimated that Sister Matylda succeeded in rescuing several hundred Jewish children. For doing so, she was accused by some people of unnecessarily endangering the lives of non-Jewish orphans in the homes of the Order. Her reply was that 'by virtue of the Jewish children's presence, God would not allow any harm to befall the other children'. Whenever a Gestapo raid on one of the orphanages was believed imminent, Sister Matylda took those Jewish children who looked 'too obviously' Jewish into temporary shelter elsewhere. When there was not enough time to do this, those particularly Jewish-looking children would have their heads or faces bandaged as if they had been injured.[10]

Wladyslaw Kowalski was a retired colonel in the Polish army at the time of the German invasion of Poland. As the Warsaw representative of the Dutch-owned Philips Company, he was given freedom of movement in Warsaw by the occupying forces, a privilege he exploited

[9] Mordecai Paldiel, 'Zabinski, Jan (b. 1897)', *Encyclopedia of the Holocaust*, volume 4, pages 1723–4.
[10] Mordecai Paldiel, 'Getter, Matylda (d. 1968)', *Encyclopedia of the Holocaust*, volume 2, pages 578–9.

to the full in his many successful attempts to save Jews. His first rescue effort was made in September 1940, when he saw a ten-year-old Jewish boy wandering in the streets of 'Aryan' Warsaw. He took the boy to his own home, fed him and obtained a new identity card for him, as well as a permanent home with one of his friends. In February 1943, after the first Jewish revolt in the ghetto, Kowalski bribed the Polish guards at the ghetto gate to allow seven Jews to leave, and then found safe havens for them on the 'Aryan' side. That November he helped a family of four living near Izbica – whose ghetto was a staging post for deportation to the death camp at Belzec – to reach Warsaw, where he found them a hiding place, once more with his friends.

After the Jewish ghetto revolt in April 1943, Kowalski gave refuge in his own home to twelve Jews, buying material with which they were able to construct an underground shelter. The fugitives made wooden toys that Kowalski was able to sell in the city, helping to cover the cost of feeding and maintaining his 'guests'. At the time of the Warsaw Uprising in August 1944, Kowalski converted the basement of a ruined building into a hiding place for himself and forty-nine Jews. Their daily ration consisted of three glasses of water, a small quantity of sugar, and vitamin pills. They remained there in hiding for 105 days, until liberation. After the war Kowalski married one of the Jewish women he had saved; together they moved to Israel.[11]

Jozef and Helena Biczyk lived in the basement of a building in 'Aryan' Warsaw. Here they gave shelter to two Jewish girls, Alicja Fajnsztejn (aged thirteen) and her sister Zofja (aged seven). Before the war Jozef had been the superintendent of one of their father's properties in the city, and, later, the girls' parents joined them

---

[11] Mordecai Paldiel, 'Kowalski, Wladyslaw (1895–1971)', *Encyclopedia of the Holocaust*, volume 2, pages 828–99.

in hiding. The Biczyks continued to live in the basement, while the four Fajnsztejns lived in the laundry room in the attic, joined at times by other Jews in search of a place to hide.[12] They remained there for a year and a half, until liberation.

Before the war, Genowefa Olczak, known as Genia, worked in Lodz as a housekeeper for Roma and Aleksander Rozencwajg and their small son Gabriel. After the outbreak of war the family moved to Warsaw, taking Genia with them. Aleksander Rozencwajg joined the Polish army, and with several thousand other officers was killed by the Soviets at Katyn in 1940 after having been interned. When non-Jews were ordered to leave the ghetto, Genia had to go, but still brought food to the Rozencwajgs until the ghetto was completely sealed. 'One day they marched us all to another part of the ghetto in order to take the children and old people away – shoot them or send them to camp,' Roma Rozencwajg's niece, Bianka Kraszewski, recalled. 'I was "camouflaged" to look much older than I was, but my aunt and Gabriel had no chance – we made a hole in the wall of the "shop" and took out bricks and hid them there, not knowing if we would come back or find them alive.' This 'shop' was one of several dozen German-run workshops in the ghetto where Jews were put to work making clothes and other items for the German army.

It was Genia Olczak who came to the rescue, making hiding places for the Rozencwajgs in her small apartment. 'In a niche behind an armoir two people could stand, and behind a false wall in the toilet – one person,' Bianka Kraszewski recalled. 'My aunt, my uncle Karol and his wife Estka and my little cousin Gabriel left the ghetto and went to stay with Genia. She prepared

---

[12] 'Alicja and Zofja Fajnsztejn . . . pose with their rescuers . . .', United States Holocaust Memorial Museum, Photo Archive, Worksheet 82303.

false papers for each of them, but for Gabriel prepared a false birth certificate as her son out of wedlock. She went to work every day to help support them and if anyone knocked on the door the three adults would go to their hiding places. Gabriel stayed home under the pretext that he had TB.'

Bianka Kraszewski's account continued: 'Genia also was instrumental later on (November 1942) in getting my mother and me out of the ghetto, getting papers for us and finding us hiding places. Later on she did the same for my father (April 1943). When the workers of our "shop" were moved to the Poniatowa camp – they took everyone, including my brother, cousins, another uncle, four aunts and my best friend – except my father whom they ordered to keep an eye on the "shop".'

At one of the Schultz workshops in Warsaw, the largest in the ghetto, it was the German manager, Fritz Schultz, who carried out an act of kindness. As Bianka Kraszewski wrote: 'Mr Schultz forcefully put my father in the trunk of his car and drove him to the Aryan side of Warsaw (where I and my mother were). My grand-father committed suicide – before they could take him to Auschwitz. I don't know about the others, but my nineteen-year-old brother was later taken to the Trawniki camp. Inmates of both camps were killed in November 1943. Genia kept finding places for *us* to hide – as it was too dangerous for us to be together with my parents. (On 1 February 1944 they were denounced and shot together with their host Mr Przybysz.) Soon after that someone denounced Genia and she had to get rid of my uncle and two aunts. They were hidden after that in the Old Town district of Warsaw and after the Warsaw Uprising ended unsuccessfully and they had nowhere to go, they too committed suicide.'

Genia Olczak continued to do all she could; taking the young Gabriel Rozencwajg to her village, where she looked after him until liberation. Bianka Kraszewski added: 'About ten years ago, Genia was awarded a medal of Righteous Among the Nations, and travelled to Israel and saw a tree being planted in her name in Yad Vashem. She never married – her young years were devoted to trying to save us all and especially to Gabriel whom she loves like her own son.' Genia, she wrote, 'who risked her life for us for years, thinks she only did what she should have done and certainly does not consider herself in any way heroic. However, this good, kind, wonderful woman is loved by everyone and if angels would walk this would have been one of them.'[13]

Each story of rescue reveals different aspects of the courage of the rescuers. William Donat was just five years old when he was smuggled out of the Warsaw Ghetto. 'I had already survived many hours in the bunker my parents and their neighbours had fashioned,' he later wrote, 'and I had just been rescued from *Umschlagplatz*, the infamous railhead the Germans had set up to transport Warsaw's Jews to Majdanek and Treblinka. My father had managed to persuade a Ghetto policeman to snatch me out of that place of terror. That close call had been so chilling that my parents began a massive effort to place me on the Aryan side. It was difficult enough to place a girl, but to find someone willing to take a boy was unheard of. I had blond hair and blue eyes, and we spoke only Polish at home, but still, I was a Jewish boy bearing the sign of the covenant.'

William Donat's account continued: 'My parents reviewed their entire list of Christian friends and business acquaintances and, after exhaustive communications, they found an older couple, active in the underground, who might be willing to take me. Before the war, the man had worked for my father's newspaper as an editor. His wife, who was to become my "Auntie Maria", came to see me at the printing shop where my

---

[13] Bianka Kraszewski, letter to the author, 15 August 2001.

father worked. The shop was outside the Ghetto walls, making this meeting possible. She felt that I could "pass" and arrangements were quickly made: my mother taught me the "Hail Mary" and "Our Father" prayers; I learned my new last name and got my first haircut; I was to forget the Ghetto and to remember that my mother was in the country and my father in the army. I had been living with Auntie Maria and Uncle Stefan for about a month when one of the neighbours betrayed me to the local Polish police. Auntie Maria stood up to the pistol-waving policemen, deftly bargaining for my life with the American $20 gold pieces that my father had given her, while reminding them that one day the war would end. A deal was struck – they would not take me to the Gestapo, but she could no longer keep me with her.'

Several days later, William Donat was sent across the Vistula to an orphanage in Otwock which was run by nuns. 'Shortly after my arrival in this strange and inhospitable place, I was approached by a young nun who said to me, "Admit you're a Jew and I'll help you." I persisted in denying what must have been obvious to all the nuns, until one day, feeling particularly lonely and melancholy – I even remember thinking that it must be my birthday – I confessed my terrible secret, but only after the nun promised to keep the confidence. She told me not to worry, she could fix everything. She arranged to have me baptized and I threw myself into daily prayers, going to mass, asking God for more food. This went on for two years . . .'

William Donat's mother and father both survived deportation and the camps. After the war, he recalled, people in Warsaw would point them out as 'an unusual sight, a Jewish family where all the members had survived'.[14]

---

[14] William H. Donat, 'Could I Still Be a Little Catholic Deep Inside?', *Hidden Child* newsletter, Fall/Winter 1997.

*   *   *

The rescue of Jews by Poles was, is and will remain a controversial topic. The historian Yisrael Gutman, who was himself in the Warsaw Ghetto – and later in the camps at Majdanek and Auschwitz – has written: 'Thousands of Jews escaped to the "Aryan" side of Warsaw and its vicinity at the time of the mass deportation, and it is estimated that between fifty and twenty thousand Jews were in hiding beyond the ghetto during the period. Even if these figures account for only five percent of Warsaw's Jewish population at its height, they nonetheless represent a substantial number in absolute terms. Despite the fact that the Polish public was rife with elements that exposed Jews and turned them in to the Nazis, and gangs of Polish extortionists (szmalcownicy) were the bane of Jews in hiding or living under false identities, it is obvious that the concentration of such a large number of fugitives in a single area could not have been possible without the active involvement of a good number of Poles.'

Gutman goes on to reflect that there are 'many facets to this ardent involvement. One particular sector of the intelligentsia – comprising both men of progressive views and devout Catholics who worked with unrelenting devotion to rescue Jews – was of singular importance. At first these people attempted to help Jews with whom they were personally acquainted – primarily assimilated Jews – but in the course of time, the aid and rescue of Jews per se became an all-consuming mission. These circles were the seed that eventually blossomed into Zegota.'[15]

Zegota – the Polish acronym for the Council for Assistance to the Jews – was set up on 27 September 1942. Its establishment was to prove a turning point in

---

[15] Yisrael Gutman, *The Jews of Warsaw, 1939–1943*, page 265.

the history of the Righteous. The originators of the Council were two women, Zofia Kossak and Wanda Filipowicz.[16] They knew full well that any Pole who helped a Jew, and was caught, could expect no mercy. Before the First World War, Wanda Filipowicz had been active, within the Socialist movement, for Polish independence. Between the wars, Zofia Kossak had been head of the Catholic Front for the Reborn Poland, which believed Poland would be a better place without Jews. She was also a best-selling novelist, having made a pilgrimage to Jerusalem in 1933 and written three historical novels about the Crusades: one of them, *Blessed Are The Meek*, had become a best-seller in the United States.

Zofia Kossak's past known anti-Jewish stance, and her fame, made her wartime advocacy of helping the Jews a powerful one. In spite of her anti-Semitism she had been repelled by the savagery of the Nazi persecutions of the Jews, and her human instincts drove her to use her organizational skills to do something about it. Her opposition to the occupation regime would lead to her being sent to Auschwitz – to the Polish section of the camp, itself a centre of torture and terror. She survived her incarceration there, and was in due course recognized in Israel as one of the Righteous Among the Nations.[17]

A month before the establishment of Zegota, Zofia Kossak wrote the appeal issued by the clandestine Front for the Rebirth of Poland. Headed 'Protest!' it declared: 'What is occurring in the Warsaw Ghetto has been occurring for the past half year in various smaller and larger cities of Poland. The total number of Jews killed already

---

[16] Wladyslaw Bartoszewski and Zofia Lewin, *Righteous Among Nations,* page 362. Bartoszewski was a member of the Council for Assistance to the Jews.

[17] Zofia Kossak was recognized by Yad Vashem on 13 September 1982. Yad Vashem Righteous Among the Nations Archive, file 577.

exceeds a million, and the number enlarges with each passing day. Everyone dies. The wealthy and the impoverished, the elderly, women, men, youth, infants, Catholics dying in the name of Jesus and Mary, as well as Orthodox Jews, all of them faulted for the fact that they were born of the Jewish race, condemned to extermination by Hitler.'

The Polish 'opponents of Jews', the appeal stated, 'demonstrate a lack of interest in a matter, which is foreign to them. The dying Jews are solely surrounded by Pilates washing their hands of any fault. This silence cannot be tolerated any longer. Whatever its motives, they are despicable. In the face of crime, one cannot remain passive. Who remains silent in the face of slaughter – becomes an enabler of the murderer. Who does not condemn – then consents.'

Bizarrely, yet honestly, Zofia Kossak went on to note that the feelings of Catholic Poles towards Jews 'have not changed. We have not stopped considering them the political, economic and conceptual enemies of Poland'; but the 'consciousness of these feelings does not free us of the responsibility of condemning the crime. We do not wish to be Pilates. We do not have the ability actively to forestall the German slaughter, we cannot change anything, and save anyone – yet we protest from the depth of our hearts, which are encompassed with pity, indignation and anger. God requires this protest from us, God who does not allow murder. It is required of a Catholic conscience. Each being, calling itself human, has a right to brotherly love. The blood of the innocent calls for vengeance to the heavens. He, who does not support this protest – is not Catholic.'[18]

Zofia Kossak then threw all her energy into her work with Zegota. In its first two months, its members took

---

[18] Andrzej Krzysztof Kunert (editor), *Poles–Jews, 1939–1945*, pages 212–16.

care of an estimated 180 Jews, mainly children. At first Zegota's activities were almost entirely limited to Warsaw, where it opened three safe houses in which Jews could be hidden at any time. It also distributed documents, cash and clothing. But within a few months, branches of Zegota were opened in Cracow, Brest-Litovsk and Siedlce. Contacts were also made, and help given, in Kielce, Bialystok, Radom and Bochnia, as well as in Lublin and a number of localities in the Lublin region, including Zamosc. Eventually Zegota's rescue efforts extended to the Eastern Galician city of Lvov. Liaison between these towns and Warsaw was undertaken by Ferdynand Arczynski, who was also Zegota's treasurer.

Active in Zegota from its earliest days was Wladyslaw Bartoszewski. As an eighteen-year-old underground activist in 1940, he had been imprisoned by the Germans in Auschwitz for seven months. On his release he was among the founders of Zegota – and later one of the first Poles to be recognized by Yad Vashem.[19] Many years later he was to recall that in the pre-war years his parents had Jewish friends and business associates who would visit them at home. 'Even though my family was Catholic, we had a very liberal outlook towards the world. What was important for me is not a person's religious beliefs, but whether a person is a good human being.'[20]

Irena Sendlerowa headed the children's section of Zegota. Before the war she had been a senior administrator in the social welfare department of the Warsaw municipality, and before the establishment of Zegota she had used her connections in the municipality to place

[19] Yad Vashem Righteous Among the Nations Archive, file 29.
[20] Etgar Lefkovits, 'A Lifetime Friend Comes to Visit', *Jerusalem Post*, 30 November 2000 (an article about Wladyslaw Bartoszewski, who was then Polish Foreign Minister).

Jewish families on the welfare rolls, using fictitious Christian identities; to get apartment superintendents to register them as tenants; and to get social workers to report, falsely, that they were afflicted with contagious diseases so they would not be inspected. In time, more than three thousand Jews were receiving assistance through her connections. After the sealing of the ghetto she obtained special passes from physicians in the epidemic control department that allowed her and her co-conspirator, Irena Schultz, to enter the ghetto at will. The two women made daily visits with food, medicine, clothing and money. They were able to bring substantial quantities of these items into the ghetto with the help of plumbers, electricians and other Polish workers who were allowed to bring their trucks into the district.

As the situation in the Warsaw Ghetto deteriorated, with starvation rampant, and deportations intensifying, Irena Sendlerowa and Irena Schultz began to help get children out of the ghetto. At the end of 1942 they were contacted by Zegota, and their network was incorporated into the new organization. As head of the children's section of Zegota, Sendlerowa placed more than two and a half thousand Jewish children in orphanages, convents, schools, hospitals and private homes. She provided each child with birth and baptismal certificates and a new identity. In addition, she carefully recorded in code the original names of all the children and where they were being placed, so that after the war they could be claimed by surviving relatives. In autumn 1943 she was arrested by the Gestapo and sent to the Pawiak prison. Though subjected to severe torture that crippled her for life, she did not reveal her networks of rescue.[21]

---

[21] 'Portrait of Irena Sendlerowa', United States Holocaust Memorial Museum, Photo Archive, Worksheet 89130 (also 90079); Yad Vashem Righteous Among the Nations Archive, file 153.

The chairman of Zegota, Julian Grobelny, working closely with his pre-war Jewish Socialist colleagues, organized the provision of medical help, secure hiding places and transport out of the ghetto, until he was arrested in March 1944. He was imprisoned for a month, suffering a relapse of his earlier tuberculosis. The Polish underground managed to smuggle him out of prison, but ill health forced him to give up his rescue activities.[22]

Henryk Wolinski was another leading activist in Zegota. Before the war he had worked in the Warsaw administration; during the German occupation he joined the underground and became head of the Jewish affairs section of the Delegatura, the Home Delegation of the Polish Government-in-Exile in London. In autumn 1942 the Jewish Fighting Organization in Warsaw contacted him, seeking to obtain arms and instructions in their use. Wolinski pleaded the Jewish cause before the Home Army command, obtained some arms for them, and played a leading role in relaying to the West the news about the fate of the Warsaw Ghetto in 1943. In addition to his liaison work, Wolinski headed a Zegota cell that protected 280 Jews in hiding.[23]

Those who helped Zegota came from many different walks of life. One of them was Jan Dobraczynski, a writer, who before the war had been a member of a Catholic nationalist party with anti-Jewish tendencies. He undertook to help Zegota's Children's Section. Working as a senior administrator in the Warsaw municipality's Department of Health and Social Welfare, he automatically signed every placement form for a Jewish child, and made arrangements with a number of convents so that, whenever they came across a child with a special recom-

---

mendation from him, they would know that the child was Jewish and required special treatment. He later dismissed his own work as 'nothing', citing the much more difficult task of those who carried the children from the ghetto through the sewers, or retrieved them from hiding places and brought them to safety.[24]

Stanislaw Dobrowolski, head of the Cracow branch of Zegota, helped many individual Jews in hiding, as well as distributing food to Jewish workers in the various factories in the area.[25]

Members of Zegota took a personal part, and a personal risk, in helping Jews, even hiding them in their own homes. One of those whom, collectively, they saved was Maurycy Gelber, a Jew from Lvov, who was masquerading as an Aryan Pole. Most of the Polish staff in the bookshop where he worked were strong anti-Semites, and some of them began to suspect that Gelber – who was using the 'Aryan' name Alexander Artymowicz – was Jewish. In fear that he would be handed over to the Gestapo ('being afraid and shaky', as he later expressed it), Gelber approached one of the other men who worked in the shop, Krzysztof Dunin-Wasowicz. 'I had confidence because his acting towards everybody had been nice and correct, and I told him that I am Jewish and in trouble.' Dunin-Wasowicz answered: 'I don't care who you are, for me you are a human being.'

Gelber was soon fired from the bookshop. Dunin-Wasowicz's family invited him to their home each day, fed him and, in his words, 'encouraged me to fight to survive'. Every night, Dunin-Wasowicz hid Gelber in a different Polish home, until he was able to find him a permanent place to live, in Zofia Kossak's home. 'In this

---

[24] Irene Tomaszewski and Tecia Werbowski, *Zegota: The Council for Aid to Jews in Occupied Poland, 1942–45*, page 62.
[25] 'Postwar portrait of Stanislaw Dobrowolski', United States Holocaust Memorial Museum, Photo Archive, Worksheet 90068.

place,' Gelber recalled, 'which I occupied for about six months by myself, never leaving the house, once a week girls from the underground brought me food – and leaflets which I folded for them for distribution to the people. From time to time they left with me a Jewish child, or woman, for a short time.'

When Zofia Kossak was arrested, Gelber had immediately to leave her home. Dunin-Wasowicz gave him the address of Adam Rysiewicz, another Polish member of Zegota, who 'kept eleven Jewish people' in his home. 'I became the twelfth.'[26] There, Gelber's food and lodging was paid for by Krzysztof Dunin-Wasowicz and Wladyslaw Bartoszewski. 'On top of that they gave me pocket money every month.'[27]

Not only Krzysztof Dunin-Wasowicz, but also his brother and his father were active in the Polish resistance. All three were arrested, and sent to Stutthof concentration camp.[28] Writing in his diary, Tuvia Borzykowski, in hiding in 'Aryan' Warsaw, commented: 'Some of the finest personalities of the Polish people are members of Zegota.'[29]

Zegota had to operate against a background of constant blackmail and betrayal. In March 1943, and again in January 1944, with the support of the Polish Government-in-Exile in London, it issued warnings that acts of extortion against Jews would be considered crimes, punishable in accordance with the law of the pre-war Polish Republic. 'Several verdicts were handed

---

[26] Adam Rysiewicz was an active member of the Council for Assistance to the Jews.
[27] Maurycy Gelber, letter to Yad Vashem, 18 June 1980, Yad Vashem Righteous Among the Nations Archive, file 1028.
[28] Krzysztof Dunin-Wasowicz became a distinguished Polish historian, and an expert on the war years. In 1960, when he was a professor at the Catholic University of Lublin, I had several talks with him during his sabbatical at St Antony's College, Oxford.
[29] Tuvia Borzykowski, *Between Tumbling Walls*, diary entry for 19 May 1943, page 123.

down and executed in 1944,' writes the American Jewish
historian Lorraine Justman-Wisnicki, 'yet the Council
was dissatisfied, as these sentences were not announced
on street posters to be read by the entire population, but
only in the underground press. The failure to punish the
extortionists led to an increase of their criminal activities. As more and more Jews made their way to the Aryan
sector, the plague of blackmail became much worse. The
hostile climate was reinforced by the political changes
in the Polish underground.' Still, even in these unpro-
pitious circumstances, Zegota continued with its work
until liberation, deserving, she writes, 'a special gold-
written chapter in the history of mankind during the
tragic years of Hitler's inferno'.[30]
   Even after the Polish Uprising in Warsaw had been
crushed in late 1944, Zegota continued to exist, moving
its headquarters to the town of Milanowek, twenty miles
west of Warsaw, and doing whatever it could, in the few
months before liberation.[31]
   In addition to Zegota, writes Yisrael Gutman, 'a
substantial number of common people took part in the
rescue work as well, usually out of profound religious,
ideological, or humanitarian convictions. These people,
in many cases villagers and townsfolk, risked their lives
to help Jews escape the jaws of the Nazi death machine.'
Yet Gutman adds that 'almost certainly the majority' of
those rescued were concealed by Poles 'in exchange for
what amounted to a ransom. Some of these Poles
behaved honorably, that is, they earned the payment by
attempting to protect the Jews under their care. But a
portion of them were eager to extort Jewish property as

[30] Lorraine Justman-Wisnicki, 'The Righteous of Nations: "Zegota" –
the Council for Aid to Jews', manuscript, sent to the author 20 August
2001.
[31] Irene Tomaszewski and Tecia Webowski, *Zegota: The Council for
Aid to Jews in Occupied Poland, 1942–45.*

quickly as possible, and when these resources were exhausted, they did not hesitate to evict the Jews from their hiding places and even went as far as turning them directly over to the Germans.' He also notes that while 'the clergy and members of certain religious institutions also engaged in the rescue and concealment of Jews, particularly children . . . these efforts were not undertaken on a broad scale and were certainly not free of proselytical motives.'[32]

Despite the need to exercise caution, even scepticism, in so many cases, individual stories of rescue can be uplifting. 'Betrayal and greed were facts of life he had to learn to live with,' Allan Levine writes in his review of Jankiel Klajman's memoirs, 'but ultimately his survival was dependent on the kindness of many strangers, among them even one soft-hearted Nazi officer.'[33]

In north London, fifty-six years after the end of the Second World War, Jerzy Lando commented: 'If it wasn't for Polish Christians I wouldn't be here today.'[34] At the age of twenty, having managed to leave the Warsaw Ghetto with the false papers of a non-Jew, Jerzy Lando had made his way to the shop owned by the mother of one of his pre-war Christian friends, Boguslaw Howil. Lando later recalled that a sign inscribed with *Galanteria Skorzana* – Leather Goods – *Helena Howil* (Bogus' mother) hung above the imposing store at the corner of Marszalkowska and Aleje Jerozolimskie, probably the busiest junction in the heart of Warsaw. 'Its large windows were packed with suitcases, ladies' handbags, briefcases and other leather articles,' he recalled. 'German police, SS and military in their green, olive and black uniforms stood out from the dense

---

[32] Yisrael Gutman, *The Jews of Warsaw, 1939–1943*, page 265.
[33] Allan Levine, 'A boy's gripping story of survival in wartime Warsaw,' *National Post* (Toronto), 23 September 2000.
[34] Jerzy Lando, conversation with the author, 16 August 2001.

crowd of civilians. Warsaw was the centre of communications for men and supplies destined for the Eastern front, and the main railway station was only a few hundred yards away . . . For a long while I stood outside the store, staring at the multitude of leather objects, a few of them known to me from my workshop days in the Ghetto.'

Jerzy Lando continued: 'I was still undecided. I hesitated until I saw the familiar figure of Bogus standing close to the glass partition. He was a handsome, tall, athletically built man with a round open face, some thirty years old. As I entered through the door, he took a look at me and his expression froze, as if he saw an apparition, probably not trusting his eyes. "Jesus Maria, what are you doing here?" He tried to keep his voice down. The shop was some fifteen feet wide and eighty feet deep. The left-hand wall was lined with shelves, reaching all the way up to the ceiling, all packed with merchandise. A few salesmen stood behind the long counter extending throughout the length of the premises; they were serving a dozen or so prospective customers, mainly women. Before I could reply, Bogus asked me to follow him to his office at the far end of the shop. This windowless room contained a small oak desk, several filing cabinets and a couple of revolving office chairs. As soon as we sat down Bogus asked me:

"How is your father?"

"He's all right, he sends his regards."

"And your mother?"

"Surviving" – this was meant to be taken literally.

"Plomniks? Morgensterns?"

"I saw them a couple of times at the Toebbens' factory. They were busy, sewing."

He then got the point.

"Why are you here?"

"I planned to see Wolowski, but he's away." I paused to take a deep breath. "Can I ask *you* to help me? I need somewhere to live. I need a job. I had learnt book-keeping. I can type fast. I know shorthand." So many words to convey a simple plea, Please save my life . . .'

For Jerzy Lando, this was the beginning of a saga of hiding, and also participation in the Warsaw Uprising of August 1944, which brought him, alive, to the war's end. As for almost every Jew in hiding, it was to be a long, dangerous and uncertain road.

Little did Lando know that Boguslaw's mother was already hiding a Jewish child. Only four days after he had been taken in by his friend, a blackmailer sent Howil an unsigned, typewritten threat: 'I know that your mother is harbouring a Jewish child in her flat in Cracow. I am about to pass this information to the Gestapo in Warsaw and in Cracow, unless you hand over 100,000 zloty (about £4,000). The exact amount, wrapped in a news-paper, is to be placed inside the waste bin located twenty steps to the right of the main entrance to the Principal Post Office in Plac Napoleona at 8 p.m. today.'

The note spelt danger for Lando, and although his presence at Boguslaw Howil's flat in Warsaw was unknown to the blackmailers, he could not risk staying there any longer. Howil told him: 'My mother has already made arrangements to find another home for the Plomniks' little girl, away from her flat.' Lando set off in search of another haven.[35] In order that he could survive – as for so many Jews who survived in hiding – five, ten, even more rescuers had to be willing to risk their lives: sometimes just for minutes, sometimes for a few hours, but often for weeks and months at a time.

In January 1943 the Jews in the Warsaw Ghetto resisted the continuing depletion of their ranks through deport-

---

[35] Jerzy Lando, *Saved By My Face: A True Story of Courage and Escape in War-Torn Poland*, pages 126–8; see also Mordecai Paldiel, *Saving the Jews*, pages 100–3.

ation, attacking the Germans who came into the ghetto in search of victims and driving them out. After this act of defiance, Josef Sack, a member of the Jewish Fighting Organization, went into hiding with his wife and daughter in the suburb of Praga, just across the Vistula from the city. There, they were helped by Wladyslaw Liszewski, who had earlier helped Jews by smuggling food into the ghetto.[36]

'Our arsenal grew after the January revolt,' recalled Zivia Lubetkin, one of the leaders of the Jewish resistance in Warsaw. 'We received a new shipment of arms from the Aryan side. The Armia Krajowa, the official Polish underground, sent fifty pistols, fifty hand grenades and a large quantity of explosives. We used the latter to construct mines, which we later planted on the main streets and in the houses which stood at the intersections through which the Germans had to pass as they entered the ghetto. Many Germans were killed by the mines during the April uprising. We received instructions on improvising other weapons from Polish experts.'[37]

On 18 April 1943, three months after the January act of defiance, the Warsaw Ghetto revolt began – a high point of Jewish resistance in Europe. When the revolt was crushed a month later, and tens of thousands of Warsaw's surviving Jews were sent to their deaths, the need for help from non-Jewish Poles became urgent for those who sought to evade capture. Several hundred did what they could to help, among them Wladyslaw Liszewski and his friend Jan Kaluszko, both of whom provided Jews with forged papers and money, built hideouts, extricated Jews from apartments that had been

[36] Yad Vashem Righteous Among the Nations Archive, file 3698. Josef Sack's daughter later became a well-known Israeli novelist, Yonat Sened.
[37] Zivia Lubetkin, *In the Days of Destruction and Revolt*, page 165.

discovered, arranged alternative hiding places, and sometimes escorted Jews who left Warsaw by train. Liszewski equipped one girl's hideout with everything she needed, and when he visited her, he escorted her to a park outside the city so she could breathe some fresh air and be slightly less lonely. Liszewski had grown up in a deeply religious family, and both he and his parents had had Jewish friends before the war. At the height of the German occupation and terror, backed by his parents and sisters, he 'risked his life to rescue Jews for no material reward'.[38]

A member of the Jewish Fighting Organization in Warsaw, David Klin, wrote of two non-Jewish sisters who gave persistent help to the Jewish fighters. One, living in Wola, a suburb of Warsaw, was Anna Wachalska, the widow of a railwayman. Klin recalled: 'She was living with her sister Maria Sawicka, a socialist leader and a sportswoman. Their home was the meeting point of special couriers of the Jewish Fighting Organization and of the Bund in the ghetto, with the group acting on the Aryan side.' The Bund was the Jewish Social Democratic Workers Party, which had been at the forefront of Eastern European and Russian Socialism since the turn of the century. 'These women never considered the dangers to which they were exposed; whenever it was necessary to go somewhere, to carry something to warn someone, to pass a code message, letter or newssheets, they just went. When it was necessary to organize the stay of a few leaders of the Jewish Fighting Organization or the Bund on the Aryan side, it was they who looked for a safe hideout, hired apartments in their own names, and organized them not only as a hideout for these leaders, but also as a point of undercover activity and contacts with the Polish socialist underground movement. To bring material

[38] Yad Vashem Righteous Among the Nations Archive, file 3698.

196

assistance to Jews in hiding was their normal daily occupation.'³⁹

The two sisters had a nephew, Stefan Sawicki, who
was seized by the Gestapo because of his contact with
the Jewish Fighting Organization. 'I was unaware of the
arrest,' wrote Simcha Rotem, 'and I came to their apartment half an hour after the Gestapo had searched their
apartment in Stefan's presence. Despite this, I asked if I
could stay there for the night. Anna answered: "If you
think it's not dangerous for you, please stay." I stayed
there since I had no other choice. Although Stefan was
executed several days later, the sisters did not retreat
and they continued to work for the Jewish Fighters
Organization.'⁴⁰

In another life-saving act, Stanislawa Busold, a
Catholic midwife, with links to the Polish underground,
helped smuggle out of the Warsaw Ghetto a newborn
Jewish child. The baby was named Elzbieta (Elizabeth).
Her parents did not survive the war. Mrs Busold, who
never revealed the secret, treated Elzbieta as her own
child and gave her a Catholic upbringing. Only after the
midwife's death did Elzbieta find out about her origins.
Shortly thereafter, she learned that some of her relatives
were living in the United States. In 1978 Elzbieta visited
her great-uncle in Miami.⁴¹

Alex and Mela Roslan hid three Jewish children from
the Warsaw Ghetto. The three boys, Jacob, Shalom and

---

³⁹ David Klin, *For Your Freedom and Ours*, page 77; Yad Vashem
Righteous Among the Nations Archive, file 78.
⁴⁰ Simcha Rotem, letter to Yad Vashem, 20 May 1964, Yad Vashem
Righteous Among the Nations Archive, file 78. Anna Wachalska and
Maria Sawicka were among the first Poles to be honoured at Yad
Vashem by the planting of a tree in the Avenue of the Righteous, on
27 April 1965. Yitzhak Zuckerman, one of the leaders of the Jewish
Fighting Organization, was among those who submitted testimony on
their behalf.
⁴¹ Lucjan Dobroszycki, *Survivors of the Holocaust in Poland*, pages
29–30.

David Gutgeld, had been left in the care of their Aunt Janke when their father had fled to Russia in the first weeks of the war, hoping to pave the way for the family to escape to Palestine. Their mother had died before the war. The Roslans brought the children into their home shortly before the Warsaw Ghetto revolt in 1943. They treated the children like their own and made every sacrifice for them, including moving apartments to ensure their safety. When Jacob and Shalom came down with scarlet fever, Alex made arrangements to have them smuggled into a hospital – where Shalom died. The following year, during the Warsaw Uprising of August 1944, the Roslans' own son was killed by a German sniper.

After the evacuation of Poles from Warsaw in October 1944, Alex and Mela Roslan wandered with their charges from place to place for six months until the liberation. The family then moved to Germany in the hopes of being able to emigrate from there to the United States. In Berlin the Roslans discovered that the boys' father had indeed reached Palestine, and since the British would grant Palestine immigration certificates only to the boys, the Roslans had to part company with them in 1947. Alex, Mela and their daughter later emigrated to the United States. It was not until 1963 that they saw Jacob again, and not until 1980 that they were reunited with David. The following year Alex and Mela were recognized by Yad Vashem as Righteous Among the Nations.[42]

As the Polish national uprising of 1944, in which more than a thousand Jews had fought, was crushed, those survivors who had not been captured and deported were

---

[42] 'Jacob Gutgeld, a Jewish child . . . in hiding', United States Holocaust Memorial Museum, Photo Archive, file 01067; Gay Block and Malka Drucker, *Rescuers: Portraits of Moral Courage in the Holocaust*; Mordecai Paldiel, *The Path of the Righteous*, pages 225–7.

forced into hiding once more. There were still non-Jews who, at grave risk, gave them shelter. In November 1944 a Polish doctor, Stanislaw Switala, took into his hospital and sheltered seven of the former leaders of the Jewish Fighting Organization, among them Tuvia Borzykowski, Yitzhak Zuckerman and his girlfriend Zivia Lubetkin.[43]

Michael Zylberberg was in hiding with his wife in 'Aryan' Warsaw. 'We had been recommended to a religious Catholic family,' he later wrote. 'They were very poor but kind and anxious to help. The members of the family were an eighty-year-old grandmother, her daughter Mrs Klima, in her fifties, and a grandson aged about twenty-five. Their home, one room and a kitchen, was in a small house in the middle of a common, not far from the main street in the district. The rear of the house was occupied by a woman and her two daughters who often held wild parties. They entertained very dubious people, including uniformed Germans.

'Our poor family', Michael Zylberberg recalled, 'were keen to have us without rent at a time when people were taking enormous sums to hide Jews. They had no previous knowledge of us but felt they had a sacred duty to shelter anyone in need. Of course, our existence had to be a closely guarded secret. During the daytime we crept on all fours so that no one should see us through the window of the little home. During the two months we were there, my wife and I scarcely spoke to each other, so that strange voices might not be heard by the neighbours. Mrs Klima had to buy food for us in a different shop from the one she normally used. Her own grocer and milkman would have guessed that she was buying for more than the usual three people. Both the grandmother and her daughter prayed frequently that

---

[43] 'The Seven from Promyka Street', a reminiscence of Dr Stanislaw Switala, *Binletyn* (Warsaw), nos 65–66, pages 207–8.

God would help them and us. When we were worried that something might happen, they always assured us that they would stand by us and protect us. Their compassion was outstanding.'

As Easter drew near, a new problem arose. As Michael Zylberberg wrote: 'Mrs Klima said she had to go to confession and that she had to tell the whole truth. That included telling about us. She was afraid that the priest might not approve and regard this procedure as dangerous; she was at a loss what to do, and asked me for advice. I begged her to let us know what day she was going to confession, so that we could stay out of the house all day. Thus she would not need to mention us and would have a clear conscience. We kept out of the house that day, as promised, but Mrs Klima confessed everything to the priest! Happily for us and for her, however, the priest assured her that she was performing a noble service in helping those in danger. She returned home overjoyed.'

Circumstances in hiding were 'so hard', Michael Zylberberg wrote, 'and got so much harder as the days lengthened, that we decided that I would leave and my wife would stay. I went to Skolimow near Warsaw to work with friends, taking a job as a gardener. Nevertheless, my wife's stay was also short-lived, for the following reason. One day, when only the grandmother and my wife were in the house, sitting as quiet as mice, Henrietta heard a conversation through the wall. The neighbour, Mrs Kaminska, and a relative of hers were talking. Mrs Kaminska said she had a feeling that a Jewess was hiding next door. The relative said she should inform the Germans at once, and they would soon find out if it were true. When my wife heard this she ran out of the house in terror and never went back. The grandmother, old and deaf, had not heard the conversation, and seeing Henrietta jump up, signalled to her not to go outside. Henrietta quietened her by whispering in her ear that she would soon return. This was their only farewell. The next day the house was searched, and nothing was found.'[44] Michael Zylberberg was never to see his wife again.

In April 1943 Maria Wagman, having escaped from the ghettos of both Kolomyja and Lvov, reached Warsaw on the second day of the Warsaw Ghetto revolt. The ghetto was completely sealed off. Seeking somewhere to hide in 'Aryan' Warsaw, she was directed by a Polish acquaintance to Walentyna Bialostocha, who gave her sanctuary; she also sheltered a young Jewish writer, Marcin Sarna, and his sister. Sarna was later arrested by the Germans and executed, but his sister survived. It is apparent from subsequent testimonies that a number of other Jewish fugitives were given refuge or assistance by Walentyna Bialostocha. These included two women from Chelm who hid in her apartment; a lawyer named Weinryb, who lived next door to her until his arrest and subsequent execution; Mieczyslaw Nojar, who was saved by her help; and Rysiek Radziejowski, who was caught in her house and executed. Walentyna Bialostocha was herself arrested and sent to Ravensbrück concentration camp north of Berlin, where she died in 1945, shortly before liberation.[45]

Within Warsaw, individual churchmen also risked their lives to save Jews. Marceli Godlewski had been the priest at All Saints Church on Grzybowski Place since 1915. Among the Jews whom he saved was Ludwig Hirszfeld, a leading professor of medicine. Godlewski's church was at the edge of the ghetto; he opened its crypt up to Jews making their way out of the ghetto, provided false papers, and hid small Jewish children under his robe to get them away to safety. Ironically, he had been known before the war as a member of the National Party,

---

[44] Michael Zylberberg, *A Warsaw Diary, 1939–1945*, pages 87–8.
[45] Yad Vashem Righteous Among the Nations Archive, file 2398.

and was regarded as being close to the anti-Semitic movements of those years. In 1945, after the end of the war, Godlewski was killed while trying to clear the rubble of the part of his church that had been destroyed.[46]

The testimonies submitted to Yad Vashem by those who were saved reveal the extraordinary determination of ordinary people to do what they could. Roma Eisenberg, who was saved in Warsaw, wrote forty years after liberation, on being asked for her testimony, that Jan Potrzebowski and his daughter had during the war years saved the lives of many Jews, including herself and her cousin Natalia. 'He hid us in the attic, in the elevator pit. He treated us as a very good father, and he saved our lives.'[47]

Following the Warsaw Ghetto revolt of April 1943, several hundred Jews managed to escape to the woods east of the city, in the region just to the west of the River Bug. Yitzhak Zuckerman, one of the leaders of the revolt, later recalled: 'The people hiding in the woods were saved by a simple gentile, a member of Armia Krajowa, whom we called "chlop" (the Polish for peasant), and whose real name was Kajszczak. One day, one of the fighters left the woods to look for something to eat and came upon that gentile, a born and bred peasant who owned a flourmill. Later, we learned he was a member of Armia Krajowa, a sergeant or something in the underground. This man truly risked his life for us. We gave

---

[46] Information provided by Jan Hoser, letter of 11 June 1997, based on the unpublished history of All Saints Church.
[47] Letter of 12 May 1984, Yad Vashem Righteous Among the Nations Archive, file 2466. After receiving affidavits from nineteen Jews who were saved as a result of the efforts of the Potrzebowski family, on 6 June 1984 Yad Vashem recognized Jan Potrzebowski, his wife Natalia, and their daughters Helena (Klepacka-Donalis) and Krystyna (Koslowska) as Righteous Among the Nations.

him money and he brought food and water. He also kept our people from getting shot. As I recall, his brother was mayor of the village; he didn't tell his brother anything, but he always got information from him about what the Germans were planning to do. One day he came to warn us that people in the village were starting to complain about the Jews hiding in the woods. Once when I was there, there was an alarm; but it turned out to be nothing but peasants going out to gather branches. It was very dangerous there. You could be discovered and captured even by accident. We had to liquidate the hideout. That gentile managed to arrange a hideout in the village for Leyzer Levin, his son and brother-in-law.'

The editor of Zuckerman's memoirs, Barbara Harshav, adds of Bronislaw Kajszczak: 'He hid Leyzer Levin and his relative in his home. He was denounced to the Germans who burned down his cottage. The fighters helped him reach Warsaw.' A member of the Jewish Fighting Organization described him as 'a good, warm-hearted peasant'. He agreed 'to supply food for the comrades. We would give him money and he would arrange his purchases in various places so as not to make the storekeepers suspicious. In the evening, he would hitch his horse to his wagon and bring them food. On his own initiative, he would always add something to drink, sometimes it was hot soup he cooked in his own home; he would bring the food and hot soup to the forest with the help of his children.'[48]

One of those who helped Jews, Helena Balicka-Kozlowska, was the daughter of Zygmunt and Jadwiga Balicki, pre-war activists in the Polish Socialist Party. From the earliest days of the German occupation of Warsaw their apartment had served as a haven for their

[48] Yitzhak Zuckerman ('Antek'), *A Surplus of Memory: Chronicle of the Warsaw Ghetto Uprising*, edited by Barbara Harshav, page 389, note 16.

Jewish acquaintances. After the ghetto uprising, a member of the Jewish Fighting Organization, Sara Biderman, sought refuge with them. She had been shot and wounded by a German policeman, and her condition was pronounced grave by a doctor who was called in to examine her. The Balickis succeeded in getting Sara transferred to a nearby hospital where she was admitted under the pretence of being a Christian. An operation was performed which saved her life.[49]

Maria and Zygmunt Rewkowska were professional actors in the pre-war years. In awarding them the designation Righteous Among the Nations at a ceremony in London in 1980, the Israeli Consul-General, Ehud Lador, spoke of how 'the couple selflessly risked their lives – and the life of their small daughter, Joanna – to shelter, for several weeks in 1943, a Jew who had managed to escape from the Warsaw Ghetto. The risk was enormous – should that Jew have been discovered by the Nazis, either through denunciation or by accident, it would have meant almost certain death for the Rewkowskas and their little daughter. Yet they took the risk, and helped that man – today a professor living in Sweden. And there were others, too. Even after the Warsaw Uprising in 1944, when her husband was taken prisoner by the Nazis, Maria Rewkowska continued to risk her own, and Joanna's life, by sheltering Jewish fugitives.'[50]

Inside Warsaw, survivors of the ghetto revolt tried to live on the 'Aryan' side as non-Jews, with false papers, hoping their looks would not give them away either to the Germans or to Poles who might betray them. Others found refuge with non-Jewish families who knew they

---

[49] Yad Vashem Righteous Among the Nations Archive, file 3136. In 1956 Helena Balicka-Kozlowska published her memoirs, *Mur mial dwie strony* ('The wall has two sides'). I was shown it during my first visit to Warsaw three years later.
[50] 'Presentation by Consul-General Ehud Lador', 9 October 1980, Embassy of Israel press release.

were Jews but took the risk of hiding them. An internationally renowned chemist, Professor Mieczyslaw Centnerszwer, was sheltered by non-Jews who knew of his work. But later he was denounced to the Germans, who executed him. Another leading pre-war figure in the world of science and academia, the economist Ludwig Landau, was also hidden by non-Jews, but then denounced and executed. In both cases the rescuer and the denouncer alike were Polish non-Jews. As Yitzhak Zuckerman, a leader of the Warsaw Ghetto revolt, reflected in his memoirs, 'You can't generalize about the Poles. There were decent and pure people among them as among other nations, people who risked their lives and sacrificed their safety fully conscious of why they were doing that. Although there were also Poles whose motive was money and who took large sums for sheltering Jews, there were also people who knew that their job was to rescue, that that was their human obligation. Some of them were simple folk who were content to receive pennies and saved Jews simply out of human kindness; and even when the Jews ran out of money, they went on supporting them. And there were others who kept Jews as long as they could pay, extorted their last cent, and then turned them over to the Germans. Some were in cahoots with the Polish police, others were blackmailers who sucked the marrow of the Jews. There were all kinds of Poles.'[51]

Forged documents were vital for Jews masquerading as non-Jews. The Jewish forgers were helped by both the Polish underground organizations, the Communist Armia Ludowa (People's Army) and the London-based Armia Krajowa (Home Army; an integral part of the Polish Government-in-Exile), as well as by Zegota. In his memoirs, Yitzhak Zuckerman recognized this. 'At a certain stage,' he wrote, 'we were forging documents

---

[51] Yitzhak Zuckerman, *A Surplus of Memory*, page 421.

ourselves, in cooperation with the AK cell that was willing to help us with that. So, with help from AL, as much as they could give, and Zegota, which did a lot in that area, we made our own stamps in 1944: we got forms from Waclaw for forged documents and we also made documents in the name of dead people or those who had sold their documents. We could get documents from the Polish underground. I got my document, for example, from the Armia Krajowa . . .'[52]

Bernard Goldstein was fifty years old when Germany invaded Poland. A leader of the Bund, he had twice been arrested and sent to exile in Siberia under the Russian tsarist regime. In independent Poland he became a leading trade unionist with the Transport Workers Union. In November 1942 he managed to leave the ghetto for 'Aryan' Warsaw, where he found refuge with the Chumatowski family. Not long afterwards, however, a gang of Polish blackmailers, discovering his whereabouts, extorted a high ransom from him, and he had to find somewhere else to hide. He did so in an apartment at 29 Grzybowska Street that had once been part of the small ghetto where the Germans had rehoused non-Jews after the Jews had been driven out – most to their deaths at Treblinka.

The apartment consisted of two rooms: a kitchen and a former photographer's darkroom. Its new owner, Janina Pawlicka, had worked for many years before the war as a servant in the home of an Orthodox Jewish family in the town of Zgierz, near Lodz. She spoke Yiddish, and out of a sense of loyalty to her employers had moved with the family from Zgierz to the Warsaw Ghetto in 1940. They had been deported when the small ghetto was wound up. She gave sanctuary to three other Jews as well as Goldstein, who later recalled: 'The neighbours knew that Janina Pawlicka lived in a darkroom and made a living knitting sweaters. About the rest of us, of course,

---

[52] Yitzhak Zuckerman, *A Surplus of Memory*, page 486.

no one was permitted to have the least suspicion. Our apartment was the small room, the former darkroom of the photographic laboratory, in which there was space for only a small bed and a tiny table. We slept on the floor, crowded together. Pawlicka gave up her bed to the old woman and slept on the floor with the rest of us. All of us, except Janina, remained locked in a little dark hole, forbidden to see the light of day.'[53]

Goldstein continued his account: 'Janina had a difficult time buying food for five adult people. To do her marketing near Grzybowska would arouse suspicion. She was known to be a poor woman who lived alone, and such heavy purchases of food would be sure to excite local curiosity. She had to do her shopping in the more distant parts of the town, at illicit marketplaces, taking a chance on German raids against black marketeers. Preparing and cooking the food presented a similar problem. Too large a pot or too heavily laden a platter of food could betray us. She was on her guard not only against neighbours and chance visitors but also against the inquisitive little child who loved to follow her wherever she went. A pot of half-cooked food and our silverware and dishes would often descend into the cellar because someone had knocked at the apartment's door.'[54]

Goldstein survived the war. In his memoirs he wrote of the woman who had saved him, and those in hiding with him: 'She carried her burden as though it were a holy religious duty. She contributed her share to all the expenses, categorically refusing to allow us to maintain her. We were horribly filthy, crawling with lice. We did not have enough clothing or underwear. Janina washed, repaired, and patched our clothes. From her things, and

---

[53] Bernard Goldstein, *The Stars Bear Witness*, page 213.
[54] Bernard Goldstein, *The Stars Bear Witness*, page 216.

from the proceeds of her knitting, she would give presents to our landlady to keep her happy.'[55]

Another astounding act of rescue took place at 11 Wielka Street, a house adjacent to the ghetto. In her five-room apartment there, another Janina, Janina S. – her surname is not given in Bartoszewski and Lewin's book – hid up to seventeen Jews at any one time. She was the wife of a Polish army officer. Their daughter Eliza helped in this collective act. Eliza also took one of those in hiding, Hanka Peiper, the daughter of a Jewish barrister from Lvov, to a clandestine summer camp for Polish girls, to work there as a gardener. The other girls in the camp knew that she was Jewish, but said nothing.

Among those hidden at 11 Wielka Street was Salomon Jusym – whose surname means 'orphan' in Yiddish. Bartoszewski and Lewin write that he hid for nearly a year 'in a bunker made of hampers in a recess in the flat. During his stay great precautions were taken since more than a dozen people (up to seventeen) lived in Wielka Street at the same time, without being registered. Usually a lookout was kept on the front balcony to watch for a car with the Gestapo that used to come very often after the destruction of the ghetto, sometimes every second night. When the Gestapo car stopped in front of the gate, Jusym was warned and would leave his niche through an aperture above the wardrobe in the adjoining room, wearing socks, and, if there was enough time, silently hide in the garret. At night he usually managed to reach there since it was quite some time before the porter woke up and unlocked the gate for the Gestapo. During daytime visits, he usually stayed behind the hampers, but knowing the danger, he maintained absolute silence, even holding his breath.'[56]

---

[55] Bernard Goldstein, *The Stars Bear Witness*, page 217.
[56] Wladyslaw Bartoszewski and Zofia Lewin, *Righteous Among Nations*, page 176.

Two other Jews who found shelter at 11 Wielka Street were Anna Rotman from Lvov and her daughter Iza. Fifteen years after the end of the war, in 1960, Iza Rotman, then living in London, made a formal declaration about her time in hiding: 'I testify that during the Nazi occupation Janina S. and her daughter helped countless people of Jewish origin to the best of their modest abilities. Fully aware of the possible tragic consequences of what they did, they never hesitated to come to the rescue and give shelter in their own flat. On several occasions my mother and I availed ourselves of their hospitality, and at other times their moral support gave us strength to endure and thus to survive. It is difficult to describe in a few sentences that period of fear, despair and hopelessness. If my testimonial will help to direct attention to what these two wonderful women did, my debt of gratitude will have been in some small part repaid.'[57]

In his book on Polish–Jewish relations published after the war, Emanuel Ringelblum wrote of the individual Poles who had helped him, among them Teodor Pajewski, a railway worker who had helped to get him out of Trawniki, and Mieczyslaw Wolski, the gardener in whose hideout he had lived in 'Aryan' Warsaw, and who was shot by the Germans after the refuge had been discovered.[58] He also noted, with some bitterness, in the spring of 1944, that in the whole of Poland, including Warsaw, 'there are probably no more than thirty thousand Jews hiding'.[59]

---

[57] Wladyslaw Bartoszewski and Zofia Lewin, *Righteous Among Nations*, page 180.
[58] Joseph Kermish and Shmuel Krakowski (editors), *Emanuel Ringelblum: Polish–Jewish Relations during the Second World War*, page xxx.
[59] Joseph Kermish and Shmuel Krakowski (editors), *Emanuel Ringelblum: Polish–Jewish Relations during the Second World War*, pages 247–9.

Jan Cabaj was an officer in the Polish army. Before the war, while living in Eastern Galicia, his two daughters had befriended two Jewish girls who went to the same school. After the German conquest of Poland, Cabaj, who then lived in the town of Garwolin, near Warsaw, was active in the resistance. By chance, the eldest of his daughters' two Jewish friends, Miriam Gruenberg, was being deported from Warsaw to Treblinka when she managed to jump from the train not far from Garwolin. Making her way to the Cabajs' home, she appealed to them for refuge. Miriam had an 'Aryan' identity card that had been obtained for her by friends, and she needed a roof over her head in order to find work in the city. Despite the risk, the Cabajs invited Miriam to stay. She remained with them until January 1943. Later that year, Jan Cabaj was arrested by the Germans and executed for his underground activities.[60]

In the autumn of 1943, to deter Poles from giving shelter to Jews, the Germans intensified their searches and arrests. 'As a sort of object lesson,' Vladka Meed recalled, they set fire to a house in Kazimierz Square in Warsaw, 'killing the entire Gentile family living there because they had given asylum to Jews'.[61] Vladka Meed also recorded how a Pole called Dankiewicz, living in Pruszkow, south-west of Warsaw, hid a Jewish woman named Zucker in a large tile stove. The stove was hollow, and could be entered from the top, which 'masqueraded' as a metal flue. Despite frequent searches, the hiding place was never discovered.[62]

From the moment that the Warsaw Ghetto was established in 1940, Janina Kwiecinska, an actress, made her home available to Jewish acquaintances from the theatre who had escaped from the ghetto and used her connections with the Polish underground to provide Jewish

---

[60] Yad Vashem Righteous Among the Gentiles Archive, file 4990.
[61] Vladka Meed, *On Both Sides of the Wall*, page 205.
[62] Vladka Meed, *On Both Sides of the Wall*, page 290.

refugees with permanent hideouts and 'Aryan' papers. Her three young daughters – Janina, Maria and Hanna – helped their mother by keeping her activity secret and by repeatedly performing dangerous missions, such as escorting refugees to hideouts that had been found for them in Warsaw and out of town. Zygmunt Keller spent nearly two years in hiding in Kwiecinska's apartment and was given friendly, devoted, and unfailing care. Kwiecinska protected Helena Nowacka and her toddler son Seweryn in the same way between August 1942 and the beginning of the Polish uprising in Warsaw in August 1944: two years of unflagging support in an atmosphere of increasing fear and danger. After the insurgents surrendered and the population of Warsaw was expelled, Kwiecinska moved among nearby villages with her daughters and her Jewish wards for more than four months, until the Soviet army liberated the area in January 1945.[63]

Whole families hid Jews in 'Aryan' Warsaw, and whole families were saved there. Because of the testimony of Jerzy and Aniela Krupinski, Yad Vashem gave an award to Ryszard Jachowicz, his mother Natalia (who had since died), and his fiancée, later his wife, Edyta (*née* Nestorowicz). Jerzy Krupinski had been at school with Ryszard Jachowicz. 'When I arrived at his apartment,' he recalled, 'he did not recognize me until I told him my name. When I asked him whether he could help us, he consulted immediately with his mother, who said that she intended to sublet one room to a married couple, a daughter of her fellow worker. She offered the room to us for the same monthly rent, which was less than our people used to pay weekly for safe accommodation. When I suggested a higher rent, she refused, stressing that she takes us because we are in need. "The other couple will find a place." Following this short

---

[63] Yad Vashem Righteous Among the Nations Archive, file 4210.

conversation we moved in and lived in their apartment at Raszynska Street for almost two years without registration, unknown to the neighbours and to the house caretaker.'

Jerzy Krupinski went on to note that Aniela (going by the name of Pauline, which she took to sound less Jewish) very rarely left the flat 'because her fear made her easily recognizable. I also limited my outings so that nobody would realize that an unregistered person was living in Jachowicz's apartment.' When Aniela had to see a doctor, 'Mrs Natalia Jachowicz offered to escort her, indicating that a young woman with an elderly lady looks much less suspicious than in the company of a young man. She and her daughter-in-law, Edyta, also did all our shopping. They had to be very careful not to raise suspicions that they were buying food not only for their own family.'

A quite unexpected problem arose when, in Jerzy Krupinski's words: 'One day Ryszard arrived very embarrassed, telling us that he was getting married. His fiancée, Edyta Nestorowicz, was of German extraction, but her father had been sent to Auschwitz – for not signing the register of Ethnic Germans. Nevertheless, we understood that he could not expose her to such a danger, and assured him that we were very grateful for the help we had received up to now, and that we would look for another hideout. After a few days Ryszard came home beaming with joy. He spoke to Edyta (currently Mrs Olszewska) and she asked him crying: "How can we ask them to leave? How do we know whether they have a place to go?" So we stayed with them for almost two years, treated not as Jews or even tenants, but as members of the family.'

Jerzy Krupinski also noted: 'Pauline asked once Ryszard's mother why she exposed herself, her son and her daughter-in-law to such a mortal danger. She answered: "Men can do so little one for another, and it

is, therefore, his duty to do so for those who need help."
The whole Jachowicz family helped us not because we
were friends or because they liked us. We were strangers
in need. They believed that they should help those who
are persecuted.'

In his letter to Yad Vashem, Dr Krupinski ended with a
bitter reflection, similar to those expressed in his diary by
Ringelblum: 'If many more people would behave as
Natalia, Ryszard and Edyta Jachowicz, your Department
for the Righteous would be overwhelmed with work.
Without their help we would not survive. In those times
helping only one Jew was punishable by death. And if the
punishment for helping only one was the same as helping
many so the reward should be the same.'[64]

[64] Dr Jerzy Krupinski (*né* Szwarcwald) and Aniela Pauline Krupinska
(*née* Gaslaw), letter of 27 April 1988, from Australia, to Mordecai
Paldiel, Yad Vashem Righteous Among the Nations Archive, file
4596.

CHAPTER SEVEN

Western Galicia

The Jewish community of Cracow, in southern Poland, numbering at least sixty thousand at the outbreak of war, was proud of its traditions, which went back five centuries in a history distinguished by great rabbis, writers, teachers and doctors, among others. The coming of war, the establishment of the ghetto, the repeated deportations and the final liquidation of the ghetto in March 1943 destroyed that community, as the Holocaust destroyed all the Jewish communities of Poland.

In Cracow as elsewhere, without those non-Jews who risked their own lives, and those of their families, to save Jews, even a fragment of Polish Jewry could hardly have survived. Each Jewish family seeking to survive in hiding faced repeated risks and dangers, and was dependent on the goodwill, determination and bravery of a few courageous people. Janina Fischler-Martinho, in search of refuge at the time of the destruction of the Cracow ghetto, found herself in Olsza, a poor working-class suburb. She first sought help in a grocer's shop from which Jews used to buy food. She remembered the young Pole in charge of the shop as 'well disposed and helpful, always cheerful and smiling'. But when he saw her: 'An expression of utter repugnance came over his face. He motioned, with his head, towards the door, as one might towards a filthy, importuning beggar or a mangy stray dog. I crept out. It was piercingly cold; the air as sharp as a whip.'

At the bottom of the pathway leading to the shop stood a man well known in Olsza. Janina herself had seen him many times. 'We knew each other by sight.' Locally, he was known 'to be a bit simple. And maybe he was.' He took her to his tiny ground-floor room. Not knowing what his intentions were, she was 'rigid with fear'; but in fact she had found a rescuer: 'He had some provisions on a shelf. He filled a mug from a kettle on the stove and flavoured the boiling water with a spoonful of jam. He brought the mug over to me. He then sat down on his bed by the stove. "I've got some bread here on the shelf. I'll cut you a slice." I shook my head. My vocal cords would not, could not, function. I closed my hands round the mug, trying to warm them against its sides. I sipped the scalding liquid very slowly, through clenched teeth – unable to unclamp them. He drew an enamel basin from under his bed, filled it with hot water from the kettle on the stove, added some cold water from the bucket, tested it with his hand and, judging it right, brought it over to where I was sitting, placed a sliver of laundry soap and a greyish cloth by it and said, "I'll be off now." He left the room. Nobody, ever, has done me as great a courtesy as that man did on the evening of 13 March 1943.'[1]

Rachel Garfunkel was nine years old when German troops entered Cracow in September 1939. Her sister was only nine months old. 'We were given over to a nanny for safekeeping,' she later wrote. 'As the war progressed and all of Cracow became "Judenrein", the situation became more dangerous. The Nazis were determined to find every last Jew in hiding. The man of the house, in a drunken fit of fury, yelled out the windows that there were two Jews here. I left that same day. By ringing doorbells in the neighbourhood, I succeeded in obtaining employment as a charwoman and a nanny to two very

---

[1] Janina Fischler-Martinho, *Have You Seen My Little Sister?*, pages 224–5.

small children. My wages were a bowl of cabbage and bean soup once a day. I was twelve years old then. My four-year-old sister remained with the nanny and her husband. She and their own daughter were the same age and looked alike. They passed as twins. I hold no grudge for these people. I would not have had their courage even for one day.'[2]

Courage was needed both to take in Jews, and to hand over a loved one to the care of someone willing to take them in. A Jewish couple in Cracow, Moses and Helen Hiller, decided that whereas, as a young couple, they might possibly survive deportation, their two-year-old son Shachne would surely perish. They had already made contact with two Catholics, Josef Jachowicz and his wife, in the nearby town of Dabrowa, and on November 15, Helen Hiller managed to leave the ghetto with her son, and to reach the Jachowicz home.

The Catholic couple agreed to take the child. Helen Hiller gave them three letters. One asked the couple to return their son 'to his people' in the event of their death. The other was addressed to Shachne himself, telling him how much his parents loved him, and that it was this love that had prompted them to leave him alone with strangers, 'good and noble people'. The second letter also told Shachne of his Jewishness and expressed the hope that he would grow up to be a man 'proud of his Jewish heritage'. A third letter contained a will written by Helen Hiller's mother, addressed to her sister-in-law in the United States, in which she asked her sister-in-law to take the child to her home in Washington should none of the family in Poland survive, and to reward Josef Jachowicz and his wife – the 'good people', as she described them.

As Helen Hiller handed the three letters to Mrs Jachowicz, she pleaded: 'If I or my husband do not return

---

[2] Rachel Garfunkel, letter to the author, 14 November 2001.

when this madness is over, please post this letter to
America to our relatives. They will surely respond and
take the child. Regardless of the fate of my husband or
myself, I want my son brought up as a Jew.' Mrs
Jachowicz promised that she would fulfil the requests.
The two women embraced, and Helen Hiller returned to
Cracow.[3] She was never to see her son again; for Moses
and Helen Hiller were among those deported from
Cracow to their deaths. At the time of the deportation,
their young son was in the safe hands of Josef Jachowicz
and his wife in Dabrowa.

The historian of this episode, Yaffa Eliach, has written
of how, when the young Shachne cried out for his father
and mother, as he often did, Jachowicz and his wife
feared that their neighbours would betray them to the
Gestapo. 'Mrs Jachowicz became very attached to
the little boy, loved his bright inquiring eyes, took great
pride in her "son" and took him regularly to church.
Soon, he knew by heart all the Sunday hymns.'

A devout Catholic, Mrs Jachowicz wanted to have
Shachne baptized. With this in mind, she went to see a
young parish priest, Karol Wojtyla, who had a reputation
for wisdom and trustworthiness. Revealing the secret of
the boy's identity, Mrs Jachowicz told the priest of her
wish that Shachne should become a 'true Christian' and
devout Catholic like herself. Wojtyla listened intently to
the woman's story. When Mrs Jachowicz had finished,
he asked: 'And what was the parents' wish, when they
entrusted their only child to you and to your husband?'
Mrs Jachowicz then told him that Helen Hiller's last
request had been that her son should be told of his
Jewish origins, and 'returned to his people' if his parents

---

[3] Testimonies of Shachne Hiller (Stanley Berger) and Anne Wolozin,
September 1977–October 1981, Yaffa Eliach, *Hasidic Tales of the
Holocaust*, pages 142–7. The story of Shachne Hiller was published
as a news item, 'Pope and Jewish Child', by Joseph Finklestone,
Jewish Chronicle, 28 May 1982.

died. Hearing this, Wojtyla replied that he would not perform the baptismal ceremony. It would be unfair, he explained, to baptize the child while there was still hope that, once the war was over, his relatives might take him.

Shachne Hiller survived the war and was eventually united with his relatives in the United States. Karol Wojtyla, the young priest who had ensured that the boy remained Jewish, was later to become Pope John Paul II.[4]

Maria Klepacka was a Catholic woman living in Cracow throughout the war. At the time of the mass deportations in Poland in 1942, she had made her way to the city of Radom to collect a Jewish child whom she had offered to take back to her home and shelter. A young girl living in Radom at the time, Alicja-Irena Taubenfeld, later recalled how her mother, knowing that Maria Klepacka's own child had already been murdered by the Germans, had approached 'the totally unknown to her Mrs Klepacka' and begged her to take with her in that child's place 'my (female) cousin and myself, aged respectively ten and twelve. Mrs Klepacka, in spite of the menace of death looming for those who sheltered Jews, agreed and took us with her and put us up in her half-a-room where she lived in Cracow.' That half-a-room was in fact no more than a partitioned landing, 'lacking sanitary equipment, with no facilities except for two folding beds. Mrs Klepacka assured all our needs receiving no remuneration but for a minimal reimbursement for our daily expenses. Following my mother's wishes, she gave us Christian religious instruction, to enable us to pass for such.'

After a few months, Mrs Klepacka, 'in order better to shelter us', put the two girls in the care of nuns in a nearby convent. 'An uncle of ours, still alive at that time, paid the nuns for our upkeep during all this period. However, when he, too, perished and no more monies

[4] Yaffa Eliach, *Hasidic Tales of the Holocaust*, pages 142–7.

218

were forthcoming, the nuns, claiming that they had received anonymous letters, denouncing their sheltering of Jews, commanded us to leave. In utter despair, not knowing anybody else, we returned to Mrs Klepacka, who in the meantime had hidden – against remuneration – two elderly Jews and consequently had no place available for all five of us. It was then that her magnanimous nobility showed itself outstandingly: she urged the elderly couple to leave: they were old and had sufficient financial means to pay for another hiding place. Her duty was (thus she argued) to shelter first of all the two children who had nothing and *could not pay*. This she had promised to my late mother.'

The elderly couple found someone else willing to take them in, for payment. Both survived the war – as did the two girls. Alicja-Irena later wrote that on a recent 'pilgrimage' to Poland she visited Maria Klepacka's grave. 'I would like to add that one of Mrs Klepacka's sisters also sheltered Jews in Cracow and was for this "crime" sent to a concentration camp. She survived it, albeit her health has been gravely compromised.'[5]

Janek Weber recently wrote of his own rescuers both inside and outside Cracow: 'I came from a well-to-do family, and my father built a small apartment house, which was completed just as the war started. The caretakers of the house were a Polish couple by the name of Ludwig and Aniela Nowak. For the duration of the ghetto, whenever it was perceived that there might be danger for me, I was smuggled out of the ghetto and spent time with the Nowaks until it was felt that it was safe for me to return. This was also the case during the two major deportations when thousands of people were sent to their deaths in Belzec. It was particularly dangerous for the Nowaks to hide me as the whole building had been

[5] Ilana Feldblum (Alicija-Irena Taubenfeld), letter to the author, 27 May 2001.

taken over by the Germans and turned into a military dental clinic. Some of the officers knew me from the days when I lived there with my parents before the establishment of the ghetto. It was difficult for the Nowaks to hide me as their living quarters consisted of just one room.'

Towards the end of 1942, when Janek Weber was nine years old, the Germans began the construction of Plaszow concentration camp. It was feared that in the near future the Cracow ghetto would be destroyed and its surviving inhabitants murdered. 'In view of this,' he recalled, 'my parents discussed the possibility of hiding me with another Polish couple called Michal and Anna Wierzbicki, if and when the ghetto would cease to exist. By way of background; Mr Wierzbicki was the head of the planning department in the town hall in Cracow, and my father had dealings with him relating to the plans and construction of the apartment building. They lived just outside Cracow in a secluded villa.'

Like so many others, Janek Weber's parents were caught unprepared on 13 March 1943 when the ghetto was surrounded by the SS, as a prelude to the deportation of the last two thousand Jews living there to Auschwitz. A few hundred Jews were taken to the slave labour camp at Plaszow; during the round-up, seven hundred more were shot down in the streets. 'Due to my parents' ingenuity,' Weber wrote, 'I was smuggled out of the ghetto in a suitcase, and escaped in miraculous circumstances.' His father had persuaded a German wagoner to take a heavy suitcase out of the ghetto, not knowing what was inside it, and had bribed a German guard to let the boy out of the suitcase once the wagon was beyond the ghetto gate, when the driver was not looking. The last time Janek Weber saw his father was through the air holes that his father had cut in the suitcase.

The young boy was totally dependent for his survival on the Christian couple to whom his parents had sent him. 'My parents told me to make my way to the Nowaks, and to remain with them, which I did. They took me in without question, and whenever there was a knock at the door, I would hide under the bed. After a week or so, my parents, who were both transferred from the ghetto to Plaszow, started to go out of the camp to their places of work. They made contact with the Wierzbickis, and one evening Mrs Wierzbicki came and took me to their home. The family consisted of two daughters (who were slightly older than me) and a son who was younger. They decided to conceal from their son my presence in the house. They felt that their son might talk to people about me and this could raise suspicions. I was therefore locked in a room which had belonged to a grandmother recently deceased. The boy was told that out of respect to the grandmother's memory, the room would remain locked. It was imperative that I should remain quiet at all times, and never to approach the window. My food was brought to me at night, and I had a night pot in the room. I was in total isolation for almost two years, until Cracow was liberated by the Red Army in January 1945.'

Although Janek had 'few memories as to how he spent those dark two years', a British journalist, Sharon Jaffa, wrote, 'he recalls reading the same couple of books over and over again, and sometimes simply remaining in bed. Even as an eight-year-old, he was acutely aware of the danger of his situation. He was so disciplined about keeping quiet that for a time he forgot how to speak.'[6]

After the war, Janek Weber found out that his father had been taken from Plaszow to Gross Rosen concentration camp, where he was murdered. His mother had been evacuated from Plaszow, and was eventually liberated in Bergen Belsen, by the British army, in April 1945. She was the only surviving member of his family. 'I was

---

[6] Sharon Jaffa, 'Saved by the Kindness of Others', *London Jewish News*, 8 June 2001.

reunited with her in Cracow in the summer of 1945.'[7]

Janek Weber and his mother kept in touch with both the families who had rescued them, helping them materially when they could. In Cracow fifty years later, on 19 June 1995, Michal and Anna Wierzbicki, and Ludwig and Aniela Nowak, were presented with their medals as Righteous Among the Nations. 'Among my family present', wrote Janek Weber, 'were my wife, my two daughters, my son-in-law and my brother and sister-in-law.'[8] The medal was presented by the Israeli Ambassador to Poland, in the recently established Jewish Centre of Culture. 'I was recently in Cracow,' Janek Weber wrote on 24 September 2001, 'and spent time with Wanda Wierzbicki (her older sister died a few years ago) and with Mrs Nowak who will be celebrating her ninetieth birthday later this year. Mrs Nowak retired as the caretaker some time ago, but she still lives in our building in the same room she occupied during the war. Wanda lives in the same house which was my hiding place.'[9]

Many rescuers took in whole families, with the added dangers, costs and difficulties that this entailed. Anna Zellner (then Tauber) was fifteen when, along with her parents and brother, she made her way back to Cracow from a village in Western Galicia, where hiding had become even more difficult than ever, in the hope of finding a safe hiding place. The family was taken in by Tadeusz Sosin – a cello and trombone player – and his wife Zofia, and hidden until the Russians liberated the city on 18 January 1945. The Sosins' apartment consisted of one bedroom, a kitchen and a bathroom. 'The Sosins lived in the bedroom,' Anna Zellner recalled; 'we lived in the kitchen where there was one bed on which

---

[7] Janek Weber, letter to the author, 24 September 2001.
[8] Janek Weber, letter to the author, 28 October 2001.
[9] Janek Weber, letter to the author, 24 September 2001.

my mother and myself slept. There was one mattress under the bed, which was moved every night and occupied by my father and brother. Mr Sosin constructed a hiding place in the pantry – building a false ceiling, which served as a floor in time of peril.'

When anyone knocked at the door, Anna Zellner recalled, 'we climbed the shelves and all four of us crouched in the hiding spot. My father gave them some jewelry items to sell in order to buy groceries and necessities. They literally and sincerely wanted to save us. Knowing well that they are endangering their lives. The only ones who knew about us were Mrs Sosin's sister and her brother, who were supplying us with food in order not to arouse suspicion in the neighbourhood by buying large quantities of groceries. Mr Sosin went to work daily. His wife Zofia was cooking and also worked part time. Son Otton attended high school and was tutoring me in many subjects.'[10] Anna Zellner is among the many Jews – as many as eight hundred each year – who seek to have their rescuers acknowledged as Righteous Among the Nations.

Another Cracow teenager, Marcel Jarvin (then Fleischer), was fifteen years old when he escaped, in August 1942, from a German labour camp in central Poland, and made his way back to Cracow. There, Marian Wlodarczyk, his father's former janitor, hid him in his apartment, together with Marcel's brother and his wife. When a former Gentile schoolfriend confronted him in the street and demanded a large ransom not to denounce him, all three realized they must leave their hiding place immediately: a few hours later Polish police, working for the Germans, came looking for them.

Some time later, Marcel Jarvin was arrested in the street, on suspicion of being Jewish. 'Despite my denial,'

---

[10] 'Data on Rescue Story', submitted to Yad Vashem, 22 June 1999 (copy sent to the author by Anna Zellner, 5 July 2001).

he later recalled, 'I was brought before a Gestapo officer who demanded that I expose myself. Being circumcised, the officer hit me in the face for lying that I was not Jewish. Nonetheless I kept on vehemently denying it, so much so that this Gestapo officer decided that I should be examined by a German doctor. In due course a German doctor looked at my penis, looked me in the eyes and pronounced: "No circumcision." I was released to live another day. However, what must be pointed out is that it was a *Polish* Gentile policeman who arrested me in the first instance in the street. It may interest you to know that Polish Gentiles were able to recognise Jews much more readily than the Germans.'[11]

Twenty-five miles east of Cracow, Abraham and Malka Schoen, and their children Tania, Alice and Meyer, had left the ghetto of Bochnia and found a hiding place with a farmer and his wife, Wladyslaw and Stanislawa Lacny, and their daughter Irena. 'All of us were hidden there for one week,' Alice Schoen (later Sally Wiener) recalled; 'then we had to leave because the neighbours were spreading rumours that Jews were being hidden there. My boyfriend Henry and his family had also gone into hiding and eventually wound up in the Bochnia ghetto. The decision was made that my family should also go to the Bochnia ghetto, which was about five miles away, but that I should remain in hiding in order to supply them with food. In the beginning I was able to send them food into the ghetto, but it eventually became too dangerous.'

Wladyslaw Lacny, with whom Alice Schoen was hiding, 'took all precautions', she recalled, 'to hide me from outsiders, regardless of who they might be. For the first year I was hidden underground, under the wooden floor. At that time there were rumours that the Polish underground Home Army, the Armia Krajowa, were searching for hidden Jews, and killing them when they

---

[11] Marcel Jarvin, letter to the author, 31 October 2001.

found them . . . One day they came unexpectedly to the farmer's house and started to search the premises, but fortunately didn't find anything. Eventually it became so dangerous that I had to escape. I headed to the Bochnia ghetto, but lost my way and hid in the woods when I heard shots. I buried myself under the leaves and tore up my birth certificate because it indicated that I was Jewish. At the lowest point of my life I recited the Shema (Hear O Israel, our God is One). When the shots ceased, I picked myself up, and, stricken with fear, I spotted a light in a far away house. I went to the house and knocked lightly at the window. When a man came out, I told him I had lost my way. He looked at me and told me that I should not be afraid, that during World War I a Jewish family had saved his life by hiding him in their barn, and dressing him as a milk maid to mislead the soldiers looking for him.'

The new rescuer hid Alice Schoen under the straw in his barn, and told her once more not to be afraid. 'He didn't want to tell me his name, in case I might reveal it if I were captured. But he did tell me that he had eight children and twelve cows. I stayed hidden there for one day and one night, and the next night the man showed me the way back to the Lacny family's village. I had decided to go back there because I had been told that the Bochnia ghetto was in the process of liquidation, and that many Jews there had already been killed, or sent out by train, destination unknown. My farmer and his family rejoiced when they saw me; they thought I had been killed during the shooting I had hidden from, which had indeed been the sounds of Jews being killed. At that point they decided to build a double wall for me. It was 23 October 1943.'

The new place of rescue was tiny. 'The width of my hiding place was the width of my body, and there was a small hole for the intake of food, and the outtake of refuse. Once I was inside the wall I didn't see any light until I was liberated on 12 January 1945. I could tell when it was morning by the sounds of the birds chirping, and the rooster. I could tell the nights by the sounds of occasional shots, knowing that another Jewish life was lost. Sometimes the mice were creeping on my body.'

Betrayal, of both rescuer and rescued, was an ever-present risk. 'One day the German and Polish police came together saying that they were informed that my farmer was hiding a Jew. Their German shepherd dog began sniffing at the hole I was hidden in. I held my breath, and covered myself in the hope that the dog would not smell me. At that point my farmer distracted the dog with salami, and the policemen with vodka, and eventually they left. After that, the rumours about the farmer hiding Jews ceased.'

When, at liberation, the farmer pulled Alice Schoen out of her hiding place, 'they were shocked at what they saw: a living skeleton of about eighty-five pounds with long fingernails, unable to walk or see. It took me about five weeks to walk properly, and three months to get my vision back.'

Alice's boyfriend Henry Wiener had also survived – one of the twelve hundred Jews saved by Oskar Schindler in his factories. They were married in a displaced persons' camp at Fürth, near Nuremberg, 'the first wedding in the DP camp'.[12]

The story of a family in the town of Chmielnik, just over fifty miles from Cracow, shows one of the many different kinds of help that were needed, and how it might be found in unexpected places. The biographer of Sonia Garfinkel, Suzan Hagstrom, has written: 'Some adults with a deep sense of foreboding tried to pass for

---

[12] 'This is the story of Sally Wiener during the Tragic Years of World War II', manuscript enclosed with a letter from Henry Wiener to the author, 13 June 2001.

non-Jew during the German occupation. This was a slim possibility for individuals with financial resources, political connections, and a supposedly Aryan appearance.' To save Sonia in such a way, her parents 'asked Mr Opalka, a Pole in Chmielnik's city hall, to make a false identification card for her. Sonia describes Mr Opalka as a kind man who offered to draft papers for all the sisters and other Jews. The Germans later gunned him down in the street.'[13]

Some twenty miles from Cracow, in the village of Sieciechowice, a fourteen-year-old Jewish girl, Roza Kfare (later Dr Rose Kfar), was in hiding, sent there by her parents after the mass deportation of more than sixty thousand Jews from Lvov to Belzec in August 1942. At Sieciechowice she lived with a Polish schoolteacher, Krystyna Moskalik. After the war Rose went to Cracow, to live with friends of her rescuer. There she learned of the fate of her family. Her mother had escaped from a deportation train to Belzec and returned to Lvov, but had died of typhus in February 1943. Her father had escaped from Janowska camp in Lvov, but also died of typhus a month later. 'I was devastated by the news,' she recalled. 'I asked Krystyna why hadn't she told me about my parents' deaths. She explained that she feared I might become despondent and lose the will to survive, and she was determined to have me survive.'[14]

The help given to Jews by non-Jews in Cracow prompted the Germans to set up an increasing number of special courts to try Poles accused of helping Jews – in spite of a report of the German chief of police in the General-Government, dated 7 October 1943, recommending that cases of Poles helping Jews should be dealt with summarily by the police 'without the necessary delay of

---

[13] Suzan E. Hagstrom, *Sara's Children*, page 77.
[14] Rose Kfar, 'Reuniting With My Family (1945–1948)', *Hidden Child* newsletter, Summer 2001.

court hearings'.[15] On 29 January 1944, in Cracow, a special court sentenced five Poles to death for helping Jews. One, Kazimierz Jozefek, as earlier described by Philip Friedman, was hanged in a public square.[16]

The final liquidation of the Bobowa ghetto took place on 14 August 1942. Of the five thousand Jews in the ghetto, one of the few who survived was twelve-year-old Samuel Oliner, who had been urged by his grandmother to escape from the ghetto into the countryside. After walking for two days, he found refuge with a friendly peasant woman who risked her life by teaching him how to pass as a non-Jew. The young Oliner was given a new name and different clothes, and was taught to read in Polish and recite the catechism. When he was ready, Samuel left her home to seek work in a village where he was not known. He found a job tending cows on a farm occupied by a Polish couple who had moved from the city and rented the formerly Jewish-owned farm from the Germans. They knew little about farm work and needed help. Samuel lived there for three years, and survived the war.[17]

In the city of Tarnow, in the centre of Western Galicia, Dr Maximilian Rosenbusz, the principal of the main Polish Jewish high school, had before the war befriended the district inspector for the Polish Education Ministry, Wladyslaw Horbacki. In June 1940, Rosenbusz had been among the first group of Jews sent to Auschwitz – not then an extermination camp – to work at forced labour in the expansion of the camp. He died soon afterwards, his ashes being returned (for payment) to his family in Tarnow. Soon after the establishment of the Tarnow

---

[15] Report of 7 October 1943, Cracow, in Wladyslaw Bartoszewski and Zofia Lewin, *Righteous Among Nations*, page 602.
[16] Wladyslaw Bartoszewski and Zofia Lewin, *Righteous Among Nations,* page 603.
[17] Simon Wiesenthal Centre, 'Children of the Holocaust' website, www.graceproducts.com.

228

ghetto, and the start of the deportations that were to lead to the total destruction of the city's Jewry, Dr Rosenbusz's wife and daughter escaped from the ghetto and sought sanctuary with the Horbackis. There, Dr Rosenbusz's daughter Zofia found herself among friends: Wladyslaw Horbacki taught her physics and mathematics, and his wife Milica taught her English. 'Every slice of bread, each drop of milk or soup was equally shared between rescuers and rescued,' she later recalled.[18]

In Przemysl, a Catholic teenager risked her own life, and that of her younger sister, to save thirteen Jews. Stefania Podgorska was sixteen years old when her father died, and her mother and brother were taken off to a German labour camp, as were so many hundreds of thousands of Poles. For the next two and half years she hid thirteen Jewish men, women and children in the attic of her family home. 'I just did what I thought I should do,' was her post-war comment.[19]

Also in Przemysl, in the Convent of the Sacred Heart, a ten-year-old Jewish girl, Maria Klein, was given refuge. She later recalled 'thirteen very frightened' other Jewish children accepted, like her, 'with grave risk'. The fact that she was Jewish was known only by three of the nuns: Sister Amelia (the Mother Superior), Sister Ligoria and Sister Bernarda. They gave her a key to the church so that 'if the Germans made a search, I was to hide inside the altar where the Holy relics were kept'.[20]

On 1 January 1967 a Polish weekly newspaper published a letter from Roza Reibscheid-Feliks, a Polish

---

[18] Yad Vashem Righteous Among the Nations Archive, file 2696.
[19] Documentaries International, Washington DC, video documentary, *The Other Side of Faith*, 1991.
[20] Maria Klein, testimony recorded on 15 February 1986, in Ewa Kurek, *Your Life is Worth Mine: How Polish Nuns Saved Hundreds of Jewish Children in German-Occupied Poland, 1939–1945*, pages 188–90.

Jewish woman then living in Tel Aviv. She wrote: 'my conscience would not leave me alone if I kept silent about the deeds of these "Righteous". Some helped me for a whole year, others for two months, some for a few days only, but I shudder to think what would have happened if they had not held out their helping hand just for those few days! Even he who gave me shelter for one night only – may he be blessed! I should be grateful to you, sir . . . if in any way open to you, you would transmit my thanks to my saviours.'[21] Roza Reibscheid-Feliks then listed nine individuals and two families, each of whom had helped her to survive. Among them were two churchmen: Canon Wojciech Bartosik from the village of Wawrzenczyce, near Miechow, and the Revd Dr Ferdynand Machay, from Our Lady's Church in Cracow.

Tragically, many of those who gave shelter to Jews were caught – usually through betrayal – and killed, as were those whom they sheltered. Nobody can calculate the numbers, but some evidence of such betrayal and execution has survived. In September 1944, shortly before Soviet forces entered Przemysl, a Jewish survivor, Yosef Buzhminsky, saw in a courtyard in the city 'a little girl six years old playing there. Gestapo and SS men arrived, surrounded the courtyard. It was a Polish family consisting of eight people. They began whipping the girl, and then they executed all of them right there in the courtyard.' This Polish family had hidden the Jewish girl.[22]

The balance of fear, indifference, betrayal and rescue is hard to measure; the scale of the rescue efforts less so.

---

[21] The newspaper was *Tygodnik Powszechny*, quoted in Kazimierz Iranek-Osmecki, *He Who Saves One Life*, page 284.
[22] Testimony of Yosef Buzhminsky, Eichmann trial, 2 May 1961, session 24.

Yehuda Bauer, a pioneer of research and writing on the Holocaust, tells a story from his personal experience in Israel after the war which throws light on this. 'On my kibbutz,' he writes, 'there lives a man whom we shall call here Tolek. All he knows about himself is his name. He was born near Cracow, or in Cracow, prior to World War II, and he was three when the war broke out. He was in an orphanage, probably because his father had died and his mother could not support him. A Polish woman took this circumcised man-child to her home and raised him there during the Nazi occupation, in alliance with a Catholic parish priest. When the Nazis came searching Polish homes for hidden Jews, the woman used to hand over Tolek to the priest. Tolek still remembers how, at the age of five and six, he used to assist the priest at Mass, swinging the incense around, walking behind the priest through the church. They survived the war, and when liberation came, the woman took Tolek to a Jewish children's home and said, "This is a Jewish child, I have kept him throughout the war, he belongs to your people, take him and look after him". Tolek does not know the name of the Polish woman, nor does he know the name of the priest. There are not very many such women, and there are not very many such priests, and therefore there are not a great many Toleks around. But there are some of each.'[23]

---

[23] Yehuda Bauer, *The Holocaust in Historical Perspective*, pages 92–3.

CHAPTER EIGHT

Germany and Austria

In Germany, the central fortress and ideological base of Nazism, hundreds – perhaps thousands – of 'ordinary' Germans helped Jews to survive the war. More than three hundred have been recognized by Yad Vashem in Jerusalem.[1]

Countess Maria von Maltzan, one of whose brothers was in the SS, lived in Berlin. As Hitler imposed increasingly repressive measures against the Jews, the Countess made contact with members of the Swedish Protestant church in Berlin who were systematically smuggling Jews out of Germany. She forged visas, ration books and other official documents and drove vegetable lorries full of refugees out of Berlin. Her relaxed, aristocratic manner helped her to hoodwink officials and to outwit the Gestapo, who frequently called her in for questioning. After the start of the Second World War, she began hiding Jews in her own home, among them the writer Hans Hirschel, who hid inside a hollowed-out sofa when the police searched the house.

During one search, the Gestapo told von Maltzan that they knew she was hiding somebody and that they

---

[1] 'Righteous Among the Nations – per Country & Ethnic Origin,' 1 January 2002, Yad Vashem Department for the Righteous Among the Nations (list sent to the author on 29 January 2002). The exact German figure, by 1 January 2002, was 358.

would turn the house upside down until they found him. When they threatened to shoot with their revolvers, she laughed – and warned that she would insist on full compensation for the damage done. 'I told them I wanted that set out in writing first and then watched as they backed down. People like that are always terrified of overstepping their position,' she later recalled.[2]

Another German aristocrat, Marie Therese von Hammerstein, was the daughter of a general. Her son Gottfried later recalled that, as the dangers intensified in pre-war Germany, 'my mother began to warn Zionist friends of hers who were about to be arrested. She would take Jews to Prague.'[3] In 1934 she married Joachim Paasche, who was Jewish. She did so, her son writes, 'in part as an act of defiance to the new Nazi order'.[4] The couple then left Germany for Palestine. In old age, Marie Therese lived in a Jewish Old Age Home in San Francisco, only the second non-Jew to be admitted there, in what one of her obituarists called 'a testimony to her family's history of helping Jews in Germany'.[5]

In Berlin, Pastor Heinrich Grüber, Dean of the Protestant Church in the capital, set up a rescue operation in the city in 1935, from which he organized escape routes for Jews to cross into the Netherlands. It became known as the 'Grüber Office' by those Jews seeking to use it to leave Germany. 'The valiant churchman preached by day against Hitler's Jewish policies and operated escape routes for the Jews by night,' wrote Henry Walter

---

[2] Denis Staunton, 'In defiance of fascism' (obituary), *Guardian*, 18 November 1997. Countess von Maltzan later married Hans Hirschel, the man whom she had saved. A film of her wartime adventures was made in 1985: *The Forbidden*, directed by Anthony Page.
[3] Gottfried Paasche, interview in *Maclean's* magazine (Toronto), 28 February 2000.
[4] Gottfried Paasche, letter to the author, 4 March 2002.
[5] Jonathan Curiel, 'Maria Paasche, Daughter of German General Who Helped Jews Escape Nazis' (obituary), *San Francisco Chronicle*, 5 February 2000.

Brann, on the twenty-fifth anniversary of the outbreak of the Second World War, when Grüber was made an honorary citizen of Berlin.[6]

On 15 February 1940 the Germans deported a thousand Jews from the Baltic port of Stettin. In Berlin, Heinrich Grüber was determined to do what he could to protect as many of those Jews as possible. Twenty years later, as a witness in the Eichmann trial in Jerusalem, he recalled: 'That same night a courier brought me news of what had happened. I would like to state that I had branches in all the major German cities, confidential agents, men and women, who did work for me throughout the country, and so the same night I was notified of what had happened. I assume that the Court is aware of those events. As soon as I heard that, I went to all the offices to which I had access. I went to the Führer's Chancellery. I was at the Chancellery of the Führer's Deputy, I also tried to contact Goering, but unsuccessfully, and then I wrote a very lengthy report to Goering.'

In that report, Grüber recalled, 'I tried first of all to show him that this also affected persons who had been seriously wounded in the First World War, and received high military decorations in the First World War, as well as very old people, including war widows. And I know that two people came back. One was a war cripple with an outstanding decoration, and the other was an old woman for whom we already had a visa for England. We then tried to stay in touch with these people through the supply of medicines, with letters, and so on. I would like to say that a few days later, on a Sunday, the Stettin general sent me his adjutant and asked me to make representations, because it was general knowledge in Germany that I kept taking steps in such cases. I was

---

[6] Henry Walter Brann, 'Pastor who rescued Jews is honoured', *Jewish Week*, Washington DC, 20 August 1970.

unable to stop myself from saying to the gentleman that if I had been the Stettin Commanding General, not a single carriage would have left for Poland with Jews.'[7]

Angered by Grüber's efforts, Adolf Eichmann summoned the pastor to his office. 'He said: "Why do you care about the Jews at all? No one is going to thank you for your efforts." I replied, because I believed that he, as a former Templar, had known this country: "You know the road from Jerusalem to Jericho." Then I said: "Once on that road there lay a Jew who had fallen amongst thieves. Then a man passed by, who was not a Jew, and helped him. The Lord, whom alone I obey, tells me, 'Go thou and do likewise': that is my answer."'

At the end of 1940, news reached Berlin of the conditions in the Vichy-run concentration camps in southern France, to which German Jews had been deported from the Rhineland. 'From this camp, Gurs,' Grüber recalled, 'we had – in Berlin – very bad news, even worse news than reached us from Poland. They did not have any medicaments or any sanitary arrangements whatsoever.' Grüber added: 'With the help of two friends from the Counter-Intelligence, Colonel Oster and Hans von Dohnanyi – both of whom were hanged after the July 20 attempt on Hitler's life – I was able to send money, medicines and so on via foreign countries to the Camp de Gurs. Using documents which the Counter-Intelligence would get for me, I wanted to go by a roundabout route to the Camp de Gurs, in order to be close to the people.'[8]

Grüber's attempt to reach Gurs – 'perhaps that will give the people some strength' – failed; instead he was arrested and sent as a prisoner first to Sachsenhausen and then to Dachau. In 1943, after a serious heart attack,

---

[7] Testimony of Heinrich Grüber, Eichmann trial, Jerusalem, 16 May 1961, session 41.
[8] Testimony of Heinrich Grüber, Eichmann trial, Jerusalem, 16 May 1961, session 41.

he was released. He survived the war, to give evidence at the Eichmann trial.[9]

Since Kristallnacht in November 1938, the pastor of St Hedwig's Cathedral in Berlin, Bernhard Lichtenberg – who had been a military chaplain in the First World War – closed each evening's service with a prayer 'for the Jews, and the poor prisoners in the concentration camps'. On 23 October 1942 he offered a public prayer for the Jews who were being deported to the East, calling on his congregants to observe the Biblical commandment 'Love thy neighbour' with regard to the Jews.

Lichtenberg was denounced to the authorities, arrested, put on trial and sentenced to two years in prison. He was sent to Dachau, but died 'on the way'.[10]

In the summer of 1942 Admiral Wilhelm Canaris, the chief of the Abwehr – the military intelligence service of the High Command of the German army – and his deputy, Hans von Dohnanyi, managed to save the lives of fourteen German Jews by sending them to Switzerland, on the pretext that they were being used as counter-intelligence operatives. To save these fourteen had taken a year of careful planning and subterfuge, culminating in persuading the Gestapo chief, Heinrich Müller, that the departure of these Jews was in the German national interest.[11]

Adolf Althoff, the head of the Althoff Circus, was approached by a Jewish woman seeking refuge at the time of the deportation of German Jews in 1942. He gave her a job walking elephants, and also helped hide her mother and sister. 'I had to help them. I could not leave

---

[9] Yad Vashem Righteous Among the Nations Archive, file 75.
[10] H. D. Leuner, *When Compassion was a Crime*, page 10; Zvi Bacharach, 'Lichtenberg, Bernhard (1875–1943)', *Encyclopedia of the Holocaust*, volume 3, page 868.
[11] Ger van Roon, *Widerstand im Dritten Reich: Ein Überblick* (Munich, 1980), cited by Egon Larsen, 'Resistance in Nazi Germany'.

them to the Nazis,' he said. 'To be honest, I have no idea how I did that. Others knew they would be fired if they talked.'[12]

At the end of November 1942, a total of 179 Jews from Pomerania, most of them from Stettin and Stolp, were rounded up and deported to Auschwitz. Only a few Pomeranian Jews were not deported. They owed their survival, writes the historian of Pomeranian Jewry, Stephen Nicholls, 'either to the loyalty of their Christian partner or to the bravery of those who were prepared to hide single Jews. For example, Joachim Pfannschmidt, vicar of Gross Kiesow near Greifswald and an active member of the German Confessional Church, hid Gertrud Birnbaum in his vicarage from 1939–1944. This pharmacist from Berlin survived the war.[13]

In December 1942 Maria Nickel, a devout Catholic, was shopping in Berlin, pushing her baby son in his pram, when she saw a pregnant woman with a yellow star sewn to her coat. Maria couldn't help thinking of her own namesake, the Virgin Mary, with no room at the inn. 'Let me help you,' she whispered, pushing her pram up behind the woman; but the woman, afraid, ran away. The next night, Maria saw her again, and again the woman ran off. Merely talking to a German could get a Jew into trouble. Gradually Maria won her trust and learned that her name was Ruth. She gave Ruth the telephone number of the bakery where she worked.

A few weeks later, Ruth's sister Ella came to see her, to warn that the Gestapo were rounding up men and women on their street to be taken for forced labour. Ella was captured on her way back to her apartment.

[12] Masha Leon, *Forward*, 14 July 2000, reviewing the documentary film *Treason or Honour* by Sy Rotter (president of the Documentary Film and Video Foundation), interviews with Jewish survivors and their German rescuers.
[13] Stephen Nicholls, *From Fortune to Misfortune*, page 14.

The writer Barbara Sofer has described the sequel:

'Ruth cut the yellow stars off her own coat and her husband Walter's. They walked out briskly, like a German couple out for a stroll. Ruth went bareheaded in the hope that her blond hair and blue eyes would keep the Gestapo from asking for papers. When the temperature turned sub-zero, Ruth and Walter huddled in a phone booth. Suddenly Ruth felt cramps. Don't let it be tonight, she begged fate. The Berlin Jewish hospital was still open, but Ruth had heard the rumours that newborns were taken away by the Nazis to be gassed. In desperation, she and Walter retraced their steps to their silent apartment.'

Any moment the SS could return. 'Walter tried to deliver the baby himself, but he was no doctor. He risked going to a phone booth and calling a physician. Amazingly, one agreed to come. In those darkest of times, Ruth gave birth to a beautiful girl, Reha. But their only chance of survival would be to go underground. For that they would need a new identity. Walter dialed the bakery.'

Maria Nickel agreed to help. 'With aplomb she went to the post office, asked for internal travel papers and handed the clerk Ruth's photograph. When the clerk questioned the photo, she didn't miss a beat. "I looked different when I was pregnant," she said. Carrying Maria Nickel's ID card and Willy Nickel's driver license, Ruth and Walter made their way to the train station, pushing a baby carriage they'd found in a bombed building. Inside, their newborn daughter sucked on a wine cork.'

The metal wheels creaked in the snow. 'With every sound, Ruth feared they were attracting attention. The station was crowded with Germans fleeing the bombing and with Nazi soldiers. As they got on the train, a soldier leapt to his feet. Ruth nearly keeled over. "For you, Fraulein, and the baby," the soldier said.'

With Maria's continued help, Ruth, Walter and the baby survived the war.[14]

On 6 March 1943 Josef Goebbels was indignant that when the deportation began of Berlin Jews from an old age home, there were what he called 'regrettable scenes . . . when a large number of people gathered and some of them even sided with the Jews'. Three days later, Goebbels wrote in his diary again: 'The scheduled arrest of Jews on one day failed because of the shortsighted behaviour of industralists who warned the Jews in time.'[15]

From Freiburg, Gertrud Luckner, a member of the long-banned German Catholic Peace Movement, organized the despatch of food packages to Jews who had been deported to Poland. She also travelled by train to many German cities, including Berlin, bringing such help as she could to Jewish families in need. During one of her train journeys the Gestapo arrested her; she was imprisoned for the rest of the war at Ravensbrück concentration camp.[16]

Protest reached the German authorities in Berlin even from the General-Government in Cracow. On 25 March 1943 an anonymous letter, written by a German, was forwarded by the head of the General-Government, Hans Frank, to Hitler's Chancellery in Berlin. In the letter, the writer described with disgust the liquidation of an eastern ghetto, and told of how children were thrown to

---

[14] Barbara Sofer, 'An angel named Maria', *Jerusalem Post*, 2 February 2001.
[15] Louis P. Lochner (editor), *The Goebbels Diaries*, page 209.
[16] Elizabeth Petuchowski, 'Gertrud Luckner: Resistance and Assistance. A German Woman Who Defied Nazis and Aided Jews', in *Ministers of Compassion During the Nazi Period*, Institute of Judaeo-Christian Studies, Seton Hall University, South Orange, New Jersey, 1999.

the ground, and their heads deliberately trampled on with boots.[17]

The situation of Jews in Berlin was both precarious and special: precarious because the headquarters of the Gestapo, of Eichmann's office, and of the SS were all in the city; special, because there were thousands of non-Jews in Berlin willing to take the risk of hiding Jews. While a hundred and seventy thousand of Berlin's pre-war Jewish population either emigrated or were deported and killed, it is estimated that some two thousand survived the war in Berlin itself – almost all of them with the help of non-Jews. In a recent article, Peter Schneider noted that Ludwig Collm, a teacher who went into hiding in October 1942, remembered twenty hiding places. Inge Deutschkron recalled that she and her mother changed hiding places twenty-two times. Konrad Latte, who after the war became the conductor of the Berlin Baroque orchestra, named fifty non-Jews who had protected him at different times. Peter Schneider wrote: 'We will never know how many Berliners had the decency and courage to save their Jewish co-citizens from the Nazis – twenty thousand, thirty thousand? We don't need to know the number in order to pay homage to this untypical, admirable minority. While many individual Germans have been honoured for protecting Jews, thousands of ordinary Germans have remained generally unrecognized in the city where many of them did their good deeds.'[18]

Thirty years before the publication of this article brought the story of the rescuers of Berlin to a wide public, Inge Deutschkron had written to Yad Vashem in

---

[17] Letter received in the Reich Chancellery on 25 March 1943, International Military Tribunal, Nuremberg, document NG-1903.
[18] Peter Schneider, 'The Good Germans', *New York Times Magazine*, 13 February 2000.

15. Jacky Borzykowski with his parents in Brussels.

16. The attic of the Belgian farmhouse of Franz and Maria Julia van Gerwen, where the five-year-old Jewish boy Jacky Borzykowski hid whenever danger threatened.

17. Annette and Margot Lederman in the village of Rumst, in Belgium.

18. Isaac and Bernard Lajbman, on a farm in Belgium.

19. Mimi Anciaux with the two Jewish children, Annie and Charles Klein, whom her parents were sheltering in Belgium.

20. Sara Lamhaut (*left*) at her First Communion in a convent school near Brussels. She was living under the assumed name of Jeannine van Meerhaegen.

21. Father Bruno with five of the Jewish children he was sheltering in Belgium.

22. Six Jewish girls living as Christians in the Dominican convent of Lubbeck in Belgium. *Front row, left to right*: Anna Zaidel, living under the name Yvonne; Lucy Brygier, who had no assumed name. *Back row, left to right*: Paula Ingelscher, who also took no assumed name; Thea Wazschal, whose assumed name was Jeanine Jausson; Sarah Brygier, whose assumed name was Suzanne; unnamed.

23. Rachelle Silberman in the garden of the Convent of the Franciscan Sisters in Bruges, on her fifth birthday.

24. Marcq Dincq holds Marguerite-Rose Birnbaum, whom his parents had rescued in Belgium.

25. Semmy Woortman Riekerk with
Lientje, the nine-month-old Jewish girl
whom she was hiding.

26. Three snapshots of Tina Strobos (*right*),
a Dutch girl who, with her mother and
grandmother, saved many Jews in their
home in Holland. She is seen here with
one of those whom the family saved,
Tirzah van Ameringen.

27. A Dutch policeman looks out of the entrance hatch of the hiding place discovered by the Germans a day earlier.

28. A hiding place in Holland, discovered by the Germans. All twenty-three Jews hiding in it were deported and killed.

29. Heinz Thomas Stein, a German Jewish boy in hiding, in a pasture on a farm at Swolchen, in Holland.

30. Two Dutch farmers, Willem and Johannes Bogaard, with two of the Jewish children whom they hid on their farm.

Jerusalem recalling 'the people who risked their heads to help us'. Emma Gumz and her husband 'were the first to take us in. They hid us for four weeks, continued to give us food throughout the two years and four months of our underground life. I also worked in her laundry as an ironer during that time.' Another rescuer was Lisa Holländer. 'She hid us for over nine months. Her husband was Jewish – Paul Holländer – and was killed in concentration camp, long before the deportations started.' Then there was Käthe Schwarz, who both hid another Jewish woman and 'for some months supplied us with food'. Another German couple, Walter Rieck and his wife, 'were more or less in charge of our underground living. Whenever we did not know where to turn he helped out. The Riecks looked after us ever since 1938 when we needed someone to hide things or help us in other difficulties. It is also hard to describe in a few lines what Walter Rieck has done for us.' Among other things, Walter Rieck employed Inge Deutschkron's mother, 'although he knew that she lived underground. He also gave her rations cards.'[19]

In a German television documentary in 1973, Albert Jurgens, a former Berlin policeman, spoke of how he had given shelter in his home to a Jewish couple ('I had met the man at the railway station, and we got to talking'). He procured false papers for them, and travelled with the couple to the Swiss border where he smuggled them across. Jurgens lost his job as a result of this act of compassion. Lili Bat Aharon, an Israeli journalist, noted that he 'recounted his tale with utter simplicity, as if his actions had been quite ordinary'.

In the same television programme, Bruno Motzko spoke of how he had hidden Jewish families in his home in Essen, procuring falsified documents for them. Also shown on the programme was Helen Jacobs. In answer

---

[19] Inge Deutschkron, letter to Yad Vashem, 9 October 1969, Yad Vashem Righteous Among the Nations Archive, file 671.

to the question 'Why did you do it?' she replied: 'To defend democracy and to fight against discrimination – of which the Jews were the greatest victims.' She had hidden Jews in her home and sent packages to people in concentration camps – with her return address on them. She had provided those hidden by her with food, clothes and necessary documents.[20]

Among the many testimonies of Jews who were saved in Berlin is one from Ruth Gumpel, who was seventeen when war broke out. She wrote of her family's rescuers, Max and Anni Gehre: 'The Gehres had been patients of my father's for many years. During that time their daughter had recovered from diphtheria, for which they were very grateful.'

When it was time for her family to think of going into hiding, 'Mrs Gehre was instrumental in finding hiding places for all of us. As a matter of fact the Gehre family kept my father hidden in a pantry of their small apartment from 9 January 1943 till the end of the war in May 1945. Mrs Gehre also arranged often new hiding places for me and my now sister-in-law Ellen Arndt, when it became necessary for us to move. The Gehres shared their meagre ration cards with all of my family. They did not accept any money from us. As ordinary working-class people, the Gehres were motivated by human decency to help Jews, with no expected rewards or remuneration. Many of our personal belongings were hidden in their apartment and returned to us at the end of the war. None of the neighbours knew about my father's presence in the apartment. During air raids he stayed there while the Gehres had to go to the shelter. Of course whenever they had company, my father kept out of sight.'[21]

---

[20] Lili Bat Aharon, 'Forgotten life-savers on German TV', *Jerusalem Post*, 10 September 1973.
[21] Testimony of Ruth Gumpel, 16 May 1988, Yad Vashem Righteous Among the Nations Archive, file 5505.

Other Berliners who risked their lives to save Ruth Gumpel and her family were Gustav and Anni Schulz, who took in her mother on several occasions, and also hid her father's medical instruments. Then, as she recalled, there were 'Mr and Mrs Max Koehler and their son Hans, and Ernst and Maria Treptow', of whom Ruth's younger brother Bruno, who was seventeen in 1943, wrote: 'I went into hiding on 30 January 1943 (three months after my mother was deported to Auschwitz). When my hiding places became unusable in April 1943, I remembered the Treptows and went there. They took me and my friend Joachim S., who was also in hiding, into their apartment. Since Mr Treptow was in the scrap and recycling business, there was a storage basement in the same house and we both slept there on bales of rags. Joachim S. was caught in a police dragnet on the streets of Berlin and was never heard from again. I stayed with the Treptows till their apartment house was destroyed during an air raid in May 1944. They moved to their one-room cottage in the suburb of Rangsdorf near Berlin and took me along. When neighbours became suspicious and started to ask questions, I had to move out.' Bruno Gumpel then found refuge with another German friend, Erich J. Arndt.[22]

Rudolf Horstmeyer was not Jewish, but his wife Felicia was. Although the Nazi authorities encouraged non-Jewish husbands to divorce their Jewish wives, he refused to do so. Both were teachers: when the Gestapo came to arrest them, former pupils who had later joined the Nazi Party interceded, and protected them. When deportation was imminent they were tipped off and escaped to the countryside, where they were hidden, and survived.[23]

---

[22] Testimony of Bruno Gumpel, 30 November 1987, Yad Vashem Righteous Among the Nations Archive, file 5505.
[23] Conversation with Rudolf and Felicia Horstmeyer's granddaughter, Nicky Gavron, 23 March 2002.

Evy Goldstein was only one year old when war broke out. Her father Ernst was among several thousand Berlin Jews deported to Auschwitz and killed in 1943. She and her mother Herta survived in Berlin thanks to the help given them by two rescuers, Dr Elisabeth Abegg and Hildegard Knies.[24] In the Holocaust Museum in Washington, Evy Goldstein's photograph is part of the photo archive, with a note that for the last part of the war she was hidden on the estate of the Baroness von Huellensen in East Prussia.[25]

Beginning on 27 February 1943, in Berlin the Gestapo rounded up 4,700 Jewish men who were married to non-Jewish women. They were taken to a collection and detention centre in the Rosenstrasse, from which they were to be deported to their deaths. In front of this building, however, an estimated two thousand of the non-Jewish wives gathered to demonstrate – as close as they could to where their husbands were being held – and demand the men's release. Their protest began on a Sunday morning. By nightfall as many as two thousand more wives had joined them. They stayed in the street for a whole week, refusing to leave until their husbands were set free. At midday on Monday, March 6, Dr Goebbels, the Minister of Propaganda and one of the most actively anti-Jewish members of Hitler's inner circle, gave in. Suddenly the Jews who had been about to be deported became 'privileged persons': free men who, the official announcement explained, 'are to be incorporated in the national community'. The 4,700 Jewish husbands thereby survived the war, living in Berlin. Their wives' protest is a little-known tale of courage – and of successful defiance.

These wives had a choice. They could have opted

---

[24] Evy (Goldstein) Woods, letter to the author, 16 August 2001.
[25] 'Portrait of Evelyn Goldstein as a hidden child . . .', United States Holocaust Memorial Museum, Photo Archive, Worksheet 05780.

to end, by divorce, the increasing discrimination, deprivation and danger which they had endured since Hitler had come to power ten years earlier. Instead, they chose to risk their lives to remain with their husbands. Charles C. Milford – then Klaus Mühlfelder – whose mother was one of those German spouses, noted: 'Couples who divorced in the belief this would improve the lot of their children, inadvertently condemned the Jewish spouse to death, as these were to be deported and killed when the systematic extermination of German Jews got under way.'[26]

The stories of mixed marriages often contain great heroism. Peter Gruner, a non-Jew, was inseparable from his Jewish wife. Margit Diamond, his niece by marriage wrote: 'He remained with his wife throughout the war, saving her life and exposing himself to untold dangers when he could have had a much easier time by leaving her. He and his wife were not allowed in the air raid shelter during the bombing of Berlin, they received starvation rations, both had to do slave-type labour . . . he could have avoided all the hardships had he left his Jewish wife. Both barely survived the war.'

Margit Diamond also recalled a second uncle, Paul Saloschin, who was married to another aunt. 'The Holocaust records show that he was transported from Berlin to Lodz along with his wife, and then "liquidated",' she writes, and then adds: 'When I told this to some survivors who knew my family intimately, I found out for the first time that my "uncle" Paul was *not* Jewish! Thus it appears that he, too, refused to abandon his Jewish wife and went to his death with her.'[27]

Otto Weidt, a German pacifist, had a small brush

---

[26] Charles C. Milford, letter to the author, 29 July 2001. The historian Nathan Stoltzfus entitled his book on the Rosenstrasse protest *Resistance of the Heart*.
[27] Margit A. Diamond, letter to the author, 2 May 2001.

factory in a courtyard in the centre of Berlin. Blind himself, he took in several dozen Jews, most of them blind, or deaf and mute, and, in his discussions with the deportation authorities, insisted that the work they did for him was essential for the German war economy.[28] Today, at the entrance to his courtyard, a plaque notes: 'Many men thank him for having survived.'[29]

Every attempt to rescue a Jew was fraught with danger. Emmy Erdmann, from Trier, gave her identity card to a Jewish friend, who thereby survived the war, and helped other Jews escape across the border into Holland. For these humane acts, she was eventually arrested and executed.[30]

From the moment of the German annexation in 1938, Austria's identity was merged with that of Germany: even the geographical term 'Austria' was replaced by smaller regions. In 1943, in a declaration issued from Moscow, the Allies stated that Austria was the first victim of Nazism, as a result of the annexation. Austrian anti-Semitism had been strong, and many of the cruellest concentration camp commandants and guards were Austrian-born, but there were many individual Austrians, like individual Germans, who opposed the Nazi persecution of the Jews and suffered as a result; some tried to help save Jewish life, despite the great risks. Eighty-three Austrians have been recognized as Righteous Among the Nations.[31]

One such Austrian was Lambert Grutsch. The life he saved was that of a young woman, Helena Horowitz, who

[28] Yad Vashem Righteous Among the Nations Archive, file 671.
[29] Martin Gilbert, *Holocaust Journey*, page 31, 'Day 2: Berlin'.
[30] United States Holocaust Memorial Museum, Photo Archive, Worksheet 05772.
[31] 'Righteous Among the Nations – per Country & Ethnic Origin,' 1 January 2002, Yad Vashem Department for the Righteous Among the Nations (list sent to the author on 29 January 2002).

on 15 December 1942 ran away from the ghetto in the Polish town of Debica, 'without a name, without any identification papers', as she later recalled. 'I wound up, as "Sypek, Julia", in Biezanow near Plaszow, working in Firma Stuag, a Viennese construction firm.' It was there that Lambert Grutsch, an overseer in the firm, offered to help her by getting her out of Poland. 'He knew that I was Jewish, but when he went with me to the Arbeitsamt in Cracow, to apply for me to serve as a maid and farmhand for his wife, I was officially working for his Firma Stuag and I also had a bona fide Arbeitskarte.

'I arrived in Tyrol on February 6, 1944. He was going home for a three-week vacation and he officially took me out of Poland as a slave-worker. He didn't say a word to anybody. I worked on his parents' farm all through 1944 till after the Liberation. The sons were all in the army and Adelheid and I did all the necessary farm work. I was "die Polin" Julia and got accepted as a cherished member of the family. They had absolutely no idea what was going on in the world. I worked hard, but I was in paradise.'[32]

Lambert had taken Helena to his family home at Jerzens, in a remote valley high in the Austrian Tyrol – a narrow valley ending in the glaciers that mark the Austro-Italian border. He then returned to Poland.[33]

Aram and Felicia Taschdjian were part of a small Armenian community in Vienna, refugees from the massacres of their compatriots in Turkey after the First World War. One night in 1942 Valentin Skidelsky, who had escaped from a train taking him to a concentration camp, came to their door in search of a safe haven. They took him in, and hid him in their attic until the end of the war.[34]

---

[32] Helena Horowitz, letter to the author, 26 January 2001.
[33] Yad Vashem Righteous Among the Nations Archive, file 9607. The award to Lambert Grutsch was made on 24 February 2002.
[34] Yad Vashem Righteous Among the Nations Archive, file 4962.

Ella Lingens-Reiner was an Austrian doctor. In 1942 she hid a Jewish girl called Erika in her flat in Vienna. 'We had to nourish her,' she recalled, 'but to get food, one needed ration cards. Friends of ours, a couple of teachers who were in charge of distributing these cards, put some of them aside for Erika. When Erika needed surgery for appendicitis, we could not bring her to the hospital without papers. It was our own maid who did not hesitate to give her the papers, so that she could be treated in the hospital. The last month Erika was with us, she took a sunbath on the roof of our house. Some people in the house opposite saw her and informed the police. A policeman rang at the door. Erika kept quiet. But the policeman said: "I know there is someone inside. I will fetch a man who will open the door by force." When he went away, Erika was in panic. Suddenly, the door opened and there came a girlfriend of my brother-in-law who had given her a key. Erika informed her of her situation. Ten minutes later when the policeman rang again, a girl opened and told him: "I am sorry, I did not open the first time, but I was so ashamed for being seen naked." The policeman fined her for her indecency. This girl, whom she had never seen before or afterwards, saved Erika's life.'

Ella Lingens-Reiner adds: 'All these people would have been killed if discovered. None of them ever claimed to be a hero. Yad Vashem does not even know their names. But my husband and I could not have helped anybody without their assistance. For anyone who is honoured today for saving Jewish lives, there were ten or more who did the same.'[35]

In 1942 Ella Lingens-Reiner helped another Jew

---

[35] Dr Ella Lingens-Reiner, speech at the Israel President's House, 6 May 1998, Yad Vashem Righteous Among the Nations Archive, file 1730.

escape from Austria. For her determination to help, she was arrested and sent to Auschwitz, but survived.[36]

Several Austrians enabled Lorraine Justman-Wisnicki to avoid recapture after she and her friend Marysia Fuchs-Wartski had escaped from a prison in Innsbruck in January 1945, before the area was liberated. The first to help was Rudl Moser. 'We found refuge, compassion and understanding,' Lorraine later recalled. 'Strangers became close family. They were deeply concerned, they cared. What an elated feeling after ten months in prison! "Don't worry, doves! I will protect you from the Nazi-swines!" – Rudl's voice sounds a bit high-flown now. A good-natured chap, he was happy for us and proud of his part in our escape.'

Being a member of the Sanitation Department of the Kripo (Criminal Police) and a frequent guest in the prison kitchen, Rudl Moser 'was quite aware of our presence and questionable fate. He tried to reassure us, by expressing his personal animosity towards the regime and – by promising help. Sitting now in the cozy dining room with Frau Maria Stocker and Rudl Moser, we gratefully acknowledged our good fortune. We slept that night in Mrs Stocker's bedroom, and remained there in hiding the next day. "The girls aren't too safe here," sighed Moser, when he returned from work. "We have to secure another shelter."'

On the following day the two girls met Frau Stocker's lifelong friend, Frau Maria Petrykiewicz, and her daughter Wanda. 'Full of admiration for our daring escape from under the noses of the Nazis, they resolved to take us into their home.'

---

[36] She was sent to Auschwitz Main Camp, also known as Auschwitz I, which had been set up in 1940 for Poles and other non-Jews, as a punishment camp of extreme hardship. Much later, she was to write a book about Auschwitz Main Camp: Ella Ringens-Reiner, *Prisoners of Fear* (London: Quill Press, 2000).

Rudl Moser came to see them each night to make sure that all was well. When the Allied bombing drove the inhabitants of Innsbruck into their shelters, 'we implored Frau Petrykiewicz and Wanda to join their neighbours. But, they wouldn't hear of leaving us alone in the fourth floor apartment. They believed strongly that God will protect us, and as well them, from evil.'

Eventually their Austrian rescuers managed to get the two girls false papers, so they could set off on their own, masquerading as foreign workers. 'The moment of parting arrived. In the apartment of Frau Petrykiewicz, on a small table, in front of a picture of Saint Antony, patron of fugitives, candles flickered. The women prayed, as they felt fit to turn to God for the protection of their new adopted, two Jewish girls ... We kissed Frau Maria Stocker and Frau Maria Petrykiewicz, and we all shed tears. Apprehension hung in the air, as our lives were again in deadly danger.'

Wanda Petrykiewicz and Rudl Moser brought the two girls to the deserted station of Rum, a small town near Innsbruck. 'It seemed safer this way, since the police and the Gestapo of Innsbruck diligently proceeded with their hunt for us.' Their last words were: 'Goodbye, Herr Moser, and thanks for all!'

The two girls survived the next few months on the move with their false papers. With the coming of the Allied armies in the first week of May 1945, they returned to Innsbruck, to the Petrykiewicz apartment. 'There was rejoicing and jubilation.'[37]

---

[37] Details appear in Lorraine Justman-Wisnicki's memoir, to be published shortly, *Quest for Life – Ave Pax* (extracts enclosed in a letter to the author, 14 August 2000). Her story is also told in Steve Schloss, 'Reader Remembers: Holocaust Victim is Surprised as Rescuers are Honoured in Jerusalem'.

CHAPTER NINE

Germans beyond Germany

Tens of thousands of Germans lived and worked in the occupied areas beyond the borders of the Third Reich during the Second World War – as soldiers and administrators, businessmen and factory owners. There were also the Volksdeutsch, the local, German-speaking Ethnic Germans who had long lived as minorities throughout eastern Europe, and who expected to be among the main beneficiaries of German rule.

The Germans living outside Germany included many who had no sympathy for the Nazi regime. Some were former Communists or Socialists; most were ordinary decent human beings, repelled by the murder of Jews. In the West Galician town of Drohobycz, a German army major, Eberhard Helmrich, was put in charge of a farm at the Hyrawka labour camp nearby. His job was to supply food for the German army. More than half his almost three hundred workers were Jewish, many of them teenage girls. At the time of the deportations from Drohobycz – on 6–8 August 1942, when two thousand Jews were deported to Belzec in three days and killed, and again on August 17 when a further three thousand were rounded up and murdered – Major Helmrich hid some of his workers in his home, and secured the release of others who had already been rounded up for deportation by insisting that they were needed 'for the proper functioning of the farm'.

There was a third deportation from Drohobycz in October, when another two thousand Jews were arrested. The ghetto was then almost empty. In an effort to save as many of his remaining workers as he could, Helmrich and his wife Donata – who had remained in Berlin – devised a plan to get some of the girls out of Poland altogether. Having provided them with false papers, which Helmrich prepared himself, the women were sent to Germany in the guise of Ukrainian and Polish housemaids, to work for German families inside the Reich. In Berlin, Donata Helmrich made sure that the Jewish women were not placed in domestic positions near 'real' Polish and Ukrainian women who might suspect their true origins.[1]

In Vilna, Major Karl Plagge was in charge of the large workshops where German military vehicles were repaired, the HKP (Heeres Kraftfahrpark or Army Motor Vehicle Repair Park). In the First World War he had fought on the Western Front in the battles of the Somme, Verdun and Ypres, before being taken a prisoner of war by the British. A pharmacologist by profession, he joined the Nazi Party in 1932, before Hitler came to power, hoping for better work and pay, but was soon disillusioned by Nazi ideology, and allowed his Party membership to lapse before the outbreak of war. After Kristallnacht he had shown his contempt for the racial laws of Nazi Germany by becoming godfather to the son of a friend of his, Kurt Hesse, whose wife Erika was Jewish.

On the outbreak of war in 1939, Plagge was drafted into the German army, becoming an engineer officer with the rank of major. According to some sources, one of the first things he did on reaching Vilna – and seeing the harsh situation of the Jews in the ghetto there – was

---

[1] Mordecai Paldiel, 'Helmrich, Eberhard', in *Encyclopedia of the Holocaust*, volume 2, page 654.

to ask his superiors if he could set up a special labour camp for his Jewish workers next to his Motor Vehicle Repair Park, in order to protect them from the regular raids on the ghetto, and the frequent deportations to the death pits at Ponar, a few miles outside the city.

Word spread through the ghetto, recalled Perela Esterowicz (later Pearl Good), then fourteen, that Plagge 'went all the way to Berlin with this request. And that he had argued the war effort needed his skilled Jewish workers. He was much loved and respected, because we knew if not for Major Plagge, we would be dead in concentration camps.' In the work camp he 'saw to it we were treated decently and had food'. Pearl Good was certain she and her parents, Ida and Samuel Esterowicz, and many others, owed their lives to Plagge.[2] Heinz Zeuner, the German who was Plagge's deputy in charge of food distribution, recalled how his boss 'was very worried about the food rations and whether all his people were really satisfied and so I met with him almost daily . . . I observed especially his great sense of justice, he always required that there would not be any injustice in his park, particularly when it was against Jews.' With his knowledge, Jewish men, women and children hid in the Motor Vehicle Repair Park for weeks at a time.

Another of the Germans who worked under Plagge, Christian Bartolomae, later testified about him: 'During my time serving in Vilna in September 1941, he gave me the order to liberate the Jews Zablocki and Trananricz from the Lukiszki prison. A few days later I got the order to free the parents of two Jewish haircutters from the SD prison. During the same time he accommodated thousands of Jews with wives and children in the park territory. He fed them and protected them from death and persecution. After that he gave them "passage

---

[2] Ruby Gonzales, 'Recognition sought for man who defied Nazis', *San Gabriel Valley Tribune*, 13 May 2001.

tickets" in order to have the liberty to go to the city without fearing persecution. The Jewish doctor Wolfson and his father were employed as workmen in order to save them from execution. Doctor Wolfson was thus able to continue his work as a physician.'

Another of Plagge's German employees, Lieutenant Alfred Stumpff, recalled how an SS sergeant at the Repair Park who had threatened a Jewish worker and physically attacked him was reprimanded by Plagge, who then transferred the sergeant to a section of the workshops where he would not come in contact with Jewish workers. Lieutenant Stumpff also testified that Plagge employed Jews in the repair workshops as barbers, shoemakers, tailors and cooks, cleaning workers and gardeners: 'naturally, the Park wasn't allowed to employ such people, and Mr Plagge could have got into serious trouble by doing so. The people were camouflaged to the outside as professional workers of the Motor Vehicle Repair Park.'[3]

Three days before the liquidation of the Vilna ghetto, Plagge took a thousand people out of the ghetto to a work camp on the outskirts of the city. There they remained under his command, safe from deportation, and well treated, from September 1943 to July 1944. Only when the SS took over the workshops was Plagge's protection stripped away; thereafter he was no longer able to help them. His last act was to call them all together, as recalled by William Begell, one of his Jewish workers. 'Plagge said that we all must have heard that the front line is moving west' and that the Motor Vehicle Repair Park's assignment was to always be a certain number of miles behind the front line. It was therefore being moved away from Vilna. As a result, Plagge told them, 'you the

---

[3] Testimonies of Major Plagge's German employees, 'Translation of Transcript of the Denazification File of Karl Plagge', State Archive, Hesse. Provided to the author by Pearl Good.

Jews and workers will also be moved. It is natural to think that since all of you are highly specialized and experienced workers in an area of great importance to the German Army, you will be reassigned to a Motor Vehicle Repair Park unit. I cannot assure you that it will again be my unit, but it will be a Motor Vehicle Repair Park unit. You will be escorted during this evacuation by the SS which, as you know, is an organization devoted to the protection of refugees. Thus there is nothing to worry about.'

Begell went on: 'This is my recollection of the speech. I have repeated it to myself hundreds of times over the years. I also remember thinking that this overt warning to us that we were about to be killed (by mentioning the SS as an organization for the protection of refugees) was made with a human stroke of the pen, so to say, because – and I repeat – because he didn't have to say it at all. These thoughts have been in my mind since that time and I stand by them. What is important now, I believe, is that Plagge tried to communicate the impending danger to the HKP Jews during his speech. That, again in my opinion, is a proven fact. Plagge had warned us in no uncertain terms. I know that the group of us (about three dozen) who escaped through the window in the machine shop knew exactly what we are escaping from and we were totally aware of Plagge's role in warning us.'

Two days later, the SS entered the camp and began to kill all the prisoners. As a result of Plagge's warning, however, between a hundred and fifty and two hundred of his workers and their families, including Pearl Good and her parents, were able to hide in specially prepared hiding places – known as malines – or escape from the camp altogether. 'These survivors and their descendants', writes Pearl Good's son Michael, 'are certain that Karl Plagge, a man whom they knew to be decent and caring, had saved them twice from almost certain death: first when the ghetto was being liquidated in September

1943, and again in the days before liberation when he warned them again of the impending arrival of the SS.'[4]

In Vilna, a German army sergeant, Anton Schmid, was in charge of a camp near the main railway station where German soldiers awaited reassignment to new units. A large number of Jews from the Vilna ghetto were assigned to various labour duties in Schmid's work-shops: upholstering, tailoring, locksmithing and shoe-mending. Schmid, who had been shocked by what he had learned of the mass killings at Ponar, decided to do whatever he could to help Jews survive. His many good deeds included securing the release of Jews in-carcerated in the city's prison, and surreptitiously supplying food and provisions to Jews inside the ghetto.

In three houses in Vilna that were under Sergeant Schmid's supervision, Jews were hidden in the cellars during various 'Actions'. Schmid also became person-ally involved with the leaders of the Jewish underground and co-operated with them. He helped some of them reach Warsaw and Bialystok (where they reported on the mass killings at Ponar) by transporting them over long distances in his truck. Some of these underground fighters met, planned activities and slept in his home. He sent other Jews to ghettos that were relatively more secure at that time, including Lida and Grodno.

Anton Schmid was arrested in January 1942 and sentenced to death by a military tribunal. He was executed on 13 April 1942.[5]

'My boss was a fine, middle-aged German army man, named Baker,' wrote Mania Salinger. In charge of a labour camp factory in Radom, where thirty Jewish women worked outside the ghetto, he was 'a warm,

[4] Michael Good, letter to the author, 27 February 2001.
[5] Mordecai Paldiel, 'Schmid, Anton (1900–1942)', *Encyclopedia of the Holocaust*, volume 4, page 1333.

caring person who a while later saved our lives. He patiently taught me office procedures, corrected my German, my typing. He was a great friend.' Baker shared his lunches and food parcels from Berlin with his Jewish labourers. 'This kind of generosity was, of course, forbidden.' Baker called his workers 'my children'.

After she had acquired a forged Polish passport, Mania Salinger consulted Baker. Several of her friends had escaped to other cities posing as Christians; should she attempt the same thing? 'Mr Baker was all for it; he strongly advised me to take advantage of it, even offered counsel where it was best to go, how to act.'

Baker learned in advance about the imminent second deportation from Radom, 'and without any explanations, ordered us to get home, pack a few belongings, valuables, and ordered us to return to work immediately. He claimed emergency work orders at early morning hours so he ordered us to stay at work for the night.'

All thirty girls stayed overnight in a deserted warehouse. 'Mr Baker stood outside all night with a shotgun in his hand, guarding our safety. We kibitzed and teased him about his over-concern. Little did we know that he practically stole us without any orders or permission, defying instructions from higher echelons and risked his life to save ours. About 5 a.m. we started hearing shots and screams coming from the ghetto area. Our first instinct was to run back to our families, but Mr Baker forced us to stay and to keep silent. Thousands were killed that night, or taken by train to what turned out to be the gas chambers of Treblinka. If I had been in the ghetto that night, I would definitely have gone with my mother to Treblinka.'

Shortly after this, Mania Salinger and several others from her work group were transferred to a safer work environment – a farm in Wsola. 'Mr Baker visited us there, I am sure he arranged the transfer. Hard to believe – a German soldier! I tried to find him after the war ended, but I was unsuccessful. I regret to this day never seeing him again and getting to express my gratitude.' Baker, she added, was 'exceptional, but there were other Germans with whom we were in contact while working in Radom, Wsola, or later in Pionki, that were warm, friendly, understanding and helpful. Even much later while in Germany in concentration camp, we encountered many incidents of concerned German civilians, especially women, who openly showed us compassion and contempt for their country's regime.'[6]

Arnold Boden was an Ethnic German whose family had lived in Poland for many generations. Yehudis Pshenitse – whose rescue by a Catholic priest was recounted in chapter 5 – later recalled the grim conditions in the ghetto of Rembertow, where she and her parents were living: 'Conditions grew steadily worse, my father lay sick in bed and my mother was swollen from hunger. That was when I became the breadwinner for the family. Bearing a sack and a letter from my father to Arnold Boden, asking him to help us out with some food, I set off along various paths for Nowy Dwor,' a distance of twenty-five miles.

Her quest was not in vain. 'Arnold Boden was a good friend of my father. I gave him the letter, and he responded with sincere concern. He filled my sack with food, and I started back to my parents, who awaited me impatiently. Unfortunately, my route back was impeded. The German guards detained me, took my sack of food, gave me a few heavy blows, and sent me back to Nowy Dwor. Once again I went to see Arnold Boden; once again he gave me food, and this time he accompanied me back to Rembertow.'

Three years later, at the time of the liquidation of the ghetto, the young girl – by then eleven years old – was being driven with hundreds of other Jews towards

---

[6] Mania Salinger, manuscript, sent to the author 18 July 2000.

specially dug pits when she saw Arnold Boden again. 'He said to me, "Leave your grandmother here. She is old already, but you are still a small child. I want to get you out of here." At first I didn't want to follow him, preferring to stay with my grandmother, but eventually he convinced me and led me away. Suddenly before my eyes I saw ditches being dug, and people being thrown in alive. When I saw my grandmother being pushed, I burst out weeping and tried to run to her, but Boden dragged me away by force. I don't even remember how I made it back to Nowy Dwor.'[7]

Ben Guterman was thirteen when war broke out. After the establishment of the Piotrkow ghetto, he worked in the headquarters of the city's German police. There he befriended a German soldier, Private Gerhard Wurl. On several occasions, Wurl even went into the ghetto to Guterman's home, where he got to know the whole family. As conditions in the ghetto worsened and the fate of the Jews became more uncertain, the soldier warned Guterman that 'terrible things are going to happen,' and that he, Wurl, would like to help him. He then issued Guterman with a certificate giving him a new name, Jan Stepian, born in the town of Sieradz, some sixty miles away. Wurl wrote on the certificate that 'the Pole, Stepian' had been working in the German headquarters for a long time, had been 'very reliable, conscientious and hard working', and that he should be given every help wherever he found employment. Wurl then took Guterman to Warsaw and found him a job in a factory employing Poles.

Soon afterwards Private Wurl was sent to the Russian front. From Warsaw, Guterman maintained a regular

---

[7] Yehudis Pshenitse, 'Wanderings of a Child', Pinkas Novy-Dvor (Nowy Dwor memorial book), quoted in Jack Kugelmass and Jonathan Boyarin (translators and editors), *From a Ruined Garden: The Memorial Books of Polish Jewry*, page 177.

correspondence with him. The Poles in the factory had begun looking at Guterman with great suspicion, and this was exacerbated when one day they discovered that he was corresponding with a German soldier. There were whispers that Guterman was a Jew who had been specially planted among the Poles to spy on them. When Guterman informed Wurl about these suspicions, his benefactor arranged to come back to Warsaw on leave. He told Guterman that he had decided to take him to a friend's farm in Germany, but in order to get into Germany, Guterman had to go through a medical examination, as did every Polish worker who volunteered to work in the Fatherland.

As a Polish doctor examined Guterman, Wurl hovered nearby. Noticing that Guterman was being questioned more thoroughly than others had been, he immediately went up to the Polish doctor, and asked if anything was wrong. The Polish doctor said, 'I think he is a Jew,' whereupon Wurl shouted at him: 'I have no time to mess around here. This man is going to work on my friend's farm. You had better sign quickly, before I do something to you.' Cowed, the Pole signed the certificate.

On the way to the farm Wurl told him, 'Whatever you do, you are the Pole, Jan Stepian. Never divulge to anybody who you really are, not even to my father, and definitely not to my brother.' Wurl's brother was a keen Nazi. Guterman worked on that farm for about two years, until the area was liberated by the Russians. After liberation, he returned to Piotrkow, where he met his sister, who had also survived with papers that had been provided for her by Wurl, enabling her to work in Cracow for a high-ranking Gestapo officer as a nanny for his children.[8]

---

[8] I am grateful to Ben Helfgott for the story of Guterman and Wurl: Ben Helfgott, in conversation with the author, 11 January 2002.

*   *   *

A German army officer, 51-year-old First Lieutenant Albert Battel, a veteran of the First World War who had been a member of the Nazi Party since 1933, was stationed in the Polish city of Przemysl, on the border between Western and Eastern Galicia. On the morning of 26 July 1942 an SS and German police detachment was about to cross the bridge spanning the River San, which separated the ghetto from the rest of the city. Their task was to round up the Jews in the ghetto for deportation to Belzec. But Battel ordered the sergeant-major commanding the soldiers at the bridge not to let them cross. The sergeant-major brandished his revolver and threatened to order his men to open fire unless the SS men retreated. They did.

Lieutenant Battel had heard of the SS plans to send most of the ghetto population to a death camp. Only one day before the bridge encounter, he had used German army trucks to take Jewish workers and their families – between eighty and one hundred people – out of the ghetto to the other side of the river and house them under direct army supervision. In later arguments with the SS, there would be snide remarks about the German army 'protecting Jews so that they could polish the boots and clean the quarters of its sergeants'.

As the deportation grew imminent, Lieutenant Battel persuaded his superior, Major Liedke, to declare a state of emergency, which would allow him to control all movements in the town. Although the Jewish population was normally under the jurisdiction of the SS, the army could assert its authority under certain conditions. Early that same afternoon, however, high-ranking SS officers arrived to persuade the army to open the bridge. Lieutenant Battel could do nothing against superior authority. The deportation of 3,850 men, women and children – the majority of the ghetto population at that time – took place the following day.

261

Two months earlier, Battel had already tried – unsuccessfully – to prevent the deportation of a thousand Jews who worked for the German army. Although there had been complaints against him, no official action was taken by the SS, 'in order to preserve good relations' with the army. 'In the long run, of course,' wrote Ernie Meyer, a journalist who had studied Battel's file in Yad Vashem, 'Albert Battel could not keep even the small number of Jews who continued working for the Wehrmacht in Przemysl out of the hands of the SS. No action was taken against him immediately, apart from a mild reprimand from his commanding officer.' Not long afterwards, however, the story reached the highest level of the SS hierarchy, whereupon the head of the SS, Heinrich Himmler, wrote a letter to Martin Bormann, the head of the Reich Chancellery, saying that 'right after the war Battel should be arrested'. Fortunately the power of the SS finished with the end of the war.

In the 1970s, Michael Gilad-Goldman, who during the war was a youngster in the Przemysl ghetto, recalled Lieutenant Battel's activities. 'I remember well hearing about the clash between the Wehrmacht and the SS on the bridge. The day was my sixteenth birthday, and although I never saw Oberleutenant Battel, we Jews knew that we had a protector in him. A few of the people he took out of the ghetto survived the war and are in Israel now.'[9]

In August 1942, at the height of the deportations from the ghettos in Poland, an SS officer, Lieutenant Kurt Gerstein, who had witnessed the gassing of several thousand Jews at Belzec a few days earlier, was on a night train from Warsaw to Berlin. So shaken was he by what he had seen that he described the whole mass murder process to a Swedish diplomat, Baron Göran van Otter,

---

[9] Ernie Meyer, 'German Officer – and Gentleman', *Jerusalem Post*, 26 April 1982.

who was on the same train. Gerstein begged the diplomat to pass the information on to the Swedish government, and to ask them to make it known publicly, in an attempt to alert the whole German population to what was happening. Were the German people to know the truth, Gerstein believed, they would demand a halt to such horrendous mass murder. The Swedish diplomat passed on the information as asked, but the government in Stockholm decided, almost certainly in order not to damage its good relations with Nazi Germany, to keep the terrible information secret. Gerstein continued to do the work with which the SS had entrusted him, arranging for the shipment of poison gas to the death camps, including Auschwitz. But in the course of supplying the gas, he was able, certainly on one occasion, to delay and even divert a shipment.

In a book about Gerstein, the historian Saul Friedlander, a former hidden child whose parents were murdered at Auschwitz, wrote that had there been in Germany thousands, even hundreds, of Gersteins – people in the Nazi apparatus who were prepared to divert or damage the shipment of the poison gas to the camps – 'then surely hundreds of thousands of the intended victims would have been saved. But there were none save Gerstein.'[10]

The historian Reuben Ainsztein has written of how, in Bialystok, there were a number of Germans and Austrians who helped Jews to survive. One of these, Arthur Schade, who had been a Social Democrat when Germans were free to choose their political allegiance, was the manager of a textile mill. Through a group of Jewish girls, led by Maryla Rozycka, Schade maintained contact with the Jewish resistance organization inside the ghetto and with the Jewish partisans in the forests,

---

[10] Saul Friedlander, *Counterfeit Nazi: the Ambiguity of Good*, pages 18–19 and 22.

supplying them with arms, clothes and valuable information. After the liquidation of the ghetto he hid twelve Jews in his factory. All twelve survived until the arrival of the Red Army.[11]

Other Jews were saved by Schade at his home. In recommending him for an honour after the war, Shamai Kizelshtein, then an Israeli citizen, wrote to Yad Vashem that Schade had 'performed a humanitarian deed of the highest degree by providing a hideout for my family – myself, Shamai, my father Beryl, my mother Raizel, my sister Mina, my cousin Mary, as well as for the Goldstein family that numbered three people – a couple with a child – on the roof of his house, and fed us and took care of us during our exceedingly difficult situation. After the "Action" in the ghetto ended and the danger passed, he brought us back in a truck hidden under raw materials delivered to a textile factory in the ghetto. In this way he saved us from cruel dangers at least for some period of time. Unfortunately, only I, my sister and my cousin survived, after much suffering.' Kizelshtein added: 'I must emphasize that Arthur Schade put his own life at risk as well as the life of his family in order to save us in that critical time.'[12]

Shamai Kizelshtein's sister Mina recalled: 'Once, Schade asked my father to find him a good housekeeper. I offered myself as a housekeeper, and since that day I saw Mr Schade every day and I had the opportunity to talk to him. One day Mr Schade ran into the kitchen and shouted in German: "I am ashamed of being a German!" When I heard these words from him, it occurred to me that this was a man who could help us.'

Mina Kizelshtein told one of the young leaders of the

---

[11] Reuben Ainsztein, *Jewish Resistance in Nazi-Occupied Eastern Europe*, pages 535–6.
[12] Letter dated 22 January 1995, Yad Vashem Righteous Among the Nations Archive, file 6619.

Jewish resistance in Bialystok, Haika Grossman, about this incident: 'She asked me to check if Mr Schade would be willing to give her a letter confirming that she worked in his office. She would only use this letter to obtain an identity card of a Polish woman. Schade agreed, and thanks to him Haika received her Polish identity card.'

During the first anti-Jewish 'Action' in Bialystok, when Schade hid Mina Kizelshtein and her family, Mina recalled that 'he personally cooked for us and brought the food to the attic where we were hiding. During the second "Action" he hid Mary Kaplan and me. After the summer "Action", a German called Bole brought his Jewish wife to Schade, and Schade allowed her to stay at his place for a few weeks. The partisans from the woods came to him too, and he gave them food. I remember how the late Chaim Lapchensko left his house with a bag full of foodstuffs on his back.'

Several times, Schade drove to the woods in the factory truck, carrying under the bonnet weapons, ammunition, medications and food for the Jewish partisans. 'Everything was wrapped in rags,' Mina Kizelshtein recalled. 'In order to avoid inspection, Schade wore a Nazi Party badge. In his house, meetings of the underground anti-Nazi cell were held, chaired by Haika Grossman, in which participated Otto Beneschek, Bole, and Arthur Schade. When the Germans retreated from Bialystok, Schade didn't go with them, but joined the partisans instead.' All the actions he took, she added, 'were at great personal risk, out of his own humanitarian principles, and out of respect for human life'.[13]

As Mina Kizelshtein noted, another German who joined the anti-Nazi underground was Otto Beneschek, a Sudeten German and a Communist, who was in the city hiding from

---

[13] Testimony of Mina Doron, 12 January 1995, Yad Vashem Righteous Among the Nations Archive, file 6619.

the Gestapo under a false identity. As manager of another textile mill situated on the border of the ghetto, he employed both Jews and Poles, and was instrumental in making it possible for Jews to smuggle arms into the ghetto. Beneschek also provided Jews with false documents and money, and introduced another Sudeten German, Kudlatschek, to the Jewish resistance organization.[14]

It was Kudlatschek who was in charge of the motor pool of all the textile mills in the city. A number of Jews left Bialystok in Kudlatschek's own car, drove to partisan territory, and transported arms to the Jewish resistance organization in the ghetto, as well as making contact with Jews in Grodno and other distant, and for Jews, inaccessible towns.

The Jews of the Bialystok ghetto were also helped by a number of German soldiers stationed in the city, from whom they obtained a few weapons and several radios. Arms also reached the ghetto from Walter, a Viennese, and Rischel, a German, both of whom worked as store-keepers in the *Beutenlager*, or 'booty stores'. Until they were posted to a front-line unit, they enabled the Jews working for them in the stores to take arms back into the ghetto. Two other Germans in Bialystok were sentenced to death for helping Jews.[15]

Another German, Otto Busse, was in charge of a painting shop attached to the Waffen SS units in Bialystok. Some of his employees were Jews from the ghetto; through them he learned what was happening to the Jews, and helped them to smuggle food and clothing into the ghetto. Later he recalled how one of his Jewish workers, Hassia Bornstein, had been terrified when he first told her that he believed her to be a disguised Jew,

---

[14] Testimony of Shamai Kizelshtein, Yad Vashem Righteous Among the Nations Archive, file 7307.
[15] Reuben Ainsztein, *Jewish Resistance in Nazi-Occupied Eastern Europe*, pages 898–9.

and how she subsequently wept in relief when he told her that he would help her and her friends. He also recalled how Hassia Bornstein and Haika Grossman had smuggled rifles concealed in old stove pipes to the partisans in broad daylight: 'Together we faced death and extermination every day.'

When the Bialystok ghetto was liquidated, Busse supplied arms and medicines to Jewish partisans in the forests outside the city. As the Red Army approached the city in 1944, the partisans offered him their protection, but he declined to seek refuge from the Soviet victors, telling those who were keen to help him: 'There is a collective German guilt, and I do not want to be an exception.' Taken into captivity by the Soviets, he spent five years in a forced labour camp near Kiev before being repatriated to Germany.

Disillusioned with life in West Germany, in 1969 Busse moved to Israel, settling in a village in Galilee whose inhabitants were mostly Swiss Christians. In an interview with the *Jerusalem Post*, he revealed that after his story had been published in Germany some eight years earlier, 'I was denounced as a traitor to the fatherland and Jew-lover.' Things got 'so bad', he said, especially his treatment by ex-soldiers, that he had to give up his position as department manager in a Darmstadt store and leave the city.[16]

In Holland two Germans, Hans-Georg Calmeyer and Dr Gerhard Wander, conspired to cheat the Third Reich of one of its cherished aims: a Dutch population that would be freed from Jewish blood so that the Dutch people could take their place as the closest 'Aryan' nation to Germany and be an integral part of the 'superior' race. In 1933 Calmeyer, who had been barred from practising law in Germany for a year because he

---

[16] Ya'akov Friedler, 'Nazi spirit not dead in Germany, rescuer of Polish Jews says', *Jerusalem Post*, 21 October 1969.

had refused to dismiss a Jewish employee, was invited in 1942 by a friend in the German administration in Holland to join the General Commissariat for Administration and Justice, and to work there examining disputed racial cases. At that point in time, someone with only two Jewish grandparents, although deprived of many rights, would not be deported. Calmeyer was willing to accept all sorts of dubious documents, and to allow individuals who were entirely Jewish to assert, for example, that one of their Jewish parents had not been their actual parent, or to claim that a grandparent who was in fact entirely Jewish from cradle to grave had been converted to Christianity.

Calmeyer's helper in this work of deception, Dr Gerhard Wander, was a fellow lawyer, whose job in Holland was to assess which firms and businesses were Jewish-owned. Those deemed to be Jewish-owned would be transferred to non-Jews. Wander, like Calmeyer, made every effort – assisted by his wife Jacoba who, in the words of their son Gerhard, 'shared and risked it all' with his father – 'to introduce doubt and ambiguity. He would accept the most spurious of claims, such as that of a Mrs Polak, who claimed that none of her four children by her late husband were in fact his, but were the illegitimate offspring of "a certain Muller", a non-Jew, who was probably dead.' There were so many such cases, all of which Wander and Calmeyer accepted, that on one occasion Wander remarked: 'I never suspected that Jewish women were so unfaithful.'[17]

In a statement to Yad Vashem, Julia Henriquez Senior, who was in Amsterdam in 1942 with her husband and three children, wrote: 'Dr Wander spontaneously offered his help to protect my family and myself from the anti-Jewish measures of the Nazis. Consequently he changed our Jewish ancestry to such an extent that our names

[17] Yad Vashem Righteous Among the Nations Archive, file 925.

could be placed on the "Calmeyer-list", thereby seriously endangering himself. Through his intermediary an examination was made by a German professor concerning the "racial characteristics" of our family; afterwards the above-mentioned professor declared that we possessed "no distinctive Jewish racial characteristics".[18]

Calmeyer managed to continue with his deception to the end. By January 1944 he had investigated 4,787 'doubtful' racial cases, of which he declared an astonishing 2,026 to be 'only' half-Jews and a further 837 to be quarter-Jews. All these were thereby saved from deportation. The historian of the fate of Dutch Jewry, Jacob Presser, writes: 'He went to endless trouble to prove helpful to all petitioners. There is no doubt that hundreds of Jews owe their lives to him.'[19]

Calmeyer was helped in this task not only by Dr Wander, but also by another German, Heinrich Miessen, who worked in his office. Wander eventually fell foul of the German authorities that had entrusted him with the task of helping with the 'purification' of the Dutch race, and was recalled to the army and sent to the Russian front. He deserted from his unit, returned to Holland and joined the Dutch underground. He was killed in January 1945, shortly before the Allied liberation of Holland, during a Gestapo ambush in Amsterdam. Calmeyer survived the war. In a letter to Jacob Presser in 1965, he wrote: 'Every action – whatever we did to help, was too little, too little . . . I am to this day filled with despair.'[20]

The story of Calmeyer and Wander is one that Mordecai Paldiel, head of the Department of the Righteous at Yad Vashem, considers of particular power, subtitling the chapter on Calmeyer in one of his books:

---

[18] Letter to Yad Vashem, Yad Vashem Righteous Among the Nations Archive, file 925.
[19] Jacob Presser, *Ashes in the Wind*, pages 298–9.
[20] Yad Vashem Righteous Among the Nations Archive, file 4997.

'How a German Official Saved 3,000 Dutch Jews Under the Noses of the SS'.[21]

Another story that attracted the special attention of Dr Paldiel – who is familiar with the details of many thousands of cases – is that of Alfred Rossner, a German factory owner in the ghetto of Bedzin, in south-western Poland. Through the years of German occupation and Nazi rule, Rossner did his utmost to save the Jews who worked under him, producing German army uniforms and boots. During the three principal SS raids into the Bedzin ghetto to seize Jews for deportation, Rossner personally intervened to try to save as many Jews as possible; sometimes by claiming they were part of the 'essential' workers of his factories; at other times by adding them to the roll-call of his workers.

At the start of the second major 'action', in summer 1942, Rossner had himself driven, in his horse-drawn carriage, through the streets of the Jewish neighbourhood, shouting in Yiddish: 'Jews don't be stupid; don't go when they call you!' During another SS raid into the ghetto, Rossner stood alongside the marching Jews. 'When he saw me pass,' Yocheved Galili recalls, 'he pointed me out to the SS man as one of his "essential" workers.' Yocheved then seized her sister's hand, she did the same to her cousin, and so on, until six women formed a chain. A heated debate then ensued between Rossner and the SS man, who insisted that only Yocheved be allowed to go. As she left the column, she dragged with her the other five women. During the melee of pushing and beatings, the six were able to sneak away. 'To this day, I don't understand how this all happened,' Yocheved Galili said. 'Rossner's men covered our escape, and we fast found ourselves hidden in Rossner's offices.'

During a third and final 'action' in the Bedzin ghetto,

---

[21] Mordecai Paldiel, *Saving the Jews*, pages 119–25.

in August 1943, Karola Baum hid with her family in a coal cellar. Somehow, luck was with her, and although her family were taken and deported, she was not caught. After sunset she tried to leave, but was inhibited by the sight of the streets filled with soldiers, and the pavements littered with the corpses of Jews. She was finally able, when the soldiers had gone, to sneak out of the ghetto, barefoot, and went to the non-Jewish side of the city. 'I was left on the street. I then decided to sneak away and head to Rossner's home. I looked terrible: dirty, with leg wounds, and frightened.'

The Polish governess of Rossner's children allowed Karola Baum into the house. Hardly had she done so when Rossner stepped out of his room and said she was welcome to join the other Jews hiding in his factory. 'In simple words, he said that I could wash up and eat, and asked his governess to help me.' After a night's stay in Rossner's home, she was taken by him to the factory.

During the same Nazi action, Cesia Rubinstein had been rounded up and was standing in line to be deported. Suddenly Rossner appeared, with a German assistant, and the two men began taking out young Jews, including Cesia, whom they quickly moved into the factory, where they were safe from harm.

Also on Rossner's orders, several trucks loaded with fabric were sent into the Bedzin ghetto. On the return journey to the factory, people were hidden under the layers of clothes, and smuggled into Rossner's two factories. After the final liquidation of August 1943, there were only six hundred Jewish slave labourers left, out of an original ten thousand. In his efforts to find and protect Jews, Rossner was persistent and heroic. His fate was sealed; at the end of 1943 he was arrested by the SS, and hanged. By the time of his execution, there were only fifty Jews left under his protection.[22]

---

[22] Mordecai Paldiel, *Saving the Jews*, pages 126–32.

*   *   *

In the East Galician town of Zolkiew, Valenti and Julia Beck and their daughter Aleksandra were typical of hundreds of thousands of Ethnic Germans whose forebears had settled in what later became Poland and Ukraine. When Germany occupied Zolkiew they registered as Ethnic Germans; this gave them a higher status than the local Poles and Ukrainians, and also made it seem impossible to the German occupation forces that they might have any sympathy for Jews. Indeed, Aleksandra often invited German soldiers to her home in order to help camouflage the family's rescue activities.

Sixteen Jews who escaped from the Zolkiew ghetto before the first deportation in November 1942 were hidden by Valenti in a bunker underneath the floor of his apartment. In April 1943, during the final liquidation of the ghetto, seven-year-old Zygmund Orlender and his four-year-old sister also sought refuge. Despite the opposition of those already hiding in the bunker, who protested against the increased overcrowding, Valenti and Julia Beck stood firm and took in the children. In spite of the heavy economic burden, the Becks supplied the needs of all their eighteen charges, of whom only a few could contribute to their upkeep. The fugitives remained in hiding until the area was liberated in July 1944.[23]

In the former Polish province of Volhynia, a German engineer, Herman Friedrich (Fritz) Graebe, the manager of a construction company, did his utmost to protect the Jews in the Zdolbunow region of eastern Poland, from which his workers were drawn. In the words of his Polish secretary, recalling the summer and autumn of 1942: 'During this period the extermination of the Volhynia Jews proceeded apace. The Jews of Zdolbunow county held out a little longer, namely until October,

---

[23] Yad Vashem Righteous Among the Nations Archive, file 2687.

thanks only to Graebe. Arguing that he must carry out important construction work (the maintenance and proper operation of the Zdolbunow railroad junction which was of decisive importance for the operations of the German army at the north-Ukrainian front), he kept the Jews alive as long as he could.'[24]

By deliberately exaggerating the importance of the work his factories were doing for the German army, Graebe built a reputation with the local SS commanders, which he was then able to use when intervening on behalf of the Jews. To ensure that his efforts were as effective as possible, he sought the advice of the chairman of the Zdolbunow Jewish Council. As a result of Graebe's efforts and influence, the Jewish poll tax and levy on food were abolished, as were other fines imposed on the Jews. He also used his influence to persuade other companies to accord fair treatment to their Jewish workers.

Graebe did not hesitate to take great risks to intervene on behalf of the Jews and protect them from the 'actions'. On Saturday, 11 July 1942 he informed his German manager in Rovno that he had heard from his contacts in the German army that a liquidation 'action' against the Rovno Jews was to take place in two days' time. Graebe had a hundred and fifty Jews – mostly from the nearby town of Zdolbunow – working for him in Rovno; they lived in several houses in the Rovno ghetto. Immediately he told them that they would have a day off on the Sunday and return on Monday to Zdolbunow.

On the morning of the Monday, Graebe learned from the second most senior Nazi official in Rovno that the ghetto would be sealed at ten o'clock that night, and the 'action' begun. He at once demanded from the official, and obtained, a document that read: 'The Jewish labour

---

[24] Letter of 29 December 1958, quoted in Shmuel Spector, *The Holocaust of Volhynian Jews, 1941–1944*, page 185.

force employed by your company is not included in the "Action". They must transfer to a new place of work until Wednesday, 15 July 1942, at the latest.'

With this document, Graebe hurried to Rovno. There, brandishing a pistol, he guarded his Jewish workers against the Ukrainian policemen who were even then assembling ghetto residents before marching them to the railway station. Graebe witnessed the 'action' and saw the resistance put up by the Jews. Later that night the SS commander told him to remove his Jews until morning. Having obtained an SS soldier as an escort, Graebe did not wait for the trucks to come to take them away, but marched them out of the city himself on foot, leading the column, pistol in hand, to deter Ukrainian policemen. All 150 Jewish workers reached Zdolbunow unharmed.

The historian of the wartime fate of Volhynian Jewry, Shmuel Spector, has recorded that Graebe 'went to great lengths to fight against the "Final Solution"'. It appears that it was he who advised the chairmen of the Ostrog, Zdolbunow and Mizocz Jewish Councils 'to get organized and bribe the Germans. He succeeded in delaying the liquidation of the Jews in these three localities and they were the last to be liquidated (in mid-October 1942).' By that time, as Graebe's Polish secretary expressed it, 'he had run out of possibilities to act'.

After the liquidations in Volhynia, in which a quarter of a million Jews were murdered, Graebe continued to employ twenty-five Jews, whom he had supplied with 'Aryan' papers. When it became clear that if they stayed in Volhynia any longer their lives would be in danger, Graebe set up a branch of his company in the southern Ukrainian city of Poltava, and sent them there. He maintained this branch at his own expense, and often visited the Jews there, to give them money and furnish them with documents.

After the war, at the Nuremberg Trials, Graebe was one

of the most powerful witnesses to German atrocities.[25] The fact that he gave testimony, writes Shmuel Spector, 'created widespread animosity against him in Germany, and with the help of Jewish organizations he emigrated to the United States, settling in California.'[26] Echoing rescuers everywhere, Fritz Graebe disclaimed any special virtue, telling his biographer: 'I did what anyone could have done, should have done.'[27]

Franz Fritsch had been sent to Tarnow in Poland to set up a workshop making tailored uniforms. As shop director, he asked for Jewish workers and thus saved many from the concentration camps and certain death. 'Do you recall,' asked one of those whom he saved – a man called Oesterweiler – 'how you went to the Gestapo in Tarnow and asked for a list of people to be taken out of the transport? They gave you fifty names. You made it a list of two hundred and fifty names – and made it look official.'[28]

An Austrian factory owner, Julius Madritsch, was also entrusted by the German authorities in the occupied eastern regions with production for the German war effort. In his textile factory in Cracow, which was managed by his fellow Austrian, Raimund Titsch, he employed many Jews who had no professional experience or training. To maximize the numbers of Jews he could protect, by insisting that their work was essential, he put three workers on every machine, although only one was needed. By this means he was able to employ eight hundred Jewish workers, enabling them to avoid deportation. He and Titsch also provided materials to

[25] Shmuel Spector, *The Holocaust of Volhynian Jews, 1941–1944*, pages 254–5.
[26] Shmuel Spector, 'Graebe, Hermann Friedrich (1900–1986)', *Encyclopedia of the Holocaust*, volume 2, pages 599–600.
[27] Douglas K. Huneke, *The Moses of Rovno*, page xvii.
[28] Lili Bat Aharon, 'Forgotten life-savers on German TV', *Jerusalem Post*, 10 September 1973.

keep another garment factory open, thereby employing another thousand Jews.

Those who worked for Madritsch and Titsch stressed the extent to which these two men did their best to provide humane and comfortable working conditions. Every person received enough bread each day to enable him to sell part of it and buy other food items. They allowed Jews to make contact with Poles outside the factory. The kitchens fed more than a thousand Jewish workers with special food unobtainable in any other factory or labour camp. One kitchen was kosher and the other was 'half-kosher'. This was made possible through the financial resources of the factory itself.

Madritsch and Titsch bought up to a hundred extra loaves of bread a day, which were passed on by their Jewish workers to other Jews in a nearby labour camp, who needed food desperately but could not leave the confines of their factory.[29]

Madritsch was also helped in his attempts to save Jews by Oswald Bosko, a police sergeant from Vienna. Bosko had managed to get a job as a member of the Cracow ghetto guard while his regiments was in Kolomjya, killing Jews. When the order was given to 'take away' all Jewish children from the Cracow ghetto, Bosko smuggled men, women and children through barbed wire and into the Madritsch factory: 'Small children were anaesthetized and put in rucksacks so that they could not be endangered by crying,' Madritsch later wrote. Many Poles, he added, 'were prepared to hide the children' in their homes, and 'even men from the Wehrmacht, who were heading to Tarnow, took women and children with them', to Madritsch's factory there, where they were given protective employment.[30]

---

[29] 'Summary' dated 25 November 1963, Yad Vashem Righteous Among the Nations Archive, file 21.
[30] Julius Madritsch, *Menschen in Not!* ('People in distress!'), page 16.

Oswald Bosko was held in high regard by the Cracow ghetto inmates. As Yaakov Sternberg, who worked in Madritsch's factories, wrote in his testimony: 'Thanks to his straight character and sense, food was brought into the ghetto through all kinds of tricks. Lots of Jews survived thanks to Bosko by escaping from the ghetto before the deportations. Whenever they felt that something was bound to happen, Bosko made it possible for them to flee to Polish residents.' In the end, Sternberg added, 'The Gestapo found out about his help to the Jews. Bosko fled but was caught and executed. He was one of the World's Righteous.'[31]

Beginning on 25 March 1943, only twelve days after the liquidation of the Cracow ghetto, Madritsch and Titsch transferred as many of their Jewish factory workers as they could by train to Madritsch's factories at Bochnia, twenty miles to the east, and Tarnow, a further thirty miles away. Not only men and women, but also children, were taken to the new workplaces, where they lived in the Bochnia and Tarnow ghettos. Whenever they could, Madritsch and Titsch also smuggled individual workers out of the ghetto and into 'Aryan' Cracow, and even to 'Aryan' Warsaw. They were helped in this task by Dr Adolf Leenhardt, another Viennese then working in Cracow.

At the end of August 1943 the fate of the surviving Jews in the Tarnow ghetto was sealed by Amon Goeth, the sadistic commandant of the Plaszow slave labour camp. Having supervised the liquidation of the nearby Cracow ghetto, Goeth turned his attention to Tarnow, then the largest surviving ghetto in Western Galicia.

In an attempt to stop Madritsch's intervention on behalf of his workers, or his taking the sort of steps he had taken earlier to save Jews from the Cracow ghetto,

---

[31] Letter of 4 July 1963, Yad Vashem Righteous Among the Nations Archive, file 23.

Goeth hit upon a simple stratagem. On September 1 he invited Madritsch and Titsch to visit him at his house in Plaszow. 'They went with mixed feelings,' Madritsch later recalled (casting his account in the third person), 'and indeed both of them were welcomed with the words "to the success of the evacuation of all Jews from the district of Cracow and you have to stay as guests here until tomorrow". Madritsch and Titsch were not even given the possibility to answer because Goeth excused himself and left them with two SS officers to keep them "company". These hours were a real torment since they could not even show or talk about their pain.'

The two men were not released until five o'clock the following morning. Madritsch managed to enter the ghetto, and there saw his co-worker, Dr Leenhardt, as well as Goeth, who assured him that nothing would happen to 'his people'. Dr Leenhardt then separated the Madritsch workers from the mass of deportees being sent to a slave labour camp in Silesia, and, when they reached that camp, which was attached to a synthetic oil factory, put them to work building new workshops for the SS. Madritsch undertook this construction job, so that his workers could be kept alive.

Some of the other workers were smuggled out of the camp in the trucks destined for the depot that was providing building materials. Leaving Tarnow, the trucks made a detour through another of Madritsch's factories, at Piwnicza, from where the Jews were able to flee southward to the Slovak border, fifty miles away, and then make their way into Hungary. (At that time, Hungarian Jews were not yet being deported.) Other Jews were smuggled out when they were brought to Madritsch's factories for the day: some, instead of going back to the camp, stayed at the factory and, at the right moment, set off, also via the factory at Piwnicza, for Slovakia.

On 14 September 1943 Madritsch was authorized to move his factories to Plaszow slave labour camp, where he took on two thousand Jewish prisoners as workers. Again he determined to help them as much as possible, providing them with food, clothing and shoes. This involved his having to pay the SS for the food and other supplies.

When Amon Goeth learned that almost a quarter of those employed by Madritsch were over the maximum age for slave labourers, he tried to reduce Madritsch's workforce accordingly. Madritsch successfully insisted that these older people 'were the most valuable ones'.[32]

Yaakov Sternberg, who worked at the Madritsch factory in Plaszow, recalled the help which Madritsch's manager, Raimund Titsch, gave to the Jewish workers. First there was the distribution of a loaf of bread at least once a week, which helped not only Madritsch's workers but also the ten thousand other Jewish prisoners at Plaszow, because it lowered the price of bread. Second, Titsch passed on information on the Allied military successes from British radio broadcasts – listening to which was a serious offence. Third, he made food supplies available to Jews outside the camp, as well as facilitating the changing and transferring of money. Fourth, as much as he could, he tried to prevent the deportation of those working for Madritsch.[33]

In May 1944 the SS declared that Plaszow was no longer a forced labour camp but a concentration camp. They then began to transfer the prisoners in Plaszow to Auschwitz. As part of the transformation, they announced that doctors were no longer needed in Plaszow. Madritsch acted immediately to save one of

---

[32] Julius Madritsch, *Menschen in Not!* ('People in distress!'), pages 20–22.
[33] Letter of 4 July 1963, Yad Vashem Righteous Among the Nations Archive, file 21.

them, Dr Haim Wachtel, by getting him transferred to his factory as a works doctor. In his affidavit on behalf of Madritsch, Dr Wachtel later wrote: 'The factory employees were given special conditions in the camp. The meals were much better and everyone received an amount of bread, which made it possible for them to sell part of it and buy margarine and sausages instead.' Nearly all the food was smuggled into the factory in Madritsch's trucks, hidden under bundles of cloth. 'Madritsch and Titsch knew about it and only asked them to be careful.'

Dr Wachtel remembered the occasion when 'a Jew called Leopold Lemensorf who was among us at the camp and worked at the storeroom – one day, he addressed himself to Madritsch, asking if he could enable a meeting with his daughter, who resided with Christians outside the camp. Madritsch found her, brought her to the camp and employed her as a clerk.' During the periodic SS selections of Jews to be sent to other camps, Madritsch and Titsch 'checked that nothing bad was to happen to the employees'.[34]

Eventually the SS closed down the factories in the Cracow area, and deported all their Jewish workers to Auschwitz and Gross Rosen. Madritsch had no factories further west, and therefore nowhere to send his Jewish workers in order to continue to protect them himself. But he and Raimund Titsch were on good terms with a fellow German factory owner in Cracow who was about to open a munitions factory at Brunnlitz, in the Sudetenland, a hundred miles to the west. This man, Oskar Schindler, agreed to take sixty of Madritsch's workers with him, together with his own workers.[35] Schindler, perhaps the

---

[34] Letter of 15 March 1963, Yad Vashem Righteous Among the Nations Archive, file 21.
[35] 'Julius Madritsch', List, October 1944. The list names forty men and twenty women. Robin O'Neil, private archive.

best known of all the Righteous, was, like Madritsch, a person for whom the German need for war supplies represented an opportunity to wield considerable protective power for his Jewish workers.

Not far from Plaszow, in the Cracow suburb of Zablocie, was an enamel works which manufactured kitchen utensils. It had belonged to a Jew, but was on the verge of bankruptcy; shortly after the German occupation, Schindler bought it. Like all the German factory owners in the German-occupied Poland, including Madritsch, he was allowed to employ Jewish workers. Like Madritsch, he knew that the Jews in Plaszow camp were being subjected to the sadistic whims of the camp commandant Amon Goeth, and that thousands had been murdered, or died of maltreatment and exhaustion. Schindler, whose relations with the Gestapo were outwardly amicable, even cordial, used his good connections with high German officials in the Armaments Administration to set up a branch of the Plaszow camp inside his own factory compound. There, he brought in nine hundred Jewish workers, including many unfit and unqualified for the labour production needs.[36] In the months ahead, fewer than two hundred were transferred elsewhere.

Among the remarkable features at Schindler's factory was the infirmary. Abraham Zuckerman, who worked for Schindler for a while, later wrote: 'If anyone was sick, Herr Schindler saw to it that he was given good medical care, as much as was possible. In the other camps where I had been interned, this did not exist. If you went to the infirmary, you were a dead person. If you were not well enough to work, the Nazis would kill you. My friend Yekel Fuhrer became very sick at Plaszow. If it were not

---

[36] Mordecai Paldiel, 'Schindler, Oskar (1908–1974)', *Encyclopedia of the Holocaust*, volume 4, pages 1331–2.

for his being in Herr Schindler's Emalia camp, I don't know whether he would have survived.'[37]

When the Gestapo tried to transfer some of Schindler's workers to Plaszow, he was able, by bribery and persuasion, to keep them. In the summer of 1944, seven hundred Jews were under his protection.[38] As the Russian army advanced into Poland, and the German army began pulling back, these men were evacuated, on German orders, to the concentration camp at Gross Rosen, in German Silesia. In an attempt to save them from the cruelties of Gross Rosen, Schindler asked for them to be sent instead to his factory in Brunnlitz, in the Sudetenland. He submitted a list of seven hundred to the SS, noting against each name some impressive but purely fictional skill, describing them as engravers, locksmiths and technicians. This was 'Schindler's List', immortalized in book and film.[39]

The women from Schindler's Cracow factory, three hundred in all, had been evacuated not to Gross Rosen but to Auschwitz. Schindler at once sought their release, going personally to Auschwitz and bribing the Nazi officials there to let him take the three hundred women to his Sudetenland factory. There they were able to rejoin their menfolk. Thus wives, daughters and mothers were saved.

'Every day from 18 October 1944 to 8 May 1945 at midnight,' Moshe Bejski later recalled, 'Schindler helped. "I will not leave you until the last SS man has left the camp,"' he told the Jews. 'If a Jew lost his glasses,' Bejski added, 'Schindler went and bought glasses.'

---

[37] Abraham Zuckerman, *A Voice in the Chorus: Memoirs of a Teenager Saved by Schindler*, pages 80, 82.
[38] Documents concerning Oskar Schindler, Yad Vashem Righteous Among the Nations Archive, file 20.
[39] Including, in addition to Thomas Keneally's novel and Steven Spielberg's film, Abraham Zuckerman's *A Voice in the Chorus: Memoirs of a Teenager Saved by Schindler*, and Dr David Crowe's *Oskar Schindler: A Life*.

Above the camp ration of a hundred grammes of bread, a bowl of so-called soup, and two cups of ersatz coffee each day, he provided extra rations. When a young Jewess became pregnant, an 'offence' punishable by death, Schindler went to the city of Brno, forty miles away, 'and bought the necessary surgical equipment, and the doctor in the camp performed an abortion'.[40]

On 29 January 1945, Schindler was told, by a friend of his who worked with the railways, of a locked goods wagon at Svitavy, the station nearest to his armament factory at Brunnlitz. The wagon was marked 'Property of the SS', and had been travelling on the railways for ten days, covered in ice. Inside were more than a hundred Jews, starving and freezing: Jews from Auschwitz who had been sent from there to the labour camp and quarry at Golleschau; Jews who had once lived in Poland, Czechoslovakia, France, Holland and Hungary.

Schindler's friend told him 'that no factory would take these poor devils'.[41] Schindler himself had no authority to take the wagon. But he asked a railway official to show him the wagon's bill of lading, and while the official was momentarily distracted, wrote on it: 'Final destination, Brunnlitz'. Schindler then pointed out to the official that the wagon was intended for his factory.[42]

After Schindler had ordered the railway authorities to transfer the wagon to his factory siding, his Jewish workers broke open the locks. Sixteen of the Jews had frozen to death. The camp commandant ordered the bodies to be incinerated. At the request of the Jews

---

[40] Judge Moshe Bejski, in conversation with the author, 1985.
[41] Oskar Schindler, 'Report on activities and expenditures for the rescue of Jews during the years 1939 to 1945 . . . ', Buenos Aires, 30 October 1955, Yad Vashem Righteous Among the Nations Archive, file 20.
[42] Information based upon the official bill of lading (Yad Vashem archives, file 0–1/164); provided by Dr J. Kermisz, Director of Archives, Yad Vashem, letter to the author, 19 October 1977.

already in the camp, Schindler stopped this, and made arrangements to allocate a special plot in the local Christian cemetery for their burial. 'They were laid to rest in accordance with Jewish funeral rites,' Moshe Bejski recalled. 'Rabbi Menashe Lewartow, who was with us, recited the Kaddish. Oskar Schindler was concerned even with paying last respects to the dead.'[43]

The rest of the Jews in the wagon were taken to a hall next to the factory, which was emptied in order to house them. 'All, or at least most, of this transport were starving,' Moshe Bejski wrote, 'as they had been on the road for many days in sealed wagons without any food. It was Mrs Schindler who took it upon herself to prepare each day cereal in large pots for these persons, in order not to feed them the coarse food available for the inmates in the general kitchen. To the best of my knowledge, several more of these inmates whose strength was depleted due to physical exhaustion, died soon thereafter; however, most of them regained their strength within a few weeks, and were even assigned light labour duties' – as demanded by the camp commander, an SS Obersturmführer.[44]

Not one of the survivors had weighed more than eighty pounds when Schindler rescued them. Those Jews already in the camp who saw the rehabilitation of the newcomers later stressed the help given to Schindler by his wife Emilie, who provided beds on which they could be nursed back to life. 'She took care of these Golleschau Jews,' Moshe Bejski later recalled. 'She prepared food for them every day.'[45]

---

[43] Eulogy delivered on 28 October 1974, quoted in Moshe Bejski, 'Oskar Schindler and Schindler's List'.

[44] Judge Bejski, letter to Steven Spielberg's office, 27 September 1993, Yad Vashem Righteous Among the Nations Archive, file 20. SS Obersturmführer is the SS equivalent of a first lieutenant in the American army (lieutenant in the British army).

[45] Information provided by Judge Moshe Bejski, 1985.

GERMANS BEYOND GERMANY

Schindler himself recognized his wife's extraordinary efforts on behalf of the Golleschau Jews. 'My wife Emilie,' he later wrote, 'in spite of the cold' – the temperature was 16 degrees below zero – 'went to Mährisch-Ostrau (300 km) to barter vodka against ointments, medicine and vitamins.'[46]

Judge Bejski later told the film-maker Steven Spielberg that the Golleschau incident (which was not included in the film *Schindler's List*) 'represents Schindler's greatest rescue and humanitarian deed, as well as of Mrs Schindler'.[47]

Schindler had one further act of protection to perform. As he himself described it: 'I was trying to get permission for evacuating a Marine depot from the frontier into my factory, with the intention to supply my Jewish protégées at the end of the war with clothing. This permission I obtained with the help of some gifts. Eighteen big truckloads full with best worsted yarn, woollen material, material for underwear and accessories, enabled me to present every single man of my people with two suits, coats, underwear, etc., so that they may be properly equipped when taking the first steps into freedom.'[48]

Between 1943 and 1945, Oskar Schindler had saved more than fifteen hundred Jews by employing them in his factories, and treating them humanely.

In Piotrkow, Mr Christman took boys as young as five into his factory, saving them from deportation. Among

[46] Oskar Schindler, 'Report on activities and expenditures for the rescue of Jews during the years 1939 to 1945 . . .', Buenos Aires, 30 October 1955, Yad Vashem Righteous Among the Nations Archive, file 20.
[47] Judge Moshe Bejski, letter to Steven Spielberg, 7 April 1994, Yad Vashem Righteous Among the Nations Archive, file 20.
[48] Oskar Schindler, 'Report on activities and expenditures for the rescue of Jews during the years 1939 to 1945 . . .', Buenos Aires, 30 October 1955, Yad Vashem Righteous Among the Nations Archive, file 20.

them was five-year-old Israel Lau, a future Chief Rabbi of Israel. Another, Ben Helfgott, then twelve, later reflected: 'Christman employed boys when no one else would. He saved our lives.'[49]

In Lvov, Max Kohl ran a factory making leather coats for the Gestapo. He employed about fifty Jews – including Lili Stern's mother Cecylia – often bribing high-ranking Gestapo officers with leather coats, to spare 'his' Jews. Lili Pohlmann also recalled Irmgard Weith, a secretary in the local Nazi administration, who hid Lili, her mother, and another Jewish couple, for more than a year. Even when a high-ranking Gestapo officer unexpectedly came to stay, she kept them in her tiny larder for two weeks. 'Had he found us he would have shot us all on the spot,' Lili wrote. She and her mother were the only survivors of a family of more than a hundred. 'I do not know "why we two?" – but what I do know is to whom we owe our lives and to whom our gratitude is eternal. They are our "unsung heroes".'[50]

[49] Ben Helfgott, in conversation with the author, 25 June 2000
[50] Lili Pohlmann, recollections, sent to the author, 1995.

286

CHAPTER TEN

Central Europe and the Balkans

A Jewish boy living in Prague, Frantisek Brichta, recalled a family who lived in the same apartment block. The mother and daughter were sent with one of the first transports from Prague to the Lodz ghetto; the father, a former Austro-Hungarian soldier, had died before the war. 'A fellow officer who felt it was his duty to protect them volunteered to go with them. I am reasonably sure that he wasn't Jewish. Such was the sense of duty of that generation.'[1]

Also in Prague under German rule, Henry Wilde had a schoolfriend whose mother, Katerina Rieger, helped him and his mother. 'Her husband was a German Army intelligence officer and must have had grave reservations about the war. He was later killed in action on the western front.' Katerina Rieger warned the family of the imminent Final Solution and made various suggestions for their escape – a very courageous thing to do at that time even for a widow of a senior German army officer'. She also gave her ration coupons to Wilde's mother.[2]

A young Christian woman in Prague, Libuse Fries, put on a yellow star in order to smuggle food and clothes into

---

[1] Frank Bright (Frantisek Brichta), letter to the author, 29 November 2000.
[2] Henry Wilde, letter to the author, 23 June 2001.

the Theresienstadt ghetto for her Jewish friend Egon Sejkorov. She also gave Egon's sister Erna her own Czech identity card, which she altered in order to enable Erna to travel to Vienna. The deception was discovered, and both women were arrested. Libuse was imprisoned; Erna was eventually sent to Theresienstadt, and from there to Auschwitz. Both women survived the war.[3]

Among the Czechs who helped Jews in Prague was Zdenek Urbanek. His apartment was one of the few centres in the city from which food parcels were posted to Theresienstadt. At the time of the deportations he also took in a family of three. 'They were so scared they did not tell me or my wife their names. I only recognized during the long nervous evenings he had been an assistant professor of comparative literature, she a nurse. I was asked to call him Pavel, and her Katia. Shamefully I forgot the name of their little girl. After a stay of three weeks in our rooms they were offered shelter at a farm in southern Bohemia, and left. I am happy to say they survived.'[4] In the town of Eger, where all eighteen hundred Jews were confined in a ghetto, the local bishop, Czapik Gyula, forbade his parish priests to assist in the persecution and deportation. When the Jews were rounded up for transfer to Auschwitz in June 1944, the bishop saved eight women by giving them work in his kitchen.[5]

One of the most remarkable of the Czech non-Jews who risked his life to save Jews was Premysl Pitter, head of the Milis Institute for abandoned children. A Czech Jew, Uta Ginz, later testified that, during the German occupation of Prague, 'for a long time he sent a supply

[3] Gay Block and Malka Drucker, *Rescuers: Portraits of Moral Courage in the Holocaust*, page 208.
[4] Letter of 8 January 1993, Yad Vashem Righteous Among the Nations Archive, file 5474.
[5] 'Eger', in Shmuel Spector (editor in chief), *The Encyclopedia of Jewish Life Before and During the Holocaust*, volume 1, A–J, page 355.

of milk to the Jewish orphanage on Belgium Street. Someone passed this information to the Gestapo and an investigation was opened against Mr Pitter but this did not prevent him from continuing to send milk for the children.' Pitter also managed to obtain food that he sent to Jewish addresses known to him in concentration camps. 'He requested addresses from us and he often brought us boxes of Swiss canned food to send to our relatives and others that we knew in the camps.'

'Mr Pitter preached at the church of the Bohemian Brothers in Smichov – always to several hundred people who were present and he asked them not to forget their Jewish brethren and to remember that the Jews get very little food. He requested their help and urged them to share the little food they had. Once I was secretly present at one of his sermons and I witnessed his brave requests from the congregation, which certainly put him in great danger, as well as his other deeds that he took upon himself to help the Jews. I remember very well that he once said, "Trees don't grow to the sky, and better days are ahead and you will be rewarded from heaven for all you have done for the Jews." Mr Pitter visited Jewish families, and came to us as well, to cheer us up and to support us. He always gave us news reports, which he heard over Allied broadcasts over the radio. He showed us on the map, which he carried in his pocket, the places from which the Germans were retreating.'

Pitter recommended Uta Ginz to a book publishing company where she worked under an assumed name. Before the war ended, she recalled, 'children of mixed marriages were supposed to be sent to concentration camps, but he warned these families not to send their children to these camps and some of these children he hid in the Milis Institution.'[6]

---

[6] Uta Ginz, 'Statement', Yad Vashem Righteous Among the Nations Archive, file 93.

Suse Lotte Tieze, to whose sister, Liese Karpe, Pitter gave the use of his premises after her own school for dancing and gymnastics was closed down, wrote: 'After my sister was deported to Lodz in October 1941, Mr Pitter regularly visited my parents in order to comfort them and give them strength.' During the German occupation he 'visited regularly many Jewish families in Prague, specially with small children, and brought fruit, sweets and milk to them, all things Jews were deprived of at that time.'[7]

When questioned by the Gestapo about the Jewish children he had taken into his school in Prague, Pitter claimed that they were not Jewish, and then smuggled them out of Prague to a children's home in the village of Myto. In all, Pitter and his assistant Olga Fierz saved a hundred Jewish children from deportation; thirty-five of them live today in Israel. On 13 October 1964, Pitter and Olga Fierz were recognized at Yad Vashem as Righteous Among the Nations. Three decades later the Czech Republic issued a stamp in Pitter's honour. Hana Greenfield, originally from the Czech town of Kolin, writes: 'There were so very few that helped and they did not get enough recognition.'[8]

David Korn was just one year old when his family fled from Czechoslovakia, following the German entry into the Sudetenland in October 1938. The family lived in the small Slovak town of Spiska Stara Ves until May 1942, when the Slovak government, which – led by a Roman Catholic clergyman, Father Tiso – was closely allied with Germany, ordered the deportation of Slovak Jews to German-occupied Poland. The Slovak government even paid the Germans 55 marks for each Jew deported.

[7] Suse Lotte Tieze, testimony of 17 April 1963, Yad Vashem Righteous Among the Nations Archive, file 93.
[8] Hana Greenfield, letter to the author, 14 February 2001. The stamp was issued on 1 February 1995.

Only the Lutheran Evangelical Church in Slovakia protested against the deportations, describing them publicly as a violation of justice and humanity.

In the First World War, David Korn's grandfather had fought for the army of Austria-Hungary, of which Slovakia was then part. In 1942 his widow, David's grandmother, was deported to Auschwitz, where she was murdered. David's uncle Martin managed to escape deportation, and found refuge in the forests. David and his elder brother Jacob were taken to a Lutheran Evangelical orphanage in the nearby town of Liptovsky St Mikulas, run by Pastor Vladimir Kuna.

On the way to the orphanage, David remembers passing a public garden at the entrance to which was a sign reading 'Jews and dogs not allowed'. His account continues: 'By entrusting my brother and me to the care of Pastor Kuna our parents felt that even if they would not be able to escape deportation and death, at least we will have a chance to survive. Thanks to the efforts of Pastor Kuna and his dedicated and courageous staff we quickly joined the activities of our Gentile fellow students. We attended school, worked in the garden and went to church on Sunday mornings. In the church I did not listen to the prayers, instead I positioned myself near the organ and listened to the beautiful music.'[9]

Of the seventy children in the orphanage, twenty-six were Jewish children in hiding. 'Our lives in the orphanage were as any other child's life during the war,' David Korn later wrote. 'We went to school, ate each day and played with Gentile children who were fully aware of our religious origins.' The orphanage staff, he recalled, were in constant danger of being exposed to the local Gestapo, as hiding Jews was punishable by death. Indeed in November of 1944 Pastor Kuna was

---

[9] David Korn, letter to the author, 21 August 2001.

taken for interrogation. The charges were "assisting Jews and partisans". They did not succeed in extracting from him any information about us. He was miraculously discharged; another Pastor had less luck and was executed.'[10]

Because of the lack of food and warm winter clothing, David Korn caught pneumonia. 'Medical treatment was not available to Jewish children,' he recalled. 'When a Jewish child had to be taken to hospital Pastor Kuna requested the hospital office not to report the admission and not to send the bills for the treatment to the municipal agency. In a previous case, however, somehow a hospital bill landed in the Town Hall. Pastor Kuna miraculously escaped imprisonment. The only remedy to lower my high fever was cold towels, applied by Sister Maria on an hourly basis twenty-four hours around the clock. Fearing that I may die, Pastor Kuna contacted my Uncle Martin hiding in nearby woods to come and see me before I died. In the middle of the night, risking his life, my uncle sneaked in. Seeing a close relative and the devoted care by Sister Maria gave me the strength to overcome my grave situation.

'The possibility of betrayal was a constant threat. When a strange person entered our room we were told to go to the window and look outside, as if our Jewishness was written in our foreheads.'

At the end of 1944, Liptovsky St Mikulas was liberated by Czechoslovak troops commanded by Pastor Kuna's brother, General Kuna. The pastor, along with those he had sheltered, was saved.

David Korn was eight years old at the time of liberation, his brother fifteen. His parents did not survive the war. Having escaped from Slovakia to Hungary, they

---

[10] Letter of 22 July 1991, Yad Vashem Righteous Among the Nations Archive, file 721.

were almost certainly deported from Hungary to Auschwitz in the early summer of 1944.[11]

Other Slovak pastors also extended a helping hand to Jews in distress. Jana Tanner has written that, in the Slovak capital Bratislava, 'the Lutheran Pastor Jurkovic (I think that was his name), although he knew he was not making converts, baptized many Jewish families in the hope that it would protect them, and at least it meant that the children could attend school. As far as my family was concerned, he baptized my parents first, so that when my brother and I were baptized he could state on our certificates of baptism that our parents were of the Lutheran religion.

'During the last year of the war my parents arranged for me (I was then 14 years old) to be hidden in the Lutheran orphanage in Modra in Slovakia. The head of the orphanage was the local Lutheran Pastor, Julius Derer. To my knowledge there were at least six and probably more Jewish girls there at any one time; one Jewish youth was employed in the garden, and a Jewish woman working as a seamstress. In the same town was a Lutheran boarding school for girls where there were also several Jewish girls. However, these were informed on and arrested. Pastor Derer pleaded with the authorities saying he considered himself in loco parentis, thus putting himself and his family in danger, but to no avail. Those of us hiding in the orphanage remained safe. The nuns who ran the orphanage treated us no differently from the other children, although our presence endangered their safety and must have made a difference to their housekeeping as they could not draw rations for us "illegals".'[12]

---

[11] David Korn, letter to the author, 21 August 2001. Pastor Kuna's story, about which David Korn submitted testimony, is in Yad Vashem Righteous Among the Nations Archive, file 721.
[12] Jana Tanner, letter to the author, 27 July 2001.

Across central Europe, courageous individuals did what they could. In Bratislava, Joseph Jaksy hid three Jewish women in his urology clinic.[13] In the Slovenian city of Maribor, Uros Zun, a policeman, helped save the lives of sixteen Jewish girls who were about to be deported to Germany. A German Jewish woman, Recha Freier, who was in charge of the emigration of young Jews to Palestine, arranged for them to be smuggled across the border from Slovenia into Italy, where they survived the war.[14] In the Croat capital, Zagreb, as a result of intervention by the Papal Nuncio, Giuseppe Marconi – a Benedictine Father from Italy – on behalf of Jewish partners in mixed marriages, a thousand Croat Jews married to Catholics survived the war. Across Croatia, forty thousand Jews were murdered. The Cardinal Archbishop of Zagreb, Aloysius Stepinac, who in 1941 had welcomed Croat independence, subsequently condemned Croat atrocities against both Serbs and Jews, and himself saved a group of Jews in an old age home.[15]

It was only in the year 2000 that a professor in Croatia, Branko Horvatinovic, learned, after the death of the couple he knew as his parents, that he was not their child, and that he was in fact Jewish. His real parents had asked a Croat woman, Bosilijka Barudija-Horvatic, to watch over him while they attended a wedding at the church. 'The vicar locked the church in which my parents took refuge and, betraying them, delivered them to the police.' His mother was beaten and murdered. His

---

[13] United States Holocaust Memorial Museum, Photo Archive, Worksheet 89116.

[14] The girls were taken to Nonantola (see chapter 15).

[15] Information provided by Mordecai Paldiel, Yad Vashem Righteous Among the Nations Department, notes for the author, 25 April 2002; International Catholic–Jewish Historical Commission, 'The Vatican and the Holocaust: A Preliminary Report', October 2000, page 11.

father was believed to have survived. 'He looked for me but, since I have a new name and ended up in Zagreb, he could not find me.'[16]

In the Croat town of Susak, on the Adriatic, a Roman Catholic woman, Mathilda Nitsch, had a small boarding house. 'I could not understand why they killed Jews, who were innocent people,' she later recalled, 'so I helped them escape. I stole false passports from the chief of police himself.' She hid Jews in her boarding house, 'gave them the false passports I had stolen, and then I took them to other friends in Fiume,' where 'most of the Italians – though not the Secret Police – are much better to the Jews than the Nazis. So at night, in Fiume, we put the people on boats, which took them across the Adriatic to other parts of Italy, where we hoped Italian peasants would hide them.' Arrested by the Italian secret police in Fiume, she was interrogated and tortured. They wanted to know who had worked with her in these acts of rescue. 'I wouldn't give out their names. I wouldn't tell anything.'[17]

In the Serb town of Bijeljina, Risto Ristic went early one morning to the home of a Jewish woman, Rahela Altara, waking her up with the news of a pending round-up of Jews. Rahela, her mother, aunt, three brothers and sisters fled to the house of a neighbour, where they were hidden. After making certain Rahela and her family were safely hidden, Risto went to warn other Jewish families. That night he was able to save about twenty Jews from deportation.

Rahela and her family managed to escape to territory that was under the control of Yugoslav partisans. Risto

---

[16] 'Looking For . . .', *Hidden Child* newsletter, volume 9, number 1, Spring 2000.
[17] Ruth Gruber, *Haven: The Unknown Story of 1,000 World War II Refugees*, page 72.

visited them a number of times, bringing with him food, other things they needed – and hope.[18]

In the Bosnian capital, Sarajevo, Mustafa Hardaga, a Muslim, was the owner of a building in which Josef Cavilio, a Jew, had a factory manufacturing steel pipes. Hardaga and his wife, and her father Ahmed Sadik, sheltered Cavilio and his family – defying the order proclaimed on posters on the streets of Sarajevo warning its citizens not to give shelter to Communists and Jews. After six weeks in hiding, Josef Cavilio, with his wife and children, managed to escape over the mountains to Mostar in the Italian zone.[19]

Tova Kabilio-Grinberg was three and a half years old when Susic Zayneba and his family gave shelter to her father in Bosnia: 'They insisted that he stay, but to harbour a Jew was terribly dangerous. The Nazi head-quarters were across the street from them and on the other side was the synagogue, which had been burnt down. My father realized how he was endangering the family so he soon fled and eventually met up with us on the Adriatic coast, where the Italians interred us until we were able to escape and join the partisans.' Susic Zayneba also helped other Jewish families, 'once pulling Jews off a death train, and another time giving a Jew a veil to disguise himself as a woman.'[20]

When the German army occupied Sarajevo in 1941, the city's new commandant asked Dervis Korkut, the Muslim director of the city museum, to head the collab-

---

[18] Information provided by the Jewish Foundation for the Righteous, New York, on its website. In the year 2002, Risto Ristic, then in his seventies, living in the Serbian town of Zemun, was in receipt of financial help from the Foundation.

[19] *Yad Vashem News* (Jerusalem), June 1984, pages 11–12. On 29 January 1984 the State of Israel recognized Mustafa Hardaga and his wife as Righteous Among the Nations.

[20] Batsheva Tsur, 'Sarajevo family finds refuge with Israelis they saved in WWII', *Jerusalem Post*, 13 February 1994.

orationist Muslim community – which was to provide a Bosnian Muslim SS Division. Korkut refused. Not long afterwards, one of the receptionists at the museum announced that a high-ranking German officer wished to view the famous fourteenth-century *Sarajevo Haggadah*, a priceless ancient manuscript describing the Jews' flight from Egypt. Sensing danger, Korkut hid the document under a display.

'Alas,' Korkut told the German colonel, 'I regret to tell you that the book vanished two years ago.'

Less than a year later, a museum caretaker brought a young woman to see Korkut. Her name was Mira Papo, he said, and she had been in with the partisans. 'Now with winter coming, Mira desperately needed sanctuary. Barely out of high school, she had no home, no identity papers or family. And she was Jewish.' Korkut took her to his home. 'She will be staying with us for a while,' he told his wife, Servet. 'We can say she is household help. She will pose as a Muslim and her name will be Amira.'

Servet knew that families harbouring Jews suffered the same penalty as the Jews – death. Nevertheless she agreed. 'So Mira the Jewish girl began living the routine of Muslims. She had lost religion by then – she had become a communist – but she respected the Korkuts' faith. Finally, as the war in Yugoslavia turned against the Nazis, the resistance reorganized. Mira bade her protectors farewell in mid-1943, when she joined the partisans.'[21]

South-east of Yugoslavia, across the Danube, Romania was never occupied by Germany, but its leader, the dictator Marshal Ion Antonescu, headed a regime that was sympathetic to Germany, in terms of both mutual territorial ambitions and ideology. Of the eight hundred thousand Jews in Romania before the war, nearly half

---

[21] Rudolph Chelminski, 'A Debt Repaid', *Reader's Digest*, September 2000.

– three hundred and seventy thousand – were murdered, some by Romanian Fascist troops and Iron Guardists, others by German Nazis after the Romanians had deported them eastward. In the summer of 1941, in an outbreak of vicious Romanian anti-Semitism, five thousand Jews were packed into a goods train in the city of Jassy, and then sent southward, the doors sealed, without water or food. For eight days these Jews were kept locked in the train's cattle trucks, as they were shunted from station to station. At one station, Roman, a local Christian woman, Viorica Agarici, head of the regional Red Cross, had the courage to insist that the German soldiers guarding the sealed train open the doors and allow her to bring the Jews water and food. A thousand were allowed off the train altogether; most of them survived. When the train journey came to an end at Kalarash, more than two thousand of its occupants were dead.

In 1994 a book was published in Romania about Viorica Agarici, entitled *The Gentile who Saved a Thousand Jews*. It is estimated that several hundred Jews survived because of her rescue efforts.[22]

In Czernowitz, then the capital of the Romanian province of Bukovina, the mayor, Dr Traian Popovici, was the only senior Romanian official to protest openly against the establishment of a ghetto in the city. He also spoke out, endangering both his public office and his personal safety, when expulsion of the Czernowitz Jews, and their transportation to Transnistria to be slaughtered, were decreed. He addressed letters and memoranda to his superiors, pointing out the credit due to the Jews of Bukovina, and of Czernowitz in particular, for their massive contribution to the province's cultural,

---

[22] The author of the book was Maius Mircu. Additional details have been provided by Leonid Saharovici, letter to the author, 22 February 2002.

industrial and communal development. He pleaded tire-
lessly with the Romanian authorities to persuade the
Germans to modify the order of expulsion to exempt
doctors, engineers, lawyers and judges, pensioners and
others. On 15 October, a countermand came from
Bucharest allowing about twenty thousand Jews,
members of the learned professions listed by Popovici,
to stay on in Czernowitz: this was their reprieve from
certain death.

The mayor's office was always crowded with Jews
seeking help. He authorized payment to Jewish
pensioners of the full sums that they had been given
before the war. Daringly, he added thousands of names
to official rolls of Jews declared exempt from transportation; as one of those who testified on his behalf
wrote: 'Dr Popovici saved souls wherever possible, in
the full knowledge of the danger to which such actions
exposed him.'[23]

The Papal Nuncio in Romania, Archbishop Andrea
Cassulo, appealed directly to Marshal Antonescu to
limit the deportations planned for the summer of 1942.[24]
His appeal was ignored; hundreds of thousands of
Romanian Jews were deported to Transnistria.

Following the deportations, and the killings that
accompanied them, the Queen Mother of Romania,
Queen Elena, made repeated efforts to have Jews brought
back from the extreme perils of the labour and concentration camps in which they had been incarcerated.
Elena was a Greek princess who had married the
Romanian King Carol, from whom she was divorced in
1930. When she learnt of the plight of the deportees she

[23] Testimony in Yad Vashem Righteous Among the Nations Archive,
file 499, quoted in 'The Mayor of Cernauti', in Arieh L. Bauminger,
The Righteous, pages 74–7.
[24] International Catholic–Jewish Historical Commission, 'The
Vatican and the Holocaust: A Preliminary Report', October 2000,
page 10.

immediately sent them food – as many as a third of
the deportees died of starvation. In October 1942, when
yet another group of Jews were about to be deported, one
of them, the famous Romanian philologist Barbu
Lazareanu, asked a well-known doctor, Victor Gomoiu,
for help. The doctor knew Queen Elena and appealed to
her. It is said that she told her son Mihai, who had
succeeded his father as King, that she would leave the
country if this new deportation took place. Mihai
secured the Jews' release.[25]

Albania, on the Adriatic Sea, had a Jewish population
of about three hundred in the interwar years. In February
1939 a hundred Jewish refugees arrived from Vienna.
King Zog and his government allowed all of them to stay.
When a further ninety-five Jewish families – three
hundred Jews in all – arrived in March 1939, the King
again gave them permission to stay.

In April 1939 the Italians invaded Albania; King Zog
was overthrown and Italian rule imposed. Soon afterwards the Italians asked the Albanian puppet
government to expel all foreign-born Jews – the four
hundred or so refugees. The Albanian administration, in
a brave display of independence, refused. Indeed, as
many as four hundred more refugees arrived from
Yugoslavia and Poland in the following years.

In April 1941, the Italian rulers of Albania took advantage of the German conquest of Yugoslavia to annex
Yugoslavia's Kosovo province, inhabited mostly by
Ethnic Albanians. Four hundred Jews had fled there as
the German troops drove through Yugoslavia.

In Pristina, the capital of the annexed region, the local
authorities complied with German demands and gaoled
sixty Jewish men. But a sympathetic local doctor, Spiro
Lito, persuaded the mayor not to let the Germans take

---

[25] Information provided by Pearl Fichman, letter to the author,
19 March 2001.

the sixty Jews to Poland and certain death. He also convinced the German authorities that the Jewish prisoners had typhus and that it was necessary to send them to hospitals in Albania to avoid an epidemic. The Jews were taken to Berat, given false documents and found refuge around Albania, mostly with friends of Dr Lito in Lushnja, Shijak, Kavaja and Kruja.

When Italy surrendered to the Allies in July 1943, German troops moved into Albania. From that moment the SS, determined to begin deportations from a new region, asked the Albanian government for a list of all the Jews in the country. The government refused, as it had refused to give up the Jews during the Italian occupation, and the Jews were taken into hiding.[26] In the occupied province of Kosovo, however, the Germans paid no heed to the Albanian authorities, seizing all four hundred Jews who had fled there from other regions of Yugoslavia two years earlier, and sending them by rail to Belsen; only a hundred survived the war.

In Albania proper, successful efforts were made by individual Albanians, both Christians and Muslims, to protect Jews from deportation and death. Refik Vesili was sixteen years old when, in November 1943, he sought his parents' permission to hide all four members of the Mandil family, as well as four of their cousins, in the family's home in the mountain village of Kruja. His parents agreed, and all eight Jews were hidden there until liberation eleven months later.[27]

In Vlora, Nuro Hoxha hid seventeen Jews in his house. He also dug a ditch in which all seventeen could hide as precaution against a possible German raid. In the village of Zall-Herr, Hoxha Ferri found places of rescue for eighty Jews and Italian soldiers who had escaped when

---

[26] Harvey Sarner, *Rescue in Albania*, frontispiece.
[27] United States Holocaust Memorial Museum, Photo Archive, Worksheet 24722.

301

Italy surrendered. Nadire Bixhiu took more than eighty Jews into her home and found places of safety for them. One of several refugees from Germany who were saved from deportation, Irene Grunbaum, wrote in her memoirs that one day she would tell the world how the Albanians 'protected a refugee and wouldn't allow her to be harmed even if it meant losing their lives. The gates of your small country remained open, Albania. Your authorities closed both eyes, when necessary, to give poor persecuted people another chance to survive the most horrible of all wars. We thank you.'[28]

The Albanians remained true, despite German pressure, to their ancient tradition of hospitality: the person who seeks your help becomes your honoured guest, to be guarded and protected. The most recent encyclopaedia of the Holocaust recognizes the achievements of the Albanian people with regard to the rescue of Jews, noting that the residents of the town of Berat protected all the hundred or so Jewish refugees who found shelter there, and that others were saved in Elbasan, Valona, Debar and Shkoder, and in Tirana, where many were disguised as Muslims.[29] An 'overwhelming majority of the Albanian population,' wrote Mordecai Paldiel, 'Muslim and Christian, gave refuge to two thousand Jews in their midst, resulting in the almost total rescue of this Jewish community.'[30]

In the spring of 1943 the Germans began the deportation of more than forty-five thousand Jews from northern

---

[28] Irene Grunbaum, *Escape Through the Balkans: The Autobiography of Irene Grunbaum*, page 139.
[29] Shmuel Spector (editor in chief), *The Encyclopedia of Jewish Life Before and During the Holocaust*, volume 1, pages 26–7.
[30] Mordecai Paldiel, quoted in the magazine *Martyrdom and Resistance*, International Society for Yad Vashem, January–February 1999.

Greece, which had been under German occupation for almost two years. The Greeks, for whom the German occupation was a harsh burden, did what they could to try to help Jews avoid deportation. Nikos Kilessopoulis, assistant mayor of the town of Katerini, was at the municipality building late one night with the other town officials when a telegram arrived from the SS instructing them to arrest the local Jews. Without hesitation he hurried to the Jewish houses and urged the Jews to escape to the mountains. Thirty Jews left. The few who could not endure the harsh conditions in the mountain villages returned, and were deported. The majority survived in the mountains.[31]

In reporting that deportations to Poland were continuing, Guelfo Zamboni, an Italian diplomat in Greece added: 'Lately Jewish children have been given out for adoption to Greek citizens and foreigners.'[32]

On 22 September 1943, SS General Jürgen Stroop, who five months earlier had destroyed the Warsaw Ghetto and crushed the Jewish uprising there, was appointed Chief of Police in Greece. His task was to carry out the registration and deportation of all Jews. His first instruction included the order: 'Any Christian who hides a Jew will be shot.'[33]

The will to help could not always be turned into action. In the town of Janina nineteen hundred Jews were seized. Only five managed to escape deportation. An eyewitness recalled: 'The Christian people of the city

---

[31] Information provided by Yitzchak Kerem, historian of the Jews of Greece, 16 July 1989: Yad Vashem Righteous Among the Nations Archive, file 4128.
[32] Telegram from the Italian consul-general, Guelfo Zamboni, to the Italian diplomatic mission in Rome, 3 April 1943, Daniel Carpi, *Italian Diplomatic Documents on the History of the Holocaust in Greece (1941–1943)*, page 151.
[33] Greek National Archives.

were deeply moved on the day of deportation,' but they were powerless.[34]

In Athens, General Stroop summoned Archbishop Damaskinos, and asked for his co-operation in deporting the Jews. Damaskinos left Stroop's office and immediately ordered the Greek Orthodox religious leaders to hide Jews, and not turn them over to the occupiers. The Jews were also helped by many Italian soldiers in the city, who were regarded by the Germans as traitors to the Axis. Thanks to their support and that of the archbishop and his church, most of Athenian Jewry was saved.[35]

Among those who did what they could to shelter Jews in Athens was Princess Alice of Greece, a great-granddaughter of Queen Victoria (and the mother of Prince Philip). She gave refuge in her own house in the centre of the city – opposite that of the archbishop – to Rachel, the widow of Haimaki Cohen, and to Rachel's young daughter and son Michel. Princess Alice also helped Rachel Cohen's other three sons, Jacques, Alfred and Elia, to escape from Greece and join the Allied forces. 'She not only saved the lives of our mother, sister and Michel, but also the lives of all the rest of us,' Alfred Cohen later wrote, 'because we would never have dared to flee Greece while knowing the rest of the family were left behind totally unprotected.'[36]

The Princess's Greek staff said nothing about those who were in hiding: their loyalty was not in doubt. The greatest danger came when, as a matter of courtesy,

---

[34] Dr Rachel Dalven, 'The Holocaust in Janina', in Solomon Gaon and M. Mitchell Serels (editors), *Sephardim and the Holocaust*, New York: Jacob E. Safra Institute of Sephardic Studies, Yeshiva University, 1987, page 62, n. 22.
[35] Benek (Baruch) Sharoni, 'Man's Humanity to Man', *Mizkor*, October 2000.
[36] Richard Kay, 'Revealed: Secret Heroism of Prince Philip's Mother', *Daily Mail*, 26 July 1993.

German officers came to call on the Princess. But her secret was kept, and Rachel and Michel Cohen survived the war, as did Jacques, one of those whom she enabled to escape to Turkey.[37]

Also in Athens, Roger Milliex, director of the French Institute in the city, hid two Jews in the Institute itself.[38] In Salonika, a Greek couple, Lina and Vittoria Citterich, gave a safe haven to Rena Shaki after the deportation of her parents. Later they enrolled her in a Roman Catholic convent school in the city, the Sisters of Saint Joseph. Her parents, taken to Auschwitz, never returned.[39]

At the time of the German occupation of Athens, the Levis family had been warned by a pre-arranged signal from Dimitrios Vlastaris, Director of the Aliens Department of the Greek police, who was a friend of the family.[40] As a result of his warning, wrote Jeff Levis (then Pepos Levis), 'my whole immediate family went into hiding. We remained in hiding during thirteen months, until the liberation of Athens by the Allies in 1944. We were fortunate enough to be in the small minority of Greek Jews who survived. We owe our survival, by and large, to Greek Christian friends of the family who either hid us in their homes or arranged for us to hide in other places.'

The principal rescuer of the Levis family was Michael Mantoudis, the Director of the Department of Culture and Fine Arts in the Greek Ministry of Education. His wife, Adamantia, was Mrs Levis's best friend. Jeff himself was hidden in the study of their home. 'During the

[37] Jacques Cohen was to become a member of the Greek Foreign Ministry, and a consultant (in 1993) to the Greek delegation to NATO.
[38] 'Noulis Vital and Sam Levy . . . in hiding from the Germans in the French Institute Athens', United States Holocaust Memorial Museum, Photo Archive, Worksheet 61661.
[39] 'Rena Shaki in hiding with her rescuers . . .', United States Holocaust Memorial Museum, Photo Archive, Worksheet 45911.
[40] Avi Sharon, 'A Youth in Hiding', The Greek American, 29 November 1997.

thirteen months that we were in hiding,' he writes, 'we had various close escapes from the German army and the SS, as well as from Greek Quisling units.'[41]

At Volos, on the Aegean coast of mainland Greece, Rabbi Pessah, through his contact with the resistance, obtained shelter for more than 752 Jews in the mountain villages east of the town. When the Germans came to deport them, only 130 were found. In nearby Trikkala, 470 Jews found refuge with Greek villagers in the mountains; only fifty were captured. In Patras, the German consul wrote to his superiors that 'after the newspapers announced the obligatory registration of all Jews, they disappeared.'[42]

On the Greek island of Zante, sixty miles from Corfu, the Mayor, Lucas Karrer, and the leading churchman, Archbishop Crysostomos, not only alerted the Jews to danger but sent 195 of them to remote villages in the hills. Unfortunately sixty-two Jews, all of them elderly, who could not make the sudden journey into the rough terrain, were seized by the Gestapo in Zante and taken to the port. 'If the deportation order is carried out,' Crysostomos declared, 'I will join the Jews and share their fate.'[43] But by a remarkable chance, when the boat arrived from Corfu it was already so packed with Jews that it did not stop.[44]

More than forty-eight thousand Jews were living in Bulgaria when war broke out. A further seven and a half thousand came under Bulgarian rule in 1941 in

[41] Jeff M. Levis, letter to the author, 26 December 2001.
[42] Joseph Matsas, *The Participation of the Greek Jews in the National Resistance (1940–1944)*.
[43] Sam Modiano, 'Island's Jews Saved by Greek Archbishop', *Jewish Chronicle*, 3 November 1978.
[44] Yad Vashem Righteous Among the Nations Archive, file 1868. All 1,800 Jews living on Corfu were taken to Auschwitz, where all but 200 were murdered.

Bulgarian-occupied Macedonia, and four thousand more in Bulgarian-occupied Thrace. During 1941 the Bulgarian government sent many Jews to labour camps inside Bulgaria. Although there was no question of deporting them to Germany, conditions in the camps were harsh. When, on 24 May 1942, there was a mass round-up of Jews in Sofia for deportation to the camps, a young Bulgarian, Rubin Dimitrov, hid twenty Jews in his grandmother's bakery, sheltering them until the raid was over. When the Bulgarian police learned what he had done they beat him so severely that his eyesight was permanently damaged.[45]

On 22 February 1943 the Bulgarian government agreed to a German request to deport the Jews from Bulgarian-occupied Thrace and Macedonia: eleven and a half thousand men, women and children, from twenty-three communities, were deported to Treblinka and murdered. On February 28 one of the leading Bulgarian churchmen, Metropolitan Stefan of Sofia, was on a visit to the town of Dupnitza when he saw the arrival of deportation trains, carrying Jews from Thrace to Treblinka. He protested to King Boris.[46] A few days later, the Germans prevailed upon the Bulgarian government to issue a deportation order for all the forty-eight thousand Jews of Bulgaria proper. On March 10 the seizure of Jews began in the city of Plovdiv, home of the Metropolitan Kiril: fifteen hundred Jews were arrested that night. The historian Uriel Tal has described how Kiril 'got up early in the morning when it was still dark and rushed to the rescue of the arrested Jews'.[47]

---

[45] Shmuel Spector, letter of 21 January 1963, Yad Vashem Righteous Among the Nations Archive, file 12.
[46] Michael Bar-Zohar, *Beyond Hitler's Grasp: The Heroic Rescue of Bulgaria's Jews*, pages 168–9.
[47] Uriel Tal (editor), *The Grey Book: A Collection of Protests Against Anti-Semitism and the Persecution of Jews issued by Non-Roman Catholic Churches and Church Leaders During Hitler's Rule*, page 193.

Again, Metropolitan Stefan wrote at once to the King: 'The cries and the tears of the slighted Bulgarian citizens of Jewish origin are a lawful protest against the injustice done to them. It should be heard and complied with by the King of the Bulgarians.'[48] In the northern part of Bulgaria, farmers threatened to lie down on the railway tracks to prevent passage of the deportation trains. Speaking at a session of the Bulgarian Holy Synod three weeks later, Metropolitan Kiril told the church dignitaries about the Jews seized in Plovdiv: 'They were detained in a school and had to be transported to Poland, just like the Jews from the newly liberated territories and Aegean Thrace. In the morning I was told what had happened. I did not know what was going on and thought that maybe the Jews in the whole country had been arrested that night. A special train to transport them was expected to arrive at the station. The citizens' indignation was enormous.'

Kiril went on to stress that the internment that had started as a prelude to deportation 'is extremely unjust and cruel. It should be underlined that the Holy Synod is unanimous in its position on that issue. I hope the head of state will be notified of our attitude. As a last resort, we could express our view from the pulpit and could instruct the parish priests what to do.'

Speaking after Kiril, Metropolitan Stefan noted that it was the duty of the Bulgarian Orthodox Church to 'bring consolation to all who suffer'. Whenever Jews sought shelter within the confines of the Church, 'we cannot turn them back. Their suffering is inhumane.' When someone 'comes to your house and tells you to pack up things in two hours and be ready to leave for some place unknown – this is unheard of and unseen in our country.' As well as Kiril and Stefan, eight other senior

---

[48] Michael Bar-Zohar, *Beyond Hitler's Grasp: The Heroic Rescue of Bulgaria's Jews*, page 194.

churchmen, among them the highly respected Neofit of Vidin, signed a formal protest to the King on behalf of all the Jews of Bulgaria.[49]

The Vice-Speaker of the Bulgarian parliament, Dimiter Peshev, angered by the earlier deportations from Bulgarian-occupied territory, on German orders, organized a petition on March 17, opposing the deportation of the Jews from Bulgaria proper. Fifty members of parliament signed, whereupon the government rescinded its order of a week earlier and released those Jews who had already been taken into custody. Their release came to be known in Bulgaria as a 'miracle of the Jewish people'.[50]

Hitler did not have the means to occupy Bulgaria and organize the deportation using German troops and police. Thus the Jews of Bulgaria survived the war. In a report to Berlin on 7 June 1943, Adolf-Heinz Beckerle, the German Ambassador to Sofia, looking back on the failure of the German deportation plans two and a half months earlier, lamented the fact that the Bulgarian people 'lacked the ideological enlightenment that we have', and that the Bulgarian man in the street 'does not see in the Jews any flaws justifying taking special measures against them'. Fifteen years later, when Beckerle was on trial for wartime crimes, German jurists acting for him noted that 'in Bulgaria there was no anti-Semitism in the conventional sense of the word.'[51]

---

[49] 'Minute no. 4 of the session on April 2/March 20 of the old-style Julian Calendar in the year 1943', Yad Vashem Righteous Among the Nations Archive, file 9375.
[50] Nissan Oren, 'The Bulgarian Exception: a Reassessment of the Salvation of the Jewish Community', *Yad Vashem Studies* (Jerusalem), volume 7, pages 83–106.
[51] Michael Bar-Zohar, *Beyond Hitler's Grasp: The Heroic Rescue of Bulgaria's Jews*, pages 259–60.

CHAPTER ELEVEN

Norway, Finland and Denmark

On the outbreak of war in September 1939 there were seventeen hundred Jews living in Norway, most of them in the capital, Oslo. Two hundred of them were German and Austrian refugees who had found sanctuary in Norway after 1933. In April 1940 the German army invaded Norway; two months later the Norwegian army surrendered, and power passed to the German Reichskommissar, Josef Terboven. At his beck and call, as Minister-President, was a former Norwegian army officer, Vidkun Quisling, the head of the pre-war Norwegian fascist movement. The first anti-Jewish action took place in April 1941, when the synagogue in Trondheim, in northern Norway, was seized and vandalized. Immediately afterwards, the leading churchman in the city, Dean Arne Fjellbu, privately warned the local Norwegian Nazis that if the synagogue action presaged a general persecution of Jews, 'I can assure you that the Church will sound the alarm from one end of the country to the other. Here the Norwegian Church stands one hundred percent united. Such a thing we will not tolerate.'

The head of the Methodist Church in Trondheim, Pastor Einar Anker Nilsen, offered the Trondheim Jews the church attic for their synagogue services. The two Torah scrolls that had not been vandalized were transferred there. So that nobody could see that Jews congregated in the church, comments the historian of Norwegian Jewry during the war, Samuel Abrahamsen, 'members of the congregation were instructed to arrive and leave the church one by one, or not more than two together in order not to attract undue attention. This functioned very well, although it was dangerous.'[1]

The first mass arrest of Jews in Norway took place on 25 October 1942. One of the Norwegian non-Jews active in helping Jews avoid deportation was Sigrid Lund. She has described in her memoirs how she and a friend learnt the news: 'On October 25, the telephone rang. A male voice said: "It will be a large party tonight. But we only want to have the large packages." Then he hung up. At first I was in doubt as to what it meant. Myrtle and I spoke about it for quite some time. Then we said almost simultaneously: "This must be about the Jews. And the large packages must be the men." They were at risk of being arrested immediately.'

The two women agreed that they should warn as many men as possible 'without daring to use the telephone. The problems were how to locate the men and obtain access to their homes. Many Jews were warned but did not believe persecutions could happen in Norway on any large scale. For others the warning came too late. The Norwegian police had already been there.'[2]

Einar Follestad was an active member of the Pentecostal movement. When he learnt on October 26 of the arrest in Oslo of his friend Josef Raskow, a Jewish shop-owner, he immediately went to the house of Raskow's brother, Herman, and his wife Fanny, who was then six months pregnant, in order to help them. From that moment, the whole Follestad family – Einar, his wife Agnes, her parents and her sister – became

---

[1] Samuel Abrahamsen, *Norway's Response to the Holocaust*, page 17.
[2] Quoted in Samuel Abrahamsen, *Norway's Response to the Holocaust*, page 18.

actively involved in preparing the rescue of their two friends. An escape route was worked out whereby the Raskows were able to cross into Sweden. Four Norwegians had taken part in this single act of rescue.'[3]

In Norway, as elsewhere, people under occupation could choose to collaborate with the authorities or help the Jews. Two Norwegian policemen arrested a Jewish schoolboy, Selik Mahler, in his classroom at the Cathedral High School in Trondheim on October 27; but two farmer's sons lent his brother Salomon a pair of skis and accompanied him to the Swedish border two days later.[4]

In February 1942, all seven bishops of the Norwegian Lutheran Church had resigned in protest against the isolation and persecution of the Jews in Norway. Following the deportations of October, all seven sent a letter, dated 10 November 1942, to Norway's Minister-President, Vidkun Quisling – whose name had by then become synonymous with betraying one's own people. In the letter they stated that for the previous ninety-one years the Jews had possessed a legal right to reside and earn a livelihood in Norway. But under Quisling's rule, the bishops noted, the Jews were being deprived of their properties without warning, and being punished as the worst criminals 'wholly and solely because they were Jews'.

The seven bishops reminded Quisling that he had on various occasions emphasized that his party would protect the basic Christian values. One of those values, the bishops pointed out, was being endangered: the

---

[3] Testimony of Fanny Raskow, 3 January 1999, Yad Vashem Righteous Among the Nations Archive, file 8611.
[4] Samuel Abrahamsen, *Norway's Response to the Holocaust*, page 107. The boys' mother and sister Mina were arrested on 25 November 1942, imprisoned, and then deported to Auschwitz, where they were murdered.

Christian commandment to 'love thy neighbour', which they described as 'the most elementary legal right for any human being'. The bishops went on to say that they were motivated in writing by the deepest dictates of conscience; they did not want the Church, by silence, to be 'co-guilty' in 'legalized injustice' against the Jews. 'The Church has God's call and full authority to proclaim God's law and God's Gospel. Therefore, it cannot remain silent when God's commandments are being trampled underfoot. And now it is one of Christianity's basic values which is being violated; the commandment of God which is fundamental to all society . . . Stop the persecution of Jews and stop the race hatred which, through the press, is being spread in our land.'

This protest from the bishops was supported by many respected theologians, nineteen church organizations and six non-state church religious societies. A total of over sixty signatures from all sections of Norway's Protestant communities endorsed the letter. On two consecutive Sundays, November 15 and 22, prayers were said for the Jews from the pulpits, and in most cases the text of the protest letter was read. The pulpits of the Protestant churches had become an effective means of anti-Nazi communication during the occupation.[5]

On November 25 the administrator of the Oslo Jewish Children's Home received a warning about the impending arrest of both the children and their guardians. She immediately contacted members of the Norwegian resistance, among them Ingebjorg Sletten and Tove Tau, who managed to take all the children to a villa in the suburbs. Later they were smuggled across to neutral Sweden, and safety, by a route north of Kongsvinger, to the east of Oslo. Among these children were thirty-seven Czech refugees whom Sigrid Lund had helped bring

---

[5] Samuel Abrahamsen, *Norway's Response to the Holocaust*, pages 141–3.

across Europe from Prague in October 1939.

The first deportation of Jews from Norway to Auschwitz took place on the night of 26–27 November 1942 from Oslo, when 523 Norwegian Jews were taken by ship to Stettin, and then on by train. At the quayside, many Norwegians had gathered, hoping somehow to help the Jews, but stood powerless as men, women and children were forced on board.[6] Many Norwegians, however, took part in smuggling Jews across the border between Norway and Sweden. Among them was Odd Nansen, the son of the polar explorer and friend of refugees, Fridjof Nansen. Odd Nansen was arrested by the Gestapo, incarcerated near Oslo, and deported to Sachsenhausen concentration camp north of Berlin. He survived the war.[7]

Several hospitals in Oslo, and also in Lillehammer, had become centres for hiding Jews until rescue could be arranged. Doctors, nurses and hospital administrators falsified the records of these 'patients' and failed to report the release of Jewish patients to the state police, as ordered by the Quisling government. Even Jews who had been hospitalized with legitimate illnesses were spirited safely across the Swedish border on stretchers. The Carl Fredriksen Transport Organization used two trucks five evenings a week from October 1942 to January 1943, rescuing hundreds of Jews.[8]

On the night of December 3, Henriette Samuel, the wife of the Chief Rabbi of Norway, and her children were among forty Jews taken in two trucks to the Swedish frontier. As the trucks were officially meant to be carrying potatoes, the escapees had to look like tubers covered by tarpaulins, and to keep strictest silence lest the Germans discover them in routine searches along the

---

[6] Per Kristian Sebak, letter to the author, 9 January 2001.

[7] Samuel Abrahamsen, *Norway's Response to the Holocaust*, page 17.

[8] Samuel Abrahamsen, *Norway's Response to the Holocaust*, page 21.

way. The children were given sleeping pills, the adults forbidden to speak. The last stage of the transit, led by the Norwegian resistance, was impassable to trucks and had to be undertaken on foot, with the temperature down to twenty degrees below freezing. The children were woken up and all forty Jews were then smuggled across the border into neutral Sweden.[9]

On December 21 another thirty-four Norwegian Jews crossed into Sweden, assisted by Norwegians who had provided them with food and clothing. A United States Office of Strategic Services report, sent secretly from Sweden eight days later, stated: 'The Norse are infuriated by the anti-Jewish attitude of the Germans and Quislings, and in order to frustrate the maltreatment of Jews risked their own lives. In one case, that of Dr Henri Zellner, 74-year-old escapee, he stated that his wife, who was paralysed, refused to leave Norway, and she was carried across the border bodily by the Norwegians.'[10]

Samuel Abrahamsen comments: 'Sweden was not easily accessible on foot. The border patrolled by German troops was an area of thick forest, mountainous terrain, difficult to cross in snow and frost.'[11] In his book *Justice in Jerusalem*, Gideon Hausner, the chief prosecutor at the Eichmann trial, expressed his and Israel's appreciation of the Norwegian underground's efforts in transporting eight hundred Jews across Norway to safety in Sweden 'under especially perilous circumstances'.[12]

---

[9] Arieh L. Bauminger, *The Righteous*, pages 64–6 (based on Bauminger's conversation with Mrs Samuel on 10 November 1968).
[10] Report of 29 December 1942, Office of Strategic Services, Washington DC, quoted in Samuel Abrahamsen, *Norway's Response to the Holocaust*, page 11.
[11] Samuel Abrahamsen, *Norway's Response to the Holocaust*, page 12.
[12] Gideon Hausner, *Justice in Jerusalem*, page 256. In 1997 Yad Vashem issued a collective certificate of honour to all members of the Norwegian Resistance: Righteous Among the Nations Archive, file 616a.

Perhaps forty Jews managed to survive the war inside Norway, living with false 'Aryan' papers in hospitals, nursing homes and homes for old people. One lived through the war in a small cabin in a remote forest.[13]

In Finland, several hundred local Jews – whose families had lived there since the time Finland had been part of the Tsarist Empire – had been joined after 1933 by a further two thousand refugees from Germany and Austria. In August 1942, at the request of the SS, eight of these refugees were deported to Germany, and then sent on to Auschwitz. All but one of them were murdered. The SS then demanded that all the remaining German- and Austrian-born Jews in Finland be handed over. Protests were immediate, from senior clergymen and from the minority Social Democratic Party. The Finnish Cabinet, which that August had agreed to deport Finland's Jews to Germany during a private visit to Finland of the SS chief, Heinrich Himmler, changed its mind and refused to allow any further deportations. Thus two thousand Jews were saved.[14]

A similar public protest took place in Denmark, where the SS were also cheated of their prize – one they had coveted for more than a year and a half, since the Wannsee Conference of January 1942, when Denmark's seven thousand Jews had been designated for deportation and death in the lists meticulously prepared by Adolf Eichmann. Following the occupation of Denmark in the spring of 1940, the Germans had pursued a policy of co-operation and negotiation with the Danish authorities. As a result, the Jews had

---

[13] Information provided by Leif Arne Mendelsohn, Oslo, letter to the author, 10 May 2000.
[14] Hannu Rautkallio, *Finland and the Holocaust: The Rescue of Finland's Jews.*

been left unmolested. But growing Danish resistance to the German occupation slowly undermined any chance of continued co-operation, and on 28 August 1943 the Germans declared martial law.

The SS hoped to use this opportunity to deport Denmark's Jews. They were forestalled by the actions of a German diplomat, Georg Ferdinand Duckwitz, who had joined the Nazi Party in 1933 and been posted to Denmark before the German conquest by German military intelligence. Following the German conquest of Denmark he had made contact with the leaders of the Danish Social Democrat Party, with whom he was on good terms. Learning of the deportation plans on 11 September 1943, Duckwitz flew to Berlin two days later to try to have the plan set aside, but was told it had already been approved by Hitler. On September 25 he flew to the Swedish capital, Stockholm, saw the Swedish Prime Minister, Per Albin Hansson, and discussed with him the possibility of Denmark's Jews being smuggled across the narrow belt of water to Sweden. Returning to Copenhagen on September 28, Duckwitz passed on details of the imminent deportation, and the possibility of a safe haven in Sweden, to three of the leaders of the Social Democrat Party (one of them a former Prime Minister, the other two future post-war Prime Ministers). The information he gave them was precise: the round-up would take place on the Friday and Saturday night of that very week.[15]

Forewarned of the planned deportation, Danes and Jews took immediate action, as did Per Albin Hansson, who had promised Duckwitz that the Swedish government would help in the effort to rescue Denmark's Jews. As Leni Yahil, the historian of the rescue of Danish

---

[15] Eichmann trial, testimony of 10 May 1961.

Jewry, has written, 'all groups of the Danish population went into action in order to save the Jews. Dozens of protests poured into the offices of the German authorities from Danish economic and social organizations; King Christian X expressed his firm objection to the German plans; the heads of the Danish churches published a strong protest and used their pulpits to urge the Danish people to help the Jews; and the universities closed down for a week, with the students lending a hand in the rescue operation. The operation went on for three weeks, and in its course all 7,200 Jews and some 700 non-Jewish relatives of theirs were taken to Sweden. The costs of the operation were borne partly by the Jews themselves and to a large extent by contributions made by the Danes. The Danish resistance movement grew in size and strength as a result of the successful rescue effort and was able to keep open a fairly reliable escape route to Sweden.' When Rolf Gunther, Adolf Eichmann's deputy, travelled from Berlin to Copenhagen to organize the deportation of the Jews, the Danish police not only refused to co-operate with him but issued an order prohibiting German police from breaking into apartments in order to arrest Jews.[16] The Germans did not have the personnel to enforce martial law.

Among individual Danish rescuers was Dr Jorgen Gersfelt, a physician in Rungsted, who helped more than a thousand Jews across The Sound from the harbour at Snekkersten. One of those whom Dr Gersfelt helped rescue, Sam Besekow (later a well-known Danish theatrical personality), recalled how Gersfelt 'mobilized all available fishing boats and motor launches, even row boats were not spurned. Jorgen discovered the whereabouts of my parents – he was as dear to them as he was

---

[16] Leni Yahil, 'Denmark', in *Encylopedia of the Holocaust*, volume 1, page 364.

to me – picked them up himself and saw them on to the train to Snekkersten. This train was so crammed with Jews that, at a glance, anyone would have guessed what was going on, what with heavy luggage, children crying in the arms of frightened mothers – a Gypsy caravan on rails.' During the first few days, eleven hundred people were saved; 'then the Gestapo got the idea and arrests and captured ships followed. Jorgen was magnificent, turning his private home into a bedlam of refugees on the run, sleeping everywhere on the floors and in the hallways – and he personally escorted my parents to the coast of Sweden, just as he dispensed sedatives to the children to prevent them from making noises that might arouse the suspicions of the Germans.'

Another of those who gave significant help was Fanny Arnskov, a leading figure in the Danish Women's League for Peace and Freedom. She not only helped Jews during the October days, but later took charge of sending parcels to those who had been seized and sent to Theresienstadt. The Danish government insisted on the Danish Jews in Theresienstadt being given special protection, and food parcels. Almost all the other inmates of the camp, mostly German, Austrian and Czech Jews, tens of thousands in all, were starved to death or deported to Auschwitz and murdered.[17]

Starting on the eve of the planned deportation from Denmark and continuing for three weeks, Danish sea captains and fishermen – some members of the resistance, others simply public-spirited – ferried a total of 5,919 Jews, 1,301 part-Jews (designated Jews by the Nazis) and 686 Christians married to Jews to neutral Sweden. Among those saved in this way was Niels Bohr, the atomic scientist, who was to put his expertise at the

---

[17] Leo Goldberger (editor), *The Rescue of the Danish Jews: Moral Courage Under Stress*, pages 130, 163.

disposal of the Americans. Two of those who helped organize the crossings were Ole Helweg and Bent Karlby, architects who left their jobs in order to form the Danish–Swedish Refugee Service, also known as the Ferrying Service. They were helped by a Danish naval lieutenant, Eric Staermose.[18]

The Danes' support for the Jews was remarkable. On one occasion, when a Jew was discovered by a Danish Nazi in the street in Copenhagen, an angry crowd forced him to hand the Jew over to the Danish police, who later helped him to escape.[19] One would-be safe haven failed, however. The eighty Jews hidden in the attic of the church at Gilleleje, awaiting transfer to a boat, were found by the Gestapo and deported to Theresienstadt.[20]

On 1 October 1943, the second day of the Jewish New Year, the Germans found only five hundred Jews remaining in Denmark. All were sent to Theresienstadt; of them, 423 survived the war. On 14 April 1945 the Swedish Red Cross negotiated their release.[21]

The Danish Jews who had been ferried to Sweden survived the war unmolested, as did a further three thousand Jewish refugees who had reached Sweden before the outbreak of war, from Germany, Austria and Czechoslovakia. Reflecting on the rescue of so many Jews in such a short time by a whole nation acting in unison, the historian Leni Yahil concludes: 'The Danish people's resolute refusal to discriminate against their Jewish fellow citizens and to surrender them, or the refugees among them, to the Germans; the rescue

[18] 'Members of the Danish resistance involved in the rescue of Danish Jewry', United States Holocaust Memorial Museum, Photo Archive, Worksheet 62168.
[19] United States Holocaust Memorial Museum, Photo Archive, Worksheet 82643.
[20] 'Church attic in Gilleleje church . . . ', United States Holocaust Memorial Museum, Photo Archive, Worksheet 62165.
[21] Norah Levin, *The Holocaust*, page 706.

launched to transfer the Jews to a safe haven in Sweden; and the unwavering support and protection they gave to the Theresienstadt deportees – all represent an exercise of high moral and political responsibility, outstanding and exceptional for the time in which it took place.'[22]

[22] Leni Yahil, 'Denmark', in *Encylopedia of the Holocaust*, volume 1, page 364.

CHAPTER TWELVE

France

Following the French capitulation in June 1940, France was divided into two zones: the Occupied Zone, which included the Channel and Atlantic coastal areas, and the Free Zone ('Zone Libre'), also known as the Unoccupied Zone, ruled from Vichy by a French collaborationist government headed by Marshal Pétain. His 'Vichy France' was eager to accede to German demands with regard to the isolation, and eventual deportation, of Jews, both foreign-born and French-born.

The first deportation of Jews from Paris to Auschwitz took place on 27 March 1942. Most of those taken were Polish-born Jews living in Paris, within the Occupied Zone. The deportations continued throughout April, May and June. On July 16 and 17 a mass round-up led to the incarceration and eventual deportation of Jews from Paris, elsewhere in the Occupied Zone, and even from the 'Free Zone', under sole control of the Vichy regime. Helping Jews required the combined effort of many people, each individually at risk, but seeking – and finding – strength in joint action. A high point came in late August 1942, as the deportations of foreign-born Jews – and in particular children – intensified. Senior church figures took a leading role: just south of Lyons, Protestant and Catholic clerics, including Cardinal Gerlier, the Archbishop of Lyons, joined forces with Jewish resistance groups to find hiding places for five hundred adults and more than a hundred children from a camp in Vénissieux, from which the local Prefect had ordered their deportation. Not only Cardinal Gerlier, but also his Secretary, Monseigneur Jean-Baptiste Maury (later Bishop of Reims), were honoured for their acts of rescue.[1]

The Night of Vénissieux, as it became known, also saw the birth of the 'Circuit Garel', the first clandestine network in the south of France set up to protect Jewish children. Jews and Christians participated equally in the work of rescue. Elisabeth Maxwell, a French Protestant who has studied this period, writes that it was 'the first episode in France when ecumenism truly worked, and when all forces of goodwill and decency combined' – to thwart a Vichy order to deport six hundred Jews to the transit camp at Drancy, in a suburb of Paris, for deportation to 'the East'.[2]

Georges Garel was a French Jew who owned a small electrical appliance shop in Lyons. 'His name was impeccably French,' noted the historian Yehuda Bauer; 'he had never been connected with any Jewish causes; he was completely unknown; and he had all the human qualities essential for such an undertaking.'[3] Among Christians who helped in this particular effort to deny the Germans their prey during the Night of Vénissieux, and for two years after that, was Abbé André Payot.

'We did what we had to do,' was his comment when one of those he had helped across the border suggested some special honour.[4]

Eighty-three deportations took place by rail from France to Auschwitz and other death camps in the East.

---

[1] Yad Vashem Righteous Among the Nations Archive, file 1769.
[2] Elisabeth Maxwell, 'The Rescue of Jews in France and Belgium During the Holocaust', *The Journal of Holocaust Education*, Summer/Autumn 1998.
[3] Yehuda Bauer, *American Jewry and the Holocaust*, page 246.
[4] Alexander Rotenberg, *Emissaries*, page 257.

When an engine driver, Léon Bronchart, was ordered to drive a train of deportees from the town of Montauban, he refused – the only engine driver known to have done so – and wrote to Marshal Pétain to protest against the order he had been given. No one followed his example. A month later he smuggled a Jew in his locomotive from Brive to Limoges, and then on to the safety of the Italian Zone in south-eastern France. Denounced to the Gestapo, he was deported to the concentration camp at Sachsenhausen, north of Berlin, and later to the slave labour camp at Dora. There, until liberation, he was a source of moral strength to his fellow prisoners.[5]

On 28 August 1942, as the deportations from France continued, the Germans ordered all Catholic priests who sheltered Jews to be arrested.[6] Those taken included a Jesuit who had hidden eighty Jewish children destined for deportation.[7]

In the British House of Commons, on September 8, Winston Churchill referred to the deportations from France during the course of a comprehensive survey of the war situation. The 'brutal persecutions' in which the Germans had indulged, he said, 'in every land into which their armies have broken', had recently been augmented by 'the most bestial, the most squalid and the most senseless of all their offences, namely the mass deportation of Jews from France, with the pitiful horrors attendant upon the calculated and final scattering of families'. Churchill added: 'This tragedy fills me with astonishment as well as with indignation, and it illustrates as nothing else can the utter degradation of the Nazi nature and theme, and the degradation of all who

---

[5] Marianne Picard, 'Il fut le seul . . .', *Memoire Vive*, March 2002.
[6] International Military Tribunal, Nuremberg, document NG-4578 (1) of 28 August 1942.
[7] International Military Tribunal, Nuremberg, document NG-5127 of 2 September 1942.

lend themselves to its unnatural and perverted passions.'[8]

In the days following Churchill's speech, *The Times* continued to report the deportation of Jews from France, and to stress the opposition of the French people to the collaboration of the Vichy government in these measures. On September 9, it published news of the dismissal by the Vichy authorities of General de St-Vincent, the Military Governor of Lyons, who had 'refused to obey Vichy's order' on August 28 'to co-operate in the mass arrests of Jews in the unoccupied zone'. General de St-Vincent had, it appeared, refused to place his troops at the disposal of the authorities in order to round up Jews.

The news item of September 9 also reported the Vichy order of August 28 for the arrest of all Roman Catholic priests who were sheltering Jews in the Unoccupied Zone. 'Some arrests', it added, had already been made. In reply to these arrests, Cardinal Gerlier issued a 'defiant refusal' to surrender those Jewish children whose parents had already been deported, and who were being 'fed and sheltered' in Roman Catholic homes.[9] Two days later, a news item in *The Times* on September 11 reported 'popular indignation' in Lyons following the arrest and imprisonment of eight Jesuit priests who had refused to surrender 'several hundred' children for deportation; children whom they had kept hidden 'in buildings belonging to the religious order'. *The Times* also reported that the Papal Secretary of State, Cardinal Maglione, had informed the French Ambassador to the Vatican 'that the conduct of the Vichy government towards Jews and Foreign refugees was a gross infrac-tion' of the Vichy government's own principles, and was

---

[8] Winston Churchill, speech of 8 September 1942, *Hansard* (Parliamentary Debates, Commons), 8 September 1942.
[9] *The Times*, 9 September 1942.

'irreconcilable with the religious feelings which Marshal Pétain had so often invoked in his speeches'.[10]

The rescue efforts made by individuals in France were remarkable. Near Paris, Germaine Le Henaff hid a number of Jewish children in the Château de la Guette children's home, of which she was the director, giving them false, non-Jewish-sounding names, and enabling them to blend in with the 120 Christian children already in the home. She was the only person in the home who knew that the newcomers were Jewish.[11]

A French farmer, Albert Masse, held out the hand of rescue to nine-year-old Karl Haussmann, who later recalled: 'The French family who took me into their home in the Ardèche region of France were poor farmers who lived on a parcel of rocky land. They had at that time one cow that was used for ploughing and to pull the wagon. Also some goats and chickens and rabbits that were raised for food. These were the people who hid me from the German occupiers and saved me from the fate that befell my family.'

Karl Haussmann was born in a small German town near Mannheim, and deported with his family to Gurs in October 1940. His parents and older brother had been deported from France to Auschwitz on 11 September 1942, and gassed. He had been fortunate to be taken out of Gurs and sent to a children's home, then to the farmer. 'I am the lone survivor of my family and probably the only survivor from the Jewish community from the town where I was born.'[12]

When a Jewish family came to the farm of Pierre and

[10] The Times, 11 September 1942.
[11] 'View of the Château de la Guette children's home', Holocaust Memorial Museum, Photo Archive, Worksheet 04962.
[12] Carl Hausman (Karl Haussmann), letter to the author, 20 December 2001.

Louise Hebras, at Romanet, near Limoges, and sought shelter, mother, son and two young daughters were found a hiding place on the farm itself, while the father, to reduce the risk of detection, was taken to the village and hidden in the attic under the farmhouse roof. The villagers kept the secret.[13]

In the tiny village of La Caillaudière, in the Indre region, Juliette and Gaston Patoux saved a Jewish girl, Felice Zimmern, from deportation. 'I was in a terrible condition when I arrived. I was very small, thin, and had sores all over my body, which, no doubt, was a result of malnutrition.' Born in Germany on 18 October 1939, she too was taken with her parents and sister Beate to Gurs in October 1940. Her parents were then deported to Auschwitz and killed. Juliette and Gaston Patoux were farmers – a typical French peasant couple, and yet not typical. 'They took care and protected me as if I was their own child. I lived with them for approximately three-and-a-half years, until I was five and a half. Through their loving care, I learned to think of them as my mother and father.'[14]

Felice recalled: 'When I asked Madame Patoux years later how I came to be placed in their home she answered: "Oh, I don't know, someone came out of the forest and asked me if I wanted to take in a little Jewish girl; and I answered yes." From the beginning, they treated me wonderfully. They made me feel as if I was their child. I slept in the same room with them as they diligently nursed me back to health.'

Felice Zimmern added: 'M. Patoux put together a doll's carriage, which was customized for me; it had very small wheels to match the carriage to my height. My charming little carriage had a bonnet on top to protect it

---

[13] Gilbert Blum (the boy who was saved), 'De vrais amis', *Memoire Vive*, March 2002.
[14] Felice Zimmern Stokes (Felice Zimmern), letter to the author, 17 December 2001.

against the weather and a little skirt around the sides. They also provided me with a lovely little doll, which I cherished and called my "ya-ya". On my fifth birthday they made me feel very special. They stood me up on a chair in front of them and gave me a present of a bouquet of flowers as the family clapped and cheered.'[15]

Rescue had constant dangers: 'Because of me, the Patoux were always afraid of being caught by the Nazis and were always ready to run. To prepare for that eventuality, Madame Patoux always slept in her slip.' But the villagers connived in the life-saving deception: 'The people of the village treated me as the Patoux child. I went to church with the Patoux. No one gave me away, and I did not know I was Jewish.'

At the end of the war, Felice Zimmern, then just five and a half years old, was reunited with her sister, who had been in hiding elsewhere. A Jewish organization placed them in Jewish orphanages in France, to get them back into Jewish surroundings. 'The separation from the Patoux was very painful for me as they were my "Mémé" and "Pépé".'[16]

In Poitiers, an employee in the town hall gave the Hoffnung family – refugees from Metz, near the German border – false identity cards, deliberately leaving out the Jewish stamp. Later, a non-Jewish classmate of the young Martha Hoffnung warned the family of an imminent round-up, and insisted that the Hoffnungs go to her parents' home for safety. Then the family was taken to the border between German-occupied and Vichy France. 'Other townsfolk watched Martha and her mother push

[15] Felice Zimmern Stokes (Felice Zimmern), letter to the author, 31 January 2001.
[16] Felice Zimmern Stokes (Felice Zimmern), letter to the author, 17 December 2001. In 1970 Felice Zimmern Stokes submitted the details of the life-saving deeds of Gaston and Juliette Patoux to Yad Vashem. As a consequence, they were recognized as Righteous Among the Nations.

Martha's grandmother across the border on a bicycle without denouncing them.'[17]

In Solignac, a French Jewish girl, Inès Dreyfus (later Vromen), and her mother were helped by several non-Jews in turn. Inès later recalled the days after her father's arrest on 1 September 1943, when, at the railway station in Roanne, 'my mother, in desperation, bought train tickets for Limoges. We spent a terrible night on the train, switched train in Limoges, arrived at Solignac early morning. Mme Schenherr was going to early Mass. I met her on the road, and she simply said: "Your parents have been arrested, haven't they? You were right to come to me." (My mother and grandmother, exhausted, were trudging behind with the suitcases.) The Schenherrs were living in two rooms – the husband always in bed – on the second floor, no running water, you had to get it from the pump. After a couple of days we found a room to sleep, in the village of Solignac, but spent the day at their place, cooking and washing together, and trying to get enough food for eight people, running to remote farms, gathering wood, apples, chestnuts.'

Inès Vromen recalled that a priest from Alsace, Robert Bengel, 'had our papers forged so that our name would be Diener instead of Dreyfus'. He then registered Inès with a Catholic correspondence course so that she could continue with her studies: 'I was fourteen at the time. He always kept in touch with us, even when we had left Solignac, which we did between Christmas 1943 and New Year: we had to leave, we were endangering the Schenherrs.'

Inès Vromen and her mother moved to the village of Panazol in the Haute-Vienne. A farmer, Monsieur Faye, who was also the mayor of the village, rented them an

---

[17] Narrated in *Past Forward* (the Newsletter of the Shoah Foundation), Spring/Summer 2001.

abandoned farm on his estate, 'and issued for us new "clean" identity papers (much safer than ours)'.[18]

In Montauban, near Toulouse, as the mass deportation of Jews from throughout France was being carried out, a French Catholic woman, Marie-Rose Gineste, rode her bicycle many miles, carrying with her a clandestine pastoral letter from the Bishop of Montauban, Pierre-Marie Théas, denouncing 'the uprooting of men and women, treated as wild animals', and calling on Catholics to protect Jews. She began her ride on Friday, 28 August 1942, and, cycling for two days from dawn to dusk, ensured that the letter could be read out in more than forty parishes during the Sunday morning service.

The French resistance ensured that the text reached London, from where it was relayed back to France over the BBC's *Ici Londres* daily broadcasts, which were listened to on tens of thousands of hidden radios. The impact was immediate. 'Historians now see it as marking a turning point in the Catholic Church's earlier passive attitude towards the Vichy regime,' Mordecai Paldiel told the journalist Philip Jacobson, who went on to recount how, as the deportation of Jews continued, Marie-Rose Gineste accepted the mission of finding safe houses for Jewish fugitives in the Montauban diocese. Dr Paldiel noted that she was also responsible for pilfering food ration cards from the authorities (sometimes aided by sympathetic officials for use by underground Jewish organizations).

'Like all those who resisted the Germans,' notes Philip Jacobson, who had just interviewed her for the *Sunday Telegraph*, 'Mrs Gineste was in constant danger of being denounced by an informer and interrogated under torture, but her profound faith never wavered.'[19]

---

[18] Inès Vromen, letter to the author, 3 September 2001.
[19] Philip Jacobson, 'Rusty bike shipped to Israel to honour wartime heroine', *Sunday Telegraph*, 25 March 2001.

At the Convent of Aubazine, near Brive in the Corrèze region, the Mother Superior, Sister Marie-Gonzague Bredoux, provided Sabbath candles – taken from the convent chapel – and set aside special Passover dishes, for the twelve Jewish girls between the ages of six and twelve, and one pregnant Jewish woman, under her care.[20]

In Paris itself, Mother Maria – Elizabeth Skobtsova, a Russian Orthodox nun – made use of her small convent to hide Jews who were on their way to more secure hiding places. This was only a small portion of her multifaceted rescue operation. Working closely with a fellow Russian émigré, the Russian Orthodox priest Father Klepinin, she collected food and clothing for Jews who were interned in the housing complex at Drancy, in a Paris suburb, where Jews were brought from all over France before deportation. She connived with the French garbage collectors to smuggle several children out of Drancy in garbage bins. She also supervised the production of false documents, and established contact with other groups to facilitate rescue. Father Klepinin issued false baptism certificates for those seeking new identities as non-Jews.

On 8 February 1943 Mother Maria and Father Klepinin were arrested by the Gestapo. Maria readily admitted to the charge of helping Jews elude the round-ups. She was sent to Ravensbrück concentration camp, where she died from exhaustion on 31 March 1945, a few days before the camp was liberated. Father Klepinin had perished earlier, in February 1944, in the Dora-Mittelbau slave labour camp.[21]

Like Mother Maria, Sofka Skipwith was also an émigré

---

[20] Yad Vashem Righteous Among the Nations Archive, file 5380.
[21] Mordecai Paldiel, 'Skobtsova, Elizaveta (Mother Maria; 1891–1945)', *Encyclopedia of the Holocaust*, volume 4, pages 1362–3.

from Russia. Married to an Englishman, she had lived between the wars in both England and France. During the war she was interned as an enemy civilian in the spa town of Vittel, in one of the resort hotels. Some 250 Polish Jews, brought from Warsaw early in 1943, were also interned there, in much harsher conditions, although they held passports and visas for various Latin American countries: among them were the Jewish poet Yitzhak Katzenelson and his son Zwi.

On one occasion Sofka Skipwith was asked to help save a baby boy whose parents had just been taken away in the first deportation of Vittel Jews, on 18 April 1944. 'We had been told', recalled Madeleine White, her friend and fellow internee, 'where we should take the baby and we cut the barbed wire the day before as usual. It was a place away from the hotels, quiet, among bushes and trees and we knew the time schedule of the sentinels. Sofka had fetched the baby at the last minute from the hospital asleep in a cardboard box, which had contained food sent by the Red Cross. I never knew whether it was a boy or a girl. At the appointed place we saw a woman hiding behind a tree; she gave a signal. I crawled under the wires (because I was smaller than Sofka) and over the space in between the three rows of barbed wire, pushing the box in front of me. I pushed it towards the waiting hands. After the war Sofka received news through the Red Cross that the baby had safely arrived and was being brought up in a kibbutz.'

Madeleine White recalled other cases where Sofka Skipwith was active in rescue work. One concerned a child of ten who was 'smuggled out and hidden in Paris until the liberation; her upkeep was paid for; her father managed to jump from the train in which he was being taken with the others to Drancy and later joined her.' Another was a baby only weeks old, 'taken out through the barbed wire and entrusted to a person outside. Later the child reached Israel. (For these exits through barbed wire Sofka had a pair of wire cutters hidden in her mattress).' Then there was Felix Eisenstadt, who was officially sent by the Germans to the American hospital in Paris to be operated on. 'With the help of a French doctor we knew in Paris, he was hidden after the operation and awaited the liberation in hiding.'[22]

Another of those whom Sofka Skipwith helped to survive was a Polish Jew, Hillel Seidman, who, Madeleine White recalled, 'never slept two nights running in the same room between the second deportation and the liberation of Vittel camp in September 1944. Sofka, myself and others did what we could to save him and his friends.'[23]

Sofka Skipwith also managed to smuggle out of Vittel an appeal for help to the British Foreign Office, with a list of Jewish internees. She wrote the list in tiny handwriting on flimsy cigarette paper, so that if the courier were caught he could swallow the list. As a result of her efforts the British government made ninety Palestine certificates available for Jews at Vittel, and asked the Swiss government to forward them. One of the Jews on her list was Katzenelson. Unfortunately, when the certificates arrived on 15 July 1944, the Jews had gone. The second and final deportation had been on May 16, back to Poland, and to Auschwitz.[24]

In a letter to Yad Vashem when her case for an award was being considered (it was finally granted, as a result of the persistence of a British Jewish scholar, Dr Oppenheim, after her death), Sofka Skipwith wrote: 'Sadly my efforts in the internment camp of Vittel did

[22] Madeleine Steinberg (*née* White), letter to Yad Vashem, 14 June 1998, Yad Vashem Righteous Among the Nations Archive, file 4349.
[23] Madeleine Steinberg (*née* White), letter to Yad Vashem, notarized on 13 December 1985, Yad Vashem Righteous Among the Nations Archive, file 4349.
[24] Dr A. N. Oppenheim, letter to Yad Vashem, 13 February 1998, Yad Vashem Righteous Among the Nations Archive, file 4349.

not succeed in saving Jewish lives, but I feel proud to be among those who attempted.'[25]

A number of French villages acted collectively to take in Jewish children and to shield them from deportation. The story of these villages is a high point in the narrative of rescue. Following the round-up of Jews in Paris on 16 July 1942, more than forty children were given sanctuary in the village of Chavagnes-en-Paillers, in the northern Vendée. One of them, Odette Meyers, later recalled: 'Although we kept our Eastern European Jewish names, we were passed off as children of Catholic prisoners of war, sent to the nuns' school. We learned to say our prayers and not to pay attention to the many German soldiers in the priests' seminary across the street. We were treated well and we had as normal a Catholic childhood as children separated from their Jewish parents could have. After the war, we were fetched back to Paris.' She added: 'It did not occur to us that we had not been the only Jewish children to be saved by local families.'[26]

The most remarkable of all the village rescues took place in and around Le Chambon-sur-Lignon, in south central France. Le Chambon is part of a group of villages, mostly Protestant, on the Vivarais–Lignon plateau. Most of the inhabitants were the descendants of Huguenots who had known long periods of persecution and massacre at the hands of the King of France and their compatriots; but devout Roman Catholics, and those whose Christian belief was minimal, shared with the Protestant majority in the acts of rescue. The three thou-

---

[25] Sofka Skipwith, letter of 14 October 1985, Yad Vashem Righteous Among the Nations Archive, file 4349. Sofka Skipwith published an account of her time in Vittel in her book *Sofka* (London, Hart Davis, 1968).
[26] Odette Meyers, 'A Long-Delayed Public Thank You to Chavagnes-en-Paillers', *Hidden Child* newsletter, volume 9, no. 1, Spring 2000.

sand inhabitants of Le Chambon, like those of the surrounding villages, were asked by two Protestant pastors, André Trocmé and Edouard Théis, to offer shelter to Jews even at the risk of their own lives. In those villages, whose own population together did not exceed five thousand, as many as three and a half thousand Jews were given sanctuary at different times, and survived the war.

An active and outspoken pacifist, Pastor Trocmé had been posted in 1934 to the remote region by his church, the Eglise Reformée de France, which hoped thereby to restrict his influence. A year before the outbreak of war he had founded the first secondary school on the plateau, based on principles of tolerance and internationalism, and had brought in Théis to be the headmaster.

Trocmé's wife Magda, of mixed Italian and Russian parentage, whom he had met while studying theology in New York in 1926, gave immediate help to any refugees who came to their door, and then put them in contact with those in the village, and in other villages on the plateau, who could give them shelter.[27]

Several homes were set up on the Vivarais–Lignon plateau under the auspices of different Christian relief organizations for Jewish children, including four institutions run by Secours Suisse aux Enfants (Swiss Children's Aid). Other children were placed in private homes and boarding houses in the villages, and on farms in the surrounding countryside.

Built in 1938 to accommodate fourteen local children, the College of Cévenol saw its student body expanding hugely with the arrival of 220 Jewish refugees fleeing from the internment camps to the south. The children, like their parents and other adults, were welcomed without hesitation. They were housed on farms or in

---

[27] Quoted in Carol Rittner and Sondra Myers (editors), *The Courage to Care: Rescuers of Jews During the Holocaust*, page 102.

hotels and were hidden in the countryside whenever the Germans came through. 'As soon as the soldiers left, we would go into the forest and sing a song,' recalled August Bohny, who ran a boarding house for Jewish students. 'When they heard that song, the Jews knew it was safe to come home.' Whenever possible, the refugees were sent by means of a well-organized underground network to safety in Switzerland or Spain.

When the Vichy police began rounding up Jews in August 1942, the hitherto legal assistance to refugees provided by relief workers and local residents turned swiftly into undercover resistance activity. Refugees were hidden during round-ups. False identification papers, birth certificates and ration cards were produced. Groups of Jews were moved secretly at night to the Swiss border and smuggled across.[28]

On one occasion, when the Vichy Minister of Youth came to the Cévenol school to urge the students to participate in Vichy's Hitler-Youth-style student organization, the students refused, informing the Minister: 'We feel obliged to tell you that there are among us a certain number of Jews. But we make no distinction between Jews and non-Jews. It is contrary to the Gospel teaching. If our comrades, whose only fault is to be born in another religion, received the orders to let themselves be deported, or even examined, they would disobey the orders received, and we would try to hide them as best we could.'[29]

Hiding them was exactly what was done. 'The Gestapo came looking for Jews,' one villager later told the American writer Robert Daley. 'They came with three buses, and the buses left empty. We told them there were

---

[28] Alexandra Tuttle, 'Marking a Blessed Conspiracy', *Time* magazine, 5 November 1990.
[28] Alexandra Tuttle, 'Marking a Blessed Conspiracy', *Time* magazine, 5 November 1990.

no Jews here.' The woman added: 'Everyone participated. Everyone agreed they had a moral obligation to
help. The Protestant pastors, about a dozen of them,
played a very important role. They had a network. They
used a code. They'd call each other up and say, "I'm
sending you three Old Testaments." '[30]

In January 1943, Trocmé, Théis, and the director of the
Cévenol school, Roger Darcissac, were arrested by the
Vichy authorities and interned at the St Paul d'Eyjeaux
camp for political prisoners near Limoges. They were
released four weeks later.[31]

Mordecai Paldiel commented: 'Almost all the people
of the plateau were involved in saving these Jews, and
no one said a word.'[32] Juliette Usach, a physician, was
in charge of La Guespy children's home in Le Chambon-
sur-Lignon. Another medical doctor, Dr Roger
Leforestier, and his wife Danielle, gave essential
medical care to those in hiding who fell sick. Dr
Leforestier had spent a year helping Albert Schweitzer
at his leper hospital in central Africa. On 4 August 1944,
only a few days before the liberation of the plateau,
Leforestier was arrested in Le Puy and jailed at the Fort
Montluc prison in Lyons. Three weeks later, on August
20, he was among the group of Frenchmen killed at St
Genis-Laval on orders from Klaus Barbie.[33]

Henri and Emma Héritier gave shelter in their small
farm on the plateau to a succession of Jewish children
over four years. One of those children, Pierre Sauvage,

---

[30] Quoted in Alan Riding, 'Jews Found Haven in French Town', *New
York Times*, 31 October 1999. Robert Daley had just published a
novel, *The Innocents Within*, which included a similar scene.

[31] 'Portrait of Pastor André Trocmé', Holocaust Memorial Museum,
Photo Archive, Worksheet 22341.

[32] Quoted in Alexandra Tuttle, 'Marking a Blessed Conspiracy', *Time*
magazine, 5 November 1990.

[33] 'Studio Portrait of Dr Roger and Danielle Leforestier', caption,
Holocaust Memorial Museum, Photo Archive, Worksheet 40339.

later made a film, *Weapons of the Spirit*, about the plateau, and about his own rescuers. The Héritiers were among those taking the greatest risks, Pierre Sauvage noted, 'for they knew full well that among the Jews they had taken in was a teenager who had become the village forger, spending his nights making false identity papers for all who needed them. Towards the end of the war, German soldiers were stationed smack in the middle of the village. Monsieur Héritier is a beekeeper. His response to the increased threat: he hid the forger's paraphernalia in his beehives.'[34]

Among those running Le Coteau Fleuri refugee home near Le Chambon was Pastor Marc Donadille, who had earlier helped get Jews out of the Vichy internment camps and sent them to the plateau. On one occasion he foiled an attempt by the French Vichy police to round up the Jews in the home for deportation; and at his own home in the village of Saint Privat-de-Vallongue, in Lozère, Pastor Donadille and his wife gave shelter to a young Jewish girl, Eva Ahlfeld.[35]

Hermine Orsi, a Frenchwoman living in Marseilles, hid Jews in her own home, including a Polish-Jewish journalist, Benjamin Feingold. She also provided Jews with false papers, and arranged for a number of Jewish children to be taken to Le Chambon.[36]

In La Garneyre, a hamlet near Le Chambon, seven-year-old Hélène Federman and her twelve-year-old brother Henri were given shelter from the storm. They had been born in France, their parents in Poland. 'Madame Mendon took me in', she later wrote. 'The Verillacs took care of my brother. There were two other

[34] Pierre Sauvage, ' "Weapons of the Spirit": A Journey Home', *The Hollywood Reporter*, 17 March 1987.
[35] 'Eva Ahlfeld, a Jewish child in hiding, poses with the two children of Pastor Marc Donadille', Holocaust Memorial Museum, Photo Archive, Worksheet 01110.
[36] Yad Vashem Righteous Among the Nations Archive, file 3211.

farms in the hamlet. The Picots took in two of my cousins, Annette and Micheline Federman.' Another Jewish child was taken into the third farm.[37]

Hélène Federman (later Resnick), who emigrated to the United States after the war, later reflected about her rescuer: 'I'm not sure how much she knew of the danger she was risking by keeping me. Her pastor had asked for help in shielding children from the Germans and she, along with many others, opened her home and her heart to us. The Germans never got there. They did get to the nearest town and arrested many people, but as isolated as we were, with no roads that could accommodate cars or trucks, we managed to stay safe until the end of the war.'

The young girl's parents survived the war in hiding in a cellar in Avignon. Soon after the end of the conflict, Hélène recalled, 'they came to get us. My mother was horrified at the thought that we were saying Christian prayers and quickly enrolled my brother and me in a Jewish organization. She was, of course, grateful that we had made it alive.'[38]

Near the hamlet of Chavagniac was a château that had belonged to the Marquis de Lafayette, a hero of both the American and French revolutions. Gisele Feldman was among the Jewish children given shelter there. 'I will always remember these tranquil landscapes,' she later wrote, and she added: 'Because of what the "Righteous Gentiles" did for me, because of their ultimate sacrifice, besides mere gratitude, I also feel the need to be the best human being that I can be. I want to be deserving of their sacrifice. I feel that I have to give, to share, to teach love

---

[37] Helen Resnick (Hélène Federman), letter to the author, 24 October 2001.
[38] Helen Resnick, 'I was almost eight in 1942, when we arrived at La Garneyre . . . ', manuscript, enclosed in letter to the author, 30 August 2001.

339

and tolerance. My mission in life is to help make the world a better place in which to live, even in a minute way.'

On a visit to the château a few years ago, Gisele Feldman found out 'that I had been hiding a few hours away from Le Chambon-sur-Lignon. I found this very exciting, and not surprising. My "Righteous Gentiles", though Catholics, showed the same high moral values and character as the people of that little Protestant village, just like so many people of Auvergne.'[39]

German-born Irene Freund was ten years old when she and her family were sent to Gurs. Two years later she was given shelter in a Catholic convent, where thirteen other Jewish girls were in hiding. 'I became Irene Fanchet and studied under Sister Theresa. One day, the SS came to our convent looking for hidden German-Jewish children. One of our girls, who was fluent in French, did the talking for us. It worked. The Germans left and we were safe.'[40]

During 1942 another German-born Jewish girl, Rita Goldstein, then aged fourteen, was placed in hiding under the name of Renée Gordon at a Catholic orphanage in Millau. She was there for only a few months before being sent to a boarding school in Mende (Lozère) in the south of France. In June 1944 Rita developed scarlet fever and was sent to live with Sister Jeanne Françoise in Rhule, near Villefranche-de-Rouergue. She survived the war, as did her brother and mother, who were in a German labour camp; her father was deported to Auschwitz, where he was killed.[41]

---

[39] Gisele Feldman, letters to the author, 12 March and 2 May 2001.
[40] 'Name: Irene Freund', Holocaust Memorial Museum, Photo Archive, Worksheet ID2191.
[41] 'Rita Goldstein poses with a group of girls at a Catholic orphanage in Millau, where she was hidden during the war', Holocaust Memorial Museum, Photo Archive, Worksheet 99369. Rita Goldstein later married Roger Waksman, who had been given shelter for more than a year by the Lefèvre family, near Grenoble.

Like so many of those saved by non-Jews, Nadine Fain owed her survival to several rescuers. She was first hidden, at the age of eleven, with her two elder sisters, in the Sainte Marguerite Catholic boarding school in Clermont-Ferrand. They were accepted there with the permission of the Bishop of Clermont-Ferrand, Gabriel Piguet. Their mother survived the war, but their father was deported from Paris to Sobibor, where he was murdered.[42]

Monsignor Piguet was arrested in his cathedral by German police on 28 May 1944, for helping a priest wanted by the Gestapo, and was held in prison at Clermont-Ferrand until he was deported to Dachau at the beginning of September. When he returned after the war he had lost thirty-five kilogrammes. Broken in body, though not in spirit, he died seven years later, at the age of sixty-five.[43]

Nadine Fain's rescuers included Marthe Guillaume, a pharmacist in La Tour d'Auvergne, who took the Fain sisters in during the Easter holiday of 1943; Mother Marie-Angélique Murt, the Mother Superior of the Sisters of St Joseph, who supervised the hiding of both Jewish and resisters' children; and Mademoiselle La Farge, directrice of the boarding school. Also honoured were Bishop Piguet and Sister Marthe de la Croix, one of the instructors at Sainte Marguerite.[44] The bishop's acts of rescue were all the more extraordinary, as he had been a political supporter of the ruler of Vichy France, Marshal Pétain. He had refused to allow politics to impinge on morality.[45]

---

[42] 'Audrée Fain and her three daughters . . . ', Holocaust Memorial Museum, Photo Archive, Worksheet 95947.
[43] Martin Randanne and Marc-Alexis Roquejoffre, *Monsignor Piguet, un évêque discuté*.
[44] Yad Vashem Righteous Among the Nations Archive, file 6968.
[45] 'French bishop honoured for Holocaust action,' *Jerusalem Post*, 25 June 2001.

On 15 September 1942 Perla Lewkowitz and her two-year-old son Michel were deported from the northern French town of Valenciennes to Auschwitz, where they were murdered with almost a thousand other French Jews, of whom 264 were children, on that single deportation train, Transport No. 84. Her two other children, Berthe and Jacques, were not deported: they had already been given a safe home by a French Christian couple, Victor and Josephine Guicherd, on their farm in the village of Dullin. Berthe was seven years old and her brother Jacques was five when they reached Dullin after what the young girl later remembered as 'a long and difficult journey in the hold of a coal-carrying barge and then by train to Lyons. The second stage was another train journey from Lyons to Lepin le Lac, a tiny rural station, and then a climb by foot up a long steep hill to the village. Victor and Josephine Guicherd looked after us from September 1942 until the end of the war.'[46] Under the un-Jewish-sounding surname Leroy, the children were taught in the local school by nuns and monks, and helped around the farm.[47]

Dullin was only three miles from Izieu, and the French collaborators who had told Klaus Barbie there were Jewish children in hiding at Izieu also told him that Jewish children were hiding in other hamlets in the area, Dullin among them. As a result, immediately after the round-up in the children's home at Izieu, SS units under Barbie's command scoured the nearby countryside looking for other Jews in hiding. 'For five days', Berthe Lewkowitz's future husband, David Eppel, reported, 'while a German armoured personnel carrier patrolled the footpaths and the soldiers knocked on the doors at

---

[46] Betty Eppel (formerly Berthe Lewkowitz), letter to the author, 10 February 2002.
[47] 'Berthe Lewkowitz, and her brother, Jacques, with their rescuers . . .', Holocaust Memorial Museum, Photo Archive, Worksheet 04993.

Dullin – it had, as it has today, some ninety inhabitants – Victor Guicherd concealed Berthe and her brother Jacques in a hollow table of the kind French peasants use to store bread and flour. To meet and talk with these unpretentious farmers, long after it was all over, was truly to understand the meaning of the term "righteous". No political or religious ideology compelled their actions. So why did they do it? "Why do you ask?" they answered.'

Victor and Josephine Guicherd were, in fact, running their own private resistance movement. Long after the war, sitting at the same table in which he had hidden the children, Victor Guicherd told his secret. There were three other Jews in hiding on his farm. The harvest 'labourers' at his table had, in fact, been Jews trying to escape across the mountains into Switzerland.[48]

In Carcassonne, within sight of the foothills of the Pyrenees, a French Jewish widow, Madeleine Dreyfus, and her three young sons, refugees from Paris, owed their lives to Juliette Bonhomme. One of the three sons, later Professor Amos Dreyfus, who was nine years old in 1942, writes that their rescuer's husband 'was a collaborator, out of opportunism, and she was in the resistance. Her underground companions called her fondly Caquet – meaning "chatterbox" – a name which fitted quite well her colourful language and her juicy Gallic humour.' Her lover, Captain Edmond Ancely, was also a member of the French resistance.

At the beginning of 1944, recalled Professor Amos Dreyfus, 'Caquet's morale-lifting activities were not sufficient any more. Jewish friends with whom mother had kept contact were disappearing. The situation worsened every day. Through her underground links with the police, Caquet learned that we were on the list

---

[48] David Eppel, 'Key to righteousness', *Jewish Chronicle*, 28 July 2000.

of a forthcoming dispatch of Jews to Auschwitz. That little woman decided that it would not happen, and in fact risked her and her family's life in order to save us. She actually did not know exactly what Jews were (I suspect that even when she died, more than fifty years later, she still was not sure about that). But to her, such knowledge was irrelevant. Her reasoning was simple: you do not kill people because of their race, religion, colour, etc., whichever they may be. And she was brave enough to act on the basis of her belief.'

An attempt was made to smuggle Madeleine Dreyfus and her three sons into Spain, but the clandestine network was uncovered by the Gestapo, and the escape road to Spain temporarily closed. Among those caught was Captain Ancely's son, who was sent to a concentration camp, where he died. Not long after the Gestapo success, wrote Professor Dreyfus, a woman from Corsica died in Carcassonne, and, 'by a strange stroke of luck, this woman had three sons with the same first names as ours, in the same order (names such as Gerard, François and Jean-Louis were extremely common). Somehow, I do not know the exact details, her death was not declared to the authorities, and with a little work by specialists, her identity card was used to transform the Dreyfus family into the Sourbe family, a good Christian family from Bastia, Corsica. We, the children, kept our first names, and mother became Anne-Marie instead of Madeleine.'

When the police came to arrest the Dreyfus family, 'they found that we had disappeared. At 4.30 in the morning we had left home, boarded a train to Toulouse (the big town fifty-five miles from Carcassonne), and from there, accompanied by Caquet, we were taken in a lorry to the very small and remote village of Vacquiers (about 250 inhabitants in 1944, far from the main road). In Vacquiers we were lodged in the "Castle", an old big house which once had belonged to the seigneurs of the village and currently belonged to an epileptic landlord. Refugees from everywhere were everywhere; everyone was used to the presence of unknown strangers and our presence was by no means out of the ordinary.'

Living with the Jewish widow and her sons in one part of the castle were 'a French Catholic colonel with his wife, daughter and son, a young French lieutenant, and a Moslem man, all very nice people, who apparently had their own reasons to hide there.' At first Juliette Bonhomme visited them, but then stopped coming 'because it had become too dangerous'. The other part of the castle was occupied by a family of refugees from Lorraine. 'They had children, with whom we played more or less every day.' Precautions were essential. 'We had strict instructions never to undress in the presence of anyone but the people who knew the truth about us, and not to pee in the presence of children. On the other hand, in spite of being allegedly Corsican, we could admit that we had always lived in Paris, since our accent had remained, through the years, unequivocally Parisian.' At the castle, 'We were outwardly good Catholics. Every Sunday we went to church. Because mother was known under the name of Anne-Marie, she was asked to decorate the Virgin's statue on May 15, and did it very nicely. I remember that, one day, one of our neighbours' children asked her mother (the woman from Lorraine) what Jews were. She answered: "I have never seen one, but I know they are very bad people." We did not know how to react.'[49]

Raoul Laporterie helped to smuggle as many as two hundred Jews across the line from German-occupied to

---

[49] Professor Amos Dreyfus, 'A Young Widow with Three Children', manuscript, enclosed with letter to the author, 21 February 2001. Juliette Bonhomme (then Juliette Bazille) was awarded a Diploma of Honour by Yad Vashem on 23 March 1995. During the war, Professor Dreyfus (now living in Israel and named Amos) was named François.

Vichy France. A historian of the Righteous, Peter Hellman, has described him as 'the most selfless of the Righteous Gentiles whom I came across, in the sense that he willingly helped people he had never seen before and would never see again.'[50]

Living on the occupied side of the line, and owning a clothing store on the Vichy side, Laporterie had the ideal cover for his rescue activities. 'Laporterie not only crossed the line daily and was familiar with the guards and their schedules,' writes the journalist Mary Stewart Krosney, 'but as mayor of the small village of Bascons, he had access to the obsolete papers of deceased citizens, which he forged into new papers for the refugees. Jews on the run, hearing about Laporterie's efficient help, came to his clothing store, where the mayor decked them out with new identities as Bascon residents and drove them across the border. He usually waited until the end of guard shifts, when the Germans were impatient to be relieved of their posts and therefore less attentive to their duties. Once across, he sheltered them, at great danger to himself and his family, until it was possible to send them on their way.'[51]

A Jewish student in Paris, Moussia Erlihmann, owed her life to Daniel Mornet, Professor of Literature, who had already ignored the German laws against Jews by allowing her to study. 'Of course,' her husband later wrote, 'a police raid at the entrance to the Sorbonne was a risk, because a girl with a "Juive" identity card had nothing to do there. Raids were frequent in Paris in May 1942. Among other reasons: the Germans looked for a

---

[50] Peter Hellman, letter to Yad Vashem, 29 November 1979, Yad Vashem Righteous Among the Nations Archive, file 1032. Hellman's book, *Avenue of the Righteous*, contains a chapter on Laporterie.
[51] Mary Stewart Krosney, 'Gallant Christian Honoured on Remembrance Hill', press release, Holyland Features, Christian News from Israel, August 1980.

supply of prisoners to be shot as hostages when the French underground forces killed Germans.'

Thus, her husband recalled, 'Moussia was arrested while leaving Sorbonne, and put into a dark cellar together with a lot of other unfortunate people. For the warders they no longer had names. Sitting along the wall around the cellar, each held his neighbour's hand, waiting. They knew when the dawn came because then the warders were taking out at random a number of prisoners. The warders were French, but the order "Fire!" coming through the wall was German.'

Moussia Erlihmann did not know that Professor Mornet was a member of the French resistance, that he had been informed of her fate and that he would act in order to save her. 'All of a sudden, a warder entered the cellar and asked for Moussia Erlihmann, a name! Her neighbours pressed her hands for courage, and the huge guy – remaining silent – drew her along corridors, through iron gates, up to a small back door; he opened it and pushed Moussia outside. It was night and, unbelievably, she was free!' Making her way to the Free Zone, beyond direct German control, she reached Marseilles, and on 1 November 1942 she crossed from France into Switzerland, and safety. Five months earlier, her mother had been interned at Drancy, from where she was deported to Auschwitz and murdered.[52]

Several thousand Jewish children were smuggled across the French border into Switzerland. Two French women, Marinette Guy and Juliette Vidal, helped in this way, starting with three sisters.[53] At the children's home in Chamonix which they headed, these two women saved 250 Jewish children and adults. In the summer of

---

[52] Harry Zeimer (Moussia Erlihmann's husband), letter to the author, 11 June 2001.
[53] Yad Vashem Righteous Among the Nations Archive, file 518.

1943, assisted by several non-Jewish counsellors, they provided recreation and relaxation in a children's holiday home known as 'Camp of the Ants'.[54]

Jeanne and François Golliet, who worked at the bus depot in Thônes, were active in enabling Jews to escape over the border into Switzerland. Among those they helped smuggle across from France were Isidore and Régine Lowenthal, Polish-born Jews who at the beginning of the war had fled to France from their home in Belgium, for whose two children they had provided false papers and new identities. One of the Golliet sons, Pierre, an eyewitness of the Lowenthals' escape, recalled 'an enormous lorry' full of furniture arriving, according to a prearranged plan, at two o'clock one morning. 'We had to remove the furniture, leave enough space for two people, and replace the furniture. Of course the village was sleeping. At one moment a light came on and we were very anxious, but luckily it soon went off. Mr and Mrs Lowenthal were able to cross the Swiss frontier before daylight. No one suspected my parents. So they hid another elderly Jewish family.'[55]

Jeannette Maurier (later Madame Brousse), from Annécy, also provided Jews with safe havens and false identity cards, and arranged for them to be smuggled across the border into Switzerland. Several dozen families owed their escape to her.[56] Thirty-five years after the end of the war, Madame Brousse recalled the way in which, while working in the administration in the Prefecture in the Haute Savoie, she had been responsible for Jewish refugees expelled from German-annexed Alsace-Lorraine. 'I was faced with a number of painful, tragic situations. Nothing was organised at the begin-

---

[54] 'No Child's Play: Children in the Holocaust – Creativity and Play', exhibition at Yad Vashem, opened 13 October 1997.
[55] The Reverend Pierre Golliet, letter to the author, 9 April 2001.
[56] Yad Vashem Righteous Among the Nations Archive, file 804.

ning. We had to find individual solutions case by case – quickly. It was so risky. My family and I were faced with impossible problems and we had to think of ideas, subterfuge and ruses to save these refugees. One also had to be alert to Trojan Horses, people who had infiltrated, who could lead to our immediate arrest.'[57]

Another Frenchwoman, Geneviève Prittet, arranged for Jews to cross from France into Switzerland at St Julien en Genevois. She was helped in this by a Roman Catholic priest, Father Marie-Jean Viollet.[58] Another priest, Abbé Simon Gallay, helped by his curate Albert Simond, and by a fellow-priest, Pierre Mopty, hid Jews in and around the French lakeside town of Evian-les-Bains and also arranged for them to be smuggled across the border into Switzerland. The curates of two of the parishes closest to the border, Abbé Marquet at Annemasse and Jean Rosay at Douvaine, gave whatever help they could. Abbé Rosay was later arrested and deported to Germany: he did not return. Also killed by the Germans – he was arrested and shot – was Yves Roussey, one of the *passeurs* who took the refugees to the border.[59]

Among those whom Abbé Simon Gallay helped cross into Switzerland was Marcus Wajsfeld. He was six years old when he entered Switzerland in 1943, crossing the border with his Polish-born parents, his sisters Anna, Rachel, Lea and Frieda, and the eight-month-old twins Mania and Simon. Thirty-nine years after the family's escape, Marcus Wajsfeld, then Mordecai Paldiel, was appointed head of the Department of the Righteous at Yad Vashem, and was to spend the next twenty years

[57] 'Les Raisons de l'Engagement de Mme J. Brousse, Annecy, 1979': sent by Madame Brousse to the author, 27 May 2001.
[58] Yad Vashem Righteous Among the Nations Archive, file 5960 (Prittet); file 5752 (Viollet).
[59] Note by Abbé Gallay, 19 November 1984. Yad Vashem Righteous Among the Nations Archive, file 4363.

ensuring that as many rescuers as possible were given recognition.[60]

In the spring of 1941 a hundred Jewish children had found refuge, under the care of the Secours Suisse aux Enfants (Swiss Children's Aid), at the Château de La Hille, an abandoned, derelict property near the town of Foix, in the Pyrenees. Born in Germany and Austria, the youngsters, aged between four and sixteen, had been sent by their families shortly before the outbreak of war to two separate refugee homes in Brussels. When Germany invaded Belgium in May 1940 they escaped by train to southern France; most of their parents and relatives were later deported either from Germany, or from France and Belgium, and murdered. In France the children lived at first in the barns of a large farm estate at Seyre, near Toulouse. Then they were taken to La Hille.

The director at La Hille was a Swiss national, Roesli Naef, who had earlier been a nurse at Albert Schweitzer's hospital in Africa. She was helped at La Hille by four other Swiss citizens of the Secours Suisse: Maurice and Eléonore Dubois, Eugen Lyrer and Emma Ott. In the summer of 1941 she was able to arrange, through the American Friends Service Committee – a Quaker organization – for the emigration of twenty of the younger children to the United States. In August 1942, French police, under Nazi orders, arrived at La Hille and arrested forty boys and girls over the age of fifteen. They were imprisoned at Le Vernet internment camp, thirty miles away, with hundreds of Jewish and other 'undesirable' foreign citizens.

Roesli Naef was at first unsuccessful in seeking the release of her children from Le Vernet. She then appealed to her superior in Toulouse, Maurice Dubois,

---

[60] Mordecai Paldiel, in conversation with the author, 27 December 2001.

who travelled to Vichy and demanded an interview with the Vichy French Minister of the Interior and Chief of Police. After Dubois threatened to close all the Swiss-run camps in France, the Minister agreed to free the forty teenagers, who returned to La Hille; they were the only Le Vernet internees to escape deportation. Some weeks later all the remaining Jewish internees at Le Vernet were loaded onto freight trains and deported to the death camps in the East.

Contrary to the wishes of the Swiss authorities, Roesli Naef then urged all the older La Hille teenagers to scatter and hide, and she assisted their attempts to escape to Spain and Switzerland. Several of the Swiss camp counsellors and teachers working at La Hille helped to smuggle the older children to safety across the Swiss border. A few succeeded only after repeated attempts. Some of these children, however, were caught or turned back by the Swiss, and deported to Auschwitz. Others attempted to flee across the Pyrenees on foot. A number succeeded, but several were betrayed by their paid guide and turned over to the Gestapo.[61] Ninety of the children of La Hille survived the war. Ten were caught by the Gestapo and deported to Auschwitz, where only one survived.

Walter H. Reed, one of the youngsters at La Hille, wrote: 'For these acts' – protecting the Jewish youngsters, obtaining their release from Le Vernet, and enabling many to escape into Switzerland – Roesli Naef 'was summoned before the chief of the Swiss Legation in Vichy and dismissed from her post at La Hille'.[62]

One of the teachers who remained at La Hille after

[61] Walter Reed, 'Children Protected by Swiss Red Cross', *Aufbau* (German refugee newspaper, New York City), 21 September 1999.
[62] Walter H. Reed (born Werner Rindsberg in northern Bavaria in 1924), letter to the author, 10 January 2001. His parents and two younger brothers were deported in March 1942 from Germany to Poland, where they were murdered.

Roesli Naef's dismissal was Anne-Marie Imhof Piguet. She helped twelve children flee illegally across the border into Switzerland in the winter of 1942–3.

Sometimes the work of many heroic rescuers was undone by a single betrayal. On 23 March 1944 sixteen Jewish children, orphans who had been hidden in various safe houses in the village of Voiron for the previous two years, having been refused entry into Switzerland by the Swiss border police, were betrayed by a local villager and handed over to the Gestapo. All sixteen were taken first to Grenoble, then to Drancy, and finally to Auschwitz, where they were murdered.[63]

Many individual French clergymen and women are to be found among the names of the Righteous. Greta Herensztat was six years old at the outbreak of war in 1939. She had been born in Paris; her parents were immigrants from Poland. After the German invasion of France in May 1940, the family made their way to Nice, in the South of France, in the Unoccupied Zone. For two-and-a-half years, life was relatively free from danger. But in November 1942, after the successful Allied landings in French North Africa, when the Germans occupied the whole of central and southern France, Greta's parents decided to place her in the safety of a convent that was known to be willing to take in Jewish children. Greta was then eight years old. Her mother told her that they were on their way to see a priest. '"A priest?" "Yes," my mother said, "and please do not talk unless he asks a question, and be careful how you answer it. This man, this priest, is going to help us. Just remember that you are Jewish." Squeezing my hand, she smiled a smile without cheer, a hopeless smile.'

The priest was Monsignor Paul Remond, Archbishop

---

[63] Serge Klarsfeld, *Memorial to the Jews Deported from France*, page 642.

of Nice, who allowed his bishopric to be used for underground activities, and helped hide Jewish children in
convents until they could be placed with Christian
families.

Greta later recalled her first meeting with Paul
Remond: 'The priest looked at me and spoke in a muffled
voice: "You are now Ginette Henry. You were born in
Orange and your parents are dead. You are going to stay
in a convent until we locate your godparents. Then you
will go to live with them as soon as possible. Do you
understand? You cannot tell where you were born, and
you cannot talk about your parents. Now repeat your
name and your birthplace to me." I probably stood there,
speechless, throat constricted with fear. I shook my
head; I could not answer. The priest spoke up with
urgency: "Talk to me. You must repeat what I told you.
I have to be sure that you understand the gravity of the
situation. Repeat, please." Finally, with a trembling
voice, I repeated the unthinkable, my new name, my new
place of birth. My parents were dead, and I was going to
stay with my godparents. Who were those people? I
never knew I had godparents. What was a godparent? I
was afraid to ask.

'The priest told me to sit down. Someone was coming
to take me to a convent in Nice, actually a cloister, a
secluded order, "The Clarisses." Again the nagging questions, "What was a convent? What was a cloister?" I
waited for my new life to commence. A new life? What
had happened to my previous life, the only life I knew?
Where was my family? I waited silently without crying.
My mother had told me not to.'[64]

Greta's father, who had been born in Poland, was deported from France to Auschwitz, where he died. Her elder

---

[64] 'Looking For. . . ', *Hidden Child* newsletter, volume 9, no. 1, Spring
2000.

brother, also Polish-born, a member of the French resistance, joined the American army after the Normandy landings and marched into Paris as a liberator.[65]

In January 1943 a French Carmelite priest in Avon, Lucien-Louis Bunel, better known as Père Jacques of Jesus, hid three Jewish boys in the boarding school where he was headmaster. In the hope of avoiding any embarrassing or dangerous enquiries, which might inadvertently reveal that the boys were Jewish, he confided their true identity to the newly arrived students in the three upper classes, confident they would be mature enough not to betray their three classmates. His confidence was well-founded: not one student betrayed the trust that had been placed in them.

In January 1944, however, a former student of the school who had been arrested after joining the resistance was interrogated and tortured by the Gestapo; he revealed that Père Jacques had helped him to make contact with the resistance. Père Jacques was arrested, and sent to Mauthausen. When the camp was liberated in May 1945, Père Jacques, although desperately malnourished and suffering from tuberculosis, was still alive; but he died twenty-eight days later. The three Jewish students, found by the Gestapo during their raid on the school, were also taken away. They too did not survive.[66]

Louis Malle's film *Au Revoir les Enfants*, released in 1987, was made as a tribute to Père Jacques. Many priests and nuns, and Catholic institutions, throughout France, did what they could to save Jews from deportation. In Valence, the convent of the Sisters of the Good Shepherd, Le Refuge, took in Lucie Dreyfus, the widow of Captain Alfred Dreyfus, arguably the most famous

---

[65] Greta Herensztat, letter to the author, 8 October 2001.
[66] Francis J. Murphy, *Père Jacques: Resplendent in Victory*, pages 90–2.

French Jew of modern times, and a symbol of the need to stand up against injustice.

In the convent Lucie Dreyfus lived under the name Madame Duteil. 'The experience', wrote Lorraine Beitler, who has devoted many years to the story of Alfred Dreyfus, 'was fraught with difficulties. The Mother Superior of La Refuge was the only person aware of "Madame Duteil's" true identity. One of the women with whom Lucie shared refuge and even meals at the convent – the sister of the local Commissioner on Jewish questions – was outspokenly anti-Semitic and given to tirades against Jews.' Lucie Dreyfus wrote to one of her granddaughters: 'It is so tragic. The world has gone insane. All these massacres are perpetrated in the midst of a general indifference.'[67]

Lucie Dreyfus survived the war. Her granddaughter Madeleine Lévy was murdered in Auschwitz in January 1944, at the age of twenty-five.[68]

A Jewish couple, Elli and Jan Friedländer, crossed into Switzerland from Novel, but were turned back by the Swiss authorities. Czechoslovak Jews, they had managed while refugees in France to find their son Saul a safe haven with Catholic nuns. On 5 October 1943 the Friedländers were taken by train from the internment camp at Rivesaltes to the deportation centre at Drancy. From the train they threw out a letter, addressed to the director of the Catholic boarding school to whom they had entrusted their son for baptism and for survival. 'Madame, I am writing you this in the train that is taking us to Germany,' the letter read. 'At the last moment, I send you, through a representative of the

[67] Lorraine Beitler, 'Lucie Dreyfus, the Sisters of the Good Shepherd, and the Holocaust', manuscript, sent to the author, 17 December 2001.
[68] Information provided by the Beitler Family Foundation (sponsors of a permanent Dreyfus Exhibition), Lorraine Beitler, letter to the author, 18 January 2002.

Quakers, 6,000 francs, a charm bracelet, and, through a lady, a folder with stamps in it. Keep all of this for the little one, and accept, for the last time, our infinite thanks and our warmest wishes for you and your whole family. Don't abandon the little one! May God repay you and bless you and your whole family. Elli and Jan Friedländer.'[69]

Jan and Elli Friedländer were deported from Drancy to Auschwitz. Of the thousand deportees in their transport, only four men, and no women, survived. The Friedländers were among those who perished. Their son Saul survived, saved by Catholic nuns.

Rosa Liwarek's parents were Polish-born. Her father had moved first to Germany – where he served in the German army in the First World War – and then to France. Rosa's mother died in childbirth, leaving her to the care of her elder sisters. She was eight years old when war broke out. During the war, the concierge of their apartment in Paris would warn them when a round-up was imminent. They would then go for safety to the Italian Andriolo family, who let them stay in their small apartment until the round-up was over. But on 3 September 1943 Rosa's father was arrested; the French Commissioner of Police who came to arrest him caught sight of Rosa's sixteen-year-old brother, but instead of taking him away too, with a swift gesture of his hand he warned him to disappear. He was later to find refuge in southern France. Their father was never seen again.

Rosa was by this time being looked after in Paris by her father's non-Jewish accountant, to whom her father had paid an annual sum. Not long after her father's arrest, she was told to leave: she was ten years old. 'The accountant said my father had been arrested, that my board and

---

[69] Saul Friedlander, *When Memory Comes*, page 90.

lodging was only paid up until Christmas, and that I had three months to look for a new place.' A friend of her father in Brittany, a Roman Catholic, sent her a train ticket and she left Paris by train for Brittany. 'We were about ten to eleven people in a compartment on the last train to leave Paris,' she recalled. 'It was bombed by the British. I was the only one to survive because I was wedged between two large ladies who fell on me.'[70]

From the wreckage of the train, the young girl made her way to Brittany, where Pauline Bohic took her to her home in the village of Pleyber-Christ. 'Her parents could not read or write. They did not speak French, only Breton. I don't think they knew what a Jew was,' Rosa reflected half a century later. 'They would have saved anybody, they were good people. They didn't know the risk they were taking.' It was decided that, to save her life – and her soul – she should be baptized. 'The priest knew I was Jewish. While I was being baptized he said that he was pleased to do so; the Jews had killed Christ but I would be forgiven.' For the next year, the church services gave her a sense of belonging. Thirty-two members of her family were murdered. Four aunts survived in hiding in southern France, and one in Poland, hidden with her husband in a graveyard, living in a tomb, underneath the stone slab, which Righteous Poles would lift up to bring them food. As to Pauline Bohic, her own rescuer, Rosa commented: 'She was a heroine without knowing it.'[71]

On 10 June 1944, four days after Allied forces landed on the Normandy beaches, the SS massacred 642 villagers at Oradour-sur-Glane. There were seven Jews hiding among their victims: adults and children who

---

[70] 'Saved by the corpse on top of me', *Hampstead and Highgate Express*, 26 March 1993.
[71] Lady Lipworth (Rosa Liwarek), in conversation with the author, 24 March 2002.

had earlier found refuge in the village, and of whose presence the Germans were unaware. Along with the Christian villagers, the seven Jews were locked in the village church and then killed, as a reprisal for the killing of an SS man by French partisans in a distant village which happened to bear the same name.

Of the Jews murdered at Oradour, 45-year-old Maria Goldman had been born in Warsaw, and ten-year-old Raymond Enciel in Strasbourg. The youngest were two boys, Simon Kanzler, aged nine, and Serge Bergman, aged eight, both born in Strasbourg.[72] All had found protection in the village against deportation. The Germans did not know or care that on this occasion there were Jews among those they had decided to kill in revenge.

Not far from Oradour, in the village of Lesterps, Josephine Levy was being protected by Sister Saint Cybard, director of the Roman Catholic convent school in the village. Her parents had left her there with the warning that she should never reveal her real identity. Under the name Josie L'Or, she stayed in the convent school for seven months, until the liberation of Paris in August 1944, when she was reunited with her parents. Fifty-six years later, she reflected on the fact that more than two hundred thousand of France's wartime population of some three hundred thousand Jews survived: 'That could not have been done without the help of many French people, who perhaps sheltered a Jew for one night, or transmitted a message, or performed some similar act of decency.'[73] As of 1 January 2002, more than two thousand French men and women had been

---

[72] Serge Klarsfeld, *Memorial to the Jews Deported from France*, pages 642, 645.
[73] Josie Martin (Josephine Levy), quoted in Tom Tugend, 'French village honours "hidden child" survivor of Holocaust', *Jewish Chronicle*, 24 November 2000.

recognized at Yad Vashem as Righteous Among the Nations, the third largest national group after Poles and Dutch.[74]

The Channel Islands are British sovereign territory, but the largest island, Jersey, is only fifteen miles from the coast of France, and seventy-five miles from Britain. In June 1940 the islands were invaded by Germany and overrun within hours: they were the only part of Britain to come under Nazi rule. Even there, on the Atlantic Ocean, the Germans searched for Jews to deport to the death camps. When an arrest party came to the home of a Dutch-born Jewish woman, Mary Richardson (*née* Olvenich; she was married to a retired British sea captain, a non-Jew), she managed to escape out of the back of the building while her husband feigned senility to keep the Germans waiting at the front door.[75] Mary Richardson was taken in and hidden by Albert Bedane, a physiotherapist, who had fought against the Germans in the First World War. Bedane hid her in his clinic in the island's capital, St Helier.

Twelve islanders were registered as Jews during the war, and deported to the camps. Had it not been for Albert Bedane, Mary Richardson would have been the thirteenth. One of the many French forced labourers on the island, Francis Le Sueur, to whom Bedane had given shelter for two weeks, recalled that he had also 'sheltered a Dutch Jewess in his home for two-and-a-half years and he must have known during all that time that he would be shot if he was caught. He took a long calculated

[74] 'Righteous Among the Nations – per Country & Ethnic Origin,' 1 January 2002, Yad Vashem Department for the Righteous Among the Nations (list sent to the author on 29 January 2002). The exact French figure is 2,171.
[75] Douglas Davis, 'Quiet saviour on the island of Jersey', *Jerusalem Post*, 30 January 2000.

risk and he must have needed a great deal of sustained courage.'[76]

The French lawyer and historian Serge Klarsfeld, a hidden child during the war, whose father was deported to Auschwitz and perished there, has stressed that the war against the Jews in France was more than anything a war against children. Between 1942 and 1944, 11,402 French children aged seventeen and under (some tiny babies) were deported, many of them without their parents. Only three hundred of those children survived.[77] These harsh facts make the acts of rescue that did take place all the more remarkable, while also raising the ever-present question: What if more people had been able to take the risk of hiding Jews?

---

[76] Testimony of Francis Le Sueur, Yad Vashem Righteous Among the Nations Archive, file 8718. [77] Serge Klarsfeld, *French Children of the Holocaust: A Memorial.* New York: New York University Press, 1996, page 8.

[77] Serge Klarsfeld, *French Children of the Holocaust: A Memorial.* New York: New York University Press, 1996, page 8.

CHAPTER THIRTEEN

Belgium and Luxembourg

As of 1 January 2002 a total of 1,322 Belgian citizens had been honoured as Righteous Among the Nations at Yad Vashem in Jerusalem.[1] Ninety-four per cent of all Jews in Belgium at the outbreak of war were recent immigrants, some ninety thousand from Poland in the aftermath of the First World War, and a further twenty thousand from Germany after 1933. In spite of this, an astonishing proportion – almost half of them – managed to survive in hiding.

In the First World War, Belgium had experienced four years of German occupation. Partly as a result, although there was a Belgian fascist movement, and even a volunteer Belgian SS division, dislike of Germany and Nazism was widespread and strong. Jewish self-help was also well-organized: the Comité de Défense des Juifs (CDJ) was able, with the help of Belgian non-Jews throughout the country, to place between three and four thousand Jewish children in hiding, and as many as ten thousand adults, many of whom entered the Belgian resistance movement.

In September 1942, as the deportation of Jews from Belgium to Auschwitz gathered momentum, the

---

[1] 'Righteous Among the Nations – per Country & Ethnic Origin', 1 January 2002, Yad Vashem Department for the Righteous Among the Nations (list sent to the author on 29 January 2002).

clandestine journal *Indépendence*, the magazine of the underground Independence Front, circulated an appeal on behalf of the Jews. It was headed: 'For the sake of that which you hold dearest, rescue the Jewish children who are dying abandoned.' The article exhorted all Belgians: 'The children are abandoned. Let us not allow them to starve but let us take them into our homes, care for them and save them from a miserable fate. Let us hide all those for whom the Gestapo are searching. Let us save them from torture, from suffering and from death in prisons and concentration camps. Contact the Independence Front (FI). It does all it can to hide and support Hitler's victims. Make your contribution – give what you can. Think of those you love and who, thanks to the generosity of each of you, would themselves be rescued if they were ever persecuted.'[2]

The response of the Belgian population was vexatious to the German occupation authorities. On 24 September 1942 the German Minister of Foreign Affairs, Joachim von Ribbentrop, received a telegram from his representative in Brussels, stating that many Jews had left their homes to avoid the round-ups and 'made efforts to find shelter with Belgian Aryans'. Ribbentrop was also told: 'These efforts are being sustained by a considerable section of the Belgian population.'[3]

Paul Duysenx and his wife Jeanne le Jeune hid a nineteen-year-old Jewish boy, Benjamin Helman, from the summer of 1942 until the liberation of the city in September 1944. Like so many of those who were rescued in this way, the young man had originally been taken in for only two days; it was the willingness of his

[2] *Indépendence*, September 1942.
[3] Herr von Bargen (delegate of the German Ministry of Foreign Affairs to the German military governor of Brussels), telegram dated 24 September 1942, quoted in Lucien Steinberg, *La Comité de Défense des Juifs en Belgique, 1942–1944*, page 79.

rescuers to continue to hide him for what turned out to be more than two years that enabled him to escape deportation. His older sister, Gdula, was hidden by another family and, like him, survived; but their father and mother, as well as their five-year-old sister, Gitta, were given shelter by a Belgian family who decided not to keep them, and were deported and killed.[4]

Alphonse and Emilie Gonsette's only son, active in the Belgian resistance, had been arrested by the Gestapo and imprisoned. Defiant, they suggested to his fellow resistance members that they take a Jewish child into their home in the town of Gosselies. The boy who was brought to them, Simon Weissblum, was only two years old. His parents were active in the underground; his mother was captured by the Gestapo and sent to Auschwitz. She survived, and was reunited with her son when the war ended. The Gonsettes refused to accept any payment for their act of rescue.[5]

Léon Platteau, General Secretary of the Belgian Ministry of Justice during the German occupation, used his position to obtain from the occupying authorities the release of Jews from Dossin detention camp at Malines (in Flemish, Mechelen), and the annulment of their deportation orders to Auschwitz. He also transferred money to the Committee for Jewish Defence to enable it to maintain two thousand people every month.[6]

More than four and a half thousand Belgian Jewish children were found safe homes with Christian families, convents, boarding schools, orphanages and even sanatoriums, as a result of the efforts of Yvonne Nèvejean, the director of the National Agency for Children. On several occasions she was able to rescue children of whose

---

[4] Yad Vashem Righteous Among the Nations Archive, file 1025.
[5] Yad Vashem Righteous Among the Nations Archive, file 329.
[6] Yad Vashem Righteous Among the Nations Archive, file 229.

whereabouts the Germans had become aware, just a few hours before they were to be deported.[7]

One of those whom Yvonne Nèvejean helped to save was Berlin-born Bronia Veitch, then five years old. She was living in a Jewish children's home when, on 30 October 1942, 'we were rounded up by the Gestapo, and all fifty-six children and the Jewish staff were taken to Caserne Dossin, Malines. However, the train due to transport us was delayed by some hours, awaiting another transport from France. The non-Jewish house-keeper at the Home telephoned Yvonne Nèvejean, who was clandestinely involved in the civilian resistance movement, the Front de l'Indépendence (FI), which had taken the Jewish resistance movement under its wing and had established the Committee for the Defence of Jews (CDJ). She contacted the Queen Mother of Belgium, Queen Elisabeth, who during most of the day and half the night interceded with the German High Command. A huge ransom was also paid by a member of the CDJ and we as "lone children" were released during the night a very short time before the transports departed. Eight children who had been left behind alone in Caserne Dossin when their families were deported, were released along with us. The transport of 1,800 people, which left for the "East" that night, included 137 children under sixteen. All were gassed on arrival at Auschwitz/Birkenau.'

There was a 'constant danger', Bronia Veitch wrote, 'that we might be raided again at any time. The major Belgian civilian resistance movement, the Front de l'Indépendence (FI), was an umbrella movement which included priests, nuns, communists, social democrats, liberals, monarchists and people of no political or religious affiliation. They placed as many as three thousand children in hiding in 128 institutions – convents,

---

[7] Yad Vashem Righteous Among the Nations Archive, file 99.

sanatoria, homes for delicate children, and seven hundred private foster homes, all over the country. All children were given false identities and birth certificates and were cross-referenced in four secret notebooks kept in four different locations to enable the children to be traced after the war.'[8]

A Belgian Christian couple, Henri and Gabrielle Bal, gave Bronia Veitch a safe haven in their home in St Niklaas. After she had been with them for eight months an Austrian officer, Wolfgang Bachata, was billeted in the house. At the dinner table, Bronia Veitch later recalled, the representative of the enemy 'unburdened his feelings about the war to us. I recall the occasion vividly. He was distressed at Austria's loss of independence and had been very unhappy to be called up. He was soon to be sent with his unit to Italy. We were all sitting around the dining room table and immediately my foster family set about persuading him to give himself up, as a prisoner of war, as soon as he could after reaching Italy. The conversation, in French, has remained with me all my life.'

When, early in 1944, a Dutch Jewish family was also given refuge by Henri and Gabrielle Bal, 'they could not adjust to being hidden', Bronia Veitch has written. 'As we were obliged to billet German officers at any time it was dangerous for all of us for them to remain with us for long. Although they had been found a safe hiding place with a widow deep in the country, they adamantly wanted to be smuggled to Switzerland. After the war we learned that they were caught on the Swiss border and perished. In the early 1970s, when she was over seventy, my foster mother told me that she had tried desperately to dissuade the couple from taking their children Sera and Jaap, who were two and four years older than I, with

---

[8] Bronia Veitch, recollections, enclosed with letter to the author, 18 August 2001.

them. She tried to reason with them that although they were free to risk themselves they had no right to endanger their children's lives, and she tried to assure them that they would be reunited when the war was over. After all those years, she would often wake up in the night crying that, if only she could have pleaded harder, Sera and Jaap would have been alive.'[9]

When, in mid-1943, the deportation began of Jews with Belgian nationality – a mere 6 per cent of the total number of Jews in the country at the outbreak of war – Henri and Gabrielle Bal paid the expenses of the Litvin family when they went into hiding in Brussels.

Bronia Veitch noted: 'My late foster parents not only saved my life but gave me unconditional love, a wonderful childhood and were ready to risk everything for me. They were fully aware of the dangers throughout the time I was with them until the liberation. They were living examples of "good will to all".'[10]

Chawa Schneider was arrested on 7 October 1942 and deported to Auschwitz. Her husband Munisch and their six-year-old daughter Nicole (later Nicole David) were out for a walk when the Germans came to Profondeville, the small town where they were living, to arrest them. Earlier, Nicole had been looked after by nuns in the St Jean Orphanage in the town of St Servais, which, she later recalled, 'had taken in Jewish children and treated us all equally'.

After her mother's arrest, young Nicole was found another couple, Gaston and Josephine Champagne, who took her in. Five of their ten children were still living at home, but her hosts accepted the risk without hesitation. Her father, who had remained in Profondeville after his wife's arrest, was in imminent danger. The local Belgian

---

[9] Bronia Veitch, letter to the author, 18 August 2001.
[10] Bronia Veitch, recollections, enclosed with letter to the author, 18 August 2001.

resistance advised him to go to a nearby hamlet, Besinne-Arbre, where, helped by the mayor, Jules Clobert, and the local priest, he was found a family, that of Jules and Marie Adnet, who hid him until liberation. Nicole David wrote: 'Jules Adnet, who worked in the local Debras quarry, and Marie who took in laundry, had one daughter Josiane who was born in October 1936. Despite the difficulties in obtaining food they always shared everything with my father. In this small and isolated village there were only a few hundred inhabitants. They all knew that my father, who called himself Monsieur Albert, as "the Jew who was hiding at the Adnets". If anyone saw or heard of anything suspicious they would advise Maurice Pochet who was the owner of the only village shop, he in turn would come to warn my father.'

Nicole David also recalled how Maurice Pochet and his wife Maria, who had three children, 'would often take in my father and hide him in a dugout in their garden when there was fear of the Germans coming to the village. Sometimes the rumours or the fears were unfounded. However, in July 1944 a Jewish woman (who was put on the last train to leave Malines for Auschwitz) was arrested in the next village, Lesve. For three days my father stayed in the dugout in the garden of Mr and Mrs Pochet as the Germans were searching all the surrounding villages in the hope of finding more Jews. Mrs Pochet whom I visited three years ago, she was about ninety-three then, remembered this episode, the terrible fear my father was in, and his refusal of coming into the house to sleep for fear of endangering their lives even more.'

Reflecting on her father's rescue, Nicole David writes of how the Adnet, Clobert and Pochet families, as well as the local priest, 'were very aware of the dangers they put themselves and their families in. The Germans were constantly looking for Jews who might be in hiding, and the Belgian population was constantly warned of the dangers they were in by helping Jews. Nevertheless, all told us after the war that they could not have done anything differently knowing the danger my father was in. After the liberation and at the end of the war Marie and Jules Adnet took me in for many months while my father was trying to rebuild his life. After the war Maurice Pochet helped my father financially by asking him to help sell his stamp collection. This helped my father to re-establish himself in business'.[11]

On 24 September 1942, in Brussels, Cardinal van Roey, head of the Catholic Church in Belgium, and Queen Elisabeth of the Belgians, the Queen Mother, both intervened with the German occupation authorities after the arrest of six leading members of the Jewish community. As a result of their intervention, five were released. The sixth, Edward Rotbel, Secretary of the Belgian Jewish Community, was not a Belgian but a Hungarian citizen; thus Belgian intervention could not save him. He was deported to Auschwitz two days later.[12]

Cardinal van Roey encouraged several institutions under his jurisdiction to open their gates to Jewish children, one of them being the orphanage of St Joseph. He also approved a means to save a number of Jewish women. One of the children given sanctuary at the St Joseph orphanage, Alexander Levy, has written of how his mother was saved as a result of a device thought up by the Cardinal, who among his other acts of rescue had opened a geriatric centre in which Jews were given shelter: 'As these elderly Jews "required" kosher food, and Christian cooks would be unable to prepare such a specialized diet, he required Jewish cooks to do the job. These Jewish cooks were given special passes protecting

[11] Nicole David, letters to the author, 29 October, 6 November 2001.
[12] Maxine Steinberg, 'The Trap of Legality: the Association of the Jews of Belgium', in *Patterns of Jewish Leadership*, page 369.

them against deportation, and my mother was one of these cooks.'[13]

The Queen Elisabeth Castle in Jamoigne was a home for the children of Belgian soldiers, sailors and airmen. It was run from day to day by Marie Taquet, an army officer's wife. In 1943 she took into the home and under her wing eighty Jewish children. All their names were changed to Christian-sounding ones, and they were dispersed among the other children in the home, without any of the other children knowing that they were Jewish. All of them were saved.[14]

The Lajbman brothers, eleven-year-old Isaac and four-year-old Bernard, had already been in hiding with families in Wilrijk (near Antwerp) and Marcinelles (near Charleroi) when lack of food and sanitation in their foster homes forced them to seek sanctuary elsewhere. Reaching Tourinnes-St-Lambert, Isaac was taken in by Alphonse and Marie Quintin, and Bernard by the Ravet family. Both families treated the boys as their own sons.[15]

In an essay on the rescue of Jewish children in Belgium during the Second World War, Mordecai Paldiel has recorded the story of an entire village that served as a refuge for fleeing children. This was Cornement-Louveigné, a hamlet of ten families near Liège, where each family sheltered one or more Jewish children and was supported by the local mayor in this effort. The area in which this tiny hamlet was located was an important centre of resistance activity, and the Germans were constantly looking for members of the underground – besides 'dropping by' to pick up fresh

[13] Alexander Levy, letter to the author, 9 December 2001.
[14] Gay Block and Malka Drucker, *Rescuers: Portraits of Moral Courage in the Holocaust*, page 108.
[15] United States Holocaust Memorial Museum, Photo Archive, Worksheet 99706.

milk and eggs. Thus, there was real danger here; but no one informed on the Jewish children or their guardians.

Paldiel also writes of a private, non-religious Belgian institution in Ottignies in which Jewish children were sheltered. Before the war it was a private boarding school for psychologically disturbed children, headed by René Jacqumotte, 'who gradually emptied the school of its Gentile boarders and replaced them with about twenty Jewish children. The Jewish youngsters received private tutoring, with the underground covering their maintenance expenses.'[16]

In October 1942 the Gestapo ordered all Jews in Belgium to register with the police. Many parents took immediate steps to place their children in the care of non-Jews willing to take the risk of harbouring them in their homes, often in remote villages. Sometimes whole families were able to find a secure hiding place. Charlotte Birnbaum was five years old in October 1942 when she and her mother, elder brother, grandparents and an aunt fled from Antwerp to the Ardennes, where they stayed with an elderly couple. They remained with them until September 1944 when that part of Belgium was liberated by the United States army. The elderly couple, Joseph and Leonie Morand, did their utmost to help them without any reward other than the rent for the accommodation provided.[17]

German-born Beatrice Muchman and her cousin Henri were given a safe haven by two Catholic sisters in the Belgian village of Ottignies. Nine years old at the time, she later recalled: 'Henri and I owed our lives to

---

[16] Mordecai Paldiel, 'The Rescue of Jewish Children in Belgium During World War II', in Dan Michman (editor), *Belgium and the Holocaust: Jews, Belgians, Germans*, Jerusalem: Yad Vashem, 1998.
[17] Information provided by Janek Weber, letter to the author, 28 October 2001. Janek Weber had been saved by non-Jews in Cracow (see chapter 7). He met Charlotte Birnbaum in Antwerp in 1959 and married her a year later, settling in London.

Marianne and Adèle, but we also owed our lives to the whole village. Almost everyone in Ottignies knew our secret and the secrets of the other Jewish children hidden there, but no one reported us to the German soldiers who patrolled the area. (Out of 4,000 Jewish children hiding in Belgium, 3,000 were saved precisely because of this kind of quiet, unsung heroism.) My parents, of course, made the ultimate sacrifice – giving up their only child. But, being a child, I had no idea what an agonizing decision it was for them. I thought they were abandoning me when in reality they were saving me. Like so many others who lost loved ones during the Holocaust, I learned very little about what happened to my parents.' Neither, in fact, survived the war.[18]

Sara Lamhaut was eleven years old when the Gestapo arrested her parents, members of the Belgian resistance. She first found sanctuary with the Sisters of Saint Mary near Mons, then in an abandoned convent in Sugny, and finally at the convent school of the Sisters of Saint Mary in Wezembeek-Oppem, near Brussels. There, under the assumed name of Jeannine van Meerhaegen, she took her First Communion.[19]

The Spiessens were Belgian farmers in the small town of Boom, near Antwerp. The couple offered shelter on their farm to two Jews, Cecile Seiden and her mother, from Antwerp. The Spiessens' son Harry and his wife Joss took them from Antwerp to Boom hidden in a hay cart. Cecile Seiden later recalled: 'Along the way we passed many patrols that examined Harry and Joss's papers. We were hidden under hay and vegetables in his little open truck. At one of the checkpoints they rifled the hay looking for contraband and anything else that

---

[18] Beatrice Michman, *Never to be Forgotten: A Young Girl's Holocaust Memoir* (excerpted in *Imprimis, Because Ideas Have Consequences*, volume 28, no. 4, April 1999).
[19] United States Holocaust Memorial Museum, Photo Archive, Worksheet 04792.

they could confiscate. When the rifle entered the hay, it went past my mother's ear and she whimpered. The guard snarled: "What do you have there?" Harry answered, "A pig, he must have grunted!" Lucky for us, he believed Harry. They let us pass and didn't confiscate the pig. Joss and Harry risked their lives for us, they could have been shot.'

The Spiessens' daughter Natalie, who lived in a nearby village with her husband, was not told that the newcomers were Jewish. 'Mrs Spiessen concealed the fact that she was hiding a Jewish woman and child from her own daughter. Many times at the dinner table, the conversation turned to the subject of Jews and Natalie would chime in – "They deserve what they get!" Being a young child I was not aware of these conversations but many times the food got stuck in my mother's throat, as Natalie would speak.

'For appearance sake, I attended the local Roman Catholic Church communion class. The Spiessens were devout Catholics. The local priest and I became good friends and I tried to learn my catechisms. After being on the farm for many months, I developed a medical problem because of malnutrition from the war. The closest medical help was a Convent in Malines, which was the deportation center for all Jews from Belgium to concentration and death camps. We waited for many hours in the crowded outer office until our turn came. I was put onto a table and the sisters proceeded to remove my scabs and treated the wounds. The pain was terrible and I was brave by not screaming too much. While this operation was going on, Mrs Spiessen overheard two nuns speaking to each other.

"Sister, did you see the huge lines of children waiting to be put on the trains? They looked so frightened, so scared!"

"Sister, don't worry, they are not ours, they are only Jewish children!"'

Cecile Seiden recalled how Mrs Spiessen 'could not believe what she heard, tears came to her eyes, she bit her lip she wanted to cry out. She suddenly became silent. All the way home, she didn't say one word but just squeezed my hand very tightly. Why didn't Mrs Spiessen speak to me, I felt that I had been so brave. That evening at the dinner table, there was not too much talk.'

Later, Cecile Seiden and her mother were to make their way to Switzerland. Her father, taken from Belgium to Auschwitz, was one of the few Belgian deportees who survived.[20]

Many of the rescuers in Belgium, as in other countries, were people with few means: hard-working farmers like the Spiessens. It was a 'fairly poor socialist family, living in the miners' county (Borinage) of Belgium' that sheltered the young Goldschläger boy. That boy's younger brother Alain, born after the war, later wrote: 'My father in his naiveté had given my brother the name Christian in 1939, thinking that the Germans would not pursue a child with that name! The Socialist Party had a strong tradition of anti-racism and anti-persecution.' Alain Goldschläger added: 'Belgium has a remarkable record of saving children. I think it was perceived as a way to fight the Germans. Anti-Semitism was also not as rooted as in some other countries like Holland. The organization for helping Jewish children in Brussels was quite admirable and extended, involving a large number of non-Jews and established services. A Catholic newspaper summed up the position quite well: "Even if we do not like Jews, they do not deserve the persecution." There was a basic "good will" that manifested itself either by active participation in the rescue, or more often

---

[20] Cecile Seiden, 'In Honour of My Righteous Rescuers', part of the New Jersey Holocaust Curriculum, under the heading 'To Honour All Children: From Prejudice, to Discrimination, to Hatred . . . to Holocaust'.

by a passive non-involvement in the persecution which gave room and time for others to act.'[21]

In Brussels, Father Anton de Breuker, the pastor of St Marie Scharbeeck church, gave shelter to ten-year-old Dora Londner-Conforti, after her parents had been taken to the deportation centre at Dossin, from where they were deported to Auschwitz and their deaths. To protect the girl's identity Father Anton adopted her, and, a year later, moved her to a Carmelite convent 'that had been specially instructed to conceal Jewish girls'.[22]

Elisabeth Maxwell has recorded the story of Madame Ovart, who ran a home where Jewish children were hidden. 'One Whitsun, the Christian children had gone back home and only the Jewish children were left. The Gestapo raided the building and, having terrified the children, took them away for deportation. They also arrested Mme Ovart. When they expressed surprise as to why a Christian would hide Jewish children, she answered, "I am a Belgian . . . Here, we do not ask for children's identity to teach them to read and write!" She died in Ravensbrück and her husband, who was also arrested, died in Buchenwald.'[23]

Shortly before being deported to Auschwitz, Chana and Benjamin Borzykowski managed to place their four-year-old son Jacky in a kindergarten in Brussels. There he was cared for by Andrée Geulen, a member both of the Belgian underground and of the Committee for the Defence of the Jews. She entrusted him to two sisters, Madeleine and Marcel de Meulemeester, also members of the resistance. They, in turn, brought Jacky to their brother and sister-in-law, John and Josiane de Meulemeester. He hid with them from 1943 to 1944 until

---

[21] Alain Goldschläger, letter to the author, 6 August 2000.
[22] 'No Child's Play: Children in the Holocaust – Creativity and Play', exhibition at Yad Vashem, opened 13 October 1997.
[23] Elisabeth Maxwell, 'The Rescue of Jews in France and Belgium . . .'.

it became too dangerous, when the de Meulemeester sisters took him to Father de Wolf Desirée in the village of Buggenhout. The priest arranged for Jacky to stay on the farm of Franz and Maria Julia van Gerwen. The boy lived with the van Gerwens and their two daughters, Maria Desirée and Amelie, for over two years; during this time he was baptized a Catholic, and lived and worked as part of the family.

Chana and Benjamin Borzykowski were murdered at Auschwitz. Jacky's aunt found him after her own liberation from Dachau; later he went to Israel with a group of other orphans.[24]

As in France, the Catholic and Protestant churches in Belgium were both active in helping Jews. A French Protestant leader, Pastor Marc Boegner, issued clear instructions to his flock that they should help persecuted Jews, and himself helped large numbers of Jews to find sanctuary in France. One institution to which he sent Jews for safety was the Adventists' Seminary at Collognes, in Haute Savoie, not far from the Swiss border.[25]

Many Belgian nunneries and convents also gave sanctuary to Jewish children and pretended they were Christian. In Namur, Father Joseph André, an abbot, found room within his monastery and in monasteries and nunneries elsewhere for as many as a hundred children. After liberation he brought them all to the Jewish community leaders.[26] Nor was this the sum total of his efforts on behalf of Jews. An American rabbi, then a chaplain with the United States forces, Captain Harold

---

[24] Information provided by Jacky Barkan (Borzykowski), United States Holocaust Memorial Museum, Photo Archive, Worksheet 04992.

[25] Yad Vashem Righteous Among the Nations Archive, file 2698.

[26] Benek (Baruch) Sharoni, 'Man's Humanity to Man', *Mizkor*, October 2000.

Saperstein, told the *New York Times* shortly after the war of how Father André 'got local Catholic families to hide Jews in their households. He gave up his own bed to Jewish refugees, and during the entire period slept on the floor of his study. He carried food to families in hiding, and messages from parents to children. All this was done from his own home, next door to the hotel used as Gestapo headquarters, now taken over for our billet. During the final months of Nazi occupation he was compelled to go into hiding himself, his own life being endangered. During the course of two years he saved more than two hundred lives.' Rabbi Saperstein also reported that, with liberation, Father André made sure that orphaned Jewish children who had been hidden in Catholic institutions were given into the charge of Jewish people, 'who could ill afford the additional loss of small numbers of Jewish children after their over-whelming losses of recent years'.[27] Also among the institutions that hid Jews were the Convent of the Franciscan Sisters in Bruges, the Protestant orphanage at Uccle, and the convent of the Sisters of Don Bosco, in Courtrai, where fourteen Jewish children were hidden. Only two of the nuns here were aware that any of the children were Jewish; even the Jewish children them-selves, among them eight-year-old Leon Fischler, did not know that any of the other children were Jewish.[28]

Four Jewish girls were given refuge at the Sisters of Saint Mary convent school in the village of Wezembeek-Oppem, near Brussels; six were saved from deportation at the Dominican convent of Lubbeek, near Hasselt, hidden in the cellar by the Mother Superior when the

---

[27] '200 Jews Owe Life to Belgian Priest', *New York Times*, 28 December 1945.
[28] Information provided by Jehuda Yinon (Leon Fischler), United States Holocaust Memorial Museum, Photo Archive, Worksheet 05695.

Gestapo came to the convent in search of Belgians to deport for forced labour.[29]

When Ursula Klipstein's German-born parents, Irma and Leo, were arrested – also German-born, she was then twelve years old – she approached a Christian friend of the family, who found her a hiding place in a convent near Braine-l'Alleud. Run by the Sisters of Saint Mary, the convent was home to twenty-five students, half of whom were Jewish children in hiding. Ursula, who was given the name Janine Hambenne, stayed at the convent from June 1943 until the liberation in September 1944.

After their arrest, Ursula's parents were taken to the transit camp at Malines. One evening the inmates were allowed a cultural evening, which was attended by the German staff as well as the prisoners. At this event, Irma Klipstein read out a poem she had written about camp life. The camp commandant, who recognized by her accent that she was from the same part of Germany as himself, was impressed by her poem, and in appreciation arranged for her and husband to be employed in the camp, rather than be deported to the East. Irma continued to work in Malines as a maid, and Leo as a carpenter, until liberation.[30]

The smallest of Jewish children were in danger: each deportation from Belgium, as from France and Holland, contained young children, often deported without their parents. A Christian nurse who worked at the Brussels hospital where Marguerite-Rose Birnbaum was born on 4 February 1943, arranged for her parents to hide in an abbey in Limbourg, with a priest, Armand Elens. The priest spoke with his sister, Marie-Josephe Dincq,

---

[29] Information provided by Thea Rothenstein, one of the girls who was saved, United States Holocaust Memorial Museum, Photo Archive, Worksheet 78027.

[30] Information provided by Janine Gimpleman Sokolov (Ursula Klipstein), United States Holocaust Memorial Museum, Photo Archive, Worksheet 99696.

saying, in code, that he had a suit and dress (that is, Lazar and Frida Birnbaum) and a small dress (Marguerite-Rose). He added that he would keep the suit and dress, and asked his sister to pick up the small dress. Madame Dincq picked up seven-month-old Marguerite-Rose and brought her to her home in Arendonk, where she lived with her husband Pierre and three children, aged between ten and six. Marguerite-Rose was baptized in St Joseph's church as the godchild of Pierre and Marie-Josephe Dincq. Pierre Dincq, a member of the Belgian resistance, was arrested in the spring of 1944 and died in Dachau. In the summer of 1945 the Birnbaums retrieved their daughter, by that time a healthy two-year-old.[31]

Annette Lederman was born in 1940, her sister Margot in 1941. When the round-ups of Jews in Brussels began, Annette's mother made contact with the Belgian underground through a Catholic priest. Annette was placed in hiding with a Christian family, but she was so homesick that her rescuer returned her to her parents. On 31 October 1942, Annette's father was deported to Auschwitz. Her mother then resolved to hide both girls with a Christian family. She made contact with Clementine and Edouard Frans van Buggenhout, who lived in the village of Rumst, halfway between Brussels and Antwerp. The van Buggenhouts had three older children. Their two sons, Roger and Sylvan, were away most of the time in forced labour battalions, but their teenage daughter, Lydia, helped care for the Lederman sisters.

While Annette and Margot were in hiding, their mother was deported to Auschwitz on the penultimate transport from Belgium in 1944. After learning that both parents had been killed, Clementine and Edouard van Buggenhout sought to adopt the girls, but the village

---

[31] Information provided by Marguerite Birnbaum, United States Holocaust Memorial Museum, Photo Archive, Worksheet 09409.

priest would not sanction the adoption 'since there was no formal indication that this would have been the wish of the parents'. In due course the two girls were found a home with a Jewish family in the United States.[32]

As more and more 'Hidden Children' began to tell their stories, the courage of Father Bruno – the Reverend Henri Reynders – became more and more well known. For those he saved he was a true 'hero'.[33] He helped find places of safety for 320 Jewish children, dozens of whom have given testimony to his courage.[34]

Father Bruno, a Benedictine monk, had paid a visit to Germany in 1938 and had been distressed by what he saw. 'I was strolling in a busy street,' he later recalled. 'Everywhere I saw insulting signs: "Jude = Judas", "Juden heraus" or "Hier sind Juden nicht erwünschen". It shocked me greatly, but what truly revolted me was the following incident: I saw an old man arriving, bearded, dressed in a caftan, wearing an old black hat, in short the stereotyped Jew. This old man walked stooped, not daring to raise his eyes, hiding his face with his hand. Passersby walked away from him as if he had the plague, or they bullied him, or pointed a finger and sneered at him. This really upset me, this segregation, this contempt, this arrogance, this cruel stupidity, no . . . it was unbearable! It still lingers in my memory and makes me nauseous.'[35]

While serving as a Belgian army chaplain in 1940, Father Bruno was wounded, captured and made a prisoner of war. It would be a year before he was released. In 1942 he was sent by the Father Superior of his order

---

[32] Information provided by Annette Lederman Linzer, United States Holocaust Memorial Museum, Photo Archive, Worksheet 89342.
[33] Flora M. Singer, letter to the author, 25 September 2001.
[34] Yad Vashem Righteous Among the Nations Archive, file 84.
[35] Michel Reynders, 'Father Bruno (Henry Reynders), His Life, His Work, Biography of a Righteous', manuscript, Yad Vashem Righteous Among the Nations Archive, file 84.

to take up the post of chaplain at a small Catholic institution, the Home for the Blind at Hodbomont. 'He quickly finds out', as his nephew Dr Michel Reynders later wrote, 'that the director, a Mr Walter Bieser, can see as well as he, and so does an elderly couple from Vienna, the Ashkenazys, and a Mr Silbermann. It is, in reality, a front for the true mission of the Home: to hide Jews in danger of being arrested. The management and most of the guests, including five or six genuinely blind children, are all Jews.'

The children at the home had recently been transferred there from L'Hospitalité, a charitable institution run by the Catholic Church to provide holiday camps for disadvantaged children, sponsored by the Diocese of Liège, and under the leadership of a lawyer from Liège, Albert Van den Berg. 'That house had, for some time, sheltered Jewish families,' Michel Reynders wrote, 'but the parents had just been arrested in a Gestapo raid (according to Father B none came back alive from Birkenau). For some unknown reason, the Nazis ignored the children, who were at once removed to Hodbomont. Upon his arrival, Father Bruno takes them under his care.'

Towards the end of 1942, Albert Van den Berg and Father Bruno decided that the Hodbomont house was no longer safe. In the words of Michel Reynders: 'Villagers know about the true situation and a careless, even inadvertent word can trigger a tragedy. Indeed, many arrests are reported in the area: adults and children must be dispersed, shelters must be found . . . thus begins the monk's rescue operation.'

Michel Reynders, then a teenager, played his own part in his uncle's rescue endeavours, serving, he writes, as 'an occasional letter carrier or escort for a brief trip within the city of Brussels'.[36]

---

[36] Dr Michel Reynders, letter to the author, 28 February 2002.

Father Bruno's work began on a small scale. In January 1943 he found ten families, some with between four and ten children of their own, willing to shelter Jews: these included the Bodarts, the Bertrands and the Martens of Louvain, and other families in Jodoigne, Ciney, Brussels, Namur and Bouge. To place Jews in these families, Michel Reynders noted, 'requires relentless work, constant and laborious travel (Father B most often rides his bicycle: at war's end he will have pedaled forty to fifty times as much as bicycle racers of the tour of Belgium!) but he never finds a closed door.' At first, there was no organization: 'Everything must be improvised, food supplies, clothing, false identification papers, new "aryanized" names, not to mention financial needs. Mr Van den Berg generously spends his own money, but, being a monk, Father Bruno owns nothing and must depend on gifts from friends and relatives. Besides, the children must be kept occupied and must pursue their studies. Fortunately, this can be arranged through school managers all over Belgium.'

In April 1943 Father Bruno found shelter for another sixteen Jewish children and adults; in May for a further seventeen; and in July for eighteen more. By the time his office in the abbey at Mont César was being raided by the Gestapo, he was handling his 159th rescue. He managed just in time to hide the incriminating documents, including lists of the non-Jewish-sounding names under which the children were being hidden. He then continued with his work of rescue, living at different addresses, first in Louvain and then in Brussels. In Brussels, he lived in the house next door to the office of an SS captain of the Office of Jewish Affairs. From that house, Father Bruno organized 150 rescues, and even hid Jews for several hours in the house itself before they were taken to their safe haven. His nephew Michel writes that, supported by Bishop Kerkhofs of Liège and in co-operation with Van den Berg, 'the priest places "his" children in numerous

381

religious institutions: the Sisters of Bellegem, the Home of Leffe, the Benedictine Abbey of Liège where his own sister (Mother Thérèse) is stationed, St Mary's boarding house at La Bouverie, the Jolimont Clinic, the nuns of Don Bosco in Courtrai, and many others.'

For his part, Van den Berg continued to place Jewish children in the three Capuchin Banneux homes, where Father Jamin and the monks Avelin, Fulbert and Jaminet cared for them. Among those sheltered in the Banneux homes were the Grand Rabbi of Liège, Joseph Lepkifker, and his elderly parents. The old couple were eventually caught and deported, to their deaths; Rabbi Lepkifker survived the war, leaving the homes with what Michel Reynders calls 'the memory of a deeply religious man, open to good relations with Christianity'. He adds: 'An exceptional man, true apostle of kindness, Albert Van den Berg is arrested in April 1943, given a light sentence but, when freed from jail, is re-arrested by the Gestapo and sent to the Neuengamme concentration camp where he was to die on the eve of liberation.'

Just before the German withdrawal, Father Bruno performed a final act of rescue in Brussels, in the Place du Chatelain. There he brought, and then found a home for, three children who had escaped the possibility of a last-minute deportation and spent the previous night in the Forest of Soignes: 'I never saw', Father Bruno recalled, 'children so eager to let themselves be scrubbed and cleansed in my basement, and with such exuberance!' He took the three children, aged eight and ten, to the Daughters of Charity in Asse, eight miles from Brussels, after which he returned to Brussels on foot, just in time to see German troops leave the city, never to return.'[37]

---

[37] Michel Reynders, 'Father Bruno (Henry Reynders), His Life, His Work, Biography of a Righteous', manuscript, Yad Vashem Righteous Among the Nations Archive, file 84.

In 1992, fifty years after Father Bruno began his rescue efforts, nine of those who owed their lives to him held a commemoration in a private home in Maplewood, New Jersey. A journalist who was present, Joseph Berger, recorded their stories for the *New York Times*. 'I think he was one of the very few good people,' said Jack Goldstein, the host of the reunion. 'He saw what was being done was wrong. Were it the reverse situation, I don't know how many people would have done what he did. Père Bruno, as he was known, was a slender, gentle man in his thirties with sharp eyes twinkling out from behind the spectacles of a scholar. A university teacher, he was an expert on the early Christian communities, which were made up of people who called themselves Jews but adhered to the teachings of Christ.'

Rachelle Goldstein was two and a half years old when she and her elder brother Jacques, aged nine, were found a hiding place in a Protestant orphanage in Uccle in July 1942. They stayed there, with several cousins, for eight months, until another child ran away from the orphanage and threatened to denounce the Jewish children. It was Father Bruno who found them other places to go. Rachelle was found sanctuary in the Convent of the Franciscan Sisters in Bruges, under the name of Lily Willems.[38] When Rachelle learned she would be staying there, she burst into tears. Some months later a woman member of the resistance came to the convent and left her a doll, a present from her mother. 'She told me my parents knew where I was,' Rachelle Goldstein recalled. 'It meant everything to me.'

A year later, after the liberation of Belgium, Rachelle was playing in the convent garden when a man and woman came to see her. She did not recognize them until the woman embraced her. 'When I went close to

---

[38] United States Holocaust Memorial Museum, Photo Archive, Worksheet 30789.

the woman, I recognized my mother by her scent.'

Jack Goldstein was nine years old when his mother took him and his twin brother to a train station to meet Father Bruno. He immediately gave them new names and new identity papers. They stayed the night with a doctor who, the next day, hid them under a blanket in the car. The doctor and Father Bruno talked their way through several German roadblocks to a convent, where the children spent the next six months. 'I didn't know if I would ever see my parents again,' said Jack Goldstein. 'I lived in fear. I studied Christianity. I went to church every morning, but I knew of my Jewish heritage.'

Many of Father Bruno's children made their way to the United States, where a remarkable quirk of destiny brought two of them together. Rachelle and Jack Goldstein did not know each other as children; they met in 1955 at a dance. Rachelle inquired about Jack's European accent, and the tale he told led to the discovery that they had been saved by the same man.

Another young boy, Bernard Rotmil, was hidden on a farm as a teenager and recalled that Father Bruno used to ride for many miles on a bicycle to visit him in hiding, to try to relieve his homesickness. Ultimately, he said, Father Bruno 'is best described by the simple Yiddish word for a decent person. He was a mensch.'

Flora Singer was helping her mother by taking jobs packing soap powder and assisting a dressmaker 'when Père Bruno stopped by and asked whether she would rather go to school. Her mother said that in order to eat they needed the money Flora brought in, so Père Bruno offered to bring the family food if Flora went to school. He then arranged for her to be hidden safely, for eleven months.[39]

---

[39] Joseph Berger, 'A Monk, a Saviour, a Mensch: Nine Jews Gather in New Jersey to Remember the Man Who Rescued Them From the Nazis', *New York Times*, 5 July 1992.

In recent years, Flora Singer frequently talks about
Father Bruno when she gives lectures in the United
States about the Righteous. 'I hold him up as an example
of what a human being should be', she has written; 'he
was certainly a model to be emulated.'[40]

'The last time I saw Père Bruno', wrote Paul Silvers,
one of the 320 youngsters for whom Father Henri
Reynders found a safe haven in Belgium, 'was shortly
after the liberation of Belgium. It was during the Jewish
High Holidays of 1944. The Dutch Synagogue in Brussels
was packed with worshippers. The Rabbi suddenly
halted the service and announced that Père Bruno had
just come in for a final visit with "his children" before
joining the Belgian troops as a chaplain. The reception
given Père Bruno by the congregation was tumultuous.
Kids were clinging to his arms and tearful parents were
showering him with thanks and blessings. It took a long
time for decorum to return to the synagogue and for the
services to resume. When I looked for him, Père Bruno
had quietly slipped out.'[41]

In Belgium, as in every German-occupied country, and
in Germany itself, it often took many non-Jews, working
together or at different times over several years, to save
a single Jew. Martin Glassman and his younger brother
Gary left Italy in April 1939 with their Polish-born
maternal grandparents to comply with an Italian law that
all foreign-born Jews must leave Italy. Their destination
was Brussels. After the German invasion of Poland in
September 1939, they were interned by the Belgian
authorities, as foreign aliens, at Camp Marneffe. There,
having reached the age of thirteen, Martin Glassman had

---

[40] Flora M. Singer, letter to the author, 12 October 2001.
[41] Paul Silvers (writing from Boulder, Colorado), 'Remember Père
Bruno', manuscript, Yad Vashem Righteous Among the Nations
Archive, file 84.

his barmitzvah. After the German invasion of Belgium in May 1940 they were released, and set off in the direction of Namur, but the German forces soon overran the whole country and they returned to occupied Brussels.

The first help given to Martin Glassman by a non-Jew came when he reached the age of fifteen and required his own identity card. A forged card was provided by Dr Thys, a member of the Belgian resistance who later took part in an attack on a deportation train – the twentieth train that left Malines for Auschwitz.

On the run from the forced labour decree issued by the Germans at the end of May 1942, Martin Glassman and his brother Gary were taken in by Madame Holland and her son Paul in their boarding house in Rhode St Genese outside Brussels. Their uncle Arthur Hellman was also found sanctuary, by Dr Thys and Madame Holland, in a tuberculosis clinic; later he returned to his home. The boys' grandparents, Emelie and Heinrich Hellman, were caught and arrested, then deported to Auschwitz and their deaths.

Later, Frère Luc de Bisshop, the Brother Director of the Institut St Nicolas in Anderlecht, took in the two brothers, registering them as Catholic students. He alone knew that they were Jewish. Martin Glassman later recalled: 'The Institut permitted students in good standing to exit Saturday afternoon and re-enter on Sunday evening. This created a need for a secure place for one night. Uncle Arthur forbade us to come to his house for fear of being denounced by one of his German tenants. Soon after the start of the school term, a spinster lady named Bile Durant became the liaison between our uncle and us. She visited us frequently, brought us clothing, school supplies, sweets and some pocket money. She would also take us along to her residence. Her sister, a physician, was married to a Jew of Russian ancestry who was also a physician. Their names were Drs Alechinsky, their offices and residence were on rue

Franz Merjay 43. We were given frequent shelter at this location. Summer vacations presented special problems because of the lengthy period during which the school was closed. During that long recess the Alechinskys permitted us to use their summer residence, the "Maison Rose" in the village of Sauvagemont. During those stays, Mademoiselle Durant would be our guardian. She would keep us busy with house chores, learning English and freehand drawing. In the fall we would resume our classes.'

Betrayal led to the arrest of Arthur Hellman. He was taken to the Gestapo fortress at Breendonk, tortured, and executed on 28 February 1944. He was thirty-seven years old. But his young nephews, Martin and Gary, were in safe hands. When Allied bombing raids led to the closure of the Institut, 'Mademoiselle Durant came to the rescue by securing us shelter in a Boy Scout camp in Momignies near the Franco-Belgian border. The camp shared facilities belonging to Trappist monks who generously provided this shelter for young men irrespective of origin to escape forced labour for the Germans. By the end of August the Germans had sustained heavy casualties; they requisitioned the facilities for their wounded and ordered us out within twenty-four hours. For the remainder of the occupation I was hidden in the Alechinsky residence, Gary in an orphanage until our liberation on September 3, 1944.'

Martin Glassman adds: 'It should be noted that there were many anonymous individuals who gave aid and comfort who wished to remain nameless or whose encounter was too brief for any introduction. I'll give you two examples. An Italian seamstress who at one time had been an employee of my uncle, spent hours in the street of his residence to intercept me should I go near the premises to warn me of his arrest. On one of the many religious holidays when I needed shelter, I was put up in the plundered offices of a physician who had been arrested for her activities with the resistance. I remained several days in the basement of the premises. My food was brought to me nightly by a Spaniard who himself was a wanted man because of his anti-Franco activities.'[42]

Cirla Italiaander was eight years old when her father Jaap was deported: he and all four of her grandparents were killed at Auschwitz. Her mother gave her into the care of a Christian couple, Jean-Louis and Betty Liem. The first thing the child had to do was to change her name to something less foreign: she became 'Suzy'. Then she was carefully coached in what she must do if the Gestapo came. 'There was a procedure we were to follow. I would pretend to be deaf and dumb and not speak whatever happened. We had no secret hiding places, but when Madame Liem's brother visited, we stayed upstairs; we were fed in advance and the brother and sister-in-law and their children didn't know. I was told "Suzy, don't make a noise because so-and-so is visiting."'

Recalling that during the Allied bombing raids against German military targets in Belgium, Madame Liem would pray, Cirla commented: 'I must say, when she made the sign of the Cross, I felt God would protect me. Her actions were guided by the knowledge that we were human beings and God would not approve of the Nazis. She was a very devout Catholic and felt that nobody should be killed because of race or religion. She took it on her that it was her mission in life.'[43]

Cirla remained in hiding with the Liems for eighteen months. After the war, she and her mother emigrated to Britain.[44]

---

[42] Martin Glassman, letter to the author, 5 September 2001.
[43] Shyam Bhatia, 'My saviours in the Holocaust' (Cirla Lewis's story), Observer, 14 September 1997.
[44] Yad Vashem Righteous Among the Nations Archive, file 7465.

Any act by a non-Jew, no matter how small or incomprehensible, could be the critical one in the story of a Jew's survival. Three-year-old Susan Preisz and her mother had been taken to Gestapo headquarters at the Avenue Louise in Brussels, 'amidst a crowd of Jews of all ages', the young girl's cousin Walter Absil later wrote, 'some crying, others praying. A scene straight out of Dante's Inferno.' What happened next was as life-saving as it was unexpected: 'A tall SS officer approached the grilled door, he asked in a loud commanding voice "to whom does this child belong", pointing at little Susan. Susan's mother gathered her child in her arms: "To me," she managed to say. "Come with me, Jewess," ordered the officer. He supplied the trembling mother with a pail, brush and water, ordering her to wash the stairs leading out of the cellar. This done, he ordered her out of the building. Holding her child, blinking at the bright sunlight filtering through the canopy of the tall chestnut trees lining the avenue, she walked slowly home.'

Walter Absil went on to ask: 'What caused the miracle? Did the officer see his own child in Susan's face? No one will ever know.' Susan Preisz and her mother survived the rest of the war in the Belgian countryside, 'helped and hidden', Walter Absil writes, 'by those brave people risking their lives without hesitation. Other countries had some righteous humanitarians helping under extremely dangerous conditions, but the Belgians and Danes, above all of the German occupied countries, behaved as real civilized Europeans.'[45]

Walter Absil was himself saved from deportation by a Belgian family who adopted him, and then by Belgian resistance fighters in the forest.[46]

*   *   *

[45] Walter Absil, 'Miracle at Avenue Louise', manuscript sent to the author, 25 October 2001.
[46] Walter Absil, letter to the author, 5 September 2001.

The principality of Luxembourg was overrun in May 1940 as German troops moved through it to conquer Belgium. Two of its citizens had worked to save Jews, but neither had been active in Luxembourg itself. One, Abbé Mat, had carried out his acts of rescue in neighbouring Belgium; the other, Victor Bodson, in neutral Spain.[47]

After describing the deportation of 674 Jews from Luxembourg between 1941 and 1943, the historian Ruth Zariz writes: 'Luxembourg became *judenrein* ("cleansed of Jews") except for a few Jews who had gone into hiding or were married to non-Jews. Once the deportations started, the chances of Jews being saved were poor. The country was small; it had a relatively large German population; the Luxembourgers were indifferent to the fate of the Jews, and while there were few instances of open hostility or informing, neither were there many efforts to hide Jews or otherwise help them.'[48]

Indifference, even betrayal, constitute many of the stories that emerge in every country; but in every country there are also many examples of risk and rescue; even tiny Luxembourg had Abbé Mat and Victor Bodson, albeit beyond its borders.

---

[47] Yad Vashem Righteous Among the Nations Archive, file 648.
[48] Ruth Zariz, 'Luxembourg', in *Encyclopedia of the Holocaust*, volume 3, page 928.

CHAPTER FOURTEEN

Holland

By 1 January 2002, Dutch citizens had received the second largest number of Righteous Among the Nations awards given by Yad Vashem in Jerusalem: 4,464 in all, second only to Poles.[1] This reflects the courage of many individual members of a small nation that was itself suffering the rigours of German rule. It was a nation which had a tradition of religious tolerance going back to the time when it rejected the Inquisition, and welcomed many thousands of the Jews who had been expelled from Spain in 1492. Wartime rescue efforts were also remarkable because Holland, ruled for almost five years by a Reich Commissar responsible directly to Berlin, contained a significant element in its social fabric sympathetic to the Nazi ideology. As a result, compared with Belgium's nearly 50 per cent, less than 20 per cent of Holland's Jews managed to find hiding places during the war, and many of these – including Anne Frank and her family – were betrayed. Of Holland's hundred and forty thousand Jews when war broke out (including twenty thousand refugees from Germany and Austria), a hundred and seven thousand were deported to their deaths.

---

[1] 'Righteous Among the Nations – per Country & Ethnic Origin,' 1 January 2002, Yad Vashem Department for the Righteous Among the Nations (list sent to the author on 29 January 2002).

The first test of Dutch reaction came on 22 and 23 February 1941, after Dutch fascists who attacked Jews in Amsterdam were met by a vigorous Jewish self-defence, during which one Dutch fascist was killed and a German policeman injured. In reprisal, the Germans seized 425 Jews, mostly youngsters, who were later deported to Buchenwald and Mauthausen concentration camps, and murdered. In reaction to the arrests, what the Dutch Jewish historian Louis de Jong has called the 'powder keg of indignation' against German occupation and Dutch collaboration 'was full to the brim'. The Dutch Communist Party called a general strike for February 25. The personnel of the Amsterdam municipal tramways, writes de Jong, 'set a fine example and within a few hours the strike was more or less general. It continued for two days. When as a result of indiscriminate shooting nine Amsterdam citizens were killed and forty-five wounded, and when, moreover, the Germans threatened serious reprisals, the workmen returned to the wharves and factories and the shop-keepers reopened their doors.'

De Jong goes on to ask: 'Does the history of the Diaspora offer another example of a non-Jewish group protesting against the persecution of Jews living in their midst by carrying out a general strike? Without doubt, patriotic sentiments played an important part in the strike movement, but one would fail to appreciate the true importance of this magnificent manifestation if one did not find the strongest motives in human sympathy and in indignation caused by the brutal behaviour of Jew-hunters.'

On 2 May 1942 the Germans ordered all Jews over the age of thirteen to wear a yellow star on their clothing. Louis de Jong notes that there were a few cases, 'altogether perhaps several dozens throughout the country – of non-Jews expressing their protest by wearing the Jewish star; some of these were imprisoned, others were sent to the concentration camp of Amersfoort. It was much more general to sympathize with the Jews in ways which did not attract the attention of German or Dutch Nazis. The Jews had been branded.'[2]

A turning point for the Jews of Holland came on 14 July 1942. That day a special issue of the Jewish weekly newspaper contained an ominous notice, based on information provided by the Gestapo: 'Some 700 Jews have been arrested today in Amsterdam. Unless the 4,000 Jews who have been assigned to labour camps in Germany report this week for transportation, these 700 hostages will be sent to a concentration camp in Germany.' The notice was signed by the two chairmen of the Jewish Council of Amsterdam.

A seventeen-year-old Dutch girl, Edith van Hessen (later Velmans), later wrote that it was this declaration that 'galvanized' her older brother Jules into action. 'He had come to the conclusion that the only thing to do now was to "dive under" – i.e. to assume a new identity – before the dreaded summons arrived for him. He convinced Father and Mother that they should let me go too.'[3] Edith van Hessen was fortunate that a Dutch couple, Tine and Egbert zur Kleinsmiede, 'had been following the predicament of the Jews with mounting dismay. They lived in Breda, a provincial town in the south of the country, with their only child, Ineke, who was four years older than me.' Tine zur Kleinsmiede, or 'Mrs z K, as I called her, was in her mid-forties. She was a formidable, proud, attractive woman with prematurely white hair and a determined set of the jaw. Her husband was fourteen years older, big, bulky and jovial, a retired high-school headmaster. They seemed nice, serious and thoughtful people. I immediately felt at ease with them.

---

[2] Louis de Jong, 'Jews and Non-Jews in Nazi-Occupied Holland', in Max Beloff (editor), *On the Track of Tyranny*, pages 145–7.
[3] Edith Velmans, *Edith's Book*, pages 93–4.

It was decided that very evening. The z Ks would take me in.'[4]

In Amsterdam, Anne Frank's family had gone into hiding on 9 July 1942, when her sister Margot received a call-up notice. The Van Daan family, with whom the Franks shared their hiding place for three years, went into hiding with them five days later. Those who helped the Franks and the Van Daans included Miep Gies, who acted as a go-between with the outside world, providing the family with information and going on errands for them. When the family first arrived at their hiding place, it was Miep Gies who, Anne Frank wrote in her diary, 'took us quickly upstairs and into the "Secret Annexe". She closed the door behind us and we were alone.'[5] Almost exactly a year later, Anne Frank wrote: 'Miep is just like a pack mule, she fetches and carries so much. Almost every day she manages to get hold of some vegetables for us and brings everything in shopping bags on her bicycle.'[6]

On 14 July 1942 an official declaration warned that any Jew who did not respond to the summons for forced labour would be arrested and sent to Mauthausen concentration camp. The same punishment was in store for any Jew who was caught not wearing a star or changing residence without notifying the authorities. From everywhere in Holland, Jews were sent by train to the detention camp at Westerbork, close to the German border. From there, starting on 15 July 1942, they were deported by train, some to Auschwitz, others to Sobibor, and murdered.

---

[4] Edith Velmans, *Edith's Book*, pages 96–7. Edith remained hidden under a false identity at the zur Kleinsmiedes' until Breda was liberated in September 1944. Her parents and brother did not survive.
[5] Diary entry, 10 July 1942, *Anne Frank, The Diary of a Young Girl*, page 17.
[6] Diary entry, 11 July 1943, *Anne Frank, The Diary of a Young Girl*, page 76.

Non-Jewish families throughout Holland risked their own safety by taking Jews into their homes and pretending they were Christians, thus keeping them safe from deportation. One of the most daring and committed rescuers was Johannes Bogaard, a devout Dutch Calvinist farmer in Nieuw Vennep. Towards the end of 1941, after his father had been detained briefly by police for his public condemnation of German anti-Semitic policy, Johannes Bogaard resolved to do all he could to rescue the Jews. He began travelling to Amsterdam, Rotterdam and other cities to find Jews in need of protection, and to bring them back to his farm. As the number of Jews on the farm increased, he dispersed them among the farms of his brothers and other Calvinist friends in the area. On his frequent trips to the city he also obtained money, ration cards, identification papers and other necessities for the Jews in hiding under assumed Christian identities.

In addition to hiding Jews, the Bogaard family also hid members of a Dutch resistance on a nearby farm, in a series of underground bunkers. In autumn 1944 a Dutch policeman accidentally discovered these hiding places and was shot and killed by the resistance. In response the SS raided the farm. Most of those in hiding managed to escape before the raid, but thirty-four adults were captured and seven others were murdered in a nearby forest. Willem Bogaard, Johannes' son, escaped during the raid, taking twenty children with him. They hid in a nearby canal until the SS had gone. Despite the arrests, Johannes Bogaard continued his rescue mission. It is believed that he saved more Jews than any other single Dutch rescuer.[7]

---

[7] United States Holocaust Memorial Museum, Photo Archive, Worksheet 15120; also Yad Vashem Righteous Among the Nations Archive, file 28. The story of the rescue work of the Bogaards is among those recounted in Debórah Dwork, *Children with a Star*.

In Amersfoort, Jan Kanis not only took in several Jewish families to his home, but found places of refuge for large numbers of Jews, both children and their parents. He also procured ration cards for those whom he had placed in hiding. Arrested by the Gestapo, he betrayed none of those whom he had helped to hide. While he was imprisoned in Dachau for a year and a half, his wife Petronela (Nel) Kanis took over his work of rescue.[8]

The hostility that could be found towards Jews in Holland made hiding much more difficult than, for example, in neighbouring Belgium, and the work of the rescuers that much more risky. The Austrian-born Victor Kugler, who hid Anne Frank and her family in Amsterdam (he appears as Mr Kraler in her diary), later recalled the moment of betrayal, what he called 'that terrible day' of 4 August 1944. 'On that fateful Friday, while working in my office, I heard an unusual commotion. I opened my office door and saw four policemen. One was a uniformed Gestapo man, the other three were Dutch.' One of the Dutch policemen was a notorious collaborator who was executed after the liberation.[9]

Betrayal was a constant danger. Albert Steenstra was a commander in the Dutch resistance. He and his wife Louisa hid as many as ten Jews in the large attic of their home in Groningen. But then the Steenstras were forced by the local authorities to house a Dutch couple, who realized that Jews were hiding in the attic and informed the authorities. In January 1945 Germans raided the house, killing Albert Steenstra and all the Jews. Louisa Steenstra managed to escape with her daughter and go into hiding.[10]

---

[8] Yad Vashem Righteous Among the Nations Archive, file 0655.
[9] Eda Shapiro (editor), 'The Memoirs of Victor Kugler, the "Mr Kraler" of the "Diary of Anne Frank"'.
[10] Yad Vashem Righteous Among the Nations Archive, file 1790.

In Amsterdam, after the war, forty-six Dutchmen and women were honoured in a single ceremony for their part in saving Jews from deportation. 'They came from Friesland in the north and from Limburg in the south, from Amsterdam and The Hague,' wrote the Amsterdam correspondent of the *Jerusalem Post*, 'and even more of them were from tiny villages. Some were Calvinists, some Roman Catholics and some had no religious affiliations. There were clergymen, doctors and peasants among them. Two of the women had been matron and assistant matron of a children's holiday home and had hidden over thirty Jewish youngsters from the Nazi occupiers. The legendary "Uncle Piet," whose real name was Wybenga and who had been the resistance leader in Friesland, was also there.'[11] Peter Wybenga, a high-school teacher, saved many Jews in the northern province of Friesland, where he was an active resistance leader.[12]

German-born Heinz Thomas Stein was an eleven-year-old refugee when the deportations began from Holland. A Dutch nurse, Hannah van der Fort, a member of the Dutch resistance, found him a hiding place, on his twelfth birthday, with the Lutjen family on their farm at Swolchen. There he worked as a farmhand, sleeping in the barn. When SS troops occupied the barn in the summer of 1944, he continued to work on the farm, slipping away each night to sleep in the nearby woods.[13]

When a Jewish woman, Leesha Rose, published her account of the work she did with Dutchmen and women who helped Jews go underground or smuggled them across the North Sea to Sweden, Alexander Zvielli, a Polish-born survivor, wrote contrasting the

---

[11] 'Postscripts', *Jerusalem Post*, 17 January 1977.
[12] Yad Vashem Righteous Among the Nations Archive, file 926.
[13] United States Holocaust Memorial Museum, Photo Archive, Worksheet 97262.

Dutch and Polish experiences: 'Except for a small gang of traitors who were carried away by German racist propaganda, the overwhelming majority of the Dutch remained faithful to their crown, church, ideals and their Jewish neighbours. They drew their encouragement from the pulpit during Sunday church services and regarded assistance to Nazi victims as the humane thing to do.'[14]

Shortly after the German conquest of Holland in May 1940, Wilhelmina Willegers made a purchase from the Amsterdam shop of Coenraad Polak, a Jewish textile merchant. They struck up a conversation and, as she left, Mrs Willegers told Mr Polak to contact her if he ever needed help. Two months later he did so, asking if her offer still stood. When the violence that had broken out in Amsterdam's Jewish quarter between Dutch fascists and Jewish defence units led to hundreds of Jewish men being sent to the camps, the Willegers family hid Coenraad Polak and a business associate of his in their home in Bussum, ten miles from Amsterdam. The day after taking them there, and without telling them, Wilhelmina Willegers and her daughter Bettina returned to Amsterdam and brought back the men's wives.

The two couples stayed with the Willegers family for six weeks before deciding to return to Amsterdam. From there, they escaped to Switzerland, through Belgium and France. Bettina Willegers (later, Elizabeth Browne) helped them with their plans, making contact with smugglers on the Dutch–Belgian border, and then travelling there with them. During the journey, German officers boarded the train to check passengers' papers, whereupon she accused one of the officers of making

---

[14] Alexander Zvielli, 'The price of courage', *Jerusalem Post*, 2 March 1979.

HOLLAND

improper advances to her, thereby saving the Polaks from detection in the ensuing chaos.[15]

Jan Schoumans, a non-Jew, was the manager of a Jewish-owned vegetarian restaurant in Amsterdam. While at work he met Rosa Ehrenzweig, a Jewish refugee from Germany. In 1942 all Jewish-owned restaurants were ordered to close, and Rosa feared she would be sent to a concentration camp. Jan Schoumans told her: 'You are not going! You leave it to me,' and provided false identification papers for her and her best friend, Temi Lowy. He then found a home in the countryside where they hid for three years while working in domestic service. 'I took the risk,' he said, 'because I am a humanist.'[16]

Eelkje Lentink-de-Boer was the first Dutch person to be designated Righteous Among the Nations. Living in Amsterdam during the war, she hid twelve Jews. She also helped others who were in trouble. S. Abrahams-Emden recalled how, after her husband was arrested, Eelkje Lentink-de-Boer 'put in safety me, my sister and her husband with the family Pap in Nunspeet. But it was not safe there. After a raid by the SS, we were on the run in a wood. During this escape, we lived in this wood for two months. Mrs Eelkje Lentink-de-Boer visited us every week. One day she told me that she would be bringing me to their home, but I was afraid, because she had still twenty refugees at home. I refused to go with her. I wanted to stay by my family in the wood. After a few

[15] Karen Glaser, 'Wartime heroics of Dutch woman are recognized', *Jewish Chronicle*, 21 July 2000. Elizabeth Browne had just received the Righteous Among the Nations award on behalf of her parents, at the Israeli Embassy in London. Yad Vashem Righteous Among the Nations Archive, file 8808.
[16] Desmond Brown, 'Israel honours two Toronto war heroes', *National Post*, 9 February 1999. The other honorand was Sandor Tonelli (see chapter 16).

days I heard from the resistance movement that all the people in the house of Mrs Lentink, including Mrs Lentink were arrested.[17]

Eelkje Lentink-de-Boer had been betrayed. She was sent to Ravensbrück concentration camp, where she was subjected to callous medical experiments, which left her 90 per cent paralysed.[18]

Another of those whom Eelkje Lentink-de-Boer had helped save was Selma Klass-Aronowitz, who later recalled how, at the beginning of 1943, her parents 'started looking for a hiding place for me first. Mrs Eelkje Lentink-de-Boer, who was working for the underground, got a place for me and they told my parents that I would be brought to the southern part of the country with a childless couple, Mr and Mrs Hein and Jeanne Oolbekking, in the city of Heerlen. After that my parents found a place for themselves in a small hamlet. I remember staying with my foster parents who were very good to me. My foster father was a chief mining engineer. They had a big house and did everything for me to make me happy. In that little town where I was there were about thirty Jewish children brought for hiding by several families.

'One day, at the end of 1943, the Germans got on the trail and decided to round up all the Jewish children in that village. My foster father, however, got notice beforehand, and took me away. Fifteen minutes later the Germans came in and asked my foster mother where the Jewish child was. My foster mother said she didn't have a Jewish child, but they started to interrogate the maid, and the maid got scared and told them there was a Jewish child. They took my foster mother to a concentration

---

[17] Testimony of S. Abrahams-Emden, 25 April 1977, Yad Vashem Righteous Among the Nations Archive, file 5.
[18] Yad Vashem Righteous Among the Nations Archive, file 5.

31. Eva Ahlfeld (*centre*), with the
two children of Pastor Marc
Donadille, her
rescuer, France, 1943.

32. Pastor André Trocmé, a French
Protestant rescuer.

33. Juliette Usach, director of a children's home in Le Chambon-sur-Lignon, France, with a group of Jewish youngsters under her care.

34. Dr Roger and Danielle Leforestier. Dr Leforestier provided medical care for Jewish children hiding in Le Chambon-sur-Lignon. He was executed by the Germans in 1944.

35. Rita Goldstein (*second from left*) with a group of girls at a Catholic orphanage in Millau.

36. Audrée Fain and her three daughters (one of them Nadine), in Souillac. The girls were hidden in a Catholic boarding school in Clermont-Ferrand.

37. Refik Veseli, a sixteen-year-old Albanian Muslim (*right*), plays in the snow with Irena and Gavra Mandil, two of the Jewish children whom his family hid, together with their parents and several cousins.

38. Marion Kaufmann (*centre*), with the Gypsy family who hid her on the Dutch–German border for a month.

39. Aleksey Aleksandrovich Glagolyev, a Russian Orthodox priest who saved five Jews in Kiev.

40. Remond Dufour, a Dutchman in the town of Aerdenhout, with his own son (*left*) and Bernard Geron (*right*), a Jewish child in hiding.

41. Alicja Pinczewska (*third from right in last row that includes girls*), hidden under the assumed name of Alicja Woloszczuk, at a convent in Wawer, outside Warsaw. Several other children at the convent were also Jewish children in hiding. This photograph was taken at the time of the children's First Communion.

42. Lea Kalin (*seated second from right*) with her Polish fellow forced labourers, at an ammunition factory in Germany. Although the others knew she was Jewish they kept her identity secret.

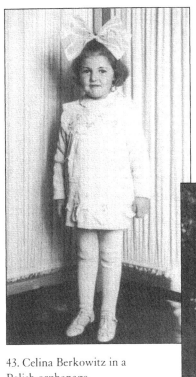

43. Celina Berkowitz in a Polish orphanage.

44. Ursula Selig, a German Jewish refugee in Italy, who was hidden with her family by Father Schivo and a fellow Roman Catholic priest in a convent.

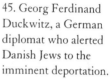

45. Georg Ferdinand Duckwitz, a German diplomat who alerted Danish Jews to the imminent deportation.

46. The attic of Gilleleje church, where eighty Jewish refugees in Denmark were caught by the Gestapo and deported to Theresienstadt.

camp; but I was very happy after the war to hear that the Germans let her free after a year in the camp.'

Hein and Jeanne Oolbekking tried to get another place for Selma, and found one with a Catholic family in Venlo. 'I was brought to Mr and Mrs Jan and Tinie van Dyk. He was a tailor. They had one daughter, my age, and they wanted very much to have more children, but couldn't get them. They were very good to me. In some way or another, during the transfer from my original foster parents to the other foster parents' home, I lost all memory of my real parents. My second foster parents were very religious and they told everybody that I was a relative; and only the church knew the truth.'

Selma's grandmother and her uncle were both hidden in Amsterdam by a young woman, Willie Dhont, from March to December 1943, 'at which time they were discovered by the Gestapo. My grandmother and uncle were sent to Auschwitz and perished there. Because my parents were on the same list, the Gestapo tried to get from the girl my parents' hiding place, but the girl kept saying she did not know.' Willie Dhont and Selma's parents survived the war.[19]

The parents of Gerda and Doris Bloch did not survive: from Westerbork they were deported to Theresienstadt, and from there to Auschwitz. The two girls were first given sanctuary by the Van Lohuizen family, resistance leaders in the town of Epe. Eventually Gerda went to live with the family of Reverend Adriaan and Ank Faber in Kampen, while Doris was taken to the farm of Carl-Johann and Helene Derksen in Lobith-Tolkamer in eastern Holland. For a time the Derksens also sheltered a young Dutchman who was in danger of being sent to Germany for forced labour, as well as two Allied airmen who had been shot down.

---

[19] Testimony of Selma Klass-Aronowitz, 12 July 1977, Yad Vashem Righteous Among the Nations Archive, file 5.

401

For most of the time Doris Bloch lived openly, under the assumed name of Dorothea Blokland, but her hosts prepared two hiding places in the event of a raid. One was behind a wall in their home, the other in the hayloft of the barn. Doris remained with the Derksens until the end of the war, when she learned that her parents had perished in Auschwitz.[20]

Aart and Johte Vos hid several Jewish families in their house on the outskirts of Amsterdam. At one point there were thirty-six Jews hidden there. From under the house they dug a tunnel that led into the nearby woods, and whenever warnings came of a Gestapo raid, the Jews fled through the tunnel. These advance warnings were relayed to the Vos couple by a personal friend – the local Dutch police chief. All the Jews hiding with them survived the war.[21]

A Dutch district nurse, Sister Ewoud, gave a place to hide to Steffi Tikotin, a nineteen-year-old German Jewish refugee from Dresden. Sister Ewoud sheltered her Steffi two and a half years, until the hiding place was betrayed; she was then given haven by Thames Commandeur, a widower with six daughters and a son. 'They treated me as one of the family,' she later wrote. 'It restored my faith in humanity.'[22]

The father and stepmother of a future Dutch Minister of Foreign Affairs, Max van der Stoel, also saved a Jewish life. When a round-up was feared to be imminent in Rotterdam, Hetty van der Stoel took an infant boy, Micha Wertheim, into her home in the village of Voorschoten, near The Hague. Her husband Martinus was the village physician. They explained the sudden arrival of a baby

---

[20] United States Holocaust Memorial Museum, Photo Archive, Worksheet 99723.
[21] United States Holocaust Memorial Museum, Photo Archive, Worksheet 90666.
[22] Steffi Robertson (*née* Tikotin), letter to the author, 25 October 1994, quoted in Martin Gilbert, *The Day the War Ended*, page 224.

with the story that he had been left as a foundling on their doorstep. Hetty van der Stoel later told a friend how, one day when she was strolling in the street in Voorschoten with the toddler, walking past a group of German soldiers, she overheard one of them saying: 'There goes Frau Doktor, with her Jewish little boy' – whereupon she deemed it prudent to leave her home for a while. The infant Micha survived in her care.[23]

Marion van Binsbergen was a student social worker when Germany invaded Holland. In 1941 she was arrested and imprisoned for seven months after German police raided a gathering at a friend's apartment, where the students were listening to Allied broadcasts and making copies of what they heard for distribution. In 1942 Marion was working in a rehabilitation centre when the director asked her to take home a two-year-old boy, Jantje Herben, the son of a Jewish couple who were about to be deported. She kept him in her home for several months, until she was able to find a safer shelter for him outside Amsterdam. Later that year she witnessed a brutal deportation action at a Jewish children's home in Amsterdam; and from then on she made rescue work her priority. Among the many Jews for whom she found shelter were Freddie Polak and his three small children. She moved them into a house in the country that was owned by a woman friend. At first she joined them only at weekends, but in 1943 she moved there full-time in order to take care of the children while their father worked on his thesis.

One night the house was raided by German and Dutch police. At the time of the raid the Polaks were hiding in the basement, and escaped detection, but when the Dutch policeman returned alone a short time later, the children were upstairs. To prevent them from being

---

[23] Information provided by Krik Arriëns, letters to the author, 31 January, 12 March 2002.

taken away, Marion van Binsbergen shot and killed the policeman with a revolver that a friend had given her. She fled, hid and survived the war, as did those for whom she had found a hiding place.[24]

Also in Amsterdam, Tina Buchter, a twenty-year-old medical student, her mother, Marie Buchter, and her grandmother, Marie Schotte, hid more than a hundred Jews on the top floor of their family home in Amsterdam, in groups of five at a time. In an interview given to her local newspaper in the United States, fifty years after the first deportations from Holland to the death camps, she spoke of how her best friend in Amsterdam was a young Jewish woman who worked as a cook in an orphanage. That young woman, her sister and her brother-in-law became the first people Tina and her mother hid.

Tina Buchter and her mother spoke to each other only once about what they were doing, and its dangers. 'We're hiding people. There are posters all over the city announcing the *death penalty* for helping or hiding Jews. Do you know we can be killed?' the mother said to her daughter. 'Yes,' the daughter replied. They never discussed the matter again. 'We knew we couldn't just stand by while Jewish people were killed,' Tina later reflected.

The goal was to shelter Jews and move them from one sympathetic home to another. Some were then smuggled to neutral Spain and Switzerland – walking, for three months, at night; others were sent to homes in the remote Dutch countryside, where there were fewer Dutch police and even fewer Germans – and more food. Those in hiding spent their days and nights as quietly as possible on the top floor of the Buchters' home. 'We talked to our Jewish friends and we stayed with them to try to make their terrifying lives just a little more bearable,' Tina

---

[24] United States Holocaust Memorial Museum, Photo Archive, Worksheet 89823.

recalled. When the Gestapo came, eight times, searching for Jews, mother and daughter insisted that they were hiding no one. Despite repeated searches, 'not one of the more than one hundred Jews hiding in our house was caught; three were caught outside.'

Tina and her mother appeared to have a friend in the Gestapo headquarters, who often telephoned before a Nazi raid to warn: 'You're going to have visitors.' This gave the Jews in hiding time to escape to other homes. Tina never discovered the identity of the caller: 'I just know he helped us a great deal.' If the friend did not telephone, the Jews were saved by a special bell that connected the first and second floors to the Jewish hiding place on the third floor. When the Germans rang the front door bell, Tina and her mother rang the second bell – and the Jews on the third floor left the house through the back doors and back windows to the roof. If there was no time to leave, the Jews would crouch in a tiny secret attic compartment that had been built by a carpenter who was a member of the Dutch underground.[25]

On nine occasions Tina was arrested and interrogated: once she was thrown against the wall by the Gestapo interrogators until she was nearly unconscious. She betrayed none of those whom she had helped.[26] At social gatherings, she stole people's identity cards, which the underground turned into life-saving documents for Jews.[27] She also obtained the release from prison of a Jewish friend, Dr Abraham Pais, by pleading in person with a high Nazi official. Pais later became a distinguished nuclear physicist, and the biographer of both Niels Bohr and Einstein.

[25] Interview with Dr Tina Strobos, *Gannett Suburban Newspapers*, 5 March 1992.
[26] United States Holocaust Memorial Museum, Photo Archive, file 90231.
[27] Eva Fogelman, *Conscience and Courage: Rescuers of Jews during the Holocaust*, page 81.

In recalling the activities of her grandmother, Tina (later Tina Strobos) has written: 'She hid Dr Henri Polak – the founder of the Diamond Workers Union and a well-known journalist – and his wife and many others until May 1945. She is the only person I know who scared the Gestapo. On one of their visits and interrogation at her house, she said to the one interrogating her, "Did not I see you looting a Persian rug out of the Mendlessohns' apartment next door a few nights ago?" He quickly grabbed his dossier on her and said he had to go. Imagine: she grabbed his arm and looked him straight in the eye. She showed me how! Her eyes sparkled with anger even in the retelling.'[28]

Tina's greatest fear was that she would not rescue enough Jews.[29]

Joop Woortman and his wife Semmy not only took a Jewish girl into their home, but were active in the rescue committee which Joop had established. This committee found foster homes, hiding places and false papers for many other Jewish children. Arrested in July 1944, Joop is thought to have died in Belsen. After his arrest, his wife took charge of the committee's work.[30]

Juliette Zeelander, in hiding in Holland at the age of four, recalls an incident after she had been placed with a Christian family. 'I had to change my surname to theirs, mine was a Jewish name. I knew I had to hide my identity. It was instilled into me what my new name was. But one day, I must have been about five and a half years old, I went shopping with the lady of the house. I see myself clearly in front of a display cabinet, with a lady in black,

---

[28] Tina Strobos, *The Book of Courage: The First Annual Act of Courage Awards*, Victims Assistance Services Brochure, Hudson River Museum, New York, 4 May 2001.
[29] Roberta Hershenson, 'Dutch Rescuer to Give Talk', *New York Times*, 26 March 1995.
[30] United States Holocaust Memorial Museum, Photo Archive, Worksheet 90790.

me looking up, and the lady asking me in a friendly tone, "Dear, what is your name?" And I said quite cheerfully: "My name is Juliette van Tijn, but my real name is Juliette Zeelander." Neither adult responded, but I realized that I had said something not right. I think as a little child I put this lady's life in danger several times. I mean real danger.'[31]

Violette Munnik took three-year-old Robert Krell into her family home in The Hague. Her friends often visited, 'and to all of them', Robert's interviewer, André Stein, later wrote, 'she told the truth about her new houseguest. A quiet conspiracy therefore followed to hide the boy's true identity from outsiders: what is amazing is that he was not betrayed. Robbie and the Munniks were most fortunate that the neighbourhood wove a net of secrecy around them, safeguarding them from the authorities' – and from a well-known collaborator, a member of the Dutch National Organization, who lived across the street. Violette Munnik's husband Albert would bring home wood and busy himself making toys for his new 'son' who had arrived at his new home without any. 'Robbie's favourite was a wooden dog that moved its legs and wagged its tail, which he has to this day. And when he was finished making toys, Albert would sit Robbie on his lap and read to him. Or he would sit at the piano and play simple melodies he had taught himself.' Indeed, writes Stein, Albert Munnik 'was a man of many talents, and he put all of them to the task of cheering up the little boy who had been forced to live in captivity without the company of friends.'[32] Robert Krell adds: 'My new ten-year-older "sister", Nora Munnik, spent her after school

---

[31] 'Juliette', in Paul Valent, *Child Survivors of the Holocaust*, page 130. Paul Valent was himself hidden as a child in Budapest with his parents.
[32] André Stein, *Hidden Children: Forgotten Survivors of the Holocaust*, pages 4, 7.

hours teaching her little Jewish brother to read and write.'[33]

'I was five years old when my parents turned me over to strangers in Amsterdam,' Lore Baer recalled. 'This couple could not keep me because they were of mixed marriage and neighbours became suspicious when they suddenly had a five-year-old child. They brought me to North Holland where the underground placed me with a very caring family. I lived with the Schouten family for two years from 1943 to 1945. I used an assumed name there, and even went to a Catholic school.'[34]

Cornelia Schouten was in her mid-twenties when she took the five-year-old into her home and made her part of the family. 'I really think she thought of me as her child and was heart-broken when my parents came to claim me after the war,' Lore Baer wrote. 'The feeling was mutual.'[35]

Remond Dufour and his family gave sanctuary in Aerdenhout to five-year-old Bernard Geron, whom they brought up with their own son, as if the two boys were brothers. After the war Bernard was reunited with his father and his own brother; his mother had not survived.[36]

In his introduction to the Netherlands volume of Yad Vashem's Lexicon of *Righteous Among the Nations*, Dr Jozeph Michman writes of 'entire groups of helpers', including a group of teachers at Alkmaar and The Hague, and a team of tax experts in Maastricht, who undertook to divide among themselves the task of providing the various facilities needed in order to maintain Jews in hiding: identity cards, means of transport from hiding

---

[33] Professor Robert Krell, letter to the author, 1 May 2002.
[34] Lore Baer, letter to the author, 6 August 2001.
[35] Lore Baer, letter to the author, 2 December 2001.
[36] United States Holocaust Memorial Museum, Photo Archive, Worksheet 05043.

place to hiding place, food supplies, and, in case of emergencies, trustworthy doctors and other specialists, such as those who could construct hiding places. 'The going into hiding which forced enervating passivity on the Jews demanded constant activity and vigilance on the part of their helpers.'[37]

Based at their isolated house near Bilthoven, Henk Huffener, his sister Ann and their younger brother Joep helped smuggle Jews to Switzerland, and later to Spain. Early in 1942 Henk was introduced to Loekie Metz, a young Jewish woman who was staying at a Zionist kibbutz at Loosdrecht farm, many of whose members were young Jewish refugees from Germany. 'In March 1942 a tip came that they had less than a month to fold up the kibbutz and get out. The Germans were very fond of the idea of "way folk", as they were then called – young people going up country, hikers and bikers.' So Huffener and others would go unnoticed as they cycled through the countryside, accompanied by one or two members of the kibbutz. It was an audacious and dangerous mission. On one occasion Huffener was stopped by German soldiers while escorting an obviously Jewish-looking girl who spoke no Dutch. He kissed her, explained to the Germans that they must be off or they would be in trouble with their parents, and got away with it.'[38]

A Dutch Christian Socialist, Joop Westerweel, who headed a group of twenty like-minded Dutch patriots who smuggled Jews from Holland across Belgium and France to Switzerland and to Spain, helped all the remaining seventy members of the 'kibbutz' at

---

[37] Dr Jozeph Michman, introduction to *Righteous Among the Nations Lexicon*, volume 1: *Holland*.
[38] Grace Bradberry, 'Surrey's own Oskar Schindler', *The Times*, 1 March 1999. After the war, Henk Huffener moved to Britain, where he became a British citizen. He was the thirteenth Briton to be honoured by Yad Vashem.

Loosdrecht farm to escape when, in August 1942, they were warned that their deportation was imminent. Westerweel's group spirited them away to safe havens throughout Holland. One of those safe havens, the Roman Catholic village of Sevenum, was hiding several hundred Jews in the village and surrounding farms by the end of the war.

Westerweel's wife, Wilhelmina, and their two daughters, also actively participated in the work of rescue. One day they were caught on the Belgian border. Wilhelmina was sent to the concentration camp at Ravensbrück, where she survived the war. Joop Westerweel was sent to Vught concentration camp in Holland, where he was tortured for several months, and then killed.[39]

It is estimated that Westerweel and his group smuggled as many as two hundred Jews out of Holland into France, including the seventy Palestine pioneers.[40]

The Streekstra family hid a seventeen-year-old Jewish girl, Katow, on their farm in Friesland. Wybren Streekstra later recalled: 'She stayed with us for the whole winter. She never came outside in the daytime; it was too dangerous, and she looked too Jewish. At different times we would get a signal that something was going to happen. It was night and curfew, but I knew the fields and creek, and I had long rubber boots. I took Katow on my back and carried her over the creek. Then I would take her across the fields to a place where we could sleep in the straw. Just before it got light in the morning we went back home. This happened ten or fifteen times. You know, you don't really sleep on those nights.'[41]

---

[39] Benek (Baruch) Sharoni, 'Man's Humanity to Man', *Mizkor*, October 2000; Yad Vashem Righteous Among the Nations Archive, file 67.
[40] Jozeph Michman, 'Westerweel, Joop (1899–1944)', *Encyclopedia of the Holocaust*, volume 4, page 1648.
[41] United States Holocaust Memorial Museum, Photo Archive, Worksheet 87556.

Those in hiding knew that they could not expect leniency or reprieve if they were discovered, either for themselves or for those who had taken them in. Thea van Oosten, whose parents took in a Jew, Joop Schijveschuurder, wrote to him after the war: 'What a risk my parents took by taking you into our home. I never asked them why they had done so. It just did not occur to them not to help people in need. It was a deed of neighbourly love. It was not just to sabotage the Germans.'

Joop Schijveschuurder, who together with his brother Loek was saved by several Dutch families, wanted to put the facts of such rescue activities into their true perspective, writing in his memoirs: 'I have to get the following off my chest. Of the approximately 25,000 Jews who were in hiding in Holland, 16,000 survived in their hiding places. The rest were betrayed or found . . . If one betrayed Jews, one was paid five or 7.50 Dutch guilders.'[42] For every Dutch person who helped a Jew, there was another seemingly ready to betray the rescuers.

Typically for Jews in hiding, in Holland as elsewhere, several families and individuals enabled Joop Schijveschuurder and his brother to survive: among them the Van Oostens, the Ides, the De Graafs, and Marius Beerman, a Dutch plainclothes policeman (known as Bob) who had warned of an imminent arrest and deportation in Haarlem. 'We were phoned by the Germans that they were going to arrest Jews in the Wagenweg,' he later recalled, in a letter to Joop Schijveschuurder. 'I raced like a hare to the address they had given, and warned the people. When the phone call about you came, it was already late in the evening, I

---

[42] Joop Schijveschuurder, *My Miracle: Haarlem, 1940–1945*, pages 103–4.

raced by bicycle like mad to the Wagenweg: we banged on the door, and I must have called, "It's Bob." I went in myself to help you. My partner warned me at a given moment. When we heard the German motors in the distance, we rode back to the station by a roundabout way.' Bob's partner was never seen again.

Bob later wrote to Joop: 'When later you were imprisoned in the police station in the Smedestraat, I went to fetch the keys to the cell one evening. As a plainclothes policeman, I was able to do this. I spoke to your mother in the cell, and later I phoned the duty doctor. We arranged that your mother should scream in pain. You know the result. By the way, it was not that your mother should simulate appendicitis. Dr Ruiter diagnosed an ectopic pregnancy. Your mother was not suffering from either. But on advice from Dr Ruiter, your mother was transferred to hospital, and not operated upon when there. Had it really been appendicitis, one would have had to operate; not to operate under those circumstances would have led to questions in the hospital. Even there, there were betrayers.'[43]

Fifty years after the first round-ups in Haarlem, in a ceremony honouring those who rescued the Schijveschuurder brothers, the Mayor of Haarlem commented: 'In contrast to those Haarlemers who stood by actionless, there were also officials who resisted. And then, for example, I think of the two teachers who refused to sign the Aryan document, and I think of the governors of the union of the school for disadvantaged children, who refused to divulge the names of Jewish children under their care, and consequently lost their subsidies. And I am reminded of the clerk who lost his job because he wore the Jewish star (although he wasn't

---

[43] Joop Schijveschuurder, *My Miracle: Haarlem, 1940–1945*, page 165.

Jewish), and I think of those officials of the state, who falsified identity cards.'[44]

In the town of Alkmaar, Laurens Vis helped hide Jewish people in safe farms around the town until they could be taken to other places of safety. His son Rudi, later a member of the British House of Commons, recalled how, at his father's funeral in 1952, 'hundreds of Jewish people came to pay their respects.'[45] In Groningen, Marguerite Mulder regarded it as her religious duty to help the persecuted. She therefore took into her home two young Jewish sisters, Vreesje and Sonia Slager, whose parents had already been deported, and arranged for them, when danger threatened, to be kept with her parents and other members of her family.[46] In Rotterdam, a Protestant priest, Dr Brillenburg-Wurth, and his wife concealed and cared for a Jewish couple in the loft of his church for more than a year.[47]

A member of the Royal Dutch Police Force, Karst Smit, undertook rescue efforts that marked him out as extra-ordinary. Only twenty-five years old in 1942, he risked his life again and again to help as many as a hundred and fifty Jews escape from Holland. With a central collecting point in the southern town of Tilburg, he and the group around him travelled with Jews from The Hague, Amsterdam and other towns, moving them south across the Dutch border with Belgium, and on to Antwerp and Brussels. From there, some went into hiding in Belgium, others made their way south to Switzerland.

One of those whom Karst Smit helped, Gertrude

[44] Elizabeth Schmitz, speech of 6 July 1992; Joop Schijveschuurder, *My Miracle: Haarlem, 1940–1945*, page 176.
[45] Rudi Vis, letter to the *Jewish Chronicle*, 25 May 2001.
[46] United States Holocaust Memorial Museum, Photo Archive, Worksheet 01055.
[47] 'Yad Vashem Honour for Dutch Couple', *Jerusalem Post*, 3 February 1978.

Mann, had been in hiding since July 1942 at several addresses in The Hague. At the end of May 1943, he told her and a friend with whom she was in hiding 'that he could help me to pass the frontier into Belgium and that I could so go on to Brussels. After talking this over with my friend and coming to the conclusion that Belgium was safer than Holland (true), we decided that I should go with KS. We sent him word that I was ready to go with him.'

Karst Smit took Gertrude Mann by train – forbidden to Jews by order of the Germans – to Tilburg, and from there to a house in Hilvarenbeek 'of a family called Vos where I hid for the night. The next morning one of the daughters brought me to a pub in Baarle-Nassau where KS told me and several other Jews, to wait for a "passeur" who would pass us over the frontier while KS (who was then a member of the frontier police) would help us to avoid German patrols. The crossing took place without any trouble. No financial conditions were asked. From Weelde in Belgium we took the tram to Antwerp and from Antwerp I took the train to Brussels. In Brussels I was given an address to hide, but as there were at least fifteen other Jews and young men hiding there, I felt that this house was a very dangerous place and so one of the above mentioned friends found another address for me to feel at home. They treated me as their second daughter and told their neighbours I was their niece. I stayed with them until the end of the war.'

On one occasion, Karst Smit travelled to Brussels to bring Gertrude Mann money and clothes that had been given to him by her friend; and 'in September 1943 he helped my friend to pass the Belgian frontier to meet me.'[48]

---

[48] Gertrude Krol-Mann, testimony submitted on 7 December 1977 to Yad Vashem Righteous Among the Nations Archive, file 1228.

After eighteen months the German secret police broke Karst Smit's network. Its members managed to flee and go underground, as so many Jews were doing. Three were later arrested by the Germans and shot: Adrianus van Gestel, Gradus Gerritsen and Cornelius Keurhorst. Smit himself was captured while on a mission to France, imprisoned, and then sent to a number of concentration camps, among them Buchenwald and Dora. He returned to Holland at the end of the war.

Another of the group, Josephus Cornelius van der Heijden, had been arrested together with his son Eugene while accompanying a Jewish woman and her child across the border into Belgium. He died in a German concentration camp, as did two of his sons, Marcel and Gustaaf. Such details were unknown to those rescued, even after liberation. 'After the war it was almost impossible for our Jewish friends to trace us back,' Karst Smit later wrote. 'During their flight they travelled by night, so they did not know where they crossed the Dutch–Belgian frontier and they did not know the names of their passeurs.'[49]

Karst Smit's brother Romke also took part in the work of the group. Sometimes he would act as a courier, collecting jewellery in Amsterdam for its onward passage to Paris. After the liberation of Paris he joined the Dutch Brigade that was formed there in late 1944, fighting in both Belgium and Holland. He was killed on Dutch soil on 26 April 1945, nine days before the Germans in Holland surrendered.

Jaap Penraat, the son of a master printer, was another Dutchman who smuggled Jews out of Holland. The route which he helped organize went via the French city of Lille, and then south to the Pyrenees and the Spanish frontier. Penraat's original speciality was making false

---

[49] Karst Smit, letter of 5 August 1973, Yad Vashem Righteous Among the Nations Archive, file 1228.

415

identity cards that enabled Jews to pass as non-Jews. Once the escape route was established, his ability to prepare false papers was tested to the utmost. Travelling to Paris, and posing as the representative of a German construction company, he persuaded the German authorities there, at the central clearing office for all work permits and licences, to issue permits for Dutch labourers wanting to work with a construction company in France, working on the Atlantic Wall defences. The company did not exist, but the papers, genuine, and with the necessary official stamps, provided a base for repeated forged permits, facilitating the rescue operation.

The first rescue journey took place in December 1942. The ten young Jews whom Jaap Penraat accompanied by train as far as Lille each had a forged 'Aryan' identity card that he had made for them, and travel papers to match. A second group followed within three weeks. In all, more than four hundred Jews were moved out of danger in this way.[50]

The risks taken by those who gave refuge to Jews often spanned many months, even years; but again and again the recollections of those in hiding show that they were borne calmly. Alex Meijer was hidden, together with his parents and two sisters, by a Dutch farmer and his family, for two years and eight months. Reading the diary that he kept, his future wife was 'impressed by the integrity and ingenuity of his hosts and the good relations that existed between their two families throughout'.[51]

However, for many Jews the Christianity of their hosts was a problem; an especial concern was the effect on young children, many of whom quickly became drawn

---

[50] Hudson Talbott, *Forging Freedom: A True Story of Heroism During the Holocaust.*
[51] Donya Meijer, letter to the author, 7 May 2001.

into the ambience of Christian worship. Some children found homes where religion did not become an issue. Ilana Tikotin, who was only four years old in 1942, writes of Willem and Jeanne Maurits, the first couple who took her and her three-year-old sister in: 'They were a jolly Catholic family with (at the time) nine children, later 12. My father took us on a sunny day to their home and told us that as a treat we were to spend the summer with all those children and animals on the farm. He did not explain anything to us, but told me to be good, not to cry and to take care of my sister, who was always naughty, a lot of responsibility to give to a four-year-old girl. We slept on straw in the cowshed, which was clean and shiny and attached to their large kitchen/living room. The cows were outside in the meadows. Behind a blanket lived a family with two children (probably also Jewish, but I do not remember them). We adapted easily to the new religion and it was fun to ride to church with the other children in a horse-drawn carriage on Sunday. The pictures, the statues, the costumes, the singing, the incense – the whole show – were very entertaining. I have very warm memories of our stay there. The family risked their lives to save us, but never made us feel uncomfortable. We felt we belonged and received the same love and attention as their own children. We helped with the work, but it was like play. My parents must have believed that the war would soon be over, because at the end of October when frost set in and the cows returned we had to leave. To me it appeared utterly normal, that we had to vacate our lodgings to make room for the animals.'

The time had come for Ilana Tikotin and her sister to move on elsewhere. 'Most of the other families we stayed with were Protestant and we did not enjoy their religious practices at all, but never showed it. The long Bible readings after the meals were sheer torture while we had to sit still and repeat the last word to show that we had listened intently. The church too, was stark and the service long and boring. The families usually had an organ in their parlour, but we were never allowed to 'play' on it, it was only used for solemn Psalms. We were never told in so many words that we were a burden, but often felt it nevertheless. We had to show constant gratitude and often had to perform quite a lot of chores. For instance, bringing in water from the pump outside, whitewash the wooden shoes of the entire family on Saturday afternoons, so that they would look nice for the Sunday or rake the yard in a special pattern in preparation of the Sunday.'

A final home for Ilana and her sister was with Dirk and Neels van der Vaart. Their 'sole motive', Ilana writes, 'was love of their fellow humans and hate of the German invaders. They were simple but wonderful people. They hid many other Jews for shorter or longer periods of time. One little boy stayed with them for almost three years. I remember how they celebrated my birthday. I knew when it was supposed to be, so they arranged a party for me with the children of the neighbours. They said it was my five and a half year birthday, because if they had told me the truth that I was six years old that day, I would have wanted to go to school. I remember the gift I got. It was a large ball sewn together from pieces of an old sheet, decorated with crayon drawings, filled with old newspapers. Of course it did not bounce, but one could throw and catch it. I stood in the middle of a circle and tossed the ball back to all the children around me. While they got one turn to throw, I got many – it was the happiest day of my life!'

Ilana added: 'My memories do not give sufficient credit to those wonderful heroes who risked their lives to save those of their fellow human beings. At the time I did not realize the danger they were exposed to and thus this is not reflected in the above. Now I know the enormous risks they took jeopardizing their lives and those of their family, but my story is that of a little girl who did not grasp the scope of the calamity.'[52]

Near Eibergen, the manager of the privately owned Hoones Forest allowed two Jewish brothers to build an underground hideout deep in the woods. Two non-Jewish builders brought the materials, dug the hole and assembled the shelter. It had two rooms and a primitive stove. Initially only the brothers hid there, but as times grew more desperate, twenty-three Jews were concealed in the bunker. On 27 March 1943 a Dutch informer led the Germans to the site. All twenty-three were arrested and sent to Westerbork. From there they were deported to Sobibor and killed. After the war the informer was identified and tried as a collaborator.[53]

In Utrecht, Geertruida van Live and her companion Jet van Berlikom ran a home for children born out of wedlock. The home was under the protection of the city's German commandant. This gave the couple the idea of a daring scheme: to take in Jewish babies as if they were Christian waifs. When a Jewish woman, Alida Natkiel, was ordered to report to the railway station for the journey to Westerbork, she took her one-year-old daughter Siny to the home. A local doctor, Hans Mayer, and his wife Nel, a nurse, volunteered to oversee the health care of the children in the home. The young couple had no children of their own and eventually adopted Siny, telling the Germans that Nel had given birth to Siny before her marriage. Siny remained with them from 1942 until the Natkiels returned to claim her in the autumn of 1945. Alida Natkiel and her husband both survived the war, unlike so many parents of children in hiding. Alida, having escaped deportation, had

[52] Ilana Drukker-Tikotin, letter to the author, 10 September 2001.
[53] United States Holocaust Memorial Museum, Photo Archive, Worksheet 25307.

been hidden by the Beimer family in Friesland, but all twelve of her brothers and sisters had perished.[54]

On 3 June 1945, less than a month after the end of the war in Europe, the *New York Times* reported that in the first days of liberation, an American soldier, Ernest Stock, on reaching the Dutch city of Utrecht, discovered his own father, Leo Stock. Ernest had managed to leave Europe for the United States in 1940, at the age of fifteen, with his sister. His mother reached the United States later, on her own. On meeting his father in 1945, he learned how he had survived. 'He says if it wasn't for the wonderful helpfulness of the Dutch people there wouldn't be a single Jew left up there.'[55] To his wife, Leo Stock wrote of Henny Terlouw, who had hidden him for two and a half years, 'I have been living here since 15.11.42 and can truly say that I ultimately owe my life to this extraordinarily brave woman.'[56]

Jacoba van Tongeren had been born in the Dutch East Indies. In The Hague, she was active in local church affairs. She was also active in the Dutch resistance, as was her friend Dr Nicolette Bruining. It was Dr Bruining who first took under her wing a seventeen-year-old Dutch Jewish girl, Elisabeth Waisvisz (later Edna Heruthy), and her sister. Tante (Auntie) Co, as Elisabeth knew her, arranged a hiding place for her in Amsterdam until her false papers could arrive. 'After that, Tante Co saw to it that I was included in a group of youngsters from Amsterdam, who through their church were sent to the north of Alkmaar for a "health vacation" of six weeks. Only the local minister knew about me.'

After six weeks, at the beginning of September 1942,

[54] United States Holocaust Memorial Museum, Photo Archive, Worksheet 42667.
[55] 'US Soldier Finds Father in Holland', *New York Times*, 3 June 1945.
[56] Letter of 6 June 1945, provided to the author by Leo Stock's son, Dr Ernest Stock.

Edna Heruthy recalled, 'Tante Co waited for me at the station of Alkmaar and we returned by train to Amsterdam. During the trip she explained to me that from now on I would live with her and her friend, Tante Nel, and that she had prepared for me a small attic-room. She added that my "new" identity card was being readied by a good friend of hers. All I had to do was go to a "safe" photographer for passport pictures. Due to Tante Co I received the best forged identity card one could hope for – a fact that subsequently saved my life many times over.'

In December 1942 a member of the Dutch Nazi Party recognized Elisabeth when she was walking in the street: he had known her as a child, when she had bought her pencils and copy books in his shop. He was unable to catch her, as she was on a bicycle, and rode briskly away. But he immediately circulated her real name and description to the Dutch police. That evening, Edna Heruthy recalled, 'a "good" policeman who happened to be a neighbour, informed my landlady that I had to leave Amsterdam immediately. Having no spare address outside Amsterdam, "Tante Co" advised me to go to my parents for a few days and disclosed where they were. I travelled that same evening – cold and dark – stayed with my (surprised but pleased) parents in The Hague until after a few days, at the beginning of January 1943, Dr Bruining came to take me to Hilversum.'

In Hilversum, Jacoba Covens took the young girl to her own parents' home in Baarn. Henricus and Maria Covens's younger daughter Henriëtte, who worked in Amsterdam as a graphic artist and was also active in the resistance, came home at weekends. 'I stayed with the Covens family for one and a half years,' Edna Heruthy recalled, 'during which time all of them took great risks on my behalf. Besides the parents who were already over sixty-five years old, grandmother Wijsman – over ninety years old – was living with them. Since both daughters were working, the task of finding additional food to add to our meagre rations fell on Mr Covens. The resistance provided me with the necessary ration-cards, but the Covens family never received money for my upkeep. They not only gave me a safe home, but also a loving one – which during those years was quite an exception.'

When the German army requisitioned the Covenses' villa, and moved them to a house next door, Henriëtte Covens took Elisabeth to The Hague, to stay for a while with her parents. 'A week later she came back to pick me up. I still see her entering my parents' room with an enormous bouquet of spring flowers for my mother in her arms! It was the last time I saw my parents.' It was Dr Bruining who, one Sunday in April, 'came straight from a church-service', Edna wrote, 'to me to tell me that my parents had been betrayed; first they were taken to Westerbork concentration camp in Holland and shortly afterwards to Sobibor. To our sorrow she had to repeat such black tidings about other dear ones many more times.' Elisabeth's mother and father were murdered at Sobibor on 28 May 1943.

On their way back to Baarn, Henriëtte Covens told her charge that another problem awaited them there. The new villa was so big that the Germans had ordered another family to move in. 'That family was unknown in the neighbourhood, and it was not certain that they could be trusted as far as my presence was concerned. As it turned out they were very friendly and helpful at critical moments, and to our relief they had no young children who in their innocence could have given the show away.'

Jacoba Covens once took 'an incredible (and additional) risk: in the summer of 1943, after my parents' deportation, she decided to take me with her as a fourth "youth-leader" of a summer camp for Protestant youth which she directed near Arnhem. She wanted me to "be away from it all", but the "Grüne" – the German Green

Police – found the farm where the camp was held and inspected everybody present, children, youth-leaders and all. My foolproof identity card saved the day! But for this unpleasant intrusion, those were truly wonderfully carefree weeks.'[57]

As in every country under German occupation, so in Holland, local priests played a major part in rescuing Jews. Cecile Kanner (later Kahn) was a schoolgirl at the time of the round-up of Jews in Amsterdam on 21 June 1942. From her home in Scheveningen she, her grandparents and her parents were ordered by the Germans to go to Amsterdam and report. Before they left, a priest arrived and took her away to a non-Jewish family in Oegstgeest, near Leiden. 'The grandparents objected to my leaving; my father simply said, "I cannot protect her anymore", and with a little bag of money around my neck and the frantic blessings of my grandfather I left with the priest.'[58]

Cecile never learned the priest's name. At Oegstgeest she was taken in by Frans and Maria Briër, a husband and wife with three young daughters, the youngest a baby. It had been intended for her to stay for just three days, but after the first day Maria Briër said to her: 'Child, you can remain with us till the war is over.' After a short while, Maria Briër went to Amsterdam to bring back Cecile's parents, but they had already been arrested – in the street – and imprisoned. Once more Maria Briër returned to Amsterdam, to bring back Cecile's grandparents, but when she reached their house she spotted German uniforms through the window. She almost fell into their hands herself.

Not long afterwards, Cecile's parents escaped from

[57] Edna Heruthy, letter to the author, 2 January 2002.
[58] Cecile Kahn-Kanner, letter to the author, 6 May 2001.

prison and made their way to Oegstgeest. 'Mr Briër made three hiding places for us. For my father one under the roof, for my mother one under the ground floor, and for me under the staircase. Mrs Briër bought food with the ration coupons she received from the underground. The three of us were in a room on the first floor always ready to leave no trace and to run to our hiding places. Mr Briër took us sometimes for a walk at night. And so the days went on and on. Till one day an underground man came by the name of Reinier Kampenhout. He said to me, "You are too young to remain all day in one room." He arranged an identity card by the name of Corry Verschoor, took me to a photographer and with this new identity brought me to an old age home in Heemstede (near Haarlem), where a maid was needed. From now on nobody knew who I really was until the end of the war. Kampenhout himself was caught by the Germans and killed.'[59]

Cecile Kahn's parents survived the war, having also been found another hiding place. Her grandparents were taken to Westerbork and then to Auschwitz, where they arrived on 31 August 1943. They were murdered there within three days.

'It should be stressed that though I was assimilated, for Queen and Fatherland, with Dutch Christian friends aplenty,' Cecile Kahn reflected, 'it took a long time to find help. People were so fearful that they even declined to hide their own sons when the Germans ordered them to work in Germany. They were so fearful that all the family albums I gave a classmate were destroyed by her parents. Only with the prevailing fear in mind can the few righteous helpers be appreciated.'[60]

The level of local support for the Jews varied from

---

[59] Cecile Kahn-Kanner, letter to the author, 6 May 2001.
[60] Cecile Kahn-Kanner, letter to the author, 6 May 2001. In 1947 Cecile Kahn emigrated from Holland to Israel. Just over a year later, during the second truce called in the War of Independence, her husband was killed in an Arab attack on the town of Modiin.

place to place. In the small town of Winterswijk, near the German frontier, hiding places were found for thirty-five Jews of the 270 who lived in the town. Eight miles away, at Aalten, of the eighty-five Jews of the town, fifty-one were hidden by non-Jews and survived the war.[61] Albert Douwes took 120 Jewish children out of Amsterdam to the village of Nieuwlande, arranging for all of them to be hidden with the farmers of the village. All the children survived; many later settled in Israel, where their rescuer also lived for many years.[62] Nieuwlande was later awarded, as a village, the designation Righteous Among the Nations.[63]

Acts of individual rescue have been recorded in Holland on virtually every day of the war. Gustel Mozes, a Jewish teenager who had left Germany for Holland after Kristallnacht, found refuge in Roermond with the Roman Catholic Thomassen family, which had twelve children, six of whom were still living at home. Two of the daughters went to meet Gustel Mozes at the train station: the family had let it be known that she was the new seamstress. 'The very first thing she had to learn was to make the sign of the cross! That, because next day, a seamstress was expected, and Gustel should not arouse any suspicion by not knowing how to make the sign of the Cross, during dinner times. During the day she never left the house. She also had to learn to eat non-Kosher food. The family had good relations with the bishop, who knew about Gustel's Jewishness. The secretary of the bishop, called Pief van Odyk, visited the family every day. Two other Jews were also introduced into the family. Gustel stayed with the family

[61] Louis de Jong, 'Jews and Non-Jews in Nazi-occupied Holland', in Max Beloff (editor), *On the Track of Tyranny*, page 150.
[62] Benek (Baruch) Sharoni, 'Man's Humanity to Man', *Mizkor*, October 2000.
[63] The award was made in 1987. Yad Vashem Righteous Among the Nations Archive, file 1148.

Thomassen until the liberation. She called the mother, Maria, "mother", and was surrounded by love.'[64]

A Christian Dutch woman, Jo Jansen, persuaded her mother, Klaasje Geuzebroek-Zein, to go to the Dutch authorities and bear false witness that a Jewish friend, Helena de Vries, was her illegitimate daughter. Had the deception been found out, mother and daughter would have faced severe punishment, possibly death. So too would Helena and her children. The young Maurits de Vries, who was saved, with his mother, sister and twin brother, as a result of this deception about their parentage, has written of Jo Jansen: 'Her motive for saving us must have been purely humane and humanitarian, she was not religious, hated the Nazis.'[65]

The question of motive, and of character, is one on which almost all of those who were saved often reflect. 'I must mention', writes Jehoedah Troostwijk, one of those who was saved, 'that all our rescuers were holding us without making any special profit out of it. They were all heroes for humanity reasons, they never tried to convert us or something of the kind.' Among those 'heroes' were Adriaan and Annie van Eerd-Mutsaers. Adriaan was captain of a football team, Annie the daughter of an archbishop.

To save and to destroy: as always the dark side lurked. Jehoedah Troostwijk also remembered that it was a Dutch policeman who arrested one of his brothers, Menno, a former soldier in the Dutch army, who was deported to Sobibor. There he took part with other former soldiers in the death camp revolt, and was shot.[66]

Yet one of the heroes was another Dutch policeman, Constable Gerrit van der Putten, who found himself

[64] Gustel (Augusta) Mozes, story communicated by Maurits Eduard de Vries, letter to the author, 27 January 2002.
[65] Maurits Eduard de Vries, letter to the author, 1 June 2001.
[66] L. I. (Jehoedah) Troostwijk, letter to the author, 2 June 2001.

present during a deportation. Among the Jews to be deported from Utrecht that day, 14 March 1943, were Caroline Kanes and her tiny baby Levie, who had been born less than two months earlier, on January 25. More than half a century later, Levie Kanes set down what he had pieced together of his story. As he described it: 'Gerrit could not remember seeing such poverty-stricken people before; he had never seen so many in such a state of complete indignity. Everywhere he could hear children crying as their mothers were told they would be sent to a labour camp. Mothers clung to their babies in desperation as they realized how little value a small child would be to a camp where they would all be expected to "labour", and they all worried about what this could mean as to the fates of their children.'

As Gerrit van der Putten watched, he saw Grietje Verduin, a nurse he knew from the resistance, enter the railway car and look towards Caroline Kanes and her baby son. Levie Kanes's account continues: 'Caroline approached her immediately. She whispered, "Please smuggle my baby out of here, he will die if he comes with me!!" Grietje had no idea who Caroline was, and she could not determine how she had known it was safe to approach her about the baby, but Caroline knew who was "safe" because of her own work in the resistance . . . Grietje saw that the police were busy bringing the new passengers on board. Wordlessly she picked up the baby and hid him in her basket of clean gauze and wound dressings. Before Caroline could even think to be grateful to her, Grietje left the train. Caroline ran back to the window to try and follow the nurse's movements through the crowds at the station. She watched as Grietje put the basket into a Dutch policeman's arms, then turned away to be lost among the people surrounding her. The last Caroline saw of the baby, and the police officer, was what she saw before he disappeared into the shadows of the nearby buildings.'

Kanes's account continued: 'Gerrit realized he had a living baby in the basket, and snapped to attention. He went into action. He moved quickly away from the train and back into the shadows of the buildings behind him. He tried to be as natural as possible with his cargo, so as not to bring attention to himself during his rescue. The whistle blew and the train pulled out of the station before Gerrit judged that he had covered enough distance to allow himself to catch his breath. He had to think fast: he would leave by the gate behind the buildings that were guarded by his colleagues. Not all of the other policemen were "trustworthy" men these days, so he knew he had to be extremely cautious. He spotted Hank Janssen at the gate, and allowed himself to feel a small amount of relief.'

Hank Janssen was a Dutch police officer Gerrit had known for a long time: 'He would never think twice about seeing him carry a basket home from work. Gerrit took a deep breath and walked by Hank and the control while holding the basket close to him as he passed. He saluted, and said, "Hello, Hank!" Hank saluted back and watched him walk away. Gerrit smiled merrily as he kept moving toward his bike, and announced, "I must be getting too busy – I forgot my laundry yesterday!" as he motioned to the basket with his eyes. Hank smiled and immediately went back to his other duties while Gerrit walked toward his bicycle, a few metres from the train station, where he would be free of the suspicions of his colleagues. Gerrit tied the basket firmly on the back of his bike, as if it truly was just a basket full of clothing, then rode quickly away.'

Gerrit van der Putten knew a contact address where he could go; he pedalled there with the baby in the basket, parked his bike, and rang the bell. Joop Wortman opened the door. His work as a taxi driver made it possible for him eventually to pass the baby to a courier in The Hague. 'Gerrit held the basket up for Joop to peek into, and Joop lifted the linen sheet so he could see the baby. It was the first time Gerrit could take a look for himself, and he was growing quite curious. Inside, they found the dark-haired baby, wrapped solely in a diaper and the little blanket provided by the hospital. He still had his identity bracelet on his arm. "Levie Kanes, 25-1-43", read Gerrit aloud. "Name and date of birth."'

Commented Joop: 'I guess we have a little baby boy with a Biblical name. Remember, Moses, in Exodus, was also saved in a similar basket.'

'Yes, that's true.'

'You have done very well. I will take care of little Levie now, but thank you for thinking so sharply.'[67]

Several Dutch men and women, as well as a Gypsy family, helped save German-born Marion Kaufmann from deportation. She was not yet four years old when, in May 1940, her parents fled with her into Holland, hoping to escape the advancing German army. But on reaching the Dutch city of Arnhem they found the Germans already there. Marion's mother went to see a Catholic priest, who put her in touch with a Dutch lawyer, Max Knapp, and his wife Ans, a doctor. She then placed her daughter with one of the leaders of the Dutch underground in Amsterdam, Boy Edgar, and his wife Mia.

Marion Kaufmann stayed with the Edgars from

---

[67] Levie Kanes, manuscript (sent to the author on 27 December 2001). Levie Kanes's grandfather, also named Levie, and his wife Ester Hamburg, perished on 23 April 1943, having been deported to Sobibor. Their eldest son, Maurits Kanes, together with his wife Rebecca Winnik and their two small children, were murdered at Auschwitz on 29 July 1942. Their daughter Anna Kanes and her husband Ezechiel Bruinvelds were also killed at Sobibor. Levie Kanes's father, Salomon Kanes, was murdered on 16 January 1944 in Auschwitz. In all, only five members of the baby's extended family of several hundred survived the Holocaust. One of them was his mother, who survived Auschwitz, returned to Holland and regained her son.

October 1942. Every six weeks, Mia took Marion to a friend who bleached her hair. In March 1943, while en route to the friend's house, the police stopped Mia and asked her why she had a Jewish child with her. They released Mia but arrested Marion, who was sent to the creche, where Jewish children were held before their deportation. With the help of the Dutch underground, and a co-operative German soldier, the Edgars smuggled Marion (to whom they gave the name Renie) out of the creche. Mia brought her to the train station, and Boy took her by train to a convent where she stayed for two weeks, until she was brought to a farm owned by Jan and Wilhelmina Beelen. The Beelens had three older boys, and two younger girls, Rie and Grada, who became Marion's friends. She remained with the Beelens until liberation by the Canadians in September 1944. A few weeks later, however, the Germans reoccupied the area. The Beelens then arranged for Marion to be hidden with a Gypsy family until the area was liberated again that October. Following the second liberation, Marion remained with the Beelen family until December 1945, when she was reunited with her mother through the International Committee of the Red Cross.[68]

Leendert Overduijn is known to have saved at least 461 Jews. He is one of those whom Mordecai Paldiel chose for an individual entry in *The Encyclopedia of the Holocaust*. A Dutch pastor, Overduijn headed a rescue organization of more than forty people in the town of Enschede, helping Jews to find hiding places throughout the region. 'The division of labour was such', writes Paldiel, 'that Overduijn stayed at home most of the time while his daughter and other helpers travelled in different localities to seek suitable places of hiding.

[68] United States Holocaust Memorial Museum, Photo Archive, Worksheet 05722.

Nevertheless, Overduijn frequently visited Jews in hiding, bringing ration cards, cigarettes, and most important of all, news from friends and relatives. His comings and goings were noticed by the authorities, and he was eventually taken in for questioning and imprisoned for an extended period.'[69]

Secret escape lines enabled Allied airmen who had been shot down over German-occupied Europe, or escapees from German prisoner-of-war camps, to reach neutral Switzerland or Spain. Jewish refugees were also the beneficiaries of these lines, one of which was run by a Dutch Seventh Day Adventist, John Weidner. He arranged for many Allied airmen as well as Jews to be moved from Holland to Switzerland. There they were safe for the rest of the war, although the airmen were unable to get back to Britain and fly in combat again.

But the cost of this operation was high. An estimated 150 people assisted Weidner in operating the route of his 280-mile-long evading line. Forty of them were arrested by the Gestapo and killed, among them Weidner's sister Gabrielle.[70]

The 4,464 Dutch men and women who are known to have helped Jews in Holland during the war years were remarkable in many ways, not least because they had to fight against the passivity of so many other Dutch citizens. Speaking to the Israeli parliament in 1995, Queen Beatrix noted that although some of her compatriots had offered brave resistance, 'they were the exceptional ones'.[71]

[69] Mordecai Paldiel, 'Overduijn, Leendert (1901–1976)', *Encyclopedia of the Holocaust*, volume 3, page 1100.
[70] Yad Vashem Righteous Among the Nations Archive, file 1228.
[71] Simon Kuper, 'Tarnished glory', *Jewish Chronicle*, 23 February 2001.

CHAPTER FIFTEEN

Italy and the Vatican

'Throughout my years of confinement in various camps during the war years in Italy,' wrote Polish-born Dr Salim Diamand, 'I never found racism in the Italians. Of course there was militarism; but throughout the war years, I never found any Italians who approached me, as a Jew, with the idea of exterminating my race.'[1] Before the German occupation of central and northern Italy in the autumn of 1943, Italian Jews, and the Jewish refugees who had made their way from the German-dominated areas of Europe to Italy since 1933, were safe from deportation. The Italian Fascist regime headed by Mussolini had introduced anti-Jewish legislation before the war, restricting the professions in which Jews could practise; but it did not seek their deaths, or co-operate with Germany, its Axis partner, in demonizing and segregating them.

On 18 July 1942, in the northern Italian village of Nonantola, Don Arrigo Beccari, a priest at the local Roman Catholic seminary, witnessed the arrival of seventy-four Jewish children and their adult helpers. Forty-three were the children of German, Austrian and Polish Jews whose parents had already been deported and killed. Together with eighteen Jewish girls who had

---

[1] Dr Salim Diamand, *Dottore! Internment in Italy, 1940–1945*, page 10.

escaped from Austria to Slovenia, and another thirteen Yugoslav Jewish children, they had been taken by a Zagreb Jew, Josef Indig, from Croatia into the Italian-occupied region of Yugoslavia. From there they had crossed into Italy.[2]

On seeing the children in his village, Father Beccari persuaded the local authorities to let them stay in a large, empty house, the Villa Emma. There they learnt to build their own furniture and worked the fields, in preparation for kibbutz life in Palestine, whither they had been on their way at the outbreak of war. They could only guess at their parents' fate. Postcards that a few parents managed to send from their home towns in Poland simply said they had to 'go away'.[3]

On the battlefields of Europe and North Africa, Italy was Germany's military ally. Italian soldiers fought alongside the Germans on the Eastern Front and were part of the occupation forces in Poland. There, to the fury of the Germans, Jews in both Lvov and Brody had acquired arms from Italian troops stationed in the town. To the distress of German occupation forces in the east, the Italians seemed to lack entirely any hatred of the Jews; for their part, Italians called anti-Semitism 'the German disease'.

On 13 December 1942 Josef Goebbels, Hitler's Propaganda Minister, wrote in his diary: 'The Italians are extremely lax in the treatment of the Jews. They protect the Italian Jews both in Tunis and in occupied France and will not permit their being drafted for work or compelled to wear the Star of David. This shows once again that Fascism does not really dare to get down to fundamentals but is very superficial regarding problems of vital importance. The Jewish question is causing us a

---

[2] Yehuda Bauer, *American Jewry and the Holocaust*, page 285.
[3] John Follain, 'Village hid Jews from Nazis', *Sunday Times*, 18 January 2001.

433

lot of trouble. Everywhere, even among our allies, the Jews have friends to help them.'[4]

The Vatican also distressed the Nazi hierarchy. After Pope Pius XII's Christmas message in 1942, the German bureau in Berlin responsible for the deportation of the Jews (the Reich Security Main Office) noted angrily: 'In a manner never known before, the Pope has repudiated the National Socialist New European Order . . . Here he is virtually accusing the German people of injustice towards the Jews and makes himself the mouthpiece of the Jewish war criminals.'[5] At the beginning of 1943, the Germans urged the Italians to allow them to deport the Jews living in the Italian-occupied zone in France, but the Italians refused to 'co-operate', and on January 13 the senior SS representative in Italy, SS Lieutenant-Colonel Knochen, telegraphed to the Chief of the Gestapo, SS Lieutenant-General Heinrich Müller: 'Although the number of Italian Jews (in France) is comparatively small, the privileges accorded to them have been a constant source of serious difficulty because it is impossible to understand why our Axis partner should refuse to align himself with us on the Jewish question.'[6]

News of the Italian obduracy reached the head of the SS, Heinrich Himmler, who wrote to the German Foreign Minister, Joachim von Ribbentrop, on 29 January 1943 to stress 'the grave security problems' which Italian resistance to the Final Solution was creating throughout the territories under Axis control. He wanted Italian Jews 'and other foreign nationals of Jewish race to be removed from the Italian-occupied area in France'. The continued presence of the Jews in the Italian sphere of influence 'provides many circles in France and in the

[4] Goebbels diary, 13 December 1942, Louis P. Lochner (editor), *The Goebbels Diaries*, page 181.
[5] Quoted in the *New York Times*, in a reader's letter, 17 August 2000.
[6] Meir Michaelis, *Mussolini and the Jews*, page 306.

rest of Europe with a pretext for playing down the Jewish question, it being argued that not even our Axis partner Italy sees eye to eye with us on the Jewish issue'.[7]

On February 2, Knochen forwarded to Müller a secret report that described in detail how the Italians in the Alpes-Maritimes department had 'prevented the enforcement of all anti-Jewish measures which have been ordered by the French Government'. On February 12, after a conversation with Eichmann in Paris, Knochen wrote again: 'The best of harmony prevails between the Italian troops and the Jewish population. The German and Italian conceptions seem here to be completely at variance.' If the anti-Jewish measures throughout France were to succeed, 'they must also be applied in the Italian zone. Otherwise the influx of Jews into this zone – an influx which is only in its initial stage – will assume formidable dimensions, and the result will be mere half-measures.'

From the SS perspective, worse was to come. On February 22, Knochen informed Müller that the Italian military authorities had compelled the police chief of Lyons to cancel an order for the arrest of several hundred Jews who were to have been sent to Auschwitz 'for labour service'. Knochen was indignant, telling Müller: 'The French who were notoriously reluctant to tackle the Jewish question had been confirmed in their resistance by the measures of the Italian authorities. Above all, it was utterly intolerable that the final solution of the Jewish question should be rendered more difficult by an ally who had proclaimed his adherence to the racial gospel.'

Three days later, Ribbentrop raised the matter personally with Mussolini, urging him to check the 'pro-Jewish zeal' of his underlings in France. Ribbentrop was 'well aware', he told Mussolini, 'that Italian military circles, and sometimes the German army itself lacked a proper

---

[7] Meir Michaelis, *Mussolini and the Jews*, page 335.

435

understanding of the Jewish question. That was the only possible explanation of the order by the Italian High Command to annul the anti-Jewish measures that the French authorities had taken in the Italian zone at Germany's request.' Mussolini denied the accuracy of the information, ascribing it 'to the desire of the French to sow discord between Germany and Italy'. Ribbentrop ended by stating that the Jews in the occupied territories were 'more dangerous than English agents'.[8]

On March 6, SS Lieutenant Heinz Röthke, in a letter to Eichmann, recapitulated all the unfulfilled Italian promises, adding that the Italian Fourth Army had even used force to free Jews arrested by the French police at Annecy. But even repeated German protests failed to persuade the Italian authorities in Italian-occupied France to hand over the Jews in their zone. On March 11, a senior Italian diplomat in Rome, Count Pietromarchi, noted that the Italian Embassy in Berlin had reported 'macabre details of mass executions of Jews concentrated at the places of massacre from all the occupied territories', and he added: 'The only ones to be saved are the Jews who put themselves under our safeguard. Our military authorities, it may be admitted to their credit, maintained a firm opposition to the brutal measures of the Germans. In France they demanded the local authorities to cancel all the instructions against the Jews, such as the duty to wear "the Star of Solomon", conscription for forced labour and the like. This is perhaps the only action earning us respect among the French. The same happens in Croatia and in Greece. The Germans manifest strong disappointment.'

Ribbentrop had expressed that disappointment in a diplomatic note of protest, in which, Count Pietromarchi wrote, 'are enumerated all the attitudes taken by our authorities in occupied countries on behalf of the Jews',

[8] Meir Michaelis, *Mussolini and the Jews*, pages 306–7.

and in which Ribbentrop added that such behaviour on Italy's part 'encourages other governments to behave in the same way'.[9]

Italy continued to refuse to follow the German lead: on May 24, Gestapo headquarters in Berlin received the copy of a letter written by the senior representative of the Italian High Command in Vichy, General Carlo Avarna di Gualtieri, in which the General had written: 'The Italian High Command requests the French Government to annul the arrests and internments of the Jews whose place of residence is in the zone occupied by us.'

As anti-Axis feeling in Italy grew, Italian resistance to the Final Solution also stiffened. On June 23, in a telegram to the Reich Security Main Office headquarters in Berlin, Knochen complained that Italian sabotage was 'endangering the application of the measures against the Jews'. Four days later, Vatican Radio was reported to have broadcast a papal injunction: 'He who makes a distinction between Jews and other men is unfaithful to God and is in conflict with God's commands.'[10]

On July 21, Heinz Röthke, in a memorandum to the Reich Security Main Office on 'the present state of the Jewish question in France', declared: 'The Italian military authorities and the Italian police protect the Jews by every means in their power. The Italian zone of influence, particularly in the Côte d'Azur, has become the Promised Land for the Jews in France. In the last few months there has been a mass exodus of Jews from our occupation zone into the Italian zone.' The escape of the Jews, Röthke noted, 'is facilitated by the existence of thousands of flight-routes, the assistance given them by the French population and the sympathy of the authorities, false identity cards and also by the size of

[9] Daniel Carpi, *Between Mussolini and Hitler*, page 121.
[10] Quoted in the Catholic League for Religious and Civil Rights, advertisement, *New York Times*, 10 April 2001.

the area which makes it impossible to seal off the zones of influence hermetically.' Röthke added that although about twenty reports on this subject had been sent to the Reich Security Main Office, there had so far been no sign of any change in the Italian attitude.[11]

The Italian zone of Greece was also a place of sanctuary sought by Jews living in the German zones. In the first weeks of 1943, the Germans prepared for the deportation of Jews both from Salonika, home of fifty-six thousand Jews, and from Macedonia, including the capital, Skopje, where a further five thousand Jews lived. The Italian consulates in both Salonika and Skopje were already protecting those Jews who could claim Italian citizenship; now, as deportation became imminent, both consulates issued passports to Jews who were not Italian citizens. A senior SS official in Greece complained to Berlin on February 8 that 'many Jews had become new Italian citizens'.

The Italian consular officials were not deterred by German complaints. On March 6, Ernst Kaltenbrunner, head of the German government's deportation authority – the Reich Security Main Office in Berlin – protested directly to Rome, urging the Italian government to warn its consular officers in Greece and Macedonia to cease issuing new passports and to repudiate the validity of the passports they had already issued. Kaltenbrunner urged the Italian diplomatic service to stop taking any interest in Jews who held Italian citizenship, 'since their deportation was inevitable'. Despite this pressure, the Italian consuls in Salonika and Skopje refused to allow the deportation of Jews holding Italian passports, whether or not they were in reality Italian citizens.[12]

---

[11] Meir Michaelis, *Mussolini and the Jews*, pages 306–7.
[12] Alexandar Matkovski, *A History of the Jews in Macedonia*, pages 197–200.

The Italian Consul in Salonika, Emilio Neri, saved many Jews by physically transferring them from the German to the Italian zone of Greece. One of those rescued, Madame Malach, later recalled: 'He put us in contact with Greek railway workers who, either for small amounts of money or just out of sympathy, would hide Jews in transport cars carrying potatoes or other goods to Athens.' In the Italian zone, she adds, 'all Jews were helped and even issued falsified documents without Semitic names.'

Emilio Neri would frequently travel from Salonika to the border of the Italian zone, where he put Jewish refugees on military convoys and even dressed them in Italian military uniforms in order to transfer them to the Italian zone. Working closely with Neri was an Italian officer, Captain Lucillo Mersi, who would also make the journey to the border between the two zones. When the Jews of Salonika were taken to the Baron Hirsch camp as a prelude to deportation, a Jewish woman who managed to escape from the camp asked Captain Mersi to get out her two sons: 'He got my sons out and eight others as well. He rescued all of those who had even very distant ties to some Italian family. To one Jewish woman, Buena Sarfati, he gave a passport under the name of Maria Tivoli and thus saved her from deportation.'

Emilio Neri's successor as Italian Consul in Salonika, Guelfo Zamboni, also did what he could to transfer Jews out of the city, which was under strict German rule, to the Italian-occupied zone, where they would be safe from deportation, and could even receive financial assistance from Italian government funds earmarked for refugees. As a result of a German protest, Zamboni was removed from his post; but his successor, Aldo Gastruccio, continued to try to save Jews from deportation. In an attempt to enlist the help of the Italian army in rounding up Jews for deportation, the German commander in Greece, General Alexander von Lehr, asked the senior Italian general in Salonika, General Carlo Gelozo, to provide soldiers, but Gelozo refused. When Lehr turned to another senior Italian officer in the city, General Tripiccione, he received the same answer.[13]

In mainland Italy, Cardinal Elia Della Costa was among many clergymen who tried to help Jews. Mario Lattes, one of those who benefited from his concern, recalled how, in Florence, the Cardinal 'was organizing forces to help the Jews, either to leave Italy, or to find shelter in convents'.[14]

In July 1943, in a dramatic palace revolution in Rome, Mussolini was overthrown. Twenty years of Fascism were at an end. To forestall the new Italian government's defection from the Axis, German troops entered Italy from the north, occupying Rome. The Italian government, having fled southward to avoid being seized by the Germans, informed the Allies on September 1 that it had accepted an armistice. Two days later, Allied forces, which had already conquered Sicily, landed south of Naples and began the long, hard struggle northward. Even as the German army imposed its occupation regime, SS experts arrived from Berlin, their task to secure the rapid deportation by train to Auschwitz of Jews in all areas of Italy that were under German military rule.

In Nonantola, the seventy-four Jewish children who had lived for the previous year untroubled at the Villa Emma were suddenly at risk. Determined to find the children sanctuary, Father Beccari went from door to door asking the villagers to hide them. Within a few hours, all of them were found homes. Among the villagers who hid Jews in Nonantola was Giuseppe

---

[13] Alexandar Matkovski, *A History of the Jews in Macedonia*, pages 197–200.
[14] Mario Lattes, letter to the author, 9 April 2002.

Moreali; one of those whom he had saved later wrote of 'this unique example in humanitarian behaviour'.[15] Beccari also persuaded the initially reluctant rector of the Benedictine abbey to let the youngest children hide in the abbey. Within forty-eight hours the Villa Emma was empty.

German-controlled radio was warning each day that anyone hiding either partisans or Jews would be shot. 'I just carried on as quietly as I could,' Beccari later recalled. 'I tried to receive as few people as possible and I kept the kids locked in.'[16]

Father Beccari's young charges were hidden for five weeks, until forged documents could be made which allowed them to cross into Switzerland. 'We made them ourselves,' he recalled. 'A town hall clerk gave us the cards. We stuck the pictures on and we made our seals from a bolt head.' Before the children could set off, one of them, fifteen-year-old Salomon Papo, was taken to hospital, suffering from tuberculosis. While in hospital he was identified as Jewish – as he had been circumcised – and was deported to Auschwitz. The other seventy-three children made their way to Switzerland, and survived.[17]

In October 1943, having established their presence in Rome, the SS were determined to deport the city's five thousand Jews to the death camps. In an attempt to forestall the deportation, the Vatican clergy opened the sanctuaries of the Vatican City to all 'non-Aryans' in need of refuge. Catholic clergymen throughout Rome acted with alacrity. At the Capuchin convent on the Via

[15] Letter of 26 February 1996, Yad Vashem, Righteous Among the Nations Archive, file 36.
[16] Quoted in John Follain, 'Village hid Jews from Nazis', *Sunday Times*, 18 January 2001.
[17] Quoted in John Follain, 'Village hid Jews from Nazis', *Sunday Times*, 18 January 2001.

Siciliano, Father Benoit, under the name of Father Benedetti, saved large numbers of Jews by providing them with false identification papers. He was helped in doing this by members of the Swiss, Hungarian, Romanian and French Embassies in Rome, and also by a number of Italians, including Mario di Marco, a senior police official, who was later tortured by the Gestapo but did not disclose what he knew.[18]

By the morning of October 16, a total of 4,238 Jews had been given sanctuary in the many monasteries and convents in Rome. A further 477 Jews had been given shelter in the Vatican and its enclaves. Later that day, SS troops combed the houses and streets of Rome in search of Jews; all they found were taken, regardless of age, sex or state of health, to the Collegio Militare. As a result of the Church's rapid rescue efforts, only 1,015 – fewer than one-fifth – of Rome's 5,730 Jews were seized that morning. Deported to Auschwitz, only ten of them survived.

The convent of Our Lady of Zion stood on a Roman hilltop. The Mother Superior, Virginie Badetti, and her close associate Sister Emilia Benedetti took in more than a hundred Jews. One of them, Ruth Weinberg, who was given shelter together with her uncle, recalled how the nuns 'shared their slim rations, and gave up their own beds for the people they were protecting – though so many had been sheltered in the convent that many had to sleep on the floor'. When someone knocked on the door, she said, the nuns rang a special alarm bell that warned their 'guests' to hide.[19]

Also in Rome, Pietro Palazzini, who was later made a Cardinal, had, in the words of a Yad Vashem represen-

[18] Philip Friedman, *Road to Extinction*, page 418.
[19] Ruth Gruber, 'Wartime bravery of nuns recognized by Yad Vashem', *Jewish Chronicle*, 13 March 1999.

tative, 'endangered his life' and gone 'above and beyond the call of duty to save Jews during the Holocaust'.[20]

On October 18 the Gestapo in Rome protested to the Gestapo chief in Berlin about the frustration of its designs against the Jews of Rome: 'The behaviour of the Italian people was outright passive resistance which in many individual cases amounted to active assistance. In one case, for example, the police came upon the home of a Fascist in a black shirt and with identity papers which without doubt had already been used one hour earlier in a Jewish home as someone claiming them as his own. As the German police were breaking into some homes, attempts to hide Jews were observed, and it is believed that in many cases they were successful.' The report went on to protest: 'The anti-Semitic section of the population was nowhere to be seen during the action, only a great mass of people who in some individual cases even tried to cut off the police from the Jews.'[21]

Professor Umberto Franchetti was an Italian Jew, a distinguished physician, who, when the Germans occupied Florence, moved with his family to their country home, Il Bigallo, on the outskirts of the city. One of his three daughters, Luisa, then aged fifteen, later recalled how, on 6 November 1943, while her parents were in Florence for the day, 'a Jewish friend informed my mother that Jews had been arrested that same morning in the city. My parents hurried back to Il Bigallo, and summoned the peasant – a Catholic named Matassini – who worked the farm attached to our home; they told him that we were in danger, and asked for his help.

---

[20] Lisa Davidson (Yad Vashem spokeswoman), quoted in an Associated Press obituary of Cardinal Palazzini, *Globe and Mail* (Toronto), 16 October 2000. Palazzini was appointed Cardinal in 1973. He was recognized as a Righteous Among the Nations in 1985.
[21] Meir Michaelis, *Mussolini and the Jews*, pages 367–8.

Matassini found us a house some distance away, occupied by one single woman, where we would be able to stay through the night. Additionally, he made arrangements for another peasant to take us even farther away, into the mountains, the following morning. We realized that with the winter coming we would need additional supplies, and so after arriving at the house walked back to Il Bigallo to gather blankets and heavier clothing.'

Luisa added: 'Within fifteen minutes of our arriving back at Il Bigallo, Matassini rushed in to tell us that German soldiers were at the villa of the Barone Franchetti, which was only twenty minutes away by foot. There were no telephones in the homes of the peasants of the area. The information had been passed by word of mouth with extreme haste, as its importance was quickly grasped: the Barone had been arrested. He was not Jewish and it took only a short time until he was released; what seemed quite clear was that the Germans had been looking for my father and stumbled upon the Barone's villa by error. We fled into the woods immediately, gathered our winter gear, and returned to the house where we were to spend the night. The next morning we left.'

On the advice of Father Achille, a Franciscan priest whom Professor Franchetti had known before the war, the Franchetti family went to the mountains, to the Valle Santa. 'After three difficult days during which he struggled with deep snow,' Luisa recalled, her father succeeded in renting a small house in Giampereta, 'from Mr Ciuccoli, a good friend of Father Achille. It was a most primitive and humble place, with no running water and no toilet. The money that my father gave to Mr Ciuccoli covered the provision of wood for heating and cooking as well as the rent. There was a fireplace in the kitchen that provided all the heat we had in the house. We would carry water from the fountain located in the centre of the village, and do our laundry there as well.'

Giampereta was no more than a hamlet of some twenty houses, set close together, and a church. 'The priest would come once a week, from a nearby village,' Luisa remembered. 'There were no shops, no pharmacy, no police station, and no main road. There was a one-room school (without toilet or heating) and a club where men would meet to listen to the news over the radio and buy wine.' The family's cover story was 'that we had left Florence because of the aerial bombings (the first one in Florence had been on 25 September 1943), but it was obvious that a more serious reason had brought us to such a far away place and such a simple house. No questions were asked.'

Luisa remembered the day when her father returned home 'after having gone to see Mr Ciuccoli to pay the monthly rent. He reported that Mr Ciuccoli had told him that if my father could not pay the rent, there was no need for him to do so, and if we should have no means to buy food we would be invited to his table and the table of all the other Giampereta families – each day being the guests of another family in turn.'

Such good deeds took place all over German-occupied Italy. There were also other deeds, less noble. Not far from Giampereta, Luisa later learned, 'in a place called Rimbocchi, a young couple, Florentine Jews, had been hiding with their two-year-old daughter in the house of a local peasant. He kept requesting more and more money from them and telling them that the Germans would come and arrest them. He so frightened them that they suffocated their small daughter and took their own lives.'

The Ciuccoli family continued to shelter the Franchettis, even when searches for Jews intensified, and the SS came to the valley, searching for Italian partisans. Luisa's family were constantly reassured that they would not be asked to leave. The Ciuccolis 'were surely aware of the risks they incurred by allowing us to stay,

445

and yet they protected us'. Nor was there any question 'but that the whole village was involved. In a village as small as Giampereta, it would have been impossible for the Ciuccoli family to give us assistance unless all the villagers were prepared to accept us as well.'[22]

Adriana Luzzati was in hiding with her family in the countryside outside Asti. 'Not only were our own lives in great danger,' she later recalled, 'but also the lives of those who gave us hospitality, because they risked being shot if the Germans had found us with them.'[23]

In Milan, when six hundred Jews were seized and deported by train to Auschwitz, more than six thousand were given shelter in Christian homes and survived. In the village of Valle Stura, not far from the border with France, between forty and fifty Jews were given refuge by the local villagers.[24] Near Varese, thirty-year-old Giuliana Basevi and her mother, Emma de Angelis Basevi, from Turin, were given refuge in a convent for almost a year. When the Germans came to the convent, the nuns insisted that there were no Jews among them. Giuliana's father, arrested in Verona in November 1944, was taken to Bolzano and then deported to Flossenbürg concentration camp, where he died a few months before liberation.[25]

In Turin, Cardinal Fossati asked the Villata family, who lived in the town of Moncalieri, to hide the Szwajcer family, Jewish refugees from central Europe. They did so, and in spring 1944 hid, in the house next door, a baby boy born to the Szwajcers while they were in hiding. There could be no guarantee of survival: when

[22] Luisa Naor (*née* Franchetti), 'Italian Jews at Risk during WWII', manuscript, sent to the author on 27 February 2002.
[23] Adriana Luzzati, testimony sent to the author, 12 March 2002.
[24] United States Holocaust Memorial Museum, Photo Archive, Worksheet 37984.
[25] Bat-Sheva Savaldi-Kohlberg (Giuliana Basevi's daughter), in conversation with the author, 24 December 2001.

another Jewish refugee, Alfred Spietz, who was also being hidden in Moncalieri, decided one day to go for a walk in the village, he was captured by Italian Fascists and deported to Auschwitz, where he perished.[26]

In Modena, the Mitrani-Andreoli family gave shelter to Zdenko Bergl, a twelve-year-old Jewish boy from Croatia who had escaped across the border into Italy. The local church authorities provided him with false papers. A year later he moved on to Florence, where Neila Fussi and her family gave him a safe haven.[27]

In the Adriatic resort town of Bellaria, Ezio Giorgetti provided shelter in his boarding house to thirty-eight Jews. 'After the Germans occupied the place and ordered the evacuation of the whole quarter where the house was situated,' one of the Jews, Dr Ziga Neumann, a refugee from Zagreb, later recalled, 'it was Ezio who looked for another place and organized the transfer to another place in the town with all the risks involved. When here again the same happened Ezio went to the village in the vicinity and eventually found a big farm in the hills above the town of Pesaro, at a small place called Nuovo. Ezio undertook all the financial obligations towards the owners of the farm for our lodging and food. Without his help and courage we would not have been able to escape to that place. After some time the Germans ordered the farm to be converted into a military hospital and we had again to flee before the Nazis. It was again Ezio who helped us to save our lives. He used his good personal connections with some peasants in the hills further on to accept and hide us in the more remote small village of Pugliano Vecchio. Here we remained until September 1944 when the Allied Forces liberated the area and we

---

[26] 'Testimonianze dell'Olocausto: Documentary Evidence of the Holocaust', Italian Immigrants Association, Israel, factsheet.
[27] United States Holocaust Memorial Museum, Photo Archive, Worksheet 02470.

could descend from the hills to Pesaro where we were received by the Allied troops stationed there.

'During all the time Ezio was always available for advice and active help. Despite the rigid control of the Germans he would visit us at the distant places of our hiding in the hills and would care for everything.'[28]

The Herczog family, father, mother and two children, were living in Trieste, having been expelled by the Italians from Fiume, where they had lived between the wars. Dr Bela Adalberto Herczog, a medical doctor, had been born in Hungary in 1901, a citizen of the Austro-Hungarian Empire. On 3 September 1943 German troops entered Trieste, and the family decided to flee. One of the children, eleven-year-old Dora, later recalled: 'The first stage of our escape was a big village called Pieris, not far from Trieste. In this village lived with her family our former maid, Maria de Luisa, who had lived in our house and was very fond of us, until she too had been forced to leave because of the same racial laws. We remained in Pieris for about three months in the house of relatives of Maria, until we felt that it was too dangerous to live near the city.'

The de Luisas again helped the Herczog family by arranging for them to stay with distant relatives in the small village of San Lorenzo, near Friuli. Their new landlords, Dora recalled, were a middle-aged peasant couple without children, Giovanni and Speranza Chiesa. 'The man was an old Fascist, the foremost representative of the Fascist party in the village, who had no idea of the Jewish problem. To our father it was important to let him know that we were Jews and that it was forbidden, and therefore dangerous, to help us. Nevertheless, this family assisted us with all their heart, with loyalty and concern for our problems until the end of the war.'

[28] Dr Ziga Neumann, 'Solemn Declaration', 24 September 1963, Yad Vashem, Righteous Among the Nations Archive, file 51.

Dr Herczog worked as a general practitioner in the village. Being the only physician in the area, Dora recalled, he was repaid with farm products. 'He relied on his intuition on the nature of human beings; more than once he told unfamiliar people whom he trusted that we were Jews, luckily without dire consequences. We were in need of fake papers: once our father was called to another village nearby to visit an important local official, who was of course one of the chiefs of the Fascist party in the place. My father after the consultation disclosed our secret and asked him for help: within half an hour he received fake documents for the whole family.'

There was a bizarre moment 'when the local German Command asked my father to replace their doctor who was going on vacation for a week. My father could not refuse and so he spent that week from morning to evening in the company of German officers. He, who could speak German fluently, pretended not to understand a word, and used an interpreter.'

Dora recalled how, one morning, a woman whom the Herczogs did not know came to the village, and told them she had been sent by a family friend, Margherita Grunwald, who had been arrested by the Germans in Venice. The woman was a worker in the prison where Margherita Grunwald was being held. In her belongings the Germans found a photograph of the four Herczogs. 'Brutal questioning followed in order to obtain our address, which our friend knew exactly, having visited us some months earlier. When the brave lady feared she would be unable to resist torture, she had asked the prison worker to come to us and to urge us to flee. In exchange she had given her a precious ring she had managed to hide, instructing her to show us the ring as a proof of her telling the truth. After the war we sadly learnt that Mrs Grunwald had perished in the concentration camp of Ravensbrück.'

The Herczog family was at grave risk. 'The danger for

us of being seized could have been immediate,' Dora recalled. 'My parents and the landlords consulted with a couple of neighbours called Masutti (both of them school teachers), and they proposed to send us to Udine to their relatives. Therefore the nephew of our landlords, Elio Chiesa, took us immediately on his horse driven cart to Udine.'

In Udine the Herczog family was hidden safely. Eventually they learned, as Dora recalled, 'that nobody had been looking for us in San Lorenzo, and that the Chiesas would be happy to have us back again with them. In February 1945 our friend Elio Chiesa took us on his cart back to San Lorenzo, and I remember that we had the feeling of coming home. On April 25 we were freed by the Italian partisans' uprising. It turned out that Giovanni Chiesa had been put on the lists of the Fascists to be killed by the partisans in revenge for his previous actions. He was saved because of his activities in our favour.'[29]

Don Beniamino Schivo was rector of the seminary in Città di Castello. With his help a Jewish refugee, Ursula Korn Selig – born in Breslau and educated in Potsdam before fleeing Germany with her parents – was sent for safety to the Benedictine convent, 'where the nuns loved me. One of them, my philosophy teacher, introduced me to her family from Naples. They became my second family.' Later her father and mother joined her. 'We had no freedom, and little to eat, but I had the Monsignor and the nuns.'

When the Germans came to Città di Castello, Ursula and her parents were arrested and taken to the SS in Perugia, the last stage before deportation to Auschwitz, 'But the prisons were full,' Ursula recalled, 'and they returned us to Città di Castello. We knew we had to run away, so the Monsignor and the Bishop prepared our

---

[29] Dora Herczog Levi, letter to the author, 2 March 2002.

escape. Monsignor Schivo and another young priest took off their clerical garb and marched us during the night for eight hours up into the mountains to a summer residence of the Salesian nuns. We broke down the door to the church and entered. There was no food, no beds, and we had only what we were wearing. The caretaker knew about us and every second night he brought us some soup, but we were slowly going mad.'

In due course the Germans arrived, 'and we were hidden in an oven for three months, and the Monsignor hid my father in another place. We had to run again. My mother and I joined the partisans in the woods. Città di Castello was in the German defence line and was mined. We were hidden in the Convent of the Sacred Heart and dressed as nuns per order of Monsignor Schivo. As the Allies advanced, there were terrible bombardments and fighting. We were locked in a room and only the Mother Superior knew. Finally, one day, 22 July 1944, all was quiet, no fighting – the Eighth British Army had liberated the town. We were free . . .'[30]

In Azzanello di Pasiano, in north-eastern Italy, Alessandro and Luisa Wiel took in Marcello Morpurgo and his family, and provided them with false documents and new identities.[31] In Cuorgné, the villagers provided several dozen refugees from Yugoslavia with lodgings and furnishings. On the day before the German occupation an Alpine guide, Gimmy Troglia – later a Partisan commander – took them all to Switzerland.[32]

In the remote village of Canale d'Alba, in Piedmont,

---

[30] Ursula Korn Selig, 'My name is Ursula Korn Selig . . .', manuscript, enclosed with letter to the author, 5 December 2001; United States Holocaust Memorial Museum, Photo Archive, Worksheet 15810. Father Schivo was honoured as a Righteous Among the Nations in 1986.
[31] Dr Marcello Morpurgo, letter to the author, 30 December 2001.
[32] Marek Herman, letter to the author, 20 December 2001. Marek Herman was himself hidden by Italians, and later fought as a partisan.

Matteo Raimondo, a 'sturdy farmer', his wife Marietta, his son Beppe and his daughter Juccia protected five Italian Jews from Genoa: Giuseppe Levi, his wife Bettina, and their three children, Ida, Elia and Pia. Betrayal was always a danger, as the Germans offered rewards to those who would reveal Jews in hiding. 'Everybody in the village knew of our being Jews,' writes Elia Levi, who was ten at the time. 'Our fate would have been concluded, and we would have appeared as a few lines in the book of Memory.' One evening, at the end of September 1943, Beppe Raimondo, Matteo's oldest son, 'a strong fellow then in his early twenties', told the Levi family 'to get ready early the following morning with a minimum luggage: he had thought of everything, where to bring us and how. They had simply guessed that by ourselves we were unable to find a way out, and decided they could not wait idly for our end to happen. In their mind it was a pity we were so inadequate and helpless to care for ourselves in those dangerous times: therefore they decided to act out of pure altruism and not without real danger for themselves.'

Elia Levi's account continued: 'Beppe had secured the help of a friend with a small car and brought us to his uncle's orphanage, in a very small village not very far off, but where nobody, hopefully, knew us as Jews. In the meantime the Fascists had come to their house, at least once, looking for the Jews to deport: the Raimondo family told them they knew nothing of our whereabouts. We stayed, under an alias, in the parsonage of the uncle priest for a few months until Beppe decided that the place was unsafe, and so he transferred us to a lonely farmhouse belonging to one of his cousins, again in a radius of a few tens of kilometers. We felt that the Raimondo family was still protecting us throughout the whole period: Juccia used to come over to us now and again, riding on her bicycle, to bring us money and news. We stayed there and in the area, with a deal of good luck, until the end of April 1945, when, after the end of the war and the collapse of Nazi Germany, we could finally go back first to Canale, then to Genova.'

Many years later, as Elia Levi recalled, 'we learnt of yet another honest deed of this generous family of friends: before going into the hiding, our Mother had entrusted to Marietta a box containing cash, money and family jewels, asking her to keep it for us. But, as she understood the dangers ahead, we told her that should we not come back, that is should we be deported, she should keep all of it. It goes without saying that the box, which had been buried somewhere in the property, was returned to our Mother after the war as the most natural thing.'[33]

Reflecting on the family's experience, Elia Levi wrote: 'For us the striking thing is that the Raimondo family, who hardly knew us, being simply our landlords, got involved at great risk to themselves and saved our lives. We can presume that at the end of our stay, in the isolated farmhouses where we found refuge (in the surroundings of Ceresole d'Alba) at least some of the simple farmers around knew or suspected that we were Jews (just by observing our way of life and our improbable cover-story), without running to denounce us.' This, Elia Levi added, 'is not exceptional. In a small book relating a different rescue experience, the author, Aldo Zargani, reports that the villagers used to call, in their local dialect, the place where the family lived, "the house of the hidden Jews".'[34]

In southern Italy, in San Giovanni Rotondo, Father Pio Abresch hid a Jewish refugee from Hungary, Gyorgy Pogany, whose mother had been deported from Hungary to Auschwitz and killed. Mother and son had both

---

[33] Elia Levi, letter to the author, December 2001.
[34] Elia Levi, letter to the author, February 2002. The book was Aldo Zargani's *Per violino solo* (Edizioni Il Mulino).

converted to Roman Catholicism, and Gyorgy was a priest; but, under the Nazi racial laws and perceptions, both were Jewish. The local Italians knew of Gyorgy's Jewish origins, but did not disclose this information.[35]

In Assisi, the birthplace of St Francis, two clergymen saved the lives of three hundred Jews. The first was the senior clergyman in the city, Bishop Nicolini; the second was the Abbot of the Franciscan monastery, Father Rufino Niccaci. At the bishop's request, Father Niccaci took care of the Jews, provided many of them with false identity papers, and, on one occasion, when German searches came too close, helped them escape disguised as monks. Such was his devotion to the well-being of the refugees that at one point Assisi could boast 'the only convent in the world with a kosher kitchen'.[36]

The hub of rescue efforts was Father Niccaci's monastery, San Damiano. Every few days, he later recalled, 'I would visit the Abbeys of Vallingegno and San Benedetto, the Hermitage, Montefalco, Gubbio, Spello. All the monasteries and churches in Assisi and the surrounding countryside were filled with Jews disguised as monks or nuns, or hiding behind the double grilles of the Enclosure, or living with false papers in the pilgrims' guesthouses attached to these houses.'

In Perugia, Father Federico Don Vincenti was the 'Father Guardian', as Father Niccaci called him, of more than a hundred Jews in hiding, some in the church's outhouse, others in private homes.

On 26 February 1944 the Gestapo entered the quiet precincts of the convent of the Poor Clares of San Quirico, in Assisi, where many Jews were hiding. Father Niccaci, having been forewarned of the raid, had

---

[35] Michael Posner, 'O brother, where art thou?', *Globe and Mail* (Toronto), 30 December 2000.
[36] S. T. Merhavi, 'Earthbound angel', *Jerusalem Post*, 10 November 1978.

arranged for the Jews to leave the convent through a secret tunnel, along which he followed them, even as the Germans were searching the room from which the tunnel led: 'After a while all sounds faded behind me. I had to stoop or crouch down, groping with my hands to find my way. Occasionally, I could hear panting or would bump into someone. Finally I discerned the outline of a man's bowed back and a small sliver of light ahead told me I was nearing the end of the passage. A moment later I crawled out in a barren, wintry field, where part of my Jewish flock awaited me in the huge shadows of the ancient, gnarled olive trees. I turned my head. In the pale moonlight I could see silhouettes of many men already climbing the steep ground, disappearing among the rocks and undergrowth, making for the forest of Monte Subasio as we had planned.'

Those who remained 'were the elderly who were unable to climb, and they waited for me to take them to San Damiano. I knew that at this very moment other groups of Jews who had left their monasteries at the sound of the warning bells were making for the same destination, where they hoped the twenty guerrillas could offer them some protection and where they might hide in the almost impenetrable forest or find refuge with peasants. "Come, my children," I said to men twice my age. And I began to lead my group down to San Damiano, so that they could join the other Jews hiding there in monks' habits.'[37]

Leah Halevy, who reached Assisi with her parents in December 1943, having escaped the round-ups in Trieste, later recalled: 'We were placed in the Convent of Stigmatique Nuns – under the protection of the ad hoc

---

[37] Dr Alexander Ramati, as told by Padre Rufino Niccaci, *The Assisi Underground: The Priests Who Rescued Jews*, pages 100, 121. Ramati had first met Father Niccaci when, as a war correspondent attached to the Polish armed forces, he entered Assisi at the time of liberation.

self-appointed Christian Committee to save Jews.
Among those, the most prominent part was played by
Father Guardian Rufino Niccaci, who was thirty-two at
the time, and in charge of Convent St Damiano. For the
entire period until Assisi was rescued by the Allies on
16 June 1944, Father Rufino was bringing us unobtainable food, kept warning us about any possible German
searches and finally managed to provide us all with false
identity cards with Christian names. He did all this at
peril of his own life and our family was only one of
many, who were saved in convents of Assisi and even in
private houses thanks to the intervention of Father
Rufino. What is most remarkable is that as no Jews ever
lived permanently in Assisi, Father Rufino had never
met Jews before.'[38]

By the end of 2001, a total of 295 Italians – including
whole families – had been recognized as Righteous
Among the Nations at Yad Vashem in Jerusalem.[39]
Typical of such families were the Avondets, living in the
remote mountain village of Luserna San Giovanni, north
of Turin, who took in a Jewish family, the Vitales, whom
they had known before the war while holidaying in the
Avondets' mountain home. 'We went there with just two
suitcases,' Ada Vitale, then aged twenty, recalled, 'and
we lived there twenty months. They gave us everything.
We were known in the village, everyone knew that we
were Jewish.' In the valley were many other people from
Turin, non-Jews, escaping from the Allied bombing. 'Just
one word, somebody could just have made the Germans
a promise, but they never sold themselves, they never

[38] Testimony of Leah Halevy, 2 April 1974, Yad Vashem, Righteous
Among the Nations Archive, file 876.
[39] 'Righteous Among the Nations – per Country & Ethnic Origin',
1 January 2002, Yad Vashem Department for the Righteous Among
the Nations.

betrayed us, or the other Jewish families who were nearby. Why? Because they themselves had been liberated in 1848, and therefore they felt morally bound to those who were living through persecution.'

Michel and Leontina Avondet knew they could face reprisals. So, too, did their daughter Silvia and their relatives Maria and Alfredo Comba, who helped in the deception. None of them had any intention of betraying their guests. When a neighbour, frightened that the fugitives might be betrayed by someone in the village, expressed his fears that reprisals might affect the whole village, the Vitales offered to try to find somewhere else, and leave. 'The Avondets knew very well that if they had been discovered they would have been shot, and the house burned down. As they lived in a small terrace, all the houses would have been destroyed.' But Michel Avondet was adamant: "You stop here. Don't worry. We'll organize everything."' Ada Vitale commented: 'Their solidarity helped us morally and physically.'[40]

In the village of Gandino – a village which was also the Nazi regional headquarters – a local Italian official, Giovanni Servalli, issued false papers to the Löwi family, refugees from Germany. These papers enabled them to change their names to those common in the region: Mariem Löwi became Maria Loverina, her daughter Marina took the surname Carnazzi and her brother became Gilberto Carnazzi.

Marina's father, Leopold (Lipa) Löwi, had been in Belgium when war came; in 1942 he was caught in a round-up there and deported to Auschwitz. He did not survive the war. Marina was six years old when she reached Gandino; her brother was nine. Among those who gave them refuge were a teacher, Vincenzo Rudelli, and his wife Candida, parents of two grown daughters who offered them refuge in a mountain village. The

---

[40] Testimony of Ada Vitale, sent to the author, 12 December 2001.

Rudellis also gave refuge to five or six other Jewish families – in addition to several partisans whom they were sheltering.

Marina Löwi also recalled that Umberto Palomba, an Italian who had left Milan to avoid the Allied bombing, 'befriended us and forewarned us of Nazi house searches, some of which we encountered, and round-ups'. At those times he 'gave us sanctuary in his house'.[41]

Marina Löwi and her brother were eventually taken in by the Sisters of Maria Bambina in Gazzaniga, and looked after by the nuns in the boarding school they ran in the village. The Mother Superior and the local priest were the only ones to know that the two 'Carnazzi' children were Jewish – as indeed were several others in the school.[42]

In July 1944, on the German-occupied island of Rhodes, on the second and third day of the internment of the Jews of the island, food was sent into their place of incarceration by local Italians distressed by the hardships imposed upon their fellow islanders. It is said on the island that the imam of the mosque went to see the rabbi, and offered to bury the synagogue's Scrolls of the Law in the mosque garden. This was done, and the rabbi retrieved them safely after the war.[43]

Also on Rhodes, an Italian teacher from Sardinia, Girolamo Sotgiu, who was teaching literature at the local lycée, did what he could to help the Jews when the deportation was ordered. 'He started by disguising himself as a porter,' Albert Amato recalled, 'in order to bring some food and some comfort (with the news that

---

[41] Marina Löwi Zinn, 'Material Submitted to Yad Vashem'; sent to the author by Marina Zinn, 26 December 2000.
[42] Marina Löwi Zinn, letter to the author, 26 December 2000.
[43] Information communicated by Jay Shir, in conversation with the author, 31 December 2001.

there had been an attempt to kill Hitler) to the men already herded together. Secondly, he told my wife that our little daughter, Lina, then eight years old, should not go to the concentration point and he risked his life taking her and hiding her with him. Thirdly he managed to find a horse carriage (the island was under blockade and there was no petrol for the cars nor feed for the horses) and took my mother to interview the Turkish Consul in a nearby village where the consulate had been transferred, owing to the bombing of the port and the town by the Allies.'[44]

The Turkish Consul, Selahattin Ulkumen, provided protective documents, in all, for fifty-two Jews on Rhodes (and nearby Kos) who had been born on the islands before 1912, when they were part of the Turkish Ottoman Empire. All fifty-two were saved.[45] After the war, Girolamo Sotgiu returned to his native Sardinia.

In the Italian port of Fiume, which was under German control until the final months of the war, the Germans arrested a senior Italian police officer, Giovanni Palatucci. He had helped more than five hundred Jewish refugees who had reached Italy from Croatia, by giving them 'Aryan' papers and sending them to safety in southern Italy.[46] Palatucci was sent to Dachau, where he perished.[47]

---

[44] Albert Amato, letter of 12 December 1987.
[45] Eric Saul, 'Visas for Life' exhibition, 2000; Yad Vashem Righteous Among the Nations Archive, file 4128.
[46] 'Rijeka' (Italian 'Fiume'), *Encyclopaedia Judaica* (Jerusalem, 1972), volume 14, col. 185.
[47] Liliana Picciotto Fargion, 'Note biografiche dei decorati con medaglia d'oro', in Giuliana Donati, *Persecuzione e Deportazione degli Ebrei dall'Italia durante la Dominazione Nazifascista*, Milan, 1975, pages 52–3.

CHAPTER SIXTEEN

Hungary

It was not until March 1944, with the German military occupation, that the Holocaust came to Hungary, which at that time – including the areas of Czechoslovakia and Romania which Hungary had annexed in 1940 – had a Jewish population of three-quarters of a million. The Hungarian Regent, Admiral Horthy, Germany's military ally but never a slavish adherent of the Nazi racial policies, had twice refused Hitler's personal request to deport Hungary's Jews to Germany. Without the German military occupation there would have been no deportations to Auschwitz. In August 1941, however, when Hungarian troops were fighting alongside German troops on the Eastern Front against the Soviet Union, Horthy had agreed to send twenty thousand Jewish slave labourers to German-occupied Russia. Most of them were from the eastern regions of Czechoslovakia annexed by Hungary the previous year; more than fifteen thousand of them were handed over to the SS and killed, eleven thousand of them in a single day of slaughter at Kamenets Podolsk in August 1941, when several thousand local Jews were also murdered.

One of those who managed to escape that carnage, Tibor Hegedus, later wrote that he and the twenty-seven who escaped with him owed their survival to their Hungarian commanding officer, a major, 'who gave all the twenty-eight people who escaped the massacre a paper, stamped by the German Commander as well, saying that we were Hungarians, and could return to Hungary. Of course the majority of these people were Jews, and he knew it. There was a Russian lady teacher who helped three of us to hide in her flat until we received the above-mentioned paper. The Hungarian soldiers were also helpful, giving food to us. The day of the massacre they were ordered to remain in their barracks, and the killings were done by German soldiers only.'[1]

Barna Kiss was a Hungarian officer in charge of one of the slave labour units. He had 214 Jews under his command. As they marched eastward towards the Russian front, his orders were to work them to death. Instead, he looked after them, ensured they were able to bathe their feet each day, and provided medical help for those who fell sick. The majority of them survived.[2]

Throughout 1942 and 1943 the Jews of Hungary were untouched by the deportations and killings that were taking place in countries all around them. Indeed, several thousand Polish and Slovak Jews managed to escape deportation to Auschwitz by fleeing southwards and finding refuge in Hungary. But within a few days of German forces entering Hungary Adolf Eichmann arrived in Budapest with a special SS Commando of 'experts', determined to deport all of Hungary's Jews without delay. The first stage of this operation was to order all Jews to leave their homes and move into specially designated ghettos, often located in brickworks or factories or a run-down part of the town. The historian of the Jews of Bonyhad, Leslie Blau – who had earlier been taken away from the town to serve as a forced labourer – has described how, in a gesture of sympathy

---

[1] Tibor Hegedus, letter to the author, 22 February 2001.
[2] *Album of Rescuers*: Humboldt State University, website: www.humboldt.edu.

for the incarcerated Jews, a number of local Gypsies threw freshly baked bread over the ghetto fence. The leaders of the local Catholic, Evangelical and Reform churches also tried to help. But the final stage, when it came, in Bonyhad as in all Hungarian towns and villages outside Budapest, was swift and cruel: deportation to Auschwitz, and the destruction of a whole community.[3]

In the town of Kassa a nun, Ida Peterfy, hid several of her Jewish friends and their families, and organized a network of like-minded Hungarians to hide others.[4] In Miskolc, Sandor Kopacsi – later one of the leaders of the 1956 Hungarian revolt against Communist rule – hid seven Jews in the cellar of a house that he had rented, saving them from deportation.[5] In Munkacs, a Roman Catholic couple, Jozsef and Margit Strausz, saved a Jewish boy, Amos Rubin, from deportation. 'I only wore my Star of David for twelve days,' he later wrote, before being taken by his parents to his new home. The neighbours were told that he was a relative who had come from a small town. 'One day Mr Strausz told me that the Germans had issued a decree in town that whoever was found hiding a Jew in his house would be severely punished. If found harbouring a Jew, he faced the possibility of death, his family would be killed, or at the very least he would lose his job. However, Mr Strausz comforted me and assured me that everything would end well.'[6]

Elie Wiesel, whose articulate writings on the Holocaust brought it to the consciousness of a wide

[3] Leslie Blau, *Bonyhad: A Destroyed Community*.
[4] 'Ida Peterfy, Nun Who Helped Save Jews, 77' (obituary), *Jerusalem Post*, 18 February 2000.
[5] 'Hungarian hero fought Nazis, Soviet', *Globe and Mail* (Toronto), 5 March 2001.
[6] Testimony of 'The Only Jewish Child in Munkacs', *Encyclopaedia of the Diaspora* (in Hebrew), volume 7 (Tel Aviv, 1959), pages 499–502; Righteous Among the Nations Archive, file 88.

public, has recalled how, in Sighet, after the establishment of the ghetto, 'Maria – our old housekeeper, wonderful Maria who had worked for us since I was born – begged us to follow her to her home. She offered us her cabin in a remote hamlet. She would have room for all six of us, and Grandma Nissel as well. Seven in one cabin? Yes, she swore it, as Christ is her witness. She would take care of us, she would handle everything. We said no, politely but firmly. We did so because we still didn't know what was in store for us. This simple, uneducated woman stood taller than the city's intellectuals, dignitaries, and clergy. My father had many acquaintances and even friends in the Christian community, but not one of them showed the strength of character of this peasant woman . . . It was a simple and devout Christian woman who saved her town's honour.'[7]

Frantiska Prva was nanny to two Jewish girls in Ungvar. As the deportations from the Ungvar region began in April 1944 she agreed to take the girls, then aged six and seven, to another town where they would not be recognized as Jews, and where she could look after them. Their parents were deported to Auschwitz and murdered.[8]

In Satoraljaujhelyen, a seventeen-year-old Calvinist girl, Malvina Csizmadia, together with her two sisters and her mother, helped Jewish men interned at a forced labour camp next to her home to maintain contact with their families. She also helped the men by smuggling food into the camp, and eventually, together with her family, over a period of five months organized the escape of twenty-five Jewish men to previously arranged hiding places on various farms.[9]

---

[7] Elie Wiesel, *Memoirs: All Rivers Run to the Sea*, page 63.
[8] Information provided by Renate Schonberg Winston (one of the two girls saved), United States Holocaust Memorial Museum, Photo Archive, Worksheet 45879.
[9] Mordecai Paldiel, *The Path of the Righteous*, pages 310–11.

In April the Gestapo arrested a British subject, Jane Haining, who had been looking after four hundred Jewish girls in a school in Budapest belonging to the Church of Scotland Mission in the city. Among the charges against her were having 'worked amongst the Jews', and having 'wept when putting yellow stars on the girls'.[10] Jane Haining was deported to Auschwitz on April 28, from the concentration camp in the town of Kistarcsa to which she had been sent. Within three months she was dead. One of the young girls who saw her taken away from the Church of Scotland Mission in the Gestapo car later recalled: 'The days of horror were coming and Miss Haining protested against those who wanted to distinguish between the child of one race and the child of another. A long time later I realised that she died for me and for others.'[11]

The deportations from Hungary to Auschwitz were carried out with brutal swiftness. Starting on 15 May 1944, within less than two months 437,402 Hungarian Jews were taken by train to Auschwitz from more than sixty towns and villages: 381,000 of those deported were murdered there, most within a few hours of their arrival.

Individual Hungarians tried to save Jews from deportation. A Hungarian army officer, Kalman Horvath, systematically drafted into his Labour Battalion Jews who would otherwise be deported. One survivor recalled how Horvath 'conscripted both children and elderly people', although the age range for Labour Battalions was between eighteen and forty-eight.[12] Another survivor, Paul Friedlaender, later described the moment in June

---

[10] Reverend David McDougall, *Jane Haining, 1897–1944*, page 26.
[11] Quoted in Joe Quinn, 'Honour for Scots Holocaust heroine', *Express*, 23 November 1997. On 8 December 1997, in Glasgow, Jane Haining was posthumously granted Righteous Among the Nations status. Her sister, Agnes O'Brien, received the award on her behalf.
[12] Testimony submitted to Yad Vashem Righteous Among the Nations Archive, file 5012.

1944 when 'we were rounded up at the brick factory of Miskolc-Diosgyor. My mother and sister and hundreds of fellow Jews were made to wait there to be deported. The Gendarmerie treated us very roughly. It was a frightful night. Shooting, shouting, cattle wagons arriving. In the morning a miracle happened. An army officer named Captain Kalman Horvath (I only learned his name at a later date) ordered every man – from the age of fifteen to sixty-five – to gather in the courtyard. About forty of us were there, and had to form a soldier-like company. At this moment the commanding officer of the Gendarmes reprimanded Captain Horvath, threatening him for interfering with "his Jews!!" The miracle was that Captain Horvath ordered his soldiers to surround our Company, with rifles drawn, ready to protect us, shouting back to the Gendarme commander: "These men are enlisted to the Army's Labour Force..." Turning to us, he gave the order: "Quick march! toward the exit gate!" '[13] Among those whom Horvath saved in this way, Friedlaender recalled, were even 'three generations' in one family: a grandfather, father and son.[14]

Itzhak Steinberger recalled: 'I was sixteen, thin, small, with big glasses and a limp. When my turn came to face Horvath, he asked me about my occupation. I was a high school student, but I claimed being a cobbler's apprentice. Horvath did not even blink and let me enlist. My late father came next. He told the truth about being a merchant. Horvath asked him, surprised: You do not want to enlist? My father answered that he would leave that to fate. He stayed with my mother. They were both murdered a few days later in Auschwitz.'[15]

---

[13] Paul Friedlaender, testimony submitted to Yad Vashem Righteous Among the Nations Archive, file 5012.
[14] Pal Foti (Paul Friedlaender), conversation with the author, 24 March 2002.
[15] Itzhak Steinberger, testimony submitted to Yad Vashem Righteous Among the Nations Archive, file 5012.

Randolph Braham, the historian of the fate of Hungarian Jewry, writes of how 'many national governmental and military leaders, as well as many local commanders, aware of the realities of the ghettoization and deportation programme and motivated by humanitarian instincts, did everything in their power to rescue as many Jews as possible.' One of the 'most praiseworthy' of these military figures, Braham adds, was Colonel Imre Reviczky, the commander of a labour battalion, under whose direction 'all Jews who appeared for service at his headquarters were immediately inducted and provided with food and shelter, irrespective of age or state of health.'[16] During the retreat of the labour battalions from the Russian front, Reviczky encouraged his Jewish conscripts to escape.[17]

The actions of those brave Hungarians who had the will or the means to help could not save more than a fragment of Hungarian Jewry outside Budapest. Having cleared the rest of Hungary of its Jewish population, Eichmann and the SS turned their attention to the capital. Eichmann planned to begin the deportation of all hundred and fifty thousand Jews from Budapest in the second week of July, as the culmination and conclusion of the destruction of Hungarian Jewry. Even as his plans were being prepared, however, there were those in the non-Jewish community willing to take action to try to save Jews from the imminent deportation. On June 21, as rumours circulated of the mass murder of Hungarian Jews at Auschwitz, the Christian clergymen of Budapest were criticized by the Hungarian Ministry of the Interior for saving Jews by issuing false baptismal certificates, but the pattern of protest and rescue was intensifying.

---

[16] Randolph Braham, *The Politics of Genocide*, volume 1, page 340.
[17] Mordecai Paldiel, *Sheltering the Jews*. Reviczky was posthumously granted a Righteous Among the Nations award, Yad Vashem Righteous Among the Nations Archive, file 72.

On June 26, information brought by four Jewish escapees from Auschwitz exploded on the Allied and neutral world: their report, smuggled out of the death camp itself, made it clear that all previous deportees to Auschwitz over the previous two years had been murdered there and that the Hungarian deportees were even then being gassed. The Jewish leadership in Budapest appealed to diplomats of neutral countries to do what they could to save the Jews of the capital from deportation. In an immediate response, the Spanish Minister in Budapest, Angel Sanz-Briz, and the Swiss Consul-General, Carl Lutz, joined forces to issue protective documents. Sanz-Briz distributed 1,898 such documents, using Spanish Legation writing paper.[18] Lutz issued protective documents for 7,800 Jews, offering the holder the protection of the Swiss government; many of the documents, on Swiss Legation writing paper, were signed by him personally.[19] On June 29 the German Embassy in Budapest protested to Berlin about these documents, but the head of the Swiss Legation, Maximilian Jaeger, a Swiss career diplomat, put his full authority behind what Lutz had done, and gave him freedom of action to continue with his rescue activities.[20]

The Swedish Legation in Budapest was also a focal point of Jewish appeals for help. 'We were besieged by Jews who suspected what was coming and pleaded for help,' recalled the Second Secretary at the Legation, Per Anger. Provisional Swedish passports were issued to Jews who had some personal or business connection with Sweden. In 'rather a short time' the Legation issued

---

[18] 'Portrait of Angel Sanz-Briz . . . ', United States Holocaust Memorial Museum, Photo Archive, Worksheet 45684, citing Eric Saul, 'Visas for Life' Exhibition, February 2000.
[19] Yad Vashem Righteous Among the Nations Archive, file 46.
[20] 'Portrait of Maximilian Jaeger . . . ', United States Holocaust Memorial Museum, Photo Archive, Worksheet 45654, citing Eric Saul, 'Visas for Life' Exhibition, prospectus, November 2000.

'no fewer than seven hundred provisional passports and certificates. The rumour of our work spread, and the host of supplicants swelled day by day.' Everyone in the Swedish Legation, headed by the Minister, Carl Ivar Danielsson, 'worked day and night during these months. When it became clear that our strength would be insufficient for this new enterprise, the Minister approached our Ministry of Foreign Affairs about reinforcing the Legation staff. A new appointment was made, specifically to head a rescue effort for the Jews.' The holder of that appointment would be Raoul Wallenberg. In 1936 he had spent six months at a branch of his family's bank in Haifa, where he came into contact with many Jewish refugees from Nazi persecution. On his return to Sweden he became an executive of an import–export firm headed by a Hungarian Jew.[21] He was due to arrive in Budapest on July 9.

Despite the international outcry after the Hungarian deportations to Auschwitz became public knowledge, the deportations from the outer suburbs of Budapest continued. However, on July 4, Admiral Horthy told Berlin's senior representative in the city, SS General Veesenmayer, that the deportations must end. He cited protests from the Vatican – recently liberated by the Allies – King Gustav VI Adolf of Sweden, and the International Committee of the Red Cross. Horthy also knew, from intercepted diplomatic messages, that the Allies intended to bomb government buildings in Budapest unless the deportations stopped.

On July 6 almost two thousand Jews were deported to Auschwitz from the southern Hungarian city of Pecs. The Hungarian Prime Minister, Dome Sztojay, immediately summoned SS General Veesenmayer and reiterated that Horthy had ordered a halt to all further deportations to Auschwitz. Two days later the imminent round-up

[21] Mordecai Paldiel, *The Path of the Righteous*, page 320.

468

and deportation of all hundred and fifty thousand Jews from Budapest itself – which Eichmann had planned to begin within a few days – was suspended. On the following day, July 9, Raoul Wallenberg arrived in Budapest. He brought with him a list of 630 Hungarian Jews for whom Swedish visas were available.

Wallenberg's list of 'protected' Jews was given to the Hungarian government at the same time that Carl Lutz submitted a Swiss list of seven hundred Jews whose emigration to Palestine had been approved by the British government. Later, that list grew to eight thousand numbered certificates, and when Lutz continued to issue them beyond the original eight thousand he deliberately began numbering them again from number one, to avoid arousing Hungarian suspicions. A number of 'protected' houses were set aside for those in possession of these Swiss and Swedish certificates, each house being marked with either a Swiss or a Swedish diplomatic emblem.[22]

Eichmann's SS Commando, thwarted in its work of despatching Budapest Jewry to Auschwitz, returned to Germany. However, danger to the city's Jews persisted in the threat of attack by the violently anti-Semitic Hungarian Arrow Cross movement. To offer some protection from this peril, on July 24 Carl Lutz extended the Swiss Legation's protection to a small department store, the Glass House, at 29 Vadasz Street, which was declared to be the 'Swiss Legation Representation of Foreign Interests, Department of Immigration'. Several hundred Budapest Jews were able to register there as Swiss-protected persons.[23]

During August and September 1944, the Jews of Budapest felt a degree of safety. Then danger returned:

---

[22] Randolph Braham, *The Politics of Genocide*, volume 2, pages 788–9.
[23] Lutz papers, Yad Vashem archive, file 46.

on October 15 the Arrow Cross, under the leadership of Ferenc Szalasi, seized power. Eichmann and his SS Commando returned to Budapest. Facing the combined anti-Jewish ferocity of the newly empowered Arrow Cross and an SS Commando earlier cheated of its prey, Wallenberg and Lutz intensified their efforts to extend the number of protected safe houses. Other foreign diplomats in Budapest also gave what protection they could. At the Swiss Embassy, Dr Harald Feller hid several Hungarian Jews in his residence, and on one occasion managed to send fourteen Jews to safety in Switzerland, two of whom he had first to get out of the Kistarcsa concentration camp.[24]

As Arrow Cross terror continued, the Spanish diplomat Angel Sanz-Briz rented several buildings in Budapest in which he housed Jews with Spanish protective documents. 'On all buildings', he wrote, 'we put signs in German and Hungarian, "Ex-territorial buildings belonging to the Spanish Embassy." And although this seemed absolutely impossible, the Hungarian nationalists, the Arrow Cross, honoured these buildings.'[25] On October 23, Sanz-Briz put Giorgio Perlasca, an Italian businessman in Budapest, whom he knew and respected, in charge of the Spanish safe houses in the city.[26]

The Portuguese Chargé d'Affaires in Budapest, Carlos de Liz-Texeira Branquino, received permission from his government to issue five hundred protective documents to Jews who had relatives in Portugal, Brazil or any Portuguese colony. In fact he issued more than eight hundred. These Jews were given refuge in safe houses

---

[24] 'Portrait of Dr Harald Feller . . . ', United States Holocaust Memorial Museum, Photo Archive, Worksheet 45652, citing Eric Saul, 'Visas for Life' Exhibition, February 2000.
[25] Yad Vashem Righteous Among the Nations Archive, file 121.
[26] Ernie Meyer, ' "Italian Wallenberg" to be Honoured for Saving Jews', *Jerusalem Post*, 22 September 1989.

established by the Portuguese Legation.[27] As the killings
by the Arrow Cross continued, Friedrich Born, Director
of the International Committee of the Red Cross in
Budapest, issued more than three thousand Red Cross
letters of protection and more than four thousand
employment certificates to Jews in the capital, and established Red Cross safe houses to protect those who held
these documents. These included more than sixty institutions belonging to the Jewish community, among them
hospitals, old age homes and research institutes. Marked
with the Red Cross insignia, these buildings became
additional protected houses for Jewish residents.[28] With
Arrow Cross members killing Jews in the streets of
Budapest, Angelo Rotta, the senior Vatican representative in Budapest, took a lead in establishing an
'International Ghetto' consisting of several dozen
modern apartment buildings to which large numbers of
Jews – eventually, twenty-five thousand – were brought,
and on which the Swiss, Swedish, Portuguese and
Spanish Legations, as well as the Vatican, affixed their
emblems.

Individual churchmen were also active. Father Jakab
Raile, Prior of the Jesuit College, saved 'close to 150 Jews'
at the Jesuit Residence in the city.[29] Father Jozsef
Janossy, head of the Holy Cross Society, oversaw the
rescue of Jews who had been given false baptismal
certificates by Father Raile. One of the leaders of the
Holy Cross Society, Margit Slachta, secured protective
documents for one of the great Polish Jewish religious
leaders, Aaron Rokeach, the Belzer Rebbe, whose

[27] 'Portrait of Carlos de Liz-Texeira Branquino', United States
Holocaust Memorial Museum, Photo Archive, Worksheet 45665,
citing Eric Saul, 'Visas for Life' Exhibition, February 2000.
[28] 'Portrait of Friedrich Born', United States Holocaust Memorial
Museum, Photo Archive, Worksheet 45659, citing Eric Saul, 'Visas
for Life' Exhibition, February 2000.
[29] Randolph Braham, *The Politics of Genocide*, volume 2, page 1123.

entire family, including his seven children, had been murdered by the Nazis in the southern Polish city of Przemysl.[30]

The historian Eugene Levai has given a comprehensive listing of the rescue efforts of Christian organizations and institutions in Budapest, and of the terrible risks involved. For example, the monks of the Champagnat Institute of the Order of Mary, a Budapest monastic institution, took in a hundred Jewish pupils as boarders, together with fifty of the children's parents. An *agent provocateur*, an SS man from Alsace, who pretended to be a French soldier in hiding, denounced the monks. As a result, they were surrounded one night by forty members of the Gestapo, who dragged six monks, two-thirds of the children and most of the adults away. The monks, after prolonged torture, were released; the Jews were killed. Those adults and children who had managed to find places to hide during the raid were saved.

In the nunnery of the Sisters of the Divine Saviour, a hundred and fifty children found refuge, but Arrow Cross members who were billeted in the neighbourhood found them and dragged them away. Sixty-two were driven to the banks of the Danube and killed. Elsewhere in the city, the Sisters of the Order of Divine Love hid more than a hundred Jewish refugees, but they were also discovered by members of the Arrow Cross, who were billeted on the other side of the road. They attacked the convent, dragging away and killing all the refugees with the exception of five who managed to escape through the roof.

The Convent of the Good Shepherd hid 112 girls, who twice escaped the Arrow Cross by hiding in neighbouring houses while the convent was being searched. In the home of the Sisters of Mercy of Szatmar, twenty

[30] Kinga Frojimovics, Geza Komoroczy, Viktoria Pusztai and Andrea Strbik, *Jewish Budapest: Monuments, Rites, History*, page 344.

Jews were hidden, and although the inhabitants of the house – which was part of a large tenement building – knew that the nuns were hiding Jews, all were saved. In the Convent of Sacré Coeur two hundred women and children survived. Eleven Jews were hidden in the small premises of the Charité. One night the manager was arrested, interrogated and threatened, but he did not betray those in hiding, and all of them were saved. The Josephinum – the Society of the Virgin Mary – only a few hundred yards from the Arrow Cross headquarters, hid sixty children and two adults. Twenty Jews found refuge in the small hospital of the Sisters of the Eucharistic Union. They were discovered and taken away by the Arrow Cross, who tortured the prioress, but set her free with a warning that they would kill her if they caught her hiding Jews again. After her escape she immediately contacted a prelate, Dr Arnold Pataky, who put his four-room apartment at her disposal. Using it as a hiding place, the prioress again gave sanctuary to as many persecuted Jews as she could.[31]

An Armenian doctor in Budapest, Ara Jeretzian, set up a medical emergency clinic in a private house, and took in forty Jewish doctors and their families, as well as other Jews – four hundred people in all. In the building he fed them, used his own funds to buy them medicine, and arranged forged papers for them. Dr Jeretzian was helped in this work of rescue by his Hungarian assistant, Laszlo Nagy, of whom Yad Vashem noted: 'He could have quietly walked away from these dangers and risks, because he was disabled. He received no remuneration.'[32]

A Hungarian army captain, Laszlo Ocskay, who commanded a Labour Battalion in Budapest, protected approximately fifteen hundred Jews by taking them into

---

[31] Eugene Levai, *Black Book on the Martyrdom of Hungarian Jewry*.
[32] Yad Vashem Righteous Among the Nations Archive, file 2002 (Jeretzian), 2002a (Nagy).

473

his company's labour camp inside the city. Two-thirds of those whom he protected were women and children. More than two dozen survivors testified to the fact that they had been saved by Ocskay, who also provided manpower from the company to help the work of the Red Cross in the city, supplying food and medicine to children's homes and orphanages in which Jews were hiding. He also hid Jews in the cellar of his own home.[33] In one incident, when a group of Arrow Cross soldiers were threatening a group of women in Ocskay's labour company, he was immediately informed, and alerted a friend of his in the SS, a certain Weber, who brought a group of German soldiers to protect the women from the Arrow Cross.[34] In a letter to Yad Vashem seeking Righteous status for Ocskay, who had died in the United States in 1966, Dan Danieli (formerly Denes Faludi) wrote: 'Myself and my family survived, together with about a thousand relatives of the Labour Company members; relatives who had no legal right to be in the compound and survived only due to Ocskay's deeds.'[35]

Individual Hungarians in Budapest sought various means to save Jews. Gusztav Mikulai, who before the war had founded an all-female orchestra, and who was married to a Jewish woman, not only provided his wife and in-laws with false identity papers, but also found hiding places for other Jews all over the city, smuggled families out of transit camps, and even managed to pull some off the trains. Eighty Jews, including many children, were saved as a result of his efforts.[36]

---

[33] Dan Danieli, *Captain Ocskay, A Righteous Man.*
[34] Mordecai Paldiel, letter to Dan Danieli, 1 September 1997, Yad Vashem Righteous Among the Nations Archive, file 7587.
[35] Exchange of letters between Mordecai Paldiel and Dan Danieli, June and July 1997, Yad Vashem Righteous Among the Nations Archive, file 7587.
[36] United States Holocaust Memorial Museum, Photo Archive, Worksheet 90791.

Vilmos Racz, who had run for Hungary in the 1908 London Olympics, and fought in the First World War, hid sixteen Jews in the basement of his house in Buda. One – a humorist in better times – stayed there for more than six months; when he eventually ventured out to cross the river, he was shot on the Chain Bridge. Racz hid four more Jews on his country estate.[37] Oszkar Szabo, a deserter from the Hungarian air force, saved the lives of twenty-eight Hasidic Jews by hiding them. He also provided false identity papers for his Jewish fiancée and her parents.[38] A medical doctor, Sandor Tonelli, arranged for forty Jews to hide in the basement of an abandoned hospital in Budapest during the German occupation. He and his staff obtained extra food rations and shared them with those in hiding. He kept the Jews safe from raids and searches of the building, and certified papers for them to find refuge in the International Ghetto.[39]

On 26 October 1944, within two weeks of the Arrow Cross seizing power in the city, the newly appointed Hungarian Minister of Defence agreed to Eichmann's request to deport Jews to Germany for forced labour. Twenty-five thousand men and twelve thousand women were rounded up in a week. Most were sent on foot westwards towards the Austrian border – a distance of more than a hundred miles. On October 28, while the round-ups were under way, the Arrow Cross seized a Roman Catholic priest, Ferenc Kallo, who had been helping Jews with life-saving certificates of baptism. They killed him at dawn on the following day.

---

[37] Anna Porter (Vilmos Racz's granddaughter), *The Storyteller: Memory, Secrets, Magic and Lies*, pages 187, 194.
[38] United States Holocaust Memorial Museum, Photo Archive, Worksheet 05820.
[39] Desmond Brown, 'Israel honours two Toronto war heroes', *National Post*, 9 February 1999. Tonelli, then aged eighty-five, was living in Toronto. The other honoree was Jan Schoumans (see chapter 14).

Seeking a means to help Jews faced with the resurgent Nazi threat and the deportations to Austria, Angelo Rotta obtained permission from the Vatican to issue protective passes to Jewish converts to Catholicism. Eventually, he was to issue more than fifteen thousand such passes, instructing his staff not to examine the credentials of the recipients too closely. Rotta also encouraged other church leaders in Budapest to help their 'Jewish brothers'.[40] Among his compassionate acts was an instruction to one of his priests, Tibor Baranszky, to approach the Jews on the forced marches and distribute letters of immunity to as many of them as possible, in order to save them.[41]

Even within Hungarian official circles the anti-Jewish violence of the Szalasi regime did not go unopposed. On 4 November 1944 the police chief of Budapest, Janos Solymossor, intervened to save ninety residents of a Jewish old people's home from being murdered by the Arrow Cross. Nevertheless, on November 8 the first few thousand of the twenty-seven thousand Jews in captivity were ordered to march towards the Austrian border, forced to walk eighteen to twenty miles a day. On November 9 the Arrow Cross seized a further ten thousand Jews throughout the city and took them to a brick factory in the suburbs, where they were held prisoner, without food or fuel, in freezing conditions. The historian of the Swiss Righteous Gentiles, Meir Wagner, writes: 'As many of these Jews were in possession of protective letters, Carl and Gertrude Lutz drove to the brick factory several times in order to personally free Jews holding these documents. Gertrude stood in the

---

[40] 'Portrait of Monsignor Angelo Rotta . . . ', United States Holocaust Memorial Museum, Photo Archive, Worksheet 45669, citing Eric Saul, 'Visas for Life' Exhibition, February 2000.
[41] Information collected by Sara Reuveni, in charge of the Hungarian section of the Righteous Among the Nations Department at Yad Vashem Righteous Among the Nations Archive, file 7690.

freezing cold for many hours checking the papers, and demanding the rights that the holders were entitled to.'[42] Representatives of the International Committee of the Red Cross and the Swedish Legation, and several individual Hungarian army officers, also took documents to the brickworks that enabled some Jews to leave.

On November 15 the Hungarian government established a 'Big Ghetto' (also known as the 'Sealed Ghetto') for sixty-nine thousand Jews in the centre of the old Jewish quarter; a further thirty thousand Jews, who held protective diplomatic documents, went to the area designated as the International Ghetto, finding sanctuary in the apartment blocks under the protection of the Red Cross and the Swedish, Swiss, Spanish, Portuguese and Vatican diplomatic authorities.

The Swiss Vice-Consul, Franz Bischof, personally hid more than thirty Jews.[43] The director of the International Committee of the Red Cross in Budapest, Friedrich Born, obtained the release of five hundred children from the Big Ghetto after they had been taken there in violation of Red Cross protection. In all, Born and his staff saved between eleven thousand and fifteen thousand Jews. Though Born was initially criticized by his Red Cross superiors in Geneva for exceeding his authority in his rescue activities, a post-war Red Cross report exonerated him.[44]

Working closely with Born and his Red Cross colleagues was an Evangelical minister, Pastor Gabor Sztehlo, leader of the Protestant Good Shepherd organization. Acting without concern for his own safety,

[42] Meir Wagner, *The Righteous of Switzerland*, page 181.
[43] 'Portrait of Franz Bischof', United States Holocaust Memorial Museum, Photo Archive, Worksheet 45660, citing Eric Saul, 'Visas for Life' Exhibition, February 2000.
[44] 'Portrait of Friedrich Born', United States Holocaust Memorial Museum, Photo Archive, Worksheet 45659, citing Eric Saul, 'Visas for Life' Exhibition, February 2000.

Sztehlo placed 905 Jewish children and 635 Jewish adults in the thirty homes under his authority. In the pre-war years his organization had been primarily concerned with converting Jewish children to Lutheranism, but when the question of rescue arose, he at once made it clear that conversion was no longer his aim, nor did he pursue it in any way.

Paul Friedlaender was one of the Jews who had earlier been saved from deportation from the Hungarian provinces to Auschwitz by Captain Kalman Horvath's protective device of enlisting them in his Labour Battalion. In mid-November 1944 he made his way to Budapest, with false papers. He was eighteen years old. 'I was lucky, nobody asked for my papers. During the day I wandered in the streets and even went to the cinema. I slept in doorways or cellars and heard the Arrow Cross gangs round up Jews and shoot them on the banks of the Danube. One night I slept in the annexe of the Dohany Street Synagogue, where I heard of a priest by the name of Gabor Sztehlo who gave shelter to Jewish children. On a late November afternoon I arrived in his office in Buda, only to be stopped by a fat doorman. We exchanged a few loud words, when an elegantly dressed young, but grey-haired man appeared. It was the Pastor, who smilingly invited me into his office. When, recovered from my surprise, I confessed my Jewishness, he said he would send me to a children's home.' The pastor then gave the young man a document, which he signed, on Red Cross writing paper, stating that the bearer was employed as a messenger by the Red Cross. Paul Friedlaender then went to the children's home on a hilltop in Buda.[45]

An eleven-year-old boy who was protected in one of Pastor Sztehlo's homes later recalled: 'We had Bible

---

[45] Pal Foti (Paul Friedlaender), 'The survivor's tale: 50 years ago the Holocaust reached Hungary', *AJR Information*, April 1994.

readings and prayer every evening. Pastor Sztehlo made no attempt to convert us, but he knew that faith in God was absolutely essential in helping us to overcome our sense of abandonment and terror. Quite naturally, he shared with us the religion he professed, Christianity. Although I never converted, I have retained a deep gratitude for the spiritual comfort that I received, which was critical to my survival and that of my friends during those horrible times. In the meantime, many of the homes were subjected to Arrow Cross raids, and Sztehlo himself was taken to an Arrow Cross district headquarters for questioning.'[46]

Gabor Vermes, another of the boys whom Sztehlo saved, recalls that the pastor was 'more concerned about the Arrow Cross than the Wehrmacht, and to use the latter as a potential shield he befriended several German officers. Sometimes these officers came to the part of the basement where we Jewish children were staying, and we sang them German songs. Sztehlo told me, after the war, that one of these officers told him that he knew who we were, but could not care less. We were lucky that it was him, and not a well-known sadistic SS officer who recognized us, because that SS officer also frequented our quarters at certain times.'[47]

Another of those whom Pastor Sztehlo saved was David Peleg. He later recalled that 'a family friend worked at a day care centre in an Evangelical Church which was under the auspices of the Red Cross. A wonderful priest was the head of the institution. I was accepted for day care as a Christian refugee. The priest gave me forged documents. After being there for about two weeks, the day care centre was attacked in the

---

[46] Manuscript sent to the author by a friend of David Peleg, 1 September 2001.
[47] 'Gabor Vermes', note sent to the author by Gabor Vermes, 8 March 2002.

bombings and we were forced to leave the church. The Germans demanded our eviction. Where were we to go in the middle of the war? Once again, the same wonderful man came to our aid. He took us in, thirty-three Jewish children with forged documents to his private home in the basement where he hid us together with his family.'[48]

Among those who helped Pastor Sztehlo were two fellow Lutheran pastors: Albert Bereczky, whose church was just beyond the northern end of the International Ghetto, and Emil Koren, of the German Lutheran church on Castle Hill. Sztehlo often worked inside Koren's church to organize his rescue efforts.[49]

Sandor Ujvari, a Red Cross official, suggested to the Apostolic Delegate Angelo Rotta that Rotta should prepare letters of safe conduct, signed by himself in advance, but with no names filled in; with the help of these blanks, an attempt would be made to keep a watch on the road from Budapest to Hegyeshalom and to rescue the most needy, sick and exhausted people from the Arrow Cross. When Ujvari admitted that he was using forged identity cards and baptismal certificates to help Jews, Rotta – according to Ujvari – made the following reply: 'What you are doing, my son, is pleasing to God and to Jesus, because you are saving innocent people. I give you absolution in advance. Continue your work to the honour of God.' On Rotta's instructions his secretary then issued a pile of ready-stamped blank letters of safe conduct and the necessary authorization for Ujvari.[50]

On November 19, diplomats representing the five neutral powers – Sweden, Spain, Portugal, Switzerland and the Vatican – issued a second collective appeal to

---

[48] David Peleg, letter to Yad Vashem, received 18 May 1971, Yad Vashem Righteous Among the Nations Archive, file 722.
[49] Yad Vashem Righteous Among the Nations Archive, file 722.
[50] Jeno Levai (editor), *Hungarian Jewry and the Papacy*, pages 44–5.

47. Raoul Wallenberg, the Swedish diplomat at the centre of international rescue activities that saved the lives of tens of thousands of Jews in Budapest.

48. Angelo Rotta, the senior Vatican representative in Budapest, who enabled many Jews to survive.

49. (*Above left*) Angel Sanz-Briz, the senior Spanish diplomat in Budapest, who helped save many Jews in the city.

50. (*Above right*) Giorgio (Jorge) Perlasca, an Italian citizen who took charge of the rescue activities of the Spanish Legation in Budapest.

51. Peter Zürcher, a Swiss businessman who, while in charge of Swiss interests in Budapest, helped prevent the destruction of the Big Ghetto.

52. Friedrich Born, Director of the International Committee of the Red Cross (ICRC) in Budapest; the protective documents he issued saved several thousand Jews.

53. Franz Bischof, the Swiss Vice-Consul in Budapest, who participated in the international rescue efforts, and personally hid more than thirty Jews.

54. A temporary branch of the Swiss Legation in Budapest, located in the Glass House (*right*) on Vadasz Street, with Jews waiting for Swiss documents that would protect them from deportation.

55. Carl Lutz, a Swiss diplomat in Budapest who was at the centre of rescue efforts, seen here at the entrance to the Swiss Legation.

56. Oszkar Szabo, who saved the lives of thirty Jews in Budapest.

57. Malvina Csizmadia, who helped save twenty-five Jews in Hungary in 1944.

58. Pastor Gabor Sztehlo, who helped rescue hundreds of Jewish children in Budapest.

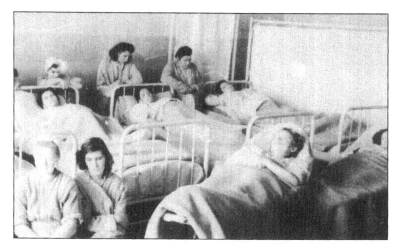

59. Jewish patients in one of the infirmaries established by the Royal Swedish Legation in Budapest as a means of saving Jews from deportation. This photograph was one of several sent by Raoul Wallenberg in December 1944 in a letter to the Swedish Ministry of Foreign Affairs in Stockholm.

60. Jews saved from deportation after being given protective documents by Raoul Wallenberg at the Jozsefvaros railway station in Budapest. This photograph was taken from Wallenberg's car as he was driving back into the city.

61. Swedish Red Cross buses (known as the White Buses) taking concentration camp prisoners from Ravensbrück to Sweden in the last weeks of the war.

62. A Red Cross transit point into Switzerland for concentration camp prisoners being transferred by train from Mauthausen to Switzerland on 9 April 1945, a month before the end of the war.

63. Seven orphaned Jewish children reach New York in May 1946; German farmers had hidden them during the war.

64. Oskar Schindler (*standing, second from right*) at a reunion in Munich in 1946 with six of the more than fifteen hundred Jews whom he had rescued during the war.

the Hungarian government, asking that 'all decisions appertaining to the deportation of the Jews be withdrawn and the measure in progress be suspended, thus rendering it possible for the unfortunate persons dragged from their homes to return there as soon as possible.'[51] As a result of this appeal the Hungarian government forbade any further 'death march' deportations from Budapest. But the situation actually prevailing in the capital was now approaching anarchy; Arrow Cross units were becoming a law unto themselves, and were all too willing to facilitate Eichmann's work.

On November 21 new deportations began. Auschwitz had ceased to operate. These new deportees were sent by train from Jozsefvaros station to Ravensbrück and Mauthausen. More than three thousand Budapest Jews were murdered in Mauthausen. On November 23, Raoul Wallenberg went to Jozsefvaros station with protective documents that enabled several dozen Jews to leave the train. He returned to the station five days later, and was able to secure further releases. At the same time, first on November 23 and again four days later, representatives of the Red Cross drove from Budapest towards the Austrian border. Eventually they reached the marchers who had been forced to leave the city just over two weeks earlier. Finding them exhausted, and tormented by brutal guards, they issued as many protective documents as they could. Under the emblem of the Red Cross, truck convoys were organized to pass out food to those being deported. Wallenberg, taking the same road, drove as far as the Austrian border to bring documents to the marchers. At his initiative, checkpoints were set up on the roads leaving Budapest, as well as at the border with Austria, to hinder the deportation of Jews holding the

---

[51] Eugene Levai, *Black Book on the Martyrdom of Hungarian Jewry*, pages 358–9.

protective passports. By this means, an estimated 1,500 Jews were saved and returned to Budapest.[52]

Rose Rosner was twenty years old when she found herself on one of the marches from Budapest towards the Austrian border. During the march, a Hungarian soldier, one of the guards, gave her his cross and his Bible, and told her to go to his parents in the country. He then let her slip away from the march.[53]

On November 30 the head of the Spanish Legation, Angel Sanz-Briz, was ordered to leave Budapest for his safety. His friend Giorgio Perlasca, the Italian whom he had earlier put in charge of the Spanish 'safe houses', became Spanish Chargé d'Affaires, taking the Spanish name Jorge. In this capacity he issued three thousand protective documents on the writing paper of the Spanish Legation. Nor was this all he did. A young Hungarian Jewish boy, Avraham Ronai, later recalled how Arrow Cross men broke into the Spanish-protected house in which he had found refuge, seizing a group of Jews, in order to march them down to the Danube, where they would be shot in the neck – 'a not uncommon sight in those days'. Because of his comparative youth, Avraham was spared, but his mother and sister were in the group about to be led away. The youngster recalled: 'Suddenly out of nowhere appeared Perlasca, and began berating the Arrow Cross commander, threatening to cable and report to Madrid this violation of Spanish rights, an act which would have grave consequences for Spanish–Hungarian relations and cause damage to the career of the Hungarian officer in charge. The ploy worked, and all those assembled were released and allowed to return to the Spanish-protected house from

---

[52] Per Anger, *With Raoul Wallenberg in Budapest*, pages 68–9.
[53] Judy Stoffman (Rose Rosner's daughter), in conversation with the author, 12 February 2002.

which they had been taken to what had been intended to be their deaths.'[54]

On December 10, Wallenberg went for the third time to Jozsefvaros railway station with protective documents for those who were about to be deported to Austria by train.

In the second week of December, Pastor Sztehlo learned that there would be a raid on his homes in a few days' time, on December 18. 'I rushed to the homes in Buda,' he later recalled, 'and tried to doctor the records. We prepared false school reports and certificates of baptism.' Other documents were written out on Red Cross writing paper. 'The most difficult thing', Sztehlo wrote, 'was to teach the small children their new names and what they were to say about their parents. It took a lot of time to make a frightened small child memorise who he or she was supposed to be. And even then we couldn't be sure they would give the right answer if interrogated. How much fear and terror these little ones had behind them and how much more they were still to endure! These days were disheartening, all homes were seized by panic. I repeated everywhere that it was already a sign of the love of God that we had been spared so far.'

He was grateful, Sztehlo added, 'to the nurses who cherished hope and faith in God and transplanted it to the children. The young people were brave and calm, the big boys the same as the girls. When I got telephone calls on the morning of December 18 that there were blue-coated municipal policemen standing at the gates of the homes, I tried to encourage those who called, saying in a fearless voice that God was with us. I expected a miracle to happen. The most frightened were those

---

[54] Speech by Mordecai Paldiel, Yad Vashem, 25 September 1989, in awarding Giorgio Perlasca a Medal of the Righteous. Yad Vashem Righteous Among the Nations Archive, file 3911.

whom I had not been able to inform in detail previously, namely the people of the small homes with only five or six children and a few adults. I tried to prepare them for the approaching raid. Strangely, everybody reported that the policemen did not want to enter the houses or flats, but asked for chairs and sat down outside.' And there was a miracle: the Arrow Cross never arrived.[55]

On December 22, with Soviet forces drawing nearer, Eichmann left Budapest by air. On the following day all the neutral diplomats left the city, with the exception of Rotta, Wallenberg, Perlasca, Lutz, and Lutz's Vice-Consul, Peter Zürcher. Two days later Wallenberg went to Jozsefvaros railway station for a fourth time with protective documents. It was the last deportation train from Budapest to Austria. Wallenberg managed to have it halted after it had left the platform, and to get people off it. On the following day – Christmas Day – Budapest was surrounded by the Russians and besieged.

On December 27 the Arrow Cross executed two Hungarian Christian women, Sister Sara Salkhazi and Vilma Bernovits, who had hidden Jews. Three days later, having entered the hitherto protective confines of the International Ghetto, they marched 170 Jews to the Danube, and killed fifty of them. On the following day they attacked the Glass House, killing three Jews. A Hungarian military unit then intervened, and the remaining Jews were saved.

On 3 January 1945, as Russian troops drew closer to Budapest, and the sound of artillery could be heard throughout the city, a German officer entered one of Pastor Sztehlo's Good Shepherd homes, a hilltop villa in Buda, and told the deaconess house-mother to vacate the villa at once: it was needed as a heavy gun position. Paul Friedlaender, one of the oldest boys in the home, later recalled: 'We arranged by telephone to go to Pastor

---

[55] Gabor Sztehlo, *In the Hands of God*, pages 121–2.

Sztehlo's house. We woke the younger children and filled up our pockets with sugar cubes. The nurses packed some first aid equipment in case of casualties. About thirty children and ten adults, we walked silently through deep snow in single file. In front and at the back German soldiers, guns at the ready, escorted us, helping to carry sleeping Jewish toddlers. At the door Pastor Sztehlo and his young wife were waiting for us. In their flat we sat where we could. After a short time Mrs Ilona Sztehlo served us steaming hot caraway-seed soup, and we ate up all her family's reserve food that morning.' Many years later, recalling his rescuer, he reflected: 'Ilona Sztehlo was a heroine as well.'[56]

Paul Friedlaender noted in his testimony on the Pastor's behalf that the Sztehlos had two young children of their own, and that in addition 'their flat already sheltered the fat doorman and his wife, as well as a Communist writer on the wanted list of the Arrow Cross. Days passed and the firing got closer, but the proximity of the Sztehlos gave me a secure feeling that I could only perish by accident of war like any other person.'[57]

One of the youngsters who was transferred to the Sztehlos' villa recalled: 'We did a lot of singing, and several times, we, a bunch of Jewish children, sang German songs to the German officers visiting in the basement, where wartime conditions were forcing us to live. We were lucky. The commander of that section of the front was a major who became very friendly with the Sztehlos.'[58] In his memoirs (written in the third person), Sztehlo described the major as 'sad and resigned, fully aware of the futility of war'; he once revealed 'that he

[56] Pal Foti, in conversation with the author, 24 March 2002.
[57] Pal Foti (Paul Friedlaender), 'The survivor's tale: 50 years ago the Holocaust reached Hungary', *AJR Information*, April 1994.
[58] Manuscript sent to the author by a friend of David Peleg (who was also saved by Pastor Sztehlo), 1 September 2001.

485

knew who these children were, but he hated any form of racism and wished Pastor Sztehlo and all of us well. Before being transferred, he warned Sztehlo about an SS lieutenant whose major preoccupation was the hunting down and killing of Jews.'[59]

The German major, whose name does not survive (he may well have been killed in the fighting in the city a few days later) was also recalled by Paul Friedlaender. 'On one occasion,' he wrote, 'an older officer, a doctor from Hamburg, indicated that he guessed who the children Sztehlo was sheltering were and expressed his admiration for him. The same officer assured Sztehlo that no Hungarian Fascist was allowed to set foot in his sector of the front. He gave us practical help in the form of an army truck and driver to collect food from the Swiss Red Cross stores in Buda Castle.'[60]

At one moment, as the battle raged around them, a shell embedded itself in the villa roof. It did not explode, and Sztehlo went up to the roof to remove it and bring it down. He then buried it under a lilac tree in the garden.[61]

On 6 January 1945 the Arrow Cross renewed their systematic raids inside the International Ghetto, once more driving many Jews from the protected houses to the Danube, where they killed them. On the following day, Lutz, Perlasca and Wallenberg obtained a hundred Hungarian soldiers to protect the International Ghetto. On January 8, Peter Zürcher learned of an imminent Arrow Cross plan to order the evacuation of all Jews from the Swiss safe houses in the International Ghetto and to kill them. He immediately intervened with a represen-

[59] Gabor Sztehlo, *In the Hands of God*, pages 139, 147.
[60] Pal Foti (Paul Friedlaender), 'The survivor's tale: 50 years ago the Holocaust reached Hungary', *AJR Information*, April 1994.
[61] Pal Foti, in conversation with the author, 24 March 2002.

tative of the Arrow Cross government, denouncing the plan as a violation of international law and demanding an immediate end to Arrow Cross attacks on the safe houses. The government representative finally yielded, and the thousands of Jews who were living under protection were spared.[62]

But this protection could no longer be relied upon in the face of increasing fascist aggression. On January 8, all 266 Jews who had been given sanctuary at the Swedish Legation food-supply building were taken out by the Arrow Cross and murdered. Still the protectors persevered. That same day, after 161 Jews were seized by Arrow Cross men and taken to the Danube to be shot, Wallenberg intervened, and they were given sanctuary in another Swedish-protected building. Four days later, on January 12, learning of a planned Arrow Cross massacre of all sixty-nine thousand Jews in the Big Ghetto, Wallenberg went to see a senior German SS officer in Budapest to urge him to prevent it, warning him that retribution for war crimes was imminent. The massacre was averted.[63]

On 16 January 1945 Soviet troops reached the International Ghetto. The twenty-five thousand Jews in its safe houses were freed. That day Wallenberg was seen in Budapest for the last time; for reasons that are still not clear, he was then seized by the Russians and taken to Moscow. He was never seen again.[64]

Two days later the Big Ghetto was liberated by Soviet troops, and within a week Pest followed. In Buda, where fighting continued until mid-February, many Jews found a safe haven in the bomb shelter in the basement

[62] Eric Saul, 'Visas for Life' exhibition, prospectus, November 2000.
[63] Per Anger, 'Introduction', in Raoul Wallenberg, Letters and Dispatches, 1924–1944, page 229.
[64] Ingrid Palmklint and Daniel Larsson (editorial group), Raoul Wallenberg: Report of the Swedish-Russian Working Group.

of Lutz's Legation: the building above was reduced to a ruin.[65]

Of the hundred and fifty thousand Jews who had been in Budapest when the German army and the SS arrived in March 1944, almost a hundred and twenty thousand survived to the moment of liberation at the beginning of 1945. Of those survivors, more than sixty-nine thousand were in the Big Ghetto, twenty-five thousand in the International Ghetto, and another twenty-five thousand in hiding in Christian homes and religious institutions. As a result of the collective efforts of many individuals – both local Hungarians and foreign diplomats – the SS were denied a final victory.

---

[65] Agnes Hirschi (who was among those in the shelter), in conversation with the author, 28 April 2002.

CHAPTER SEVENTEEN

In the Camps and on the Death Marches

Within the many hundreds of labour camps in which the Germans enslaved their captive peoples, some kindnesses were offered to Jews even by the German supervisors who ran them. Polish-born Lea Goodman was seven years old when her parents were taken to Kostrze camp and factory near Cracow. Had she not been able to go with them, she would almost certainly have been deported to Auschwitz. The head of the camp, and owner of the light engineering factory where the inmates worked, was a German, Richard Strauch. 'He was willing to have children with their parents for a while,' Lea Goodman wrote. 'These kind people made a difference, it was life instead of death.' When children could no longer be kept at the camp, she was taken back to Cracow, to a Christian family, Mr and Mrs Soltisowa, who took her in without payment.[1]

In the Pawiak prison in Warsaw, a place of torture and execution, Julien Hirshaut recalled two of the Ukrainian guards. One, he wrote, was violent and cruel, but of the other he stated: 'Barczenko was a true friend, a decent Gentile.'[2]

One of the most savage labour camps in German-occupied Poland was Skarzysko-Kamienna. Yet even

---

[1] Lea Goodman, letter to the author, 13 August 2001.
[2] Julien Hirshaut, *Jewish Martyrs of Pawiak*, page 109.

489

here there was someone who tried to help: a factory manager named Laskowski, an Ethnic German who was employed by the SS. One of the Jewish prisoners at Skarzysko later recalled: 'Laskowski wasn't so bad. He never beat me. I never saw him beat anyone. Other Meisters were beaters. People in other divisions were beaten a lot.'

Despite his slight stature, Laskowski looked intimidating. 'He never smiled. He came to inspections a lot of times. He never looked at a person straight in the face. He looked at you sideways.' Another inmate at Skarzysko, Etka Baumstick, commented: 'He didn't do anything for anybody personally as far as I know, but I didn't see him hit anybody. If he was around, I would thank him now.'

To protect the women from the blows of the guards, Laskowski placed them in a barracks and instructed them to look busy and to start sweeping and cleaning if any guards or Nazi officials came by. When he found the women weeping during the first few days, 'Laskowski came in and explained to us that we shouldn't cry, that we should work. He said that he didn't have it so good. He said his wife died, he had two sons on the front. He gave us a little hope. He said maybe the war would end and we would be free.'[3]

One of the most feared German concentration camps was Lvov-Janowska, on the outskirts of Lvov, where thousands of Jews perished as a result of the harshness of slave labour and the brutality of their guards. Elias Gechman, who was practising medicine in Lvov when war broke out, was put to work at Janowska loading coal on to trains bound for the Eastern Front. 'We were allowed one bath in three weeks,' Dr Gechman later recalled. 'One day the camp commandant upbraided me for being a dirty Jew and – as a doctor – setting a bad

---

[3] Suzan E. Hagstrom, *Sara's Children*, page 122.

example for the other prisoners. He sentenced me to be hanged the next day.' Before the sentence could be carried out, Polish workers in a neighbouring camp gave Dr Gechman some of their clothing. He removed his yellow star and merged with the Poles in their camp. Later he escaped from the camp altogether and was hidden by a Polish railwayman who had been his patient before the war. This man dug a hole underneath the floor of his kitchen and kept Dr Gechman in hiding there until liberation.[4]

Also at Janowska, Leon Wells recalled an SS sergeant who behaved decently. He saw him first when he entered one of the workshops in the camps, 'a whip in his hand'. He was, Wells recalled, the supervisor of the workshops, an Austrian named Czekala. 'He first turned his attention to me, the newcomer, and asked me how I had come to be here. He listened to my story with such an open expression of dejection, his head nodding in such sincere regret, that I simply could not regard it as a pose on his part. I learned later that he was a very good sort, and had never been known to strike a man in the workshop. It was only outside, in the course of inspection, that he struck out like the others, and then he did it only to save his face in the presence of the senior authorities.'[5]

In the concentration camp of Majdanek, where tens of thousands of Jews were murdered, as well as tens of thousands of Soviet prisoners of war and many Poles, there was a Polish prisoner, Stanislaw Zelent, whom Jews in the camp remembered with gratitude. One of them, Paul Trepman, later recalled: 'If a Polish prisoner was near collapse, Zelent came to his aid. If a Jewish

---

[4] Ernie Meyer, 'Saying "thanks" to Denmark', *Jerusalem Post*, 7 February 1973.
[5] Leon Weliczker Wells, *The Death Brigade (The Janowska Road)*, page 66.

inmate was in need of help, Zelent was also there. The Jews blessed him and called him "The Angel of Majdanek." He had a smile for everybody, even for the Germans, though there his smile was a little bitter, I suppose. His face radiated kindness and compassion; more than one of us confessed to an impulse to kiss him, as one would a gentle, loving father. Stanislaw Zelent, or Stasiek, as we called him, brought a ray of hope and sunshine to hundreds of sick, broken spirits in the living hell that was Majdanek.'

Stanislaw Zelent was the foreman of a labour battalion assigned to various tasks inside the camp. He was in charge of the work that had to be done on barracks, sewers and electrical installations, and also supervised the carpentry and locksmith shops. 'Most of the chores assigned to Stasiek's supervision were comparatively easy and uncomplicated, requiring no more than twenty men at a time,' Paul Trepman recalled, 'but Stasiek always requested authorization to draft 120 prisoners. He would then select his crew from among those Poles, Russians and Jews who seemed to him the weakest and therefore unlikely to survive in the battalions that did hard labour outside the camp under the clubs and whips of the Kapos.'

Zelent had been given a small hut to use as a toolshed. 'We privately called the hut "Zelent's Sanatorium," for whenever he saw a prisoner who looked especially bad, or one who was recovering from an illness, Zelent would assign him to the toolshed, officially for the purpose of cleaning the shovels, spades and picks used by the rest of the crew. At least that was the notation entered in the camp's work records. In fact, however, the only work that the prisoner would be asked to do was to light the oven in the toolshed while Zelent went to the kitchen to "organize" some ersatz coffee, potatoes, or dried peas. When Zelent returned with his loot, the prisoner would prepare soup and coffee to share with fellow inmates who would come in from the biting cold outside when the guards were not looking. In this way, again, Stasiek saved dozens of human lives.'[6]

Zygmunt Freifeld was among tens of thousands of Polish Jews in Plaszow camp. He had a job at the camp's railway station. In a letter to the Polish weekly newspaper *Tygodnik Powszechny* ('Universal Weekly'), which was published on 19 April 1964, he wrote of a vicious German railway clerk there, who 'picked me out for special discrimination during the whole day of very heavy, murderous, and often useless work. He disliked my looks and took exception to my spectacles. I was helped by a Pole, Alojzy Kramarski, aged twenty-three, a junior railway official. He persuaded the German that an additional worker was needed for checking the store of printed notices and that I, knowing German, was suitable for the job.'

The German agreed to this suggestion. 'From this moment onward my life changed a great deal for the better,' Zygmunt Freifeld recalled. 'My benefactor frequently visited me in the storeroom, keeping my spirits up and also my body, as he would bring me something to eat whenever he could. Another kindness was to allow my family (who at that time were still in Sosnowiec) to write to me under his name and address.' The German 'would always bring me their letters discreetly, almost gloating with enthusiasm, and he always cheered me up. I might add that he was rendering services to all Jewish prisoners working at the station, as did several Poles also employed there.'[7]

Among the Polish deportees in the German ammunition factory at Telgte was one Jewish girl, Lea Kalin. Although the Polish girls in her barrack knew that she

[6] Paul Trepman, *Among Men and Beasts*, pages 206–7.
[7] Kazimierz Iranek-Osmecki, *He Who Saves One Life*, pages 287–8.

was Jewish, they kept her identity secret.[8] In a labour camp in Dukla, southern Poland, one of the German truck drivers, Fritz Zachmann, was remembered by a Jewish worker, Abraham Zuckerman. 'He felt compassion for us', Zuckerman wrote, and he added: 'My strongest memory of Fritz Zachmann is from several nights after the deportation of the Jews of Dukla. I felt I could trust him, so I asked him if he would take me back to the house where my family had lived. I didn't have any clothes with me other than what I was wearing, and I wanted to get some more clothing. He agreed to drive me over in his truck. He took a chance by doing this. He ran an enormous risk, but it did not seem to concern him much. He did it, I suppose, because he thought it was the right thing to do. He was violating the rules by taking a prisoner out of the camp. If we had been stopped, we both would have been severely reprimanded or punished. We could have been killed for what we were doing.'[9]

Among the hundreds of thousand of Jews in the slave labour camps that dotted every region of Greater Germany in 1944 was Zwi Glazer, a fifteen-year-old Jewish boy from the Polish town of Zdunska Wola. He was later to set down his recollections of a moment at Ridelau, a slave labour camp in southern Germany, when death seemed very near – but when a German guard gave him the will to live. Day after day, he and those with him were marched to their place of work. 'The weather was stormy in the forest and whatever did not fall on us from heaven came from the treetops. My breath shortened, my head wobbled and I felt my toes turn numb. I could not move my fingers. I did not realize what had moved me or what had pushed me. The trees,

---

[8] 'Lea Kalin . . . ', United States Holocaust Memorial Museum, Photo Archive, Worksheet 09342.
[9] Abraham Zuckerman, *A Voice in the Chorus: Memoirs of a Teenager Saved by Schindler*, page 51.

the branches, the people around and everything seemed to me as one mixture into which I was being whipped. Thus, while I was carrying a tree trunk heavier than my body (or that was what I imagined) my fingers lost all their sensitivity, a mixture of snow and rain seeped into the cement sack that I wore over the "striped pajama", my feet sank into the mud and I was moving like a sleep-walker and dragging myself and the tree trunk with an inhuman thrust. I collapsed.

'I found myself in a wooden shack when I opened my eyes and wiped the snowflakes that were still glued to my lashes. I noticed in front of me an elderly guard, the age of my grandfather. The snow on my face started to melt. I melted inside as well. I held my guts from bursting. Then suddenly I could not hold anymore and my eyes were dripping like the clouds outside in what turned to be an outpouring that could not be stopped. My bones rattled like the trees in a storm. I cried. Unbelievable. I was not ashamed. I did not care what would happen to me and I surrendered myself to self-pity, which I had not done for years . . .

'The details of this event are carved in me like an inscription on a monument. I remember that I felt a touch on my shoulder. It was the elderly German guard. He told me to take off the paper sack and put it near the stove, which stood in the middle of the shack. After that he pointed to my shoes, to take them off as well, and the rags that were wrapped around my feet, so that they would dry. While these were steaming above the iron stove, the guard brought me hot and sweet tea in a tin mug.

'Then, when the paper sack was dry, he motioned me to take off my "striped pajamas", which were still drip-ping, and put on the sack. He was very scared in speaking. From time to time he looked out as if to ensure that he or I might be endangered. When everything was dry, including the shoes, which steamed like a boiling kettle, he took out of his haversack a slice of white bread,

495

a big piece with some spread on it, handed it to me, and motioned to eat it. I would have preferred to take away this delicacy and to indulge, chewing it slowly and licking my lips. But I realized that I had to eat it there and then, and so I did. The guard was observing me with satisfaction, as a hospital attendant looks at a patient who has come out of a coma. I finished chewing the last piece, wishing it were the first bite and not the last, and that my temporary paradise would last a little longer. I dragged myself and dressed, stood up, bowed properly and said: "Thank you so much" and left.

'To my astonishment, when I returned to work, the soldier who guarded us at work just looked upon me and said nothing. My co-prisoners told me that I was on the verge of death, and therefore I should move as little as possible and that they would take over my working quota. When you are in a jungle, humanity is sevenfold conspicuous. On that evening when I returned to the block I pondered a long while on the piece of white bread which I did not taste a long time and I was thinking about the elderly guard who saved me even before he gave me the slice of bread and the hot sweet tea. He probably has a grandson my age and the war is a cursed thing for him as well. Suddenly it occurred to me that there is a righteous man in Sodom, a German different from those that I got to know starting with the Ethnic German in my home town, Zdunska Wola, to the monsters in the concentration camps, the gas chambers and crematoria – a German with a human image, a German with a human face.'[10]

In the winter of 1944–5, Hana Lustig, who had earlier been a prisoner at Auschwitz, was working as a slave

[10] Translated by Zvi Gill (formerly Zwi Glazer) from his book *Paper Bridge*, published in Hebrew in Tel Aviv, 1996; Zvi Gill, letter to the author, 5 June 2001.

labourer at Neugraben, near Hamburg. She and her fellow prisoners had been put to work clearing rubble from bombed-out buildings in the suburbs of Hamburg, repairing frozen water pipes and labouring in brick and munitions factories. 'Because we were working in the open countryside, where there were only a few scattered houses, and since there were no toilets, we were allowed, from time to time, to run into the surrounding area to relieve ourselves among the trees and bushes. One day, while out of sight of the SS men and women who guarded us, I mustered all my courage and knocked on the door of a house – its chimney puffing smoke into the cold grey air.

'After the second knock, an old woman opened the door bewildered at what she saw, but no more frightened than I, while words pleading for food came out of my mouth. The woman, after a few moments of hesitation, during which I nearly died of fright, beckoned me in. Guiding me into her kitchen, she spoke briefly to her husband, who sat in a corner repairing shoes. She took out a soup bowl and poured some hot liquid into it. I ate in haste, not wanting to be missed by the guards, for punishment for such a breach of discipline was harsh. I thanked them both and ran. As I was leaving, the old lady whispered to me, "Come again when you can."'

A few days later, while working at the same site, Hana managed to slip away again. 'This time I knew my destination. Eagerly, I knocked on the door of the same house, with the nostalgic memory of having my shrunken stomach filled with the delicious liquid of my previous visit. Again, it was the old woman who opened the door carefully. Upon seeing the same hungry girl in a torn striped uniform with wooden clogs on her feet, she let me in quickly. After serving me a bowl of sweet thick porridge, she murmured something to her husband and handed me an old pair of men's shoes with new soles that her husband had prepared for me. The shoes were twice the size of my feet, but with old newspaper stuffed inside, I fitted them to my frozen feet and tied them up with string. I thanked them for this priceless gift, and although I would have liked to linger in their warm kitchen a little longer, fear propelled me on. I ran in my new warm shoes, my feet slowly defrosting in all that vacuum, no longer wet from the snow. The guards noticed neither my absence nor my new acquisition.'

On the following day, the slave labourers were sent elsewhere to work and did not return to that neighbourhood. 'I never learned the names of these good people nor their address, but for the rest of the winter I blessed them, while my frozen feet recovered thanks to their kindness and humanity. These were righteous gentiles.'[11]

Anna Ostrowiak and her sister worked in a slave labour camp at the German airport in Deblin. Their supervisors were two German soldiers, Lieutenant Schläde and Sergeant Schmidt. 'Both were decent men,' Anna Ostrowiak recalled: 'Schmidt never raised his voice to us. Every day at the assembly point prior to job assignments, instead of calling us he sang to us: "Come over, come over, come over to Schmidt."' Schläde appeared only from time to time: 'His huge open face was always smiling.'

The girls worked mainly outdoors, sweeping the area outside the hangars, washing military vehicles, digging ditches for storing potatoes for the winter and performing other manual tasks. When winter came, their work became much harder. 'Schläde gave us permission to eat our meager lunch soup inside the hangars, at noon. When the weather was extremely cold, he even let us clean the premises inside the heated hangars. We knew where the potato bunkers were, so soon one of us used to sneak out to steal some of the potatoes. But how could

---

[11] Hana Greenfield, *Fragments of Memory*, pages 41–3.

we eat raw potatoes? So we devised a plan. We will smuggle the potatoes into the camp and the people who worked at the Kohlenstelle will smuggle in some pieces of coal. We will cook them very primitively outside the barracks after work and share the loot. It was a risky undertaking because once in a while we were searched and several other inmates were publicly hanged for stealing. But hunger overrode that concern.'

Lieutenant Schläde found out what the women were doing, but far from punishing them, he took an astounding step: 'One day at noon he came over to us with two soldiers carrying a small, primitive stove, some coal and pipes. He took us to the second floor of the hangars into an empty room and asked the soldiers to install the stove. When the soldiers left, he gave us some matches and with a wink in his eye gave us an order: "Lunch-time Potato Stealing", then added softly: "I have a wife and two nice children, but the damned war." Then he was gone.'

In July 1944, as Soviet forces began to advance deep into German-occupied Poland, the slave labour camp at Deblin was evacuated to Czestochowa. That Christmas, Anna Ostrowiak and her fellow slave labourers were surprised to find a Christmas cake in a paper bag, left on a bench. A German soldier, who knew it was there, did nothing. 'Back to work we went,' Anna Ostrowiak later recalled, 'constantly debating the risk of consuming the delicacy. The soldier still was yelling his lungs out until darkness fell and the landing strip was cleared of snow and ice. Totally exhausted and hungry we returned to the shack to dispose of the tools. The cake was still there. "Out, out," the soldier commanded, loudly. Then, suddenly, he walked out and left us all alone. We stood speechless when one of the girls broke the silence. "Listen, all of you," she said. "There is something phony about this guy. First of all, he yelled at us too much and too loud, and now he walks out and leaves us unguarded? I don't care what you do, but I am going to take a piece of that cake and eat it right now. I am not afraid of him." Like hungry animals we all fell in line and within a minute the cake was gone. Cleaning up every little crumb we found a small note at the bottom of the pan. It said "Glory To The Highest, Peace On Earth." Silently the soldier escorted us back to the barracks, his gun still drawn, his heavy boots still loudly hitting the ground.'[12]

Within three weeks of this act of kindness, Anna Ostrowiak's brother, who was also working in the ammunition factory, came to her in desperation. His identity number had been taken away. Within hours he would be deported to his death. 'Our group supervisor', Anna Ostrowiak recalled, 'was an SS woman whom we called "Hexa No. 2" (Witch No. 2) because there was another Hexa much more brutal than ours was. Grief stricken with my brother's news, all I could do was cry with him. For a moment, my mind went blank.'

Anna Ostrowiak was jolted back to reality when she saw 'our "Hexa" leaning over me. With a soft voice I never thought she had, she asked me why we are crying. I answered that my younger brother was dismissed from his job, his tag was taken away and tomorrow he is going to go away – I don't know where. I also told her that destiny had kept us together for the last three years and perhaps I can go with him. "He is not going away from you," she told me with a decisive voice; then, turning to him, she asked him where he was working. When he told her where his place of work was, she turned to me again, and with her familiar harsh voice ordered me to start working again. Then she disappeared.

'Within several minutes she was back with three identity tags. My brother was still beside me when she

[12] Anna Ostrowiak, 'Soldier showed mercy amid brutality', *Miami Herald*, 25 December 1999.

handed him the tags and ordered him to return to work. As my brother, in bewilderment, walked away, she leaned to me again and whispered softly: "I have a young son who looks very much like your brother, in fact he has the same colour blue eyes as your brother has." I wanted to say something, but in a minute she was gone to the other end of our workplace.'

Four days later the camp was liberated.[13]

In Dachau, Dr Moses Brauns, a survivor of the Kovno ghetto and an expert on typhus – which he had helped to eliminate in the ghetto – was asked by the Germans to write a report on the deaths at Dachau. He did so, stating correctly that the cause of death of the inmates whom he had examined was starvation. Dr Brauns' son Jack, who was with his father in Dachau, recalled the sequel. 'This report had to go to Dachau main camp on a weekly basis where the top German physician in charge of all Dachau Camp had to review it. The specific day when the report arrived, the man who was the chief physician and was known to be an alcoholic was not in Dachau and the report proceeded on to Berlin. It was a big surprise in Berlin that the death certificate stated that the inmates in Dachau had died from starvation. This was not accepted by Berlin, which insisted that the rations were all calculated and provided for survival, not for death.'

A committee was sent from Berlin to investigate how a prisoner or inmate could die from starvation. What they did not know, and probably did not want to know, was that more than half the food assigned to the camp was being taken by the SS and sold on the black market. When the committee left and the German physician returned to Dachau, he was, Jack Brauns recalled, 'obsessed with the intent to kill the man who had written the report, my father'. The physician did not know Dr

---

[13] Anna Ostrowiak, letter to the author, 4 February 2002.

Brauns; but to protect the doctor, an SS man in his fifties, Private Helmanowitsch, took Dr Brauns out of the camp and to his own home. 'He felt that it would be safer for my father to be there until the storm calmed down.'[14] A few days later, when the physician's anger had abated, Dr Brauns returned to the camp. An SS man had saved his life.

Before the war, Helmanowitsch, a German from Memel, living in Kaunas, had brought his wife to be treated by Dr Brauns for typhus. Under his care, she recovered. To check on her recovery, Dr Brauns would visit her in her home. Jack Brauns recalled: 'I accompanied him on these visits. I remember Mr Helmanowitsch as very soft spoken and very respectful to my father.'[15]

In 1939, Helmanowitsch had been among several thousand German-speakers expelled from Lithuania by the Lithuanian government, in reaction to the German occupation of Memel. Driven from his home and dumped across the German border, he had joined the SS.

At Dachau's Camp Four, in nearby Kaufering, another survivor of the Kovno ghetto, Zev Birger, was working as a slave labourer, under daily threat of death. One day an electrician was required. Without hesitation he volunteered. 'I could not imagine that work in another place could be any worse,' he recalled, 'which was why I had volunteered so quickly. The worst scenario was that the Germans would soon discover I was not an electrician, and would finish me off – but that was going to happen soon anyway, I figured. An electrical engineer from AEG needed an assistant, and I was assigned to work with him. Naturally he noticed after just the first day that I had never studied this profession, but he said to me: "You are certainly no electrician, but you learn quickly, I still want to keep

---

[14] Jack Brauns, 'Memoirs' (draft), page 155.
[15] Jack Brauns, letter to the author, 21 March 2001.

you on and see if you can really work." In this way he actually gave me a chance to live. This man still had human emotions and did not just obey orders. He had sympathy for me. My previous work in the ghetto, in the locksmith's workshop, had prepared me technically for this task. I worked well and was a great help to him. He was always very satisfied with my work and therefore treated me compassionately.'[16]

In February 1943 the Russian Orthodox nun Mother Maria (Elizabeth Skobtsova), who had helped save many Jews in Paris, was arrested and deported to Ravensbrück. Even there, as Elisabeth Maxwell has recorded, 'she continued her rescue activities until her death. For nearly two years, she lived in a vermin-infested cell block with 2,500 other women, most of them Jewish. Because she was a Gentile and thus of privileged status, she survived for quite a long time, witnessing daily the dying moments of her Jewish cell-mates who were dragged to their deaths before her eyes. She helped as she could, sharing food and giving moral support when she was powerless to offer any more substantial help.' As she lay dying, 'her last act was to slip her Gentile identity card to a Jewish woman in the hope of saving her life.'[17]

By the end of April 1945, while German troops were still fighting throughout northern Europe, most members of the SS were doing their best to slip into anonymity. On April 28 – the day before Hitler committed suicide in his bunker in Berlin, with Soviet troops surrounding the German capital – the Swedish Red Cross negotiated the release of three thousand five

---

[16] Zev Birger, *No Time for Patience: My Road from Kaunas to Jerusalem*, pages 74–5.
[17] Elisabeth Maxwell, 'The Rescue of Jews in France and Belgium During the Holocaust', *The Journal of Holocaust Education*, Summer/Autumn 1998.

hundred Jewish women being held in the harshest of conditions in Ravensbrück concentration camp, north of Berlin. To ensure that the agreement was not a trap, ten were taken by bus to Sweden on April 28; the rest followed within a few days. On their way through Germany, five of the women were killed in an Allied air raid. The others reached Sweden safely, but twenty-six of them were too weak to survive, despite being given the very best of medical attention when they reached their host country.[18]

The Swedish Red Cross also arranged for a group of French Jewish women in Mauthausen concentration camp, in Austria, to be allowed to leave Mauthausen for Switzerland. The first group left on April 9, crossing the Austrian–Swiss border at Kreuzlingen. A second group reached Switzerland on April 25, when they were taken to hospital in St Gallen.[19]

Very few Jews interned in the camps escaped; but some of those who did found help outside. Following the revolt of Jewish slave labourers on 2 August 1943 at Treblinka, where they were being forced to dig up and then burn the bodies of tens of thousands of Jewish deportees from Warsaw and central Poland, most of the Jews who managed to get beyond the perimeter of the camp were hunted down by German and Ukrainian units, and killed. Others, on reaching the banks of the River Bug, were helped by a Pole, Stanislaw Siwek.[20] After a revolt of Jewish slave labourers at Babi Yar, on the outskirts of Kiev, on 29 September 1943, two of those who got away were hidden by two Ukrainian sisters, Natalya and Antonina Petrenko, underneath their

---

[18] Archives of the International Committee of the Red Cross, Geneva.
[19] United States Holocaust Memorial Museum, Photo Archive, Worksheets 66619 and 81603.
[20] Zabecki, *Wspomnienia*, page 126.

house.[21] And after escaping on 24 December 1943 during a mass breakout from the camp at Borki, where Jewish slave labourers were likewise being forced to dispose of the bodies of thousands of Jewish victims of earlier massacres, Josef Reznik was helped in hiding by a Polish priest.[22]

Henry Wilde was among the Jewish prisoners in a Waffen-SS labour camp at Semovice, in Czechoslovakia, where he worked loading and unloading artillery shells. These were kept in former farmhouses and barns, and a Waffen-SS non-commissioned officer, Wilhelm Bergmann, from Munich, was in charge of the place where Wilde worked. 'He treated me and two others detailed there like normal labour, provided from his allotment (mostly bread and margarine but also occasional apples) for us, and often came by himself to talk about his family and general matters,' Wilde later recalled. 'I felt that he was not happy with the war and his own position in it (he had been in a tank unit, was wounded on the Eastern Front and had the Iron Cross First Class on his chest). One day, towards the end of the war (winter of 44/45), he took me aside and told me in confidence that things looked bleak for all of us. The camp was to be taken over by SD people (the really bad SS security service) and there would very likely be an order to shoot all inmates if the Russians came nearer.'

Wilde added that Bergmann 'just about suggested that I make a run for it if possible. I actually did this a few days later, but not from the work site so as not to endanger him. I think he took a great risk and I never learned if I was the only one he warned. I actually got away and was free for several weeks, hiding at an old German country doctor's home near Chemnitz (a World

---

[21] Reuben Ainsztein, *Jewish Resistance in Nazi-Occupied Eastern Europe*, page 695.
[22] Testimony of Josef Reznik, Eichmann trial, 5 June 1961, session 64.

War One army friend of my father) who also took a grave risk. I was arrested there and ended up in Bergen-Belsen at the end of the war. I later learned that Dr Laurentius (my father's friend) was never arrested and that he survived the war and continued practicing at Oberlungwitz for a number of years before his death. He was a righteous man and so was his family which included several teenagers, all mandatory members of the Hitler Jugend but still able to keep a closed mouth.'[23]

At Auschwitz, Maryla Chodnikewicz, a Polish partisan who had been caught by the Germans, brought two Jewish girls into the kitchens where she worked. There they were able to survive as Polish prisoners, with less cruelty and more food. They were also able to steal hot water for some of their friends who were literally freezing in the Jewish section of the camp.[24] Recalling her own incarceration in Auschwitz, Hungarian-born Isabella Leitner wrote of 'the gentile woman from Budapest, she of noble birth, who was sent to Auschwitz because she had committed an unpardonable crime – she had helped her Jewish friends. I no longer remember her name, only her aristocratic face, drawn and hungry . . . She died in the ovens later, but now she was with us, and we loved her, and she loved us. There had not been any need for intellectual utterances for a long while now. Only the language of survival was of import here. Yet with her, on occasion, we actually talked of books. Strange must be the ways of the hungry, for even while the body is starving the mind may crave nourishment too.'[25]

---

[23] Henry Wilde, letter to the author, 23 June 2001.

[24] Information provided by Sinai Leichter, letter to the author, 20 November 2001. Maryla Chodnikewicz, like Sinai Leichter, was from the Polish town of Kielce. When she visited Israel to receive the Righteous Among the Nations award, she stayed at Sinai Leichter's home.

[25] Isabella Leitner, *Fragments of Isabella; A Memoir of Auschwitz*, page 54.

Body and mind were both nourished by one of the block leaders in Auschwitz. His name was Franz, and an eyewitness of his actions was Rudolf Vrba, who later escaped from Auschwitz and helped bring details of its gas chambers and slaughter to the West. Vrba later recalled how, as Franz shouted at his work detail, 'he swung at us with his club. To the passing SS men he looked and sounded a splendid kapo, heartless, brutal, efficient; yet never once did he hit us. In fact all the time I knew him, I never saw him strike a prisoner and that in Auschwitz was quite a record. I learned the reasons for his humanity later. In the first place he was a civilized, honourable man. Secondly he had suffered under the Nazis much longer than we had and hated them much more deeply.'

Vrba learned that Franz's battle against the Nazis 'had begun when he tried to reach Spain at the age of seventeen to fight against Franco. He never got further than the Austrian frontier, however, and when the Nazis took over his country, they sent him to Dachau concentration camp. After that came a succession of concentration camps; and when war broke out he became a kapo because experienced, hardened prisoners were needed to teach manners to the naïve newcomers who were being driven behind barbed wire in hundreds of thousands all over Europe.'

On one occasion, Franz and Vrba saw a group of starving Slovak girls who were scavenging empty food tins from the rubbish bins, 'and scraping them clean with their fingers'. Franz said to Vrba: 'Rudi, we must do something for those girls,' and proceeded to steal a box of marmalade from the camp store. After that he was known to those in his barrack as 'Franz Marmalade', a name that still attached to him after the war, where he ran a hotel in Vienna.[26]

---

[26] Rudolf Vrba (with Alan Bestic), *I Cannot Forgive*, pages 90, 100–2.

Helena Toth was the daughter of a Hungarian baron. Shortly before the Second World War she had married a Yugoslav Jew, Benjamin Elias. He was among many hundreds of Jews seized and deported in 1944 to the Baja concentration camp, inside Hungary. Helena Elias made her way to the camp, where she was received by the commanding officer and managed to convince him, without revealing that Benjamin Elias was her husband, that he was a Jew who always helped Christians. On that ground, she requested his release. It took her two and a half months of sustained effort to persuade the camp officials to release her husband and six other Jews. The very day of their release, the other Jewish captives in Baja were sent to Auschwitz. The seven who survived did so as a result of Helena Elias' persistence and persuasiveness, and her willingness to put her own life at risk.[27]

A name can be deceptive: Charles Coward was far from a coward. A British soldier in the battle for France, in 1940 he was taken prisoner by the Germans. He escaped from captivity several times, but, like so many escapees, was caught, and finally sent as a punishment to a prisoner-of-war camp attached to Auschwitz III, the slave labour camp at Buna-Monowitz, only a few miles from the gas chambers, where Jews, foreign workers and Allied prisoners of war worked in the construction of the largest synthetic oil plant in German-occupied Europe. At any one time, as many as ten thousand Jews toiled there. Two of them, Elie Wiesel and Primo Levi, later wrote about the cruel suffering endured in that place.

Norbert Wollheim, a Jewish prisoner at Monowitz, testified at the Nuremberg Trials immediately after the war that at least four hundred Jews had been able to get away from the Jewish slave labour camp at Monowitz

[27] Yad Vashem Righteous Among the Nations Archive, file 1029.

because Charles Coward had had an ingenious idea: he would collect precious chocolate from his fellow British prisoners of war and exchange it with one of the Monowitz guards – an SS sergeant-major who was open to bribery – for dead bodies, whose identities he then gave to Jews, a few each night, as they were marched back to their barracks from the I. G. Farben factories. These 'substituted' Jews were then given civilian clothing and smuggled out of the camp altogether.

On one occasion, Coward smuggled himself into Auschwitz 'and spent the night in one of the death huts searching for a British Jew, a naval officer, reputed to be languishing in the Camp.'[28]

On learning of Coward's death in 1976, Donia Rosen, then head of the Department of the Righteous at Yad Vashem, wrote to his family: 'We will long remember and will pass on to our posterity the memory of Mr Coward's heroic and selfless actions, which he rendered in service to his fellow man. Our sages were addressing themselves to men like Mr Coward when they thought: "He who saves one life, it is as if he had saved the entire world".'[29]

Starting in the autumn of 1944, and in increasing numbers into the early months of 1945, more than a hundred thousand Jews were marched, in groups of up to a thousand, from their places of incarceration in several hundred concentration and slave labour camps

---

[28] Letter from Anne Rose to the ambassador of Israel, London, 21 March 1961, Yad Vashem Righteous Among the Nations Archive, file 109.

[29] Letter of 28 December 1976, Yad Vashem Righteous Among the Nations Archive, file 109. In 1954 Charles Coward's story was the subject of a book by John Castle, *The Password is Courage*. In the film, Dirk Bogarde played Coward. Coward was helped in his rescue efforts at Monowitz by a Jewish prisoner of war there, Yitzhak Perski, who, like Coward, had served in the British army in North Africa and Greece before being captured by the Germans. One of Perski's sons, Shimon Peres, was later (three times) Prime Minister of Israel.

in the East – including Auschwitz and Monowitz – to slave labour camps and concentration camps in Germany. The Nazi aim was to prevent these Jews being liberated by the advancing Soviet forces, and to be able to continue to exploit them as slave labourers. During these 'death marches' the German guards inflicted terrible acts of cruelty on the marchers, thousands of whom were shot dead as they walked, or, too weak to continue, were shot dead as they lay on the ground unable to rejoin the march. Some Jews managed to escape from these death marches. One of them, Jakub Lichterman, had been the last cantor at the Nozyk Synagogue in Warsaw. He had been deported to Majdanek in 1943 and to Birkenau in 1944. In his group of marchers, about twenty Jews evaded the guards and slipped away. 'It was snowing,' he later recalled. 'We ate snow. Many people died. I saw a little light in a hut. I decided to knock. The others said, "It is dangerous, it might be a German's hut." But I thought, "Must I die here? Maybe they will give me something."'

Lichterman knocked on the door of the hut. 'It was an Ethnic German. He gave me hot coffee in a bottle, and bread.' Then, as Lichterman left the hut, two other escapees came up to him, desperate for a drink. 'The bottle fell out of my hand. The coffee dropped in the snow. I went back. He had no more food. He gave me a box of matches and said, "There are lots of Germans around. If they catch you, they will kill you on the spot."' The Jews wandered off, each to a different part of the wood. Lichterman knocked on another door, another small hut. 'Can you take me in?' 'How many are you?' 'Just one.' Lichterman was taken in, hidden in a shack, and fed three times a day. Eight days later, with the arrival of Soviet troops, Lichterman was free.[30]

---

[30] Testimony of Jakub Lichterman, in conversation with the author, Cape Town, 1985.

To the Jews who survived to the final months of the war, even small acts of kindness that did not put the lives of the helpers at risk could serve as a means of living through until liberation. Ilana Turner recalls that, before leaving Stutthof concentration camp for Dresden, 'I myself received from a Polish girl warm gloves and a large piece of bread.' As the girl handed over these precious gifts she whispered: 'I am so sorry that I cannot give you more.'[31]

When a Hungarian military unit was passing through Bonyhad, it included 150 Jewish forced labourers. The historian of the Jews of Bonyhad, Leslie Blau, recalled how, seizing the opportunity, the principal of the local school, Sandor Rozsa, and one of his teachers, Gustav Tomka, 'talked to the officers and advised them to let the Jews alone and try to escape. The overworked Jews were hidden at the school garret. A couple of days later the Red Army arrived and 150 Jewish lives were saved.'[32]

In January 1945 more than six thousand Jewish women, and a thousand Jewish men, were driven towards Palmnicken, a small fishing village on the Baltic Sea. On the march itself eight hundred were shot. Once in Palmnicken, the survivors were put into a disused factory. The German official in charge of the factory, seeing their plight, allocated three potatoes to each of the marchers. One of them, Polish-born Celina Manielewicz, later recalled: 'We heard that he was a humane man who had objected to us prisoners remaining in his town under inhumane conditions. A few hours later a rumour circulated that the Nazis had shot him.'

A few days later, the Jews were ordered to line up in rows of five and were marched towards the sea, where German machine-gunners mowed them down. Hardly anyone survived. Three women who did, among them

---

[31] Ilana Turner, letter to the author, 22 January 2001.
[32] Leslie Blau, letter to the author, 26 December 2000.

Celina Manielewicz, managed to make their way inland, where they found refuge with a German farmer called Voss. Later, however, Voss tried to turn them over to the Germans. Before he could do so, they were given shelter by two other villagers, Albert Harder and his wife, who fed and clothed them, and pretended they were three Polish girls. One day three German officers asked Frau Harder for permission to take the three girls on an outing. It would have aroused too many suspicions for the girls to refuse. On his way back from the outing with Celina Manielewicz, one of the officers told her, thinking her a local Polish girl, that 'Two hundred Jews had survived the night massacre, but had been handed over to the Gestapo by the population of the surrounding villages among whom they had sought asylum. They had all been killed.'[33]

Celina Manielewicz and her two friends, at least, were safe; Albert Harder and his wife continued to give them shelter until the Russians arrived. But of the more than seven thousand marched to the seashore, only ten had survived.

Thousands of other concentration camp prisoners were being transported into Germany by rail, in open goods wagons exposed to the ravages of winter. Ben Edelman managed to escape from his train. He owed his survival to a German farmer. As he recalled, 'I crawled the last half mile to the farmhouse; I was unable to walk any farther. When I reached the gate, a dog came running toward me and sniffed the blood from my wound. The farmer, who had been roused by the dog's barking, came to the gate and looked down at me. I figured I had nothing to lose by asking him to help me, for without medical attention I would surely die. I saw the farmer go through the motions of blessing himself and I thought,

[33] Testimony of Celina Manielewicz, Jerusalem, 7 November 1958; Yad Vashem Archive, 03/1108.

"Thank you, God, for people in this part of the world who still believe in you." The farmer looked around quickly and then opened the gate and pulled me in. He picked me up, carried me to the barn, and put me on the hay. "I'll be right back," he said.'

The farmer walked away, 'and I watched him disappear through the barn door. He was gone only about five minutes, but during the time I was alone a small sliver of apprehension and suspicion began to creep into my mind. I began to visualize his coming back with an SS man and, pointing his finger at me, saying: "There he is! I found him here when I came in to get my shovel. I just want you to know I had nothing to do with it." I said to myself, "What am I doing here letting a German take care of me? A Gentile would have been bad enough, but a German?" Through my wartime childhood years I had developed an emotional and psychological barrier that kept me apart from the Gentile world, a world which I feared and mistrusted as a result of my experiences. Up until now, with a couple of exceptions, my knowledge of the Aryans was linked with fear, distrust, hate, and ultimately the Holocaust.'

Ben Edelman continued: 'I was now restless and terrified and even made an attempt to leave, but as I crawled halfway to the door it opened from the outside and in walked the farmer holding a large piece of white bread in one hand and a cup of warm milk in the other. He asked me if I was Jewish, to which I nodded, believing now that he did not intend to harm me. He said I was welcome to stay, but only long enough to rest. He washed my wound and told me I had to leave in a couple of hours because SS men were checking all the farmhouses for escaped concentration camp prisoners.'[34]

On the morning of 26 January 1945 a group of ten British prisoners of war, held at night behind bars at

---

[34] Ben Edelman, *Growing up in the Holocaust*, pages 251–3.

prisoner-of-war camp Stalag 20B, near Marienburg, were at work on a German farm twenty-six miles from Danzig. Three hundred Jewish women on a death march from Stutthof concentration camp were brought to a halt near them, repeatedly beaten and brutalized by their guards. Among them was Sara Matuson, who managed to break away from the march and run into a barn, where she hid in the animals' feeding trough. 'Quite a bit of time passed,' she later recalled, 'and a man came in and I asked if he was Polish . . . he said he was British.' Later she recalled his exact words: 'Don't move, I'm English – don't be afraid,' and she added: 'English! I knew I was saved!' That soldier, Stan Wells, was also a captive of the Third Reich. 'He went into the farm house and brought me bread.'[35]

Bill Fisher, the diarist among the men, recorded the sequel: 'Stan comes to me after dinner and tells me a Jewess has got away and he has her hiding in the cow's crib. I suggest moving her to loft over camp. Plenty straw and the chimney from our fire will keep her warm. I arrange to take her to the camp. Wait till nearly dusk and go to Stan's farm, he hands over girl. I tell her to walk five paces near, on the other side of the road, and speak to no one. She is crippled, too frightened to understand me, grabs my arm. I am a bit windy as the Gerries will stop us as it is a definite "crime" for prisoner to speak or walk with women . . . No trouble at all! . . . Hot water, soap, towel, old clothes, slacks, food, rushed up to her . . . Take all clothing off kid, give her paraffin for lice in her hair and bid her goodbye. She grabs my hand and kisses it – and tries to thank me, calls me hero – I say roughly, Drop it, we are comrades, only doing what we can. Had no chance for a good look at her, judge her to be twenty-five years of age.

[35] Sara Hannah Matuson Rigler, letter of 20 October 1988, Yad Vashem Righteous Among the Nations Archive, file 5872.

'Everyone brings in food for our escapee! Hundred weight peas, ducks, hens, best part of a pig. Bread by loaves – and believe me she's ate three loaves today and five bowls of soup – somewhere around twenty-two pounds of food. She's ill now – sick diarrhoea. Suggest only milk for a few days . . .

'We had a good look at her. Her eyes are large as is usual with starvation, sunken cheeks, no breasts. Hair has not been cut, body badly marked with sores caused by scratching lice bites. Head still a bit matted and lice still obviously in. I got my forefinger and thumb around the upper part of her arm easily . . . Feet blue and raw with frostbite, the right heel is eaten away from frost and constant rubbing of badly fitting clog.'

Sara Matuson recalled Bill Fisher's arrival: 'He brought me a full length coat and put it on top of my clothes and walked with me through the town. Luckily we weren't stopped – the guards must have thought I looked like a prisoner of war. He took me to the barn and put me upstairs and made a hole in the straw. The straw was for the horses. A couple of the men came that night – one of them a medic – and they brought stuff for my feet which had frostbite, they brought me paraffin for the lice and food, I mustn't forget the food. I was so hungry and they will tell you how much I ate. They bathed me. All I had was a dress with a very big red Jewish star on the back of it, a thin coat and a blanket. I was very sick – I had diarrhoea. I was with them for three weeks and they nursed me back to health – every day I was visited with food. I only met one who would come up with food – he was Alan Edwards. After about a week the fellows decided I was to visit them. He got a sweater and coat to cover the dress shoes and stockings. I still had flannel underpants from the camp they must have washed them for me. They pushed me through a window and I met them. We all spoke German. They then pushed me back up in to the straw. They overheard that the horses were being moved away and that the straw – my home – was going. They said they would think of something – build a double wall or something but that they would save me. They were all in this together. Alan came one evening and said they were moving that night.' A Pole would look after her, she was told, but 'The fellow never showed up. The men who saved my life were moved on – it was nearly the end of the war.'[36]

The death march from which Sara had been rescued had started two weeks earlier with twelve hundred prisoners; by the time they reached the farm where the British prisoners of war were working, only three hundred were still alive. One of Sara Matuson's rescuers, Tommy Noble, a Scot, later recalled that the men would steal food and clothes from civilian Germans passing by; they had a fire in their camp, and could therefore cook. 'She gained her strength while in hiding.' Asked why they had risked their lives to hide her, he said: 'Why not? She was only a young girl. She was a very nice wee thing, she'd been treated badly, like us – they were cruel pigs.' Another of the men, George Hammond, recalled how, over the weeks, she became like 'a little sister'.[37]

After ten weeks the British prisoners of war were ordered westward. Sara Matuson stayed in the barn on her own until liberation. After the war, in a letter to Yad Vashem seeking recognition for the ten men, she wrote: 'If one of the ten had been against hiding me, I would not be alive today. This was truly a unanimous decision. It is not who of the prisoners of war brought me food, or tended my frostbite, or who applied paraffin to my hair, or bathed me or who nursed me back to health. All of

---

[36] Sara Hannah Matuson Rigler, letter of 20 October 1988, Yad Vashem Righteous Among the Nations Archive, file 5872.
[37] Interviews carried out in 1988 by Richard Woolfe, producer, BBC Television, Yad Vashem Righteous Among the Nations Archive, file 5872.

them were involved. All had to agree; all took equal responsibility and equal risk. Had I been discovered all of us would have been shot. They had all decided, despite the danger, that they would save from the Germans that poor Jewish girl who chanced into their lives.

'In the morning when the men were led to work they would bring me food under the guise of hanging laundry in the barn. They had sawn through the bars of their own prison and in the evening sneaked up to the loft to bring me food. The police station was right outside and the danger was fearful.' Had Sara been discovered, 'I would certainly have been shot together with the ten prisoners of war, all of whom had families and homes in England. I had nobody, and no one would have known had I been killed. I would just have been another one of the Six Million, but they had much more to risk and it was close to going home. They could touch freedom.'[38]

Three Jewish slave labourers who escaped from a death march near Dresden were hidden by a German husband and wife, Kurt and Hertha Fuchs. The three were Polish Jews: Roman Halter, Josef Szwajcer and Abraham Sztajer. Soon after liberation, Halter left the farm, returning a few weeks later with some gifts. 'When I arrived,' he recalled, 'I found Mrs Fuchs all in black. Her face had aged by years in those few weeks since my departure from them. She screamed when she saw me and refused to speak. Her neighbour told me that a few days after I had left, the Nazis in the village had found out that the Fuchses had sheltered Jews in their home. They then went to the house and took out Mr Fuchs, Szwajcer and Sztajer. Mr Fuchs and Szwajcer were shot. Sztajer managed to talk himself out of it. Mrs Fuchs

---

[38] Hannah Sara Rigler, letters to Mordecai Paldiel, 22 November, 9 December 1988, Yad Vashem Righteous Among the Nations Archive, file 5872.

517

dragged her husband's body back to the garden and buried him under a walnut tree.'[39]

Forty years later, remembering that terrible day of execution, Hertha Fuchs told Roman Halter: 'When I heard the shots, I knew that my lovely Kurt was dying. So I ran out into the field and took his head on my lap. He tried to speak, to say something to me. Szwajcer lay dead. Those who murdered my husband and Szwajcer were just walking away. One of them said, "We can get her now, too," but they just walked away.'[40]

Rescue and murder – the two opposite impulses – continued to exist side by side to the very last days of the war: by far the rarer, rescue was the noble face of those tragic years.

---

[39] Roman Halter, letter to the author, March 1993, quoted in Martin Gilbert, *The Boys: Triumph over Adversity*, page 269.
[40] Roman Halter, 'Before and after', *Journal of the '45 Aid Society*, number 18, December 1994.

Afterword

What were the motives of those who tried to save Jews from deportation and death? This question is raised with every account of rescue, as the reader, like the historian, wonders whether he, or she, would have behaved in such a courageous manner. First and foremost, the Righteous of this book chose to act; theirs was a deliberate decision to behave in a civilized, humane manner, rather than to do nothing, or to refuse to be involved, or to take the route of barbarism.

In the circumstances of a combination of Nazi rule, SS power and Gestapo terror, inaction motivated by fear cannot be belittled. Those who turned against the tide of terror were all the more remarkable. 'We did what we had to do'; 'Anyone would have done the same' – the words of many rescuers – mask the courageousness of the course they chose, knowing it to be full of danger, often the danger of execution of their families as well as themselves. Yet these were not foolhardy, rash or intemperate people; most of them made their choice calmly, deliberately and with full realization of the risks – risks that they faced, and took, for months and even years.

Those who put their lives in jeopardy to save Jews were often people who had known those Jews before the war. Some had been close personal friends and neighbours, others had been business partners or business acquaintances, others were teachers or fellow pupils.

Some rescuers were women who had worked in a Jewish household, or been nannies to Jewish children. Pre-war friendship and acquaintance played a significant part in many acts of rescue; but equally, many rescuers had never before seen the person, or the family, to whom they gave life-guarding shelter.

Mordecai Paldiel, head of the Righteous Among the Nations Department at Yad Vashem since 1982, has supervised the preparation of more than fourteen thousand sets of documentation about those who risked their lives to save Jews. His work brings him in contact every day with stories of incredible courage. 'Goodness leaves us gasping,' he has written, 'for we refuse to recognize it as a natural human attribute. So off we go on a long search for some hidden motivation, some extraordinary explanation, for such peculiar behaviour. Evil is, by contrast, less painfully assimilated. There is no comparable search for the reasons for its constant manifestation (although in earlier centuries theologians pondered this issue).'

Contrasting good and evil, Paldiel notes: 'We have come to terms with evil. Television, movies and the printed word have made evil, aggression and egotism household terms and unconsciously acceptable to the extent of making us immune to displays of evil. There is a danger that the evil of the Holocaust will be absorbed in a similar manner; that is, explained away as further confirmation of man's inherent disposition to wrong-doing. It confirms our visceral feeling that man is an irredeemable beast, who needs to be constrained for his own good. In searching for an explanation of the motivations of the Righteous among the Nations, are we not really saying: what was wrong with them? Are we not, in a deeper sense, implying that behaviour was something other than normal?'

Evil instincts are taken for granted; altruistic, humane behaviour appears to need special explanation. Is it possible, asks Paldiel, 'that we are creating a problem where there ought not to be one? Is acting benevolently and altruistically such an outlandish and unusual type of behaviour, supposedly at odds with man's inherent character, as to justify a meticulous search for explanations? Or is it conceivable that such behaviour is as natural to our psychological constitution as the egoistic one we accept so matter-of-factly?'[1]

Agnes Hirschi, who, with her mother, was given sanctuary in Budapest by Carl Lutz, wrote about his motivation in issuing protective documents to Jews in Budapest: 'The laws of life are stronger than man-made laws. That's how my father thought and that's how he acted. He was not born a hero, he was rather shy and introverted.' In Budapest 'it was not his task to rescue Jews, he was chief of the Swiss Legation's Department of Foreign Interests, and he was in charge of the interests of fourteen belligerent nations, among them the United States and Great Britain.' But the instinct to help was deep within him. 'He had grown up in a Methodist family in eastern Switzerland. He was the second oldest of ten brothers and sisters. His mother was a strong personality. They were poor but she helped people in trouble and sick, as much as she could. She gave an example of humanity and was deeply admired by her son Carl.' His motive was a simple one, which his stepdaughter encapsulated thus: 'Carl Lutz, as an engaged Christian, could not tolerate the Jews being pursued and killed in Budapest. He had to protect and help these people. He felt, God gave him this task, and he was persuaded He would give him also the force to fulfil it.'[2]

Those Christian values, which had first been shown when the Good Samaritan went out of his way on the road from Jericho to Jerusalem, were central to the

[1] Mordecai Paldiel, 'Is goodness a mystery?', *Jerusalem Post*, 8 October 1989.
[2] Agnes Hirschi, letter to the author, 20 March 2002.

actions of many thousands of rescuers. Good deeds do not necessarily come unsought. In 1964, when the Belgian priest Father Bruno was honoured for finding homes for as many as 320 Jews, he asked those gathered to honour him: 'Saved? But who saved? What did I do? I searched; but searching without finding is perfectly fruitless: finding is essential. But finding was not my doing ... finding meant that doors were opened, the door of a home, the door of a heart.'[3] The Baptists in eastern Poland had been motivated by their religious belief that God was testing their Christian faith by sending them Jews in distress. Nor were Jews universally regarded as the enemy by Christian Europe in the inter-war years; when asked to give details about his rescue activities in Serbia, Risto Ristic would only say: 'I did my best to save Jews because I love them.'[4] There were many practising Christians, especially in the eastern regions of Europe, who went out of their way to harm Jews; there were others, even in the midst of this primitive hostility, who risked the disapproval of their Christian neighbours to try to save Jews, and were sometimes themselves betrayed by those neighbours – betrayed and then killed.

Dislike of German occupation also motivated many rescuers: this was particularly true, for example, in Belgium, France and Holland, where helping Jews was for some an integral part of the pattern of resistance; indeed, in Holland, seven separate resistance organizations helped hide Jews. With regard to Warsaw, Zofia Lewin noted that the 'overwhelming majority' of the people who helped her survive on the 'Aryan' side of the city expressed, 'by their whole attitude towards me',

---

[3] Michel Reynders, 'Father Bruno (Henry Reynders), His Life, His Work, Biography of a Righteous', manuscript, Yad Vashem Righteous Among the Nations Archive, file 84.
[4] Information provided by the Jewish Foundation for the Righteous, New York, on its website.

their protest against the occupier. 'Not only did they not let me feel that my very presence was dangerous, they also treated me as one of themselves, a person in greater danger due only to external reasons, due to the false principles of the occupying power and not because of any essential difference on my part.'[5] Hatred of the occupier was a feature of rescue in many lands.

There were also social characteristics and patterns of behaviour that affected the reception of Jews in search of refuge. When Refik Vesili, the first of sixty Albanians to be awarded the title of Righteous, was asked how it was possible that so many Albanians helped to hide Jews and protect them, he explained: 'There are no foreigners in Albania, there are only guests. Our moral code as Albanians requires that we be hospitable to guests in our home and in our country.' When asked about the possibility of Albanians reporting the presence of the Jews to the Germans, Veseli said that while such a thing was possible, 'if an Albanian did this he would have disgraced his village and his family. At a minimum his home would be destroyed and his family banished.' The discussion was pointless as 'no Albanian disgraced us'.[6]

Whole nations could, if circumstances allowed, prevent the deportation of Jews, or enable them to escape deportation. This was true of Italy and Hungary before the German military occupations of those countries in 1943 and 1944 respectively. It was true of Denmark on the eve of full German occupation. It was true of Finland and Bulgaria throughout the war. Reflecting on the reasons why Bulgarian Jews survived the Holocaust, and on what he calls 'the fragility of goodness', the historian of Bulgarian rescue efforts, Tzvetan Todorov, after describing the actions of 'men of conscience and

---

[5] Wladyslaw Bartoszewski and Zofia Lewin, *Righteous Among Nations*, page 39.
[6] Harvey Sarner, *Rescue in Albania*, page 63.

courage' like the prelates Stefan and Kiril, has written that even the King would not have agreed to stand up to German pressure 'without the swell of public opinion against the deportation, and without the intervention of many around him'. Todorov concludes that 'the people were opposed to the anti-Semitic measures, but a community is powerless without leaders, without those individuals within its midst who exercise public responsibility – in this case, the metropolitans, the deputies, the politicians who are ready to accept the risks that their actions entailed. All this was necessary for good to triumph, in a certain place and at a certain time; any break in the chain and their efforts might well have failed. It seems that, once introduced into public life, evil easily perpetuates itself, whereas good is always difficult, rare, and fragile. And yet possible.'[7]

Dislike of Nazism and its racial doctrines; a refusal to succumb to them, a refusal to be bullied, even by superior force; an unwillingness to allow evil to triumph, despite the overwhelming military and secret police powers of Nazi Germany; contempt for prejudice, a sense of decency: each played its part in making acts of rescue possible, even desirable. When Tine zur Kleinsmiede was honoured in Israel in 1983, she told the assembled officials she had done nothing special in hiding Jews in Holland: 'Anyone would have done the same thing, in my place. Any decent person, that is.' She put a special stress on the word 'decent'.[8]

In 1988, visiting the Lithuanian town of Naumiestis from which his family had come, and where virtually the whole Jewish community had been murdered, Dr

---

[7] Tzvetan Todorov (editor), *The Fragility of Goodness: Why Bulgaria's Jews Survived the Holocaust*, page 40.
[8] Edith Velmans, *Edith's Book: The True Story of How One Young Girl Survived the War*, page 241. Tine zur Kleinsmiede died in 1994, at the age of one hundred.

Benjamin E. Lesin, a Los Angeles surgeon, asked his hosts, 'Didn't anybody help?' and then ascertained that 'dozens had'. He was told of a couple to whom a baby girl was passed through a ghetto fence; of a carpenter who saved twelve Jews; of a farmer, part of a network with two other farmers, who saved twenty-six. 'I was overwhelmed by their modesty,' Lesin recalled. 'I asked the couple who had saved the baby (now living in Wilkes Barre, Pennsylvania) why they put themselves in so much danger. Their response was, "We did the only thing a decent person would do . . . what a good Christian would do." '[9]

The response of that Lithuanian couple – 'We did the only thing a decent person would do . . .' – was almost universal among rescuers. In 1989 Vitalija Rinkevicius received the Yad Vashem Medal of the Righteous on behalf of her parents, who had helped save Margaret and Joseph Kagan in Kaunas. During the ceremony she said she was happy and grateful for this honour to her parents and thanked everyone; but above all she wanted to convey what she felt sure her father would have said on this occasion: 'I am no hero, have done nothing out of the ordinary, nothing other than any normal human being would have done.'[10]

Reflecting on the altruistic behaviour of the Righteous, Samuel Oliner, who was himself saved as a youngster, commented in 1994: 'Acts of heroic altruism are not the exclusive province of larger-than-life figures such as Mahatma Gandhi and Albert Schweitzer. Rather, they are manifestations of ordinary people whose moral courage is born out of the routine ways in which they live their lives – their characteristic ways of feeling, their perceptions of authority, the rules and examples of

---

[9] Quoted in Rob O'Neil, 'Helping Hand for Old Heroes of Holocaust', *Los Angeles Times*, 1 August 1996.
[10] Margaret Kagan, manuscript, sent to the author 10 August 2000. I was myself present on this occasion.

conduct they have learned from family, friends, religion, political leaders, their schools, workplaces, and all their associates.'[11]

Asked about his motives for saving Jews in Bialystok during the war, the German paint-shop manager Otto Busse reiterated that he was a Christian, 'and considered it his duty according to the way he interpreted his Christian conscience'. He did not belong to any denomination. 'I do not hold with the institutionalized church. We must go back to early Christianity. We should be neither crusaders nor missionaries. Instead, we should let the idea of Christ come to new life in our hearts. If this had happened earlier, there would never have been the Hitler Holocaust.'[12]

Major Helmrich and his wife, who had helped Jews in the Polish city of Drohobycz, reflected: 'We were fully aware of the risks and the clash of responsibilities, but we decided that it would be better for our children to have dead parents than cowards as parents.'[13] Major Karl Plagge – who had been a member of the Nazi Party from 1932 to 1939 – spoke of why he had protected Jews in Vilna during the war. 'There needed to be people who were doing something good for the German reputation,' he said. 'I was ashamed.'[14]

One of those who took in Jewish children in France, Marie-Elise Roger, commented: 'I did nothing unusual . . . I only took in a little guy who had just lost his parents . . . I loved him and gave him food to eat. If I had

---

[11] Samuel Oliner, untitled article in *The Month* magazine (London), January 1994.
[12] Ephraim Lahav, 'German friend settles in Israel', *Jewish Observer and Middle East Review*, 24 April 1970.
[13] Mordecai Paldiel, 'Helmrich, Eberhard', in *Enclopedia of the Holocaust*, volume 2, page 654.
[14] Yad Vashem Righteous Among the Nations Archive file 9557. (As of 2002, Major Plagge had not been recognized as a Righteous Among the Nations.)

not done this, that would not have been normal.'[15] Recalling the help given by French farmers at Dullin in hiding Jewish children, David Eppel – who later married one of those children – has written: 'To meet and talk with these unpretentious farmers, long after it was all over, was truly to understand the meaning of the term "righteous". No political or religious ideology compelled their actions. So why did they do it? "Why do you ask?" they answered.'[16]

As to her motive in helping save Jews in France, Jeannette Brousse commented: 'I felt horrified by the atrocious fate likely to befall all these innocent victims whose only "mistake" was to have been born Jewish. I did not know any Jews before these events. I discovered they were people like us, even though some influential newspapers presented them as scapegoats for all evils. I was determined to find solutions so that the greatest number of those who came to me could be saved.'[17]

In explaining the motives of those who, like herself, gave shelter to Jews, Pastor Trocmé's wife Magda, one of the French rescuers honoured at Yad Vashem, later remarked: 'Those of us who received the first Jews did what we thought had to be done – nothing more complicated. It was not decided from one day to the next what we would have to do. There were many people in the village who needed help. How could we refuse them? A person doesn't sit down and say I'm going to do this and this and that. We had no time to think. When a problem came, we had to solve it immediately. Sometimes people ask me, "How did you

[15] Odette Meyers, 'a Long-Delayed Public Thank You to Chavagnes-en-Paillers', *The Hidden Child* newsletter, volume 9, no. 1, Spring 2000.
[16] David Eppel, 'Key to righteousness', *Jewish Chronicle*, 28 July 2000.
[17] 'Les Raisons de l'Engagement de Mme J. Brousse, Annecy, 1979', sent by Madame Brousse to the author, 27 May 2001.

make a decision?" There was no decision to make. The issue was: "Do you think we are all brothers or not? Do you think it is unjust to turn in the Jews or not? Then let us try to help!"'[18]

'I took the risk because I am a humanist,' a Dutch rescuer, Jan Schoumans, commented when, at a ceremony in his home in Toronto, he was presented with a Righteous Among the Nations Award.[19]

Cecile Seiden, who was saved in Belgium, later reflected: 'After the war, my mother, father and I wondered why our righteous Rescuers had saved us. We told the Spiessens that they were true heroes and they would simply answer, "No, we were not heroes but this was the correct thing to do!" We were also so grateful to the Stettler family for giving me a home and a wonderful new family and for sharing their lives and taking such good care of me. One can never repay the kindness and courage that the righteous Rescuers demonstrated during this period of unbelievable horror and inhumanity, when one nation tried to destroy another nation with blind hatred and ferocity unequalled in history.'[20]

Michel Reynders, who as a teenager was involved with his uncle, Father Bruno, in helping to save Jews in Belgium, commented: 'Our family is proud of having its name on a tree at Yad Vashem, but we think we only did our duty as Christians: to help people in necessity or in danger is one of the prime Christian obligations.' Of those who did not heed the commands, Michel Reynders

---

[18] Quoted in Carol Rittner and Sondra Myers (editors), *Courage to Care: Rescuers of Jews During the Holocaust*, page 102.
[19] Desmond Brown, 'Israel honours two Toronto war heroes', *National Post*, 9 February 1999. The other honorand was Sandor Tonelli.
[20] Cecile Seiden, 'In Honour of My Righteous Rescuers', part of the New Jersey Holocaust Curriculum, under the heading 'To Honour All Children: From Prejudice, to Discrimination, to Hatred . . . to Holocaust'.

reflects: 'We are sad an[
sheep" and hope that futu[
the message of love and c[

Flora Singer, one of t[
asked him many years lat[
not his goal, he had riske[
dren. He told her, 'Flora, v[
did what I'm supposed to [
such risks to hide the ch[
Father Beccari comment[
still living in the village: 'It was simple. They were children in danger. What would you have done?'[23]

Given the dangers faced by every person who hid or sheltered a Jew, given the ever-present prospect of severe punishment, of execution, and of the execution of one's whole family, the number of those for whom evidence of rescue has been ascertained is indeed high. By the beginning of 2000 the Yad Vashem committee set up to commemorate those 'who risked their lives to save Jews' had located seventeen and a half thousand such people. A former member of the committee, Baruch Sharoni – who had left Poland for Palestine before the war – has asked: 'Is the number 17,500 a final one? Not at all. First, the committee's work is not done. Not all the names of these wonderful people have been submitted to it. Many died alongside the survivors. Others passed away without anyone to remember them. Still others have requested, for reasons known only to themselves, not to be revealed.'[24]

---

[21] Dr Michel Reynders, letter to the author, 28 February 2002.
[22] Joseph Berger, 'A Monk, a Saviour, a Mensch: Nine Jews Gather in New Jersey to Remember the Man Who Rescued Them from the Nazis', *New York Times*, 5 July 1992.
[23] Quoted in John Follain, 'Village hid Jews from Nazis', *Sunday Times*, 18 January 2001.
[24] Benek (Baruch) Sharoni, 'Man's Humanity to Man', *Mizkor*, October 2000.

perative in remembering and recog-
k of the Righteous is also an important
ir story, for without the determination to
eyewitnesses and record their stories the
s would not have been accorded their true place
tory. During his two decades of work at Yad
hem, Mordecai Paldiel has followed up information
d requests from all over the world from those who
want to honour their rescuers. 'I must confess', he has
written, 'that I have always viewed the work I perform
here, within the framework of the "Righteous Among the
Nations", as a moral duty which we, the generation of
the Shoah, have toward those within the non-Jewish
population of German-dominated Europe who exerted
themselves to save Jews, and thereby rescued the
spirit and idea of man, as expressed in the best Biblical
tradition.'[25]

Recognition and remembrance continue into the
twenty-first century, even as the number of those
rescued, and the number of surviving rescuers, declines.
When the Holocaust is finally beyond living memory,
the desire to remember and honour those who extended
a helping hand will remain. This is a question not only
of recognizing individual bravery, but of providing a
reminder that it is possible for human beings, in situations where civilized values are being undermined, to
find the strength of character and purpose to resist the
evil impulses of the age, and to try to rescue the victims
of barbarity. Long after the Righteous the Second
World War have died, they will serve as models of the
best in human behaviour and achievement to which
anyone may choose to aspire. As Pierre Sauvage, one of
the youngsters saved in the French village of Le
Chambon-sur-Lignon, explained when he made a film

---

[25] Mordecai Paldiel, letter to the author, 17 January 2002.

about the village, he wanted his son 'to learn that the stories of the righteous are not footnotes to the past'.[26] Above all, the stories of the Righteous emphasize, in the words of Mordecai Paldiel, 'the belief that man, if he is to be appreciated as a unique creature, is indeed endowed with a great capacity for goodness; for moral and ethical behaviour. This bright and shining side of man, if put to full use, is more than enough to offset the other, and darker, side of man's behaviour.'[27]

The many survivors who have written to me about their rescuers feel strongly that these individual, selfless acts – the acts whereby they were saved – have not entered sufficiently into the general histories of the Holocaust, or indeed of the Second World War. Put succinctly, as they see it, and as the material presented in this book surely underlines, human decency was also an integral part of the war years; and it was a decency that, had it been on an even larger scale, had it permeated even more deeply into the societies of that time, could have saved many more lives – thousands, even tens of thousands. The story of the Righteous is not only a story of the many successful individual acts of courage and rescue; it is also a pointer to what human beings are capable of doing – for the good – when the challenge is greatest and the dangers most pressing. Each of the nineteen thousand and more known stories – like each of the several hundred stories in these pages – must lead each of us to ask: 'Could I have acted like this, in the circumstances; would I have tried to, would I have wanted to?' One can only hope that the answer would have been – and would still be, if occasion rose – 'yes'.

---

[26] Pierre Sauvage, ' "Weapons of the Spirit": A Journey Home', *The Hollywood Reporter*, 17 March 1987.
[27] Mordecai Paldiel, letter to the author, 26 April 2002.

Maps

showing the places mentioned in the text

1. Western France

2. Central France and Switzerland

3. Belgium

4. The Brussels region

5. Holland

MAPS

6. Germany

539

7. Central Europe

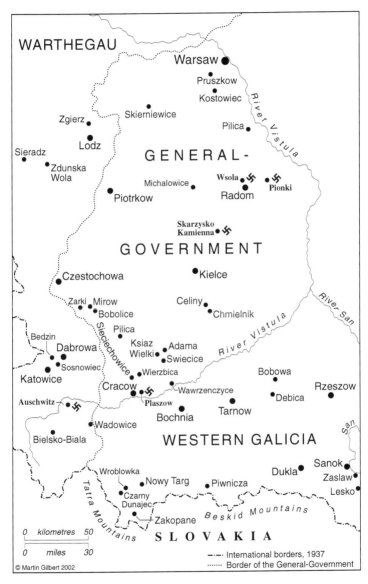

8. Western Poland

541

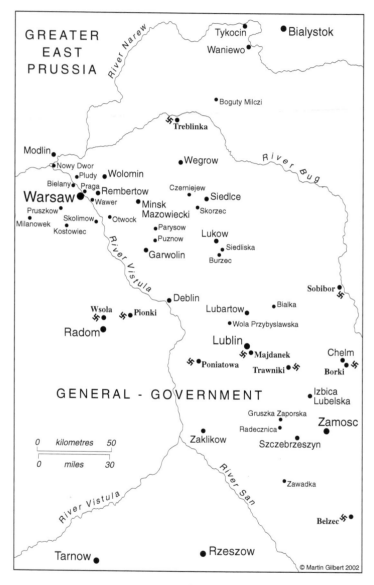

9. Central Poland

10. Lithuania, Eastern Poland, Byelorussia

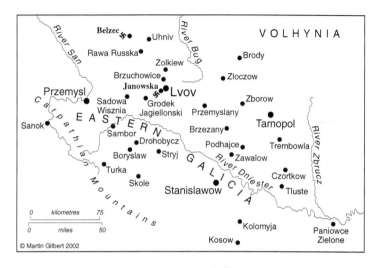

11. Eastern Galicia

12. Slovakia and Hungary

544

13. From the Baltic Sea to the Black Sea

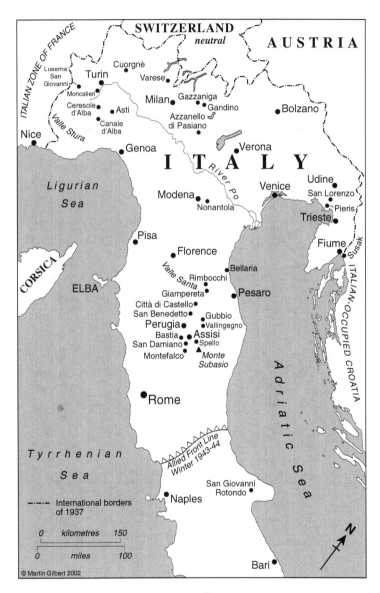

14. Italy

15. The Balkans

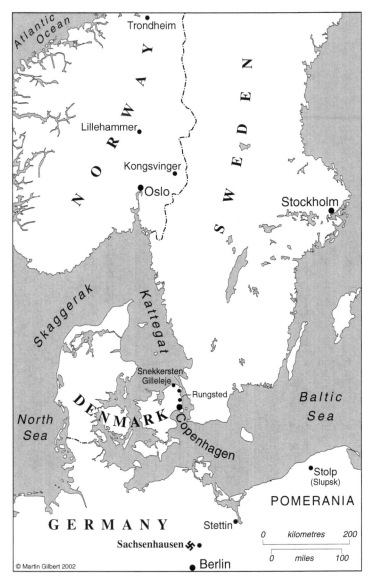

16. Norway and Denmark

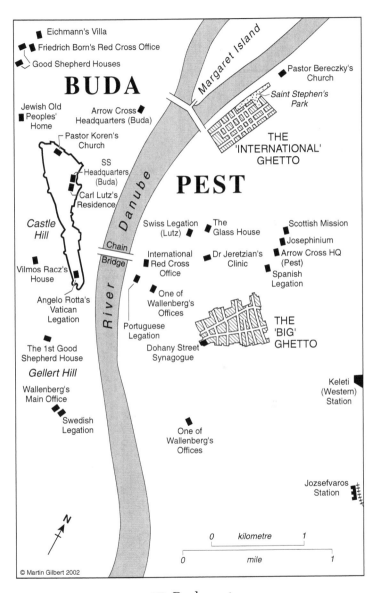

Eichmann's Villa

Friedrich Born's Red Cross Office

Good Shepherd Houses

BUDA

Jewish Old Peoples' Home

Arrow Cross Headquarters (Buda)

Pastor Koren's Church

SS Headquarters (Buda)

Carl Lutz's Residence

Castle Hill

Vilmos Racz's House

Angelo Rotta's Vatican Legation

The 1st Good Shepherd House

Gellert Hill

Wallenberg's Main Office

Swedish Legation

Margaret Island

Danube

Pastor Bereczky's Church

Saint Stephen's Park

THE 'INTERNATIONAL' GHETTO

PEST

Swiss Legation (Lutz)

The Glass House

Scottish Mission

Josephinium

Arrow Cross HQ (Pest)

Chain Bridge

International Red Cross Office

Dr Jeretzian's Clinic

Spanish Legation

River

One of Wallenberg's Offices

Portuguese Legation

Dohany Street Synagogue

THE 'BIG' GHETTO

Keleti (Western) Station

One of Wallenberg's Offices

Jozsefvaros Station

N

| 0 | kilometre | 1 |

| 0 | mile | 1 |

© Martin Gilbert 2002

17. Budapest

549

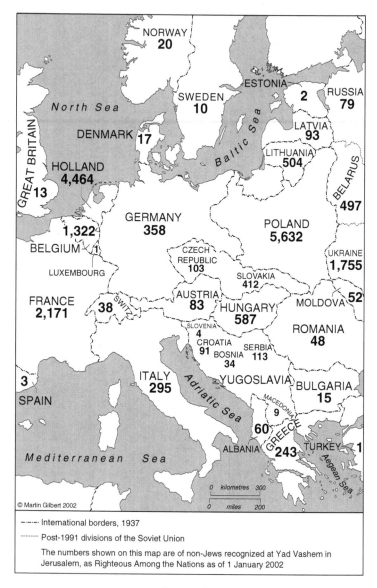

NORWAY
20

SWEDEN
10

ESTONIA
2

RUSSIA
79

North Sea

Baltic Sea

LATVIA
93

DENMARK **17**

LITHUANIA
504

HOLLAND
4,464

GREAT BRITAIN
13

BELARUS
497

GERMANY
358

POLAND
5,632

1,322

BELGIUM **1**

CZECH
REPUBLIC
103

UKRAINE
1,755

LUXEMBOURG

SLOVAKIA
412

SWITZ.
38

AUSTRIA
83

HUNGARY
587

MOLDOVA **52**

FRANCE
2,171

SLOVENIA
4

CROATIA
91

BOSNIA
34

SERBIA
113

ROMANIA
48

3

SPAIN

ITALY
295

Adriatic Sea

YUGOSLAVIA

BULGARIA
15

MACEDONIA
9

GREECE

ALBANIA
60

243

TURKEY **1**

Mediterranean Sea

Aegean Sea

© Martin Gilbert 2002

0 kilometres 300

0 miles 200

—·—·— International borders, 1937

·········· Post-1991 divisions of the Soviet Union

The numbers shown on this map are of non-Jews recognized at Yad Vashem in Jerusalem, as Righteous Among the Nations as of 1 January 2002

18. The Righteous

Works Cited

Books specifically about non-Jews who helped Jews during the Second World War

Per Anger, *With Raoul Wallenberg in Budapest: Memories of the War Years in Hungary.* New York: Holocaust Library, 1981.

Per Anger, 'Introduction', in *Raoul Wallenberg, Letters and Dispatches, 1924–1944.* New York: Arcade Publishing, 1995.

Michael Bar-Zohar, *Beyond Hitler's Grasp: The Heroic Rescue of Bulgaria's Jews.* Holbrook, Massachusetts: Adams Media Corporation, 1999.

Wladyslaw Bartoszewski and Zofia Lewinowna, *Ten jest z Ojczyzny mojej: Polacy z pomoca Zydom, 1939–1945* ('He is my fellow countryman: Poles giving assistance to Jews, 1939–1945'). Cracow: Wydnawnictwo Znak, 1966.

Wladyslaw Bartoszewski and Zofia Lewin (editors), *Righteous Among Nations: How Poles Helped the Jews, 1939–1945.* London: Earlscourt Publications, 1969.

Arieh L. Bauminger, *The Righteous.* Jerusalem: Yad Vashem Martyrs' and Heroes' Remembrance Authority 1969. Subsequent editions 1971 and 1983 as *Roll of Honour.*

Arieh Ben-Tov (compiler), *Friedrich Born, 'A Righteous Among the Nations.* Jerusalem: Yad Vashem, 1988.

Gay Block and Malka Drucker, *Rescuers: Portraits of Moral Courage in the Holocaust.* New York: Holmes & Meier, 1922.

John Castle, *The Password is Courage*. London: Chiswick Press, 1954.

Dan Danieli, *Captain Ocskay, A Righteous Man*. New York: privately printed. First edition, May 1966; second (enlarged) edition, May 1998.

Mikhail Erenburg and Viktorija Sakaite (editors), *Hands Bringing Life and Bread*. Vilnius: The Vilna Gaon Jewish State Museum, two volumes, 1997 and 1999.

Eva Fogelman, *Conscience and Courage: Rescuers of Jews During the Holocaust*. New York: Anchor Books, 1994.

Saul Friedlander, *Counterfeit Nazi: the Ambiguity of Good*. London: Weidenfeld & Nicolson, 1969. (On Kurt Gerstein.)

Philip Friedman, *Their Brothers' Keeper: The Christian Heroes and Heroines Who Helped the Oppressed Escape the Nazi Terror*. New York: Crown, 1957; Holocaust Library, 1978.

Leo Goldberger (editor), *The Rescue of the Danish Jews: Moral Courage Under Stress*. New York: New York University Press, 1987.

David Gushee, *The Righteous Gentiles of the Holocaust: A Christian Interpretation*. Minneapolis: Fortress, 1994.

Irene Gut Opdyke (with Jeffrey M. Elliot), *Into the Flames: The Life Story of a Righteous Gentile*. San Bernardino, California: Borgo Press, 1992.

Philip Hallie, *Lest Innocent Blood Be Shed: The Story of the Village of Le Chambon and How Goodness Happened There*. New York: Harper & Row, 1979.

Wilfred Harrison, *Rescuers Speaking*. Amsterdam: Harwood Academic Publishers, 1997.

Peter Hellman, *Avenue of the Righteous*. New York: Athenaeum, 1981.

Douglas K. Huneke, *The Moses of Rovno: The Stirring Story of Fritz Graebe, a German Christian Who Risked His Life to Lead Hundreds of Jews to Safety During the Holocaust*. Tiburon, California: Compassion House, 1985.

Kazimierz Iranek-Osmecki, *He Who Saves One Life: The Complete, Documented Story of the Poles Who Struggled To Save Jews During World War Two*. New York: Crown Publishers, 1971.

Thomas Keneally, *Schindler's Ark*. London: Hodder & Stoughton, 1982.

Ewa Kurek, *Your Life is Worth Mine: How Polish Nuns Saved Hundreds of Jewish Children in German-Occupied Poland, 1939–1945*. New York: Hippocrene Books, 1997.

Ellen Land-Weber, *To Save a Life: Stories of Holocaust Rescue*. Urbana and Chicago: University of Illinois Press, 2000.

H. D. Leuner, *When Compassion was a Crime: Germany's Silent Heroes*. London: Oswald Wolff, 1966.

Reverend David McDougall, *Jane Haining, 1897–1944*. Edinburgh: Church of Scotland World Mission, 1949 (updated by Ian Alexander, 1999).

Andy Marino, *A Quiet American: The Secret War of Varian Fry*. New York: St Martin's Press, 1999.

Robert Marshall, *In the Sewers of Lvov: a Heroic Story of Survival from the Holocaust*. London: Collins, 1990.

Milton Meltzer, *Rescue: The Story of How Gentiles Saved Jews in the Holocaust*. New York: Harper & Row, 1988.

Francis J. Murphy, *Père Jacques: Resplendent in Victory*. Washington DC: Institute of Carmelite Studies Publications, 1998.

Samuel and Pearl Oliner, *The Altruistic Personality: Rescuers of Jews in Nazi Europe*. New York: Free Press, 1988.

Mordecai Paldiel, *The Path of the Righteous: Gentile Rescuers of the Jews During the Holocaust*. Hoboken, New Jersey: KTAV Publishers, 1993.

Mordecai Paldiel, *Sheltering the Jews: Stories of Holocaust Rescuers*. Minneapolis: Fortress Publishers, 1995.

Mordecai Paldiel, *Saving the Jews: Amazing Stories of Persons who Defied the 'Final Solution'*. Rockville, Maryland: Schreiber Publishing, 2000.

Portuguese Ministry of Foreign Affairs, *Spared Lives: The Actions of Three Portuguese Diplomats in World War Two*, Documentary Exhibition Catalogue. Lisbon: Portuguese Ministry of Foreign Affairs, September 2000.

Dr Alexander Ramati, as told by Padre Rufino Niccaci, *The Assisi Underground: The Priests Who Rescued Jews*. New York: Stein & Day, 1978.

Hannu Rautkallio, *Finland and the Holocaust: The Rescue of Finland's Jews*. New York: Holocaust Library, 1987.

Carol Rittner and Sandra Myers (editors), *The Courage to Care: Rescuers of Jews During the Holocaust*. New York: New York University Press, 1986.

Harvey Sarner, *Rescue in Albania: One Hundred Percent of Jews in Albania Rescued from Holocaust*. Cathedral City, California: Brunswick Press, 1997.

Eric Silver, *The Book of the Just: The Silent Heroes Who Saved Jews from Hitler*. London: Weidenfeld & Nicolson, 1992.

Michael Smith, *Foley, the Spy Who Saved 10,000 Jews*. London: Hodder & Stoughton, 1999.

Tina Strobos, *The Book of Courage: The First Annual Act of Courage Awards*, Victims Assistance Services Brochure, Hudson River Museum, New York, 4 May 2001.

Uriel Tal (editor), *The Grey Book: A Collection of Protests Against Anti-Semitism and the Persecution of Jews issued by Non-Roman Catholic Churches and Church Leaders During Hitler's Rule*. Assen, Holland: Van Gorcum, 1969.

Hudson Talbott, *Forging Freedom: A True Story of Heroism During the Holocaust*. New York: G. P. Putnam's Sons, 2000.

Nechama Tec, *When Light Pierced the Darkness: Christian Rescue of Jews in Nazi-Occupied Poland*. New York: Oxford University Press, 1986.

Tzvetan Todorov (editor), *The Fragility of Goodness: Why Bulgaria's Jews Survived the Holocaust. A Collection of Texts with Commentary*. Princeton, New Jersey: Princeton University Press, 2001.

Irene Tomaszewski and Tecia Werbowski, *Zegota: The Council for Aid to Jews in Occupied Poland, 1942–45*. Montreal: Price-Patterson, 1999.

Meir Wagner, *The Righteous of Switzerland, Heroes of the Holocaust*. Hoboken, New Jersey: KTAV Publishing House, 2001.

Leni Yahil, *The Rescue of Danish Jewry: Test of a Democracy*. Philadelphia: Jewish Publication Society of America, 1983.

Memoirs

Maja Abramowitch, *To Forgive But Not Forget: Maja's Story*. London: Vallentine Mitchell, 2002.

Samuel Bak, *Painted in Worlds: A Memoir*. Bloomington and Indianapolis: Indiana University Press, in conjunction with Pucker Art Publications, Boston, 2001.

Zev Birger, *No Time for Patience: My Road from Kaunas to Jerusalem, A Memoir of a Holocaust Survivor*. New York: Newmarket Press, 1999.

Tuvia Borzykowski, *Between Tumbling Walls*. Kibbutz Lohamei Ha-Gettaot, Israel: Ghetto Fighters' House, 1972.

Jeannette Brousse, *Les Raisons de l'Engagement de Mme J. Brousse, Annecy, 1979*. Annecy: privately printed, 1979.

Dr Salim Diamand, *Dottore! Internment in Italy, 1940–1945*. Oakville, Ontario: Mosaic Press, 1987.

Doba-Necha Cukierman, *A Guardian Angel: Memories of Lublin*. East Bentleigh, Victoria, Australia: Ester Csaky, 1997.

Ben Edelman, *Growing up in the Holocaust*. Kansas City, Missouri: privately printed, 1980.

Janina Fischler-Martinho, *Have You Seen My Little Sister?* London: Valentine Mitchell, 1988.

Anne Frank, *Anne Frank, The Diary of a Young Girl*. New York: Doubleday, 1952.

Saul Friedlander, *When Memory Comes*. New York: Farrar, Straus & Giroux, 1979.

Varian Fry, *Surrender on Demand*. New York: Random House, 1945.

Bernard Goldstein, *The Stars Bear Witness*. London: Victor Gollancz, 1950.

Hana Greenfield, *Fragments of Memory: From Kolin to Jerusalem*. Jerusalem, 1990.

Irene Grunbaum (translated and edited by Katherine Morris), *Escape Through the Balkans: The Autobiography of Irene Grunbaum*. Omaha: University of Nebraska Press, 1996.

Henry Armin Herzog, *. . . And Heaven Shed No Tear*. New York: Shengold Publishers, 1996.

Jack Kagan and Dov Cohen, *Surviving the Holocaust with the*

555

Russian Jewish Partisans. London: Vallentine Mitchell, 1998.

Joseph Kagan, *Knight of the Ghetto: The Story of Lord Kagan*. Privately printed. No date.

Jerzy Lando, *Saved By My Face: A True Story of Courage and Escape in War-Torn Poland*. Edinburgh: Mainstream Publishing, 2002.

Isabella Leitner, *Fragments of Isabella: A Memoir of Auschwitz*. New York: Harper & Row, 1978.

Primo Levi, *Survival in Auschwitz: The Nazi Assault on Humanity*. New York: Collier Books, 1961.

Isaac Lewin, *Remember the Days of Old: Historical Essays*. New York: Research Institute of Religious Jewry, 1994.

Cirla Lewis, *Cirla's Story*. London: Minerva Press, 1995.

Rivka Lozansky Bogomolnaya, *Wartime Experiences in Lithuania*. London: Vallentine Mitchell, 2000.

Zivia Lubetkin, *In the Days of Destruction and Revolt*. Kibbutz Lohamei Ha-Gettaot, Israel: Ghetto Fighters' House, 1981.

Julius Madritsch, *Menschen in Not!* ('People in distress!'). Vienna: privately published, 1946; second edition, Vienna, 1962.

Vladka Meed, *On Both Sides of the Wall: Memoirs from the Warsaw Ghetto*. New York: Holocaust Library, 1979.

Beatrice Michman, *Never to be Forgotten: A Young Girl's Holocaust Memoir*. Hoboken, New Jersey: KTAV Publishing House, 1997.

Dr Jozeph Michman (editor), *Righteous Among the Nations Lexicon*, volume 1, *Holland*. Jerusalem: Yad Vashem, 2002.

Felicja Nowak, *My Star: Memoirs of a Holocaust Survivor*. Toronto: Polish Canadian Publishing Fund, 1996.

Irene Gut Opdyke, *In My Hands: Memories of a Holocaust Rescuer*. London: Anchor/Doubleday, 2001.

Anna Porter, *The Storyteller: Memory, Secrets, Magic and Lies*. Toronto: Anchor Canada, 2000.

Leesha Rose, *The Tulips are Red*. New York: A. S. Barnes, 1979.

Donia Rosen, *The Forest My Friend*. New York: Bergen-Belsen Memorial Press, 1971.

Alexander Rotenberg, *Emissaries: a Memoir of the Riviera,*

WORKS CITED

Haute-Savoie, Switzerland and World War II. Secaucus, New Jersey: Citadel Press, 1987.

Joop Schijveschuurder, *My Miracle: Haarlem, 1940–1945.* Jerusalem: privately printed, 2001.

Wiktoria Sliwowska, *The Last Eyewitnesses: Children of the Holocaust Speak.* Evanston, Illinois: Northwestern University Press, 1998.

Jacob Sloan (editor), *Notes from the Warsaw Ghetto: The Journal of Emanuel Ringelblum.* New York: Schocken Books, 1958.

Leo Spritzer, *The Culture of Memory and a Refugee from Nazism.* New York: Hill & Wang, 1998.

Gabor Sztehlo, *In the Hands of God.* Budapest: Gabor Sztehlo Foundation for the Help of Children and Adolescents, 1994 (English-language edition).

Nechama Tec, *Dry Tears: The Story of a Lost Childhood.* New York: Oxford University Press, 1984.

Samuel Lipa Tennenbaum, *Zloczow Memoir.* New York: Shengold Publishers, 1986.

Paul Trepman, *Among Men and Beasts.* London: Thomas Yoseloff, 1978.

Edith Velmans, *Edith's Book: The True Story of How One Girl Survived the War.* London: Viking, 1998.

Rudolf Vrba (with Alan Bestic), *I Cannot Forgive.* London: Sidgwick & Jackson, 1964.

David Wdowinski, *And We Are Not Saved.* London: W. H. Allen, 1964.

Leon Weliczker Wells, *The Death Brigade (The Janowska Road).* New York: Macmillan, 1963.

Elie Wiesel, *Memoirs: All Rivers Run to the Sea.* New York: Alfred A. Knopf, 1995.

Abraham Zuckerman, *A Voice in the Chorus: Memoirs of a Teenager Saved by Schindler.* Stamford, Connecticut: Longmeadow Press, 1991.

Yitzhak Zuckerman ('Antek'), *A Surplus of Memory: Chronicle of the Warsaw Ghetto Uprising*, translated and edited by Barbara Harshav. Berkeley and Los Angeles: University of California Press, 1993.

Michael Zylberberg, *A Warsaw Diary, 1939–1945.* London: Vallentine, Mitchell, 1969.

Reference Books

Israel Gutman (editor in chief), *Encyclopedia of the Holocaust*, four volumes. New York: Macmillan, 1990.

Shmuel Spector (editor in chief), *The Encyclopedia of Jewish Life before and during the Holocaust*, four volumes. New York: New York University Press, 2001.

Encyclopaedia Judaica, 16 volumes. Jerusalem: Keter, 1972.

The Trial of Adolf Eichmann: Record of Proceedings in the District Court of Jerusalem, 5 volumes. Jerusalem: State of Israel, Ministry of Justice, 1994.

Trial of the Major War Criminals before the International Military Tribunal: Official Text, 42 volumes. Nuremberg: Secretariat of the International Military Tribunal, 1947–9.

General Books

Samuel Abrahamsen, *Norway's Response to the Holocaust*. New York: Holocaust Library, 1991.

Reuben Ainsztein, *Jewish Resistance in Nazi-Occupied Eastern Europe: with a historical survey of the Jew as Fighter and Soldier in the Diaspora*. London: Paul Elek, 1974.

Yitzhak Arad, *Ghetto in Flames: The Struggle and Destruction of the Jews of Vilna in the Holocaust*. Jerusalem: Yad Vashem, 1980.

Haim Avni, *Spain, the Jews, and Franco*. Philadelphia: Jewish Publication Society of America, 1982.

Yehuda Bauer, *American Jewry and the Holocaust: The American Jewish Joint Distribution Committee, 1929–1945*. Jerusalem: Institute of Contemporary Jewry, Hebrew University; Detroit: Wayne State University Press, 1981.

Yehuda Bauer, *The Holocaust in Historical Perspective*. Seattle: University of Washington Press, 1978.

John Bierman, *Righteous Gentile: The Story of Raoul Wallenberg, Missing Hero of the Holocaust*. New York: Viking Press, 1981.

Leslie Blau, *Bonyhad: A Destroyed Community: The Jews of Bonyhad, Hungary*. New York: Shengold Publishers, 1994.

Randolph L. Braham, *The Politics of Genocide: the Holocaust in Hungary*, two volumes. New York: Columbia University Press, 1981.

Daniel Carpi, *Between Mussolini and Hitler: The Jews and the Italian Authorities in France and Tunisia*. Hanover, New Hampshire: University Press of New England, 1994.

Daniel Carpi (editor), *Italian Diplomatic Documents on the History of the Holocaust in Greece (1941–1943)*. Tel Aviv: Diaspora Research Institute, 1999.

Szymon Datner, *Walka i Zaglada Bialystockiego Ghetta*. Lodz: Central Jewish Historical Commission, 1946.

Lucjan Dobroszycki, *Survivors of the Holocaust in Poland: A Portrait Based on Jewish Community Records, 1944–1947*. Armonk, New York: M. E. Sharpe, 1994.

Deborah Dwork, *Children With A Star: Jewish Youth in Nazi Europe*. New Haven: Yale University Press, 1991.

Ilya Ehrenburg and Vasily Grossman (translated and edited by David Patterson), *The Complete Black Book of Russian Jewry*. New Brunswick, New Jersey: Transaction Publishers, 2002.

Yaffa Eliach, *Hasidic Tales of the Holocaust*. New York: Oxford University Press, 1982.

Yaffa Eliach, *There Once Was a World: A Nine-Hundred-Year Chronicle of the Shtetl of Eishyshok*. Boston: Little, Brown and Co., 1998.

Philip Friedman, *Roads to Extinction: Essays on the Holocaust*. Philadelphia: Jewish Publication Society of America, 1980.

Kinga Frojimovics, Geza Komoroczy, Viktoria Pusztai and Andrea Strbik, *Jewish Budapest: Monuments, Rites, History*. Budapest: Central European University Press, 1999.

Martin Gilbert, *The Day the War Ended: VE-day 1945 in Europe and Around the World*. London: HarperCollins, 1995.

Martin Gilbert, *The Boys: Triumph over Adversity*. London: Weidenfeld & Nicolson, 1996.

Martin Gilbert, *Holocaust Journey: Travelling in Search of the Past*. London: Weidenfeld & Nicolson, 1997.

Jan Tomasz Gross, *Neighbours: The Destruction of the Jewish Community in Jedwabne*. Princeton, New Jersey: Princeton University Press, 2001.

Ruth Gruber, *Haven: The Unknown Story of 1,000 World War II Refugees*. New York: Coward-McCann, 1983.

Yisrael Gutman, *The Jews of Warsaw, 1939–1943: Ghetto, Underground, Revolt*. Bloomington, Indiana: Indiana University Press, 1982.

Suzan E. Hagstrom, *Sara's Children: The Destruction of Chmielnik*. Spotsylvania, Virginia: Sergeant Kirkland's Press, 2001.

Gideon Hausner, *Justice in Jerusalem*. New York: Harper & Row Publishers, 1966.

Julien Hirshaut, *Jewish Martyrs of Pawiak*. New York: Holocaust Library, 1982.

Henry R. Huttenbach, *The Destruction of the Jewish Community of Worms, 1933–1945: A Study of the Holocaust Experience in Germany*. New York: Memorial Committee of Jewish Victims of Nazism from Worms, 1981.

Joseph Kermish and Shmuel Krakowski (editors), *Emanuel Ringelblum: Polish–Jewish Relations during the Second World War*. Jerusalem: Yad Vashem, 1974.

Serge Klarsfeld, *Memorial to the Jews Deported from France*. Paris: Beate Klarsfeld Foundation, 1981.

Jack Kugelmass and Jonathan Boyarin (translators and editors), *From a Ruined Garden: The Memorial Books of Polish Jewry*. New York: Schocken Books, 1983.

Andrzej Krzysztof Kunert (editor), *Poles–Jews, 1939–1945*. Warsaw: Rada Ochrony Pamieci Walk i Meczenstwa (Council for the Protection of Memory, Fighting and Martyrdom), 2001.

Eugene Levai, *Black Book on the Martydom of Hungarian Jewry*. Zurich: Central European Times Publishing Company, 1948.

Jeno Levai (editor), *Hungarian Jewry and the Papacy: Pope Pius XII did not remain silent*. Dublin: Clonmore & Reynolds, 1969.

Nora Levin, *The Holocaust: The Destruction of European Jewry, 1933–1945.* New York: Schocken Books, 1968.

Louis P. Lochner (editor), *The Goebbels Diaries.* London: Hamish Hamilton, 1948.

Alexander Matkovski, *A History of the Jews in Macedonia.* Skopje: Macedonian Review Editions, 1982.

Joseph Matsas, *The Participation of the Greek Jews in the National Resistance (1940–1944).* Janina, Greece, 1982. (Text of a lecture delivered in Athens on 2 October 1982 and in Salonika on 6 December 1982).

Joseph A. Melamed (editor), *Lithuania: The Land of Blood.* Tel Aviv: Association of Lithuanian Jews, April 2000.

Odette Meyers, *Doors to Madame Marie.* Seattle: University of Washington Press, 1997.

Meir Michaelis, *Mussolini and the Jews: German–Italian Relations and the Jewish Question in Italy, 1922–1945.* Oxford: Clarendon Press, 1978.

John F. Morley, *Vatican Diplomacy and the Jews during the Holocaust, 1939–1943.* New York: KTAV Publishing House, 1980.

Stephen Cameron Jalil Nicholls, *Jewish Life in Pomerania.* Burgess Hill, Sussex: privately printed, 2002.

Adam Nossiter, *The Algeria Hotel: France, Memory and the Second World War.* London: Methuen, 2001.

Dalia Ofer and Lenore J. Weitzman (editors), *Women in the Holocaust.* New Haven, Connecticut: Yale University Press, 1998.

Ingrid Palmklint and Daniel Larsson (editorial group), *Raoul Wallenberg: Report of the Swedish-Russian Working Group.* Stockhom: Swedish Ministry for Foreign Affairs, Department for Central and Eastern Europe, 2000.

Yitzhak Parlan (editor), *Sefer Skierniewic* (Memorial Book). Tel Aviv: Organization of the Survivors of Skierniewic, 1955. (In Hebrew).

Jacob Presser, *Ashes in the Wind: The Destruction of Dutch Jewry.* Detroit: Wayne State University Press, 1998.

Martin Randanne and Marc-Alexis Roquejoffre, *Monsignor Piguet, un évêque discuté.* Clermont-Ferrand: privately printed, 2000.

Shmuel Spector, *The Holocaust of Volhynian Jews,*

561

1941–1944. Jerusalem: Yad Vashem/The Federation of Volhynian Jews, 1990.

André Stein, *Hidden Children: Forgotten Survivors of the Holocaust.* New York: Viking, 1993.

Lucien Steinberg, *Le Comité de Défense des Juifs en Belgique, 1942–1944.* Brussels: Editions de l'Université de Bruxelles, 1973.

Nathan Stoltzfus, *Resistance of the Heart: Intermarriage and the Rosenstrasse Protest in Nazi Germany.* New York: W. W. Norton, 1996.

Paul Valent, *Child Survivors of the Holocaust.* London: Brunner-Routledge, 1993.

Susan Zuccotti, *The Italians and the Holocaust: Persecution, Rescue and Survival.* New York: Basic Books, 1987.

Published Articles (by author)

Zvi Bacharach, 'Lichtenberg, Bernhard (1875–1943)', *Encyclopedia of the Holocaust* (editor in chief Israel Gutman), volume 3, p. 868.

Lili Bat Aharon, 'Forgotten life-savers on German TV', *Jerusalem Post*, 10 September 1973.

Moshe Bejski, 'Oskar Schindler and Schindler's List', *Yad Vashem Studies* (Jerusalem), volume 24, 1994.

Joseph Berger, 'A Monk, a Saviour, a Mensch: Nine Jews Gather in New Jersey to Remember the Man Who Rescued Them From the Nazis', *New York Times*, 5 July 1992. (On Father Bruno Reynders.)

Shyam Bhatia, 'My Saviours in the Holocaust', *Observer*, 14 September 1997. (On Cirla Lewis.)

Gilbert Blum, 'De vrais amis': *Mémoire Vive*, March 2002.

Grace Bradberry, 'Surrey's own Oskar Schindler', *The Times*, 1 March 1999. (On Henk Huffener.)

Henry Walter Brann, 'Pastor who rescued Jews is Honoured', *Jewish Week* (Washington DC), 20 August 1970. (On Pastor Grüber.)

Desmond Brown, 'Israel honours two Toronto war heroes', *National Post*, 9 February 1999. (On Jan Schoumans and Sandor Tonelli.)

Rudolph Chelminski, 'A Debt Repaid', *Reader's Digest*, September 2000. (On a Muslim rescuer.)

Jonathan Curiel, 'Maria Paasche, Daughter of German General Who Helped Jews Escape Nazis' (obituary), *San Francisco Chronicle*, 5 February 2000.

Dr Rachel Dalven, 'The Holocaust in Janina', in Solomon Gaon and M. Mitchell Serels (editors), *Sephardim and the Holocaust*. New York: Jacob E. Safra Institute of Sephardic Studies, Yeshiva University, 1987.

Douglas Davis, 'Quiet saviour on the island of Jersey', *Jerusalem Post*, 30 January 2000.

William H. Donat, 'Could I Still Be a Little Catholic Deep Inside?', *The Hidden Child* (newsletter), Fall/Winter 1997.

David Eppel, 'Key to righteousness', *Jewish Chronicle*, 28 July 2000.

Liliana Picciotto Fargion, 'Note biografiche dei decorati con medaglia d'oro', in Giuliana Donati, *Persecuzione e Deportazione degli Ebrei dall'Italia durante la Dominazione Nazifascista*. Milan: La Giuntina, 1975.

Joseph Finklestone, 'Pope and Jewish child', *Jewish Chronicle*, 28 May 1982.

John Follain, 'Village hid Jews from Nazis', *Sunday Times*, 18 January 2001. (On Nonantola, Italy.)

Pal Foti (Paul Friedlaender), 'The survivor's tale: 50 years ago the Holocaust reached Hungary', *AJR Information* (published by the Association of Jewish Refugees in Great Britain), April 1994.

Frank Fox, 'A Skeleton in Poland's Closet: The Jedwabne Massacre', *East European Jewish Affairs*, volume 31, number 1, 2000.

Frank Fox, 'Endangered Species: Jews and Buffaloes, Victims of Nazi Pseudo-science', *East European Jewish Affairs*, volume 31, number 2, 2001. (On the Warsaw Zoo.)

Ya'akov Friedler, 'Nazi spirit not dead in Germany, rescuer of Polish Jews says', *Jerusalem Post*, 21 October 1969. (On Otto Busse.)

Si Frumkin, editorial, *Graffiti for Intellectuals* (magazine, Los Angeles), 3 July 2000.

John and Carol Garrard, 'Barbarossa's First Victims, The Jews of Brest', *East European Jewish Affairs*, volume 28, number 2, 1998–9.

Karen Glaser, 'Wartime heroics of Dutch woman are recognized', *Jewish Chronicle*, 21 July 2000. (On Elizabeth Browne.)

Jeffrey Goldberg, 'Latvia's Empty Gesture', *Forward*, 27 February 1998.

Ruby Gonzales, 'Recognition sought for man who defied Nazis', *San Gabriel Valley Tribune*, 13 May 2001. (On Karl Plagge.)

Ruth Gruber, 'Wartime bravery of nuns recognized by Yad Vashem', *Jewish Chronicle*, 13 March 1999.

Katia Gusarov, 'Valentina and Valik, Rescued from the Wreckage', *Yad Vashem Quarterly Magazine* (Jerusalem), volume 25, Winter 2002.

Roman Halter, 'Before and after', *Journal of the '45 Aid Society*, number 18, December 1994.

Rena Hass, 'This Is How It Is', *The Hidden Child*, volume 10, number 1, Summer 2001.

Zula Hass, 'This Is How It Was', *The Hidden Child*, volume 10, number 1, Summer 2001.

Roberta Hershenson, 'Dutch Rescuer to Give Talk', *New York Times*, 26 March 1995. (On Dr Tina Strobos.)

Terry Hokenson, 'Sabina Zimering gets students' undivided attention', *The Voice of Piotrkow Survivors*, magazine (edited by Ben Giladi), number 24 (123), October–November 2001.

Philip Jacobson, 'Rusty bike shipped to Israel to honour wartime heroine', *Sunday Telegraph*, 25 March 2001. (On Marie-Rose Gineste.)

Sharon Jaffa, 'Saved by the kindness of others', *London Jewish News*, 8 June 2001.

Louis de Jong, 'Jews and Non-Jews in Nazi-Occupied Holland', in Max Beloff (editor), *On the Track of Tyranny: Essays Presented by the Wiener Library to Leonard G. Montefiore, OBE, on the Occasion of his Seventieth Birthday*. London: Vallentine, Mitchell, 1960.

Dovid Katz, '"Radin's last Jew" recalls Nazi and Soviet Horrors', *Jewish Chronicle*, 7 November 1997.

Richard Kay, 'Revealed: secret heroism of Prince Philip's mother', *Daily Mail*, 26 July 1993.

Sam Kiley, 'Secret witness tells of Nazis' boasts', *The Times*, 3 January 2000. (On Yanis Vabulis.)

Bronka Klibanski, 'In the Ghetto and in the Resistance: A Personal Narrative', in Dalia Ofer and Lenore J. Weitzman (editors), *Women in the Holocaust*. New Haven, Connecticut: Yale University Press, 1998.

Mary Stewart Krosney, 'Gallant Christian Honoured on Remembrance Hill', press release, Holyland Features, Christian News from Israel, August 1980. (On Raoul Laporterie.)

Simon Kuper, 'Tarnished glory', *Jewish Chronicle*, 23 February 2001. (On Holland.)

Ephraim Lahav, 'German friend settles in Israel', *Jewish Observer and Middle East Review*, 24 April 1970. (On Otto Busse.)

Egon Larsen, 'Resistance in Nazi Germany', Association of Jewish Refugees from Germany, *Information* (bulletin), volume 36, number 1, January 1981.

Etgar Lefkovits, 'A lifetime friend comes to visit', *Jerusalem Post*, 30 November 2000. (On Wladyslaw Bartoszewski, then Polish Foreign Minister.)

Masha Leon, *Forward*, 14 July 2000. (On Adolf Althoff.)

Benjamin E. Lesin, 'Lithuania, the Evil and the Righteous', *Los Angeles Jewish Times*, 2 August 1996.

Isidor Levin, 'Uku Masing (11.8.1909–25.4.1985)', *Ural-Altaic Yearbook*, number 59, 1987.

Allan Levine, 'A boy's gripping story of survival in wartime Warsaw', *National Post* (Toronto), 23 September 2000. (On Jack Kajman.)

Dr S. Margoshes, 'Dr Felix Kanabus, Rescuer of Polish Jews, His Deeds of Heroism, Welcome!' *News and Views* (New York), 7 September 1965.

Elisabeth Maxwell, 'The Righteous Gentiles', *European Judaism*, volume 90, number 2. Oxford: Pergamon Press, 1990.

Elisabeth Maxwell, 'The Rescue of Jews in France and Belgium During the Holocaust', *Journal of Holocaust Education*, Summer/Autumn 1998.

Susan Meadows (publisher), *Spotlight* (magazine), March 1995.

S. T. Merhavi, 'Earthbound angel', *Jerusalem Post*, 10 November 1978. (On Father Niccaci.)

Ernie Meyer, 'Saying "thanks" to Denmark', *Jerusalem Post*, 7 February 1973.

Ernie Meyer, 'German officer – and gentleman', *Jerusalem Post*, 26 April 1982. (On Alfred Battel.)

Ernie Meyer, '"Italian Wallenberg" to be honoured for saving Jews', *Jerusalem Post*, 22 September 1989. (On Giorgio Perlasca.)

Odette Meyers, 'A Long-Delayed Public Thank You to Chavagnes-en-Paillers', *The Hidden Child*, volume 9, number 1, Spring 2000.

Beatrice Michman, 'Never to be Forgotten: A Young Girl's Holocaust Memoir', *Imprimis, Because Ideas Have Consequences*, volume 28, number 4, April 1999.

Jozeph Michman, 'Westerweel, Joop (1899–1944)' in *Encyclopedia of the Holocaust*, volume 4, p. 1648.

Sam Modiano, 'Island's Jews saved by Greek Archbishop', *Jewish Chronicle*, 3 November 1978. (On Zante.)

Keith Morgan, 'Hidden from the Holocaust', *Province* (Vancouver), 24–27 October 2000.

Samuel P. Oliner, untitled article, *The Month* (magazine, London), January 1994.

Rob O'Neil, 'Helping Hand for Old Heroes of Holocaust', *Los Angeles Times*, 1 August 1996.

Wila Orbach, 'The Destruction of the Jews in the Nazi-Occupied Territories of the USSR', *Soviet Jewish Affairs*, volume 6, number 2, 1976. London: Institute of Jewish Affairs.

Nissan Oren, 'The Bulgarian Exception: a Reassessment of the Salvation of the Jewish Community', *Yad Vashem Studies* (Jerusalem), volume 7, 1968.

Anna Ostrowiak, 'Soldier showed mercy amid brutality', *Miami Herald*, 25 December 1999.

Gottfried Paasche, interview in *Maclean's* (magazine, Toronto), 28 February 2000.

Mordecai Paldiel, 'Getter, Matylda (d. 1968), in *Encyclopedia of the Holocaust*, volume 2, pp. 578–9.

Mordecai Paldiel, 'Helmrich, Eberhard', in *Encyclopedia of the Holocaust*, volume 2, p. 654.

Mordecai Paldiel, 'Kowalski, Wladyslaw (1895–1971)', in *Encyclopedia of the Holocaust*, volume 2, pp. 828–99.

Mordecai Paldiel, 'Overduijn, Leendert (1901–1976)', in *Encyclopedia of the Holocaust*, volume 3, p. 1100.

Mordecai Paldiel, 'Schindler, Oskar (1908–1974)', in *Encyclopedia of the Holocaust*, volume 4, pp. 1331–2.

Mordecai Paldiel, 'Schmid, Anton (1900–1942)', in *Encyclopedia of the Holocaust*, volume 4, p. 1333.

Mordecai Paldiel, 'Simaite, Ona (1899–1970), in *Encyclopedia of the Holocaust*, volume 4, p. 1358.

Mordecai Paldiel, 'Skobtsova, Elizaveta (Mother Maria; 1891–1945), in *Encyclopedia of the Holocaust*, volume 4, pp. 1362–3.

Mordecai Paldiel, 'Zabinski, Jan (b. 1897)', in *Encyclopedia of the Holocaust*, volume 4, pp. 1723–4.

Mordecai Paldiel, 'Is goodness a mystery?', *Jerusalem Post*, 8 October 1989.

Mordecai Paldiel, 'The Rescue of Jewish Children in Belgium During World War II', in Dan Michman (editor), *Belgium and the Holocaust: Jews, Belgians, Germans*. Jerusalem: Yad Vashem, 1998.

Mordecai Paldiel, 'A Last Letter and a Precious "Bundle"', *Yad Vashem*, volume 26, Spring 2002.

Jolanta Paskeviciene, 'Childhood is not a dream', *Lithuania in the World* (magazine, Kaunas), 2001.

Elizabeth Petuchowski, 'Gertrud Luckner: Resistance and Assistance. A German Woman who Defied Nazis and Aided Jews', in *Ministers of Compassion During the Nazi Period*. South Orange, New Jersey: Institute of Judaeo-Christian Studies, Seton Hall University, 1999.

Marianne Picard, 'Il fut le seul . . .', *Mémoire Vive*, March 2002.

Michael Posner, 'O brother, where art thou?' *Globe and Mail* (Toronto), 30 December 2000.

David Preston, 'Horrors of Nazis recalled', *Columbia Missourian*, 23 April 1978.

Joe Quinn, 'Honour for Scots Holocaust heroine', *Express*, 23 November 1997. (On Jane Haining.)

Walter Reed, 'Children Protected by Swiss Red Cross', *Aufbau*

(German Jewish refugee newspaper, New York City), 21 September 1999.

Alan Riding, 'Jews Found Haven in French Town', *New York Times*, 31 October 1999. (On Le Chambon-sur-Lignon.)

Rose Kfar Rose, 'Reuniting With My Family (1945–1948), 'The Hidden Child, volume 10, number 1, Summer 2001.

Pierre Sauvage, '"Weapons of the Spirit": A Journey Home', *Hollywood Reporter*, 17 March 1987.

Steve Schloss, 'Reader remembers: Holocaust victim is surprised as rescuers are honoured in Jerusalem', *The Jewish Week*, New York, 27 August 1982. (On Lorraine Justman-Wisnicki.)

Peter Schneider, 'The Good Germans', *New York Times Magazine*, 13 February 2000.

Cecile Seiden, 'In Honour of My Righteous Rescuers', New Jersey Holocaust Curriculum, 'To Honour All Children: From Prejudice, to Discrimination, to Hatred . . . to Holocaust'. Trenton, New Jersey: no date.

Somini Sengupta, 'Tearful Renunion for Friends who Defied the Nazis', *New York Times*, 28 November 1997.

Eda Shapiro (editor), 'The Memoirs of Victor Kugler, the "Mr Kraler" of the "Diary of Anne Frank"', *Yad Vashem Studies* (Jerusalem), volume 13, 1979.

Avi Sharon, 'A Youth in Hiding', *The Greek American*, 29 November 1997. (On Pepos Levis.)

Benek (Baruch) Sharoni, 'Man's Humanity to Man', *Mizkor* (the newsletter of the Centre of Organizations of Holocaust Survivors in Israel), number 11, October 2000.

Barbara Sofer, 'An angel named Maria', *Jerusalem Post*, 2 February 2001. (On Maria Nickel.)

Shmuel Spector, 'Graebe, Hermann Friedrich (1900–1986)', *Encyclopedia of the Holocaust*, vol. 2, pp. 599–600.

Denis Staunton, 'In defiance of fascism' (obituary of Countess von Maltzan), *Guardian*, 18 November 1997.

Maxine Steinberg, 'The Trap of Legality: the Association of the Jews of Belgium', in *Patterns of Jewish Leadership*, in *Nazi Europe, 1933–1945*, proceedings of the third Yad Vashem International Historical Conference, 1–7 April 1977. Jerusalem: Yad Vashem, 1979.

Judy Stone, 'French Hero Who Saved 5,000 Jews From the

Nazis', *Sunday Examiner and Chronicle* (San Francisco), 19 July 1987. (On a German officer.)

Dr Tina Strobos, interview, *Gannett Suburban Newspaper*, 5 March 1992.

Nehama Tec, 'A Glimmer of Light', in Carol Rittner, Stephen D. Smith and Irena Steinfeldt (editors), *The Holocaust and the Christian World*. Beth Shalom Holocaust Memorial Center in conjunction with Yad Vashem. London: Kuperard, 2000.

Batsheva Tsur, 'Sarajevo family finds refuge with Israelis they Saved in WWII', *Jerusalem Post*, 13 February 1994.

Tom Tugend, 'French village honours "hidden child" survivor of Holocaust', *Jewish Chronicle*, 24 November 2000.

Alexandra Tuttle, 'Marking a Blessed Conspiracy', *Time* (magazine), 5 November 1990.

Rudi Vis, letter to the *Jewish Chronicle*, 25 May 2001.

Shewach Weiss, 'A 700-day nightmare', *Jerusalem Post*, 8 April 1983.

Leni Yahil, 'Denmark', in *Encyclopedia of the Holocaust*, volume 1, p. 364.

Ruth Zariz, 'Luxembourg', in *Encyclopedia of the Holocaust*, volume 3, p. 928.

Alexander Zvielli, 'The price of courage', *Jerusalem Post*, 2 March 1979 (reviewing Leesha Rose, *The Tulips are Red*).

Published Articles (no author given)

'200 Jews Owe Life to Belgian Priest', *New York Times*, 28 December 1945.

Associated Press, obituary of Cardinal Palazzini, *Globe and Mail* (Toronto), 16 October 2000.

'Eger', in *The Encyclopedia of Jewish Life Before and During the Holocaust*, volume 1, A–J, p. 355.

'French bishop honoured for Holocaust action', *Jerusalem Post*, 25 June 2001. (On Bishop Piguet.)

Haggadah Supplement. New York: Jewish Foundation for the Righteous, 2001.

'Hungarian hero fought Nazis, Soviet', Associated Press

obituary, *Globe and Mail* (Toronto), 5 March 2001. (On Sandor Kopacsi.)

'Ida Peterfy, Nun Who Helped Save Jews, 77', obituary, *Jerusalem Post*, 18 February 2000.

Interview with Jerzy Kisson-Jaszczinski, *Voice of Piotrkow Survivors* (magazine), number 5, September–October 1997.

'Looking For . . .', *The Hidden Child*, volume 9, number 1, Spring 2000.

Maariv (newspaper), Youth Supplement (Tel Aviv), Holocaust Remembrance Day, 1996.

New York Times, 'US Soldier Finds Father in Holland', 3 June 1945.

'Parczew District, Bialka', *Scenes of Fighting and Martyrdom Guide*. Warsaw: Interpress, 1978.

'Postscripts', *Jerusalem Post*, 17 January 1977.

'Rijeka' (Italian 'Fiume'), *Encyclopedia Judaica* (Jerusalem, 1972), volume 14, column 185.

'Saved by the corpse on top of me', *Hampstead and Highgate Express*, 26 March 1993. (On Rosa Lipworth.)

'US Soldier Finds Father in Holland', *New York Times*, 3 June 1945.

'Yad Vashem honour for Dutch couple', *Jerusalem Post*, 3 February 1978. (On Dr and Mrs Brillenburg-Wurth.)

Unpublished Manuscripts

Walter Absil, 'Miracle at Avenue Louise'.

Lorraine Beitler, 'Lucie Dreyfus, the Sisters of the Good Shepherd, and the Holocaust'.

Jack Brauns, 'Memoirs'.

Professor Amos Dreyfus, 'A Young Widow with Three Children'.

Pearl Good, 'Life Story of Perela Esterowicz – Pearl Good'.

International Catholic–Jewish Historical Commission, 'The Vatican and the Holocaust: A Preliminary Report', October 2000.

Margaret Kagan (Lady Kagan), recollections.

Luisa Naor, 'Italian Jews at Risk during WWII'.

Robin O'Neil, 'The Belzec Death Camp and the Origins of

Jewish Genocide in Galicia', doctoral thesis, University College, London, Department of Hebrew and Jewish Studies, London, 2002.

Shimon Redlich, 'Together and Apart in Brzezany: Poles, Jews and Ukrainians, 1919–1945'.

Michel Reynders, 'Father Bruno (Henry Reynders), His Life, His Work, Biography of a Righteous'.

Ursula Korn Selig, 'My name is Ursula Korn Selig . . .'.

'Testimonianze dell'Olocausto: Documentary Evidence of the Holocaust', Italian Immigrants Association, Israel, factsheet.

'Testimony of Ad Vitale'.

'Translation of Transcript of the Denazification File of Karl Plagge' (testimonies of Major Plagge's German employees), State Archive, Hesse.

Joseph Wisnicki, 'My Fight for Survival'.

Marina Löwi Zinn, 'To Whom It May Concern: Material Submitted to Yad Vashem'.

Exhibitions

'No Child's Play: Children in the Holocaust – Creativity and Play', Yad Vashem, Jerusalem, opened 13 October 1997.

'Visas for Life', Eric Saul, travelling exhibition, 2000–.

Index

579

Blum, Gilbert: saved, 327 n.13

Bobolice (Poland):   rescue in, 143–4

Bobowa (Poland):   a young Jewish boy from, finds refuge, 228

Bobrovski family: help Jews, 43–4

Bochnia (Poland):   Council for Assistance to the Jews in, 186; a Jewish family hidden near, 224–5; a factory in, gives shelter to Jews, 277

Bodart family (Belgium):   shelters Jews, 381

Boden, Arnold: helps a Jewish girl, 258–9

Bodson, Victor: his acts of rescue, 390

Boegner, Pastor Marc: issues clear instructions for rescue, 375

Bogaard, Johannes: a rescuer, 395; with two Jewish girls, Photo 30

Bogaard, Willem: saves twenty children, 395; with two Jewish girls, Photo 30

Bogarde, Dirk: plays a Righteous British sergeant, 509 n.29

Bogomolnaya, Rivka Lozanska: in hiding, 127–8

Boguty Milczi (Poland):   Jews hidden in, 146 n 14

Bohemia (Czechoslovakia):   three Jews given shelter in, 288

Bohemian Brothers: a preacher in the church of, 289

Bohic, Pauline: a rescuer, 357

Bohny, August: shelters Jews, 336

Bohr, Niels: saved, 319–20; his biographer, rescued in Holland, 405

Boinski (a farmer):   helps Jews, 43

Bole (a German):   his Jewish wife

helped, 265; in an anti-Nazi cell, 265

Bolzano (Italy):   a deportation from, 446

Bonhomme, Juliette: hides a Jewish mother and her three sons, 343, 345

Bonyhad (Hungary):   a gesture of sympathy in, 461–2; help during a Death March through, 511

Boom (Belgium):   rescuers in, 371

'Borek':   an assumed surname, 102

Boris, King (of Bulgaria):   church men protest to, 307, 309; the effect of public protests on, 524

Borki (Poland):   a Polish priest helps a survivor of revolt at, 505

Bormann, Martin: ordered to make an arrest, 262

Born, Friedrich (a Swiss citizen):   his rescue efforts in Budapest, 471, 477; Photo 52

Bornstein, Hassia: helped by a German, 266–7

Borowczyk (a shoemaker):   helps a Jew, 151

'Borowska':   a name in hiding, 89

Boryslaw (Eastern Galicia):   rescuers and rescued in, 97–8

Borzykowski, Chana and Benjamin: deported, 374–5

Borzykowski, Jacky: in hiding, 374; with his parents before going into hiding, Photo 15

Borzykowski, Tuvia: and some of the 'finest personalities of the Polish people', 190; given shelter, 199

Bosko, Oswald: a Viennese, helps Jews in Cracow, 276–7; executed, 277

Bosnia: Jews saved in, 11, 296

THE RIGHTEOUS

Brussels (Belgium): refugees from, find sanctuary in France, 350; help to Jews in, 362, 373–4, 380, 381, 382; a rescuer in, honoured after liberation, 385; Dutch Jews smuggled through, 413, 414

Brygier, Lucy: in hiding, Photo 22

Brygier, Sarah: in hiding, Photo 22

Brzezany (Eastern Galicia): Jews from, find a safe haven, 95, 104–7

Brzuchowice (Eastern Galicia): and a Jewish boy in hiding, 68

Bucharest (Romania): a protest to, 299

Buchenwald concentration camp: the husband of a Righteous German dies in, 374; Jews deported to, 392; a Dutch rescuer imprisoned in, 415

Buchter, Marie: hides Jews, in Holland, 404–6

Buchter, Tina (Dr Tina Strobos): hides Jews, in Holland, 404–6; with one of those in hiding, Photo 26

Budapest (Hungary): a boy and his parents in hiding in, 407 n.31; Eichmann and his SS Commando reach, 461; Eichmann turns his attention to, 466–7; acts of rescue in, 466–7; a 'gentile woman' from, helps Jewish fellow-prisoners in Auschwitz, 506; motivation of a rescuer in, 521

Budishevskaya, Floriya: saves a Jewish boy, 47

Budnowska, Sister Tekla: hides Jewish girls, 89

Budrikene, Lusia: a rescuer, 111

Budzanow (Eastern Galicia): a Jewish family saved in, 88

Bug River: flight towards, after betrayal, 149; a Pole helps Jewish escapees at, 504

Buggenhout, Clementine and Edouard Frans: Belgian rescuers, 378

Buggenhout (Belgium): a Jewish child in hiding in, 375

Bukovina: Jews from, find refuge, 53; Jews of, find a champion, 298–9

Bukovinsky (a priest): encourages an act of rescue, 37

Bulgaria: Jews of, saved from deportation, 306–9, 523

Bulgarian Orthodox Church: takes a lead, 308–9

Buna-Monowitz (East Upper Silesia): a courageous British sergeant at, 508–9

Bund, the (Jewish Social Democratic Workers Party): and 'Aryan' Warsaw, 196; a leader of, in hiding, 206

Bunel, Lucien-Louis (Père Jacques of Jesus): see Père Jacques

Burdzynski (a Pole): helps Jews, 30

Burlingis, Pawel and Wiktoria: save a Jewish baby girl, 118

Burzec (Poland): betrayal at, 169

Busold, Stanislawa: saves a new-born Jewish child, 197

Busse, Otto: helps Jews, 266–7; reflects on his 'Christian conscience', 526

Bussum (Holland): two Jewish couples given refuge in, 398

Butrin, Adam: hides Jews, 166

Buzhminsky, Yosef: witnesses the execution of rescuers, 230

Byelorussia: acts of rescue in, 45–52

582

INDEX

Byelorussians: help Jews, 43–5; help Germans, 49

Cabaj, Jan: saves a Jewish girl, 210
Cabaj, Stanislawa: shelters two Jewish girls, 146–7
California (USA): a Righteous German settles in, 275
Calmeyer, Hans-Georg: helps Jews, 267–70
'Calmeyer's List': Jews on, saved from deportation, 269
Calvinists: save Jews, 395, 397, 463
'Camp of the Ants': Jewish children find refuge at, 348
Canada: 'Visas for Life' exhibition in, 26 n.1; survivors in, 111
Canadian soldiers: liberators, 430
Canale d'Alba (Italy): Jews in hiding in, 451–2
Canaris, Admiral Wilhelm: helps Jews leave Germany, 236
Capuchin Banneux homes (Belgium): shelter Jews, 382
Capuchin convent (Rome): help for Jews in, 441–2
Carcassonne (France): a rescuer in, 343
Carl Fredriksen Transport Organization: helps Jews escape, 314
Carmelites: and the rescue of Jews, 354, 374
Carpathian Mountains: a worker from, helps a Jew, 88
Cassulo, Archbishop Andrea: appeals, in vain, 299
Castle Hill (Budapest): and a Righteous pastor, 480
Castle, John: his book about a Righteous British soldier, 509 n.29

Catholic Front for the Reborn Poland: its head, leads rescue efforts, 184
Catholic League for Religious and Civil Rights (USA): and a wartime papal injunction, 437 n.10
Catholic University of Lublin: a Polish rescuer at, 190 n.28
Cavilio, Josef: sheltered, with his family, 296
Celiny (Poland): a rescuer in, 164
Centnerszwer, Professor Mieczyslaw: sheltered, denounced, executed, 205
Ceresole d'Alba (Italy): a safe haven, 453
Chameides, Leon: in hiding, 67–9; seeks recognition for a rescuer, 72
Chameides, Zwi (later Zwi Barnea): in hiding, 67–71
Chamonix (France): Jewish children saved in, 347
Champagnat Institute of the Order of St Mary (Budapest): rescue efforts by, 472
Champagne, Gaston and Josephine: provide refuge, 366
Channel Islands: an act of rescue in, 359–60
Charaszkiewicz, Maria: saves her Jewish dentist, 77–9; further Righteous acts by, 172–3
Charaszkiewicz, Mr: and a Jewess in hiding, 77–9
Charité (Budapest): nuns of, hide eleven Jews, 473
Château de la Guette (near Paris): Jewish children hidden in, 326
Château de La Hille (France): Jews find refuge at, 350–2
Château Lafayette (France): Jews find refuge at, 339

601

Laurentius, Dr: a 'righteous man',
506
Laurysiewicz, Stefania: protects
three Jews, 173–4
Lavorishkes (Lithuania): an act of
rescue in, 136
Laxander, Walenty: saves a
Jewish child, 76–7
Lazanowski family: rescue three
Jews, 86
Lazareanu, Barbu: seeks help,
300
Lazdijai (Lithuania): a Jewish girl
saved in, 122
Laznik, Esther Rachel: saved,
159–60, 161–2
Laznik, Heinich: his daughter's
rescue, 159; finds his daughter
after the war, 162
Le Chambon-sur-Lignon
(France): Jews in hiding at,
334–8, 340; a rescuer with some
of her 'children' at, Photo 33
Le Coteau Fleuri (France): a
refugee home, 338
Le Henaff, Germaine: hides
Jewish children, 326
Le Jeune, Jeanne: hides a Jewish
boy, 362–3
Le Puy (France): a rescuer
arrested in, 337
Le Vernet (France): internment
camp at, 350
Lederman, Annette and
Margot: in hiding, 378–9;
Photo 17
Leenhardt, Dr Adolf: a Viennese,
helps Jews in Poland, 277; and
a rescue stratagem, 278
Lefèvre family: shelter a Jewish
boy, 340 n.41
Leffe, Home of (Belgium): Jews
given refuge in, 382
Leforestier, Dr Roger and
Danielle: help Jews, 337;
together, Photo 34

Lehr, General Alexander
von: fails to get Italian help,
439–40
Lehrer (a lawyer): saved, 90 n.30
Lientje (a Jewish girl): with her
rescuer, Photo 25
Leitner, Isabella: recalls a 'gentile
woman' in Auschwitz, who
helped Jews, 506
Lemecki, Mr: thanks Hitler, but
saves Jews, 100–1
Lemensorf, Leopold: helped by
an Austrian, 280
Leningrad (Russia): German drive
to, 56
Lentink-de-Boer, Eelkje: a Dutch
rescuer, 399–400
Lepin le Lac (France): a journey
to safety through, 342
Lepkifker, Grand Rabbi (of
Liège): given refuge, 382
'Leroy': an assumed surname,
342
Lesin, Benjamin: relates a story of
rescue and murder, 138–9; and
the 'modesty' of rescuers, 524–5
Lesko (Poland): rescuers in, 156
Lesterps (France): an act of
rescue at, 358
Levai, Eugene: lists Christian
rescuers in Budapest, 472–3
Levi family (from
Genoa): protected by an
Italian family, 452–3
Levi, Elia: recalls her family's
rescue, 452–3
Levi, Primo: at Buna-Monowitz,
508
Levin, Isidor: saved, 60
Levin, Leyzer: found a hiding
place, 203
Levine, Allan: reflects on betrayal
and rescue, 192
Levis family: rescued, 305–6
Levis, Jeff (Pepos Levis): and
'Greek Christian friends', 305

Levy, Alexander: recounts his
mother's rescue, 368–9
Levy, Josephine: protected, 358
Lévy, Madeleine: murdered, 355
Lewartow, Rabbi Menashe: and
'last respects to the dead', 284
Lewin, Rabbi Aaron: murdered,
66–7
Lewin, Cesia and Janek: shelter
found for, 173
Lewin, Kurt: found a place to
hide, 67
Lewin, Yechezkel: seeks support
for fellow Jews, 66
Lewin, Zofia: records Righteous
acts, 154, 155, 208; reflects on
her rescuers, 522–3
Lewit, Erna: saved, 90
Lewit, Jakov: his daughter in
hiding, 90
Lewkowitz, Berthe and
Jacques: given a safe haven,
342–3
Lewkowitz, Perl: deported with
one of her sons, 342
Leysorek, Heynoch: escapes
execution, 150
Lichtenberg, Bernhard: offers
prayers for the Jews, 236
Lichterman, Jakub: finds refuge
from a Death March, 510
Liczkowce (Eastern Galicia): a
Jewish girl hidden in, 72
Lida (eastern Poland): an escape
route through, 44; Jews sent for
safety to, 256
Liderman, Josef: seeks sanctuary,
then murdered, 41–2
Liderman, Szmuel: seeks
sanctuary, 41
Liedke, Major: agrees to a
subterfuge, 261
Liège (Belgium): and a Belgian
rescuer, 380
Liem, Jean-Louis and
Betty: rescuers, 388

Lille (France): a Dutch escape
route through, 415
Lillehammer (Norway): Jews in
hiding in, 314
Limbourg (Belgium): a Jewish girl
in hiding in, 377
Limburg province
(Holland): rescuers from, 397
Limoges (France): Jews smuggled
to, 324; a Jewish family given
shelter near, 327
Lindenberg, Renée: saved, 11
Lingens-Reiner, Ella: saves a
Jewish girl, 248; helps a Jew
escape, and punished, 249
Lipke, Alfred: helps his father
hide Jews, 56
Lipke, Janis: saves Jews, 56–7
Lipke, Johanna: helps her
husband hide Jews, 56
Liptovsky St Mikulas
(Slovakia): refuge in, 291
Liszewski, Wladyslaw: helps
Jews in hiding, 195, 196
Lithuania: paucity of rescuers in,
12; Jews flee through, 26; and
Vilna, 110; acts of rescue in,
120–39
Lithuanian Nationalists: murder
a rescuer of Jews, 139
Lithuanians: and
collaboration: 14, 27, 124
Litka (a rescuer's daughter): 50–1
Lito, Dr Spiro: intercedes on
behalf of Jews, 300–1
Litovsky, Fira: given shelter,
54–5
Litovsky, Masha: in hiding, 54–5
Litvin family: in hiding, 366
Liwarek, Rosa (Lady
Lipworth): the saga of her
rescue, 356–7
Lobith-Tolkamer
(Holland): rescuers in, 401

INDEX

613

Paasche, Joachim: and his wife's defiance, 233
Padrabé (Lithuania): rescuers in, 125
Page, Anthony: directs a film about a rescuer, 233 n.2
Pais, Dr Abraham: his release secured, 405
Pajewski, Teodor: helps a Jewish historian, 209
Palatucci, Giovanni: helps five hundred Jews, then sent to Dachau, 459
Palazzini, Pietro (later Cardinal): saves Jews in Rome, 442–3
Paldiel, Mordecai: and a Lithuanian rescuer, 122; and Polish rescuers, 177–8 ns.9, 10, 11, 194 n.35; and German rescuers, 252 n.1, 256 n.5; and a German rescuer in Holland, 269–70; and a German rescuer in Poland, 270; and the rescuers of Albania, 302; and a 'turning point' in Roman Catholic attitudes, 330; and a French rescuer, 331 n.21; and the people of Le Chambon, 337; his own rescuer, 349–50; and a Belgian village, 369–70; and a Belgian boarding school, 369–70; and a Dutch rescuer, 431 n.69; and a Hungarian rescuer, 466 n.17; and Raoul Wallenberg, 468 n.21; and an Italian rescuer, in Budapest, 483 n.54; reflects on the behaviour of the Righteous, 520–1; and the 'moral duty' of honouring the rescuers, 530–1; and the 'bright and shining side of man', 531
Palestine (British Mandate): a pre-war visit to, 65; a post-war visit to, 110; those rescued make their way to, 198; those

on way to, smuggled into Italy, 294; certificates for, sent to Vittel, 333; pioneers training for, smuggled out of Holland, 410; pioneer training for, in Italy, 433; a list of approved immigrants to, 469
Palmnicken (Baltic Sea): massacre and rescue at, 511
Palomba, Umberto: helps a Jewish refugee family in Italy, 458
Panazol (France): a safe haven in, 329
Paniowce Zielone (Eastern Galicia): a Jewish boy in hiding in, 71
Pan-Jun-Shun: a rescuer, 53
Pap family: give sanctuary, in Holland, 399
Papal Nuncio (Zagreb): intervenes, 294
Papo, Mira: given refuge, 297
Papo, Salomon: deported from hospital, 441
Parankova (Lithuania): 'noble souls' in, 126
Paris (France): deportations to Auschwitz from, 322; Jewish children hidden near, 326; a Jewish child hidden in, 333; a round-up in, 334; an arrest in, 346; a rescuer in, 347; a train ticket from, 356–7
Parysow (Poland): three Jewish sisters from, given sanctuary, 148
Paskeviciene, Jolanta: tells the story of Lithuanian rescuers, 125–6
Passover: and the Righteous, 9; and Jews in hiding, 33, 85, 331; and a precious manuscript, 297